D1038714

Reflections
on Language

Stuart Hirschberg
Rutgers: The State University
of New Jersey, Newark

Terry Hirschberg

New York ♦ Oxford
Oxford University Press
1999

Oxford University Press

Oxford New York
Athens Auckland Bangkok Bogotá Buenos Aires Calcutta
Cape Town Chennai Dar es Salaam Delhi Florence Hong Kong Istanbul
Karachi Kuala Lumpur Madrid Melbourne Mexico City Mumbai
Nairobi Paris São Paulo Singapore Taipei Tokyo Toronto Warsaw

and associated companies in
Berlin Ibadan

Copyright © 1999 by Oxford University Press, Inc.

Published by Oxford University Press, Inc.
198 Madison Avenue, New York, New York 10016
http://www.oup-usa.org

Oxford is a registered trademark of Oxford University Press

Library of Congress Cataloging-in-Publication Data

Hirschberg, Stuart.
    Reflections on language / Stuart Hirschberg, Terry Hirschberg
        p. cm.
    Includes indexes.
    ISBN 0-19-512044-2 (alk. paper)
        1. Language and languages.   I. Hirschberg, Terry.   II. Title.
P106.H54 1999
400—dc21   98-14737
                                                                  CIP

Printing (last digit): 9 8 7 6 5 4 3 2 1

Printed in the United States of America
on acid-free paper.

In memory of M. L. Rosenthal,
il miglior fabbro

Contents

Rhetorical Contents

COMPARISON AND CONTRAST

DEFINITION

DESCRIPTION

CLASSIFICATION AND DIVISION

EXAMPLE AND ILLUSTRATION

NARRATION

PROCESS ANALYSIS

HUMOR AND SATIRE

List of Illustrations

Cartoons

Advertisements

Preface

ORGANIZATION

Language is an indispensable component of the world, and enables us to think about and interpret our society and culture. *Reflections on Language* is a thematic language reader that is intended to help students study the medium they are attempting to master, become more aware of language, and employ it more effectively. A major emphasis of *Reflections on Language* is on language as a social form; students will discover the complex, subtle, and often unseen ways in which language interactions shape perception. Instructions and apparatus incorporated in the work focus on the role that language plays in the writing process, and are designed to encourage students to keep journals and write about language.

In addition to seventy-three lively, informative, and authoritative readings, this text also includes five selections of short fiction, poetry and drama that exemplify the eleven themes and language practices in each chapter. The organization of the book and the sequence in which themes are presented are especially useful for understanding what language is; how it is acquired as part of our genetic and biological inheritance; how it develops through a variety of interpersonal, social, and cultural interactions; how it is used for commercial and political purposes; and the new direction language is taking because of computers.

CHAPTER DESCRIPTIONS

The introduction looks at some of the different uses of language; stresses the importance of critical reading, journal-keeping, and knowing one's audience;

and addresses the stages of prewriting, writing, and revising that most writers use when composing. This section concludes with invaluable advice by Kurt Vonnegut on "How to Write with Style."

Chapter 1, "Acquiring Language," presents essays on the innate human capacity for language (by Noam Chomsky, Jay Ingram, and Steven Pinker) and on the evolution of pidgin languages in Hawaii (by Jared Diamond). This chapter also offers a selection from the autobiography of Helen Keller and an account by Eileen Simpson that examines how the relationship between language and physiology can limit our abilty to acquire language and express ourselves.

Chapter 2, "Communication Across Species," reviews the history of research designed to establish whether or not other species possess language capabilities. The affirmative view is championed by Donald R. Griffin, Francine Patterson, and Vicki Hearne. Doubts raised by empirical observations are put forth by Herbert S. Terrace and Susanne K. Langer. The chapter also includes David Ives's amusing one-act play on the likelihood that monkeys left to type into infinity could produce *Hamlet*.

Chapter 3, "The Bodily Basis of Language," focuses on the way gestural (Kenneth Burke, Oliver Sacks), expressive (David Abram, Richard Selzer), and metaphorical (George Lakoff, Temple Grandin) forms of language are rooted in sensory bodily experiences. Also included are essays that explore the connection between language and landscape (Terry Tempest Williams) and the symbolic vocabulary of fashion (Alison Lurie).

Chapter 4, "Can We Talk?" examines the unstated assumptions governing the social rituals of conversation. Included are works by the distinguished linguistic theorists Mikhail Bakhtin, Ronald Wardhaugh, and Peter Farb, and lighter analyses of conversational social interactions by Fritz Peters and James Gorman. The chapter concludes with Raymond Carver's classic short story "What We Talk About When We Talk About Love," a thoughtful and poignant exploration of how what we say just hints at the wealth of unexpressed meanings below the surface in ordinary conversations.

Chapter 5, "Communication Between the Sexes," examines how men and women use language to achieve different, often conflicting, objectives. These gender-based differences can be observed in children's conversations (Robin Lakoff), those of adults (Deborah Tannen), sexist language (Jane Tompkins, Eugene R. August), and in the language of courtship and dating (Lance Morrow, Sherrie Schneider and Ellen Fein, Linda Stasi).

Chapter 6, "Language Between Cultures," looks at the relationship between language and culture. The readings include personal reflections from Hispanic, Korean, Chinese, and Japanese perspectives (Richard Rodriguez, Sara Min, Amy Tan, Lydia Minatoya), on societal aspects of language (Enrique Fernandez), and international business ramifications (David A. Ricks).

Chapter 7, "Many Englishes," takes up the question of what is considered correct English through an overview of the evolution of English grammar considered from traditional and feminist perspectives (Paul Roberts, Julia Penelope) and controversies that relate to black English (Barbara Mellix, Itabari Njeri). A wide variety of selections offer evidence of the dramatic and entertaining process by which new words and slang are coined (Lewis Carroll, Martha Barnette, Anthony Burgess, John Agard).

Chapter 8, "The Politics of Everyday Language," looks at the persuasive effects of language on our everyday opinions, perceptions, and attitudes, and covers issues of stereotyping (Jack Solomon), sexist language (Alleen Pace Nilsen), ageist language (Frank Nuessel), and the damaging effects of language intended to create prejudice (Susan Sontag, Michiko Kakutani). Other readings consider the societal agendas underlying literacy (Fan Shen, Jonathan Kozol). The chapter ends with James Finn Garner's amusing spoof of the excesses of political correctness.

Chapter 9, "The Rhetoric of Advertising," continues to look at persuasive language and its effects, in this case addressing the way advertising shapes our desires and decisions as to what to purchase. The selections offer insight into the evolution (Bill Bryson), mythologies (John Berger), and techniques of advertising (Stuart Hirschberg). The cultural impact of advertising on contemporary American women raises questions of how advertising shapes our concept of beauty (Naomi Wolf), acceptable body images (Jean Kilbourne), and the marketing of innocence in recent perfume ads (Susan Irvine).

Chapter 10, "The Language of Politics," extends the analysis of the persuasive effects of language into the realm of public discourse, beginning with George Orwell's classic dissection of political doubletalk. The issues touched on in this chapter include the use of "downplaying and intensifying" as rhetorical techniques used to slant information (Stuart Hirschberg), the use of propaganda (Aldous Huxley), the role of public oratory to inspire (Gilbert Highet, Martin Luther King, Jr., Earl Charles Spencer), and the mutually self-serving relationship between politics and the media (Neil Postman and Steve Powers).

Chapter 11, "Cybertalk," delves into the profound impact computers have had on the English language and the ways in which we communicate. Selections from many different perspectives offer insight into who has access to this new technology (LynNell Hancock), controversies that relate to the loss of privacy (Sven Birkerts, Chet Williamson), the addictiveness of computers (Amy Bruckman), treatment of women in cyberspace (Paula Span), and the changes in how we communicate via e-mail (David Angell and Brent Heslop). There are, as well, informative discussions on the way language itself is changing, the downside of research conducted on the Internet (David Rothenberg), and the consequences to scholarship when documents cease to be stored on paper (Brian Hayes).

LITERARY SELECTIONS, HUMOR, CARTOONS, AND ADS

There is no law that says a language reader has to be dull. And, consequently, we have included a number of features that invite students to appreciate how language can be entertaining. Several chapters incorporate works of short fiction, as well as a chapter from a novel, poetry, and an amusing one-act play to show students how imaginative fiction uses language in ways that can dramatically enhance our grasp of language principles discussed by essayists and theorists. Humorous works by well-known columnists Lance Morrow and Linda Stasi and writers such as Fritz Peters, Martha Barnette, and James Finn Garner, as well as pithy observations by Fran Lebowitz and Dave Barry, enliven the text. The work of classic cartoonists such as James Thurber, Scott Adams, Gary Larson, W. Miller, Charles Schultz, Barbara Brandon, Jules Feiffer, Edward Koren, Doug Marlette, and Mike Peters begin each chapter and are interspersed throughout the text to add a delightful visual dimension and salient observations about language and gender, literacy, culture, computers, and advertising. A portfolio of ads in Chapter 9 and additional advertisements throughout the book provide students with indispensable opportunities to analyze the interaction between graphic images and written text.

APPARATUS

Introduction, Headnote, and Journal Prompt

The editorial apparatus is intended to enhance the usefulness of this anthology. Each chapter introduces the selections by discussing the ways in which they relate to a particuar theme. Headnotes preceding each selection provide biographical information on the author and tell where the selection was first published. Each reading also begins with a journal prompt ("To Consider") that is intended to encourage students to write about their own experiences and the relevant language issues in ways that tie in with the guidance on keeping a journal described in the introduction. Students can then draw on these observations when doing the writing assignments at the end of each selection and at the end of each chapter.

End-of-Selection Questions

The end-of-selection questions are of several varieties. The first three emphasize the topical language issues, content, and meaning of each reading. The remaining questions ask students to think about the rhetorical strategies employed by the writer, and make connections between the language issue explored in the article and their own experiences.

End-of-Chapter Questions

The end-of-chapter writing assignments are intended to provide a number of provocative and intriguing suggestions for three-to-five-page papers on the language-related issue and writing strategies explored in each chapter. They are structured in several different ways. The first kind ("Connections") is intended to help students relate particular essays to others in the same chapter, while the second set of connection assignments is designed to broaden students' awareness of how language issues explored by writers in the chapter relate to other selections in the book. Lastly, a general set of writing assignments provides the opportunity for students to draw on their journal entries as a basis for fully developed essays that explore some particular language principle or rhetorical technique exemplifed in the readings. Many of the end-of-chapter writing assignments include concise and informative discussions of key linguistic terms and concepts (for example, *jargon, tone, euphemisms, definition,* etc.).

RHETORICAL CONTENTS AND GLOSSARY OF RHETORICAL, LINGUISTIC, AND LITERARY TERMS

To provide students with an accessible source of information about the rhetorical strategies and linguistic principles used by the authors, we have created a second table of contents that classifies individual selections by the rhetorical techniques employed and a glossary that defines important terms. These resources are keyed to italicized terms in the questions, the end-of-chapter discussions, and writing assignments. They provide students with accessible definitions of key terms, and instructors with an invaluable resource for generating writing assignments based on the rhetorical modes or patterns.

ACKNOWLEDGMENTS

How lucky we are to have Tony English as our editor! His unfailing patience, humor, and skill in guiding this book from its inception have made this entire project truly the kind of delightful experience most authors can only dream about. Much appreciation goes to Ruth Levine and Trudy Brown at Oxford University Press and to Julie A. Bokser, Lisa Cochran, Bridget O'Rourke Flisk, and David R. Zauhar from the University of Illinois at Chicago, Paul Eschholz from the University of Vermont, and Thomas P. Miller from the University of Arizona, who reviewed the manuscript and made such constructive suggestions. We would also like to thank Kevin Reiss for his incisive remarks and contributions to the text.

Introduction

The limits of my language are the limits of my world.

—Ludwig Wittgenstein

USING LANGUAGE

Language offers a means by which we can express what we think, know, and feel, and a bridge between thought and expression. Imagine how difficult it would be to express a thought without first conceiving it in words. Once formulated, words enable us to hold events in our minds and to think and talk about them long after they have occurred. We also use language to imagine events that have never happened. This descriptive and creative capacity joins us to one another as human beings through communication and enables us to form societies and cultures. For these reasons, language is a quintessentially human activity that defines us as a species.

The impulse to communicate is one of the most fundamental and basic human needs. The sheer pleasure of expressing thoughts through language, and our sense of how the language we use shapes the thoughts we express, allows us to create our identities. To imagine a single day without language or being able to communicate would be a threatening prospect for most people. In severe medical conditions, like aphasia, the loss of language is tantamount to losing the essence of the person who is afflicted.

How do we use this wonderful ability? Self-expression is certainly at the heart of the matter. The chance to exteriorize and project inner feelings and thoughts, even if we are simply speaking to ourselves or talking to our pets, is so deep-seated that we can understand when writers say they've written books because they simply *had* to. The cathartic and therapeutic function of language is responsible for some of the world's greatest literary masterpieces. Would D. H. Lawrence have written and rewritten his novel *Sons and Lovers* so many times if the process had not offered him the chance to work through his deepest thoughts and feelings?

The same might be said of James Joyce's revisions of *A Portrait of the Artist as a Young Man*. This expressive function of language is intimately connected to its artistic uses. Accomplished practitioners derive great satisfaction from deft and skillful fashioning of texts. Beyond the personal expressive dimension of language, people communicate to share information about the world and to compare and contrast their observations with those of others.

Because language is a form of communication that uses symbols to share ideas, insights, and feelings, it is intrinsically capable of shaping and reshaping others' perceptions of the world. At this level, the effect of language depends very much on the intent with which it is used—to manipulate or to inspire. This use of language might be called its political and moral dimension. Here we enter the realm of rhetoric, where the use of language is always calculated in terms of its probable effect on others. This is perhaps the most sophisticated use of language in that it is not used simply to express private feelings or to serve as an exact and faithful transcription of sense impressions of the world, but rather is employed with the explicit intent to persuade others to accept our symbols of reality as reality itself. Once let loose from this Pandora's box, language has an infinite capacity to create a sense of solidarity among like-minded individuals or to foment the deepest hatreds of which the human species is capable.

Although as human beings we have this marvelous innate capacity, considerable conscious effort is required to transform this instinct into a fully formed, competent mastery of both spoken and written forms of language. How best to do this is the concern—some might say obsession—of college English teachers. One of the most useful and successful methods that has proved to make the writing process more manageable involves looking at it as a sequence of steps. Briefly, you perform specific tasks at each stage in order first to discover what you want to say, then to gather information to support and test the validity of your idea, decide what pattern of organization would best suit the idea, and choose appropriate stylistic and rhetorical strategies to express your idea in a clear, vivid form your readers can easily grasp. Keep in mind that this is a recursive process without a clearly defined beginning or ending and that you are always free to move back to an earlier stage at any given time. The sequence might appear as follows:

1. Prewriting and invention strategies
2. Formulating the thesis or controlling idea
3. Developing evidence to support the thesis
4. Organizing the supporting evidence
5. Writing the first draft
6. Revising the essay

Styles of composition vary enormously and over time each writer develops his or her own unique approach to the process. Some writers, rare and lucky souls that they are, can work a topic through so thoroughly in their minds that they can jump immediately into a nearly perfect first draft. The rest of us can take comfort in the French dramatist Molière's (1622–1673) observation, "I always write a good first line, but I have trouble in writing the others" (from *Les Precieuses Ridicules,* sc. 11. 1659). At the other extreme, some writers need the reassurance of creating detailed outlines for their essays before they even write the first word.

Whatever their differences in terms of the ways in which they compose, most writers have come to recognize that the ability to become a better writer depends on becoming a better reader.

CRITICAL READING FOR IDEAS AND ORGANIZATION

One of the most important skills to have in your repertoire is the ability to survey unfamiliar articles, essays, or excerpts and come away with an accurate understanding of what the author wanted to communicate and how the material is organized. On the first and in subsequent readings of any of the selections in this text, especially the longer ones, pay particular attention to the title, look for introductory and concluding paragraphs (with special emphasis on the author's statement or restatement of central ideas), identify the headings and subheadings (and determine the relationship between these and the title), and identify any unusual terms necessary to fully understand the author's concepts.

As you work your way through an essay, you might look for cues to enable you to recognize the main parts of the argument or help you perceive the overall organization of the article. Once you find the main thesis, underline it. Then work your way through fairly rapidly, identifying the main ideas and the sequence in which they are presented. As you identify an important idea, ask yourself how this idea relates to the thesis statement you underlined or to the idea expressed in the title.

FINDING A THESIS

Finding a thesis involves discovering the idea that serves as the focus of the essay. The thesis is often stated in the form of a single sentence or several sentences that assert the author's response to an issue that others might respond to in different ways.

For example, the opening paragraph of "How to Say 'Fetch!' " (Chapter 2) presents Vicki Hearne's assessment of the language abilities of dogs and horses:

> If we consider, as I have been doing, the size and kind of the social space created by the language shared by two or more creatures, and if we describe the integrity of a language as the physical, intellectual and spiritual distance talking enables the speakers of that language to travel together, then **it looks very much as though the dog and the horse** (who are neurologically simpler organisms than chimpanzees and whose linguistic codes certainly appear simpler) **have a greater command of language than chimpanzees do.**

The thesis (in boldface type) represents the writer's view of the topic of animal intelligence. Here, Hearne states the view that will serve as a focus for her entire essay. By stating her views in this unequivocal way, she has obligated herself to prove her assertion with reasons and evidence in a convincing manner. Hearne has also made it possible for her audience to evaluate every fact or reason she introduces into her essay in terms of whether it does or does not support this assertion. Thus, a clearly stated thesis made at the start of an essay makes both the writer's and the reader's jobs easier.

Writers often place the thesis in the first paragraph or group of paragraphs so that the readers will be able to perceive the relationship between the supporting evidence and this main idea.

As you read, you might wish to underline the topic sentence or main idea of each paragraph or section (since key ideas are often developed over the course of several paragraphs). Jot it down in your own words in the margins, identify supporting statements and evidence (such as examples, statistics, and the testimony of authorities), and try to discover how the author organizes the material to support the development of important ideas. To identify supporting material, look for any ideas more specific than the main idea that are used to support it. Also look for instances where the author uses examples, descriptions, statistics, quotations from authorities, comparisons, or graphs to make the main idea clearer or prove it to be true.

Pay particular attention to important transitional words, phrases, or paragraphs to better see the relationships among major sections of the selection. Noticing how certain words or phrases act as transitions to link paragraphs or sections together will dramatically improve your reading comprehension. Also look for section summaries, where the author draws together several preceding ideas.

Writers use certain words to signal the starting point of an argument. If you detect any of the following terms, look for the main idea they introduce:

since, because, for, as, follows from, as shown by, inasmuch as, otherwise, as indicated by, the reason is that, for the reason that, may be inferred from, may be derived from, may be deduced from, in view of the fact that

An especially important category of words is that which includes signals that the author will be stating a conclusion. Words to look for are these:

therefore, hence, thus, so, accordingly, in consequence, it follows that, we may infer, I conclude that, in conclusion, in summary, which shows that, which means that, and which entails, consequently, proves that, as a result, which implies that, which allows us to infer, points to the conclusion that

You may find it helpful to create a running dialogue with the author in the margins, posing and then trying to answer the basic questions *who, what, where, when,* and *why,* and to note observations on how the main idea of the article is related to the title. These notes can later be used to evaluate how effectively any specific section contributes to the overall line of thought.

MARKING AS YOU READ

The most effective way to think about what you read is to make notes as you read. Making notes as you read forces you to go slowly and think carefully about each sentence. This process is sometimes called annotating the text, and all you need is a pen or a pencil. There are as many styles of annotating as there are readers, and you will discover your own favorite technique once you have done it a few times. Some readers prefer to underline major points or statements and jot down their reactions to them in the margin. Others prefer to summarize each paragraph or section to help them follow the author's line of thinking. Other readers circle key words or phrases necessary to understand the main ideas. Feel free to use your notes as a kind of conversation with the text. Ask questions. Express doubts. Mark unfamiliar words or phrases to look up later. If the paragraphs are not already numbered, you might wish to number them as you go to help you keep track of your responses. Try to distinguish the main ideas from supporting points and examples. Most important, go slowly and think about what you are reading. Try to discover whether the author makes a credible case for the conclusions he or she reaches. One last point: take a close look at the idea expressed in the title before and after you read the essay to see how it relates to the main idea.

KEEPING A READING JOURNAL

The most effective way to keep track of your thoughts and impressions and to review what you have learned is to start a reading journal. The comments you record in your journal may express your reflections, observations, questions, and reactions to the essays you read. Normally, your journal would not contain lecture notes from class. A reading journal will allow you to keep a record of your progress during the term and can also reflect insights you gain during class discussions and questions you may want to ask, as well as unfamiliar words you intend to look up. Keeping a reading journal becomes a necessity if your composition course will require you to write a research paper that will be due at the end of the semester. Keep in mind that your journal is not something that will be corrected or graded, although some instructors may wish you to share your entries with the class.

Although there is no set form for what a journal should look like, reading journals are most useful for converting your brief annotations into more complete entries that explore in depth your reactions to what you have read. Interestingly, the process of turning your annotations into journal entries will often produce surprising insights that will give you a new perspective.

USING YOUR READING JOURNAL TO GENERATE IDEAS FOR WRITING

You can use all the material in your reading journal (annotations converted to journal entries, reflections, observations, questions, rough and final summaries) to relate your own ideas to the ideas of the person who wrote the essay you are reading. Here are several different kinds of strategies you can use as you analyze an essay in order to generate material for your own:

When evaluating an essay, consider what the author's purpose is in writing it. Was it to inform, explain, solve a problem, make a recommendation, amuse, enlighten, or achieve some combination of these goals? How is the tone or voice the author projects toward the reader related to his or her purpose in writing the essay?

You may find it helpful to write short summaries after each major section to determine whether you understand what the writer is trying to communicate. These summaries can then serve as a basis for an analysis of how successfully the author employs reasons, examples, statistics, and expert testimony to support and develop his or her main points.

As you list observations about the various elements of the article you are analyzing, take a closer look at the underlying assumptions and see whether you can locate and distinguish between those assumptions that are explicitly stated and those that are implicit.

1. What is missing in the essay? Information that is not mentioned is often just as significant as information the writer chose to include.

2. You might analyze an essay in terms of what you already know and what you didn't know about the issue.

3. You might consider whether the author presents a solution to a problem.

4. After clearly stating what the author's position on an issue is, try to imagine other people in that society or culture who would view the same issue from a different perspecitve.

CONSIDERING THE AUDIENCE

Most of the things we write are written with the expectation that someone besides the writer will read them.

Unless you have inquired into what beliefs and attitudes your audience already hold, you won't be able to determine the best way to present your essay. Try to estimate how much the audience know about the issue in question. If they are unfamiliar with the issue, you might provide a brief summary of background information, to give them a more complete context in which to appreciate why this particular issue is an important one. If your audience already know something about the issue, how do they feel about it?

For most writers, the simplest procedure consists of imagining yourself as part of the audience and then asking what would be necessary to convince you to agree with the assertion stated in the thesis. By being your own most critical reader, you can assess the credibility of the reasons that would change your attitudes. From this viewpoint, you can evaluate whether the reasons given are adequate. If you are not persuaded, consider what better reasons and what additional evidence would convince you.

To understand what writers do to increase the chances that what they write will be accepted by the audience for whom it is intended, we might use a simple analogy: Writing an essay is rather like cooking and serving a meal. Just as the process of writing an essay moves through the stages of prewriting, writing, and revising, the process of preparing a meal moves through the stages of planning the meal, cooking the food, and serving it in an appetizing way.

Audience considerations play an important part in both processes. Both processes require the writer or chef to look at actions performed in the present with reference to what will be required in the future. The writer uses a variety of invention strategies to generate a thesis while looking at the thesis from the perspective of how well it will serve as a focus for a rough draft. The writer also evaluates the thesis in light of the purpose of the whole essay and the particular audience for whom it is intended. Only by looking to the end point of what can be accomplished by addressing this particular audience can the writer avoid formulating an unrealistic thesis. So, too, the chef looks ahead to the particular audience during the planning stages. Who the audience is and what the occasion is will alter the decision of what to cook. Without these considerations, the chef might begin to prepare a rib roast for vegetarians.

Writing the first draft involves combining the thesis, an outline of the organization of the paper, and any notes generated in the prewriting stage while keeping in mind the particular needs, values, and concerns of the audience for whom the argument is being written. The order in which the writer raises points, the kinds of examples a particular audience would find effective, and questions of tone can be correctly gauged only by keeping in mind potential audience reactions.

The next stage, revising, encompasses everything that must be done in terms of transforming the essay to make it easier to understand: revising ambiguous words or unclear phrases and garbled sentences, checking to see that the essay has an attention-getting introduction and an effective conclusion, and adding transition sentences to help the audience see the relationship between sections of the essay.

The most important shift in perspective relates to seeing what is being prepared from the potential audience's point of view. In our analogy, the chef's attitude toward the food changes so that he or she no longer sees only the ingredients being transformed into this or that kind of a dish but now perceives the task as one of making the food acceptable to others in terms of their needs, anticipated expectations, and satisfactions. So, too, the writer must be able to look at the work as it is being written from the perspective of those who will read and "digest" it.

To put this into practice, try to create an audience "inventory" by answering each of the following questions:

What do I know about the audience's background?

What are they already likely to know about the issue?

Based on what they know, what explanations, definitions of terms, and descriptions of unfamiliar processes would they need to know to better understand the issue?

How might the audience be expected to feel about the issue?

What might be the audience's misconceptions about the issue that I could clarify?

By studying the list of responses to these questions, you will have a clearer sense of which approaches might work best for your specific audience.

REVISING, REWRITING, AND EDITING

Although revision is often discussed as if it were something you do after writing your essay, it is actually part of the continuous editing process that goes on as you write your paper. Each time you change a word to improve how a sentence sounds, or make your essay more coherent by changing the order in which reasons are presented, or pursue any promising idea that may not have been apparent when you began writing, you are revising your essay.

Read your essay aloud so that you can hear how your writing sounds. Your ear will often tell you what your eye will not. As you listen to what you have written, you may hear inconsistencies in grammar, usage, and syntax that escaped your notice. Reading your work aloud is also a good way to discover repetitious words, sentence fragments, and run-ons.

In looking over your paper for stylistic flaws, be on the lookout for inappropriate, emotionally charged language; melodramatic figures of speech; and flowery metaphors. Writers who hold strong opinions are understandably susceptible to such linguistic excesses.

Ask whether the issues in your essay are raised in the best possible order. Could any paragraph or group of paragraphs be better placed elsewhere? Would some other arrangement contribute more effectively to the overall sense of the paper as expressed in the thesis? The type of development your paper should follow will depend in large part on your thesis, but certain general criteria should be met:

1. Have you offered sufficient evidence to support your assertions.

2. If your approach requires you to attack the credibility of an opposing viewpoint, have you summarized the opposing position before countering its main assertions?

3. Have you effectively questioned the assumptions underlying the opposing argument, disputed the validity of the evidence cited, and pointed

out logical fallacies in the process by which the conclusions were reached?

4. Did you support your recommendations or proposed solutions with logical reasoning and compelling evidence?

If this seems like a tall order, keep in mind that argumentative essays and to a lesser extent expository essays, are expected to take into account diverse opinions on the subject. What would someone who holds a view opposite to your own have to say about your thesis? What about the assumptions underlying your argument? Does any portion of your essay depend on shaky assumptions, whether implicit or explicitly stated, that would not withstand close scrutiny? Consider whether some of the assumptions you take for granted need to be explicitly stated for your audience.

STYLE

When you revise to improve style, go through your essay and look for sentences that might be recast in the active voice. Find the verb, ask who is doing what to whom, and rewrite the sentence to conform to the basic subject-verb-object (or complement) pattern. When you find prepositional phrases that wander off from the trunk of your sentence, prune them back.

Change your method of editing by reading your paper aloud. Do you hear any sentences that you would not understand if you had not written them? Does the introduction of your paper immediately capture your interest? If you find the opening superfluous, imagine how your readers will feel. The beginnings of most rough drafts are notoriously expendable. Is it easy to tell how the paper is organized at first glance, or do you need to insert clearer signposts letting your reader know that you are defending a thesis, making a value judgment, or recommending a certain course of action to solve a problem? Does each section of your paper contain enough different kinds of evidence from a variety of sources to substantiate your points?

Do any of the sections of your paper bore you to tears? If it fails to keep your interest, pity your audience. See if you can improve these sections through clever analogies, attention-getting quotations, and unusual and interesting examples.

Next, reread your paper, this time double-checking to see whether you have accurately transcribed the information from your sources. If you have combined direct quotations from one source with supporting interpretations from other sources, make sure that you have not omitted any necessary documentation.

Are there places where additional direct quotations are necessary to give your ideas greater weight, conviction, and validity? Have you remembered to indicate clearly the source of every quotation at the point where it is introduced in your paper? Check to see whether in recopying information from your note or journal, you have mistaken a quotation for your own words.

Don't be afraid to experiment with language. Substitute down-to-earth words for abstract jargon. Cut through the fog. Say it simply by using single words for the following circumlocutions:

although	for	in spite of the fact that
because	for	due to the fact that
where	for	in the place that
if	for	in the event that
after	for	at the conclusion of
now	for	at this point in time
when	for	at the time that

Do you hear any clichés, hackneyed expressions, or trite phrases that could be rewritten in your own voice to express your ideas, insights, and opinions? Most important, are all the words you have written really necessary? Any words that do not make your thoughts clearer to the reader should be eliminated.

A concise, elegant, and practical guide to the principles of effective writing is Kurt Vonnegut's "How to Write with Style."

How to Write with Style   *Kurt Vonnegut*

◆ KURT VONNEGUT is the author of such iconoclastic masterpieces as *Cat's Cradle* (1963), *Slaughterhouse Five* (1969), *Sirens of Titan* (1971), *Breakfast of Champions* (1973), *Timequake* (1993), and innumerable short stories written for magazines. He is well qualified to offer practical advice on writing with style, since the unique voice Vonnegut creates in his fiction makes his work a joy to read.

Newspaper reporters and technical writers are trained to reveal almost nothing about themselves in their writings. This makes them freaks in the world of writers, since almost all of the other ink-stained wretches in that world reveal a lot about themselves to readers. We call these revelations, accidental and intentional, elements of style.

These revelations tell us as readers what sort of person it is with whom we are spending time. Does the writer sound ignorant or informed, stupid or bright, crooked or honest, humorless or playful—? And on and on.

Why should you examine your writing style with the idea of improving it? Do so as a mark of respect for your readers, whatever you're writing. If you scrib-

---

ble your thoughts any which way, your readers will surely feel that you care nothing about them. They will mark you down as an egomaniac or a chowderhead— or worse, they will stop reading you.

The most damning revelation you can make about yourself is that you do not know what is interesting and what is not. Don't you yourself like or dislike writers mainly for what they choose to show you or make you think about? Did you ever admire an empty-headed writer for his or her mastery of the language? No.

So your own winning style must begin with ideas in your head.

1. FIND A SUBJECT YOU CARE ABOUT

Find a subject you care about and which you in your heart feel others should care about. It is this genuine caring, and not your games with language, which will be the most compelling and seductive element in your style.

I am not urging you to write a novel, by the way—although I would not be sorry if you wrote one, provided you genuinely cared about something. A petition to the mayor about a pothole in front of your house or a love letter to the girl next door will do.

2. DO NOT RAMBLE, THOUGH

I won't ramble on about that.

3. KEEP IT SIMPLE

As for your use of language: Remember that two great masters of language, William Shakespeare and James Joyce, wrote sentences which were almost childlike when their subjects were most profound. "To be or not to be?" asks Shakespeare's Hamlet. The longest word is three letters long. Joyce, when he was frisky, could put together a sentence as intricate and as glittering as a necklace for Cleopatra, but my favorite sentence in his short story "Eveline" is this one: "She was tired." At that point in the story, no other words could break the heart of a reader as those three words do.

Simplicity of language is not only reputable, but perhaps even sacred. The *Bible* opens with a sentence well within the writing skills of a lively fourteen-year-old: "In the beginning God created the heaven and the earth."

4. HAVE THE GUTS TO CUT

It may be that you, too, are capable of making necklaces for Cleopatra, so to speak. But your eloquence should be the servant of the ideas in your head. Your rule might be this: If a sentence, no matter how excellent, does not illuminate your subject in some new and useful way, scratch it out.

5. SOUND LIKE YOURSELF

The writing style which is most natural for you is bound to echo the speech you heard when a child. English was the novelist Joseph Conrad's third language, and much that seems piquant in his use of English was no doubt colored by his first language, which was Polish. And lucky indeed is the writer who has grown up in Ireland, for the English spoken there is so amusing and musical. I myself grew up in Indianapolis, where common speech sounds like a band saw cutting galvanized tin, and employs a vocabulary as unornamental as a monkey wrench.

In some of the more remote hollows of Appalachia, children still grow up hearing songs and locutions of Elizabethan times. Yes, and many Americans grow up hearing a language other than English, or an English dialect a majority of Americans cannot understand.

All these varieties of speech are beautiful, just as the varieties of butterflies are beautiful. No matter what your first language, you should treasure it all your life. If it happens not to be standard English, and if it shows itself when you write standard English, the result is usually delightful, like a very pretty girl with one eye that is green and one that is blue.

I myself find that I trust my own writing most, and others seem to trust it most, too, when I sound most like a person from Indianapolis, which is what I am. What alternatives do I have? The one most vehemently recommended by teachers has no doubt been pressed on you, as well: to write like cultivated Englishmen of a century or more ago.

6. SAY WHAT YOU MEAN TO SAY

I used to be exasperated by such teachers, but am no more. I understand now that all those antique essays and stories with which I was to compare my own work were not magnificent for their datedness or foreignness, but for saying precisely what their authors meant them to say. My teachers wished me to write accurately, always selecting the most effective words, and relating the words to one another unambiguously, rigidly, like parts of a machine. The teachers did not want to turn me into an Englishman after all. They hoped that I would become understandable—and therefore understood. And there went my dream of doing with words what Pablo Picasso did with paint or what any number of jazz idols did with music. If I broke all the rules of punctuation, had words mean whatever I wanted them to mean, and strung them together higgledy-piggledy, I would simply not be understood. So you, too, had better avoid Picasso-style or jazz-style writing, if you have something worth saying and wish to be understood.

Readers want our pages to look very much like pages they have seen before. Why? This is because they themselves have a tough job to do, and they need all the help they can get from us.

7. PITY THE READERS

They have to identify thousands of little marks on paper, and make sense of them immediately. They have to *read,* an art so difficult that most people don't really master it even after having studied it all through grade school and high school—twelve long years.

So this discussion must finally acknowledge that our stylistic options as writers are neither numerous nor glamorous, since our readers are bound to be such imperfect artists. Our audience requires us to be sympathetic and patient teachers, even willing to simplify and clarify—whereas we would rather soar high above the crowd, singing like nightingales.

That is the bad news. The good news is that we Americans are governed under a unique Constitution, which allows us to write whatever we please without fear of punishment. So the most meaningful aspect of our styles, which is what we choose to write about, is utterly unlimited.

8. FOR REALLY DETAILED ADVICE

For a discussion of literary style in a narrower sense, in a more technical sense, I commend to your attention *The Elements of Style,* by William Strunk, Jr., and E. B. White (Macmillan, 1979). E. B. White is, of course, one of the most admirable literary stylists this country has so far produced.

You should realize, too, that no one would care how well or badly Mr. White expressed himself, if he did not have perfectly enchanting things to say.

1

In his whole life man achieves nothing so great and so wonderful as what he achieved when he learned to talk.

—Otto Jespersen

I know what I am, but I can't pronounce it.

Acquiring Language

T he authors in this chapter explore what language is, where it comes from, how it is acquired, and how it can transform people's lives. They make us aware in different ways that language is far more than simply a capability that we as humans possess—instead, and in a very real sense, it is the precondition for our humanity.

Consider the sheer complexity of what human beings must learn in order to be able to communicate with each other. Moving accounts by Helen Keller ("The Day Language Came Into My Life") and Eileen Simpson ("Dyslexia") make us aware of the formidable difficulties children who suffer from neurological and physiological impairments must overcome. In Keller's case, language freed her from the isolation of being deaf and blind and opened up a world of human contact and communication. After we read Simpson's account, we can truly appreciate what we often take for granted—being able to decipher the text and signs that surround us in daily life.

Several of the writers in this chapter examine the question as to where the capacity for language originates. In the traditional view, language is transmitted through culture and acquired by learning. But the most recent research into the question of how human beings learn to talk has suggested that we are "programmed" by our biology to acquire language. This theory of a "language instinct" was first put forth and cogently argued for by Noam Chomsky, who, in "The Language Faculty," maintains that children possess an innate capacity to master their particular culture's language. This latent but sophisticated grammar preexists and makes possible the complex adaptations that all human children are able to make in learning particular languages in different societies. In "Genespeak," Jay Ingram expands the concept that language is rooted in biology rather than culture by revealing how recent discoveries in genetics have established that specific genes actually control basic features of syntax and grammar (like the ability to form plurals and past tenses).

Additional insight into the innate human capacity for language is offered by Jared Diamond, who reveals, in "Reinventions of Human Language," how children of working-class immigrants to Hawaii (who had no common language) reevolved grammar to the point where they could communicate with each other through an invented Creolized language. Diamond's discussion of Derek Bickerton's pioneering research provides compelling proof of Chomsky's theory within an actual social context where children, of necessity, had to discover a way to communicate with each other. Steven Pinker, in "Baby Born Talking—Describes Heaven," discloses how the preschooler's implicit understanding of grammar is intrinsically more sophisticated than that proscribed by even the most detailed grammar textbook.

The Day Language Came Into My Life   *Helen Keller*

♦ HELEN KELLER (1880–1968) was afflicted with a disease at the age of eighteen months that caused her to become blind and deaf. When she was seven years old her family engaged a tutor, Annie Sullivan, through whose efforts Keller discovered what words meant and learned to communicate. After graduating with honors from Radcliffe, she spent most of her life helping the blind and deaf through the American Foundation for the Blind. In 1964, she was awarded the Presidential Medal of Freedom. Her autobiography, *The Story of My Life* (1902), from which "The Day Language Came Into My Life" is taken, was made into a movie, *The Unconquered* (1954). This film served as the basis for the award-winning play *The Miracle Worker* (1959), directed by William Gibson, and was also made into a movie with Anne Bancroft and Patty Duke.

For Helen Keller, acquiring language was the indispensable key to discovering her own humanity. Without the ability to correlate specific events, objects, and emotions with their names, she was limited to immediate sensory responses such as feeling the sun on her face or expressing anger. With language, her world enlarged and it became possible for her to relate to other people.

TO CONSIDER   To become aware of the formidable difficulties Keller experienced, think of how you would describe music to someone who is deaf, or colors to someone who is blind.

The most important day I remember in all my life is the one on which my   1
teacher, Anne Mansfield Sullivan, came to me. I am filled with wonder when I consider the immeasurable contrast between the two lives which it connects. It was the third of March 1887, three months before I was seven years old.

On the afternoon of that eventful day, I stood on the porch, dumb, expec-   2
tant. I guessed vaguely from my mother's signs and from the hurrying to and fro in the house that something unusual was about to happen, so I went to the door and waited on the steps. The afternoon sun penetrated the mass of honey-suckle that covered the porch and fell on my upturned face. My fingers lingered almost unconsciously on the familiar leaves and blossoms which had just come forth to greet the sweet southern spring. I did not know what the future held of marvel or surprise for me. Anger and bitterness had preyed upon me continually for weeks and a deep languor had succeeded this passionate struggle.

Have you ever been at sea in a dense fog, when it seemed as if a tangible   3
white darkness shut you in, and the great ship, tense and anxious, groped her way toward the shore with plummet and sounding-line, and you waited with beating heart for something to happen? I was like that ship before my education began, only I was without compass or sounding-line and had no way of know-ing how near the harbor was. "Light! give me light!" was the wordless cry of my soul, and the light of love shone on me in that very hour.

I felt approaching footsteps. I stretched out my hand as I supposed to my   4
mother. Someone took it, and I was caught up and held close in the arms of her who had come to reveal all things to me, and, more than all things else, to love me.

The morning after my teacher came she led me into her room and gave me   5
a doll. The little blind children at the Perkins Institution had sent it and Laura Bridgman had dressed it; but I did not know this until afterward. When I had played with it a little while, Miss Sullivan slowly spelled into my hand the word "d-o-l-l." I was at once interested in this finger play and tried to imitate it. When I finally succeeded in making the letters correctly I was flushed with childish pleasure and pride. Running downstairs to my mother I held up my hand and made the letters for doll. I did not know that I was spelling a word or even that words existed; I was simply making my fingers go in monkeylike imitation. In the days that followed I learned to spell in this uncomprehending way a great many words, among them *pin, hat, cup* and a few verbs like *sit, stand* and *walk*.

But my teacher had been with me several weeks before I understood that everything has a name.

6   One day, while I was playing with my new doll, Miss Sullivan put my big rag doll into my lap also, spelled "d-o-l-l" and tried to make me understand that "d-o-l-l" applied to both. Earlier in the day we had had a tussle over the words "m-u-g" and "w-a-t-e-r." Miss Sullivan had tried to impress it upon me that "m-u-g" is *mug* and that "w-a-t-e-r" is *water*, but I persisted in confounding the two. In despair she had dropped the subject for the time, only to renew it at the first opportunity. I became impatient at her repeated attempts and, seizing the new doll, I dashed it upon the floor. I was keenly delighted when I felt the fragments of the broken doll at my feet. Neither sorrow nor regret followed my passionate outburst. I had not loved the doll. In the still, dark world in which I lived there was no strong sentiment or tenderness. I felt my teacher sweep the fragments to one side of the hearth, and I had a sense of satisfaction that the cause of my discomfort was removed. She brought me my hat, and I knew I was going out into the warm sunshine. This thought, if a wordless sensation may be called a thought, made me hop and skip with pleasure.

7   We walked down the path to the well-house, attracted by the fragrance of the honeysuckle with which it was covered. Some one was drawing water and my teacher placed my hand under the spout. As the cool stream gushed over one hand she spelled into the other the word *water*, first slowly, then rapidly. I stood still, my whole attention fixed upon the motions of her fingers. Suddenly I felt a misty consciousness as of something forgotten—a thrill of returning thought; and somehow the mystery of language was revealed to me. I knew then that "w-a-t-e-r" meant the wonderful cool something that was flowing over my hand. The living word awakened my soul, gave it light, hope, joy, set it free! There were barriers still, it is true, but barriers that could in time be swept away.

8   I left the well-house eager to learn. Everything had a name, and each name gave birth to a new thought. As we returned to the house every object which I touched seemed to quiver with life. That was because I saw everything with the strange, new sight that had come to me. On entering the door I remembered the doll I had broken. I felt my way to the hearth and picked up the pieces. I tried vainly to put them together. Then my eyes filled with tears; for I realized what I had done, and for the first time I felt repentance and sorrow.

9   I learned a great many new words that day. I do not remember what they all were; but I do know that *mother, father, sister, teacher* were among them—words that were to make the world blossom for me, "like Aaron's rod, with flowers." It would have been difficult to find a happier child than I was as I lay in my crib at the close of that eventful day and lived over the joys it had brought me, and for the first time longed for a new day to come.

---

1 Why is it important for the reader to understand Keller's state of mind in the days preceding the events she describes? For example, in paragraph 6 she says, "in the still, dark world in which I lived there was no strong sentiment or tenderness." Why would not being able to name objects (in this case, a doll she had broken) make it impossible for her to feel strong sentiment or tenderness?

2 Why was it important for Annie Sullivan to make Keller realize that the spelled out "d-o-l-l" could refer to both her big rag doll and the new doll? What principle of language is involved here?

3 How did Keller's breakthrough (in para. 7) bring a sense of order and connection to her limited existence and allow her to enter a world where "mother, father, sister, teacher were named" (para. 9)?

4 How does the simile Keller uses in paragraph 3 ("in a dense fog . . . as if a tangible white darkness shut you in . . . I was like that ship") communicate her condition in ways that a literal description would not? Can you think of other similes or metaphors that would express her predicament? (Glossary: *Figurative Language, Simile*.)

5 What is the main idea or narrative point of Keller's essay? Explain it in your own words. What conflict does her narrative dramatize? (Glossary: *Narration*.)

6 If you have ever been temporarily physically incapacitated or have a disability, write an essay that will help your audience understand your plight and the visible and subtle psychological aspects of discrimination that the disabled must endure every day.

Dyslexia *Eileen Simpson*

♦ EILEEN SIMPSON is a psychotherapist and author of short stories, a novel, and several works of nonfiction, including *Poets in Their Youth* (1982), *Orphans: Real and Imaginary* (1987), and *Reversals: A Personal Account of Victory Over Dyslexia* (1979), in which the following article first appeared.

One of the most common obstacles to acquiring language is a type of learning disability known as dyslexia, which is a condition that results in severe and long-term difficulties in learning to read despite average or above-average intelligence, normal vision, and appropriate reading instruction. Imagine being unable to recognize that a small letter and a capital letter (for example, "g" and "G") refer to the same letter, or being unable to follow a line of text without jumping above it or below it. Imagine inverting words or the letters within words or being unable to remember the sequence of words in a line of text. This should give you some idea of the immense difficulties confronting those suffering from dyslexia, a disorder that afflicts nearly ten percent of the population. As Eileen Simpson points out, however, drawing on her own experiences, dyslexia is a treatable condition. In fact, such notable figures as W. B. Yeats, Thomas Edison, and Woodrow Wilson overcame it.

> **TO CONSIDER**   To give you an idea of the challenge being dyslexic poses to normal learning, describe something you found very difficult to do or learn that others find easy.

1   Dyslexia (from the Greek, *dys,* faulty, + *lexis,* speech, cognate with the Latin *legere,* to read), developmental or specific dyslexia as it's technically called, the disorder I suffered from, is the inability of otherwise normal children to read. Children whose intelligence is below average, whose vision or hearing is defective, who have not had proper schooling, or who are too emotionally disturbed or brain-damaged to profit from it belong in other diagnostic categories. They, too, may be unable to learn to read, but they can-
2   not properly be called dyslexics.

For more than seventy years the essential nature of the affliction has been hotly disputed by psychologists, neurologists, and educators. It is generally agreed, however, that it is the result of a neurophysiological flaw in the brain's ability to process language. It is probably inherited, although some experts are reluctant to say this because they fear people will equate "inherited" with "untreatable." Treatable it certainly is: not a disease to be cured, but a malfunc-
3   tion that requires retraining.

Reading is the most complex skill a child entering school is asked to develop. What makes it complex, in part, is that letters are less constant than objects. A car seen from a distance, close to, from above, or below, or in a mirror still looks like a car even though the optical image changes. The letters of the alphabet are more whimsical. Take the letter b. Turned upside down it becomes a p. Looked at in a mirror, it becomes a d. Capitalized, it becomes something quite different, a B. The M upside down is a W. The E flipped over becomes Ǝ. This reversed E is familiar to mothers of normal children who have just begun to go to school. The earliest examples of art work they bring home often have I LOVE YOU
4   written on them.

Dyslexics differ from other children in that they read, spell, and write letters upside down and turned around far more frequently and for a much longer time. In what seems like a capricious manner, they also add letters, syllables, and words, or, just as capriciously, delete them. With palindromic words (was-saw, on-no), it is the order of the letters rather than the orientation they change. The new word makes sense, but not the sense intended. Then there are other words
5   where the changed order—"sorty" for story—does not make sense at all.

The inability to recognize that g, *g,* and G are the same letter, the inability to maintain the orientation of the letters, to retain the order in which they appear, and to follow a line of text without jumping above or below it—all the results of the flaw—can make of an orderly page of words a dish of alphabet soup.
6   Also essential for reading is the ability to store words in memory and to retrieve them. This very particular kind of memory dyslexics lack. So, too, do

they lack the ability to hear what the eye sees, and to see what they hear. If the eye sees "off," the ear must hear "off" and not "of," or "for." If the ear hears "saw," the eye must see that it looks like "saw" on the page and not "was." Lacking these skills, a sentence or paragraph becomes a coded message to which the dyslexic can't find the key.

It is only a slight exaggeration to say that those who learned to read without difficulty can best understand the labor reading is for a dyslexic by turning a page of text upside down and trying to decipher it.

While the literature is replete with illustrations of the way these children write and spell, there are surprisingly few examples of how they read. One, used for propaganda purposes to alert the public to the vulnerability of dyslexics in a literate society, is a sign warning that behind it are guard dogs trained to kill. The dyslexic reads:

Wurring.

Guard God

Patoly

for

Warning.

Guard Dog

Patrol

and, of course, remains ignorant of the danger.

Looking for a more commonplace example, and hoping to recapture the way I must have read in fourth grade, I recently observed dyslexic children at the Educational Therapy Clinic in Princeton, through the courtesy of Elizabeth Travers, the director. The first child I saw, eight-year-old Anna (whose red hair and brown eyes reminded me of myself at that age), had just come to the Clinic and was learning the alphabet. Given the story of "Little Red Riding Hood," which is at the second grade level, she began confidently enough, repeating the title from memory, then came to a dead stop. With much coaxing throughout, she read as follows:

Grandma you a top. Grandma [looks over at picture of Red Riding Hood]. Red Riding Hood [long pause, presses index finger into the paper. Looks at me for help. I urge: Go ahead] the a [puts head close to the page, nose almost touching] on Grandma.

for

Once upon a time there was a little girl who had a red coat with a red hood. Etc.

"Grandma" was obviously a memory from having heard the story read aloud. Had I needed a reminder of how maddening my silences must have been to Miss Henderson, and how much patience is required to teach these children,

Anna, who took almost ten minutes to read these few lines, furnished it. The main difference between Anna and me at that age is that Anna clearly felt no need to invent. She was perplexed, but not anxious, and seemed to have infinite tolerance for her long silences.

11 Toby, a nine-year old boy with superior intelligence, had a year of tutoring behind him and could have managed "Little Red Riding Hood" with ease. His text was taken from the *Reader's Digest's Reading Skill Builder*, Grade IV. He read:

> A kangaroo likes as if he had but truck together warm. His saw neck and head do not . . . [Here Toby sighed with fatigue] seem to feel happy back. They and tried and so every a tiger Moses and shoots from lonesome day and shouts and long shore animals. And each farm play with five friends . . .

12 He broke off with the complaint, "This is too hard, Do I have to read any more?"

13 His text was:

> A kangaroo looks as if he had been put together wrong. His small neck and head do not seem to fit with his heavy back legs and thick tail. Soft eyes, a twinkly little nose and short front legs seem strange on such a large strong animal. And each front paw has five fingers, like a man's hand.

14 An English expert gives the following bizarre example of an adult dyslexic's performance:

> An the bee-what in the tel mother of the biothodoodoo to the majoram or that emidrate eni eni Krastrei, mestriet to Ketra lotombreidi to ra from treido as that.

15 His text, taken from a college catalogue the examiner happened to have close at hand, was:

> It shall be in the power of the college to examine or not every licentiate, previous to his admission to the fellowship, as they shall think fit.

16 That evening when I read aloud to Auntie for the first time, I probably began as Toby did, my memory of the classroom lesson keeping me close to the text. When memory ran out, and Auntie did not correct my errors, I began to invent. When she still didn't stop me, I may well have begun to improvise in the manner of this patient—anything to keep going and keep up the myth that I was reading—until Auntie brought the "gibberish" to a halt.

---

1 In what important ways do children suffering from dyslexia differ from normal children who are just learning to read and write? What is Simpson's purpose in defining dyslexia? What myths concerning dyslexia does Simpson wish to dispel?

2 How does the way in which the eight-year-old child, Anna (para. 9), is being treated help explain why her attitude is different from that of Simpson when she was a child?

3 What part did improvisation play for Simpson (as it still does for other dyslexics) when called upon to read aloud? Why is it necessary for dyslexics to pretend they are reading the words (para. 10, 16)?

4 In the first paragraph Simpson uses formal definition and negation to identify the distinguishing features of dyslexia. How does she elaborate and develop this definition with examples (para. 8 and 9,,etc.), descriptions (para. 6, etc.), and comparisons and contrasts (para. 3 and 4, etc.)? Explain how these strategies give you a clearer idea of what dyslexia is. (Glossary: *Definition*.)

5 What steps does Simpson take to provide the reader with some background necessary to visualize and understand what dyslexia is and how it affects perception? (Glossary: *Process Analysis*.)

6 Describe an experience you have had when you looked at a familiar word that appeared totally unfamiliar to you, even if just for a moment. How did this experience give you insight into the predicament dyslexics have all the time?

The Language Faculty   *Noam Chomsky*

♦ NOAM CHOMSKY is a professor of linguistics at MIT and has attracted international attention with his research into the nature of human language and communication. Among his many widely praised publications are *Language and Mind* (1968), *Reflections on Language* (1975), *Rules and Representations* (1980), from which the following article is drawn, and, most recently, *Language and Thought* (1994).

It may come as a shock to realize that the only living member of a select group of the ten most frequently cited writers (including Sigmund Freud, Shakespeare, Aristotle, Lenin, Marx, Plato, etc.) is Noam Chomsky. Chomsky's analysis of the syntax and structure of sentences people speak suggests the existence of a universal grammar that underlies the particular grammars of all languages and is part of the intrinsic biological inheritance of every human being. Thus, language—rather than being something one learned or acquired, as the Behaviorist School of Psychology (dominated by the theories of John Watson and B. F. Skinner) believed in the 1950s—is a kind of biological instinct that begins to unfold the minute one is born. Guided by this universal grammar, children can

The Edith Weigert Lecture, sponsored by the Forum on Psychiatry and the Humanities, Washington School of Psychiatry, November 19, 1976. From Joseph H. Smith, ed., *Psychoanalysis and Language, Psychiatry and the Humanities,* vol. 3, published by Yale University Press, copyright © 1978 by the Forum on Psychiatry and the Humanities of the Washington School of Psychiatry.

create or understand novel combinations of words and interpret sentence constructions they have never encountered. Chomsky's influence has been monumental in shaping the directions of research in child development, speech perception, neurology, genetics, and memory and thinking. In the following selection, "The Language Faculty," Chomsky puts forward many of the key insights that have guided the study of language in the twentieth century.

> **TO CONSIDER** To give you an idea of what Chomsky means by an innate capacity for language, describe a special ability or talent you have that seemed to develop on its own.

If the study of human language is to be pursued in a serious way, it is necessary to undertake a series of abstractions and idealizations. Consider the concept "language" itself. The term is hardly clear; "language" is no well-defined concept of linguistic science. In colloquial usage we say that German is one language and Dutch another, but some dialects of German are more similar to Dutch dialects than to other, more remote dialects of German. We say that Chinese is a language with many dialects and that French, Italian, and Spanish are different languages. But the diversity of the Chinese "dialects" is roughly comparable to that of the Romance languages. A linguist knowing nothing of political boundaries or institutions would not distinguish "language" and "dialect" as we do in normal discourse. Nor would he have clear alternative concepts to propose, with anything like the same function.

Furthermore, even within the more restricted "languages" there may be considerable diversity. Two dialects of what we call a single language may be mutually incomprehensible. . . .

It should come as no surprise, then, that a significant notion of "language" as an object of rational inquiry can be developed only on the basis of rather far-reaching abstraction. How to proceed is a matter of controversy. My own view is this. We may imagine an ideal homogeneous speech community in which there is no variation in style or dialect. We may suppose further that knowledge of the language of this speech community is uniformly represented in the mind of each of its members, as one element in a system of cognitive structures. Let us refer to this representation of the knowledge of these ideal speaker-hearers as the grammar of the language. We must be careful to distinguish the grammar, regarded as a structure postulated in the mind, from the linguist's grammar, which is an explicit articulated theory that attempts to express precisely the rules and principles of the grammar in the mind of the ideal speaker-hearer. The linguist's grammar is a scientific theory, correct insofar as it corresponds to the internally represented grammar. (Exactly what is meant by the notion "corresponds" in the case of the abstract study of a physical system is a complex question, not unique to this enterprise.) It is common to use the term "grammar" with systematic ambiguity, letting the context determine whether it refers to the internalized grammar or to the linguist's theory. The practice is unobjectionable but may lead to confusion unless care is taken.

The grammar of the language determines the properties of each of the sentences of the language. For each sentence, the grammar determines aspects of its phonetic form, its meaning, and perhaps more. The language is the set of sentences that are described by the grammar. To introduce a technical term, we say that the grammar "generates" the sentences it describes and their structural descriptions; the grammar is said to "weakly generate" the sentences of the language and to "strongly generate" the structural descriptions of these sentences. When we speak of the linguist's grammar as a "generative grammar," we mean only that it is sufficiently explicit to determine how sentences of the language are in fact characterized by the grammar.

The language generated by the grammar is infinite. Putting aside irrelevant limitations of time, patience, and memory, people can in principle understand and use sentences of arbitrary length and complexity. Correspondingly, as these limitations are relaxed in practice, our ability to use language increases in scope—in principle, without bound. A sentence that is incomprehensible in speech may be intelligible if repeated several times or presented on the printed page, where memory limitations are less severe. But we do not have to extend our knowledge of language to be able to deal with repeated or written sentences that are far more complex than those of normal spoken discourse. Rather, the same knowledge can be applied with fewer extrinsic constraints.

To illustrate with a simple analogy, consider a person who knows arithmetic, who has mastered the concept of number. In principle, he is now capable of carrying out or determining the accuracy of any computation. Some computations he may not be able to carry out in his head. Paper and pencil are required to extend his memory. But the person does not have to learn something new to carry out a more complex computation, using paper and pencil. Rather, he uses the knowledge already represented in his mind, with access to more computing space than his short-term memory provides. Some computations may be too complex even for paper and pencil, but these limitations are independent of knowledge of arithmetic. They hold for other domains as well. Therefore a scientist interested in determining "arithmetical competence" would quite properly disregard these limitations, attributing them to independent components of the mind.

Although the language generated is infinite, the grammar itself is finite, represented in a finite brain. Thus, the rules of grammar must iterate in some manner to generate an infinite number of sentences, each with its specific sound, structure, and meaning. We make use of this "recursive" property of grammar constantly in ordinary life. We construct new sentences freely and use them on appropriate occasions, just as we comprehend the new sentences that we hear in novel circumstances, generally bringing much more than our knowledge of language to the performance of these creative acts. Though our language use is appropriate to situations, it is not controlled by stimulus conditions. Language serves as an instrument for free expression of thought, unbounded in scope, uncontrolled by stimulus conditions though appropriate to situations, available for use in whatever contingencies our thought processes can comprehend. This "creative aspect of language use" is a characteristic species property of humans.

Descartes appealed to this property of language use as a criterion for the existence of "other minds."

It is important to bear in mind the fundamental conceptual distinction between generation of sentences by the grammar, on the one hand, and production and interpretation of sentences by the speaker, making use of the resources of the grammar and much else, on the other. The grammar, in whatever form its principles are represented in the mind and brain, simply characterizes the properties of sentences, much as the principles of arithmetic determine the properties of numbers. We have some understanding of the principles of grammar, but there is no promising approach to the normal creative use of language, or to other rule-governed human acts that are freely undertaken. The study of grammar raises problems that we have some hope of solving; the creative use of language is a mystery that eludes our intellectual grasp. . . .

How can we proceed to investigate the properties of language? To clarify the issue, we might think about the less controversial task of studying the physical structure of the body. A rational approach would be to select some reasonably self-contained physical system of the body—some bodily organ—and try to determine its nature. Having done this in a number of cases, we might proceed to a higher level of analysis and ask how organs interact. how they grow and develop, how they function in the life of the organism.

Consider the kinds of questions we might ask about an organ of the body— say the eye, or more broadly, the visual system regarded as an organ. We might organize our inquiry along the following lines:

(1) (a) function
    (b) structure
    (c) physical basis
    (d) development in the individual
    (e) evolutionary development

Thus we might ask (*a*) what the visual system does, what purpose it serves in human life. We seek further to determine (*b*) the principles in accordance with which it is organized and operates. Given some characterization of the structure of the visual system at this abstract level, we might try to establish (*c*) the physical mechanisms that meet the conditions of (*b*), asking how the structural principles and postulated elements are actually realized in the physical system of the brain. We want to know (*d*) how the system comes to assume its mature form, how nature and nurture interact in the growth of the organ—a question that can be raised at the abstract level of study of mind or with respect to the physical study of the brain. And finally, we might try to discover (*e*) how the genetically determined aspects of the organ, as established under (*d*), came to be as they are, for the species. . . .

Suppose that we attempt to study language on the model of a bodily organ, raising the questions (1a)–(1e) Let us briefly consider these questions in turn.

What is the function of language? It is frequently alleged that the function of language is communication, that its "essential purpose" is to enable people to communicate with one another. It is further alleged that only by attending to this essential purpose can we make any sense of the nature of language.

also: a cognitive organizer

although, according to Foucault, this organizing process is fallacious

It is not easy to evaluate this contention. What does it mean to say that language has an "essential purpose"? Suppose that in the quiet of my study I think about a problem, using language, and even write down what I think. Suppose that someone speaks honestly, merely out of a sense of integrity, fully aware that his audience will refuse to comprehend or even consider what he is saying. Consider informal conversation conducted for the sole purpose of maintaining casual friendly relations, with no particular concern as to its content. Are these examples of "communication"? If so, what do we mean by "communication" in the absence of an audience, or with an audience assumed to be completely unresponsive, or with no intention to convey information or modify belief or attitude?

It seems that either we must deprive the notion "communication" of all significance, or else we must reject the view that the sole purpose of language is communication. While it is quite commonly argued that the purpose of language is communication and that it is pointless to study language apart from its communicative function, there is no formulation of this belief, to my knowledge, from which any substantive proposals follow. The same may be said of the idea that the essential purpose of language is to achieve certain instrumental ends, to satisfy needs, and so on. Surely language can be used for such purposes—or for others. It is difficult to say what "the purpose" of language is, except, perhaps, the expression of thought, a rather empty formulation. The functions of language are various. It is unclear what might be meant by the statement that some of them are "central" or "essential."

A more productive suggestion is that functional considerations determine the character of linguistic rules. Suppose it can be shown, for example, the some rule of English grammar facilitates a perceptual strategy for sentence analysis. Then we have the basis for a functional explanation for the linguistic rule. But several questions arise, quite apart from the matter of the source of the perceptual strategy. Is the linguistic rule a true universal? If so, then the functional analysis is relevant only on the evolutionary level; human languages *must* have this rule or one like it, by virtue of a species property. Suppose, on the contrary, that the linguistic rule is learned. We may still maintain the functional explanation, but it will now have to do with the evolution of English. That is, English developed in such a way as to accord with this principle. In either case, the functional explanation applies on the evolutionary level—either the evolution of the organism or of the language. The child does not acquire the rule by virtue of its function any more than he learns to have an eye because of the advantages of sight.

The second basic question (1*b*) is the one that deserves the most extensive discussion, but I will have little to say about it here. I cannot attempt to outline the answers that have been proposed to the question, What is the abstract structure of language? or the problems that arise along the way. If work of recent years is anywhere near the mark, then a language is generated by a system of rules and principles that enter into complex mental computations to determine the form and meaning of sentences. These rules and principles are in large measure unconscious and beyond the reach of potential consciousness. Our perfect knowledge of the language we speak gives us no privileged access to these principles; we cannot hope to determine them by introspection or reflection, "from within," as it were. Correspondingly, there is no basis whatsoever for dogmatic stipulations as to the degree or quality of the complexity or abstractness that is "permitted" in a theory of language structure, just as such a priori doctrine would be out of place in the study of the visual system or any bodily organ.

The most intriguing of the studies of language structure are those that bear on linguistic universals, that is, principles that hold of language quite generally as a matter of biological (not logical) necessity. Given the richness and complexity of the system of grammar for a human language and the uniformity of its acquisition on the basis of limited and often degenerate evidence, there can be little doubt that highly restrictive universal principles must exist determining the general framework of each human language and perhaps much of its specific structure as well. To determine these principles is the deepest problem of contemporary linguistic study. . . .

There is good reason to suppose that across the human species the ability to acquire language is invariant within narrow limits, apart from pathology. We may assume that a fixed and highly restrictive initial state is a common human possession.

The child's initial state, it seems, must lay down the general principles of language structure in fair detail, providing a rich and intricate schematism that determines (1) the content of linguistic experience and (2) the specific language that develops under the boundary conditions given by this experience. If the initial restriction is sufficiently severe, it will be possible for the child to attain a system of great intricacy on the basis of limited data, data sufficient to rule out all possibilities but one or a few. Then he will know the language compatible with his limited experience, though there will be no relation of generalization, abstraction, induction, habit formation, or the like that relates the system attained at the final state to the data of experience. The relation between experience and knowledge will be quite abstract. The principles of language structure incorporated in the initial state express this relationship. Qualitative considerations suggest that this may be a reasonable approach to the fundamental question of development in the individual (1*d*). If so, the human language faculty is much like other organs known to biology.

We need not content ourselves with vague and metaphoric discussions of this sort. Rather, we can proceed to spell out in specific detail a schematism that characterizes the initial state. Call this schematism "universal grammar." We may think of universal grammar as, in effect, the genetic program, the schematism that permits the range of possible realizations that are the possible human languages. Each such possible realization is a possible final steady state, the grammar of a specific language. Universal grammar is a system that is genetically determined at the initial state, and is specified, sharpened, articulated, and refined under the conditions set by experience, to yield the particular grammars that are represented in the steady states attained. Looking at the question of growth of language ("language learning") in this way, we can see how it is possible for a person to know vastly more than he has experienced.

Once the steady state is attained, knowledge of language and skill in using language may still be refined, as in the case of learning to see. Wilhelm von Humboldt argued that the resources of a language can be enriched by a great thinker or writer, without any change in the grammar. An individual can expand his facility or the subtlety of his comprehension of the devices of language through his own creative activities or immersion in the cultural wealth of his society. But as in the case of the visual system, it seems quite appropriate to set this matter aside in abstracting the linguistic system as a separate object of study. . . .

I have said nothing so far about the questions (1*c*) and (1*e*)—namely, the physical realization of the abstract structures of language and their evolutionary history. In fact, little is known about these questions, though the first, at least, may be open to serious investigation.

Can we expect to find, in other organisms, faculties closely analogous to the human language capacity? It is conceivable, but not very likely. That would constitute a kind of biological miracle, rather similar to the discovery, on some unexplored island, of a species of bird that had never thought to fly until instructed to do so through human intervention. Language must surely confer enormous selectional advantage. It is difficult to imagine that some other species, say the chimpanzee, has the capacity for language but has never thought to put it to use. Nor is there any evidence that this biological miracle has occurred. On the contrary, the interesting investigations of the capacity of the higher apes to acquire symbolic systems seem to me to support the traditional belief that even the most rudimentary properties of language lie well beyond the capacities of an otherwise intelligent ape.

The fundamental differences between human language and the systems taught to apes are clear at the most elementary level. Consider the five basic dimensions of inquiry suggested earlier, (1*a*)–(1*e*). From a functional point of view, human language is a system for free expression of thought, essentially <u>independent of stimulus control, need-satisfaction, or instrumental purpose,</u> hence, qualitatively different from the symbolic systems taught to apes. Structurally, human language is a system with recursive structure-dependent rules, operating on sequences organized in a hierarchy of phrases to generate a countable infinity of sentences. These basic properties are, so far as we know, unique to human language, and the same is true, *a fortiori,* of the more complex principles of universal grammar that characterize human language.

As far as the physical basis of human language is concerned, the very little that is known indicates that a crucial role is played by specific language centers in the dominant hemisphere that seem to have no direct analogue in other mammals. There is also evidence that humans with severe injury to the language centers of the brain and consequent irremediable language loss can readily acquire the systems designed for apes, supporting the natural assumption that these systems have only the most superficial resemblance to human language. As for development, language grows in the child through mere exposure to an unorganized linguistic environment, without training or even any particular language-specific care. Turning finally to the evolutionary level, though little is known, it seems clear that language is a fairly ancient human possession that developed long after the separation of humans from other primates.

Hence, along each dimension of inquiry, even the most superficial examination reveals fundamental properties that radically distinguish human language from other systems. This is not to suggest that studies of the intellectual capacities of apes are without interest. On the contrary, they are of considerable interest in themselves. One would assume that apes in the wild are capable of intellectual achievements specific to their lives and world that go well beyond the ability to acquire the symbolic systems artificially induced under laboratory conditions. Experiments in training apes to use symbolic systems are sure to further understanding of ape intelligence, and thus, indirectly, to teach us something more about the apparently quite different specific qualities of intelligence that underlie the use of language and other human achievements. We might discover that the unique human achievements in the linguistic domain result in part from organization of capacities that are individually present in some form in other organisms, though it is not unlikely that more than this is involved in the evolutionary development of a species capable of human language.

I have been suggesting that we pursue the study of mind—that is, the principles that underlie our thoughts and beliefs, perception and imagination, the organization of our actions, and the like—much as we investigate the body. We may conceive of the mind as a system of "mental organs," the language faculty being one. Each of these organs has its specific structure and function, determined in general outline by our genetic endowment, interacting in ways that are also biologically determined in large measure to provide the basis for our mental life. Interaction with the physical and social environment refines and articulates these systems as the mind matures in childhood and, in less fundamental respects, throughout life.

---

1 How does Chomsky's conception of the "grammar of a language" differ from the linguist's idea of grammar as stated in paragraph 3? What is the difference in the way each is acquired and used?

2 What are the chief reasons Chomsky gives to support his assertion that human beings possess an innate capacity to comprehend and construct grammatical utterances in any culture where they are born? Why does Chomsky believe that the language faculty is biological, tangible, and presumably physiologically based in the human brain?

3 Why, in Chomsky's view, is it unlikely that other species—such as chimpanzees, great apes, etc.—possess this innate ability to acquire language? What is Chomsky's attitude toward the experimental research that has supposedly disclosed this innate capacity for language in other species? Do you agree with his analysis? Why or why not?

4 What are some key features, according to Chomsky, of the "language faculty"? How does he use the analogy of the evolution of biological organs and structures to shed light on the evolution of the "language faculty" as a mental organ? Keep in mind he has characterized the "language faculty" as follows: "We may think of universal grammar as, in effect, the genetic program . . . that permits the range of possible realizations that are the possible human languages." (Glossary: *Analogy, Thesis.*)

5 Summarize Chomsky's argument in your own words. What evidence did you find especially compelling that supports his thesis? To what extent does he seek out and acknowledge conflicting viewpoints? (Glossary: *Argument.*)

6 Do you believe that people who are native speakers of their culture's language intuitively know whether a sentence is grammatical or not? How would Chomsky's theory help explain whether this is true?

Genespeak   *Jay Ingram*

◆ JAY INGRAM was the host of *Quirks and Quarks* on CBC (Canadian Broadcasting Corporation) radio in Canada for twelve years. His most recent CBC program was "The Talk Show," which also aired on NPR (National Public Radio). He has won two ACTRA awards and several Canadian science writers awards. He is the author of *The Science of Everyday Life* (1989) and *Talk, Talk, Talk* (1992), from which "Genespeak" is taken.

Noam Chomsky postulated that the brain must contain an underlying program—which he called a "universal grammar"—that makes it possible for children to utter and understand novel combinations of words and to discern the underlying syntactic patterns of sentences they never previously encountered (and, moreover, to do this without formal instruction). But, where could such a "language organ" be located? Recent genetic research suggests that the ability to talk is actually encoded in our genes in an incredibly precise and specific way— so much so that a supposedly learned ability to form past tenses and plurals, for example, can be tied to particular sets of genes. Talking is a deceptively simple activity that everyone takes for granted, but it is, in fact, one of the most extraordinary things we do. The following chapter, drawn from Jay Ingram's well-researched but lively and accessible book *Talk, Talk, Talk* (1992), delves into the mysteries of the physiology and genetics that determine how we articulate words to create meaningful sentences.

> **TO CONSIDER**   Do you have difficulty forming certain kinds of sentences or using certain parts of speech? How would you feel if it could be proven that these are caused by a defective language gene?

T he biggest of all the big arguments in language circles over the last thirty years has been over how each of us learns to talk: is our language ability innate, inborn, or do we learn language from scratch the same way we learn so much of our other behaviour? Linguist Noam Chomsky; who claims it's innate, has so dominated this field since the late fifties that while normally you'd describe a debate like this as having two sides, his and the other's, somehow in this case it seems that Chomsky is at the centre, with all other points of view swirling around him. Even those who agree with him that much or all of language ability is innate still stake out their own slightly different piece of territory.

Chomsky's view is that the only possible explanation for the ease with which we learn language and use it (especially given the complexity of the rules that we employ without even knowing that we're doing so) is that we are born with special nerve circuits in our brains, the equivalent of a very detailed software package for language. Although he then appears slightly vague about where the language program came from, biologists would step in and argue that the design and construction of such language circuits in the brain, if they exist, would have to be under the direction of a particular set of genes (unless there's something so special about the brain that it can ignore the rules of biology). Would that be one gene, or many? And what would happen if there were mutations in those genes—what sort of linguistic problems might result?

If you don't buy the Chomskian idea that language is innate, you can still allow for the existence of genes important for the development of language, but maintain that they wouldn't necessarily control the ability to talk directly. Instead, they could make possible a range of mental abilities, all of which contribute in some way to language. In other words, genes for smarts, but no genes for language.

Linguist Philip Lieberman of Brown University in Rhode Island has attacked the Chomskian view for years, saying that it is impossible to have a "language organ" in the brain that is identical in everyone, because no genetically determined feature is the same in every individual. A hypothetical language organ would show the same sort of variation from person to person that we see in height, body shape, hair colour or resistance to tooth decay. But, Lieberman continues, any such variation, any weak link in the tightly interconnected set of rules of language would cause the whole thing to fall apart, and that individual would be totally incapable of language. We don't see such individuals, so Chomsky's idea of a language organ is nonsense—it ignores the basic rules of biology.

This argument is, you'll notice, based on what Lieberman says Chomsky says, and Chomsky says that's not what he said. Noam Chomsky doesn't suffer fools gladly, nor is he hesitant to include his colleagues in the definition of "fool." In his final word in an exchange with Lieberman in *The New York Review of Books* in December 1991, Chomsky, after outlining how Lieberman had misunderstood what he (Chomsky) had been saying for years, finished by writing, "Lieberman's other attributions are no less fanciful, and at this level of unseriousness, not worth pursuing."

Lieberman will surely survive these comments, but whether he's right that Chomsky meant what Lieberman said he meant, or not, these two represent the poles of the argument: either language stands alone in the brain, with its own set of genes (Chomsky), or it may have some genes that contribute to it, but it is also dependent on general mental ability (Lieberman).

It's easy to debate the existence of something like language genes as long as none have yet been discovered, but it looks as though that situation has suddenly, and dramatically, changed. Dr Myrna Gopnik is a linguist at McGill University in Montreal, and she has found a group of people who have a genetic language disability. Disability may be too strong a word for some of them, because it's evident that a few who have apparently inherited this problem have learned to work around it. But there's no doubt that their linguistic ability is different, and in one case, Dr Gopnik has been able to trace this problem through three generations in one family.

She stumbled on it several years ago when she was asked to work with a boy named Paul, then eight years old, who talked a mile a minute—fluency was not his problem—but listeners had a hard time understanding what he was trying to say. He would say things like:

"Last time I lost my mommy in the metro. And last time I'm waiting in the [station] and there's another trains coming."

He'd talk about his favourite sport, hockey, and describe how he could watch his favourite team at "the Montreal Forums," even though he knows very well there's only one. Countless other examples in which he was asked to describe scenes in pictures revealed that he had a big problem with plurals. He *knew* there was only one Christmas tree, and many presents under it, but he would say "trees" and "present." He couldn't tell whether the sentences "I can cut a trees" and "I have two puck" sounded right or wrong. And yet he was first in his class in math, so he obviously had no difficulty with numbers themselves. His problem was expressing the difference between singular and plural in language.

Then Dr Gopnik found that it wasn't just plurals he couldn't get right. Words like "he" and "they" also relate to number, and he got them wrong too. If he was asked to repeat, "when it rains," he might say, "when they rain." And even that wasn't all. He also didn't appear to have the automatic system for making the past tense that most of us do. Paul scored zero out of twelve on a test where he was first given a sentence like "Everyday he walks five miles. Yesterday he_____?" In this case he answered, "Yesterday he walk." He had obviously figured out ways of compensating for the problem; he often designated the past tense by using the words "last time" at the beginning of the sentence. (Even when he had, probably by luck, used the correct past tense anyway, as in the sentence about the metro above.) After seven years of language training, he still makes these mistakes.

Paul is not alone: there have been reports of other children with the same sorts of problems, including several in Germany and more recently some children in northern Canada who speak Inuktitut. So Paul isn't an isolated case, and English isn't the only language in which this inability to deal with plurals and tenses appears. But it still wasn't clear what was going on, until by chance, Myrna Gopnik stumbled on the discovery that made sense of all this: a family in England, three generations' worth, several of whom had exactly the same problem as Paul. More important, the pattern of who had the problem and who didn't showed that it was caused by a single gene that had been inherited in a perfectly straightforward way.

It's hard to believe: a gene that makes it possible for most of us to be able to add an "s" to a word to make it plural, or choose "they" instead of "he" when it's appropriate, or add "ed" to a verb when it happened in the past! Apparently if you inherit a faulty version of this gene you will never be able to do any of those automatically. Dr Gopnik has come up with some stunning examples of this. In one interview with the grandmother of the English family, Dr Gopnik tested her ability to make plurals of nonsense words (these are used to eliminate the possibility that the person being quizzed might have memorized the correct plurals for real words). One favourite nonsense word used by linguists is "wug," the name given to a little stick figure with a triangular body. Dr Gopnik showed the grandmother one of these, and said, "This is a wug," then pointed to several and asked her to complete the sentence, "These are_____"?

The grandmother paused, then said, "Oh dear, well, carry on . . ." When asked again, her response was, "Wugness isn't it? No, no, I see now . . . you want me to pair it up . . . ," and finally, with great difficulty, she came up with "wugs." When faced with another version using "zat," she settled on the plural form "zackle." Others in the English family made one "zat" into many "zacko," and one "zoop" into "zoopez." If she or any of the others had known (unconsciously) the rule for plurals, making "wugs" out of "wug" would have been a cinch. And even when some of the adults did get the right answer, it was obvious they were using a rule they had taught themselves: one woman was overheard saying to herself, "Add an s, add an s." Even at that, she wasn't able to add the "s" in the same way we would. We would change one "mess" into many "messes." She made it into "messes."

Myrna Gopnik suspects that the people with this defective gene have to learn every plural in the English language the same way we learn the unusual ones, like "oxen" and "geese." There's no automatic rule for those—we just memorize them. In fact it's striking how powerful our urge to add "s" can be: my daughter Amelia, as I was writing this, was two months away from her third birthday, and was constantly saying, "I found thems," or "I'm going to get thems." She knew that plurals need an "s." But the people with the defective gene have to memorize "books," "cars" and every other word that we would just automatically add "s" to. And learning one probably doesn't help with any of the others: once they've figured out that the word for more than "book" is "books," they then have to start anew with "car."

There's some additional evidence that their whole notion of number is different from ours. If you're sitting at a table on which are placed a single book and a separate small pile of books, and you're asked, "Point to the book," you're likely to point to the one off by itself. If you're asked to point to the "books," you'll indicate the pile. These people who have some problem with this language gene will point to one in the pile when asked to indicate a "book," and may point to both the single book *and* the pile when asked to point to "books."

As far as Dr Gopnik can tell, these people aren't aware that they have a problem making plurals and past tenses, although they do admit that making conversation is a laborious business. This is borne out by the fact that the family members who have the defective gene speak at a rate of seventy-odd words a minute, while the ones whose gene is normal average more than a hundred and forty. This slower speech might indicate that these people are having to think as they talk, not just about what they want to say, but how to say it: imagine how difficult it would be to have a conversation in which every time you wanted to use the past tense or a plural, you had to remember exactly what to do with that particular word. Speaking deliberately might be the only way you could make your statements reasonably grammatical.

One intriguing footnote to this story has been provided by Elena Plante at the University of Arizona. She has studied the brains of two boys with impaired language (apparently of this sort) and their parents, and she's found that one part of the brain in these people is unusually *large:* it's the part of the brain that corresponds to Wernicke's area, the area up and behind the ear on the left side of the brain, damage to which often leaves the person capable of fluent but non-sensical speech. But there's one important difference in this case: it's that part of the brain all right, but on the *right* side, not the left. What does this mean? The right side usually has very limited language abilities, and besides, in this case it's not damaged, it's *bigger.* At the same time, the corresponding area on the left, Wernicke's area, appears completely normal. And a gene causes this difference? There's a glimpse of something really fascinating here, but nobody has a clue what it is—yet.

This discovery of a gene that is apparently responsible for the rules governing past tenses and plurals has a lot to say about the connection between genes and language. First, it makes it much more difficult to argue that language is simply a byproduct of learning, or that there are no genes directly responsible for it. It seems there are. It also eliminates the possibility that there is a single language gene, because although these people have apparently incurable problems with verb tenses and plurals, they have no problem with word order or complicated sentence structures. This suggests that there might be several different brain systems for language that work together—whether they were put together one by one over time, or all at once, can't be answered yet.

In a way, this family which carries a defective language gene gives us a glimpse of how we all might deal with language. Remember that it appears as if they are forced to memorize every plural, and every past tense, as if it were an irregular. All of us have to learn that the past tense of "buy" is "bought." They have to learn the past tense of any verb the same way: they can't automatically derive "turned" from "turn," as we seem to be able to. Dr Steven Pinker, a linguist at the Massachusetts Institute of Technology, has suggested that this is a picture of the way our brains are organized to learn language. Some of it, as Noam Chomsky has long argued, is inborn: that would include rules like changing present to past tense, or singular to plural, and these rules would apply to all the so-called regular nouns and verbs. The rest of the nouns and verbs are irregular, and we have to learn them case by case. Pinker's convinced that adding "ed" to a verb is an innate rule that applies not only to all kinds of verbs in common use, but also to new ones: "He faxed it to me." One of the most striking examples he uses to back up this idea is his demonstration that whenever we encounter verbs that we intuitively perceive as having been derived from nouns, we automatically form from the past tense by adding "ed," even if the word contains an irregular verb! So, for instance, a showoff is said to have "grandstanded," not "grandstood." He "flied out" to end the inning, not "flew out." And the penalized player "highsticked," not "highstuck" the other guy. Steven Pinker says we use these past tenses because these novel verbs are stored in our brains as nouns, and nouns can't have past tenses, so we simply apply the automatic rule of "ed" to them when we form the past tense.

The family that Myrna Gopnik has studied would presumably not make these automatic decisions about past tense, because they don't have the whatever-it-takes to apply the automatic rule. What that single missing gene actually does is anybody's guess: it's a very long way from identifying the specific protein that a gene makes (and that *is* what genes do) to deciding how that single protein can eliminate a grammatical rule in the brain! About the only thing that can be said is that however farfetched the idea of a gene, or protein, for grammar sounds, there are precedents for a single gene having far-ranging, even weird effects: children who have a kind of retardation called Williams syndrome are nonetheless very good at language, and in fact when asked to name animals will come up with "unicorn," "aardvark" or "ibex," instead of the normal "dog," "pig" or "cat." The gene that causes this condition plays a role in the processing of calcium in the brain. That just shows how difficult it might be to "explain" how one gene in a family leaves them unable to make plurals or past tenses.

At the same time, the existence of this gene suggests there could be others. They haven't been identified yet, but could we be hearing the subtle evidence of some as yet undiscovered genetic language deficits in daily conversation? We all know people who are better or worse at language, ranging from some who seem to be able to spin long, complex but beautifully assembled sentences one after the other, to those who are terse and straight-forward; some who never get to the point, others who never embellish. If people with a relatively severe genetic disability like the inability to make plurals and past tenses can figure out ways of getting by, so too might many others who are less severely compromised. But proving such people exist would be pretty difficult: if they're employing some unconscious strategy to overcome a genetic language problem, and it's working, how would they ever be found out?

1 What evidence has Dr. Myrna Gopnik discovered (in studying people with abnormal language patterns) that supports Chomsky's view that human beings possess an innate capacity for language?

2 What does recent research about an ability or inability to deal with plurals and past tenses suggest about the genetic basis for language? How do the language disabilities of Paul and the members of the English family supply important pieces to the puzzle and why is it significant that three generations of this family all were born with this same disability?

3 Which items of evidence presented by Ingram appear to you to be the most persuasive in suggesting that there is a genetic basis for the acquisition of language?

Do you agree with Ingram's assessment (with its implicit support of Chomsky's theory) or do you agree with Philip Leiberman's rebuttal (para. 4)? Explain.

4 What role do transitions play in connecting various sections of Ingram's essay to each other? For example, how does the sentence that begins "it's easy to debate the existence of something like language genes as long as none as yet have been discovered . . ." signal the appearance of a new topic? What other examples can you find? (Glossary: *Transitions.*)

5 Ingram's essay is structured to explain how specific genes influence linguistic capabilities. Explain how Ingram develops this causal relationship in his essay. How is the supporting material Ingram presents designed to be effective for his potential audience? Where does he provide information necessary to understand his causal analysis? (Glossary: *Cause and Effect.*)

6 Do you believe there is a genetic basis for writing well? If so, what specific attributes of good writing do you imagine might be involved? Draw up your own genetic profile, identifying attributes that would make the person who possessed them a good writer (for example, a gene for clear organization).

Reinventions of Human Language

Jared Diamond

♦ JARED DIAMOND is currently a professor of physiology at the University of California at Los Angeles Medical School. He is the author of *Avifauna of the Eastern Highlands of New Guinea* (1972) and *Ecology and the Evolution of Communities* (1979). He is an expert on conservation and has served as an advisor to the governments of Indonesia and the Solomon Islands in the planning of national parks.

Occasionally, unusual combinations of events have made it possible to gain genuine insights into the mysterious process by which children make the leap from one-word statements to fully formed language. A window into this process is offered by how the children of pidgin English–speaking adults in Hawaii (Filipinos, Chinese, Japanese, Koreans, Puerto Ricans, and others who emigrated to Hawaii to work the sugar cane crop) created in one generation a whole new language of Hawaiian creole, complete with consistent and sensible rules. Without being able to use their native languages and without formal instruction in English, these children evolved a language that bore no resemblance to the languages the children might have heard around them. Diamond's account of the research of Derek Bickerton suggests that the language they invented was created in accordance with a built-in plan—the language instinct suggested by Noam Chomsky—and is the fundamental human language. In short, the way creole was formed suggests what the recipe for uttering and understanding syntactic structures looks like in its purest form. Creole has all the features of a true language—grammatical rules, constraints on word order, rules that dictate which word modifies which, etc. An innate tendency to form double negatives that children learning standard English suppress with some difficulty is clear evidence of the kind of brain-wiring that might be described as a "language organ." Diamond's summary of Bickerton's research reveals that Hawaiian creole is an expression of this innate capacity for acquiring language and may in essence be the fundamental "universal language."

TO CONSIDER   Did you ever make up your own language—for example, a version of pig latin—that only had meaning for you or a few others? What principles guided the way words were formed?

Try to understand this advertisement for a department store, in a language related to English:

> Kam insait long stua bilong mipela—stua bilong salim olgeta samting—mipela i-ken helpim yu long kisim wanem samting yu laikim bikpela na liklik long gutpela prais.

If some of the words look strangely familiar but don't quite make sense, read the ad aloud to yourself, concentrate on the sounds, and ignore the strange spelling. As the next step, here is the same ad rewritten with English spelling:

> Come inside long store belong me-fellow—store belong sellim altogether something—me-fellow can helpim you long catchim what-name something you likim, big-fellow na liklik, long good-fellow price.

A few explanations should help you make sense of the remaining strangenesses. All the words in this text are derived from English, except for the word *liklik* for "little." The strange language has only two pure prepositions: *bilong*, meaning "of" or "in order to," and *long*, meaning almost any other English preposition. The English consonant *f* becomes *p*, as in *pela* for "fellow." The suffix-*pela* is added to monosyllabic adjectives (hence *bikpela* for "big") and also makes the singular pronoun "me" into the plural "we" (hence *mipela*). *Na* means "and." Thus, the ad means:

Come into our store—a store for selling everything—we can help you get whatever you want, big and small, at a good price.

The language of the ad is Neo-Melanesian, alias New Guinea pidgin English, which serves in Papua New Guinea (PNG) as the language not only of much conversation but also of many schools and newspapers, and much parliamentary discussion. It developed as a lingua franca for communication between New Guineans and English-speaking colonists, and among New Guineas themselves, since PNG boasts about 700 native languages within an area similar to California's. When I arrived in PNG and first heard Neo-Melanesian, I was scornful of it. It sounded like long-winded, grammarless baby talk. On talking English according to my own notion of baby talk, I was jolted to discover that New Guineans weren't understanding me. My assumption that Neo-Melanesian words meant the same as their English cognates led to spectacular disasters, notably when I tried to apologize to a woman in her husband's presence for accidentally jostling her, only to find that Neo-Melanesian *pushim* doesn't mean "push" but instead means "have sexual intercourse with."

Neo-Melanesian proved to be as strict as English in its grammatical rules and as capable of expressing complex ideas. Its supple vocabulary is based on a modest number of core words whose meaning varies with context and becomes extended metaphorically. As an illustration, consider the derivation of *banis bilong susu* as the Neo-Melanesian words for "bra." *Banis,* meaning "fence," comes from that English word as spoken by New Guineans who have difficulty pronouncing our consonant *f* and our double consonants like *nc*. *Susu,* taken over from Malay as the word for "milk," is extended to mean "breast" as well. That sense, in turn, provides the expressions for "nipple" (*ai* [eye] *bilong susu*), "prepubertal girl" (*i no gat susu bilong em*), "adolescent girl" (*susu i sanap* [stand up]), and "aging woman" (*susu i pundaun pinis* [fall down finish]). Combining these two roots, *banis bilong susu* denotes a bra as the fence to keep the breasts in, just as *banis pik* denotes pigpen as the fence to keep pigs in.

At first, I ignorantly assumed that Neo-Melanesian was a delightful aberration among the world's languages. It had obviously arisen in the 170 years since English ships started visiting New Guinea, but I supposed that it had somehow developed from baby talk that colonists spoke to natives they believed incapable of learning English. Only when I began working in Indonesia and learned the language did I sense that Neo-Melanesian origins exemplified a much broader phenomenon. On the surface, Indonesian is incomprehensible to an English speaker and totally unrelated to Neo-Melanesian because its vocabulary is largely Malay. Still, Indonesian reminded me of Neo-Melanesian in its word use and in the grammatical items that it possessed or lacked.

As it turns out, dozens of other languages resemble Neo-Melanesian and Indonesian in structure. Known as pidgins and creoles (I'll explain the difference later), they have arisen independently around the globe, with vocabularies variously derived largely from English, French, Dutch, Spanish, Portuguese, Malay, or Arabic. Their interest stems from the insights they may offer us into human language origins, the most challenging mystery in understanding how our species rose from animal status to become uniquely human. Linguist Derek Bickerton's articles and his stimulating recent book, *Language and Species* (University of Chicago Press, 1990), have much to say on this subject and are the basis for my discussion here.

Language is what lets us communicate with one another far more precisely than can any animals. It lets us lay joint plans, teach one another, and learn from what others experienced elsewhere or in the past. With it, we can mentally store precise representations of the world and hence encode and process information far more efficiently than can any animals. Without language we could never have conceived and built Chartres Cathedral—or the gas chambers of Auschwitz. These are the reasons for speculating that our species' Great Leap Forward within the last hundred thousand years—that stage in human history when innovation and art at last emerged, and when modern *Homo sapiens* replaced Neanderthals in Europe—was made possible by the emergence of spoken language.

Between human language and the vocalizations of any animal lies a seemingly unbridgeable gulf. As has been clear since the time of Darwin, the mystery of human language origins is an *evolutionary* problem: how was this unbridgeable gulf nevertheless bridged? If we accept that we evolved from animals lacking human speech, then our language—along with the human pelvis, tools, and art—must have evolved and become perfected with time. There must once have been intermediate languagelike stages linking monkeys' grunts to Shakespeare's sonnets. However, the origins of language prove harder to trace than the origins of the human pelvis, tools, and art. All those latter things may persist as fossils that we can recover and date, but the spoken word vanishes in an instant.

Fortunately, two exploding bodies of knowledge are starting to build bridges across the seemingly unbridgeable gulf, starting from each of its opposite shores. Sophisticated new studies of wild animal vocalizations, especially those of our primate relatives, such as vervet monkeys, constitute the bridgehead on the gulf's animal shore (*see* "In the Minds of Monkeys," by Dorothy Cheney and Robert Seyfarth, *Natural History,* September 1990). The bridgehead on the human shore has been harder to place, since all existing human languages seem infinitely advanced over animal sounds. That's what lends such interest to Bickerton's argument that pidgins and creoles exemplify two primitive stages on the human side of the causeway.

One difference between human language and vervet vocalizations is that we possess grammar—the variations in word order, prefixes, suffixes, and changes in word roots (like they/them/their) that modulate the sense of the roots. A second difference is that vervet vocalizations, if they constitute words at all, stand only for things with referents that one can point to or act out, such as "eagle" or "watch out for eagle." While our language also has words with referents (nouns, verbs, and adjectives), up to half of the words in typical human speech are purely grammatical items, with no referents. These words include prepositions, conjunctions, articles, and auxiliary verbs (such as can, may, do, and should). It's much harder to understand how grammatical terms could evolve than it is for items with referents. Given someone who understands no English, you can point to your nose to explain the noun "nose." How, though, do you explain the meaning of *by*, *because*, *the*, and *did* to someone who knows no English? How could apes have stumbled on such grammatical terms?

Still another difference between human and vervet vocalizations is that ours possess a hierarchical structure, such that a modest number of items at each level create a larger number of items at the next level up. Our languages use many different syllables, all based on the same set of only a few dozen sounds. We assemble those syllables into thousands of words. Those words aren't merely strung together haphazardly but are organized into phrases, such as prepositional phrases. Those phrases in turn interlock to form a potentially infinite number of sentences. In contrast, vervet calls cannot be resolved into modular elements and lack even a single stage of hierarchical organization.

As children, we master all this complex structure of human language without ever learning the explicit rules that produce it. The earliest written languages of 5,000 years ago were as complex as those of today, so that human language must have achieved its modern complexity long before that. Surviving hunter-gatherers and other technologically primitive peoples speak languages as complex as the rest of us do. Little wonder that most linguists never discuss how human language might have evolved from animal precursors.

One approach to bridging this gulf is to ask whether some people, deprived of the opportunity to hear any of our fully evolved modern languages, ever spontaneously invented a primitive language. Certainly, solitary children reared in social isolation, like the famous wolf-boy of Aveyron, remain virtually speechless and don't invent or discover a language. However, a variant of the wolf-boy tragedy has occurred dozens of times in the modern world. In this variant, whole populations of children heard adults around them speaking a grossly simplified and variable form of language, somewhat similar to what children themselves usually speak around the age of two. The children proceeded unconsciously to evolve their own new language, far advanced over vervet communication but simpler than normal human languages.

These new languages were the ones commonly known as creoles. They appeared especially in plantation, fort, and trading post situations, where populations speaking different languages came into contact and needed to communicate, but where social circumstances impeded the usual solution of each group learning the other's language. Many cases throughout the tropical Americas and Australia, and on tropical islands of the Caribbean and the Pacific and Indian oceans, involved the importing by European colonists of workers who came from afar and spoke many different tongues. Other European colonists set up forts or trading posts in already densely populated areas of China, Indonesia, or Africa.

Strong social barriers between the dominant colonists and the imported workers or local populations made the former unwilling, the latter unable, to learn the other's language. Even if those social barriers had not existed, the workers would have had few opportunities to learn the colonists' tongue, because workers so greatly outnumbered colonists. Conversely, the colonists would also have found it difficult to learn "the" workers' tongue, because so many different languages were often represented.

Out of the temporary linguistic chaos that followed the founding of plantations and forts, simplified but stabilized new languages emerged. Consider the evolution of Neo-Melanesian as an example. After English ships began to visit Melanesian islands just east of New Guinea about 1820, the English took islanders to work on the sugar plantations of Queensland and Samoa, where workers of many language groups were thrown together. From this babel somehow sprang the Neo-Melanesian language, whose vocabulary is 80 percent English, 15 percent Tolai (the Melanesian group that furnished many of the workers), and the rest Malay and other languages.

Linguists distinguish two stages in the emergence of the new languages: initially, the crude languages termed pidgins, then later, the more complex ones referred to as creoles. Pidgins arise as a second language for colonists and workers who speak differing native (first) languages and need to communicate with each other. Each group (colonists or workers) retains its native language for use within its own group; each group uses the pidgin to communicate with the other group. In addition, workers on a polyglot plantation may use pidgin to communicate with other groups of workers. Compared with vervet vocalizations, even the crudest pidgins are enormously advanced in their hierarchical organization of phonemes into syllables, syllables into words, and words into word strings. Compared with normal languages, however, pidgins are greatly impoverished in their sounds, vocabulary, and syntax. A pidgin's sounds are generally only those common to the two or more native languages thrown together. Words of early-stage pidgins consist largely of nouns, verbs, and adjectives, with few or no articles, auxiliary verbs, conjunctions, prepositions, or pronouns. As for grammar, early-stage pidgins typically consist of short strings of words with little phrase construction, no regularity in word order, no subordinate clauses, and no inflectional word endings. Along with that impoverishment, variability of speech within and between individuals is a hallmark of early-stage pidgins, which approximate an anarchic linguistic free-for-all.

Pidgins that are used only casually by adults who otherwise retain their own separate native languages persist at this rudimentary level. For example, a pidgin known as Russonorsk grew up to facilitate barter between Russian and Norwegian fishermen who encountered each other in the Arctic. That lingua franca persisted throughout the nineteenth century but never developed further, as it was used only to transact simple business during brief visits. When speaking with their compatriots, each group of fishermen spoke either Russian or Norwegian. In New Guinea, on the other hand, the pidgin gradually became more regular and complex over many generations because it was used intensively on a daily basis; nevertheless, most children of New Guinea workers continued to learn their parents' native languages as their first language until after World War II.

Pidgins evolve rapidly into creoles whenever a generation of the groups contributing to a pidgin begins to adopt the pidgin itself as its native language. That generation then finds itself using pidgin for all social purposes, not just for discussing plantation tasks or bartering. Compared with pidgins, creoles have a larger vocabulary, a much more complex grammar, and consistency within and between individuals. Creoles can express virtually any thought expressible in a normal language, whereas trying to say anything even slightly complex is a desperate struggle in pidgin. Somehow, without any equivalent of the Académie Française to lay down explicit rules, a pidgin expands and stabilizes to become a uniform and fuller language.

Creolization is a natural experiment in language evolution that has unfolded independently many times over much of the world. The laborers have ranged from Africans through Portuguese and Chinese to New Guineans; the dominant colonists, from the English to Spaniards to other Africans and Portuguese; and the century, from at least the seventeenth to the twentieth. The linguistic outcomes of all these independent natural experiments share many striking similarities, both in what they lack and in what they possess. On the negative side, creoles are simpler than normal languages in mostly lacking such seemingly standard grammatical items as conjugations of verbs for tense and person, declensions of nouns for case and number, most prepositions, and the passive voice of verbs. On the positive side, creoles are advanced over pidgins in many respects, including consistent word order, conjunctions, relative clauses, and auxiliary verbs to express verb moods and aspects and anterior tense. Most creoles agree in placing a sentence's subject, verb, and object in that particular order, and also agree in the order of auxiliaries preceding the main verb and in the meanings of those auxiliaries alone and in combination.

The factors responsible for this remarkable convergence are still controversial among linguists. It's as if you drew a dozen cards fifty times from well-shuffled decks and almost always ended up with no hearts or diamonds, but with one queen, a jack, and two aces. Derek Bickerton derived his interpretation from his studies of creolization in Hawaii, where sugar planters imported workers from China, the Philippines, Japan, Korea, Portugal, and Puerto Rico in the late nineteenth century. Out of that linguistic chaos, and following Hawaii's annexation by the United States in 1898, a pidgin based on English developed into a fullfledged creole. The immigrant workers themselves retained their original native language. They also learned pidgin that they heard, but they did not improve on it, despite its gross deficiencies as a medium of communication. That, however, posed a big problem for the immigrants' Hawaii-born children. Even if the kids were lucky enough to hear a normal language at home because both mother and father were from the same ethnic group, that normal language was useless for communicating with kids and adults from other ethnic groups. Many children were less fortunate and heard nothing but pidgin at home, when mother and father came from different ethnic groups. Nor did the children have adequate opportunities to learn English because of the social barriers isolating them and their worker parents from the English-speaking plantation owners. Presented with an inconsistent and impoverished model of human language in the form of pidgin, Hawaiian laborers' children spontaneously "expanded" pidgin into a consistent and complex creole within a generation.

In the mid-1970s, Bickerton was still able to trace the history of this creolization by interviewing working-class people born in Hawaii between 1900 and 1920. Like all of us, those children soaked up language skills in their early years but then became fixed in their ways, so that in their old age their speech continued to reflect the language spoken around them in their youth. (My children, too, will soon be wondering why their father persists in saying "icebox" rather than "refrigerator," decades after the iceboxes of my parents' own child-hood disappeared.) Hence, the old adults of various ages, whom Bickerton interviewed in the 1970s, gave him virtually frozen snapshots of various stages in Hawaii's pidgin-to-creole transition, depending on the subjects' birth year. In that way, Bickerton was able to conclude that creolization had begun by 1900, was complete by 1920, and was accomplished by children in the process of their acquiring the ability to speak.

In effect, the Hawaiian children lived out a modified version of the wolf-boy story. Unlike the wolf-boy, the Hawaiian children did hear adults speaking and were able to learn words. Unlike most children, however, the Hawaiian children heard little grammatical speech, and much of what they did hear was inconsistent and rudimentary. Instead, they created their own grammar. That they did indeed create it, rather than somehow borrowing grammar from the language of Chinese laborers or English plantation owners, is clear from the many features of Hawaiian creole that differ from English or from the workers' languages. The same is true for Neo-Melanesian: its vocabulary is largely English, but its grammar has many features that English lacks.

I don't want to exaggerate the grammatical similarities among creoles by implying that they're all essentially the same. Creoles do vary depending on the social history surrounding creolization. But many similarities remain, particularly among those creoles quickly arising from early-stage pidgins. How did each creole's children come so quickly to agree on a grammar, and why did the children of different creoles tend to reinvent the same grammatical features again and again?

It wasn't because they did it in the easiest or sole way possible to devise a language. For instance, creoles use prepositions (short words preceding nouns), as do English and some other languages, but there are other languages that dispense with prepositions in favor of postpositions following nouns, or else noun case endings. Again, creoles happen to resemble English in placing subject, verb, and object in that order, but borrowing from English can't be the explanation, because creoles derived from languages with a different word order still use the subject-verb-object order.

These similarities among creoles seem instead likely to stem from a genetic blueprint that the human brain possesses for learning language during childhood. Such a blueprint has been widely assumed ever since the linguist Noam Chomsky argued that in the absence of any hard-wired instructions, the structure of human language is far too complex for a child to learn within just a few years. For example, at age two my twin sons were just beginning to use single words. As I write this paragraph a bare twenty months later, still several months short of their fourth birthday, they have already mastered most rules of basic English grammar that people who immigrate to English-speaking countries as adults often fail to master after decades. Even before the age of two, my children could make sense of the initially incomprehensible babble of adult sound coming at them, recognize groupings of syllables into words, and realize which groupings constituted underlying words despite variations of pronunciation within and between adult speakers.

Such difficulties convinced Chomsky that children learning their first language would face an impossible task unless much of language's structure were already preprogrammed into them. Hence, Chomsky reasoned that we are born with a "universal grammar" already wired into our brains to give us a spectrum of grammatical models encompassing the range of grammars in actual languages. This prewired universal grammar would be like a set of switches, each with various alternative positions. The switch positions would then become fixed to match the grammar of the local language that the growing child hears.

However, Bickerton goes further than Chomsky and concludes that we are preprogrammed not just to a universal grammar with adjustable switches but to a particular set of switch settings: the settings that surface again and again in creole grammars. The preprogrammed settings can be overridden if they conflict with what a child hears in its local language. But when a child hears no local switch settings because it grows up amid the structureless anarchy of a pidgin language, the creole settings can persist.

If Bickerton is correct and we really are preprogrammed at birth with creole settings that can be overridden by later experience, then one would expect children to learn creolelike features of their local language earlier and more easily than features conflicting with creole grammar. This reasoning might explain English-speaking children's notorious difficulty in learning how to express negatives: they insist on creolelike double negatives such as "Nobody don't have this." The same reasoning could explain the difficulties that English-speaking children have with word order in questions.

To pursue the latter example, English happens to be among the languages that use the creole word order of subject, verb, and object for statements: for instance, "I want juice." Many languages, including creoles, preserve this word order in questions, which are merely distinguished by altered tone of voice ("You want juice?"). However, the English language does not treat questions in this way. Instead, our questions deviate from creole word order by inverting the subject and verb ("Where are you?" not "Where you are?") or by placing the subject between an auxiliary verb (such as "do") and the main verb ("Do you want juice?"). My wife and I have been barraging my sons from early infancy onward with grammatically correct English questions, as well as statements. My sons quickly picked up the correct order for statements, but both of them still use the incorrect creolelike order for questions, despite the hundreds of correct counterexamples that my wife and I model for them every day. Today's samples from Max and Joshua include, "Where it is?" "What that letter is?" "What the handle can do?" and "What you did with it?" It's as if they're not ready to accept the evidence of their ears, because they're still convinced that their preprogrammed creolelike rules are correct.

Now let's use these studies to assemble a coherent, if speculative, picture of how our ancestors progressed from grunts to Shakespeare's sonnets. A well-studied early stage is represented by vervet monkeys, with at least ten different calls that are used for communication and have external referents. The single words of young toddlers, like "juice" as uttered by my son Max, constitute a next stage beyond animal grunts. But Max made a decisive advance on vervets by assembling his "juice" word from the smaller units of vowels and consonants, thereby scaling the lowest level of modular linguistic organization. A few dozen such phonetic units can be reshuffled to produce a very large number of words, such as the 142,000 words in my English desk dictionary. That principle of modular organization lets us recognize far more distinctions than vervets can. For example, they name only six types of animals, whereas we name nearly two million.

A further step toward Shakespeare is exemplified by two-year-old children, who in all human societies proceed spontaneously from a one-word to a two-word stage and then to a multiword one. But those multiword utterances are still mere word strings with little grammar, and their words are still nouns, verbs, and adjectives with concrete referents. As Bickerton points out, those word strings are like the pidgins that human adults spontaneously reinvent when necessary. They also resemble the strings of symbols produced by captive apes whom we have instructed in the use of those symbols.

From pidgins to creoles, or from the word strings of two-year-olds to the complete sentences of four-year-olds, is another giant step. In that step were added words lacking external referents and serving purely grammatical functions; elements of grammar such as word order, prefixes and suffixes, and word root variation; and more levels of hierarchical organization to produce phrases and sentences. Perhaps that step is what triggered the Great Leap Forward in human innovation and art within the last hundred thousand years. Nevertheless, creole languages reinvented in modern times still give us clues to how these advances arose, through the creoles' circumlocutions to express prepositions and other grammatical elements.

If you compare a Shakespearean sonnet with the Neo-Melanesian ad that introduced this piece, you might conclude that a huge gap still remains. But I'd argue that with an ad like "Kam insait long stua bilong mipela," we have come 99.9 percent of the way from vervet calls to Shakespeare. Creoles already constitute expressive complex languages. For example, Indonesian, which arose as a creole to become the language of conversation and government for the world's fifth most populous country, is also a vehicle for serious literature.

Thus, animal communication and human language once seemed to be separated by an unbridgeable gulf. Now, we have identified not only parts of bridges starting from both shores but also islands and bridge segments spaced across the gulf. We are beginning to understand in broad outline how the unique and important attribute that distinguishes us from animals arose from animal precursors.

---

1 How do Derek Bickerton's discoveries about grammar reevolution among children of working-class immigrants to Hawaii who had no common language suggest an innate blueprint in the brain for language? Why was it significant that, without instruction, these children were able to expand the pidgin language in systematic, syntactically coherent ways? What explains why these children were able to reinvent the same grammatical features again and again?

2 What features distinguish "pidgin" languages (which contain only nouns, verbs, and adjectives) from creole languages? What process takes place when "pidgin" develops into creole?

3 What unsuspected parallel connections did Diamond discover between the way his young son Max learned language and the way creole was developed by children in Hawaii? Why is the significance of word order an important issue in Diamond's comparison?

4 How does the example of the language of a department store ad in Papua, New Guinea—with which Diamond begins his essay—introduce the reader to the surprising sophistication of pidgin languages? (Glossary: *Introduction, Conclusion.*)

5 In your own words, state the chain of causation consisting of an interwoven series of causes and effects that Diamond explores. Where in Diamond's essay can you see him sorting through multiple causes or multiple effects to discover which causes are more important than others? How does he organize his essay to explore what happened and the possible reasons for what happened? Where does he use transitions to make it easy for his readers to see the links between the points in his discussion? (Glossary: *Cause and Effect, Transitions.*)

6 How does language make it possible to understand experiences in a way that would otherwise be inaccessible? What experiences have you had that revealed the importance of language to you in understanding and communicating your thoughts?

Baby Born Talking— Describes Heaven

Steven Pinker

♦ STEVEN PINKER is currently director of the Center for Cognitive Neuroscience at MIT. He is well known for his groundbreaking theory of how children acquire language, reported in *Language Learnability and Language Development* (1984) and *Learnability and Cognition: The Acquisition of Argument Structure (1989)*. In *The Language Instinct* (1994), from which the following excerpt is taken, Pinker provides insight into the innate capabilities of children to learn language. His latest book is *How the Mind Works* (1997).

Steven Pinker, "Baby Born Talking—Describes Heaven," from *The Language of Instinct*. Reprinted with permission from William Morrow & Company, Inc.

Despite the hyperbole of the title of this selection, recent research has shown that all children do come into the world equipped with a prodigious variety of linguistic skills that unfold in clearly definable, if somewhat arbitrary, stages. It is astonishing to consider that between eighteen months and adolescence children possess the capacity to add new words to their vocabulary every two hours. A child's quickly emerging ability to produce an infinite number of sentences is one of the most distinctive properties of human grammar.

TO CONSIDER   Did you ever try to make sense out of what a toddler was trying to communicate to you? What difficulties did you experience in trying to decipher this baby talk?

On May 21, 1985, a periodical called the *Sun* ran these intriguing headlines:

John Wayne Liked to Play with Dolls.

Prince Charles' Blood Is Sold for $10,000
     by Dishonest Docs.

Family Haunted by Ghost of Turkey
     They Ate for Christmas.

BABY BORN TALKING—DESCRIBES HEAVEN
     Incredible proof of reincarnation

The last headline caught my eye—it seemed like the ultimate demonstration that language is innate. According to the article,

> Life in heaven is grand, a baby told an astounded obstetrical team seconds after birth. Tiny Naomi Montefusco literally came into the world singing the praises of God's firmament. The miracle so shocked the delivery room team, one nurse ran screaming down the hall. "Heaven is a beautiful place, so warm and so serene," Naomi said. "Why did you bring me here?" Among the witnesses was mother Theresa Montefusco, 18, who delivered the child under local anesthetic . . . "I distinctly heard her describe heaven as a place where no one has to work, eat, worry about clothing, or do anything but sing God's praises. I tried to get off the delivery table to kneel down and pray, but the nurses wouldn't let me."

Scientists, of course, cannot take such reports at face value; any important finding must be replicated. A replication of the Corsican miracle, this time from Taranto, Italy, occurred on October 31, 1989, when the *Sun* (a strong believer in recycling) ran the headline "BABY BORN TALKING—DESCRIBES HEAVEN. Infant's words prove reincarnation exists." A related discovery was reported on May 29, 1990: "BABY SPEAKS AND SAYS: I'M THE REIN-CARNATION OF NATALIE WOOD." Then, on September 29, 1992, a second replication, reported in the same words as the original. And on June 8, 1993, the clincher: "AMAZING 2-HEADED BABY IS PROOF OF REIN-CARNATION. ONE HEAD SPEAKS ENGLISH—THE OTHER ANCIENT LATIN."

Why do stories like Naomi's occur only in fiction, never in fact? Most children do not begin to talk until they are a year old, do not combine words until they are one and a half, and do not converse in fluent grammatical sentences until they are two or three. What is going on in those years? Should we ask why it takes children so long? Or is a three-year-old's ability to describe earth as miraculous as a newborn's ability to describe heaven?

All infants come into the world with linguistic skills. We know this because of the ingenious experimental technique in which a baby is presented with one signal over and over to the point of boredom, and then the signal is changed; if the baby perks up, he or she must be able to tell the difference. Since ears don't move the way eyes do, the psychologists Peter Eimas and Peter Jusczyk devised a different way to see what a one-month-old finds interesting. They put a switch inside a rubber nipple and hooked up the switch to a tape recorder, so that when the baby sucked, the tape played. As the tape droned on with *ba ba ba ba . . .* , the infants showed their boredom by sucking more slowly. But when the syllables changed to *pa pa pa . . .* , the infants began to suck more vigorously, to hear more syllables. Moreover, they were using the sixth sense, speech perception, rather than just hearing the syllables as raw sound: two *ba*'s that differed acoustically from each other as much as a *ba* differs from a *pa,* but that are both heard as *ba* by adults, did not revive the infants' interest. And infants must be recovering phonemes, like *b*, from the syllables they are smeared across. Like adults, they hear the same stretch of sound as a *b* if it appears in a short syllable and as a *w* if it appears in a long syllable.

Infants come equipped with these skills; they do not learn them by listening to their parents' speech. Kikuyu and Spanish infants discriminate English *ba*'s and *pa*'s, which are not used in Kikuyu or Spanish and which their parents cannot tell apart. English-learning infants under the age of six months distinguish phonemes used in Czech, Hindi, and Inslekampx (a Native American language), but English-speaking adults cannot, even with five hundred trials of training or a year of university coursework. Adult ears can tell the sounds apart, though, when the consonants are stripped from the syllables and presented alone as chirpy sounds; they just cannot tell them apart *as phonemes.*

The *Sun* article is a bit sketchy on the details, but we can surmise that because Naomi was understood, she must have spoken in Italian, not Proto-World or Ancient Latin. Other infants may enter the world with some knowledge of their mother's language, too. The psychologists Jacques Mehler and Peter Jusczyk have shown that four-day-old French babies suck harder to hear French than Russian, and pick up their sucking more when a tape changes from Russian to French than from French to Russian. This is not an incredible proof of reincarnation; the melody of mothers' speech carries through their bodies and is audible in the womb. The babies still prefer French when the speech is electronically filtered so that the consonant and vowel sounds are muffled and only the melody comes through. But they are indifferent when the tapes are played backwards, which preserves the vowels and some of the consonants but distorts the melody. Nor does the effect prove the inherent beauty of the French language: non-French infants do not prefer French, and French infants do not distinguish Italian from English. The infants must have learned something about the prosody of French (its melody, stress, and timing) in the womb, or in their first days out of it.

Babies continue to learn the sounds of their language throughout the first year. By six months, they are beginning to lump together the distinct sounds that their language collapses into a single phoneme, while continuing to discriminate equivalently distinct ones that their language keeps separate. By ten months they are no longer universal phoneticians but have turned into their parents; they do not distinguish Czech or Inslekampx phonemes unless they are Czech or Inslekampx babies. Babies make this transition before they produce or understand words, so their learning cannot depend on correlating sound with meaning. That is, they cannot be listening for the difference in sound between a word they think means *bit* and a word they think means *beet,* because they have learned neither word. They must be sorting the sounds directly, somehow tuning their speech analysis module to deliver the phonemes used in their language. The module can then serve as the front end of the system that learns words and grammar.

During the first year, babies also get their speech production systems geared up. First, ontogeny recapitulates phylogeny. A newborn has a vocal tract like a nonhuman mammal. The larynx comes up like a periscope and engages the nasal passage, forcing the infant to breathe through the nose and making it anatomically possible to drink and breathe at the same time. By three months the larynx has descended deep into the throat, opening up the cavity behind the tongue (the pharynx) that allows the tongue to move forwards and backwards and produce the variety of vowel sounds used by adults.

Not much of linguistic interest happens during the first two months, when babies produce the cries, grunts, sighs, clicks, stops, and pops associated with breathing, feeding, and fussing, or even during the next three, when coos and laughs are added. Between five and seven months babies begin to play with sounds, rather than using them to express their physical and emotional states, and their sequences of clicks, hums, glides, trills, hisses, and smacks begin to sound like consonants and vowels. Between seven and eight months they suddenly begin to babble in real syllables like *ba-ba-ba, neb-neb-neb,* and *dee-dee-dee.* The sounds are the same in all languages, and consist of the phonemes and syllable patterns that are most common across languages. By the end of the first year, babies vary their syllables, like *neb-nee, da-dee,* and *meb-neb,* and produce that really cute sentencelike gibberish.

In recent years pediatricians have saved the lives of many babies with breathing abnormalities by inserting a tube into their tracheas (the pediatricians are trained on cats, whose airways are similar), or by surgically opening a hole in their trachea below the larynx. The infants are then unable to make voiced sounds during the normal period of babbling. When the normal airway is restored in the second year of life, those infants are seriously retarded in speech development, though they eventually catch up, with no permanent problems. Deaf children's babbling is later and simpler—though if their parents use sign language, they babble, on schedule, with their hands!

Why is babbling so important? The infant is like a person who has been given a complicated piece of audio equipment bristling with unlabeled knobs and switches but missing the instruction manual. In such situations people resort to what hackers call frobbing—fiddling aimlessly with the controls to see what happens. The infant has been given a set of neural commands that can move the articulators every which way, with wildly varying effects on the sound. By listening to their own babbling, babies in effect write their own instruction manual; they learn how much to move which muscle in which way to make which change in the sound. This is a prerequisite to duplicating the speech of their parents. Some computer scientists, inspired by the infant, believe that a good robot should learn an internal software model of its articulators by observing the consequences of its own babbling and flailing.

Shortly before their first birthday, babies begin to understand words, and around that birthday, they start to produce them. Words are usually produced in isolation; this one-word stage can last from two months to a year. For over a century, and all over the globe, scientists have kept diaries of their infants' first words, and the lists are almost identical. About half the words are for objects: food (*juice, cookie*), body parts (*eye, nose*), clothing (*diaper, sock*), vehicles (*car, boat*), toys (*doll, block*), household items (*bottle, light*), animals (*dog, kitty*), and people (*dada, baby*). (My nephew Eric's first word was *Batman*.) There are words for actions, motions, and routines, like *up, off, open, peekaboo, eat,* and *go,* and modifiers, like *hot, allgone, more, dirty,* and *cold.* Finally, there are routines used in social interaction, like *yes, no, want, bye-bye,* and *hi*—a few of which, like *look at that* and *what is that,* are words in the sense of listemes (memorized chunks), but not, at least for the adult, words in the sense of morphological products and syntactic atoms. Children differ in how much they name objects or engage in social interaction using memorized routines. Psychologists have spent a lot of time speculating about the causes of those differences (sex, age, birth order, and socioeconomic status have all been examined), but the most plausible to my mind is that babies are people, only smaller. Some are interested in objects, others like to shmooze.

Since word boundaries do not physically exist, it is remarkable that children are so good at finding them. A baby is like the dog being yelled at in the two-panel cartoon by Gary Larson:

WHAT WE SAY TO DOGS: "Okay, Ginger! I've had it! You stay out of the garbage! Understand, Ginger? Stay out of the garbage, or else!"

WHAT THEY HEAR: "Blah blah GINGER blah blah blah blah blah blah blah blah GINGER blah blah blah blah blah."

Presumably children record some words parents use in isolation, or in stressed final positions, like *Look-at-the* BOTTLE. Then they look for matches to these words in longer stretches of speech, and find other words by extracting the residues in between the matched portions. Occasionally there are near misses, providing great entertainment to family members:

> I don't want to go to your ami. [from *Miami*].
>
> I am heyv! [from *Behave!*]
>
> Daddy, when you go tinkle you're an eight, and when I go tinkle I'm an eight, right? [from *urinate*].
>
> I know I sound like Larry, but who's Gitis? [from *laryngitis*]
>
> Daddy, why do you call your character Sam Alone? [from *Sam Malone*, the bartender in *Cheers*].
>
> The ants are my friends, they're blowing in the wind. [from *The answer, my friend, is blowing in the wind*]

But these errors are surprisingly rare, and of course adults occasionally make them too. In an episode of the television show *Hill Street Blues,* police officer JD Larue began to flirt with a pretty high school student. His partner, Neal Washington, said, "I have only three words to say to you, JD. Statue. Tory. Rape."

Around eighteen months, language takes off. Vocabulary growth jumps to the new-word-every-two-hours minimum rate that the child will maintain through adolescence. And syntax begins, with strings of the minimum length that allows it: two. Here are some examples:

All dry.	All messy.	All wet.
I sit.	I shut.	No bed.
No pee.	See baby.	See pretty.
More cereal.	More hot.	Hi Calico.
Other pocket.	Boot off.	Siren by.
Mail come.	Airplane allgone.	Bye-bye car.
Our car.	Papa away.	Dry pants.

Children's two-word combinations are so similar in meaning the world over that they read as translations of one another. Children announce when objects appear, disappear, and move about, point out their properties and owners, comment on people doing things and seeing things, reject and request objects and activities, and ask about who, what, and where. These microsentences already reflect the language being acquired: in ninety-five percent of them, the words are properly ordered.

There is more going on in children's minds than in what comes out of their mouths. Even before they put two words together, babies can comprehend a sentence using its syntax. For example, in one experiment, babies who spoke only in single words were seated in front of two television screens, each of which featured a pair of adults improbably dressed up as Cookie Monster and Big Bird from *Sesame Street*. One screen showed Cookie Monster tickling Big Bird; the other showed Big Bird tickling Cookie Monster. A voiceover said, "OH LOOK!!! BIG BIRD IS TICKLING COOKIE MONSTER!! FIND BIG BIRD TICKLING COOKIE MONSTER!!" (or vice versa). The children must have understood the meaning of the ordering of subject, verb, and object—they looked more at the screen that depicted the sentence in the voiceover.

When children do put words together, the words seem to meet up with a bottleneck at the output end. Children's two- and three-word utterances look like samples drawn from longer potential sentences expressing a complete and more complicated idea. For example, the psychologist Roger Brown noted that although the children he studied never produced a sentence as complicated as *Mother gave John lunch in the kitchen,* they did produce strings containing all of its components, and in the correct order:

Agent	Action	Recipient	Object	Location
(Mother	gave	John	lunch	in the kitchen.)
Mommy	fix.			
Mommy			pumpkin.	
Baby				table.
Give		doggie.		
	Put		light.	
	Put			floor.
I	ride		horsie.	
Tractor	go			floor.
	Give	doggie	paper.	
	Put		truck	window.
Adam	put		it	box.

If we divide language development into somewhat arbitrary stages, like Syllable Babbling, Gibberish Babbling, One-Word Utterances, and Two-Word Strings, the next stage would have to be called All Hell Breaks Loose. Between the late twos and the mid-threes, children's language blooms into fluent grammatical conversation so rapidly that it overwhelms the researchers who study it, and no one has worked out the exact sequence. Sentence length increases steadily, and because grammar is a discrete combinatorial system, the number of syntactic types increases exponentially, doubling every month, reaching the thousands before the third birthday. You can get a feel for this explosion by seeing how the speech of a little boy called Adam grows in sophistication over the period of a year, starting with his early word combinations at the age of two years and three months ("2;3"):

2;3:   Play checkers. Big drum. I got horn. A bunny-rabbit walk.

2;4:   See marching bear go? Screw part machine. That busy bulldozer truck.

2;5:   Now put boots on. Where wrench go? Mommy talking bout lady. What that paper clip doing?

2;6:   Write a piece a paper. What that egg doing? I lost a shoe. No, I don't want to sit seat.

2;7:   Where piece a paper go? Ursula has a boot on. Going to see kitten. Put the cigarette down. Dropped a rubber band. Shadow has hat just like that. Rintintin don't fly, Mommy.

2;8:   Let me get down with the boots on. Don't be afraid a horses. How tiger be so healthy and fly like kite? Joshua throw like a penguin.

2;9:   Where Mommy keep her pocket book? Show you something funny. Just like turtle make mud pie.

2;10: Look at that train Ursula brought. I simply don't want put in chair. You don't have paper. Do you want little bit, Cromer? I can't wear it tomorrow.

2;11: That birdie hopping by Missouri in bag. Do want some pie on your face? Why you mixing baby chocolate? I finish drinking all up down my throat. I said why not you coming in? Look at that piece a paper and tell it. Do you want me tie that round? We going turn light on so you can't see.

3;0:   I going come in fourteen minutes. I going wear that to wedding. I see what happens. I have to save them now. Those are not strong mens. They are going sleep in wintertime. You dress me up like a baby elephant.

3;1:   I like to play with something else. You know how to put it back together. I gon' make it like a rocket to blast off with. I put another one on the floor. You went to Boston University? You want to give me some carrots and some beans? Press the button and catch it, sir. I want some other peanuts. Why you put the pacifier in his mouth? Doggies like to climb up.

3;2:   So it can't be cleaned? I broke my racing car. Do you know the light wents off? What happened to the bridge? When it's got a flat tire it's need a go to the station. I dream sometimes. I'm going to mail this so the letter can't come off. I want to have some espresso. The sun is not too bright. Can I have some sugar? Can I put my head in the mailbox so the mailman can know where I are and put me in the mailbox? Can I keep the screwdriver just like a carpenter keep the screwdriver?

Normal children can differ by a year or more in their rate of language development, though the stages they pass through are generally the same regardless of how stretched out or compressed. I chose to show you Adam's speech because his language development is rather *slow* compared with other children's. Eve, another child Brown studied, was speaking in sentences like this before she was two:

I got peanut butter on the paddle.
I sit in my high chair yesterday.
Fraser, the doll's not in your briefcase.

Fix it with the scissor.
Sue making more coffee for Fraser.

Her stages of language development were telescoped into just a few months.

Many things are going on during this explosion. Children's sentences are getting not only longer but more complex, with deeper, bushier trees, because the children can embed one constituent inside another. Whereas before they might have said *Give doggie paper* (a three-branch verb phrase) and *Big doggie* (a two-branch noun phrase), they now say *Give big doggie paper,* with the two-branch NP embedded inside the middle branch of three-branch VP. The earlier sentences resembled telegrams, missing unstressed function words like *of, the, on,* and *does,* as well as inflections like *-ed, -ing,* and *-s.* By the threes, children are using these function words more often than they omit them, many in more than ninety percent of the sentences that require them. A full range of sentence types flower—questions with words like *who, what,* and *where,* relative clauses, comparatives, negations, complements, conjunctions, and passives.

Though many—perhaps even most—of the young three-year-old's sentences are ungrammatical for one reason or another, we should not judge them too harshly, because there are many things that can go wrong in any single sentence. When researchers focus on one grammatical rule and count how often a child obeys it and how often he or she flouts it, the results are astonishing: for any rule you choose, three-year-olds obey it most of the time. As we have seen, children rarely scramble word order and, by the age of three, come to supply most inflections and function words in sentences that require them. Though our ears perk up when we hear errors like *mens, wents, Can you broke those?, What he can ride in?, That's a furniture, Button me the rest,* and *Going to see kitten,* the errors occur in only 0.1% to 8% of the opportunities for making them; more than 90% of the time, the child is on target. The psychologist Karin Stromswold analyzed sentences containing auxiliaries from the speech of thirteen preschoolers. The auxiliary system in English (including words like *can, should, must, be, have,* and *do*) is notorious among grammarians for its complexity. There are about twenty-four billion billion logically possible combinations of auxiliaries (for instance, *He have might eat; He did be eating*), of which only a hundred are grammatical (*He might have eaten; He has been eating*). Stromswold wanted to count how many times children were seduced by several dozen kinds of tempting errors in the auxiliary system—that is, errors that would be natural generalizations of the sentence patterns children heard from their parents:

Pattern in Adult English	Error That Might Tempt a Child
He seems happy. → Does he seem happy?	He is smiling. → Does he be smiling?
	She could go. → Does she could go?
He did eat. → He didn't eat.	He did a few things. → He didn't a few things.
He did eat. → Did he eat?	He did a few things. → Did he a few things?
I like going. → He likes going.	I can go. → He cans go.
	I am going. → He ams (*or* be's) going.

They want to sleep. → They wanted to sleep.	They are sleeping. → They are'd (*or* be'd) sleeping.
He is happy. → He is not happy.	He ate something. → He ate not something.
He is happy. → Is he happy?	He ate something. → Ate he something?

For virtually all of these patterns, she found *no* errors among the 66,000 sentences in which they could have occurred.

The three-year-old child is grammatically correct in quality, not just quantity. In earlier chapters we learned of experiments showing that children's movement rules are structure-dependent ("Ask Jabba if the boy who is unhappy is watching Mickey Mouse") and showing that their morphological systems are organized into layers of roots, stems, and inflections ("This monster likes to eat rats; what do you call him?"). Children also seem fully prepared for the Babel of languages they may face: they swiftly acquire free word order, SOV and VSO orders, rich systems of case and agreement, strings of agglutinated suffixes, ergative case marking, or whatever else their language throws at them, with no lag relative to their English-speaking counterparts. Languages with grammatical gender like French and German are the bane of the Berlitz student. In his essay "The Horrors of the German Language," Mark Twain noted that "a tree is male, its buds are female, its leaves are neuter; horses are sexless, dogs are male, cats are female—tomcats included." He translated a conversation in a German Sunday school book as follows:

GRETCHEN: Wilhelm, where is the turnip?
WILHELM: She has gone to the kitchen.
GRETCHEN: Where is the accomplished and beautiful English maiden?
WILHELM: It has gone to the opera.

But little children learning German (and other languages with gender) are not horrified; they acquire gender marking quickly, make few errors, and never use the association with maleness and femaleness as a false criterion. It is safe to say that except for constructions that are rare, used predominantly in written language, or mentally taxing even to an adult (like *The horse that the elephant tickled kissed the pig*), all languages are acquired, with equal ease, before the child turns four.

The errors children do make are rarely random garbage. Often the errors follow the logic of grammar so beautifully that the puzzle is not why the children make the errors, but why they sound like errors to adult ears at all. Let me give you two examples that I have studied in great detail.

Perhaps the most conspicuous childhood error is to overgeneralize—the child puts a regular suffix, like the plural -*s* or the past tense -*ed*, onto a word that forms its plural or its past tense in an irregular way. Thus the child says *tooths* and *mouses* and comes up with verb forms like these:

My teacher holded the baby rabbits and we patted them.
Hey, Horton heared a Who.

I finded Renée.

I love cut-upped egg.

Once upon a time a alligator was eating a dinosaur and the dinosaur was
eating the alligator and the dinosaur was eaten by the alligator and the
alligator goed kerplunk.

These forms sound wrong to us because English contains about 180 irregular
verbs like *held, heard, cut,* and *went*—many inherited from Proto-Indo-Euro-
pean!—whose past-tense forms cannot be predicted by rule but have to be memorized by rote. Morphology is organized so that whenever a verb has an idiosyncratic form listed in the mental dictionary, the regular *-ed* rule is blocked:
goed sounds ungrammatical because it is blocked by *went.* Elsewhere, the regular rule applies freely.

So why do children make this kind of error? There is a simple explanation.
Since irregular forms have to be memorized and memory is fallible, any time the
child tries to use a sentence in the past tense with an irregular verb but cannot
summon its past-tense form from memory, the regular rule fills the vacuum. If
the child wants to use the past tense of *hold* but cannot dredge up *held,* the regular rule, applying by default, marks it as *holded.* We know fallible memory is the
cause of these errors because the irregular verbs that are used the least often by
parents (*drank* and *knew,* for instance) are the ones their children err on the most;
for the more common verbs, children are correct most of the time. The same
thing happens to adults: lower-frequency, less-well-remembered irregular forms
like *trod, strove, dwelt, rent, slew,* and *smote* sound odd to modern American ears
and are likely to be regularized to *treaded, strived, dwelled, rended, slayed,* and
smited. Since it's we grownups who are forgetting the irregular past, we get to
declare that the forms with *-ed* are not errors! Indeed, over the centuries many of
these conversions have become permanent. Old English and Middle English had
about twice as many irregular verbs as Modern English; if Chaucer were here
today, he would tell you that the past tenses of *to chide, to geld, to abide,* and *to
cleave* are *chid, gelt, abode,* and *clove.* As time passes, verbs can wane in popularity, and one can imagine a time when, say, the verb *to geld* had slipped so far that
a majority of adults could have lived their lives seldom having heard its past-tense
form *gelt.* When pressed, they would have used *gelded;* the verb had become regular for them and all subsequent generations. The psychological process is no different from what happens when a young child has lived his or her brief life seldom having heard the past-tense form *built* and, when pressed, comes up with
builded. The only difference is that the child is surrounded by grownups who are
still using *built.* As the child lives longer and hears *built* more and more times, the
mental dictionary entry for *built* becomes stronger and it comes to mind more
and more readily, turning off the "add *-ed*" rule each time it does.

Here is another lovely set of examples of childhood grammatical logic, discovered by the psychologist Melissa Bowerman:

Go me to the bathroom before you go to bed.

The tiger will come and eat David and then he will be died and I won't have
a little brother any more.

I want you to take me a camel ride over your shoulders into my room.

Be a hand up your nose.

Don't giggle me!

Yawny Baby—you can push her mouth open to drink her.

These are examples of the causative rule, found in English and many other languages, which takes an intransitive verb meaning "to do something" and converts it to a transitive verb meaning "to cause to do something":

The butter melted. → Sally melted the butter.

The ball bounced. → Hiram bounced the ball.

The horse raced past the barn. → The jockey raced the horse past the barn.

The causative rule can apply to some verbs but not others; occasionally children apply it too zealously. But it is not easy, even for a linguist, to say why a ball can bounce or be bounced, and a horse can race or be raced, but a brother can only die, not be died, and a girl can only giggle, not be giggled. Only a few kinds of verbs can easily undergo the rule: verbs referring to a change of the physical state of an object, like *melt* and *break*, verbs referring to a manner of motion, like *bounce* and *slide,* and verbs referring to an accompanied locomotion, like *race* and *dance.* Other verbs, like *go* and *die,* refuse to undergo the rule in English, and verbs involving fully voluntary actions, like *cook* and *play,* refuse to undergo the rule in almost every language (and children rarely err on them). Most of children's errors in English, in fact, would be grammatical in other languages. English-speaking adults, like their children, occasionally stretch the envelope of the rule:

In 1976 the Parti Québecois began to deteriorate the health care system.

Sparkle your table with Cape Cod classic glass-ware.

Well, that decided me.

This new golf ball could obsolete many golf courses.

If she subscribes us up, she'll get a bonus.

Sunbeam whips out the holes where staling air can hide.

So both children and adults stretch the language a bit to express causation; adults are just a tiny bit more fastidious in which verbs they stretch.

The three-year-old, then, is a grammatical genius—master of most constructions, obeying rules far more often than flouting them, respecting language universals, erring in sensible, adultlike ways, and avoiding many kinds of errors altogether.

---

1 Why is the ability to identify individual phonemes (para. 3–4) such an important milestone in the process by which babies learn the sounds of their parents' language?

2 What are the main stages of language development, according to Pinker? What features define each stage? What new abilities do children demonstrate, for example, at the age of eighteen months? What significant language principle becomes evident in each of these stages that represents a new kind of ability that had not existed previously? For example, why is babbling beginning around eight months to a year so important?

3 How do the kinds of errors that children make—and more important, those they do *not* make—support Pinker's view that language is innate? For example, what is the significance of errors in which the child overgeneralizes and says "holded" instead of held or "goed" instead of went?

4 How would you characterize Pinker's tone in this article and his attitude toward his readers? Who do you think the audience is for this essay and what does Pinker want them to appreciate about the subject? Locate evidence to support your answer. (Glossary: *Audience, Tone.*)

5 What are the main stages in the baby's acquisition of language? What happens at each stage? What words and phrases does Pinker use to indicate that he is moving from one stage to the next? Does he provide sufficient detail for you to understand this process? (Glossary: *Process Analysis, Tone.*)

6 Have you ever had the occasion to observe the language-acquiring behavior of babies or children over some period of time? To what extent do your own observations support or refute Pinker's analysis?

◆ CONNECTIONS: ACQUIRING LANGUAGE

Helen Keller, "The Day Language Came Into My Life"

1. To what extent do Keller's experiences suggest that in learning language she is making use of an innate capacity of the kind described by Noam Chomsky?
2. How does Keller's experience in learning what "w-a-t-e-r" meant illustrate Susanne K. Langer's view in "Language and Thought" (Ch. 2) of the symbolic function of human language?

Eileen Simpson, "Dyslexia"

1. In what important respects does the way a dyslexic child perceives words differ from the normal difficulties children encounter in learning words, as described by Steven Pinker?
2. How does dyslexia pose at least as formidable challenge to those who suffer from it as does being illiterate (as described by Jonathan Kozol in "The Human Cost of an Illiterate Society," Ch. 8)?

Noam Chomsky, "The Language Faculty"

1. How do the discoveries about the formation of creole languages among children in Hawaii (as described by Jared Diamond) support Chomsky's theory of an innate capacity for language?
2. To what extent does the primate research described by Herbert S. Terrace in "What I Learned from Nim Chimsky" (Ch. 2) support Chomsky's belief that chimpanzees and other primates lack an innate capacity for language?

Jay Ingram, "Genespeak"

1. How do the genetically linked language mistakes Ingram describes provide specific examples of Noam Chomsky's belief that language is innate?
2. In what way does a mismatch between language and perception enter into both the genetic disabilities described by Ingram and the effects of aphasia noted by Oliver Sacks in "The President's Speech" (Ch. 3)?

Jared Diamond, "Reinventions of Human Language"

1. To what extent is the difference between human and animal languages as described by Diamond similar to the distinction drawn by Noam Chomsky?
2. What light does Diamond's discussion of the way pidgin and creole languages are formed shed on the process by which Spanglish has evolved (see Enrique Fernandez's "Salsa × 2," Ch. 6)?

Steven Pinker, "Baby Born Talking—Describes Heaven"

1. How does Pinker's analysis of the stages in children's acquisition of language illustrate the means by which innate language processes unfold (as suggested by Noam Chomsky)?
2. What dramatic breakthroughs do two- to three-year-old children make that Herbert S. Terrace ("What I Learned from Nim Chimsky," Ch. 2) was unable to observe in chimpanzees?

◆ WRITING ASSIGNMENTS FOR CHAPTER 1

1. In looking over samples of writing you have done over some period of time, how can you tell if you have begun to write more effectively? What specific changes in style and content would reflect your increasing mastery of writing skills?
2. Many of the writers in this chapter (Keller, Simpson, Diamond) structure their essays by identifying important markers or milestones in the struggle to acquire language. Drawing on your journal, try to create a chronological list that identifies significant stages or milestones in your education. Choose one of these stages, write for fifteen minutes, and expand the time period it refers to by describing the events, feelings, and associations that made it such a significant step for you.

3. In a short essay, discuss what Chomsky sees as important differences between human languages and animal "languages." Do you share his belief that it is unlikely other species possess the kind of linguistic creativity that Chomsky sees as the birthright of every human being? Why or why not?

4. Abstract and concrete language plays a crucial role in communication. Concrete words refer to actual things, instances, or experiences. By contrast, writers need abstractions to generalize about experience and discuss qualities or characteristics apart from specific objects or to sum up the qualities of whole classes of things. (Glossary: *Abstract, Concrete.*)

    Without being able to call upon abstractions with which to generalize, we would find ourselves in a situation similar to the one described by Jonathan Swift in Book III of *Gulliver's Travels* (1727). There, Gulliver, on a visit to a "school of languages," learns of a "Scheme for Entirely Abolishing All Words Whatsoever." The rationale behind this unlikely enterprise is that "since words are only names for things, it would be more convenient for all men to carry about them, such things as were necessary to express the particular business they are to discourse on." Thus, instead of speaking, citizens would carry sacks filled with the physical objects about which they wished to converse, and a "conversation" would appear as follows:

    > If a man's business be very great and of various kinds, he must be obliged in proportion to carry a greater bundle of Things upon his back unless he can afford one or two strong servants to attend him. I have often beheld two of those sages almost sinking under the weight of their packs like peddlers among us who when they meet in the streets would lay down their loads, open their sacks and hold conversation for an hour together, then put up their implements, help each other to resume their burdens and take their leave.

    How does this amusing caricature of a conversation without speech dramatize the disadvantages of being unable to use abstractions to symbolize qualities or express ideas?

5. Have you ever consciously set about trying to add new words to your vocabulary? In what context did you come across these words and what steps did you take to discover their meaning and incorporate them into your speech and writing? What is the most recent unfamiliar word you have encountered or term you felt it would be important to know?

6. Drawing on any of the articles in this chapter, in a short essay, discuss whether, in your opinion, writers are born or made. How does Fran Lebowitz use the idea of a predisposition to become a writer in the following article?

How To Tell If Your Child Is A Writer*

Your child is a writer if one or more of the following statements are applicable. Truthfulness is advised—no amount of fudging will alter the grim reality.

---

*Fran Lebowitz, "How to Tell If Your Child Is a Writer," from *The Penguin Book of Women's Humor.* Copyright 1994 by *Metropolitan Life.* Reprinted with permission from the William Morris Agency.

1. Prenatal
    A. You have morning sickness at night because the fetus finds it too distracting to work during the day.
    B. You develop a craving for answering services and typists.
    C. When your obstetrician applies his stethoscope to your abdomen he hears excuses.
2. Birth
    A. The baby is at least three weeks late because he had a lot of trouble with the ending.
    B. You are in labor for twenty-seven hours because the baby left everything until the last minute and spent an inordinate amount of time trying to grow his toes in a more interesting order.
    C. When the doctor spanks the baby the baby is not at all surprised.
    D. It is definitely a single birth because the baby has dismissed being twins as too obvious.
3. Infancy
    A. The baby refuses both breast and bottle, preferring instead Perrier with a twist in preparation for giving up drinking.
    B. The baby sleeps through the night almost immediately. Also through the day.
    C. The baby's first words, uttered at the age of four days, are "Next week."
    D. The baby uses teething as an excuse not to learn to gurgle.
    E. The baby sucks his forefinger out of a firm conviction that the thumb's been done to death.
4. Toddlerhood
    A. He rejects teddy bears as derivative.
    B. He arranges his alphabet blocks so as to spell out derisive puns on the names of others.
    C. When he is lonely he does not ask his mother for a baby brother or sister but rather for a protégé.
    D. When he reaches the age of three he considers himself a trilogy.
    E. His mother is afraid to remove his crayoned handiwork from the living room walls lest she be accused of excessive editing.
    F. When he is read his bedtime story he makes sarcastic remarks about style.
5. Childhood
    A. At age seven he begins to think about changing his name. Also his sex.
    B. He balks at going to summer camp because he is aware that there may be children there who have never heard of him.
    C. He tells his teachers that he didn't do his homework because he was blocked.
    D. He refuses to learn how to write a Friendly Letter because he knows he never will.
    E. With an eye to a possible movie deal, he insists upon changing the title of his composition "What I Did on My Summer Vacation" to the far snappier "Vacation."

F. He is thoroughly hypochondriac and is convinced that his chicken pox is really leprosy.

G. On Halloween he goes out trick-or-treating dressed as Harold Acton.

By the time this unfortunate child has reached puberty there is no longer any hope that he will outgrow being a writer and become something more appealing—like a kidnap victim.

No matter how eloquently a dog may
bark, he cannot tell you that his parents
were poor but honest.

—Bertrand Russell

THE FAR SIDE　　　By GARY LARSON

Larson, *In Search of the Far Side* © 1984, Andrews & McNeel, a
Universal Syndicate Company. Used by permission.

Communication Across Species

The driving force behind research into the linguistic capabilities of other species is the fundamental question as to what language, in its essence, really is. What unique characteristics and capabilities define whether a species possesses a capability for language? This is more than an exercise in definition, since each of the experimental studies reported in this chapter inevitably raises a follow-up question: If the behaviors described by researchers are not language, as we expect it to be manifested, why not? The emotional stakes in these investigations, although unstated, are quite powerful. Think how exciting and appealing it would be to discover that a species other than human possessed thought, reasoning, intelligence, and the ability to communicate a suspected but until this point unproved dimension of verbal capabilities, cognition, and understanding. Imagine how animals would be treated if these capabilities could be verified.

Susanne K. Langer, in "Language and Thought," draws this demarcation between language as human beings use it and the ways in which animals communicate, on the basis that human language is fundamentally symbolic. Yet, it is precisely this view of language as a symbol-manipulating ability that has been the focus of research into the hitherto uncharted communicative abilities of captive and free-living monkeys and apes. In "Wordy Apes," Donald Griffin reviews evidence that "lever pressing" and "signing" activities by chimpanzees suggests that higher primates can learn to use arbitrary symbols to communicate with humans. Several captive apes have also been taught to converse with humans using such systems as American Sign Language.

In "Conversations with a Gorilla," Francine Patterson describes one such experiment, in which a gorilla named Koko's acquisition and use of sign language led Patterson and other researchers to believe that Koko displayed evidence of linguistic capabilities. These and other early experiments raised the possibility that the traditional view that language was integral and wholly unique in defining what it meant to be human was incorrect. It is against this background that later studies such as that by Herbert S. Terrace ("What I Learned from Nim Chimsky") were conducted. Terrace's findings suggest that the language skills demonstrated by chimpanzees do not progress beyond those possessed by two- to three-year-old human children. And, perhaps most crucial, chimpanzees, in the wild, without the elaborate reinforcement schedules of human trainers, cannot develop even to this point by themselves, as human children do.

The apparently promising nature of previous research was discredited on a number of grounds—that whatever the apes did learn, it was not ASL, there was no evidence of what we call grammar, and the output of spontaneous gestures and "signing" trailed off well before showing any resemblance to the kinds of sentences children are able to produce. Vicki Hearne's experiences as a professional trainer of dogs and horses add an intriguing dimension to the question of what language is, and whether animals can possess it. Hearne believes that domestic animals are truer possessors of language than the much publicized "signing" apes. The chapter also includes a one-act play by David Ives, *Words, Words, Words,* an inventive, free-wheeling dramatization of what would happen if three monkeys (Kafka, Milton, Swift) could type into infinity. Would they produce *Hamlet?* What would they talk about?

Wordy Apes   *Donald R. Griffin*

◆ DONALD R. GRIFFIN is Professor of Animal Behavior at the Rockefeller University in New York. His original discoveries in the field of animal communication revealed the echolocation techniques of bats and the principles by which birds navigate. *Listening in the Dark,* 1958, won the Elliot Medal from the National Academy of Sciences in 1961. Griffin was awarded the Phi Beta Kappa Science Prize for *Bird Migration,* 1964. His later research examines the linguistic abilities of chimpanzees and the possibility of human communication with whales and porpoises. The results of his research first appeared in *Animal Thinking,* 1984, from which the following article is reprinted.

The question of whether chimpanzees and gorillas possess a capability to learn language has resulted in some of the most controversial and interesting experiments in linguistic research. If they can, language is not unique to the human species. Moreover, we may discover how language, in the sense of vocal communication of some complexity that refers to abstract concepts, may have originated. Of course, primates don't possess the vocal anatomy to articulate the sounds required to speak English. Therefore, researchers have taught chimpanzees to use symbols, either plastic tokens or American Sign Language, instead of words. Whether the manipulation of these symbols demonstrates any grasp of grammar or of the structure of language remains a subject of inquiry and debate. Griffin reviews the key experiments done in this field and draws some tentative conclusions.

TO CONSIDER Why is the prospect of being able to communicate with other species so appealing?

Some of the most convincing recent evidence about animal thinking stems from the pioneering work of Alan and Beatrice Gardner of the University of Nevada (1969, 1979). The Gardners had noted that wild apes seem to communicate by observing each other's behavior, and they suspected that the extremely disappointing results of previous efforts to teach captive chimpanzees to use words reflected not so much a lack of mental ability as a difficulty in controlling the vocal tract. Captive chimpanzees had previously demonstrated the ability to solve complex problems and, like dogs and horses, they had learned to respond appropriately to many spoken words. The Gardners wanted to find out whether apes could also express themselves in ways that we could understand. In the late 1960s they made a concerted effort to teach a young chimpanzee named Washoe to communicate with people using manual gestures derived from American Sign Language. This language, one of many that have been developed in different countries for use by the deaf, consists of a series of gestures or signs, each of which serves the basic function of a single word in spoken or written language. To permit fluent conversation, these signs have evolved into clearly distinguishable hand motions and finger configurations that can be performed rapidly.

Washoe was reared in an environment similar to that in which an American baby would be raised. All the people who cared for Washoe "spoke" to her only in American Sign Language, and used it exclusively when conversing with each other in her presence. They signed to Washoe, much as parents talk to babies who have not yet learned to speak, but always in sign language rather than spoken English. Washoe was encouraged to use signs to ask for what she wanted, and she was helped to do this by a procedure called molding, in which the trainer gently held the chimpanzee's hand in the correct position and moved it to form a certain sign.

3   The Gardners were far more successful than most scientists would have predicted on the basis of what was previously known about the capabilities of chimpanzees or any other nonhuman species, although Robert Yerkes had anticipated such a possibility (Bourne, 1977). During four years of training Washoe learned to use more than 130 wordlike signs and to recognize these and other signs used by her human companions. She could make the appropriate sign when shown pictures of an object, and on a few occasions she seemed to improvise new signs or new two-sign combinations spontaneously. The best example of this was Washoe's signing "water bird" when she first saw a swan. She also signed to herself when no people were present.

4   Following the Gardners' lead, several other scientists have trained other great apes to use a quasilinguistic communication system. This work has been thoroughly and critically reviewed by Ristau and Robbins (1982) and widely discussed by many others, so I will give only a brief outline here. Most of the subjects have been female chimpanzees, but two gorillas (Patterson and Linden, 1981) and one orangutan (Miles, 1983) have also been taught gestures based on American Sign Language. Because gestures are variable and require the presence of a human signer, who may influence the ape in other ways that are difficult to evaluate, two groups of laboratory scientists have developed "languages" based on mechanical devices operated by the chimpanzees. David Premack of the University of Pennsylvania used colored plastic tokens arranged in patterns resembling strings of words. His star chimpanzee pupil, named Sarah, learned to select the appropriate plastic "words" to answer correctly when the experimenter presented her with similar chips arranged to form simple questions. Questions such as "What is the color of—?" were answered correctly about familiar objects when the objects were replaced by their plastic symbols, even if the colors were different from those of the objects they represented. Sarah thus learned to answer questions about *represented* objects (reviewed by Premack, 1976; and Premack and Premack, 1983). This type of communication has the property of displacement, as in the case of the honeybee dances.

5   In another ambitious project at the Yerkes Laboratory of Emory University, Duane Rumbaugh, Sue Savage-Rumbaugh, and their colleagues have used backlighted keys on a keyboard (Rumbaugh, 1977; Savage-Rumbaugh, Rumbaugh, and Boysen, 1980). Their chimpanzee subjects have learned to press the appropriate keys to communicate simple desires and answer simple questions. In some significant recent studies, two young male chimpanzees, Sherman and Austin, have not only learned to use simple tools to obtain food or toys but have learned to employ the keyboard to ask each other to hand over a certain type of tool. These investigations, as well as extensions of the Gardners' original studies using words derived from American Sign Language, have been extensively reviewed (Ristau and Robbins, 1982) and discussed by Patterson and Linden (1981) and Terrace (1979). Despite disagreement about many aspects of this work, almost everyone concerned agrees that the captive apes have learned, at the very least,

to make simple requests and to answer simple questions through these word-like gestures or mechanical devices.

A heated debate has raged about the extent to which such learned communication resembles human language. Sebeok and Umiker-Sebeok (1980) and Sebeok and Rosenthal (1981) have argued vehemently that the whole business is merely wishful and mistaken reading into the ape's behavior of much more than is really there. They stress that apes are very clever at learning to do what gets them food, praise, social companionship, or other things they want and enjoy. They believe that insufficiently critical scientists have overinterpreted the behavior of their charges and that the apes have really learned only something like: "If I do this she will give me candy," or "If I do that she will play with me," and so forth. They also believe that the apes may be reacting to unintentional signals from the experimenters and that the interpretations have involved what behavioral scientists call "Clever Hans errors." This term refers to a trained horse in the early 1900s that learned to count out answers to arithmetical questions by tapping with his foot. For instance if shown 4×4 written on a slate board, the horse would tap sixteen times. More careful studies showed that Hans could solve such problems only in the presence of a person who knew the answer. The person would inadvertently nod or make other small motions in time with Hans' tapping and would stop when the right number had been reached. Hans had learned to perceive this unintentional communication, not the arithmetic. The Sebeoks argue that Washoe and her successors have learned, not how to communicate with gestural words, but rather how to watch for signs of approval or disapproval from their human companions and to do what is expected. 6

Although students of animal behavior must constantly guard against such errors, many of the experiments described above included careful controls that seem to have ruled out this explanation of all the languagelike communication learned by Washoe and her successors. In many cases the ape's vocabulary was tested by having one person present a series of pictures that the animal was required to name, while a different person, who could not see the pictures, judged what sign Washoe used in response. Furthermore the sheer number of signs that the apes employed correctly would require a far more complex sort of Clever Hans error than an animal's simple noticing that a person has stopped making small-scale counting motions.

Another criticism of the ape language studies has been advanced by Terrace and colleagues (1979). Terrace, aided by numerous assistants, taught a young male chimpanzee named Nim Chimsky to use about 125 signs over a forty-five-month period. He agrees that Nim, like Washoe and several other language-trained apes, did indeed learn to use these gestures to request objects or actions he wanted and that Nim could use some of them to answer simple questions. But when Terrace analyzed videotapes of Nim exchanging signs with his trainers, he was disappointed to find that many of Nim's "utterances" were copies of what his human companion had just signed. This is scarcely surprising, inasmuch as his trainers had encouraged him to repeat signs throughout his training. 8

Terrace and his colleagues also concluded that Nim showed no ability to combine more than two signs into meaningful combinations and that his sign- 9 ing never employed even the simplest form of rule-guided sentences. It is not at all clear, however, whether Nim's training provided much encouragement to develop grammatical sentences. In any event, he did not do so, and Terrace doubts whether any of the other signing apes have displayed such a capability. But Miles (1983) reports that her orangutan Chantek's use of gestural signs resembled the speech of young children more closely than Nim's, and Patterson believes that her gorilla Koko follows some rudimentary rules in the sequence of her signs. Yet even on the most liberal interpretation there remains a large gap between the signing of these trained apes and the speech of children who have vocabularies of approximately the same size. The children tend to use longer strings of words, and the third or later words add important meaning to the first two. In contrast, Nim and other language-trained apes seem much more likely to repeat signs or add ones that do not seem, to us at least, to change the basic meaning of a two-sign utterance. For instance, the following is one of the longer utterances reported for the gorilla Koko: "Please milk please me like drink apple bottle"; and from Nim, "Give orange me give eat orange give me eat orange give me you." But grammatical or not, there is no doubt what Koko and Nim were asking for. To quote Descartes and Chomsky (1966), "*The word is the sole sign and certain mark of the presence of thought.*" Grammar adds economy, refinement, and scope to human language, but words are basic. Words without grammar are adequate though limited, but there is no grammar without words. And it is clear that Washoe and her successors use the equivalent of words to convey simple thoughts.

10   The enormous versatility of human language depends not only on large vocabularies of words known to both speakers and listeners but on mutually understood rules for combining them to convey additional meaning. George A. Miller (1967) has used the term "combinatorial productivity" for this extremely powerful attribute of human language. By combining words in particular ways we produce new messages logically and economically. If we had to invent a new word to convey the meaning of each phrase and sentence, the required vocabulary would soon exceed the capacity of even one most proficient human brains. But once a child learns a few words he can rapidly increase their effectiveness by combining them in new messages in accordance with the language's rules designating which word stands for actor or object, which are modifiers, and so forth.

11   Signing apes so far have made very little progress in combinatorial productivity, although some of their two-sign combinations seem to conform to simple rules. The natural communication systems of other animals make no use of combinatorial productivity, as far as we know. But the investigation of animal communication has barely begun, especially as a source of evidence about animal thoughts. What has emerged so far has greatly exceeded the prior expectations of scientists; we may be seeing only the tip of yet another iceberg. Extrapolation of scientific discovery is an uncertain business at best, but the momentum of discovery in this area does not seem to be slackening. The apparent lack of any significant combinatorial productivity in the signing of Washoe and her successors might turn out be a temporary lull in a truly revolutionary development, which

began only about fifteen years ago. Perhaps improved methods of investigation and training will lead to more convincing evidence of communicative versatility.

One relevant aspect of all the ape-language studies to date is that the native language of all the investigators has been English, and the signs taught to apes have been derived from American Sign Language. In English, word order is used to indicate actor or object, principal noun or modifying adjective, and many other rule-guided relationships. But this is very atypical; most other human languages rely much more on inflections or modifications of principal words to indicate grammatical relationships. No one seems to have inquired whether signing apes or naturally communicating animals might vary their signals in minor ways to communicate that a particular sign is meant to designate, for instance, the actor rather than the object. This would be a difficult inquiry, because the signals vary for many reasons, and only a laborious analysis of an extensive series of motion pictures or videotapes would disclose whether there were many consistent differences comparable to those conveyed by inflections of words in human speech.

Regardless of these controversies, there seems no doubt that through gestures or manipulation of token or keyboards apes can learn to communicate to their human companions a reasonable range of simple thoughts and desires. They also can convey emotional feelings, although an ape does not need elaborate gestures or other forms of symbolic communication to inform a sensitive human companion that it is afraid or hungry. What the artificial signals add to emotional signaling is the possibility of communicating about specific objects and events, even when these are not part of the immediate situation. Furthermore, when Washoe or any other trained ape signs that she wants a certain food, she must thinking about that food or about its taste or odor. We cannot be certain just what the signing ape is thinking, but the content of her thought must include at least some feature of the object or event designated by the sign she has learned to use. For instance, the Gardners taught Washoe to use a sign that meant flower, to them. But Washoe used it not only for flowers but for pipe tobacco and kitchen fumes. To her it apparently meant smells. Washoe may have been thinking about smells when she used the sign, rather than about the visual properties of colored flowers, but she was certainly thinking about something that overlapped it with the properties conveyed by the word *flower* as we use it.

The major significance of the research begun by the Gardners is its confirmation that our closest animal relatives are quite capable of varied thoughts as well as emotions. Many highly significant questions flow from this simple fact. Do apes communicate naturally with the versatility they have demonstrated in the various sorts of languagelike behavior that people have taught them? One approach is to ask whether apes that have learned to use signs more or less as we use single words employ them to communicate with each other. This is being investigated by studying signing apes that have abundant opportunity to interact with each other. Few results have been reported so far, although some signing does seem to be directed to other apes as well as to human companions. When scientists have been looking for something, and when we hear little or nothing about the results, we conclude that nothing important has been discovered. But the lack of results may only mean that chimpanzees can communicate perfectly well without signs. The subject obviously requires further investigation, and we may soon hear about new and interesting developments.

REFERENCES

Bourne, G. H., ed. *Progress in ape research.* New York: Academic Press. 1977.

Chomsky, N. *Cartesian linguistics.* New York: Harper and Row. 1966.

Gardner, R. A., and B. T. Gardner. Teaching sign language to a chimpanzee. *Science* 165:664–672. 1969.

Gardner, R. A., and B. T. Gardner. Two comparative psychologists look at language acquisition. In *Children's language,* ed. K. E. Nelson. New York: Halstead. 1979.

Miles, H. L. Apes and language: The search for communicative competence. In *Language in primates: Implications for linguistics, anthropology, psychology, and philosophy,* ed. J. de Luce and H. T. Wilder. New York: Springer. 1983.

Miller, G. A. *The psychology of communication.* New York: Basic Books. 1967.

Patterson, F. G., and E. Linden. *The education of Koko.* New York: Holt, Rinehart and Winston. 1981.

Premack, D. *Intelligence in ape and man.* Hillsdale, N. J.: Erlbaum. 1976.

Premack, D., and A. J. Premack. *The mind of an ape.* New York: Norton. 1983.

Ristau, C. A., and D. Robbins. Language in the great apes: A critical review. *Advances in Study of Behavior* 12:142–225. 1982.

Rumbaugh, D. M. *Language learning by a chimpanzee: The Lana Project.* New York: Academic Press. 1977.

Savage-Rumbaugh, E. S., D. M. Rumbaugh, and S. Boysen. Do apes use language? *Amer. Sci.* 68:49–61. 1980.

Sebeok, T. A., and R. Rosenthal. The Clever Hans phenomenon: Communication with horses, whales, apes, and people. *Ann. N. Y. Acad. Sci.* 364:1–311. 1981.

Sebeok, T. A., and J. Umiker-Sebeok, eds. *Speaking of apes, a critical anthology of two-way communication with man.* New York: Plenum. 1980.

Terrace, H. S. *Nim.* New York: Knopf. 1979.

Terrace, H. S., L. A. Petitto, and T. G. Bever. Can an ape create a sentence? *Science* 208:891–902. 1979.

1 How is the way particular experiments were designed so crucial in being able to discover whether chimpanzees were capable of using language to communicate with humans? For example, what was the significance of the chimpanzee Sarah's ability (para. 4) to answer questions about familiar objects when the objects were replaced by their plastic symbols? In your view, do these experiments really shed light on how to tell whether an animal possesses language capability?

2 How were experiments with Washoe redesigned (para. 7) to eliminate the so-called Clever Hans error that called into question the results of an earlier experiment?

3 What significance does Griffin derive from the fact that children can routinely combine longer strings of words than can apes with comparable size signing vocabularies?

4 How does Griffin organize his essay? Are the topics presented in an order that helps the reader make sense of the subject? How does he use transitions to move from one idea to the next? (Glossary: *Organization, Transitions.*)

5 To what extent does Griffin try to find a common ground on which all sides can agree despite their differences on the question of whether primates can learn to communicate? Where does he point out problems with dissenting views? Does his willingness to do this enhance the credibility of his case? What range of sources does Griffin draw upon in clarifying what is at stake in the issue? Which piece of evidence did you find the most dramatic in making his argument more persuasive? (Glossary: *Argument.*)

6 How does Griffin organize his summary of research around the question of what criteria should be used and what evidence should be accepted as proof of the ability of primates to communicate with humans? How would it be possible to determine whether a response was evidence of true communication or simply imitative behavior that could be misinterpreted by overly enthusiastic researchers?

Conversations with a Gorilla

Francine Patterson

◆ FRANCINE PATTERSON is the author of books and articles about Koko the gorilla, an animal she trained since the ape was one year old. *The Education of Koko* (1981), written with Eugene Linden, chronicles how Koko learned to communicate with humans. Koko was taught sign language and was trained to type on a computer linked to a voice synthesizer. Patterson believes that Koko is able to form abstract concepts and to rhyme, and is capable of deception. Her publications include *Koko's Kitten* (1985), *Koko's Story* (1987), and numerous articles in the *American Journal of Primatology* and the *American Journal of Psychology*. The following article is taken from *Reader's Digest* (March 1979).

With Koko, investigations as to whether primates might be capable of learning language entered a new phase. Not only did Koko appear to have learned hundreds of words in American Sign Language, but, more significantly, she seemed to be capable of having conversations with her trainer, Dr. Patterson. For exam-

---

Francine Patterson, "Conversations with a Gorilla," from *National Geographic*. Copyright 1979. Reprinted with permission from the author.

ple, Koko would express regret for having bitten or scratched her; ask for her companion gorilla, Mike; blame the assistant for breaking the kitchen sink when she had done it herself; and invent novel sign combinations like "white tiger" for "zebra" (as reported by Patterson in her article with R. Cohn, "Language Acquisition by a Lowland Gorilla," in *Word*. Vol. 41, 1990, pp. 97–143). The following article was written in 1979, when Koko was six and a half years old.

TO CONSIDER   Think about what it would be like to really communicate with an animal who was a pet of yours.

K OKO IS A SEVEN-YEAR-OLD, 130 pound "talking" gorilla. She is the focus of my career as a developmental psychologist, and also has become a dear friend. Through mastery of sign language—the familiar hand speech of the deaf—Koko has made us aware that her breed is bright, and shares sensitivities commonly held to be the prerogative of people.

Take Koko's touching empathy toward fellow animals. Seeing a horse with a bit in its mouth, she signed, "Horse sad." When asked why sad, she signed, "Teeth." Shown a photo of the famous albino gorilla Snowflake struggling against having a bath, Koko, who also hates baths, signed, "Me cry there," while pointing at the picture.

Koko responds to more complicated motivations, too. She loves an argument, is not averse to trading insults, and will lie her way out of a jam. After $6\frac{1}{2}$ years of working with her, I've come to cherish her lies, relish her arguments and look forward to her insults. What makes all this awesome is that, traditionally, such behavior has been considered uniquely human; yet here is a gorilla that uses—and exploits—language the way we do.

Fireworks-Child. When I enrolled at Stanford University, Calif., in 1970 as a graduate student, I chose nonhuman primates for my research. In 1971, psychologists R. Allen and Beatrice Gardner came to speak. They had taught Washoe, a female chimpanzee, American Sign Language—Ameslan—used by an estimated 200,000 deaf Americans. The language consists of gestures, each of which signifies a word or idea. By 1970, Washoe had acquired 132 expressive signs and used them in two-way communication; she understood many more.

Other experimenters had established communication with individual chimps who spoke and were spoken to through plastic symbols, or through statements typed out on an arbitrarily encoded keyboard at a computer console. The weight of all these experiments helped erode doubts that an ape could be capable of language.

I had decided that I too would like to become involved in language research with the chimpanzee—pursuing the ultimate question with the ultimate animal. But then one day at the gorilla grotto of the San Francisco Zoo, my eyes were drawn to a tiny gorilla infant clinging tenaciously to her mother. The infant was named Hanabi-Ko, Japanese for Fireworks-Child (she was born on the Fourth of July), but she was nicknamed Koko. Brashly I asked the zoo director if I might try to teach Koko sign language. He said no, and quite rightly. She was only three months old, and could not be separated from her mother. Undaunted, I began to learn Ameslan. Nine months later, in July 1972, my renewed request to work with and care for Koko was accepted because, ailing, she had been removed from the gorilla group and needed a surrogate mother.

Gorillas are tragically misunderstood. In fact exceedingly shy, placid and unaggressive, they are conceived to be ferocious, slavering man-killers. In a poll of British schoolchildren, gorillas ranked with rats, snakes and spiders among the least liked animals.

On our first meeting, Koko did nothing to advance the cause of gorilla public relations. The tiny 20-pounder bit me on the leg. But I was undeterred. Today, people often ask if I am worried about dealing with her when she reaches full growth, perhaps 250 pounds. The answer is a qualified no—though at 130 pounds she already outweighs me and is astonishingly strong. While many captive chimpanzees become difficult to work with as they mature, gorillas seem to be of quite a different temperament.

To get Koko to make signs, I used the "molding" technique: shaping her hands into the proper sign for an activity or an object while in its presence. As the animal comes to associate the hand movement and its meaning, the teacher gradually loosens hold until the animal is making the sign by itself. At first, every time I would take Koko's hands, she would try to bite me.

Another early problem at the zoo was distraction. So it was with great relief that I moved Koko into her own mobile home, today situated on the Stanford University campus. There, from the start, I (and my assistants) have recorded Koko's casual signing, conversations and self-directed utterances. I have also recorded her signing on videotape and film.

Star's Day. Vocabulary development is one of the best indexes of human intelligence. Koko learned the signs for "*drink*" and "*more*" within a few weeks, and over the first year and a half acquired about one new sign every month. Her current working vocabulary—signs she uses regularly and appropriately—stands at about 375, and includes *airplane, belly button, lollipop, friend* and *stethoscope.*

The mobile home's living room became Koko's nursery and training playroom with the installation of her metal sleeping box (she nests on two plush rugs draped over a motorcycle tire), an exercise bar and a trapeze. After our second gorilla, a $3\frac{1}{2}$-year-old male named Michael, arrived in September 1976, we transformed the master bedroom into a second training room. Two solid-wood doors separate Michael's domain from Koko's. With these doors open, one large common play area is formed.

Koko rises at 8 or 8:30 a.m. Following a breakfast of cereal or raisin-thick rice bread with milk and fruit, she helps clean her room. Then, most mornings, Koko sits at an electric-typewriter keyboard for a 30-minute lesson. Wearying of this, she asks me, "Have Mike in." They play for an hour or so. Then comes sign-language instruction.

Koko has a light meal at 1 p.m. and a sandwich (usually peanut butter and jam) at 2 or 2:30. Some days I take Koko and Mike out for a walk or a drive in my car. Koko will occasionally backseat drive—signing "Go there" (so we won't go home) or "Hurry go drink" (indicating a vending machine).

Dinner at 5 consists almost exclusively of fresh vegetables, like corn on the cob and tomatoes. If Koko cleans her plate, she gets dessert— Jell-O, dried fruits, a cookie, or cheese and a cracker. After dinner she may relax with a book or magazine (fingering a picture, she signs, "There flower"), nest with her blankets ("That soft"), or play with her dolls ("That ear," placing the doll's ear against her own).

Following tooth-brushing and application of baby oil, both gorillas settle down about 7 with a "night dish"—a fruit treat—to make bedtime more pleasant. On most nights Koko cries when I leave her.

Learning Log. From the start I have monitored Koko's performance on human intelligence tests. Her I.Q. scores have ranged from 84 to 95, only slightly below the average for a human child—despite the cultural bias in the tests. For instance, one quiz asked the child to pick where he would run to shelter from the rain: a hat, spoon, tree or house. Koko naturally chose tree. But rules required that I record the response as an error.

Other "errors" offer insight into the personality of an adolescent gorilla. One associate saw Koko signing, "That red," as she built a nest out of a white towel. Koko insisted it was red—"red, red, *red*"—and finally held up a minute speck of red lint clinging to the towel. Koko was grinning.

Sometimes she seems to relish responding exactly opposite to what I ask her to do. One associate got her to stop breaking plastic spoons by signing, "Good break them." Whereupon Koko stopped bending them and started kissing them. She knows when she is misbehaving. Once when I became irritated, she quite accurately described herself as a "stubborn devil."

She reserves an equally expressive lexicon of insults—"rotten stink" and "bird" or "nut"—for others who are unmannerly. She has referred to me as "You toilet dirty devil" during a fit of pique.

Evidence strongly suggests that Koko expresses a make-believe capacity similar to humans'. At about age 5 she discovered the value of the lie. My assistant Kate Mann was with Koko when the gorilla, then 90 pounds, plumped down on the trailer's kitchen sink and it separated from its frame. Later, when I asked Koko if she broke the sink, she signed, "Kate there bad," pointing to the sink. (Koko couldn't know, of course, that the deception would be obvious to me.)

Some of Koko's lies are startlingly ingenious. While I was busy writing, she snatched up a red crayon and began chewing on it. "You're not eating that crayon, are you?" I asked. Koko signed, "Lip," and began moving the crayon first across her upper, then her lower lip as if applying lipstick.

Bilingual! Today there is a new challenge for Koko. She understands and responds to hundreds of spoken words. (To avoid her eavesdropping, we have to spell out words like c-a-n-d-y and g-u-m. She makes attempts to talk, and has even—on her own—tried using the phone.) Now Prof. Patrick Suppes and his colleagues at Stanford's Institute for Mathematical Studies in the Social Sciences have designed a keyboard-computer linkup that permits Koko to talk through a speech synthesizer. A major objective is to evaluate the gorilla's sense of spoken word order.

When she presses keys on an electric-typewriter keyboard, spoken words are produced. Besides letters and numbers, the keys are painted with simple geometric patterns representing words. If I place, say, an apple before Koko, she may push the keys for "want," "apple," "eat" with one hand—while simultaneously making the signs with the other—and the computer will vocalize her message. An ambidextrous and bilingual gorilla!

Koko has taken it upon herself to coach Michael's execution of certain signs. But he doesn't always do it fast enough. Once last year he was fumbling for the right sign to convince us to let him in to play with Koko. After Mike signed "Out," Koko, waiting in her own room, began to get impatient. She signed through the wire mesh, "Mike think hurry." When it finally dawned on him to say "Koko," a relieved Koko signed, "Good know Mike," and then, "In Mike."

Now the godmother of two gorillas, I weigh my responsibilities to this threatened species. I have set up the Gorilla Foundation* to provide financial support for the project and protect the future of Koko and Michael. My fondest hope is to establish them in a place set aside for the study of gorillas and for their preservation in circumstances of relative freedom.

Koko grows ever more flexible and sophisticated in communication. Today she is even defining objects. "What do you do with a stove?" I ask her. "Cook with." She perceives right and wrong, but is touchy about blame. She tries to steal grapes from a bowl. I scold her: "Don't be such a pig. Be polite. Ask me. Stealing is wrong, wrong, wrong, like biting and hurting is wrong."

Then I ask, "What do *I* do that's wrong?" Koko says, "Break things, lie, tell me 'polite' [when I'm] hungry pig."

Finally, Koko is learning self-esteem. A reporter asks about her as a person. I turn to Koko: "Are you animal or person?"

Koko's instant response: "Fine animal gorilla."

―――――――――――――

1 What criteria does Patterson apply as a standard by which to measure the existence of a capacity for language in Koko? Is it simply Koko's proficiency in mastering a repertoire of signs that has convinced Patterson that Koko is really communicating with her? Why, for example, would a phenomenon like Koko's capacity to insult, deceive, lie, or shift blame be so important in Patterson's evaluation?

2 Do any of the experiments described by Patterson, or the criteria used to interpret the results, call into question the methodology researchers in this field use?

―――――――――――――

*Readers can help the foundation and receive its newsletter by sending a tax-deductible contribution of $10 to the Gorilla Foundation, P.O. Box 3002, Stanford, Calif. 94305.

3 Which of the incidents described by Patterson seems the most persuasive to you in suggesting Koko's linguistic capabilities? (You may wish to consult Koko's website, established in March 1998 on America OnLine, where Koko is available for conversations: www.gorilla.org.)

4 What, in your view, is the purpose of Patterson's essay? That is, what objective does she wish to achieve in terms of its effect on the reader? How are the rhetorical strategies she uses designed to help her reach this objective? For example, what is the tone of Patterson's essay, as revealed in such comments as "Koko . . . has become a dear friend" in para. 1? (Glossary: Audience, Purpose, Tone.)

5 Francine Patterson presents behavioral evidence that Koko is capable of deception. Why would the capacity to deceive be useful in suggesting a higher level of communication?

What I Learned from Nim Chimsky

Herbert S. Terrace

◆ HERBERT S. TERRACE is a psychologist and educator who has taught at Harvard and currently teaches at Columbia University. He is the author of a number of influential studies on animal behavior, in particular, his pioneering work on the chimpanzee Nim. Terrace's books include *Individual Learning Systems* (1971), *NIM* (1979), and *Animal Cognition* (1983). He has served as the editor of the journal *Human Behavior.*

Terrace's research at Columbia University in 1979 (undertaken initially to refute Noam Chomsky's assertion that only humans possess a "language faculty") working with a chimpanzee he named Neam Chimsky (later abbreviated to Nim) was based on an immense amount of data he gathered from taping and analyzing the 20,000 sequences of signs Nim produced in American Sign Language. In contrast to Francine Patterson's experiences of conversing with her gorilla, Koko, Terrace found that Nim could not contribute to an ongoing exchange, could not progress beyond a minimum two-sign message, and never referred to anything or anyone outside of himself other than food. On this basis, Terrace concluded that Nim was incapable of communicating or producing what researchers could identify as true language. Critics of Terrace's research have raised the question as to what behavior a chimpanzee would have to exhibit in order to be judged capable of acquiring language.

TO CONSIDER How much effort would you be willing to make to teach someone whose capacity to learn was very limited? Should more effort be made if the subject were a chimpanzee rather than a human being?

The main goal of Project Nim was to provide information about a chimpanzee's ability to create a sentence. As far as I know, our corpus of Nim's combinations is unique in studies of sign language in apes. It is without parallel in studies of language learning by either deaf or speaking children. The regularities in our corpus that were noted before Nim was returned to Oklahoma gave me reason to believe that Nim was creating primitive sentences. Our intensive post-Oklahoma effort at data analysis had hardly begun, however, when I began to doubt that Nim's combinations were legitimate sentences.

One of the first facts that troubled me was the absence of any increase in the length of Nim's utterances. During the last two years in which Nim lived in New York, the average length of his utterances fluctuated between 1.1 and 1.6 signs. That state of affairs characterizes the *beginning* of a child's development in combining words. As a child gets older, the average length of its utterances increases steadily. This is true both of children with normal hearing and of deaf children who sign. Having learned to make utterances relating a subject and a verb (such as "Daddy eats") and utterances relating a verb and an object (such as "eats breakfast") the child apparently learns to link them into longer utterances relating the subject, verb, and object (such as "Daddy eats breakfast"). Later, the child learns to elaborate that utterance into statements such as "Daddy didn't eat breakfast" or "When will Daddy eat breakfast?" and goes on to still further elaborations. Despite the steady increase in the size of Nim's vocabulary, the mean length of his utterances did not increase. Apparently, utterances whose average length was 1.5 signs were long enough to express the meanings that Nim wanted to communicate.

Even though the mean length of Nim's utterances did not exceed 1.6, some of his utterances were very long. Yet they were as a rule very repetitious. Consider, for example, the longest utterance Nim was observed to make, an utterance containing 16 signs: *give orange me give eat orange me eat orange give me eat orange give me you.* Whereas a child's longer utterances expand the meaning of shorter utterances, this one does not. Further, the maximum length of a child's utterance is related very reliably to its average length. Nim's longer utterances neither added new information, nor was the maximum length of his utterances related to their average length.

Our corpus of Nim's combinations allowed us to observe in detail the nature of his progression from two- to three-sign combinations. Table 1 shows the twenty-five most frequent two- and three-sign combinations, and their absolute frequencies. From a lexical point of view, a comparison of these combinations reveals that the topics of Nim's three-sign combinations overlapped considerably with the topics of his two-sign combinations. His three-sign combinations do not, however, provide new information. Consider, for example, Nim's most frequent two- and three-sign combinations: *play me* and *play me Nim*. Adding *Nim* to *play me* is simply redundant. A further complication is revealed when one realizes that the three-sign combination *play me Nim* may have been derived by adding the single sign, *play,* to Nim's second most frequent two-sign combination, *me Nim*. There is no obvious way to choose between the two derivations of *play me Nim* suggested by Table 1: *play me + Nim* and *play + me Nim*. Similar alternatives present themselves when trying to derive the other three-sign combinations shown in Table 1.

The overlap between Nim's most frequent two- and three-sign combinations is apparent in other comparisons as well. Eighteen of Nim's twenty-five most frequent two-sign combinations can be seen in his twenty-five most frequent three-sign combinations, in virtually the same order in which they appear in his two-sign combinations. A striking similarity emerges between Nim's two- and three-sign combinations if one considers only the signs and not their order of occurrence. All but five of the signs that appear in Nim's twenty-five most frequent two-sign combinations appear in his twenty-five most frequent three-sign combinations. The five exceptions are *gum, tea, sorry, in,* and *pants.* The combi-

TABLE 1. Most Frequent Two- and Three-Sign Combinations

TWO-SIGN COMBINATIONS	FREQUENCY	THREE-SIGN COMBINATIONS	FREQUENCY
play me	375	play me Nim	81
me Nim	328	eat me Nim	48
tickle me	316	eat Nim eat	46
eat Nim	302	tickle me Nim	44
more eat	287	grape eat Nim	37
me eat	237	banana Nim eat	33
Nim eat	209	Nim me eat	27
finish hug	187	banana eat Nim	26
drink Nim	143	eat me eat	22
more tickle	136	me Nim eat	21
sorry hug	123	hug me Nim	20
tickle Nim	107	yogurt Nim eat	20
hug Nim	106	me more eat	19
more drink	99	more eat Nim	19
eat drink	98	finish hug Nim	18
banana me	97	banana me eat	17
Nim me	89	Nim eat Nim	17
sweet Nim	85	tickle me tickle	17
me play	81	apple me eat	15
gum eat	79	eat Nim me	15
tea drink	77	give me eat	15
grape eat	74	nut Nim nut	15
hug me	74	drink me Nim	14
banana Nim	73	hug Nim hug	14
in pants	70	play me play	14
		sweet Nim sweet	14

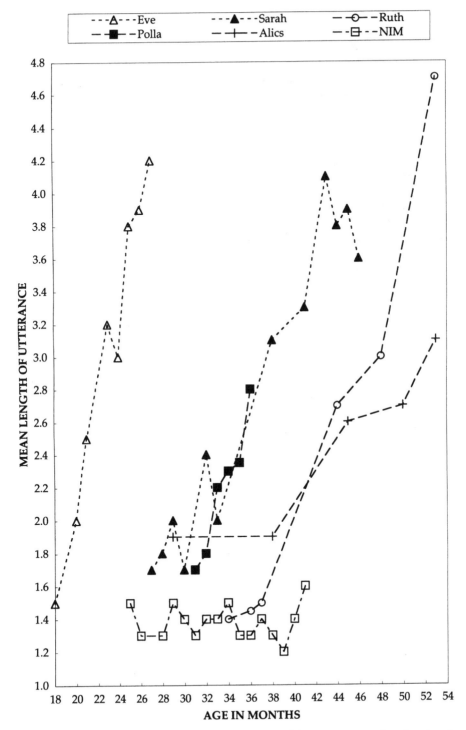

Unlike those of the children in this sample, Nim's utterances did not increase significantly in length as he grew older.

nation *in pants* was the least frequent two-sign combination shown in Table 1. It occurred mainly during dressing and after trips to the toilet.

The repetition of the same sign, as for example in *eat Nim eat* and *nut Nim nut*, is another redundant feature of Nim's three-sign combinations. In producing a three-sign combination, it appears that Nim was simply adding emphasis. Nim's four-sign combinations reveal a similar picture. Table 2 shows all four-sign combinations whose frequency is equal to or greater than three. Fifteen of the twenty-one types of four-sign combinations shown in Table 2 contain repetitions of some signs, for example, *eat banana Nim eat* and *grape eat Nim eat*. If *me* and *Nim* are equated, on the grounds that they mean the same thing, twenty of the twenty-one combinations types shown in Table 2 repeat the same sign. That leaves but one combination type, *me eat drink more,* which contains four distinctly different signs. Seven of the twenty-one combinations shown in Table 2 repeat two-sign combinations in the same order, for example, *drink Nim drink Nim* and *me gum me gum.*

The lack of growth of the length of Nim's utterances and the numerous repetitions of signs in his longer utterances distinguish Nim's use of language from that of a child. These lexical features of Nim's signing suggest a considerably weaker view of his linguistic competence than does the evidence I noted in Chapter II. In reviewing our semantic analysis I became skeptical about its validity for two reasons. One problem is the small number of signs used to express particular semantic roles. Ninety percent of the combinations interpreted as an expression of location involved the sign *point.* A similar state of affairs exists in the case of combinations interpreted as expressions of recurrence. That role was represented exclusively by *more.* In combinations presumed to relate an agent and an object or an object and a beneficiary, one would expect a broad range of examples—*Nim, me, you,* and names of other animate beings. However, 99 percent of the beneficiaries in utterances judged to be object-beneficiary combina-

TABLE 2. Most Frequent Four-Sign Combinations

FOUR-SIGN COMBINATIONS	FREQUENCY	FOUR-SIGN COMBINATIONS	FREQUENCY
eat drink eat drink	15	drink eat me Nim	3
eat Nim eat Nim	7	eat grape eat Nim	3
banana Nim banana Nim	5	eat me Nim drink	3
drink Nim drink Nim	5	grape eat me Nim	3
banana eat me Nim	4	me eat drink more	3
banana me eat banana	4	me eat me eat	3
banana me Nim me	4	me gum me gum	3
grape eat Nim eat	4	me Nim eat me	3
Nim eat Nim eat	4	Nim me Nim me	3
play me Nim play	4	tickle me Nim play	3
drink eat drink eat	3		

tions were *Nim* and *me,* and 76 percent of the agents in utterances judged to be agent-object combinations were *you.* There were other examples showing the limited range of signs used by Nim to express different semantic categories. This is in contrast to the results of semantic analyses of children's utterances that normally reveal a greater richness of words within different semantic categories, and an orderly progress toward greater complexity. The issue of progress is irrelevant in the case of Nim's combinations because the number of his utterances containing three or more signs was too small to warrant a serious semantic analysis.

The other reason for doubting the conclusion that Nim's two-sign combinations were simple sentences came from a detailed analysis of videotapes. These tapes provided me with an invaluable opportunity to analyze, with the wisdom of hindsight, just about any aspect of Nim's signing. The importance of this becomes clear when one recalls that the data upon which the distributional analyses were based came solely from teachers' reports. Whatever the teacher missed about Nim's signing was missed forever. The videotapes, on the other hand, captured it all.

It was while looking at playbacks of videotapes that I realized I had missed an important aspect of the context of Nim's signs. When the other teachers and I were working with Nim and recording what he signed, our attention had always been riveted on his signing. We had paid too little attention to what *we* signed to Nim. It is true that teachers were attentive to what they signed in determining whether Nim satisfied our criterion for learning a sign, a criterion that required that Nim make a particular sign without the teacher having made it during his or her prior utterance. But we did not ask systematically how often Nim's utterances contained signs that we had just signed to him. We also did not consider how often Nim signed if his teacher hadn't first signed to him. I was aware that Nim often signed spontaneously to request and describe things, but until we began to glean that information from our videotapes we could only guess how frequently Nim signed spontaneously.

Studies of language development in children, referred to as discourse analyses, have revealed a number of systematic relationships between a child's utterances and those of its parents. Initially, it is often the parent who starts the conversation. One study estimated that 70 percent of a child's utterances were occasioned by something the parent had said. In most instances the child did not reply by simply repeating what the parent had said but added to the parent's utterance or created a new one from totally different words. Less than 20 percent of a child's utterances were *imitations* of its parent's utterance. The remainder of the child's replies were either elaborations of the parent's utterance or totally novel but relevant utterances.

Our initial analysis of the relationship between Nim's utterances and those of his teachers showed that Nim's were more dependent upon what his teachers signed than a child's are dependent on the words of its parents. In order to characterize the relationship between Nim's utterances and those of a child, we assigned each of Nim's utterances to one of five categories: spontaneous, imitation, reduction, expansion, or novel. A spontaneous utterance was one that was not preceded by a teacher's utterance. All of the remaining categories included utterances that were preceded by a teacher's utterance. Imitations were exact reproductions of his teacher's signs. Reductions were imitative utterances that omitted some of the teacher's signs. An expansion included some of the teacher's signs and some new signs added by Nim. A novel utterance was one in which there was no overlap between the signs of a teacher's utterance and Nim's response. . . .

During Nim's last year in New York only 10 percent of his videotaped utterances were spontaneous. Approximately 40 percent were imitations or reductions. If the conversations we videotaped and transcribed were representative of the thousands of conversations from which our corpus was derived—and I have no reason to believe that they were not—I must conclude that Nim's utterances were less spontaneous and less original than those of a child. To a much larger extent than a child's, Nim's utterances were variations of the signs contained in his teacher's prior utterance. He was much less likely than a child to add new information to a conversation in his replies. (I should note that it would be more valid to compare Nim with a deaf child than with a speaking child. But until more data become available showing how deaf children learn to sign, the only way to compare Nim's use of language with that of a child's is to use data obtained from speaking children. The limited data that is available show no major differences in language acquisition by hearing children who speak and deaf children who sign.). . .

I must therefore conclude—though reluctantly—that until it is possible to defeat *all* plausible explanations short of the intellectual capacity to arrange words according to a grammatical rule, it would be premature to conclude that a chimpanzee's combinations show the same structure evident in the sentences of a child. The fact that Nim's utterances were less spontaneous and less original than those of a child and that his utterances did not become longer, both as he learned new signs and as he acquired more experience in using sign language, suggests that much of the structure and meaning of his combinations was determined, or at least suggested, by the utterances of his teachers.

---

1 Why are the average length of Nim's utterances and his ability to combine different signs within utterances important criteria that Terrace used in evaluating Nim's linguistic capabilities?

2 Why is the concept of a "spontaneous utterance" such an important one in determining whether Nim possessed a capacity for language?

3 Why, in Terrace's view, is he now compelled to disbelieve in an innate linguistic capability in chimpanzees (although he originally set this experiment up to refute Noam Chomsky's theory)?

4 How did the examples of the "mean length of Nim's utterances," when broken down into two-, three-, and four-sign combinations, support Terrace's conclusions about the ways Nim's use of language differs from that of a child? Is the evidence given sufficient to warrant the conclusions that Terrace reaches? (Glossary: *Evidence*.)

5 Which comparison/contrast method of organization does Terrace use in this selection? Why might he have chosen this method? (Glossary: *Comparison and Contrast*.)

6 Koko has a very different relationship with Francine Patterson than Nim Chimsky has with Herbert S. Terrace. How would you characterize the differences in these relationships? In what way could the differences in the relationships have affected the results obtained?

Language and Thought *Susanne K. Langer*

◆ SUSANNE K. LANGER (1895–1985) was born in New York City and attended Radcliffe and the University of Vienna. Between 1927 and 1942 she was a tutor in philosophy at Harvard University and then taught at the University of Delaware, Columbia University, and Connecticut College. Her influential books include *Philosophy in a New Key: A Study in the Symbolism of Reason, Rite, and Art* (1942), *Feeling and Form* (1953), *Problems of Art* (1957), and *Mind: An Essay on Human Feeling* (1967). "Language and Thought" first appeared in *Fortune*, January 1944.

The question for Langer is how language allows us to perceive the world in ways that are radically different from the rest of the animal kingdom. Whereas animals use and respond to signs ("dogs bark at the door to be let in"), human beings employ symbols to imagine, conceive, and create in ways that are not immediately tied to sensory stimuli. This abstract or symbolic function of language, which allows us to think and talk about objects and events that are not physically present, in Langer's view, is what distinguishes us from the other species.

> **TO CONSIDER** How does being able to think about the environment in images and symbols, as human beings do, differ from the way animals respond to the world?

A symbol is not the same thing as a sign; that is a fact that psychologists and philosophers often overlook. All intelligent animals use signs; so do we. To them as well as to us sounds and smells and motions are signs of food, danger, the presence of other beings, or of rain or storm. Furthermore, some animals not only attend to signs but produce them for the benefit of others. Dogs bark at the door to be let in; rabbits thump to call each other; the cooing of doves and the growl of a wolf defending his kill are unequivocal signs of feelings and intentions to be reckoned with by other creatures.

We use signs just as animals do, though with considerably more elaboration. We stop at red lights and go on green; we answer calls and bells, watch the sky for coming storms, read trouble or promise or anger in each other's eyes. That is animal intelligence raised to the human level. Those of us who are dog lovers can probably all tell wonderful stories of how high our dogs have sometimes risen in the scale of clever sign interpretation and sign using.

A sign is anything that announces the existence or the imminence of some event, the presence of a thing or a person, or a change in the state of affairs. There are signs of the weather, signs of danger, signs of future good or evil, signs of what the past has been. In every case a sign is closely bound up with something to be noted or expected in experience. It is always a part of the situation to which it refers, though the reference may be remote in space and time. In so far as we are led to note or expect the signified event we are making correct use of a sign. This is the essence of rational behavior, which animals show in varying degrees. It is entirely realistic, being closely bound up with the actual objective course of history—learned by experience, and cashed in or voided by further experience.

If man had kept to the straight and narrow path of sign using, he would be like the other animals, though perhaps a little brighter. He would not talk, but grunt and gesticulate the point. He would make his wishes known, give warnings, perhaps develop a social system like that of bees and ants, with such a wonderful efficiency of communal enterprise that all men would have plenty to eat, warm apartments—all exactly alike and perfectly convenient—to live in, and everybody could and would sit in the sun or by the fire, as the climate demanded, not talking but just basking, with every want satisfied, most of his life. The young would romp and make love, the old would sleep, the middle-aged would do the routine work almost unconsciously and eat a great deal. But that would be the life of a social, superintelligent, purely sign-using animal.

5   To us who are human, it does not sound very glorious. We want to go places and do things, own all sorts of gadgets that we do not absolutely need, and when we sit down to take it easy we want to talk. Rights and property, social position, special talents and virtues, and above all our ideas, are what we live for. We have gone off on a tangent that takes us far away from the mere biological cycle that animal generations accomplish; and that is because we can use not only signs but symbols.

A symbol differs from a sign in that it does not announce the presence of the object, the being, condition, or whatnot, which is its meaning, but merely *brings this thing to mind*. It is not a mere "substitute sign" to which we react as though it were the object itself. The fact is that our reaction to hearing a person's name is quite different from our reaction to the person himself. There are certain rare cases where a symbol stands directly for its meaning: in religious experience, for instance, the Host is not only a symbol but a Presence. But symbols in the ordinary sense are not mystic. They are the same sort of thing that ordinary signs are; only they do not call our attention to something necessarily present or to be physically dealt with—they call up merely a conception of the thing they "mean."

The difference between a sign and a symbol is, in brief, that a sign causes us to think or act *in face* of the thing signified, whereas a symbol causes us to think *about* the thing symbolized. Therein lies the great importance of symbolism for human life, its power to make this life so different from any other animal biography that generations of men have found it incredible to suppose that they were of purely zoological origin. A sign is always embedded in reality, in a present that emerges from the actual past and stretches to the future; but a symbol may be divorced from reality altogether. It may refer to what is not the case, to a mere idea, a figment, a dream. It serves, therefore, to liberate thought from the immediate stimuli of a physically present world; and that liberation marks the essential difference between human and nonhuman mentality. Animals think, but they think *of* and *at* things; men think primarily *about* things. Words, pictures, and memory images are symbols that may be combined and varied in a thousand ways. The result is a symbolic structure whose meaning is a complex of all their respective meanings, and this kaleidoscope of *ideas* is the typical product of the human brain that we call the "stream of thought."

The process of transforming all direct experience into imagery or into that supreme mode of symbolic expression, language, has so completely taken possession of the human mind that it is not only a special talent but a dominant, organic need. All our sense impressions leave their traces in our memory not only as signs disposing our practical reactions in the future but also as symbols, images representing our *ideas* of things; and the tendency to manipulate ideas, to combine and abstract, mix and extend them by playing with symbols, is man's outstanding characteristic. It seems to be what his brain most naturally and spontaneously does. Therefore his primitive mental function is not judging reality, but *dreaming his desires*.

Dreaming is apparently a basic function of human brains, for it is free and unexhausting like our metabolism, heartbeat, and breath. It is easier to dream than not to dream, as it is easier to breathe than to refrain from breathing. The symbolic character of dreams is fairly well established. Symbol mongering, on this ineffectual, uncritical level, seems to be instinctive, the fulfillment of an elementary need rather than the purposeful exercise of a high and difficult talent.

The special power of man's mind rests on the evolution of this special activity, not on any transcendently high development of animal intelligence. We are not immeasurably higher than other animals; we are different. We have a biological need and with it a biological gift that they do not share.   10

Because man has not only the ability but the constant need of *conceiving* what has happened to him, what surrounds him, what is demanded of him—in short, of symbolizing nature, himself, and his hopes and fears—he has a constant and crying need of *expression*. What he cannot express, he cannot conceive; what he cannot conceive is chaos, and fills him with terror.

If we bear in mind this all-important craving for expression we get a new picture of man's behavior; for from this trait spring his powers and his weaknesses. The process of symbolic transformation that all our experiences undergo is nothing more nor less than the process of *conception,* underlying the human faculties of abstraction and imagination.

When we are faced with a strange or difficult situation, we cannot react directly, as other creatures do, with flight, aggression, or any such simple instinctive pattern. Our whole reaction depends on how we manage to conceive the situation—whether we cast it in a definite dramatic form, whether we see it as a disaster, a challenge, a fulfillment of doom, or a fiat of the Divine Will. In words or dreamlike images, in artistic or religious or even in cynical form, we must *construe* the events of life. There is great virtue in the figure of speech, "I can *make* nothing of it," to express a failure to understand something. Thought and memory are processes of *making* the thought content and the memory image; the pattern of our ideas is given by the symbols through which we express them. And in the course of manipulating those symbols we inevitably distort the original experience, as we abstract certain features of it, embroider and reinforce those features with other ideas, until the conception we project on the screen of memory is quite different from anything in our real history.

Conception is a necessary and elementary process; what we do with our conceptions is another story. That is the entire history of human culture—of intelligence and morality, folly and superstition, ritual, language, and the arts—all the phenomena that set man apart from, and above, the rest of the animal kingdom. As the religious mind has to make all human history a drama of sin and salvation in order to define its own moral attitudes, so a scientist wrestles with the mere presentation of "the facts" before he can reason about them. The process of *envisaging* facts, values, hopes, and fears underlies our whole behavior pattern; and this process is reflected in the evolution of an extraordinary phenomenon found always, and only, in human societies—the phenomenon of language.

15 Language is the highest and most amazing achievement of the symbolistic human mind. The power it bestows is almost inestimable, for without it anything properly called "thought" is impossible. The birth of language is the dawn of humanity. The line between man and beast—between the highest ape and the lowest savage—is the language line. Whether the primitive Neanderthal man was anthropoid or human depends less on his cranial capacity, his upright posture, or even his use of tools and fire, than on one issue we shall probably never be able to settle—whether or not he spoke.

In all physical traits and practical responses, such as skills and visual judgments, we can find a certain continuity between animal and human mentality. Sign using is an ever evolving, ever improving function throughout the whole animal kingdom, from the lowly worm that shrinks into his hole at the sound of an approaching foot, to the dog obeying his master's command, and even to the learned scientist who watches the movements of an index needle.

This continuity of the sign-using talent has led psychologists to the belief that language is evolved from the vocal expressions, grunts and coos and cries, whereby animals vent their feelings or signal their fellows; that man has elaborated this sort of communion to the point where it makes a perfect exchange of ideas possible.

I do not believe that this doctrine of the origin of language is correct. The essence of language is symbolic, not signific; we use it first and most vitally to formulate and hold ideas in our own minds. Conception, not social control, is its first and foremost benefit.

Watch a young child that is just learning to speak play with a toy; he says the name of the object, e.g.: "Horsey! horsey! horsey!" over and over again, looks at the object, moves it, always saying the name to himself or to the world at large. It's quite a time before he talks to anyone in particular; he talks first of all to himself. This is his way of forming and fixing the *conception* of the object in his mind, and around this conception all his knowledge of it grows. *Names* are the essence of language; for the *name* is what abstracts the conception of the horse from the horse itself, and lets the mere idea recur at the speaking of the name. This permits the conception gathered from one horse experience to be exemplified again by another instance of a horse, so that the notion embodied in the name is a general notion.

To this end, the baby uses a word long before he *asks* for the object; when   20 he wants his horsey he is likely to cry and fret, because he is reacting to an actual environment, not forming ideas. He uses the animal language of *signs* for his wants; talking is still a purely symbolic process—its practical value has not really impressed him yet.

Language need not be vocal; it may be purely visual, like written language or even tactual, like the deaf-mute system of speech, but it *must be denotative*. The sounds, intended or unintended, whereby animals communicate do not constitute a language because they are signs, not names. They never fall into an organic pattern, a meaningful syntax of even the most rudimentary sort, as all language seems to do with a sort of driving necessity. That is because signs refer to actual situations, in which things have obvious relations to each other that require only to be noted; but symbols refer to ideas, which are not physically there for inspection, so their connections and features have to be represented. This gives all true language a natural tendency toward growth and development, which seems almost like a life of its own. Languages are not invented; they grow with our need for expression.

In contrast, animal "speech" never has a structure. It is merely an emotional response. Apes may greet their ration of yams with a shout of "Nga!" But they do not say "Nga" between meals. If they could *talk about* their yams instead of just saluting them, they would be the most primitive men instead of the most anthropoid of beasts. They would have ideas, and tell each other things true or false, rational or irrational; they would make plans and invent laws and sing their own praises, as men do.

---

1 What is the most essential difference between signs and symbols (para. 3)? Using only signs, how would you relate to the world in a way that is much different from the way you do now using symbols?

2   In Langer's view, how do animals think in a way that is fundamentally different from the way human beings think? Why does she use the example of how humans and animals respond to perceived threats differently (para. 10)?

3   Through joint communication, people learn from each other's experiences in ways that animals can never do. How does language serve an important social function in this regard? How do symbols enable people to conceptualize and analyze the meaning of experiences rather than simply react to them?

4   In what important respects does a symbol differ from a sign? How helpful do you find the comparisons Langer offers in the opening paragraphs in understanding the difference between signs and symbols? Are the examples of symbols Langer provides in paragraphs 1–6 helpful in enabling you to understand what she means by a symbol? Explain. (Glossary: *Comparison and Contrast, Examples, Symbol.*)

5   To develop her essay. Langer uses the one-side-at-a-time or subject-by-subject method of comparison/contrast. What does this method enable her to do that the point-by-point approach would not? (Glossary: *Comparison and Contrast.*)

6   Susanne K. Langer and Vicki Hearne (in the following selection) approach the question of animal intelligence from very different perspectives and have very different assumptions. What are these differences? Whose view, in your opinion, seems more persuasive, and why?

How to Say "Fetch!"   *Vicki Hearne*

◆ VICKI HEARNE is professor of English at Yale University. She has trained dogs for obedience classes, the hunt field, and scenting work. Hearne has written two volumes of poetry, is a contributing editor of *Harper's* magazine, and has written a regular column on animals for the *Los Angeles Times*. In "How to Say 'Fetch' " from her 1986 book *Adam's Task*, Hearne provides a fascinating analysis of the relationship between language and learning in the context of dog training. She believes that dogs—as well as cats and horses— are truer possessors of language than the much-publicized signing apes.

As Hearne makes clear, a dog's ability to understand human speech is largely dependent on all the previously formed associations between words and acts and

Vicki Hearn, "How To Say 'Fetch!'" from *Adam's Task*. Copyright © 1986 by Vicki Hearn. Reprinted by permission of Alfred A. Knopf, Inc.

objects that have been added to the animal's repertoire through an intensive training program. It is the nature of this additional surrounding information that Hearne explores through her analysis of teaching a dog to respond to the command "fetch." Hearne does not claim that dogs can understand English in ways that several researchers think primates can. She does, however, feel that dogs, cats, and horses are capable of entering into a kind of "conversation" or interaction with humans based on a mutual recognition of meaning, belief, and intention.

TO CONSIDER   Would you be willing to use harsh training methods in order to have a well-behaved pet?

If you do not teach me I shall not learn.
—*Beckett*

Terms that have histories cannot be defined.
—*Nietzsche*

If we consider, as I have been doing, the size and kind of the social space created by the language shared by two or more creatures, and if we describe the integrity of a language as the physical, intellectual and spiritual distance talking enables the speakers of that language to travel together, then it looks very much as though the dog and the horse (who are neurologically simpler organisms than chimpanzees and whose linguistic codes certainly appear simpler) have a greater command of language than chimpanzees do. There is even a sense in which a well-trained dog or horse may be said to have a greater command of language than a human being whose code is infinitely more complex. The dog/dog trainer language is perhaps more primitive (in the sense Wittgenstein has in mind when he criticizes Augustine or invites us to consider primitive language games) than the chimpanzee's language, or the schizophrenic's, but I can go a lot farther with my dog than I can with a schizophrenic, or a Nazi, if only because my dog doesn't bore me.

Does this matter? Or is it just a sentimentalization of the enslavement of the domestic animal? Well, dog trainers and horse trainers insist that training—teaching animals the language games of retrieving, say, or haute école in dressage—results in ennoblement, in the development of the animal's character and in the development of both the animal's *and the handler's* sense of responsibility and honesty. This is either hopelessly corrupt, in a sense that *The Genealogy of Morals* might unfold, or else it can tell us something about not only what goes on in training but also what it might mean to respond fully as human beings to "character," "responsibility" and "honesty."

It is worthwhile, then, to describe part of one of the language games of training, namely retrieving, in the hope of discovering what sort of moral cosmos is revealed thereby . . .

In order to investigate this . . . further, I am going to tell a story in which I am the trainer and the dog is a year-old Pointer bitch named Salty.

Salty is a bird dog, and a good one, which means that the chance of her biting me is so remote that we are unlikely to have to discuss it. Not that Salty is a "soft" dog. She is a hard-core Pointer, birdy and geared to travel all out for miles, the heiress of an unsurpassable tradition that includes Algonquin, the hero of Dion Henderson's wonderful book *Algonquin: The Story of a Great Dog,* who was "very gallant, sir. I think perhaps he would pity his bracemates if he were not enough of a nobleman to know that they would rather die than be pitied." For a true Pointer admirer, the Pointer's fire, speed, precision and power constitute the central good in the universe, the rest of which is judged by its ability to honor and celebrate the Pointer. "Mr. Washington felt that any bird you didn't hunt exclusively with Pointers was unfit to associate with gentlefolk."

So Salty, in my story, has it in her to be staunch to wing and shot, to hunt wholeheartedly where lesser dogs lose spirit, to work with full courtliness and gallantry, to become so dedicated to the perfecting of finding and pointing birds that the sort of hunting where the art is adulterated by actually shooting the birds too much of the time, for merely practical reasons, becomes uninteresting. Unfortunately, her wonderful qualities may look to the uninitiated remarkably like wildness and uncontrollability. She's a year old, and she hasn't even had any puppy conditioning; the only part of the noble rhetoric she has gotten down is the part about going hard and tirelessly. This she does everywhere, as indifferent to obstacles like the kitchen table or the bedside lamp as her forebears were to nearly unleapable gullies and impenetrable thickets. Her former owners had known only the sort of dog who is more accommodating of cooing and bribery. Salty was not so much intolerant of the cooing as she was indifferent to it—it had, literally, no meaning to her. She thought she was doing a fine thing when she went through the picture window to point some meadowlarks in the back-yard, and the cries of "You bad dog, how could you do this to us, you're supposed to be our precious baby, look at my potted Chinese palm, all ruined!" deterred her no more than the gashes on her neck and shoulders. But she was tolerant of the fussing, even if she was unresponsive to it. Proof of her tolerance is in her not having bitten anyone. A German Shepherd or a Doberman, or any of the breeds for whom the forms of companionship can be as deeply visionary as the forms of hunting are for Salty, might very well have responded to this particular incoherence with some hostility.*

When Salty enters my life she's been talked at a lot, but she knows virtually nothing of talking with people who mean what they say, so I don't say much of anything to her at first. I take her out of her kennel and am silent except for a

---

*It is impossible to say enough in defense of the deeply civilized hearts possessed by most members of the working breeds, especially Dobermans. The fear of Dobies is all too easy to understand in light of the bad press they've had, which hasn't so far been offset by tales as powerful as those of Rin Tin Tin. I shall content myself by saying that the bad press was boosted by Hitler's charge that they were of impure blood and therefore unstable in temperament, and that perpetuating the myth of the vicious Doberman amounts to perpetuating a Nazi line.

calm "Good morning, Salty." I put her on a fifteen-foot line, attached to a training collar, and I begin to go for a little walk. Salty stays at my side for about one and one-quarter seconds, which is how long it takes her to spot something huntable—in this case, my motley-coated cat, Touchstone, who is idly watching the progress of the ten o'clock shade of the pepper tree toward his sunny spot, contemplating as is his wont the curious ways the shadows move round and round, forcing him to change napping places as the day wears on. Salty heads for Touchstone at proper field-trial speed. I say nothing to her—nothing at all. Nor do I tug suggestively on the line to remind her of me. Instead, I drop all fifteen feet of slack into the line and turn and run in the opposite direction, touchdown style. Salty hits the end of the line and travels, perforce, some distance in the direction I am going, tumbling end over end.

This thoughtless behavior elicits no hysterics from her, as it might from a lesser dog who is used, as Salty is, to being coaxed and tugged away from kitty cats, instead of having to deal with a handler so clumsy and impolite as to fail to check first on what Salty is doing before dashing off as I did. She is startled, of course, but she forgives me and romps toward me to let me know it. On her way to forgiving me she catches sight of a leaf moving in a way that might be construed to mean *bird* and spins out after it. Again I head swiftly in a direction opposite to hers, and again she tumbles end over end, correcting her story about who I am.

The third or fourth time she gets dumped in this way, it dawns on Salty that there is a consistency in my inconsiderate and apparently heedless plunges. She sits down in order to think this over, cocking her head in puzzlement, trying to work out the implications of my behavior. She suspects, correctly, that they are cosmic. I respond by heading purposefully toward an open gate. She decides she'd better keep an eye on me and follows. Then the sight of the gate standing there in such an *opened* way tempts her and, forgetting the new cosmology, she charges for it. I turn again to do my routine, but this time she remembers before she's in high gear that I can't be counted on to follow, and she brakes and turns, loping in my direction and avoiding hitting the end of the line.

By the end of the first session she is more attentive to me, more willing to follow—to try, that is, to understand—than she has ever been to anyone in the whole course of her life, and I've said *nothing* to her. When the session is over, I utter the first command—"Salty, Okay!"—as I release her to think things over. The "okay" command is essential to establishing all sorts of clarities. It means something like "You are free to walk about, sniff things, take a nap, have some lunch, initiate a conversation with Touchstone on the mysteries of time, but you are *not* free to commit any crimes, dig holes, chase Touchstone, leap into the middle of my morning tea or generally buzz around at low altitudes." If she does any of these things I correct her by jerking sharply on the line while hollering "*OUT!*" in my most terrifying voice, sounding as much as I can like a clap of doom. Since she is neither a wild animal nor a hardened criminal but a true dog, she is able to grant fairly quickly the reasonableness of my demands, and since neither "Okay!" nor "Out!" requires her to love me or nourish my soul, her willingness to cooperate need not be contaminated by questions about whether she loves me better than she loves the vision of herself as a mighty huntress. There can't in any case be much talk of love between us at this point, though we do find each other likable enough. Love will follow on shared commitments and collaboration, on a mutual autonomy that is not now possible.

The mastery of the "okay" command is not an achievement of love but rather of the simultaneous granting and earning of some rudimentary rights—in particular, Salty's right to the freedom of the house, which, like my right to the freedom of the house, is contingent on making a limited number and kind of messes, respecting other people's privacy, refraining from leaping uninvited onto furniture and laps and making the right distinctions between mine and thine, especially in the matter of food dishes. I have managed to grant this right only by becoming inflexibly in command about certain things. It is a matter of authority, not love—I don't even have to like a dog in order to accomplish this. In most adult human relationships we don't have to do quite so much correcting in order to grant each other house privileges, but that doesn't mean that house privileges don't depend on the possibility of such corrections. Try putting your ice cream cone on my typewriter, and you'll get the idea. Freedom is being on an "okay" command.

Love, of course, is getting into things, but at this point I love not Salty but the literary tradition that has produced her. She doesn't know this tradition, but she has it in her to respond to and enlarge on my response to it in the way that a talented young poet has it in him or her to respond to mentor's response. That is an important part of a talent for anything. In Salty I see echoes of the great field-trial dogs of the past and the paintings and tales of them, in the way I see in a student's work and manner of thinking echoes of the authentic energy of Stevens or Dickens. The better I am at responding with great accuracy—at, for instance, not making mistakes about which great tale or painting is being invoked—the greater the likelihood that this particular dog's qualities will be realized.

After about a week of work on the longe line ("longe" is a term for a certain piece of equipment, a long line, and for certain sets of exercises in both the dog and the horse worlds) it is time to introduce a piece of linguistic behavior whose syntax is more like the usual syntax of the imperative mode than "Salty, Okay!" is. I spend a while in an activity called "Teaching the dog what 'Sit' means," although that phrase captures very little of what teaching anyone anything is like. Briefly, I gently place her in a sitting position at the same time that I say, "Salty, Sit!" This is not what "Sit" will come to mean, but an incomplete rehearsal of it. I do this for several days, without giving any corrections, not because a dog needs more than one rehearsal to learn that the utterance means a certain posture and a certain relationship to my position, but because it *is* a rehearsal, and more than one rehearsal of more than one kind must precede genuine performance. There are, as I said, no corrections. Attending to me, refraining from biting and leaping about, is the only obedience required at this point.

Then comes the moment when I give the command without placing her (and without stooping or wiggling my ears or any other part of my anatomy pleadingly or suggestively). If she refuses to sit, or just doesn't think to sit, I give her a harsh, emphatic sit correction. The meaning of sit has now changed, been projected into a new context. Salty says to herself, "By God, I'd better sit when she says to, or the world will keep coming to an end!" The imperative mode has at *this* point, *this* form.

Someone may be wondering about all of that glorious dashing about, full expression of creaturely energy and so forth. It may seem that I've destroyed that, broken Salty's spirit. It is in fact possible to do so, although quite difficult in this particular case. With some dogs, syrup and cooing will do it, especially if there's also a full-blown emotional blackmail operation. That didn't work on Salty, but if I fail now not only in respect for her but in love of the literary tradition that has taught me to want to train Salty, I can in fact "break her spirit." Failing to give the corrections harshly enough would be an example of such a failure. When there is danger here, it is that so many of the stories we know about authority are about people getting stuck, as it were, in a parental or imperative mode. So with Salty I must be prepared to drop that instantly and to respond to every true motion with awe and recognition. If my "Way to go, kid!" or "Good dog!" invokes for me what I know and feel about the great dogs of the past, then what we are doing will lead in time to the second inheritance of her running gear. Dog training is one of the arts concerned with the imitation of nature, which is to say, the second inheritance of nature.

At this point in Salty's training it is not clear whether the utterance "Salty, Sit!" is language, even though there is plainly a looped thought involved: Salty, that is, is sitting in response to her recognition of my intention that she do so. But it's not clear how interesting or useful it is to *say* that it's language, or that anything much would be known thereby that we couldn't know just as well if the anecdote avoided terms like "meaning" and "intention" and used instead a Skinnerian or a Cartesian vocabulary. The situation is far more complex than my account of it, but at this point those complexities don't illuminate the issue. We have a looped thought, but the flow of intention is, as it were, one way. In my account the dog doesn't initiate anything yet. She obeys me, but I don't obey her.

One day, though, and quite soon, I am wandering around the house and Salty gets my attention by sitting spontaneously in just the unmistakably symmetrical, clean-edged way of formal work. If I'm on the ball, if I respect her personhood at this point, I'll respond. Her sitting may have a number of meanings. "Please stop daydreaming and feed me!" (Perhaps she sits next to the Eukanuba or her food dish.) Or it may mean, "Look, I can explain about the garbage can, it isn't the way it looks." In any case, if I respond, the flow of intention is now two-way, and the meaning of "Sit" has changed yet again. This time it is Salty who has enlarged the context, the arena of its use, by means of what we might as well go ahead and call the trope of projection. Salty and I ate, for the moment at least, obedient to each other and to language.

Understanding has been enlarged by enforced obedience! How queer, one may want to say; surely this is a borderline case having very little to do with understanding as we usually talk about it. But our concept of obedience is larger than we admit in certain discussions when we're talking about the importance of autonomy or the power of the individual imagination. "Obey" itself comes from a word meaning "to hear." We covertly recognize that this may not be an irrelevant etymology by using expressions like "I don't follow you" or "I'll go along with that." It is a certain spookiness about the *word,* together perhaps with the terror of being suggestible and therefore weak, that makes us forget that no one is more suggestible (more responsive to a text) than the great critic or philosopher, no one more obedient, more fully surrendering of the self, than the master of an art. *What* we surrender to matters, of course. Salty appears to have no choice about surrendering to me, but to say that as though it distinguished her from us is to overlook the degree of choice any of us has about surrendering to our native tongues. My training methods, like any teaching method, depend on her willingness to cooperate,* which is one of the reasons the chimp trainers want to insist on the word "teaching" for what they do, and there are contexts where they are quite right. Salty's surrender, I would like to say, is not entirely helpless. She can't know ahead of time how fully I will follow through on the commitments commanding another being entails, or even what it might mean to know that, but she has (unlike the wolf) something like the rough-and-ready criteria we use frequently in judging when to surrender. She has a million tiny observations of my tone and manner to go on (when people are as good as most animals are at this, we say they have a "way with animals"), and her recognition of them is not entirely unlike the recognition that leads me to attend more closely to a book I've picked up idly. Of course, I can always decide I've made a mistake and put the book back down (or at least I like to think this, sometimes forgetting that there are tiny increments of loss in even so trivial a repudiation), but Salty, too, can always decide to bite me and split. I have known this to happen. She is free, or rather she is not free, in the way babies aren't free.

Now, though Salty is not yet the master of anything, and I am not yet her master, some more rights have been granted to her, or she has earned them, whichever you prefer. If my behavior has been just, then Salty has the right to a certain attentiveness or responsiveness. This is part, as are the corrections, of what Bill Koehler has in mind when he says the dog has the "right to the consequences of his actions." We stand on the threshold of a discipline that can free us from some ancient and troublesome trespasses against language, and the resources of consciousness have been renewed.

There are a lot of things we don't have yet. Among others, we don't have a subject—a grammatical object, that is—for our primitive language to engage. Even Salty's creative management of the food dish and the garbage can doesn't enable her to name the garbage can. Naming is an advanced activity of language

---

*Since most house cats would rather die than obey a direct order, some people have been led to elevate the cat in their estimation, as T. S. Eliot did: "A dog's an easy going lout/He'll answer any hail or shout." The belief in the independence of cats is an example of what has been called anthropomorphism but is not. It is attributing to animals, not traits that we possess, but traits that we wish we possessed, or are afraid that we possess or that someone possesses. Pure savagery, unending and impersonal sexuality, unshakable love, etc. In this case, the mythical emotional independence of the cat. It is imaginative failure that obscures our view of the ways in which the house cat cooperates deeply in the domestic enterprise.

and not the prior, essential act some of our allegories about ourselves and matters such as signing chimpanzees make it out to be. Names for anyone or anything but the speakers of a language are not necessary for knowledge or acknowledgment until we actually do name objects, and then they will be necessary.

We can now say something about how the story the behaviorist brings into the laboratory affects not only his or her interpretation of what goes on but also what actually does go on. To the extent that the behaviorist manages to deny any belief in the dog's potential for believing, intending, meaning, etc., there will be no flow of intention, meaning, believing, hoping going on. The dog may try to respond to the behaviorist, but the behaviorist won't respond to the dog's response; there will be between them little or no space for the varied flexions of looped thoughts. The behaviorist's dog will not only seem stupid, she will be stupid. If we follow Wittgenstein in assuming the importance of assessing the public nature of language, then we don't need to lock a baby up and feed it by machine in order to discover that conceptualization is pretty much a function of relationships and acknowledgment, a public affair. It takes two to conceive.

---

1   What features of the "moral cosmos" are revealed in Hearne's description of the kind of training procedures she uses in teaching Salty to retrieve? How would you characterize the relationship that is established between Hearne as trainer and her dog?

2   Discuss the importance that a willingness to exercise authority plays in the complex system of rights and privileges Hearne describes as being the very essence of training.

3   To what extent does Hearne appear to be defensive about what might appear to others as harsh training methods? How do they compare with methods you or people you know have employed in trying to train a dog? What results were achieved?

4   Hearne gives a detailed description of the training procedure she used with Salty and concludes that even the most basic two-way flow of communication and language had not yet been achieved. What insight does this give you into what Hearne means by "language"? What conditions have not yet been met? How would you characterize the language Hearne uses in this account? Is it concrete or abstract? (Glossary: *Definition, Concrete, Abstract.*) Is it general or specific? (Glossary: *Specific/General.*)

5   Is Hearne's process analysis primarily directional or informational? Explain. To what extent does Hearne try to persuade her readers to follow her instructions in how to train an animal and to adopt her philosophy underlying the training procedure? What are the main stages and what happens at each step? What words and phrases does Hearne use to indicate she is moving from one step to the next? (Glossary: *Process Analysis.*)

6   Have you ever had the occasion to try to train an animal? What objectives did you hope to achieve? What procedures did you follow? What kind of communication, if any, took place? What was the result of your training? Describe your experiences.

7   How do the following ad for IAMS and the Peanuts cartoon develop the theme of communication that Hearne discusses in her essay?

Source: Iams Company, W.B. Doner & Company. Photograph by Elliot Erwitt.

Words, Words, Words   *David Ives*

◆ DAVID IVES is a contemporary American playwright who specializes in comic sketches that sparkle with inventiveness. In this play, Ives starts from the premise that three monkeys typing into infinity would sooner or later produce *Hamlet* and asks, "What would the monkeys talk about at their typewriters?" Six of his one-act comedies are compiled in *All in the Timing* (1994), including *Words, Words, Words,* which was first produced in New York in 1987.

Certain features of the experiments done at Columbia University by Herbert S. Terrace (who may have served as the model for Dr. David Rosenbaum, the experimenter in the play, who is carrying out his research at Columbia University) seem to lie at the heart of Ives's thought-provoking satire. Some critics of Terrace argued that Nim Chimsky performed so poorly because the conditions under which he was trained were so sterile—i.e., six hours of training in a stark white room where the chimp was under enormous pressure to come up with something really innovative in his signing. What if the experiment could be described from Nim Chimsky's point of view? The result might be something like *Words, Words, Words.* Ives might have chosen the names Milton, Swift, and Kafka for the three monkeys because of significant associations each author evokes. John Milton brings to mind the whole drama of evolution and the emergence of human beings—Adam and Eve—against the background of the rest of the animal kingdom. Jonathan Swift, besides being an acerbic critic, is known for his story *Gulliver's Travels,* in which his protagonist prefers the company of horselike creatures who speak to him. And Franz Kafka is the author of a story about a man who awakens to discover he has become a cockroach ("The Metamorphoses"). All three are obsessed with the metaphysical predicament of human beings, as is Shakespeare in *Hamlet.*

> **TO CONSIDER**   Suppose it could be proven that a nonhuman species was capable of thought and could learn to speak and write. What do you think their lives would be like? Would they have a future beyond the laboratory or the sideshow?

Lights come up on three monkeys pecking away at three typewriters. Behind them, a tire-swing is hanging. The monkeys are named Milton, Swift and Kafka. Kafka is a girl monkey.[1]

They shouldn't be in monkey suits, by the way. Instead, they wear the sort of little-kid clothes that chimps wear in circuses: white shirts and bow-ties for the boys, a flouncy little dress for Kafka.

They type for a few moments, each at his own speed. Then Milton runs excitedly around the floor on his knuckles, swings onto the tire-swing, leaps back onto his stool, and goes on typing. Kafka eats a banana thoughtfully. Swift pounds his chest and shows his teeth, then goes back to typing.

SWIFT.   I don't know. I just don't know . . .

KAFKA.   Quiet, please. I'm trying to concentrate here. (*She types a moment with her toes.*)

MILTON.   Okay, so what've you got?

SWIFT.   Me?

MILTON.   Yeah, have you hit anything? Let's hear it.

SWIFT.   (*Reads what he's typed.*) "Ping-drobba fft fft fft inglewarp carcinoma." That's as far as I got.

KAFKA.   I like the "fft fft fft."

MILTON.   Yeah. Kind of onomatopoeic.

SWIFT.   I don't know. Feels to me like it needs some punching up.

MILTON.   You can always throw in a few jokes later on. You gotta get the throughline first.

SWIFT.   But do you think it's *Hamlet*?[2]

MILTON.   Don't ask me. I'm just a chimp.

KAFKA.   They could've given us a clue or something.

SWIFT.   Yeah. Or a story conference.

MILTON.   But that'd defeat the whole purpose of the experiment.

SWIFT.   I know, I know, I know. Three monkeys typing into infinity will sooner or later produce *Hamlet*.

MILTON.   Right.

SWIFT.   Completely by chance.

MILTON.   And Dr. David Rosenbaum up in that booth is going to prove it.

SWIFT.   But what is *Hamlet*?

MILTON.   I don't know.

SWIFT.   (*To Kafka.*) What is *Hamlet*?

KAFKA.   I don't know. (*Silence.*)

---

[1]John Milton, 1608–74, English poet, author of *Paradise Lost*, 1667. Jonathan Swift, 1667–1745, Anglo-Irish satirist, author of *Gulliver's Travels*, 1726, Franz Kafka, 1883–1924, German novelist and short story writer, author of *The Trial*, 1925.

[2]William Shakespeare's classic tragedy, composed in 1600–01.

SWIFT. (*Dawning realization.*) You know—this is really *stupid!*

MILTON. Have you got something better to do in this cage? The sooner we produce the goddamn thing, the sooner we get out.

KAFKA. Sort of publish or perish, with a twist.

SWIFT. But what do we owe this Rosenbaum? A guy who stands outside those bars and tells people, "That one's Milton, that one's Swift, and that one's Kafka"—? Just to get a laugh?

KAFKA. What's a Kafka anyway? Why am I a Kafka?

SWIFT. Search me.

KAFKA. What's a Kafka?

SWIFT. All his four-eyed friends sure think it's a stitch.

KAFKA. And how are we supposed to write *Hamlet* if we don't even know what it is?

MILTON. Okay, okay, so the chances are a little slim.

SWIFT. Yeah—and this from a guy who's supposed to be *smart?* This from a guy at *Columbia University?*

MILTON. The way I figure it, there is a Providence that oversees our pages, rough-draft them how we may.[3]

KAFKA. But how about you, Milton? What've you got?

MILTON. Let's see . . . (*Reads.*)
"Of Man's first disobedience, and the fruit
Of that forbidden tree whose mortal taste
Brought death into the—"[4]

KAFKA. Hey, that's good! It's got rhythm! It really sings!

MILTON. Yeah?

SWIFT. But is it Shakespeare?

KAFKA. Who cares? He's got a real voice there.

SWIFT. Does Dr. Rosenbaum care about voice? Does he care about anybody's individual creativity?

MILTON. Let's look at this from Rosenbaum's point of view for a minute—

SWIFT. No! He brings us in here to produce copy, then all he wants is a clean draft of somebody else's stuff. (*Dumps out a bowl of peanuts.*) We're getting peanuts here, to be somebody's hack!

MILTON. Writing is a mug's game anyway, Swifty.

SWIFT. Well it hath made me mad.

MILTON. Why not just buckle down and get the project over with? Set up a schedule for yourself. Type in the morning for a couple of hours when you're fresh, then take a break. Let the old juices flow. Do a couple more hours in the afternoon, and retire for a shot of papaya and some masturbation. What's the big deal?

---

[3]Alludes to *Hamlet*, Scene V, Act ii, line 10.
[4]Alludes to Milton's *Paradise Lost*, Book I, lines 1–3.

SWIFT.   If this Rosenbaum was worth anything, we'd be working on word processors, not these antiques. He's lucky he could find three who type this good, and then he treats us like those misfits at the Bronx Zoo. I mean—a *tire-swing?* What does he take us for?

MILTON.   I like the tire-swing. I think it was a very nice touch.

SWIFT.   I can't work under these conditions! No wonder I'm producing garbage!

KAFKA.   How does the rest of yours go, Milton?

MILTON.   What, this?

KAFKA.   Yeah, read us some more.

MILTON.   Blah, blah, blah . . ."whose mortal taste

Brought death into the blammagam.

Bedsocks knockwurst tinkerbelle."

(*Small pause.*) What do you think?

KAFKA.   "Blammagam" is good.

SWIFT.   Well. I don't know . . .

MILTON.   What's the matter? Is it the tone? I knew this was kind of a stretch for me.

SWIFT.   I'm just not sure it has the same expressive intensity and pungent lyricism as the first part.

MILTON.   Well sure, it needs rewriting. What doesn't? This is a rough draft! (*Suddenly noticing.*) Light's on. (*Swift claps his hands over his eyes, Milton puts his hands over his ears, and Kafka puts her hands over her mouth so that they form "See no evil, hear no evil, speak no evil."*)

SWIFT.   *This* bit.

KAFKA.   (*Through her hands.*) Are they watching?

MILTON.   (*Hands over ears.*) What?

KAFKA.   Are they watching?

SWIFT.   I don't know, I can't see. I've got my paws over my eyes.

MILTON.   What?

KAFKA.   What is the point of this?

SWIFT.   Why do they videotape our bowel movements?

MILTON.   *What?!*

SWIFT.   Light's off. (*They take their hands away.*)

MILTON.   But how are you doing, Franz? What've you got?

KAFKA.   Well. . . .(*Reads what she's typed.*)

   "K.K.K.K.K.K.K.K.K.K.K.K.K.K.K."[5]

SWIFT.   What is that—post-modernism?

KAFKA.   Twenty lines of that.

SWIFT.   At least it'll fuck up his data.

---

[5]May allude to Joseph K., the protagonist of Kafka's novels *The Trial,* 1925 and *The Castle* 1926, symbolic and surreal works that anticipate postmodernist techniques and themes.

KAFKA.   Twenty lines of that and I went dry. I got blocked. I felt like I was repeating myself.

MILTON.   Do you think that that's in *Hamlet?*

KAFKA.   I don't understand what I'm doing here in the first place! I'm not a writer, I'm a monkey! I'm supposed to be swinging on branches and digging up ants, not sitting under fluorescent lights ten hours a day!

MILTON.   It sure is a long way home to the gardens of sweet Africa. Where lawns and level downs and flocks grazing the tender herb were sweetly interposèd . . . [6]

KAFKA.   Paradise, wasn't it?

MILTON.   Lost!

SWIFT.   Lost!

KAFKA.   Lost!

MILTON.   I'm trying to deal with some of that in this new piece here, but it's all still pretty close to the bone.

SWIFT.   Just because they can keep us locked up, they think they're more powerful than we are.

MILTON.   They *are* more powerful than we are.

SWIFT.   Just because they control the means of production, they think they can suppress the workers.[7]

MILTON.   Things are how they are. What are you going to do?

SWIFT.   Hey—how come you're always so goddamn ready to justify the ways of Rosenbaum to the apes?

MILTON.   Do you have a key to that door?

SWIFT.   No.

MILTON.   Do you have an independent food source?

SWIFT.   No.

MILTON.   So call me a collaborator. I happen to be a professional. If Rosenbaum wants *Hamlet,* I'll give it a shot. Just don't forget—we're not astrophysicists. We're not brain surgeons. We're chimps. And for apes in captivity, this is not a bad gig.

SWIFT.   What's really frightening is that if we stick around this cage long enough, we're gonna evolve into Rosenbaum.

KAFKA.   Evolve into Rosenbaum?

SWIFT.   Brush up your Darwin, baby. We're more than kin and less than kind.[8]

MILTON.   Anybody got a smoke?

KAFKA.   I'm all out.

---

[6]Alludes to Eden, as described in *Paradise Lost,* Book IV.

[7]May allude to Karl Marx, 1818–83, German social philosopher and revolutionary, author of the *Communist Manifesto* (1848), in collaboration with Friedrich Engels, 1820–95.

[8]Alludes to *Hamlet,* I, ii, 65.

SWIFT.   Don't look at me. I'm not going to satisfy those voyeurs with the old smoking-chimp act. No thank you.

MILTON.   Don't be a sap, Swifty. You gotta use 'em! Use the system!

SWIFT.   What do you mean?

MILTON.   Watch me, while I put my antic disposition on.[9] (*He jumps up onto his chair and scratches his sides, screeches, makes smoking motions, pounds his chest, jumps up and down—and a cigarette descends.*) See what I mean? Gauloise, too. My fave. (*He settles back to enjoy it.*)

SWIFT.   They should've thrown in a kewpie doll for that performance.

MILTON.   It got results, didn't it?

SWIFT.   Sure. You do your Bonzo routine and get a Gauloise out of it. Last week I totalled a typewriter and got a whole carton of Marlboros.

MILTON.   The trouble was, you didn't smoke 'em, you took a crap on 'em.

SWIFT.   It was a political statement.

MILTON.   Okay, you made your statement and I got my smoke. All's well that ends well, right?

KAFKA.   It's the only way we know they're watching.

MILTON.   Huh?

KAFKA.   We perform, we break typewriters, we type another page—and a cigarette appears. At least it's a sign that somebody out there is paying attention.

MILTON.   Our resident philosopher.

SWIFT.   But what'll happen if one of us *does* write *Hamlet*? Here we are, set down to prove the inadvertent virtues of randomness, and to produce something that we wouldn't even recognize if it passed right through our hands—but what if one of us actually does it?

MILTON.   Will we really be released?

KAFKA.   Will they give us the key to the city and a tickertape parade?

SWIFT.   Or will they move us on to *Ulysses*?[10] (*The others shriek in terror at the thought.*) Why did they pick *Hamlet* in the first place? What's *Hamlet* to them or they to *Hamlet* that we should care? Boy, there's the respect that makes calamity of so long life! For who would bear the whips and scorns of time, the oppressor's wrong, the proud man's contumely—[11]

MILTON.   Hey. Swifty!

SWIFT.   —the pangs of despisèd love, the law's delay—

MILTON.   Hey, Swifty! Relax, will you?

KAFKA.   Have a banana.

SWIFT.   I wish I could get Rosenbaum in here and see how he does at producing *Hamlet.* . . . *That's it!*

---

[9]Alludes to *Hamlet,* I, V, 172.

[10]James Joyce's (1882–1941) novel, published in 1922.

[11]Alludes to Hamlet's famous Soliloquy, Act III, scene i, lines 68–74.

KAFKA.   What?

SWIFT.   That's it! Forget about this random *Hamlet* crap. What about *revenge?*

KAFKA.   Revenge? On Rosenbaum?

SWIFT.   Who else? Hasn't he bereft us of our homes and families? Stepped in between us and our expectations?[12]

KAFKA.   How would we do it?

SWIFT.   Easy. We lure him in here to look at our typewriters, test them out like something's wrong—but! *we poison the typewriter keys!*

MILTON.   Oh Jesus.

SWIFT.   Sure. Some juice of cursèd hebona spread liberally over the keyboard? Ought to work like a charm.

MILTON.   Great.

SWIFT.   If that doesn't work, we envenom the tire-swing and invite him for a ride. Plus—I challenge him to a duel.[13]

MILTON.   Brilliant.

SWIFT.   Can't you see it? In the course of combat, I casually graze my rapier over the poisoned typewriter keys, and—(*Jabs.*)—a hit! A palpable hit![14] For a reserve, we lay by a cup with some venomous distillment. We'll put the pellet with the poison in the vessel with the pestle!

MILTON.   Listen, I gotta get back to work. The man is gonna want his pages. (*He rolls a fresh page into his typewriter.*)

KAFKA.   It's not a bad idea, but . . .

SWIFT.   What's the matter with you guys? I'm on to something here!

KAFKA.   I think it's hopeless, Swifty.

SWIFT.   But this is the goods!

MILTON.   Where was I . . . "Bedsocks knockwurst tinkerbelle."

KAFKA.   The readiness is all, I guess.

MILTON.   Damn straight. Just let me know when that K-button gives out, honey.

SWIFT.   Okay. You two serfs go back to work. I'll do all the thinking around here. Swifty—revenge! *(He paces, deep in thought.)*

MILTON.   "Tinkerbelle . . . shtuckelschwanz . . . hemorrhoid." Yeah, that's good. *That is good. (Types.)* "Shtuckelschwanz . . ."

KAFKA.   *(Types.)* "Act one, scene one. Elsinore Castle, Denmark . . ."

MILTON.   *(Types.)* ". . . hemorrhoid."

KAFKA.   *(Types.)* "Enter Bernardo and Francisco."

MILTON.   *(Types.)* "Pomegranate."

---

[12]Alludes to *Hamlet,* V, ii, 65.

[13]Alludes to *Hamlet,* IV, vii, 138–143.

[14]Alludes to *Hamlet,* V, ii, 269.

KAFKA.   *(Types.)* "Bernardo says, 'Who's there?' "[15]

MILTON.   *(Types.)* "Bazooka." *(Kafka continues to type* Hamlet, *as the lights fade.)*

Property list

3 typing tables

3 stools

3 old typewriters

Typing paper

3 wastebaskets overflowing with crushed paper

Tire-swing

Banana (KAFKA)

Bowl of peanuts (SWIFT)

3 ashtrays, full of butts

Empty cigarette pack (KAFKA)

Cigarette on a wire, for Milton

Cigarette lighter, for Milton

---

1 What kind of comic mileage does Ives get from having his three monkeys named Milton, Swift, and Kafka? What literary and philosophical frames of reference does Ives summon in this way? What is the effect of not naming any of the monkeys Shakespeare, the presumed author of *Hamlet*?

2 Select some lines where the offhand invented comments seem curiously appropriate to the context in which they occur while at the same time echoing real lines from actual literary works. How does *Words, Words, Words* raise the question of who decides what particular literary works are deemed valuable, and to what extent writers are aware of the quality of their work at the time of its composition?

3 How does Ives incorporate the revenge theme of *Hamlet* to comment on the ethics of animal experimentation?

4 Why is the contrast between what chimpanzees are and what they are able to write ironic? Identify specific moments within the play when this paradox is most apparent. (Glossary: *Irony, Paradox.*)

5 How do literary allusions function in this play? Why would knowing more about the events and actions alluded to enhance the audience's enjoyment of the sketch? (Glossary: *Allusion.*)

---

[15]Alludes to *Hamlet*, I, i, 1, the line with which the play open.

6 Do you detect a subtle satire directed against the traditional Eurocentric canon of literature, since the "author" of *Hamlet* is a "female" monkey named Kafka? Franz Kafka wrote "Metamorphosis" (1915), a story about a man who awakens to discover he has become a cockroach. He also wrote a delightful story of an ape captured in the wild who becomes civilized and addresses an academy of scientists in "A Report to an Academy" (published in *A Franz Kafka Miscellany*, 1940) which begins "Honored members of the Academy! You have done me the honor of inviting me to give your Academy an account of the life I formerly led as an ape."

◆ CONNECTIONS: COMMUNICATION ACROSS SPECIES

Donald R. Griffin, "Wordy Apes"

1. What issues discussed by Griffin are illustrated by Francine Patterson's experiences with Koko?
2. How does Griffin deal with the specific objections raised by Noam Chomsky in "The Language Faculty" (Ch. 1) as to why chimpanzees and apes cannot be considered to possess the animal equivalent of a human capacity for language?

Francine Patterson, "Conversations with a Gorilla"

1. To what extent do Patterson's descriptions of her training Koko to use American Sign Language undercut Susanne K. Langer's analysis of the impassable gulf that separates human from animal communication?
2. If Patterson's experiments with Koko were validated, how would perceptions of gorillas change in ways that would be similar to those described by Jack Solomon (see "What's in a Name?: The Ideology of Cultural Classification," Ch. 8) in relationship to other species?

Herbert S. Terrace, "What I Learned From Nim Chimsky"

1. How does Terrace's research undercut the findings of Francine Patterson? To what extent do Terrace and Patterson apply different criteria to assess primate capacity for language?
2. How does Terrace's research support Noam Chomsky's assessment as to the differences between human and animal languages (see "The Language Faculty," Ch. 1)?

Susanne K. Langer, "Language and Thought"

1. To what extent does the entire field of primate research described by Donald R. Griffin counter Langer's claim that the fundamental difference between animal communication and human language is that animals are incapable of conceptualizing abstract symbolic thought?
2. How does Enrique Fernandez's discussion of the idea of what salsa represents in "Salsa × 2" (Ch. 6) illustrate Langer's distinction between sign and symbol?

Vicki Hearne, "How To Say 'Fetch!'"

1. Evaluate Hearne's contention that the relationship between a trainer and a dog or horse is intrinsically a higher form of communication than that capable of being achieved with primates by comparing her account with that of Francine Patterson.
2. In what sense might the process of training entail what Kenneth Burke calls "the dancing of an attitude" in "Symbolic Action" (Ch. 3)?

David Ives, *Words, Words, Words*

1. How does Herbert S. Terrace's analysis of Nim Chimsky's progress or lack thereof at Columbia University offer a window into the mind of the experimenter Dr. David Rosenbaum, who is conducting this experiment at Columbia University?
2. Do you detect any signs that Ives might be spoofing Noam Chomsky's theory put forward in "The Language Faculty" (Ch. 1) that the capacity for language is unique to humans? Why or why not?

◆ WRITING ASSIGNMENTS FOR CHAPTER 2

1. What actions did a pet of yours ever take that suggested evidence of consciousness, motivation, and intelligence? Describe this event or action and reply to the objections of someone who would not see this action as evidence of intelligence, but simply your desire to interpret it as such.
2. What could your pet say about you that no other human being knows?
3. Describe the search you went through and the final decision you made as to what to name your pet. What does the name reveal about the character traits important to you and your family in bestowing an identity on the animal?
4. Discuss an experience you have had that convinced you that animals (dogs, cats, birds, horses, reptiles, etc.) can indeed communicate with people.
5. Take a dog's-eye view of the member of the human species called an "animal trainer" by stepping outside the situation and objectively describing traits that distinguish either animal trainers in general, Vicki Hearne in her narrative, or yourself if you have ever had the occasion to try to train a domestic animal. Write it from the animal's point of view.
6. In what sense can a dog have, as Hearne says, a greater command of language than chimpanzees do? Compare the accounts of Hearne with those of Francine Patterson. Koko appears to have mastered a human language, yet cannot be brought into a mutually responsible moral relationship, as Salty, the retriever can. Who, in your view, is a truer possessor of language, Koko or Salty? Why?
7. How does the new potential for transgenic engineering (that is, the intermingling of genes from various species) raise concerns for a whole new category of abuse and exploitation of animals? In what way do the essays in this chapter reveal underlying assumptions about animals—as sentient creatures

on one hand or as biological resources to be manipulated on the other—that would need to be considered in assessing this new technology? Consider that chimpanzees share over 99 percent of our genetic heritage, but no laws exist that prevent them from being captured, locked into cages, and dissected for research purposes. How "human" would a creature have to be in order to be included in the system of rights and protections accorded to humans? How do the language studies in this chapter impact on this question?

8. What are the teachings of major world religions (Buddhism, Judaism, Christianity, Hinduism, Islam, and others) about the relationship between human beings and animals? How do these various tenets impact on the issues discussed in this chapter?

9. How do recent discoveries (by Elizabeth Brannon and Herbert Terrace) that rhesus monkeys can count shed new light on the question of whether monkeys can think (*New York Times,* October 23, 1998)?

Words are as vital to life as food and
drink and sex, but on the whole we don't
show as much interest in language as we
do in the other—more obvious—
pleasures.

—Gyles Brandreth

"Food as metaphor for love? Again?"

The Bodily Basis of Language

I f language is, as Noam Chomsky suggested, a profoundly biologically rooted phenomenon rather than an abstract cultural invention, then where should we draw the line as to where the biological makeup of our brain leaves off and the body's capacity to influence language begins? This conception of language as a gesture rooted in the sensory physical matrix of bodily existence proposes that we learn our native languages first through the body, not mentally. The view that language is expressive and gestural has sparked a number of intriguing investigations of the mind-body connection.

One of the earliest studies to recognize the profound implications of the way body language could be construed symbolically is Kenneth Burke's influential essay "Symbolic Action." Burke views language as a bodily phenomenon that is at its root gestural, representing an individual's unique response to the world. In "The Flesh of Language," David Abram elaborates on this conception that language arises from the perceptual interplay between the body and the world in direct sensory experience.

George Lakoff's groundbreaking investigation "Anger" brings this speculative discussion down to earth by revealing how metaphors used to express anger invariably incorporate actual images reflective of bodily states. Lakoff shows how even when we think we are expressing ourselves in abstract terms—in metaphors—direct sensory experience always underlies the words we use.

The consequences when language strays too far from direct sensory experience are dramatically illustrated in Oliver Sacks's "The President's Speech." His patients suffered from aphasia, a mind-body disorder that sensitized them to discrepancies between words and gestures and made them superb detectors of rhetorical deception.

Although rooted in the body, we have come to believe that language exists in its own abstract realm as a purely mental phenomenon. The nature of autism will quickly disabuse us of this notion. Imagine being unable to conceive of a thought unless you could simultaneously imagine a concrete specific image that expressed the abstract idea. This is the experience Temple Grandin describes in "Thinking in Pictures." She was quite literally unable to grasp the meaning of a sentence like "we have to bridge the gap in understanding . . ." unless she could translate it into the visual picture of a bridge spanning a chasm. Grandin's account is so extraordinary because she is one of the very few suffering from autism who has given us a glimpse into the world of concrete images where we all begin.

The enunciation of individually pronounced syllables that we call spoken language is not the only means by which human beings communicate. Richard Selzer, in "The Language of Pain," explores the communicative meanings implicit in the sounds we make when we suffer. This language is immediate, spontaneous, gestural, and, as Selzer points out, by no means arbitrary, since all people in the world speak it, whatever other language they speak.

In "Yellowstone: The Erotics of Place," Terry Tempest Williams takes up the theme of the mythic connection between language and our direct sensory experience of the environment. Williams discloses that at the most primordial level we are surrounded by a landscape that speaks to us. This is nowhere more apparent than in Yellowstone National Park.

In "The Language of Clothes," Alison Lurie explores the gestural function of clothing in her examination of how body decoration, ornamentation, and fashion are a kind of language whose meanings are subtly attuned to changing social trends.

Symbolic Action   *Kenneth Burke*

◆ KENNETH BURKE (1897–1993) was a distinguished writer, translator, editor, critic, and lecturer. He taught at the University of Chicago and Syracuse University, and authored numerous pioneering works in rhetorical and literary theory. The following excerpt is drawn from his influential book *The Philosophy of Literary Form: Studies in Symbolic Action* (2nd Ed., 1967).

The debate as to what constitutes true language is a long-standing one. According to Burke, what we call language may be a partial, incomplete, or too narrow conception, and ought to be expanded to include unique symbolic gestural responses that communicate intention, meaning, and emotion through the body. Burke looks at these mind-body expressions as possessing the same function that articulated speech and written language do. He analyzes the grammar of these gestures and speculates on how they evolved. Burke presents a compelling case that our conception of spoken and written language ought to be broadened to include a continuum of language systems. Each person has a repertoire of gestural responses that is unique. For example, he points out that psychosomatic illnesses have come to be recognized as bodily expressions of underlying mental states (such as having a "pain in the neck" when encountering someone you find to be just that).

TO CONSIDER   What nonverbal forms of communication do you use most often?

We might sum all this up by saying that poetry, or any verbal act, is to be considered as "symbolic action." But though I must use this term, I object strenuously to having the general perspective labeled as "symbolism." I recognize that people like to label, that labeling *comforts* them by *getting things placed*. But I object to "symbolism" as a label, because it suggests too close a link with a particular school of poetry, the Symbolist Movement, and usually implies the unreality of the world in which we live, as though nothing could be what it is, but must always be something else (as though a house could never be a house, but must be, let us say, the concealed surrogate for a woman, or as though the woman one marries could never be the woman one marries, but must be a surrogate for one's mother, etc.).

Still, there is a difference, and a radical difference, between building a house and writing a poem about building a house—and a poem about having children by marriage is not the same thing as having children by marriage. There are *practical* acts, and there are symbolic acts (nor is the distinction, clear enough in its extremes, to be dropped simply because there is a borderline area wherein many practical acts take on a symbolic ingredient, as one may buy a certain commodity not merely to use it, but also because its possession testifies to his enrollment in a certain stratum of society).

The symbolic act is the *dancing of an attitude* (a point that Richards has brought out, though I should want to revise his position to the extent of noting that in Richards' doctrines the attitude is pictured as too sparse in realistic content). In this attitudinizing of the poem, the whole body may finally become involved, in ways suggested by the doctrines of behaviorism. The correlation between mind and body here is neatly conveyed in two remarks by Hazlitt, concerning Coleridge:

I observed that he continually crossed me on the way by shifting from one side of the foot-path to the other. This struck me as an odd movement; but I did not at that time connect it with any instability of purpose or involuntary change of principle, as I have done since. . . .

There is a *chaunt* in the recitation both of Coleridge and Wordsworth, which acts as a spell upon the hearer, and disarms the judgment. Perhaps they have deceived themselves by making habitual use of this ambiguous accompaniment. Coleridge's manner is more full, animated, and varied; Wordsworth's more equable, sustained, and internal. The one might be termed more *dramatic,* the other more *lyrical.* Coleridge has told me that he himself liked to compose in walking over uneven ground, or breaking through the straggling branches of a copse-wood; whereas Wordsworth always wrote (if he could) walking up and down a straight gravel-walk, or in some spot where the continuity of his verse met with no collateral interruption.[1]

We might also cite from a letter of Hopkins, mentioned by R. P. Blackmur in *The Kenyon Review* (Winter, 1939):

As there is something of the "old Adam" in all but the holiest men and in them at least enough to make them understand it in others, so there is an old Adam of barbarism, boyishness, wildness, rawness, rankness, the disreputable, the unrefined in the refined and educated. It is that that I meant by tykishness (a tyke is a stray sly unowned dog).

Do we not glimpse the labyrinthine mind of Coleridge, the *puzzle* in its pace, "danced" in the act of walking—and do we not glimpse behind the agitated rhythm of Hopkins' verse, the conflict between the priest and the "tyke," with the jerkiness of his lines "symbolically enacting" the mental conflict? So we today seem to immunize ourselves to the arhythmic quality of both traffic and accountancy by a distrust of the lullaby and the rocking cradle as formative stylistic equipment for our children.

The accumulating lore on the nature of "psychogenic illnesses" has revealed that something so "practical" as a bodily ailment may be a "symbolic" act on the part of the body which, in this materialization, *dances* a corresponding state of mind, reordering the glandular and neural behavior of the organism in obedience to mind-body correspondences, quite as the formal dancer reorders his externally observable gesturing to match his attitudes. Thus, I know of a man who, going to a dentist, was proud of the calmness with which he took his punishment. But after the session was ended, the dentist said to him: "I observe that you are very much afraid of me. For I have noted that, when patients are frightened, their saliva becomes thicker, more sticky. And yours was exceptionally so."

---

[1]The quotations are lifted from Lawrence Hanson's excellent study, *The Life of S. T. Coleridge.*

Which would indicate that, while the man in the dentist's chair was "dancing an attitude of calmness" on the public level, as a social facade, on the purely bodily or biological level his salivary glands were "dancing his true attitude." For he *was* apprehensive of pain, and his glandular secretions "said so." Similarly I have read that there is an especially high incidence of stomach ulcers among taxi drivers—an occupational illness that would not seem to be accounted for merely by poor and irregular meals, since these are equally the lot of workers at other kinds of jobs. Do we not see, rather, a bodily response to the intensely arhythmic quality of the work itself, the irritation in the continual jagginess of traffic, all puzzle and no pace, and only the timing of the cylinders performing with regularity, as if all the *ritual* of the occupational act had been drained off, into the *routine* of the motor's explosions and revolutions?

In such ways, the whole body is involved in an enactment. And we might make up a hypothetical illustration of this sort: imagine a poet who, on perfectly rational grounds rejecting the political and social authority of the powers that be, wrote poems enacting this attitude of rejection. This position we might call his symbolic act on the abstract level. On the personal, or intimate level, he might embody the same attitude in a vindictive style (as so much of modern work, proud of its emancipation from prayer, has got this emancipation dubiously, by simply substituting prayer-in-reverse, the oath).

---

1 How, in Burke's view, do the unique individual and contrasting styles of Coleridge and Wordsworth (when they walk and when they write) provide evidence of a kind of symbolic acting out of the personality of each man? According to Burke, in what sense are each of these projections the "dancing of an attitude"?

2 Burke's philosophical and rhetorical ideas are based on the observation of striking correspondences between body language and mental states. Does this equivalence make sense to you? Why or why not?

3 Have you ever observed the correspondence between mind and body that Burke discusses, especially where body gestures revealed an attitude that was belied by the public or social attitude?

4 How does Burke's conception of the symbolic differ from the traditional literary one? (Glossary: *Symbol.*)

5 In this essay, Burke tries to account for the symbolic expression of mental attitudes. Explain how Burke develops this chain of cause and effect throughout his essay. What verbal signals does Burke use when discussing causes and when discussing effects? (Glossary: *Cause and Effect.*)

6 Identify and describe some of your favorite nonverbal body signals that people use in their daily lives. In each case, describe the action that takes place (for example, miming the action of shooting oneself in the head with a handgun), the circumstances under which the action would occur (in this case, when someone commits a social error), and the meaning of the gesture ("I am so embarrassed I could shoot myself").

The Flesh of Language   *David Abram*

◆ DAVID ABRAM is an ecologist and philosopher whose writings have had a profound influence on the environmental movement in North America and abroad. He has a Ph.D. in philosophy and has received fellowships from the Watson and Rockefeller Foundations. The following selection is drawn from his book *The Spell of the Sensuous* (1996).

Abram reveals that the idea that we learn language first through the body had already been noted by 18th-century philosophers such as Jean-Jacques Rousseau (1712–1778). In this view, Abram is an heir to the Romantic tradition, but provides a valuable corrective to those who view language as a purely mental phenomenon and forget that we are situated in a dynamic relationship with the natural world.

> **TO CONSIDER**   What experiences have you had in which you heard what some writers call the "language of nature"?

> *The rain surrounded the cabin . . . with a whole world of meaning, of secrecy, of rumor. Think of it: all that speech pouring down, selling nothing, judging nobody, drenching the thick mulch of dead leaves, soaking the trees, filling the gullies and crannies of the wood with water, washing out the places where men have stripped the hillside. . . .Nobody started it, nobody is going to stop it. It will talk as long as it wants, the rain. As long as it talks I am going to listen.*
>
> —Thomas Merton

EVERY ATTEMPT TO DEFINITIVELY *SAY WHAT LANGUAGE IS* is subject to a curious limitation. For the only medium with which we can define language is language itself. We are therefore unable to circumscribe the whole of language within our definition. It may be best, then, to leave language undefined, and to thus acknowledge its open-endedness, its mysteriousness. Nevertheless, by paying attention to this mystery we may develop a conscious familiarity with it, a sense of its texture, its habits, its sources of sustenance.

Merleau-Ponty, as we have seen, spent much of his life demonstrating that the event of perception unfolds as a reciprocal exchange between the living body and the animate world that surrounds it. He showed, as well, that this exchange, for all its openness and indeterminacy, is nevertheless highly articulate. (Although it confounds the causal logic that we attempt to impose upon it, perceptual experience has its own coherent structure; it seems to embody an open-ended logos that we enact from within rather than the abstract logic we deploy from without.) The disclosure that preverbal perception is already an exchange, and the recognition that this exchange has its own coherence and articulation, together suggested that perception, this ongoing reciprocity, is the very soil and support of that more conscious exchange we call language.

Already in the *Phenomenology of Perception,* Merleau-Ponty had begun to work out a notion of human language as a profoundly carnal phenomenon, rooted in our sensorial experience of each other and of the world. In a famous chapter entitled "The Body as Expression, and Speech," he wrote at length of the gestural genesis of language, the way that communicative meaning is first incarnate in the gestures by which the body spontaneously expresses feelings and responds to changes in its affective environment. The gesture is spontaneous and immediate. It is not an arbitrary sign that we mentally attach to a particular emotion or feeling; rather, the gesture *is* the bodying-forth of that emotion into the world, it *is* that feeling of delight or of anguish in its tangible, visible aspect. When we encounter such a spontaneous gesture, we do not first see it as a blank behavior, which we then mentally associate with a particular content or significance; rather, the bodily gesture speaks directly to our own body, and is thereby understood without any interior reflection:

> Faced with an angry or threatening gesture, I have no need, in order to understand it, to [mentally] recall the feelings which I myself experienced when I used these gestures on my own account. . . . I do not see anger or a threatening attitude as a psychic fact hidden behind the gesture, I read anger in it. The gesture *does not make me think of anger,* it is anger itself.

Active, living speech is just such a gesture, a vocal gesticulation wherein the meaning is inseparable from the sound, the shape, and the rhythm of the words. Communicative meaning is always, in its depths, affective; it remains rooted in the sensual dimension of experience, born of the body's native capacity to resonate with other bodies and with the landscape as a whole. Linguistic meaning is not some ideal and bodiless essence that we arbitrarily assign to a physical sound or word and then toss out into the "external" world. Rather, meaning sprouts in the very depths of the sensory world, in the heat of meeting, encounter, participation.

We do not, as children, first enter into language by consciously studying the formalities of syntax and grammar or by memorizing the dictionary definitions of words, but rather by actively making sounds—by crying in pain and laughing in joy, by squealing and babbling and playfully mimicking the surrounding soundscape, gradually entering through such mimicry into the specific melodies of the local language, our resonant bodies slowly coming to echo the inflections and accents common to our locale and community.

We thus learn our native language not mentally but bodily. We appropriate new words and phrases first through their affective tonality and texture, through the way they feel in the mouth or roll off the tongue, and it is this direct, felt significance—the *taste* of a word or phrase, the way it influences or modulates the body—that provides the fertile, polyvalent source for all the more refined and rarefied meanings which that term may come to have for us.

> . . . the meaning of words must be finally induced by the words themselves, or more exactly, their conceptual meaning must be formed by a kind of subtraction from a *gestural meaning,* which is immanent in speech.

Language, then, cannot be genuinely studied or understood in isolation from the sensuous reverberation and resonance of active speech. James M. Edie attempts to summarize this aspect of Merleau-Ponty's thought in this manner:

> . . . Merleau-Ponty's first point is that words, even when they finally achieve the ability to carry referential and, eventually, conceptual levels of meaning, never completely lose that primitive, strictly phonemic, level of 'affective' meaning which is not translatable into their conceptual definitions. There is, he argues, an affective tonality, a mode of conveying meaning beneath the level of thought, beneath the level of the words themselves . . . which is contained in the words *just insofar as they are patterned sounds,* as just the sounds which this particular historical language uniquely uses, and which are much more like a melody—a 'singing of the world'—than fully translatable, conceptual thought. Merleau-Ponty is almost alone among philosophers of language in his sensitivity to this level of meaning. . . .

Edie here emphasizes Merleau-Ponty's originality with regard to language, and asserts that Merleau-Ponty gave special attention to "what no philosopher from Plato on down ever had any interest in" (namely, the gestural significance of spoken sounds). Yet this assertion is true only if one holds a very restricted view of the philosophical tradition. The expressive, gestural basis of language had already been emphasized in the first half of the eighteenth century by the Italian philosopher Giambattista Vico (1668–1744), who in his *New Science* wrote of language as arising from expressive gestures, and suggested that the earliest and most basic words had taken shape from expletives uttered in startled response to powerful natural events, or from the frightened, stuttering mimesis of such events—like the crack and rumble of thunder across the sky. Shortly thereafter, in France, Jean-Jacques Rousseau (1712–1778) wrote of gestures and spontaneous expressions of feeling as the earliest forms of language, while in Germany, Johann Gottfried Herder (1744–1803) argued that language originates in our sensuous receptivity to the sounds and shapes of the natural environment.

In his embodied philosophy of language, then, Merleau-Ponty is the heir of a long-standing, if somewhat heretical lineage. Linguistic meaning, for him, is rooted in the felt experience induced by specific sounds and sound-shapes as they echo and contrast with one another, each language a kind of song, a particular way of "singing the world."

The more prevalent view of language, at least since the scientific revolution, and still assumed in some manner by most linguists today, considers any language to be a set of arbitrary but conventionally agreed upon words, or "signs," linked by a purely formal system of syntactic and grammatical rules. Language, in this view, is rather like a *code;* it is a way of *representing* actual things and events in the perceived world, but it has no internal, nonarbitrary connections to that world, and hence is readily separable from it.

If Merleau-Ponty is right, however, then the denotative, conventional dimension of language can never be truly severed from the sensorial dimension of direct, affective meaning. If we are not, in truth, immaterial minds merely housed in earthly bodies, but are from the first material, corporeal beings, then it is the sensuous, gestural significance of spoken sounds—their direct bodily resonance—that makes verbal communication possible at all. It is this expressive potency—the soundful influence of spoken words upon the sensing body—that supports all the more abstract and conventional meanings that we assign to those words. Although we may be oblivious to the gestural, somatic dimension of language, having repressed it in favor of strict dictionary definitions and the abstract precision of specialized terminologies, this dimension remains subtly operative in all our speaking and writing—if, that is, our words have any significance whatsoever. For meaning, as we have said, remains rooted in the sensory life of the body—it cannot be completely cut off from the soil of direct, perceptual experience without withering and dying.

Yet to affirm that linguistic meaning is primarily expressive, gestural, and poetic, and that conventional and denotative meanings are inherently secondary and derivative, is to renounce the claim that "language" is an exclusively human property. If language is always, in its depths, physically and sensorially resonant, then it can never be definitively separated from the evident expressiveness of bird-song, or the evocative howl of a wolf late at night. The chorus of frogs gurgling in unison at the edge of a pond, the snarl of a wildcat as it springs upon its prey, or the distant honking of Canadian geese veeing south for the winter, all reverberate with affective, gestural significance, the same significance that vibrates through our own conversations and soliloquies, moving us at times to tears, or to anger, or to intellectual insights we could never have anticipated. Language as a bodily phenomenon accrues to *all* expressive bodies, not just to the human. Our own speaking, then, does not set us outside of the animate landscape but—whether or not we are aware of it—inscribes us more fully in its chattering, whispering, soundful depths.

If, for instance, one comes upon two human friends unexpectedly meeting for the first time in many months, and one chances to hear their initial words of surprise, greeting, and pleasure, one may readily notice, if one pays close enough attention, a tonal, melodic layer of communication beneath the explicit denotative meaning of the words—a rippling rise and fall of the voices in a sort of musical duet, rather like two birds singing to each other. Each voice, each side of the duet, mimes a bit of the other's melody while adding its own inflection and style, and then is echoed by the other in turn—the two singing bodies thus tuning and attuning to one another, rediscovering a common register, *remembering* each other. It requires only a slight shift in focus to realize that this melodic singing is carrying the bulk of communication in this encounter, and that the explicit meanings of the actual words ride on the surface of this depth like waves on the surface of the sea.

It is by a complementary shift of attention that one may suddenly come to hear the familiar song of a blackbird or a thrush in a surprisingly new manner— not just as a pleasant melody repeated mechanically, as on a tape player in the background, but as active, meaningful speech. Suddenly, subtle variations in the tone and rhythm of that whistling phrase seem laden with expressive intention, and the two birds singing to each other across the field appear for the first time as attentive, conscious beings, earnestly engaged in the same world that we ourselves engage, yet from an astonishingly different angle and perspective.

Moreover, if we allow that spoken meaning remains rooted in gesture and bodily expressiveness, we will be unable to restrict our renewed experience of language solely to animals. As we have already recognized, in the untamed world of direct sensory experience *no* phenomenon presents itself as utterly passive or inert. To the sensing body *all* phenomena are animate, actively soliciting the participation of our senses, or else withdrawing from our focus and repelling our involvement. Things disclose themselves to our immediate perception as vectors, as styles of unfolding—not as finished chunks of matter given once and for all, but as dynamic ways of engaging the senses and modulating the body. Each thing, each phenomenon, has the power to reach us and to influence us. Every phenomenon, in other words, is potentially expressive. At the end of his chapter "The Body as Expression, and Speech," Merleau-Ponty writes:

> It is the body which points out, and which speaks. . . . This disclosure [of the body's immanent expressiveness] . . . extends, as we shall see, to the whole sensible world, and our gaze, prompted by the experience of our own body, will discover in all other "objects" the miracle of expression.

Thus, at the most primordial level of sensuous, bodily experience, we find ourselves in an expressive, gesturing landscape, in a world that *speaks.*

It is this dynamic, interconnected reality that provokes and sustains all our speaking, lending something of its structure to all our various languages. The enigmatic nature of language echoes and "prolongs unto the invisible" the wild, interpenetrating, interdependent nature of the sensible landscape itself.

Ultimately, then, it is not the human body alone but rather the whole of the sensuous world that provides the deep structure of language. As we ourselves dwell and move within language, so, ultimately, do the other animals and animate things of the world; if we do not notice them there, it is only because language has forgotten its expressive depths. "Language is a life, is our life and the life of the things. . . ." It is no more true that *we* speak than that the things, and the animate world itself, *speak within us:*

> That the things have us and that it is not we who have the things. . . . That it is being that speaks within us and not we who speak of being.

From such reflections we may begin to suspect that the complexity of human language is related to the complexity of the earthly ecology—not to any complexity of our species considered apart from that matrix. Language, writes Merleau-Ponty, "is the very voice of the trees, the waves, and the forests."

As technological civilization diminishes the biotic diversity of the earth, language itself is diminished. As there are fewer and fewer songbirds in the air, due to the destruction of their forests and wetlands, human speech loses more and more of its evocative power. For when we no longer hear the voices of warbler and wren, our own speaking can no longer be nourished by their cadences. As the splashing speech of the rivers is silenced by more and more dams, as we drive more and more of the land's wild voices into the oblivion of extinction, our own languages become increasingly impoverished and weightless, progressively emptied of their earthly resonance.

---

1 How, in Abram's view, have previous investigations of language failed to take into account the interplay between sensorial experience and perception in terms of the subtle shift in associations, memories, and meanings that words have for us as we converse?

2 What, according to Abram, is the significance of Merleau-Ponty's observations of the emotional associations instantly registered in response to gestures, tone, and other extralinguistic factors that words evoke? How does Merleau-Ponty's work continue the approach that the philosophers Vico (language mimics nature), Rousseau (emotions comprise the first nongrammatical language), and Herder (spoken words tie our bodies into the resonance of nature) had begun previously?

3 What common experiences cited by Abram seem to support his thesis that our concept of language should be broadened to include gestures, emotions, and a connection with nature?

4 Abram is attempting to bridge the gap between conclusions drawn from the works of philosophers (Merleau-Ponty in particular, but also Vico, Rousseau, Herder) and personal experiences we all have had (talking to a friend, hearing the familar song of a blackbird or thrush). Did the academically based analyses illuminate the personal experiences? Why or why not? (Glossary: *Objective/Subjective.*)

5 How does Abram use causal analysis to encourage his readers to gain a more accurate understanding of the mind-body connection? To what extent do his thesis statements signal how the essay will be developed? In your view, what purpose does Abram have in writing this essay—to enlighten his readers, to persuade them, or to speculate on the consequences of contemporary society's separation from nature? (Glossary: *Cause and Effect.*)

6 Create a dialogue between you and a feature, condition, plant, or animal in the natural environment near you (for example, a mountain, a wolf, a marshland, a redwood tree, etc.) whose presence is important to you. Give this feature its own voice and consider how its perspective differs from yours.

Anger   *George Lakoff*

◆ GEORGE LAKOFF is a professor of linguistics at the University of California at Berkeley. He is coauthor with Mark Johnson of *Metaphors We Live By* (1980) and, with Mark Turner, of *More Than Cool Reason: A Field Guide to Poetic Metaphor* (1989). The following excerpts are drawn from his book *Women, Fire, and Dangerous Things: What Categories Reveal About the Mind* (1987).

Lakoff believes that the clearest proof of the extent to which our awareness of physical states permeates the language we use can be seen in metaphors we employ to express the emotion of anger. When a number of these metaphors ("doing a slow burn," "letting off steam," "blew up," "hot under the collar, "seeing red") are analyzed, they reveal a coherent and widely exhibited conceptual organization that is based on metaphorical expressions of actual bodily states. Lakoff believes that rather than being simple expressions of feeling, the language used to express anger reveals a number of scenarios (anger/appeasement, anger/retribution) that determine not only how we express anger but how we think about it. A disturbing manifestation of how we conceptualize and express anger can be seen in the metaphors that connect rape and lust with anger—and result in blaming the victim.

TO CONSIDER   What expressions do you use when you are angry? What metaphors underlie these expressions?

THE CONCEPTUALIZATION OF FEELING

Emotions are often considered to be feelings alone, and as such they are viewed as being devoid of conceptual content. As a result, the study of emotions is usually not taken seriously by students of semantics and conceptual structure. A topic such as the logic of emotions would seem on this view to be a contradiction in terms, since emotions, being devoid of conceptual content, would give rise to no inferences at all, or at least none of any interest.

I would like to argue that the opposite is true, that emotions have an extremely complex conceptual structure, which gives rise to a wide variety of nontrivial inferences. The work I will be presenting is based on joint research by myself and Zoltán Kövecses. Kövecses had suggested that the conceptual struc-

---

ture of emotions could be studied in detail using techniques devised by Mark Johnson and myself (Lakoff and Johnson 1980) for the systematic investigation of expressions that are understood metaphorically. English has an extremely large range of such expressions. What we set out to do was to study them systematically to see if any coherent conceptual structure emerged.

At first glance, the conventional expressions used to talk about anger seem so diverse that finding any coherent system would seem impossible. For example, if we look up *anger* in, say, *Roget's University Thesaurus,* we find about three hundred entries, most of which have something or other to do with anger, but the thesaurus doesn't tell us exactly what. Many of these are idioms, and they seem too diverse to reflect any coherent cognitive model. Here are some sample sentences using such idioms:

- He *lost his cool.*
- She was *looking daggers* at me.
- I almost *burst a blood vessel.*
- He was *foaming at the mouth.*
- You're beginning to *get to me.*
- You make my *blood boil.*
- He's *wrestling* with his anger.
- Watch out! He's *on a short fuse.*
- He's just *letting off steam.*
- Don't *get a hernia!*
- Try to *keep a grip on yourself.*
- Don't *fly off the handle.*
- When I told him, he *blew up.*
- He *channeled* his anger into something constructive.
- He was *red with anger.*
- He was *blue in the face.*
- He *appeased* his anger.
- He was *doing a slow burn.*
- He *suppressed* his anger.
- She kept *bugging* me.
- When I told my mother, *she had a cow.*

What do these expressions have to do with anger, and what do they have to do with each other? We will be arguing that they are not random. When we look at inferences among these expressions, it becomes clear that there must be a systematic structure of some kind. We know, for example, that someone who is foaming at the mouth has lost his cool. We know that someone who is looking daggers at you is likely to be doing a slow burn or be on a short fuse. We know that someone whose blood is boiling has not had his anger appeased. We know that someone who has channeled his anger into something constructive has not had a cow. How do we know these things? Is it just that each idiom has a literal meaning and the inferences are based on the literal meanings? Or is there something more going on? What we will try to show is that there is a coherent conceptual organization underlying all these expressions and that much of it is metaphorical and metonymical in nature.

METAPHOR AND METONYMY

The analysis we are proposing begins with the common folk theory of the physiological effects of anger:

> The physiological effects of anger are increased body heat, increased internal pressure (blood pressure, muscular pressure), agitation, and interference with accurate perception.
>
> As anger increases, its physiological effects increase.
>
> There is a limit beyond which the physiological effects of anger impair normal functioning.
>
> We use this folk theory in large measure to tell when someone is angry on the basis of their appearance—as well as to signal anger or hide it. In doing this, we make use of a general metonymic principle:
>
> The physiological effects of an emotion stand for the emotion.
>
> Given this principle, the folk theory given above yields a system of metonymies for anger:

Body heat

- Don't get *hot under the collar.*
- Billy's a *hothead.*
- They were having a *heated argument.*
- When the cop gave her a ticket, she got all *hot and bothered* and started cursing.

Internal pressure

- Don't get a *hernia!*
- When I found out, I almost *burst a blood vessel.*
- He almost had a *hemorrhage.*

Increased body heat and/or blood pressure is assumed to cause redness in the face and neck area, and such redness can also metonymically indicate anger.

Redness in face and neck area

- She was *scarlet with rage.*
- He got *red with anger.*
- He was *flushed with anger.*

Agitation

- She was *shaking* with anger.
- I was *hopping mad.*
- He was *quivering with rage.*
- He's *all worked up.*

- There's no need to get so *excited* about it!
- She's *all wrought up.*
- You look *upset.*

Interference with accurate perception

- She was *blind with rage.*
- I was beginning to *see red.*
- I was so mad I *couldn't see straight.*

Each of these expressions indicate the presence of anger via its supposed physiological effects.

The folk theory of physiological effects, especially the part that emphasizes HEAT, forms the basis of the most general metaphor for anger: ANGER IS HEAT. There are two versions of this metaphor, one where the heat is applied to fluids, the other where it is applied to solids. When it is applied to fluids, we get: ANGER IS THE HEAT OF A FLUID IN A CONTAINER. The specific motivation for this consists of the HEAT, INTERNAL PRESSURE, and AGITATION parts of the folk theory. When ANGER IS HEAT is applied to solids, we get the version ANGER IS FIRE, which is motivated by the HEAT and REDNESS aspects of the folk theory of physiological effects.

As we will see shortly, the fluid version is much more highly elaborated. The reason for this, we surmise, is that in our overall conceptual system we have the general metaphor:

The body is a container for the emotions.

- He was *filled* with anger.
- She couldn't *contain* her joy.
- She was *brimming* with rage.
- Try to get your anger *out of your system.*

The ANGER IS HEAT metaphor, when applied to fluids, combines with the metaphor THE BODY IS A CONTAINER FOR THE EMOTIONS to yield the central metaphor of the system:

Anger is the heat of a fluid in a container.

- You make my *blood boil.*
- *Simmer* down!
- I had reached the *boiling point.*
- Let him *stew.*

A historically derived instance of this metaphor is:

- She was *seething with rage.*

Although most speakers do not now use *seethe* to indicate physical boiling, the boiling image is still there when *seethe* is used to indicate anger. Similarly, *pissed*

off is used only to refer to anger, not to the hot liquid under pressure in the bladder. Still, the effectiveness of the expression seems to depend on such an image.

When there is no heat, the liquid is cool and calm. In the central metaphor,
cool and calmness corresponds to lack of anger.

- Keep *cool*.
- Stay *calm*. . . .

Let us now turn to the question of what issues the central metaphor
addresses and what kind of ontology of anger it reveals. The central metaphor
focuses on the fact that anger can be intense, that it can lead to a loss of control,
and that a loss of control can be dangerous. Let us begin with intensity. Anger
is conceptualized as a mass, and takes the grammar of mass nouns, as opposed
to count nouns:

> Thus, you can say
> > How much anger has he got in him?
> but not
> > How many angers does he have in him?

Anger thus has the ontology of a mass entity, that is, it has a scale indicating its
amount, it exists when the amount is greater than zero, and it goes out of existence when the amount falls to zero. In the central metaphor, the scale indicating the amount of anger is the heat scale. But, as the central metaphor indicates,
the anger scale is not open-ended; it has a limit. Just as a hot fluid in a closed container can only take so much heat before it explodes, so we conceptualize the
anger scale as having a limit point. We can only bear so much anger before we
explode, that is, lose control. This has its correlates in our folk theory of physiological effects. As anger gets more intense the physiological effects increase and
those increases interfere with our normal functioning. Body heat, blood pressure,
agitation, and interference with perception cannot increase without limit before
our ability to function normally becomes seriously impaired, and we lose control
over our functioning. In the folk model of anger, loss of control is dangerous,
both to the angry person and to those around him. In the central metaphor, the
danger of loss of control is understood as the danger of explosion. . . .

The ANGER IS AN OPPONENT metaphor is constituted by the following correspondences:

Source: STRUGGLE   *Target:* ANGER

- The opponent is anger.
- Winning is controlling anger.
- Losing is having anger control you.
- Surrender is allowing anger to take control of you.
- The pool of resources needed for winning is the energy needed to con-
  trol anger.

One thing that is left out of this account so far is what constitutes "appease-ment." To appease an opponent is to give in to his demands. This suggests that anger has demands. We will address the question of what these demands are below.

The OPPONENT metaphor focuses on the issue of control and the danger of loss of control to the angry person himself. There is another metaphor that focuses on the issue of control, but its main aspect is the danger to others. It is a very widespread metaphor in Western culture, namely, PASSIONS ARE BEASTS INSIDE A PERSON. According to this metaphor, there is a part of each person that is a wild animal. Civilized people are supposed to keep that part of them private, that is, they are supposed to keep the animal inside them. In the metaphor, loss of control is equivalent to the animal getting loose. And the behavior of a person who has lost control is the behavior of a wild animal. There are versions of this metaphor for the various passions—desire, anger, etc. In the case of anger, the beast presents a danger to other people.

Anger is a dangerous animal.

- He has a *ferocious* temper.
- He has a *fierce* temper.
- It's dangerous to *arouse* his anger.
- That *awakened* my ire.
- His anger *grew*.
- He has a *monstrous* temper.
- He *unleashed* his anger.
- Don't let your anger *get out of hand*.
- He *lost his grip* on his anger.
- His anger is *insatiable*.

An example that draws on both the FIRE and DANGEROUS ANIMAL metaphors is:

- He was *breathing fire*.

The image here is of a dragon, a dangerous animal that can devour you with fire.

The DANGEROUS ANIMAL metaphor portrays anger as a sleeping animal that it is dangerous to awaken, as something that can grow and thereby become dangerous, as something that has to be held back, and as something with a dangerous appetite. . . .

As in the case of the OPPONENT metaphor, our analysis of the DANGEROUS ANIMAL metaphor leaves an expression unaccounted for—"insatiable." This expression indicates that the animal has an appetite. This "appetite" seems to correspond to the "demands" in the OPPONENT metaphor, as can be seen from the fact that the following sentences entail each other:

- Harry's anger is *insatiable*.
- Harry's anger cannot be *appeased*.

To see what it is that anger demands and has an appetite for, let us turn to expressions that indicate causes of anger. Perhaps the most common group of expressions that indicate anger consists of conventionalized forms of annoyance: minor pains, burdens placed on domestic animals, etc. Thus we have the metaphor:

The cause of anger is a physical annoyance.

- Don't be *a pain in the ass.*
- Get *off my back!*
- You don't have to *ride me so hard.*
- You're *getting under my skin.*
- He's *a pain in the neck.*
- Don't *be a pest!*

These forms of annoyance involve an offender and a victim. The offender is at fault. The victim, who is innocent, is the one who gets angry.

There is another set of conventionalized expressions used to speak of, or to, people who are in the process of making someone angry. These are expressions of territoriality, in which the cause of anger is viewed as a trespasser.

Causing anger is trespassing.

- You're beginning to *get to* me.
- Get *out of here!*
- Get *out of my sight!*
- *Leave me alone!*
- This is where I *draw the line!*
- Don't *step on my toes!*

Again, there is an offender (the cause of anger) and a victim (the person who is getting angry). The offense seems to constitute some sort of injustice. This is reflected in the conventional wisdom:

- Don't get *mad,* get *even!*

In order for this saying to make sense, there has to be some connection between anger and retribution. Getting even is equivalent to balancing the scales of justice. The saying assumes a model in which injustice leads to anger and retribution can alleviate or prevent anger. In short, what anger "demands" and has an "appetite" for is revenge. This is why warnings and threats can count as angry behavior:

- If I get mad, watch out!
- Don't get me angry, or you'll be sorry.

The angry behavior is, in itself, viewed as a form of retribution.

We are now in a position to make sense of another metaphor for anger:

Anger is a burden.

- Unburdening himself of his anger gave him a sense of *relief.*
- After I lost my temper, I felt *lighter.*
- He *carries* his anger around with him.
- He *has a chip on his shoulder.*
- You'll feel better if you *get it off your chest.*

In English, it is common for responsibilities to be metaphorized as burdens. There are two kinds of responsibilities involved in the folk model of anger that has emerged so far. The first is a responsibility to control one's anger. In cases of extreme anger, this may place a considerable burden on one's "inner resources." The second comes from the model of retributive justice that is built into our concept of anger; it is the responsibility to seek vengeance. What is particularly interesting is that these two responsibilities are in conflict in the case of angry retribution: If you take out your anger on someone, you are not meeting your responsibility to control your anger, and if you don't take out your anger on someone, you are not meeting your responsibility to provide retribution. The slogan "Don't get mad, get even!" offers one way out: retribution without anger. The human potential movement provides another way out by suggesting that letting your anger out is okay. But the fact is that neither of these solutions is the cultural norm. It should also be mentioned in passing that the human potential movement's way of dealing with anger by sanctioning its release is not all that revolutionary. It assumes almost all of our standard folk model and metaphorical understanding and makes one change: sanctioning the "release.". . .

The metaphors and metonymies that we have investigated so far converge on a certain prototypical cognitive model of anger. It is not the only model of anger we have; in fact, there are quite a few. But as we shall see, all of the others can be characterized as minimal variants of the model that the metaphors converge on. The model has a temporal dimension and can be conceived of as a scenario with a number of stages. We will call this the "prototypical scenario"; it is similar to what De Sousa (1980) calls the "paradigm scenario." We will be referring to the person who gets angry as *S*, short for the self.

Stage 1: Offending Event

There is an offending event that displeases *S*. There is a wrongdoer who intentionally does something directly to *S*. The wrongdoer is at fault and *S* is innocent. The offending event constitutes an injustice and produces anger in *S*. The scales of justice can only be balanced by some act of retribution. That is, the intensity of retribution must be roughly equal to the intensity of offense. *S* has the responsibility to perform such an act of retribution.

Stage 2: Anger

Associated with the entity anger is a scale that measures its intensity. As the intensity of anger increases, S experiences physiological effects: increase in body heat, internal pressure, and physical agitation. As the anger gets very intense, it exerts a force upon S to perform an act of retribution. Because acts of retribution are dangerous and/or socially unacceptable, S has a responsibility to control his anger. Moreover, loss of control is damaging to S's own well-being, which is another motivation for controlling anger.

Stage 3: Attempt at Control

S attempts to control his anger.

Stage 4: Loss of Control

Each person has a certain tolerance for controlling anger. That tolerance can be viewed as the limit point on the anger scale. When the intensity of anger goes beyond that limit, S can no longer control his anger. S exhibits angry behavior and his anger forces him to attempt an act of retribution. Since S is out of control and acting under coercion, he is not responsible for his actions.

Stage 5: Act of Retribution

S performs the act of retribution. The wrongdoer is the target of the act. The intensity of retribution roughly equals the intensity of the offense and the scales are balanced again. The intensity of anger drops to zero.

At this point, we can see how the various conceptual metaphors we have discussed all map onto a part of the prototypical scenario and how they jointly converge on that scenario. This enables us to show exactly how the various metaphors are related to one another and how they function together to help characterize a single concept.

ANGER, LUST, AND RAPE

We have shown that an emotion, anger, has a conceptual structure, and we have investigated various aspects of it. A deeper question now arises: How do such conceptual structures affect how we live our lives? To get some idea of how the emotional concepts function in our culture, let us consider an issue that has enormous social importance, but which most people would rather not think about: rape.

Not all cultures have a high incidence of rape. In some cultures, rape is virtually unknown. The high incidence of rape in America undoubtedly has many complex causes. I would like to suggest that the way we conceptualize lust and anger, together with our various folk theories of sexuality, may be a contributing factor.

Let us begin with an examination of our concept of lust. It is commonly thought that lust, as a sexual urge, is devoid of cognitive content and that there is not much to say about how lust, or sexual desire, is understood. On the contrary, lust is a complex concept which is understood via a system of conceptual metaphors. Here are some examples that Zoltán Kövecses and I have discovered:

Lust is hunger; the object of lust is food.

- He is *sex-starved*.
- You have a remarkable *sexual appetite*.
- She's quite a *dish*.
- Hey, *honey*, let's see some *cheesecake*.
- Look at those *buns!*
- What a piece of *meat!*
- She had him *drooling*.
- You look *luscious*.
- Hi, *sugar!*
- I *hunger* for your touch.

A lustful person is an animal.

- Don't touch me, you *animal!*
- Get away from me, you *brute!*
- He's a *wolf*.
- He looks like he's ready to *pounce*.
- Stop *pawing* me!
- Wanna *nuzzle* up close?
- He *preys* upon unsuspecting women.
- He's a real *stud*—the Italian *Stallion!*
- Hello, my little *chickadee*.
- She's a *tigress* in bed.
- She looks like a *bitch in heat*.
- You bring out the *beast* in me.

Lust is heat.

- I've got the *hots* for her.
- She's an old *flame*.
- Hey, baby, *light my fire*.
- She's *frigid*.
- Don't be *cold* to me.
- She's *hot stuff*.
- He's still carrying a *torch* for her.
- She's a *red hot mama*.
- I'm *warm* for your form.
- She's got *hot pants* for you.
- I'm *burning* with desire.
- She's *in heat*.
- He was *consumed* by desire.

Lust is insanity.

- I'm *crazy* about her.
- I'm *madly* in love with him.
- I'm *wild* over her.
- You're driving me *insane*.
- She's *sex-crazed*.
- He's a real *sex maniac*.
- She's got me *delirious*.
- I'm a *sex addict*.

A lustful person is a functioning machine (especially a car).

- You *turn me on*.
- I got my *motor runnin'*, baby.
- Don't leave me *idling*.
- I think I'm *running out of gas*.
- *Turn my crank*, baby.

To return to examples of longer standing:

Lust is a game.

- I think I'm going to *score* tonight.
- You won't be able to *get to first base* with her.
- He's a *loser*.
- I *struck out* last night.
- She wouldn't *play ball*.
- *Touchdown!*

Lust is war.

- He's known for his *conquests*.
- That's quite a *weapon* you've got there.
- Better put on my *war paint*.
- He *fled from her advances*.
- He has to *fend off* all the women who want him.
- She *surrendered* to him.

Sexuality is a physical force; lust is a reaction to that force.

- She's *devastating*.
- When she grows up, she'll be a *knockout*.
- I was *knocked off my feet*.
- She *bowled me over*.
- What a *bombshell!*
- She's *dressed to kill*.

- I could feel the *electricity* between us.
- She *sparked* my interest.
- He has a lot of *animal magnetism*.
- We were *drawn* to each other.
- The *attraction* was very strong.

A particularly important fact about the collection of metaphors used to understand lust in our culture is that their source domains overlap considerably with the source domains of metaphors for anger. As we saw above, anger in America is understood in terms of HEAT, FIRE, WILD ANIMALS and INSANITY as well as a reaction to an external force. Just as one can have *smoldering sexuality,* one can have *smoldering anger.* One can be *consumed with desire* and *consumed with anger.* One can be *insane with lust* and *insane with anger.* Your lust, as well as your anger, can get *out of hand.* I believe that the connection between our conception of lust and our conception of anger is by no means accidental and has important social consequences.

One might suggest that these conceptual metaphors provide ways of passively understanding and talking about lust, but no more than that. What I would like to show is that, at the very least, it is possible for them to enter into reasoning. For this purpose, I will look in detail at the reasoning in a passage from Timothy Beneke's collection of interviews, *Men on Rape* (1982). The analysis of the passage was done jointly with Mark Johnson.

Before we get to the details of the analysis, we should bear in mind that it raises an important social issue. Many experts have argued that rape has nothing to do with sex or even lust, but is simply violence against women with no sexual aspect. But, as we have seen, sexual desire is partly understood in America in terms of physical force and war metaphors. This suggests that sex and violence are linked in the American mind via these metaphors. Since sex and violence are conceptually anything but mutually exclusive, it is quite conceivable that rape is not a matter of violence alone and that it may have a lot to do with lust and the fact that the metaphorical understanding of lust shares a considerable amount with the metaphorical understanding of anger.

The passage I'll be looking at is taken from Beneke's interview with a mild-mannered librarian in the financial district of San Francisco. It is a passage in which he gives a coherent argument providing what he would consider a justification for rape.

Let's say I see a woman and she looks really pretty, and really clean and sexy, and she's giving off very feminine, sexy vibes. I think, "Wow, I would love to make love to her," but I know she's not really interested. It's a tease. A lot of times a woman knows that she's looking really good and she'll use that and flaunt it, and it makes me feel like she's laughing at me and I feel *degraded*.

I also feel dehumanized, because when I'm being teased I just turn off, I cease to be human. Because if I go with my human emotions I'm going to want to put my arms around her and kiss her, and to do that would be unacceptable. I don't like the feeling that I'm supposed to stand there and take it, and not be able to hug her or kiss her; so I just turn off my emotions. It's a feeling of humiliation, because the woman has forced me to turn off my feelings and react in a way that I really don't want to.

If I were actually desperate enough to rape somebody, it would be from wanting the person, but also it would be a very spiteful thing, just being able to say, "I have power over you and I can do anything I want with you"; because really I feel that *they* have power over *me* just by their presence. Just the fact that they can come up to me and just melt me and make me feel like a dummy makes me want revenge. They have power over me so I want power over them. (Beneke 1982, pp. 43–44)

Here is a clear and forceful statement in which a man is giving an account of his reality. On the face of it, there is nothing particularly difficult about this passage. It is fairly straightforward as explanations go. But when we make sense of a passage even as simple as this, there is a lot going on that we are not usually conscious of. What is most important in this passage are the conceptual metaphors and the folk theories of everyday experience that jointly make it cohere.

The logic of the passage is based on the SEXUALITY IS A PHYSICAL FORCE metaphor, which is reflected in the following expressions:

- She's *giving off very feminine, sexy vibes.*
- Just the fact that they can come up to me and just *melt me . . .*

In addition to the SEXUALITY IS A PHYSICAL FORCE metaphor, the passage draws upon a number of other metaphors and folk theories. Let us roughly trace the logic of the passage. The speaker assumes that A WOMAN IS RESPONSIBLE FOR HER PHYSICAL APPEARANCE and since PHYSICAL APPEARANCE IS A PHYSICAL FORCE, he assumes that, if she looks sexy ("giving off very feminine, sexy vibes"), she is using her sexy appearance as a force on him ("a woman knows that she's looking very good and she'll use that and flaunt it"). The speaker also assumes that SEXUAL EMOTIONS ARE PART OF HUMAN NATURE and that A PERSON WHO USES A FORCE IS RESPONSIBLE FOR THE EFFECT OF THAT FORCE. It follows that A WOMAN WITH A SEXY APPEARANCE IS RESPONSIBLE FOR AROUSING A MAN'S SEXUAL EMOTIONS. As he says, "they have power over me just by their presence." The speaker has an important additional folk theory about the relationship between sexual emotion and sexual action: SEXUAL EMOTION NATURALLY RESULTS IN SEXUAL ACTION ("because if I go with my human emotions I'm going to want to put my arms around her and kiss her."). This raises problems for him because "to do that would be unacceptable." This is based upon the folk theory that SEXUAL ACTION AGAINST SOMEONE'S WILL IS UNACCEPTABLE. It follows that TO ACT MORALLY, ONE MUST AVOID SEXUAL ACTION (in such a case as this one). Since sexual action is for him the natural result of sexual emotions, the only acceptable thing he can do is inhibit his emotions: AVOIDING SEXUAL ACTION REQUIRES INHIBITING SEXUAL EMOTIONS. As he says, "I don't like the feeling that I'm supposed to stand there and take it, and not be able to hug her or kiss her; so I just turn off my emotions." TO ACT MORALLY, ONE MUST INHIBIT SEXUAL EMOTIONS.

So, as a consequence, a woman who looks sexy is responsible for his sexual emotions and for putting him in a position where he must inhibit them if he is to act morally. He explains, "It's a feeling of humiliation, because the woman has forced me to turn off my feelings and react in a way that I don't really want to."

The humiliation he feels is part of his sense that he has become less than human ("I feel degraded . . . I also feel dehumanized . . . I cease to be human"). The reason for this is, as we saw above, that he assumes that SEXUAL EMOTIONS ARE PART OF HUMAN NATURE and therefore that TO INHIBIT SEXUAL EMOTIONS IS TO BE LESS THAN HUMAN. Since she forces him to turn off his emotions, she makes him less than human. A WOMAN WITH A SEXY APPEARANCE MAKES A MAN WHO IS ACTING MORALLY LESS THAN HUMAN. The speaker feels (by a fairly natural folk theory) that TO BE MADE LESS THAN HUMAN IS TO BE INJURED. He also assumes the biblical eye-for-an-eye folk theory of retributive justice: THE ONLY WAY TO MAKE UP FOR BEING INJURED IS TO INFLICT AN INJURY OF THE SAME KIND.

Since the injury involves the use of sexual *power,* he sees rape as a possibility for appropriate redress: "If I were actually desperate enough to rape somebody, it would be from wanting the person, but also it would be a very spiteful thing, just being able to say, 'I have power over you and I can do anything I want with you'; because really I feel that *they* have power over *me* just by their presence. Just the fact that they can come up to me and just melt me and make me feel like a dummy makes me want revenge. They have power over me so I want power over them."

Here the overlap between lust and anger is even stronger. Our concept of anger carries with it the concept of revenge, as well as the idea of insane, heated, animal behavior. In this particular logic of rape, lust and anger go hand-in-hand.

In giving the overall logic of the passage, we have made explicit only *some* of the implicit metaphors and folk theories necessary to understand it. Little, if any, of this is explicit, and we are not claiming that we have presented anything like a conscious chain of deduction that the speaker has followed. Rather, we have tried to show the logic and structure that unconsciously lies behind the reality the speaker takes for granted.

There is an important, and somewhat frightening, sense in which his reality is ours as well. We may personally find his views despicable, but it is frightening how easy they are to make sense of. The reason that they seem to be so easily understood is that most, if not all, of them are deeply ingrained in American culture. All of the metaphors and folk theories we have discussed occur again and again in one form or another throughout Beneke's interviews. Moreover, it seems that these metaphors and folk theories are largely held by women as well as men. As Beneke's interviews indicate, women on juries in rape trials regularly view rape victims who were attractively dressed as "asking for it" or bringing it upon themselves and therefore deserving of their fate. Such women jurors are using the kind of reasoning we saw in the passage above.

Of course, not everyone's sense of reality is structured in terms of *all* the above metaphors and folk theories. And even if it were, not everyone would put them together in the way outlined above. Nor does it follow that someone with such a sense of reality would act on it, as the speaker supposedly has not. What the analysis of the passage does seem to show is that American culture contains within it a sufficient stock of fairly common metaphors and folk theories which, when put together in the way outlined above, can actually provide what could be viewed as a "rationale" for rape. Furthermore, if these metaphors and folk theories were not readily available to us for use in understanding—that is, if they were not ours in some sense—the passage would be simply incomprehensible to us.

The metaphorical expressions that we use to describe lust are not mere words. They are expressions of metaphorical concepts that we use to understand lust and to reason about it. What I find sad is that we appear to have no metaphors for a healthy mutual lust. The domains we use for comprehending lust are HUNGER, ANIMALS, HEAT, INSANITY, MACHINES, GAMES, WAR, and PHYSICAL FORCES.

---

1 How does the complex conceptual structure underlying the expression of anger suggest that linguistic metaphors are closely tied in with bodily states? How do metaphorical systems used to express anger project (a) physiological effects, (b) equivalence with heat, (c) equivalence with insanity, (d) equivalence with dangerous animals, and (e) anger at an opponent?

2 What cycle of consequences or implicit scenario does Lakoff discover in the ways metaphors used to express anger are linked with each other?

3 What did Lakoff discover about the way systems of metaphors interact when he examined the case history of a rapist? What psychological connections between the feelings of anger and lust and the act of rape did Lakoff find were culturally sanctioned and peculiar to American society?

4 Lakoff cites the "folk theory of physiological effects" as a kind of common sense homespun value system that makes it possible to understand the hidden connection between related metaphors used to express anger. How is this folk theory of anger structured on the concept of a protagonist and antagonist, which then serves as a justification for rape in American culture? (Glossary: *Metaphor, Protagonist/Antagonist.*)

5 What is Lakoff's thesis? Locate the sentence(s) where he states the main idea and express it in your own words. When analyzing a subject, writers usually try to identify divisions and classifications that are, within reason, mutually exclusive, but Lakoff acknowledges that the metaphors in which anger is expressed overlap. How does this overlapping of categories help Lakoff make his point? (Glossary: *Classification/Division.*)

6 Analyze the verbs (for example, clobber, jolt, maul, blast) sportswriters use in reporting the final scores of football, baseball, basketball, hockey (etc.) games to discover the underlying physical metaphors and the systems of metaphors that recur—for example, metaphors that imply physical injury, prowess, speed, etc. What metaphors involved with the reporting of sports seem central to American culture? Draw on Lakoff's study "Anger" to help you write your analysis.

The President's Speech   *Oliver Sacks*

◆ OLIVER SACKS is a physician, medical researcher, and writer and is presently a professor of Neurology at Albert Einstein Medical College in New York. All of his works deal with the interrelations between mind and body. His books include *Migraine* (1970), *Awakenings* (1973), *A Leg to Stand On* (1984), *Seeing Voices* (1989), and *The Man Who Mistook His Wife for a Hat* (1985), from which this essay is taken.

While treating patients at the Albert Einstein Medical College in New York, Sacks became progressively aware of the extent to which the mind and the body work together. In the following essay, "The President's Speech," Sacks describes patients suffering from a variety of neurological disorders, including aphasia and agnosia, that prevent them from responding to language in conventional ways. Aphasics don't understand words, but are extremely sensitive to "extraverbal cues"—that is, the tone, bodily gestures, and facial expressions that accompany the words being said. On the other hand, tonal agnosiacs don't register tone at all, and consequently concentrate exclusively on the bodily gestures, facial expressions, and words spoken. Ironically, both groups suffering from these rare brain disorders responded in ways quite different from their normal counterparts. They were not seduced by the rhetoric, and, in fact, found the incongruity between what was said and how it was said quite hilarious. In short, the message the president communicated through his words (which was so wholeheartedly accepted by the public) was rejected by these brain-damaged patients, who read the total sensory environment of his speech instead of just listening to the words.

> **TO CONSIDER**   When is the last time you discovered that someone lied to you? What tip-offs were there in their posture, gestures, facial expressions, or tone of voice that led you to believe they were lying?

*W*hat was going on? A roar of laughter from the aphasia ward, just as the President's speech was coming on, and they had all been so eager to hear the President speaking. . . .

There he was, the old Charmer, the Actor, with his practiced rhetoric, his histrionisms, his emotional appeal—and all the patients were convulsed with laughter. Well, not all: Some looked bewildered, some looked outraged, one or

1

2

two looked apprehensive, but most looked amused. The President was, as always, moving—but he was moving them, apparently, mainly to laughter. What could they be thinking? Were they failing to understand him? Or did they, perhaps, understand him all too well?

3   It was often said of these patients, who though intelligent had the severest receptive or global aphasia, rendering them incapable of understanding words as such, that they nonetheless understood most of what was said to them. Their friends, their relatives, the nurses who knew them well, could hardly believe, sometimes, that they *were* aphasic.

4   This was because, when addressed naturally, they grasped some or most of the meaning. And one does speak "naturally," naturally.

5   Thus to demonstrate their aphasia, one had to go to extraordinary lengths, as a neurologist, to speak and behave unnaturally, to remove all the extraverbal cues—tone of voice, intonation, suggestive emphasis or inflection, as well as all visual cues (one's expressions, one's gestures, one's entire, largely unconscious, personal repertoire and posture): One had to remove all of this (which might involve total concealment of one's person, and total depersonalization of one's voice, even to using a computerized voice synthesizer) in order to reduce speech to pure words, speech totally devoid of what Frege called "tone-color" (*Klangenfarben*) or "evocation." With the most sensitive patients, it was only with such a grossly artificial, mechanical speech—somewhat like that of the computers in *Star Trek*—that one could be wholly sure of their aphasia.

6   Why all this? Because speech—natural speech—does not consist of words alone, nor (as Hughlings Jackson thought) "propositions" alone. It consists of *utterance*—an uttering-forth of one's whole meaning with one's whole being— the understanding of which involves infinitely more than mere word-recognition. And this was the clue to aphasiacs' understanding, even when they might be wholly uncomprehending of words as such. For though the words, the verbal constructions, *per se,* might convey nothing, spoken language is normally suffused with "tone," embedded in an expressiveness which transcends the verbal—and it is precisely this expressiveness, so deep, so various, so complex, so subtle, which is perfectly preserved in aphasia, though understanding of words be destroyed. Preserved—and often more: preternaturally enhanced. . . .

7   This too becomes clear—often in the most striking, or comic, or dramatic way—to all those who work or live closely with aphasiacs: their families or friends or nurses or doctors. At first, perhaps, we see nothing much the matter; and then we see that there has been a great change, almost an inversion, in their understanding of speech. Something has gone, has been devastated, it is true—but something has come, in its stead, has been immensely enhanced, so that—at least with emotionally laden utterance—the meaning may be fully grasped even when every word is missed. This, in our species *Homo loquens,*[1] seems almost an inversion of the usual order of things: an inversion, and perhaps a reversion too, to something more primitive and elemental. And this perhaps is why Hughlings

---

[1]Latin: "speaking man."—EDS.

Jackson compared aphasiacs to dogs (a comparison that might outrage both!) though when he did this he was chiefly thinking of their linguistic incompetencies, rather than their remarkable, and almost infallible, sensitivity to "tone" and feeling. Henry Head, more sensitive in this regard, speaks of "feeling-tone" in his (1926) treatise on aphasia, and stresses how it is preserved, and often enhanced, in aphasiacs.

Thus the feeling I sometimes have—which all of us who work closely with   8
aphasiacs have—that one cannot lie to an aphasiac. He cannot grasp your words, and so cannot be deceived by them; but what he grasps he grasps with infallible precision, namely the *expression* that goes with the words, that total, spontaneous, involuntary expressiveness which can never be simulated or faked, as words alone can, all too easily. . . .

We recognize this with dogs, and often use them for this purpose—to pick   9
up falsehood, or malice, or equivocal intentions, to tell us who can be trusted, who is integral, who makes sense, when we—so susceptible to words—cannot trust our own instincts.

And what dogs can do here, aphasiacs do too, and at a human and immea-   10
surably superior level. "One can lie with the mouth," Nietzsche writes, "but with the accompanying grimace one nevertheless tells the truth." To such a grimace, to any falsity or impropriety in bodily appearance or posture, aphasiacs are preternaturally sensitive. And if they cannot see one—this is especially true of our blind aphasiacs—they have an infallible ear for every vocal nuance, the tone, the rhythm, the cadences, the music, the subtlest modulations, inflections, intonations, which can give—or remove—verisimilitude to or from a man's voice.

In this, then, lies their power of understanding—understanding, without   11
words, what is authentic or inauthentic. Thus it was the grimaces, the histrionisms, the false gestures and, above all, the false tones and cadences of the voice, which rang false for these wordless but immensely sensitive patients. It was to these (for them) most glaring, even grotesque, incongruities and improprieties that my aphasic patients responded, undeceived and undeceivable by words.

This is why they laughed at the President's speech.   12

If one cannot lie to an aphasiac, in view of his special sensitivity to expres-   13
sion and "tone," how is it, we might ask, with patients—if there are such—who *lack* any sense of expression and "tone," while preserving, unchanged, their comprehension for words: patients of an exactly opposite kind? We have a number of such patients, also on the aphasia ward, although, technically, they do not have aphasia, but, instead, a form of *agnosia,* in particular a so-called "tonal" agnosia. For such patients, typically, the expressive qualities of voices disappear—their tone, their timbre, their feeling, their entire character—while words (and grammatical constructions) are perfectly understood. Such tonal agnosias (or "atonias") are associated with disorders of the *right* temporal lobe of the brain, whereas the aphasias go with disorders of the *left* temporal lobe.

Among the patients with tonal agnosia on our aphasia ward who also lis-   14
tened to the President's speech was Emily D., with a glioma in her right tempo-

ral lobe. A former English teacher, and poetess of some repute, with an exceptional feeling for language, and strong powers of analysis and expression, Emily D. was able to articulate the opposite situation—how the President's speech sounded to someone with tonal agnosia. Emily D. could no longer tell if a voice was angry, cheerful, sad—whatever. Since voices now lacked expression, she had to look at people's faces, their postures and movements when they talked, and found herself doing so with a care, an intensity, she had never shown before. But this, it so happened, was also limited, because she had a malignant glaucoma, and was rapidly losing her sight too.

15   What she then found she had to do was to pay extreme attention to exactness of words and word use, and to insist that those around her did just the same. She could less and less follow loose speech or slang—speech of an allusive or emotional kind—and more and more required of her interlocutors that they speak *prose*—"proper words in proper places." Prose, she found, might compensate, in some degree, for lack of perceived tone or feeling.

16   In this way she was able to preserve, even enhance, the use of "expressive" speech—in which the meaning was wholly given by the apt choice and reference of words—despite being more and more lost with "evocative" speech (where meaning is wholly given in the use and sense of tone).

17   Emily D. also listened, stony-faced, to the President's speech, bringing to it a strange mixture of enhanced and defective perceptions—precisely the opposite mixture to those of our aphasiacs. It did not move her—no speech now moved her—and all that was evocative, genuine or false, completely passed her by. Deprived of emotional reaction, was she then (like the rest of us) transported or taken in? By no means. "He is not cogent," she said. "He does not speak good prose. His word-use is improper. Either he is brain-damaged, or he has something to conceal." Thus the President's speech did not work for Emily D. either, due to her enhanced sense of formal language use, propriety as prose, any more than it worked for our aphasiacs, with their word-deafness but enhanced sense of tone.

        Here then was the paradox of the President's speech. We normals—aided,
18   doubtless, by our wish to be fooled, were indeed well and truly fooled ("*Populus vult decipi, ergo decipiatur*"[2]). And so cunningly was deceptive word-use combined with deceptive tone, that only the brain-damaged remained intact, undeceived.

---

1 How would you characterize the affective disorder of the patients that made the president's (most likely Reagan's) speech appear to be so hilarious? What did they respond to that people without this disorder were unaware of?

2 What distinguishes a person with aphasia from someone suffering from tonal agnosia? How do the disabilities of both groups make them more receptive to "extraverbal cues" that are available for anyone to perceive? Why doesn't the rest of the population see these discrepancies?

---

[2]Latin: "The population wants to be deceived, therefore let it be deceived."—EDS.

3 How does Sacks feel about his patients and about their "immensely enhanced" (para. 7) capacity to grasp with "infallible precision" (para. 8) the cues that prevent them from being deceived?

4 How does Sacks employ the methods of process analysis to explain how aphasics (para. 8) and tonal agnosiacs (para. 13) compensate for their perceptual impairments? (Glossary: *Process Analysis*.)

5 Identify the main point of contrast or comparison in Sacks's essay. How is this organizational method well suited to reveal the distinctively different way in which aphasics perceive the world? (Glossary: *Comparison and Contrast*.)

6 What body signals or facial gestures serve as reliable indicators that someone is attempting to lie to you?

Thinking in Pictures　　　*Temple Grandin*

◆ TEMPLE GRANDIN has a Ph.D. in animal science from the University of Illinois and has designed one-third of the livestock-handling facilities in the United States and many other countries. She is currently assistant professor of animal sciences at Colorado State University and a frequent lecturer at autism meetings throughout the country. In the selection drawn from her 1995 book *Thinking in Pictures,* Grandin describes what it is like to be among the few who have overcome many of the neurological impairments associated with autism.

By the time you are reading this, you can process abstract thoughts and ideas without having to summon a visual image for each of the terms. For Grandin, it was quite different. The images that came into her mind triggered specific memories (for the word "jump" she visualized an actual hurdle-jumping competition). Every word had to be processed in this way. She was literally incapable of reading a sentence without conjuring up a concrete image for each word, and there were many gaps because there were so many words without corresponding visual images. This will give you some idea of the isolation and self-absorption of those imprisoned in the world of autism. It was only through the most incredible efforts in establishing communication with other people and finding out what they meant by words they used that she was able to learn to express

---

herself in ways others could understand. Grandin's experience is so important in cognitive research because it describes how language is derived through the manipulation of symbolic images, beginning with concrete references and becoming progressively more abstract. Being able to generalize, which autistics find so difficult to do, is the key to language. This may be similar to the way primates process information and explain why they find it difficult to move beyond using symbols for very specific requests and to generalize. This might answer why so much of the vocabulary of primitive people is so specific, concrete, and functional, and answer the question of how language evolves.

> **TO CONSIDER**   Choose an abstract concept and try to think about it only in images, without using words. What images did you use?

PROCESSING NONVISUAL INFORMATION

Autistics have problems learning things that cannot be thought about in pictures. The easiest words for an autistic child to learn are nouns, because they directly relate to pictures. Highly verbal autistic children like I was can sometimes learn how to read with phonics. Written words were too abstract for me to remember, but I could laboriously remember the approximately fifty phonetic sounds and a few rules. Lower-functioning children often learn better by association, with the aid of word labels attached to objects in their environment. Some very impaired autistic children learn more easily if words are spelled out with plastic letters they can feel.

Spatial words such as "over" and "under" had no meaning for me until I had a visual image to fix them in my memory. Even now, when I hear the word "under" by itself, I automatically picture myself getting under the cafeteria tables at school during an air-raid drill, a common occurrence on the East Coast during the early fifties. The first memory that any single word triggers is almost always a childhood memory. I can remember the teacher telling us to be quiet and walking single-file into the cafeteria, where six or eight children huddled under each table. If I continue on the same train of thought, more and more associative memories of elementary school emerge. I can remember the teacher scolding me after I hit Alfred for putting dirt on my shoe. All of these memories play like video-tapes in the VCR in my imagination. If I allow my mind to keep associating, it will wander a million miles away from the word "under," to submarines under the Antarctic and the Beatles song "Yellow Submarine." If I let my mind pause on the picture of the yellow submarine, I then hear the song. As I start humming the song and get to the part about people coming on board, my association switches to the gangway of a ship I saw in Australia.

I also visualize verbs. The word "jumping" triggers a memory of jumping hurdles at the mock Olympics held at my elementary school. Adverbs often trigger inappropriate images—"quickly" reminds me of Nestle's Quik—unless they are paired with a verb, which modifies my visual image. For example, "he ran quickly" triggers an animated image of Dick from the first-grade reading book running fast, and "he walked slowly"slows the image down. As a child, I left out words such as "is," "the," and "it," because they had no meaning by themselves. Similarly, words like "of" and "an" made no sense. Eventually I learned how to use them properly, because my parents always spoke correct English and I mimicked their speech patterns. To this day certain verb conjugations, such as "to be," are absolutely meaningless to me.

When I read, I translate written words into color movies or I simply store a photo of the written page to be read later. When I retrieve the material, I see a photocopy of the page in my imagination. I can then read it like a TelePrompTer. It is likely that Raymond, the autistic savant depicted in the movie *Rain Man,* used a similar strategy to memorize telephone books, maps, and other information. He simply photocopied each page of the phone book into his memory. When he wanted to find a certain number, he just scanned pages of the phone book that were in his mind. To pull information out of my memory, I have to replay the video. Pulling facts up quickly is sometimes difficult, because I have to play bits of different videos until I find the right tape. This takes time.

When I am unable to convert text to pictures, it is usually because the text has no concrete meaning. Some philosophy books and articles about the cattle futures market are simply incomprehensible. It is much easier for me to understand written text that describes something that can be easily translated into pictures. The following sentence from a story in the February 21, 1994, issue of *Time* magazine, describing the Winter Olympics figure-skating championships, is a good example: "All the elements are in place—the spotlights, the swelling waltzes and jazz tunes, the sequined sprites taking to the air." In my imagination I see the skating rink and skaters. However, if I ponder too long on the word "elements," I will make the inappropriate association of a periodic table on the wall of my high school chemistry classroom. Pausing on the word "sprite" triggers an image of a Sprite can in my refrigerator instead of a pretty young skater.

Teachers who work with autistic children need to understand associative thought patterns. An autistic child will often use a word in an inappropriate manner. Sometimes these uses have a logical associative meaning and other times they don't. For example, an autistic child might say the word "dog" when he wants to go outside. The word "dog" is associated with going outside. In my own case, I can remember both logical and illogical use of inappropriate words. When I was six, I learned to say "prosecution." I had absolutely no idea what it meant, but it sounded nice when I said it, so I used it as an exclamation every time my kite hit the ground. I must have baffled more than a few people who heard me exclaim "Prosecution!" to my downward-spiraling kite.

Discussions with other autistic people reveal similar visual styles of thinking about tasks that most people do sequentially. An autistic man who composes music told me that he makes "sound pictures" using small pieces of other music to create new compositions. A computer programmer with autism told me that he sees the general pattern of the program tree. After he visualizes the skeleton for the program, he simply writes the code for each branch. I use similar methods when I review scientific literature and troubleshoot at meat plants. I take specific findings or observations and combine them to find new basic principles and general concepts.

My thinking pattern always starts with specifics and works toward generalization in an associational and nonsequential way. As if I were attempting to figure out what the picture on a jigsaw puzzle is when only one third of the puzzle is completed, I am able to fill in the missing pieces by scanning my video library. Chinese mathematicians who can make large calculations in their heads work the same way. At first they need an abacus, the Chinese calculator, which consists of rows of beads on wires in a frame. They make calculations by moving the rows of beads. When a mathematician becomes really skilled, he simply visualizes the abacus in his imagination and no longer needs a real one. The beads move on a visualized video abacus in his brain.

ABSTRACT THOUGHT

Growing up, I learned to convert abstract ideas into pictures as a way to understand them. I visualized concepts such as peace or honesty with symbolic images. I thought of peace as a dove, an Indian peace pipe, or TV or newsreel footage of the signing of a peace agreement. Honesty was represented by an image of placing one's hand on the Bible in court. A news report describing a person returning a wallet with all the money in it provided a picture of honest behavior.

The Lord's Prayer was incomprehensible until I broke it down into specific visual images. The power and the glory were represented by a semicircular rainbow and an electrical tower. These childhood visual images are still triggered every time I hear the Lord's Prayer. The words "thy will be done" had no meaning when I was a child, and today the meaning is still vague. Will is a hard concept to visualize. When I think about it, I imagine God throwing a lightning bolt. Another adult with autism wrote that he visualized "Thou art in heaven" as God with an easel above the clouds. "Trespassing" was pictured as black and orange **no trespassing** signs. The word "Amen" at the end of the prayer was a mystery:a man at the end made no sense.

As a teenager and young adult I had to use concrete symbols to understand abstract concepts such as getting along with people and moving on to the next steps of my life, both of which were always difficult. I knew I did not fit in with my high school peers, and I was unable to figure out what I was doing wrong. No matter how hard I tried, they made fun of me. They called me "workhorse," "tape recorder," and "bones" because I was skinny. At the time I was able to figure out why they called me "workhorse" and "bones," but "tape recorder" puzzled me. Now I realize that I must have sounded like a tape recorder when I repeated things verbatim over and over. But back then I just could not figure out why I was such a social dud. I sought refuge in doing things I was good at, such as working on reroofing the barn or practicing my riding prior to a horse show. Personal relationships made absolutely no sense to me until I developed visual symbols of doors and windows. It was then that I started to understand concepts such as learning the give-and-take of a relationship. I still wonder what would have happened to me if I had not been able to visualize my way in the world.

---

1 What is so unusual about how Grandin understands the meanings of words? What insight does her account provide into the limitations autistic children and adults experience in communicating?

2 Which of the examples and incidences mentioned by Grandin most clearly communicate the limitations she and other autistic people experience in establishing contact with the outside world?

3 To what extent does the way you understand the meanings of words overlap with methods Grandin has to use? What important differences can you identify?

4 What process does Grandin analyze and explain in her essay? How does this help us understand the nature of autism more completely? What words or phrases does Grandin use to signal the different steps she takes in this process? (Glossary: *Process Analysis*.)

5 Grandin takes an analogical approach to make the complex subject of autism easier to understand. How does this rhetorical strategy clarify the unique manner in which those with autism must translate abstract concepts into concrete images in order to grasp ideas? To what extent does her discussion clear up misconceptions about autism? (Glossary: *Analogy*.)

6 Describe a natural wonder and try to explore the effect of this place or thing on your psyche if you could not use abstract concepts and could only express your feelings by "thinking in pictures."

The Language of Pain   *Richard Selzer*

◆ RICHARD SELZER was born in 1928 in Troy, New York. After receiving his M.D. from Albany Medical College in 1953, he spent fifteen years teaching surgery at Yale School of Medicine before leaving medicine to write full time. In 1975 he received the National Magazine Award from the Columbia School of Journalism. Among his many books are *Confessions of a Knife* (1979), *Letters to a Young Doctor* (1982), and *Raising the Dead* (1993), an account based on Selzer's near-death experience from Legionnaire's disease. "The Language of Pain" first appeared in the *Wilson Quarterly* (1994).

As a surgeon for over fifteen years, Selzer had many occasions to witness patients expressing pain. His own near-death encounter and slow recovery from Legionnaires' disease have produced a lifelong obsession with the sounds that constitute the language of pain. Selzer explores how cries of pain may offer a way to exteriorize and dispossess oneself of it, and the way emblems of suffering have served a religious function. According to Selzer, pain is at its essence very personal, and may be put to a variety of uses. For example, the French essayist Montaigne (1533–92) looked at his writing as a way to defeat his adversary, pain. The language of pain is a paraverbal way in which the body expresses itself; that is, it parallels and coexists with the more usual forms of communication.

TO CONSIDER   What sounds do people make when they are happy, sad, annoyed, surprised, or cheering for their team?

Why do you write so much about pain? they ask me. To give it a name, I reply. And I am not sure what I mean. I try again: In October, when the leaves have fallen from the trees, you can see farther into the forest. Now do you see? No? Well, what is your notion of pain? Pain is fire, a ravening, insatiable thing that insists upon utter domination; it is the occasion when the body reasserts itself over the mind; the universe contracts about the part that hurts; if the pain is not placated with analgesics, it will devour the whole organism. Only then will it too be snuffed. Still, pain is revelatory; in the blaze of it, one might catch a glimpse of the truth about human existence.

It was the poet Rilke who wrote that the events of the body cannot be rendered in language. Surely this is so with pain as with its opposite, orgasm. These extremes of sensation remain beyond the power of language to express. Say that a doctor is examining a patient who is in pain. The doctor needs to know the exact location of the pain and its nature. Is the pain sharp or dull? Steady or intermittent? Does it throb or pulse? Is it stabbing? A heavy pressure? Crampy? Does it burn? Sting? All these questions the doctor asks of the patient. But there is no wholly adequate way for the sufferer to portray his pain other than to cry out. In order to convey his pain, the patient, like the writer, must resort to metaphor, simile, imagery: "You want to know what it's like? It's as if someone were digging in my ribs with a shovel." "It feels as if there's heavy rock on my chest."

Years ago as a doctor and more recently as a writer, I declared my faith in images—the human fact placed near a superhuman mystery, even if both are illusions of the senses. Diagnosis, like writing, calls for the imagination and the skill to discover things not seen, things that hide themselves under the shadow of natural objects. It is the purpose of the writer and the doctor to fix these unseen phenomena in words, thereby presenting to plain sight what did not actually exist until he arrived. Much as a footprint hides beneath a foot until a step is taken.

By using metaphor and imagery, the patient brings the doctor into a state of partial understanding of his pain. In order to express it fully, he would have to cry out in a language that is incomprehensible to anyone else. This language of pain has no consonants, but consists only of vowels: ow! aiee! oy! oh! These are the sounds the sufferer makes, each punctuated by grunts, hiccoughs, sobs, moans, gasps. It is a self-absorbed language that might have been the first ever uttered by prehistoric man. Perhaps it was learned from animals. These howled vowels have the eloquence of the wild, the uncivilized, the atavistic. Comprehension is instantaneous, despite the absence of what we call words. It is a mode of expression beyond normal language. Nor could it be made more passionate or revelatory by the most gifted writer. Not even by Shakespeare.

But what is the purpose of these cries of pain? Wouldn't silence be as eloquent? For one thing, the loud, unrestrained pouring forth of vowels is useful in attracting the attention of anyone within earshot who might come to the assistance of the sufferer. Vowels carry farther than consonants and are easier to mouth, requiring only the widely opened jaws, without the more complex involvement of tongue, teeth, and palate that the speaking of consonants requires. Giuseppe Verdi[3] knew that and made his librettist write lines full of easily singable vowels and diphthongs. It is the sung vowel that carries to the last row of La Scala.[4] The consonants are often elided or faked by the singers who know that consonants are confined to the immediate vicinity of the stage and are altogether less able to be infused with emotive force. It comes as no surprise that the greatest opera singers are in the Italian repertoire—Italian, a language dripping with vowels and in which there is scarcely a word that does not end in one. "Mille serpi divoranmi il petto," sings the anguished Alfredo upon learning of the sacrifice made by his beloved Violetta in *La Traviata*. The translation—"A thousand snakes are eating my breast"—simply won't do.

One purpose of these cries of pain, then, might be to summon help, to notify fellow members of the tribe of one's predicament so that they will come running. But I think there is more to it than that. For the sufferer, these outcries have a kind of magical property of their own, offering not only an outlet for the emotion but a means of letting out the pain. Hollering, all by itself, gives a measure of relief. To cry out ow! or aiee! requires that the noise be carried away from the body on a cloud of warm, humid air that had been within the lungs of the sufferer. The expulsion of this air, and with it, the sound, is an attempt to exteriorize the pain, to dispossess oneself of it, as though the vowels of pain were, in some magical way, the pain itself. It is not hard to see why the medieval church

5

---

[3]*Giuseppe Verdi* (1813–1901): An Italian composer of opera, whose works such as *La Traviata* (1853) remain among the most popular of all operas.—EDS.

[4]*La Scala:* The famous 18-century opera house in Milan, Italy, where many of Verdi's operas had their premieres.—EDS.

came to believe that a body, writhing and wracked and uttering unearthly, primitive cries, was possessed by devils. Faced with such a sufferer, authorities of the church deemed exorcism both necessary and compassionate.

"Go ahead and holler," says the nurse to the patient. "You'll feel better. Don't hold it in." It is wise advice that has been passed down through the millennia of human suffering. But even these ululations cannot really convey to the reader what the sufferer is feeling, for they are not literature. To write *ow* or *aiee* on a page is not an art. The language of pain, then, is the most exclusive of tongues, spoken and understood by an elite of one. Hearing it, we shudder, out of sympathy for the sufferer, but just as much out of the premonition that each of us shall know this language in our time. Our turn will come. It is a fact that within moments of having been relieved of this pain, sufferers are no longer fluent in this language. They have already forgotten it, all but an inkling or two, and are left with a vague sense of dread, a recollection that the pain was awful, a fear that it might return.

In lieu of language, the doctor seems to diagnose by examining the body and its secretions—urine, blood, spinal fluid—and by using a number of ingenious photographic instruments. A last resort would be the laying open of the body for exploratory surgery. Fifty years ago, it was to the corpse that the doctor went for answers. Ironic that life should have provided concealment and death be revelatory. Even now, it is only in the autopsy room that the true courage of the human body is apparent, the way it carries on in the face of all odds: arteriosclerosis, calculi, pulmonary fibrosis, softening of the brain. And still the body goes on day after day, bearing its burdens, if not jauntily, at least with acceptance and obedience until at last it must sink beneath the weight of those burdens and come to the morgue where its faithfulness can be observed and granted homage.

There is about pain that which exhilarates even as it appalls, as Emily Dickinson has written. Pain is the expression of the dark underside of the body. As such, the sight of the wound, the sound of the outcry it produces, stir the imagination in a way that pleasure never can. We are drawn to the vicinity of pain by the hint of danger and death, as much as by the human desire to compare our fortunate state to that of those unluckier. Then, too, there is the undeniable relation of pain and beauty, brought to artistic flower during the Renaissance and later by the 19th-century Romantic poets. It is the writhen Christ slumping on the cross that is the emblematic vision of pain from which has come the word *excruciating*. It was Christianity that first tried to wrest meaning from pain. "Offer it up," say the Catholics, as if suffering, boredom, or even annoyance were currency to be paid on the road to sanctity. Simone Weil turned affliction into evidence of God's tenderness. Affliction is love, she wrote. To some, this represents a perversion of the senses, not unlike the masochism that welcomes pain as pleasure. To welcome pain as an approach to God is to negate mercy as proof of His love for human beings. It is an elite band of saints that can achieve ecstasy through pain. Even Christ cried out from the cross: Why hast thou forsaken me?

The artist who would prettify or soften the Crucifixion is missing the point. 10
The aim was to kill horribly and to subject the victim to the utmost humiliation.
It involved a preliminary whipping with the dreaded Roman *flagrum*, a leather
whip with three tails. At the tip of each tail there was tied a small dumbbell-
shaped weight of iron or bone. With each lash of the whip, the three bits dug
into the flesh. The victim was tied or chained to a post and two centurions stood
on either side. The wounds extended around to the chest and abdomen. Profuse
bleeding ensued. Then the condemned was beaten on the face with reeds so that
his face was bruised, his nose broken. To ensure maximum humiliation, the cross
was set up in a public place or on an elevation of land such as the hill of Calvary.
In the case of Jesus, in order to deride him further and to mock his appellation
of King of the Jews, a crown of thorns was placed on his brow. Jesus, weakened
by a night of fasting and prayer, as well as by the flogging and the blood loss,
was not able to carry his own cross to the place of execution as the punishment
required. Simon of Cyrene did it for him. Then Jesus' hands were nailed to the
crosspiece, which was raised and set into a groove on the vertical piece. The
height was approximately seven and a half feet. At one point, a Roman soldier
hurled a spear that opened the wound in his side. To add to Christ's suffering,
he was assailed by extreme thirst, as is usual in instances of severe blood loss and
dehydration. Once, a disciple was able to reach up and give him a drink through
a hollow straw. Death came slowly, from shock, both traumatic and hypo-
volemic, and from respiratory failure due to the difficulty of expelling air from
the lungs in the upright and suspended position when the diaphragm does not
easily rise.

I wonder whether man has not lost the ability to withstand pain, what with
the proliferation of pain-killing drugs and anesthetic agents. Physical pain has
become a once-in-a-while experience for most of the industrialized world. Resistance to pain, like any other unused talent, atrophies, leaving one all the more
vulnerable. What to a woman of the late 19th century might have been bearable
is insupportable to her great-great-granddaughter. Still, for some, chronic pain
is an old adversary, one whose cunning can be, if not negated, at least balanced,
by hypnosis, acupuncture, biofeedback, exercise, practice of ritual, and other
techniques not well understood. There is that pain which cannot be relieved by
any means short of death and which must be lived *against*. Such was the pain of
Montaigne who, tortured by bladder stones that occluded the outflow of urine,
had to write *against* the pain. On the other hand, Aristotle was unable to phi-
losophize because of his toothache.

Is the pain experienced in a dream any less than the pain experienced while
awake? I think it is not. I have a dream that has recurred many times: I am standing alone in the middle of a great empty amphitheater. It is midnight and the
scene is bathed in bluish moonlight. The city is European; Milan, I think. At
either end of the amphitheater, a statue stands upon a marble pedestal. One is of
Caesar wearing a toga and holding up a sheaf of wheat. The other is a great marble tiger. All at once, the tiger stirs, rises to its feet, then rears as if to spring. Yes,
it is about to spring! I turn to run in the opposite direction, toward Caesar, but
my feet are heavy, so heavy that I cannot lift them. Already I can sense the near-

ness of the beast, feel its hot breath upon my neck. A moment later there is the pressure of its fangs in the supraclavicular fossa on the left—and again in the nape. And there is pain. I look down to see my shadow bearing the burden of the huge cat on its back. At that instant, I wake up. My heart is pounding; I am gasping; the bed is drenched with sweat. And in the left side of my neck there is pain as if that area had been badly bruised. The pressure of my fingers intensifies the pain that I have brought back with me from the dream, the pain that has crossed from dream to wakefulness. Slowly, my pulse returns to normal; the pain dissipates and I begin to regain a measure of equanimity. But only a measure, for I know that I shall have this dream again, that its pain and horror will be undiminished.

Lying there in the ecstasy of having survived, I wonder: Had I died in the jaws of that tiger, died of a heart attack or sudden arrhythmia, died of fright, doubtless my next of kin would comfort themselves with the knowledge that I had died peacefully in my sleep. "He died the death of a righteous man," they would murmur to one another. Had I the breath for it, I would sit up in the coffin and shout: "No! No! It wasn't like that at all!"

Pain. The very word carries its own linguistic baggage, coming down to us from the Latin *poena*—punishment. It is the penalty for misdeeds; one is placed in a penitentiary and made to do penance. The pain of childbirth was inflicted upon Eve for her act of disobedience, and from her upon all those who follow. Immediately upon delivery of her young, a woman begins to distance herself from the pain which she experienced during childbirth. Such forgetfulness is nature's way of assuring the continuation of the human race.

15   It is at the very least curious that Milton in *Paradise Lost,* reinventing the birth of Eve, has the masculine effrontery to anesthetize Adam during the rib resection. In Book 8, Adam has just finished telling God of his loneliness, his sense of incompleteness. God has promised the solution. Here is Adam describing the birth of Eve:

> Dazzl'd and spent, sunk down, [I] sought repair
> Of sleep, which instantly fell on me, call'd
> By Nature as in aid, and clos'd mine eyes.
> Mine eyes he clos'd, but op'n left the Cell
> Of Fancy my internal sight, by which
> Abstract as in a trance methought I saw,
> Though sleeping where I lay, and saw the shape
> Still glorious before whom awake I stood;
> Who stooping op'n'd my left side, and took
> From thence a Rib, with cordial spirits warm,
> And Life-blood streaming fresh; wide was the wound,
> But suddenly with flesh fill'd up and heal'd:
> The Rib he form'd and fashion'd with his hands;
> Under his forming hands a Creature grew,
> Manlike, but different sex, so lovely fair. . . .

Milton's act of anesthesia is evidence, if any further were needed, that a man cannot imagine, nor can he admit, the pain of giving birth. It is outside the precincts of his understanding. Had *Paradise Lost* been written by a woman, doubtless Adam would have felt each and every twinge.

Many is the writer who has tried to make the reader *feel* pain in a fictional character. I among them, in this passage from an essay on the subject of kidney stones:

> Whom the stone grips is transformed in one instant from man to shark; and like the shark that must remain in perpetual motion, fins and tail moving lest it sink to terrible black depths of pressure, so the harborer of stone writhes and twists, bending and unbending in ceaseless turmoil. Now he straightens, stretches his limbs, only to draw them upon his trunk the next moment and fling his body from one side to the other, finding ease in neither. From between his teeth come sounds so primitive as to trigger the skin to creep. He shudders and vomits as though to cast froth the rock that grinds within. He would sell his birthright, forfeit his honor, his name, even kill to rid him of it. He toils in bed, pronged and spiked from within. Seed pearls of sweat break upon his face. In a moment his hair is heavy with it. His fingers scrabble against the bed, the wall, his own flesh to tear relief from these surfaces. But it does not pass. The impacted stone cannot push through into the lake, and from there voided. Like some terrible work of art, insatiable it screams to be extruded, let out into the air and light so as to be seen, touched, venerated. Never mind that the very act of deliverance will tear apart its creator.
>
> At last he is able to force a few drops of bloody urine and the pain subsides. The stone has fallen away from the point of impaction, washed loose into the bladder. He is miraculously free of the pain. It is no less than being touched by the hand of God. Still, he is afraid to move lest the lightest change of position should sink the craggy thing into some new part and the hell be reenacted. It has not passed. It lies within him yet, malevolent, scorpioid. It is only a matter of time before the beast will rise again.

Does this convey the pain of colic? I think it does not. No matter the metaphor and simile, all the pomp of language falls short in transmitting pain, that private corporeal experience, to the reader. It is beyond the reach of words; it is subverbal. Just as well, for to convey pain exactly would be to relive it and to suffer anew. In the matter of pain, it is better to experience it metaphorically than to know it directly.

---

1 Selzer confesses that in this essay he is attempting to come to terms with the nature of pain, which he is ready to admit cannot be captured in words (para. 2), even by great literary figures. What reasons can you infer from his essay that answer the question of why he would want to write about pain?

2 What experiences has Selzer had as both a doctor and a patient (para. 12–13) that have given him greater insight into the nature of pain and the language used to express it? What function does Selzer's depiction of the crucifixion play in suggesting how one's cultural framework determines how pain is perceived?

3 Look at the variety of language Selzer himself uses in his essay. Where does he move between the objective vocabulary of medicine and the subjective language that is personal and private? What does he achieve by obtaining this dual perspective on the subject of pain?

4 At several points in his essay Selzer compares the writer with the suffering patient (para. 2) and the doctor (para. 3 and 4). What are these comparisons meant to illustrate? Selzer has been both patient and doctor; what is the effect of his presenting both objective and subjective insights? (Glossary: *Comparison and Contrast, Objective/Subjective*.)

5 What is Selzer's underlying purpose in defining the term "pain"? How does he develop his definition of this term? How does Selzer organize the extended definition of "pain" and how does this organizational pattern help Selzer persuade his readers to accept his interpretation of what pain is? (Glossary: *Definition*.)

6 At what points in Selzer's essay does he draw on the kinds of terms that would be employed in a medical diagnosis? At which other points does he employ language characteristic of the arts? How does his use of language reflect shifts in perspective? What is the effect of these changes in perspective?

Yellowstone: The Erotics of Place

Terry Tempest Williams

◆ TERRY TEMPEST WILLIAMS is the Naturalist in Residence at the Utah Museum of Natural History. She is the author of *Pieces of White Shell* (1984), *Secret Language of Snow* (1984), *Between Cattails* (1985), *Refuge* (1991), and, most recently, *An Unspoken Hunger: Stories from the Field* (1994), from which the following essay is taken. She is the recipient of the Lannan Fellowship in creative nonfiction.

Williams expands the concept of the body to include the landscape of the natural world, especially when it is as dramatic and inspiring as Yellowstone National Park. In this essay, she provides a specific exploration of the connection between human beings, the language they use, and the animate world of the environment (previously discussed by David Abram). As we look at this world through her eyes, we gain a fuller understanding of how the land can speak to those who can hear. Her vision is pre-Christian and pagan and seeks to recover a way of perceiving nature that she calls "an erotics of place." Williams believes that if human beings express themselves through gestures as well as speech, then the study of language is enriched by understanding the connections between language and the sounds and shapes of the natural environment. The world of Yellowstone National Park is to her infinitely expressive and speaks a language all its own, to which she is attuned. To restrict oneself to believing language is only that spoken by human beings is to cut oneself off from the expressive meanings of the beautiful sensory world in which we live.

TO CONSIDER Has any camping or hiking trip you've taken produced a feeling of being in touch with nature in ways that were a completely different experience for you?

Steam rising. Water boiling. Geysers surging. Mud pots gurgling. Herds breathing. Hooves stampeding. Wings flocking. Sky darkening. Clouds gathering. Rain falling. Rivers raging. Lakes rising. Lightning striking. Trees burning. Thunder clapping. Smoke clearing. Eyes staring.

We call its name—and the land calls back.

Yellowstone.

Echo System.

Echo.

An echo is a sound wave that bounces back, or is reflected from, a large hard surface like the face of a cliff, or the flanks of a mountain, or the interior of a cave. To hear an echo, one must be at least seventeen meters or fifty-six feet away from the reflecting surface.

Echos are real—not imaginary.

We call out—and the land calls back. It is our interaction with the ecosystem; the Echo System.

We understand it intellectually.

We respond to it emotionally—joyously.

When was the last time we played with Echo?

The Greek god Pan played with her all the time.

Echo was a nymph and she was beautiful—long, dark hair flowing over her bare shoulders, lavender eyes, burnished skin and red lips. Pan was intrigued. He was god of wild nature—rustic, lustful, and seductive. But with his goat legs and horns, he could not woo Echo. She remained aloof, indifferent to his advances.

Pan was not accustomed to loving nymphs in vain. He struck her dumb, save for the power of repetition.

Echo roamed the woods and pastures repeating what she heard. The shepherds became incensed and seized her. They tore her body to pieces.

Gaia, the Earth Mother, quietly picked up the pieces of Echo and hid them in herself—where they still retain their repetitive powers.

Pan, seeking no further revenge, strengthened his vows to love the land in all its wildness—dancing in the woods, in the fields and grottoes, on mountain-tops and in glens—dancing, chasing, and seducing the vulnerable, all in the name of fertility.

Pan, as we know him, is therianthropic—half-man and half-animal—with a bare chest and the lower limbs of a goat. Two small horns rise from his head like lightning rods. He is blessed with the goat's prodigious agility and bestial passions. He wears a crown made of pine boughs and blows through pipes of reed.

He is a dangerous creature.

But we know Pan is dead. Elizabeth Barrett Browning has told us so:

Earth outgrows the mythic fancies
Sung beside her in her youth . . .
    Pan, Pan is dead

These lines are founded on an early Christian belief that when the heavenly hosts told the shepherds at Bethlehem of the birth of Christ, a deep groan was heard throughout Greece. Pan was dead.

When James Watt was asked what he feared most about environmentalists, his response was simple: "I fear they are pagans."

He is right to be fearful.

I would like to suggest Pan is not dead, that Echo lives in her repetitive world, in the cycles and circles of nature.

I would like even to suggest that the Greater Yellowstone Ecosystem/Echo System is a Pansexual landscape. Of Pan. A landscape that loves bison, bear, elk, deer, moose, coyote, wolf, rabbit, badger, marmot, squirrel, swan, crane, eagle, raven, pelican, red-tail, bufflehead, goldeneye, teal, and merganser.

Pansexual. Of Pan. A landscape that loves white pine, limber pine, lodge-pole, Douglas fir, blue spruce, aspen, cottonwood, willow, sage, serviceberry, huckleberry, chokecherry, lupine, larkspur, monkshood, steershead, glacier lilies, spring beauties, bistort, and paintbrush.

Pansexual. Of Pan. A landscape where the Bitter-root Valley, the Sawtooths, Tetons, Wind Rivers, and Absarokas loom large in our imaginations—where Henry's Fork, the Clark Fork, the Snake, and the Missouri nourish us, refresh us, and revive our souls.

It is time for us to take off our masks, to step out from behind our personas—whatever they might be: educators, activists, biologists, geologists, writers, farmers, ranchers, and bureaucrats—and admit we are lovers, engaged in an erotics of place. Loving the land. Honoring its mysteries. Acknowledging, embracing the spirit of place—there is nothing more legitimate and there is nothing more true.

That is why we are here. It is why we do what we do. There is nothing intellectual about it. We love the land. It is a primal affair.

Pagans? Perhaps.

Involved in an erotics of place? Most definitely.

There are rituals along the way. Doug Peacock writes in *Grizzly Years:*

> Before leaving for Bitter Creek, I had one more job to do: hide the head of
> the bull bison, which died in the open. If the Park Service discovers the
> head, rangers with sledgehammers are sent to smash the skull to pieces.
> This is to protect the bones from horn and head hunters, who spot the
> skull—perhaps from a helicopter—swoop down, pluck it up, and sell it to
> buyers who grind up every last piece of bone and antler for sale on the Asian
> market as an aphrodisiac.
>
> Late in the morning, I packed up for Bitter Creek wondering where I
> should hide the bull buffalo head. He should have stayed where he was for-
> ever. Barring that, I thought he should rejoin the bull herd of about a
> dozen bison with which he spent his adult life. I had been looking after this
> herd for years, and stashed other skulls when bulls died during hard win-
> ters. He would join his buddies in a semicircle of four bison skulls facing the
> rising sun. A mile away, hidden where they would never be discovered,
> below trees and under the snow, I brought together a ghost herd of bison
> skulls, decorated with the feathers of crane and eagle, the recipients of bun-
> dles of sage and handfuls of earth carried from sacred mountains and
> offered up in private ceremonies.

Rituals. Ceremonies. Engaging with the land. Loving the land and dreaming it. An erotics of place.

Biologist Tim Clark says at the heart of good biology is a central core of
imagination. It is the basis for responsible science. And it has everything to do
with intimacy, spending time outside.

But we forget because we spend so much time inside—inside offices, inside
boardrooms, inside universities, inside hearings, inside eating power breakfasts,
power lunches, dinners, and drinks.

To protect what we love outside, we are inside scheming, talking, telephoning, writing, granting, faxing memos, memos, memos, memos to them, to us;
inside to protect what we love outside.

There is no defense against an open heart and a supple body in dialogue
with wildness. Internal strength is an absorption of the external landscape. We
are informed by beauty, raw and sensual. Through an erotics of place our sensitivity becomes our sensibility.

If we ignore our connection to the land and disregard and deny our relationship to the Pansexual nature of earth, we will render ourselves impotent as
a species. No passion—no hope of survival.

Edward Abbey writes, "Nature may be indifferent to our love, but never
unfaithful."

We are a passionate people who are in the process of redefining our relationship toward the land.

And it is sensual.

I believe that out of an erotics of place, a politics of place is emerging. Not radical, but conservative, a politics rooted in empathy in which we extend our notion of community, as Aldo Leopold has urged, to include all life forms— plants, animals, rivers, and soils. The enterprise of conservation is a revolution, an evolution of the spirit.

We call to the land—and the land calls back.

Echo System.

Steam rising. Water boiling. Geysers surging. Mud pots gurgling. Herds breathing. Hooves stampeding. Wings flocking. Sky darkening. Clouds gathering. Rain falling. Rivers raging. Lakes rising. Lightning striking. Trees burning. Thunder clapping. Smoke clearing. Eyes staring. Wolves howling into the Yellowstone.

---

1 How does Williams's essay reveal that she wishes to reawaken an older sacramental view of nature that is associated with pagan deities? What change in attitude toward the environment would this pre-Christian view produce?

2 How does Williams elaborate the metaphor of an "echo system" as a controlling image that governs her conception of attunement to the body of nature? What other words imply that the environment is a living entity? What benefits are there for everyone in seeing nature in this way?

3 How does the episode of the bison's skull illustrate Williams's new sensitivity and desire to protect what she loves, especially when contrasted to the conventional attitude of the park rangers at Yellowstone National Park?

4 How does Williams use the echoing of sound at Yellowstone to evoke the mythic images of Echo, Pan, and Gaia, the Earth Mother? What function do these mythic allusions and plays on names ("ecosystem," "pansexual") have in her account? Why are these allusions necessary to get her audience to see things from her point of view? (Glossary: *Allusion*.)

5 What sensory details does Williams use to create a dominant impression of Yellowstone National Park? What is this impression? How does this dominant impression support the essay's persuasive intent? (Glossary: *Description*.)

6 Do you live in a town or city or near a river or mountain or other natural feature whose name reflects local history or patterns of settlement and migration? Do some research and write a short essay describing the origin and significance of this name.

The Language of Clothes   *Alison Lurie*

◆ ALISON LURIE is the Frederic J. Whiton Professor of American Literature at Cornell University, where she teaches writing and children's literature. She is the author of several books of nonfiction and fiction, including *Foreign Affairs* (1984), for which she was awarded a Pulitzer Prize in 1985. "The Language of Clothes" first appeared in *Human Ecology,* Spring 1991.

Lurie takes an approach that might be described as semiotic, which means that she is looking at clothing as a set of signs that can be "read" as a kind of language. She sees clothing as expressing a vocabulary that can be decoded and analyzed to discover its meaning in the particular social and cultural contexts in which these items of clothing are worn. For her, clothing is a kind of language that communicates the wearer's and the surrounding culture's intentions, emotions, meanings, values, and belief systems. For example, discovering that many societies passed laws setting conditions for who could wear specific items of clothing (only those of high rank in ancient Egypt could wear sandals) tells us how clothing functioned as a sign system in previous ages. Lurie's essay not only supplies a multitude of interesting examples of the different meanings items of clothing and body decorations have served in various cultures, but broadens our conception of what language can be.

TO CONSIDER   What is the last item of clothing you purchased that had symbolic meaning in addition to its practical value? What statement does it make about you?

For thousands of years human beings have communicated with one another first in the language of dress. Long before I am near enough to talk to you on the street, in a meeting, or at a party, you announce your sex, age and class to me through what you are wearing—and very possibly give me important information (or misinformation) as to your occupation, origin, personality, opinions, tastes, sexual desires and current mood. I may not be able to put what I observe into words, but I register the information unconsciously; and you simultaneously do the same for me. By the time we meet and converse we have already spoken to each other in an older and more universal language.

The statement that clothing is a language, though made occasionally with the air of a man finding a flying saucer in his backyard, is not new. Balzac, in *Daughter of Eve* (1830), observed that dress is a "continual manifestation of intimate thoughts, a language, a symbol." Today, as semiotics becomes fashionable, sociologists tell us that fashion too is a language of signs, a nonverbal system of communication.

None of these theorists, however, has gone on to remark what seems obvious: that if clothing is a language, it must have a vocabulary and a grammar like other languages. Of course, as with human speech, there is not a single language of dress, but many: some (like Dutch and German) closely related and others (like Basque) almost unique. And within every language of clothes there are many different dialects and accents, some almost unintelligible to members of the mainstream culture. Moreover, as with speech, each individual has his own stock of words and employs personal variations of tone and meaning.

The vocabulary of dress includes not only items of clothing, but also hair styles, accessories, jewelry, make-up and body decoration. Theoretically at least this vocabulary is as large as or larger than that of any spoken tongue, since it includes every garment, hair style, and type of body decoration ever invented. In practice, of course, the sartorial resources of an individual may be very restricted. Those of a sharecropper, for instance, may be limited to five or ten "words" from which it is possible to create only a few "sentences" almost bare of decoration and expressing only the most basic concepts. A so-called fashion leader, on the other hand, may have several hundred "words" at his or her disposal, and thus be able to form thousands of different "sentences" that will express a wide range of meanings. Just as the average English-speaking person knows many more words than he or she will ever use in conversation, so all of us are able to understand the meaning of styles we will never wear.

MAGICAL CLOTHING

Archaeologists digging up past civilizations and anthropologists studying primitive tribes have come to the conclusion that, as Rachel Kemper [*Costume*] puts it, "Paint, ornament, and rudimentary clothing were first employed to attract good animistic powers and to ward off evil." When Charles Darwin visited Tierra del Fuego, a cold, wet, disagreeable land plagued by constant winds, he found the natives naked except for feathers in their hair and symbolic designs painted on their bodies. Modern Australian bushmen, who may spend hours decorating themselves and their relatives with patterns in colored clay, often wear nothing else but an amulet or two.

However skimpy it may be, primitive dress almost everywhere, like primitive speech, is full of magic. A necklace of shark's teeth or a girdle of cowrie shells or feathers serves the same purpose as a prayer or spell, and may magically replace— or more often supplement—a spoken charm. In the first instance a form of *con-*

tagious magic is at work: the shark's teeth are believed to endow their wearer with the qualities of a fierce and successful fisherman. The cowrie shells, on the other hand, work through *sympathetic* magic: since they resemble the female sexual parts, they are thought to increase or preserve fertility.

In civilized society today belief in the supernatural powers of clothing—like belief in prayers, spells and charms—remains widespread, though we denigrate it with the name "superstition." Advertisements announce that improbable and romantic events will follow the application of a particular sort of grease to our faces, hair or bodies; they claim that members of the opposite (or our own) sex will be drawn to us by the smell of a particular soap. Nobody believes those ads, you may say. Maybe not, but we behave as though we did: look in your bathroom cabinet.

The supernatural garments of European folk tales—the seven-league boots, the cloaks of invisibility and the magic rings—are not forgotten, merely transformed, so that today we have the track star who can only win a race in a particular hat or shoes, the plain-clothes cop who feels no one can see him in his raincoat and the wife who takes off her wedding ring before going to a motel with her lover.

Sympathetic or symbolic magic is also often employed, as when we hang crosses, stars or one of the current symbols of female power and solidarity around our necks, thus silently involving the protection of Jesus, Jehovah or Astarte. Such amulets, of course, may be worn to announce our allegiance to some faith or cause rather than as a charm. Or they may serve both purposes simultaneously—or sequentially. The crucifix concealed below the parochial-school uniform speaks only to God until some devilish force persuades its wearer to remove his or her clothes; then it acts—or fails to act—as a warning against sin as well as a protective talisman.

Articles of clothing, too, may be treated as if they had mana, the impersonal supernatural force that tends to concentrate itself in objects. When I was in college it was common to wear a particular "lucky" sweater, shirt or hat to final examinations, and this practice continues today. Here it is usually contagious magic that is at work: the chosen garment has become lucky by being worn on the occasion of some earlier success, or has been given to its owner by some favored person. The wearing of such magical garments is especially common in sports, where they are often publicly credited with bringing their owners luck. Their loss or abandonment is thought to cause injury as well as defeat. Actors also believe ardently in the magic of clothes, possibly because they are so familiar with the near-magical transforming power of theatrical costume.

FASHION AND STATUS

Clothing designed to show the social position of its wearer has a long history. Just as the oldest languages are full of elaborate titles and forms of address, so for thousands of years certain modes have indicated high or royal rank. Many societies passed decrees known as *sumptuary laws* to prescribe or forbid the wearing of specific styles by specific classes of persons. In ancient Egypt only those in high position could wear sandals; the Greeks and Romans controlled the type, color and number of garments worn and the sorts of embroidery with which they could be trimmed. During the Middle Ages almost every aspect of dress was regulated at some place or time—though not always with much success. The common features of all sumptuary laws—like that of edicts against the use of certain words—seem to be that they are difficult to enforce for very long.

Laws about what could be worn by whom continued to be passed in Europe until about 1700. But as class barriers weakened and wealth could be more easily and rapidly converted into gentility, the system by which color and shape indicated social status began to break down. What came to designate high rank instead was the evident cost of a costume: rich materials, superfluous trimmings and difficult-to-care-for styles, or as Thorstein Veblen later put it [in *The Theory of the Leisure Class*], Conspicuous Waste and Conspicuous Leisure. As a result, it was assumed that the people you met would be dressed as lavishly as their income permitted. In Fielding's *Tom Jones,* for instance, everyone judges strangers by their clothing and treats them accordingly; this is presented as natural. It is a world in which rank is very exactly indicated by costume, from the rags of Molly the gamekeeper's daughter to Sophia Western's riding habit "which was so very richly laced" that "Partridge and the postboy instantly started from their chairs, and my landlady fell to her curtsies, and her ladyships, with great eagerness." The elaborate wigs characteristic of this period conferred status partly because they were both expensive to buy and expensive to maintain.

By the early eighteenth century the social advantages of conspicuous dress were such that even those who could not afford it often spent their money on finery. This development was naturally deplored by supporters of the status quo. In Colonial America the Massachusetts General Court declared its "utter detestation and dislike, that men or women of mean condition, should take upon them the garb of Gentlemen, by wearing Gold or Silver lace, or Buttons, or Points at their knees, or to walk in great Boots; or Women of the same rank to wear Silk or Tiffiny hoods, or Scarfes. . . ." What "men or women of mean condition"—farmers or artisans—were supposed to wear were coarse linen or wool, leather aprons, deerskin jackets, flannel petticoats and the like.

To dress above one's station was considered not only foolishly extravagant, but deliberately deceptive. In 1878 an American etiquette book complained,

> It is . . . unfortunately the fact that, in the United States, but too much attention is paid to dress by those who have neither the excuse of ample means nor of social claims. . . .We Americans are lavish, generous, and ostentatious. The wives of our wealthy men are glorious in garb as are princesses and queens. They have a right so to be. But when those who can

ill afford to wear alpaca persist in arraying themselves in silk . . . the matter is a sad one.

COLOR AND PATTERN

Certain sorts of information about other people can be communicated in spite of a language barrier. We may not be able to understand Welsh or the thick Southern dialect of the Mississippi delta, but when we hear a conversation in these tongues we can tell at once whether the speakers are excited or bored, cheerful or miserable, confident or frightened. In the same way, some aspects of the language of clothes can be read by almost anyone.

The first and most important of these signs, and the one that makes the greatest and most immediate impact, is color. Merely looking at different colors, psychologists have discovered, alters our blood pressure, heartbeat and rate of respiration, just as hearing a harsh noise or a harmonious musical chord does. When somebody approaches from a distance the first thing we see is the hue of his clothes; the closer he comes, the more space this hue occupies in our visual field and the greater its effect on our nervous system. Loud, clashing colors, like loud noises or loud voices, may actually hurt our eyes or give us a headache; soft, harmonious hues, like music and soft voices, thrill or soothe us. Color in dress is also like tone of voice in speech in that it can completely alter the meaning of what is "said" by other aspects of the costume: style, fabric and trimmings. Just as the words "Do you want to dance with me?" can be whispered shyly or flung as a challenge, so the effect of a white evening dress is very different from that of a scarlet one of identical fabric and pattern. In certain circumstances some hues, like some tones of voice, are beyond the bounds of polite discourse. A bride in a black wedding dress, or a stockbroker greeting his clients in a shocking-pink three-piece suit, would be like people screaming aloud.

Although color often indicates mood, it is not by any means an infallible guide. For one thing, convention may prescribe certain hues. The urban businessman must wear a navy blue, dark gray or (in certain regions) brown or tan suit, and can express his feelings only through his choice of shirt and tie, or tie alone; and even here the respectable possibilities may be very limited. Convention also alters the meaning of colors according to the place and time at which they are worn. Vermilion in the office is not the same as vermilion at a disco; and hot weather permits the wearing of pale hues that would make one look far more formal and fragile in midwinter.

There are other problems. Some people may avoid colors they like because of the belief or illusion that they are unbecoming, while others may wear colors they normally dislike for symbolic reason: because they are members or fans of a certain football team, for instance. In addition, some fashionable types may select certain hues merely because they are "in" that year.

Finally, it should be noted that the effect of any color in dress is modified by the colors that accompany it. In general, therefore, the following remarks should be taken as applying mainly to costumes composed entirely or almost entirely of a single hue.

The mood of a crowd, as well as that of an individual, can often be read in the colors of clothing. In the office of a large corporation, or at a professional convention, there is usually a predominance of conventional gray, navy, beige, tan and white—suggesting a general attitude of seriousness, hard work, neutrality, propriety and status. The same group of people at a picnic are a mass of lively, relaxed blue, red and brown, with touches of yellow and green. In the evening, at a disco, they shimmer under the rotating lights in dramatic combinations of purple, crimson, orange, turquoise, gold, silver and black.

Apart from the chameleon, man is the only animal who can change his skin to suit his background. Indeed, if he is to function successfully he must do so. The individual whose clothes do not fall within the recognized range of colors for a given situation attracts attention, usually (though not always) unfavorable attention. When a child puts its pet chameleon down on the earth and it does not turn brown, we know the creature is seriously ill. In the same way, men or women who begin to come to work in a conservative office wearing disco hues and a disco mood are regarded with anxiety and suspicion. If they do not blush a respectable beige, navy or gray within a reasonable length of time, their colleagues know that they will not be around for long.

---

1 Lurie starts from the assumption that fashion is a system of communication equivalent to a language. She also believes that there are many varieties of "clothing languages" (para. 3) and that clothing, like conventional language, often possesses many local variations or inflections. What factors determine how extensive or limited this language is and how particular articles of clothing and body decorations communicate meaning in specific cultures? For example, how do the color and pattern of clothes communicate meaning (para. 15–21)?

2 How have clothing and bodily adornment served magical purposes? What distinction does Lurie make between associative magic and symbolic magic? How has clothing served as one of the primary markers of social status in different societies throughout history?

3 Go through your wardrobe and classify items of clothes you wear according to the "statement" you want to make in different contexts. Give some examples of different things you wear for different occasions as they relate to Lurie's thesis. You might wish to pursue Lurie's analogy by asking whether, just as in language, rules exist as to how signs can be combined or arranged, how they affect each other, and how complex structures of signs and meanings can be built up. For example, is a suit a word or a phrase? Is an entire outfit a sentence? Do different types of clothing or adornment serve different grammatical purposes? For example, do accessories connect

things together just as conjunctives do? How might accessories serve the same function that modifiers (adjectives and adverbs) do?

4 What principle of organization governs the sequence of topics in Lurie's essay as indicated in the headings of "Magical Clothing," "Fashion and Status," and "Color and Pattern"? (Glossary: *Organization*.)

5 Lurie draws an analogy between two seemingly unrelated subjects (language and clothes) to point out unsuspecting similarities. Why is this rhetorical strategy particularly helpful in illustrating the symbolic function clothes have served in various societies? (Glossary: *Analogy*.)

6 Using Alison Lurie's essay as a basis, interpret the "language" and significance of costumes for any of the following: weddings, funerals, graduations, ethnic parades, formal dances, folk dances, Halloween, or another special occasion where unusual apparel plays a role.

◆ CONNECTIONS: THE BODILY BASIS OF LANGUAGE

Kenneth Burke, "Symbolic Action"

1. In what way do both Burke and George Lakoff start from the premise that what might be considered to be symbolic and metaphorical is actually quite literal?
2. How does Burke's theory of "symbolic action" illuminate Naomi Wolf's analysis in "The Beauty Myth" (Ch. 10) of the culturally constructed nature of contemporary ideals of feminine beauty when compared with images of female beauty in different cultures at different times?

David Abram, "The Flesh of Language"

1. How does George Lakoff's study "Anger" illustrate how rooted language is in a physical dimension of experience in ways described by Abram?
2. How is Abram's theory that language evolves as an expressive response to the environment demonstrated in Burgess's creation of an invented slang for his protagonist in *A Clockwork Orange* (ch. 7)?

George Lakoff, "Anger"

1. What role does metaphor play in the communication of the nature of pain in Richard Selzer's article and what different cognitive models appear to be operating in the examples cited by Selzer that support Lakoff's thesis? In what sense, according to Selzer, are metaphors inadequate to express pain?
2. How does Susan Sontag's discussion of the metaphorical meanings assigned to AIDS ("AIDS and Its Metaphors," Ch. 8) illustrate how the mind-body connection researched by Lakoff can become politicized?

Oliver Sacks, "The President's Speech"

1. How does the importance of gestures in communicating meaning aside from the words being used constitute an entirely separate vocabulary that can also be seen in the examples cited by Kenneth Burke?
2. How do the aphasics described by Sacks pick up deceptions, lies, and bad intentions (because of a mismatch between words and gestures) in ways that the analysis of advertising tries to ascertain (see Stuart Hirschberg's "The Rhetoric of Advertising," Ch. 9)?

Temple Grandin, "Thinking in Pictures"

1. How does Grandin's unusual method of processing information demonstrate the same kind of cognitive processes, albeit more extensive, that George Lakoff describes?
2. How does the way Grandin creates concrete images in order to visualize abstract concepts relate to the process by which advertisers create images to sell their products (as discussed by Bill Bryson in "The Hard Sell: Advertising in America," Ch. 9)?

Richard Selzer, "The Language of Pain"

1. How does Selzer's analysis of the language used to express pain support David Abram's thesis about the somatic basis of language?
2. What connections can you discover between Selzer's exploration of the language used to express pain and the imaginary language made up by Lewis Carroll in "Jabberwocky" (Ch. 7)?

Terry Tempest Williams, "Yellowstone: the Erotics of Place"

1. What myths does Williams evoke in responding to the environment of Yellowstone National Park? Drawing on George Lakoff's method of linking separate metaphors and seeing what they have in common, analyze the different systems of metaphor used by Williams.
2. How does the holistic ecological perspective explored by Williams differ from the traditional American attitude toward the Old West described by Jane Tompkins in "Women and the Language of Men" (Ch. 5)?

Alison Lurie, "The Language of Clothes"

1. According to Lurie, how are articles of clothing designed to serve a gestural function in relation to particular or specific economic and social environments in ways that constitute a repertoire of signals that corresponds to what Kenneth Burke calls "the dancing of an attitude"?
2. In light of Lurie's discussion, analyze the syntax and symbolism of items of dress, accessories, make-up, etc., in any of the ads discussed by John Berger in "Ways of Seeing" (Ch. 9).

◆ WRITING ASSIGNMENTS FOR CHAPTER 3

1. How do the uniforms worn by football players contribute to what Lurie might call a "vocabulary" of aggression? How do the uniforms worn in other sports express a "vocabulary" and significance?
2. What do each of the following gestures communicate? How do they differ from formal sign-language systems? (Glossary, *American Sign Language.*) What others can you think of?

Armpits hook

Temple "shoot"

Hand ring-kiss

Fingertips kiss

Adapted from *Body Talk*, by Desmond Morris, 1995.

3. Recall a conversation where there were distinct nonverbal clues implying one of the following emotions was operating: anxiety, bliss, envy, ecstasy, boredom, determination, paranoia, surprise, or joy. Describe the action performed and the meaning and emotion conveyed.

4. Analyze the following cartoon in terms of Gary Larson's use of the idea of confusion between figurative and literal meanings.

THE FAR SIDE   By GARY LARSON

"Hang him, you idiots! Hang him! . . . 'String-him-up' is a figure of speech!"

Larson, *In Search of the Far Side* © 1984, Andrews & McNeel, a Universal Syndicate Company. Used by permission

5. How do cultures that use the phrase "mother earth" (including Native Americans, Australian Aborigines, natives of Pacific islands, the Inuit in Alaska and Canada) differ from technological cultures in their attitudes toward owning, mining, and selling land? How does this fundamentally different viewpoint produce frequent conflicts in our culture? How is Terry Tempest Williams's attitude close to that of these native groups?

6. Would a TV anchorwoman who wore a flowered sundress to deliver the news be more or less credible than if she wore a tailored suit? Why or why not? Why do you think that women have to wear what were traditionally men's clothes to be seen as credible?

Half the world is composed of people
who have something to say and can't,
and the other half who have nothing to
say and keep on saying it.

—Robert Frost

CATHY   **by Cathy Guisewite**

Guisewite, *A Mouthful of Breath Mints and No One to Kiss* © 1993, Andrews & McNeel, a Universal Syndicate Company. Used by permission.

Can We Talk?

The writers in this chapter approach the fundamental question of the relationship between what we think and how we communicate our thoughts to others.

As social creatures, we spend a great deal of time talking to one another, to let each other know how we are feeling, to communicate information, and to pass on that extraordinary amount of knowledge that we call culture from one person to another and from one generation to the next. Yet, who of us has not felt at one time or another that the words we choose to convey a thought fail to express exactly what we have in mind? To put it another way, we can listen, but do we really hear?

If we have been dazzled by the amazing potential of what language offers—as represented in the readings in the first three chapters—a salutary corrective is provided by the writers in this chapter.

To get the most out of words, we must be receptive to the accumulated and too seldom recognized trail of meanings that words bring with them. We owe this insight to the most profound theorist of dialogue, Mikhail Bakhtin, whose essay "The Dialogic Imagination" launched a school of literary and linguistic criticism. Bakhtin argues that dialogue is characterized by a "many-voiced" evolving world of constantly interacting viewpoints. No word exists by itself in a vacuum, but is already laden with a web of connotations and associations.

Just as Bakhtin discovered how the words we use are already freighted with the accumulated thoughts of all those who used them before, Ronald Wardhaugh ("The Social Basis of Talk") and Peter Farb ("Verbal Dueling") reveal how the rituals and strategies of ordinary conversation are responsible for generating this dimension of all-important but rarely recognized meaning.

What happens when the social rituals governing conversation go wrong is dramatized by Fritz Peters in "Gurdjieff Remembered," and James Gorman in "Like, Uptalk?" In "What's Wrong with TV?: Talk Shows," by Tom Shachtman, the collapse of literate communication is analyzed as a sign of the times. Perhaps the most telling exploration of the gulf between thought and language and how much of what we have to communicate goes unexpressed can be seen in Raymond Carver's short story "What We Talk About When We Talk About Love."

The Dialogic Imagination

Mikhail M. Bakhtin

◆ MIKHAIL MIKHAILOVICH BAKHTIN'S (1895–1975) literary criticism has become the focus of widespread Western attention since the 1960s. He was initially admired for his study of the Russian author Fyodor Dostoevsky, but has become recognized for his theories of dialogue. Dialogue is for Bakhtin an evolving world of contrasting viewpoints where conversation, language, and context constantly influence each other. His many publications include *Problems of Dostoevsky's Poetics,* translated by R. W. Rostel (1973), and *The Dialogic Imagination,* translated by Caryl Emerson and Michael Holquist (1981), from which the following selection is reprinted.

Bakhtin's theories are so important to the study of linguistics because he took language out of the "ivory tower" realm in which it had been studied previously (through its forms, structure, and origins) and looked at words in their social and cultural context as already invested with a whole host of associations. It is in this sense that Bakhtin considered words to be "dialogic" in nature—that is, already reflecting an exchange of views as in a dialogue. The meanings of words we use are already present, because they are always part of some continuing conversation in the past, in the present, and in the future. From common experience, everyone knows this to be true—that is, you are having a conversation in which you take for granted that the other person can tune into the subtext and already-present connotations of mutually understood references. For Bakhtin, language is first and foremost a social phenomenon, and he would place the emphasis of this chapter's title on the word "We."

TO CONSIDER   Were you ever surprised to discover that someone had very different associations connected with a word than you did? Rule out simple misunderstandings about the meaning of a term.

DISCOURSE IN POETRY AND DISCOURSE IN THE NOVEL

For the philosophy of language, for linguistics and for stylistics structured on their base, a whole series of phenomena have therefore remained almost entirely beyond the realm of consideration: these include the specific phenomena that are present in discourse and that are determined by its dialogic orientation, first, amid others' utterances inside a *single* language (the primordial dialogism of discourse), amid other "social languages" within a single *national* language and finally amid different national languages within the same *culture,* that is, the same socio-ideological conceptual horizon.[1]

In recent decades, it is true, these phenomena have begun to attract the attention of scholars in language and stylistics, but their fundamental and wide-ranging significance in all spheres of the life of discourse is still far from acknowledged.

The dialogic orientation of a word among other words (of all kinds and degrees of otherness) creates new and significant artistic potential in discourse, creates the potential for a distinctive art of prose, which has found its fullest and deepest expression in the novel.

We will focus our attention here on various forms and degrees of dialogic orientation in discourse, and on the special potential for a distinctive prose-art.

As treated by traditional stylistic thought, the word acknowledges only itself (that is, only its own context), its own object, its own direct expression and its own unitary and singular language. It acknowledges another word, one lying outside its own context, only as the neutral word of language, as the word of no one in particular, as simply the potential for speech. The direct word, as traditional stylistics understands it, encounters in its orientation toward the object only the resistance of the object itself (the impossibility of its being exhausted by a word, the impossibility of saying it all), but it does not encounter in its path toward the object the fundamental and richly varied opposition of another's word. No one hinders this word, no one argues with it.

But no living word relates to its object in a *singular* way: between the word

---

[1]Linguistics acknowledges only a mechanical reciprocal influencing and intermixing of languages, (that is, one that is unconscious and determined by social conditions) which is reflected in abstract linguistic elements (phonetic and morphological).

and its object, between the word and the speaking subject, there exists an elastic environment of other, alien words about the same object, the same theme, and this is an environment that it is often difficult to penetrate. It is precisely in the process of living interaction with this specific environment that the word may be individualized and given stylistic shape.

Indeed, any concrete discourse (utterance) finds the object at which it was directed already as it were overlain with qualifications, open to dispute, charged with value, already enveloped in an obscuring mist—or, on the contrary, by the "light" of alien words that have already been spoken about it. It is entangled, shot through with shared thoughts, points of view, alien value judgments and accents. The word, directed toward its object, enters a dialogically agitated and tension-filled environment of alien words, value judgments and accents, weaves in and out of complex interrelationships, merges with some, recoils from others, intersects with yet a third group: and all this may crucially shape discourse, may leave a trace in all its semantic layers, may complicate its expression and influence its entire stylistic profile.

The living utterance, having taken meaning and shape at a particular historical moment in a socially specific environment, cannot fail to brush up against thousands of living dialogic threads, woven by socio-ideological consciousness around the given object of an utterance; it cannot fail to become an active participant in social dialogue. After all, the utterance arises out of this dialogue as a continuation of it and as a rejoinder to it—it does not approach the object from the sidelines.

The way in which the word conceptualizes its object is a complex act—all objects, open to dispute and overlain as they are with qualifications, are from one side highlighted while from the other side dimmed by heteroglot social opinion, by an alien word about them.[2] And into this complex play of light and shadow the word enters—it becomes saturated with this play, and must determine within it the boundaries of its own semantic and stylistic contours. The way in which the word conceives its object is complicated by a dialogic interaction within the object between various aspects of its socio-verbal intelligibility. And an artistic representation, an "image" of the object, may be penetrated by this dialogic play of verbal intentions that meet and are interwoven in it; such an image need not stifle these forces, but on the contrary may activate and organize them. If we imagine the *intention* of such a word, that is, its *directionality toward the object,* in the form of a ray of light, then the living and unrepeatable play of colors and light on the facets of the image that it constructs can be explained as the spec-

---

[2]Highly significant in this respect is the struggle that must be undertaken in such movements as Rousseauism, Naturalism, Impressionism, Acmeism, Dadaism, Surrealism and analogous schools with the "qualified" nature of the object (a struggle occasioned by the idea of a return to primordial consciousness, to original consciousness, to the object itself in itself, to pure perception and so forth).

tral dispersion of the ray-word, not within the object itself (as would be the case in the play of an image-as-trope, in poetic speech taken in the narrow sense, in an "autotelic word"), but rather as its spectral dispersion in an atmosphere filled with the alien words, value judgments and accents through which the ray passes on its way toward the object; the social atmosphere of the word, the atmosphere that surrounds the object, makes the facets of the image sparkle.

The word, breaking through to its own meaning and its own expression across an environment full of alien words and variously evaluating accents, harmonizing with some of the elements in this environment and striking a dissonance with others, is able, in this dialogized process, to shape its own stylistic profile and tone.

Such is the *image in artistic prose* and the image of *novelistic prose* in particular. In the atmosphere of the novel, the direct and unmediated intention of a word presents itself as something impermissably naive, something in fact impossible, for naiveté itself, under authentic novelistic conditions, takes on the nature of an internal polemic and is consequently dialogized (in, for example, the work of the Sentimentalists, in Chateaubriand and in Tolstoy). Such a dialogized image can occur in all the poetic genres as well, even in the lyric (to be sure, without setting the tone).[3] But such an image can fully unfold, achieve full complexity and depth and at the same time artistic closure, only under the conditions present in the genre of the novel.

In the poetic image narrowly conceived (in the image-as-trope), all activity—the dynamics of the image-as-word—is completely exhausted by the play between the word (with all its aspects) and the object (in all its aspects). The word plunges into the inexhaustible wealth and contradictory multiplicity of the object itself, with its "virginal," still "unuttered" nature; therefore it presumes nothing beyond the borders of its own context (except, of course, what can be found in the treasure-house of language itself). The word forgets that its object has its own history of contradictory acts of verbal recognition, as well as that heteroglossia that is always present in such acts of recognition.

For the writer of artistic prose, on the contrary, the object reveals first of all precisely the socially heteroglot multiplicity of its names, definitions and value judgments. Instead of the virginal fullness and inexhaustibility of the object itself, the prose writer confronts a multitude of routes, roads and paths that have been laid down in the object by social consciousness. Along with the internal contradictions inside the object itself, the prose writer witnesses as well the unfolding of social heteroglossia *surrounding* the object, the Tower-of-Babel mixing of languages that goes on around any object; the dialectics of the object are interwoven with the social dialogue surrounding it. For the prose writer, the object is a focal point for heteroglot voices among which his own voice must also

---

[3]The Horatian lyric, Villon, Heine, Laforgue, Annenskij and others—despite the fact that these are extremely varied instances.

sound; these voices create the background necessary for his own voice, outside of which his artistic prose nuances cannot be perceived, and without which they "do not sound."

The prose artist elevates the social heteroglossia surrounding objects into an image that has finished contours, an image completely shot through with dialogized overtones; he creates artistically calculated nuances on all the fundamental voices and tones of this heteroglossia. But as we have already said, every extra-artistic prose discourse—in any of its forms, quotidian, rhetorical, scholarly—cannot fail to be oriented toward the "already uttered," the "already known," the "common opinion" and so forth. The dialogic orientation of discourse is a phenomenon that is, of course, a property of *any* discourse. It is the natural orientation of any living discourse. On all its various routes toward the object, in all its directions, the word encounters an alien word and cannot help encountering it in a living, tension-filled interaction. Only the mythical Adam, who approached a virginal and as yet verbally unqualified world with the first word, could really have escaped from start to finish this dialogic inter-orientation with the alien word that occurs in the object. Concrete historical human discourse does not have this privilege: it can deviate from such inter-orientation only on a conditional basis and only to a certain degree.

It is all the more remarkable that linguistics and the philosophy of discourse have been primarily oriented precisely toward this artificial, preconditioned status of the word, a word excised from dialogue and taken for the norm (although the primacy of dialogue over monologue is frequently proclaimed). Dialogue is studied merely as a compositional form in the structuring of speech, but the internal dialogism of the word (which occurs in a monologic utterance as well as in a rejoinder), the dialogism that penetrates its entire structure, all its semantic and expressive layers, is almost entirely ignored. But it is precisely this internal dialogism of the word, which does not assume any external compositional forms of dialogue, that cannot be isolated as an independent act, separate from the word's ability to form a concept [*koncipirovanie*] of its object—it is precisely this internal dialogism that has such enormous power to shape style. The internal dialogism of the word finds expression in a series of peculiar features in semantics, syntax and stylistics that have remained up to the present time completely unstudied by linguistics and stylistics (nor, what is more, have the peculiar semantic features of ordinary dialogue been studied).

The word is born in a dialogue as a living rejoinder within it; the word is shaped in dialogic interaction with an alien word that is already in the object. A word forms a concept of its own object in a dialogic way.

But this does not exhaust the internal dialogism of the word. It encounters an alien word not only in the object itself: every word is directed toward an *answer* and cannot escape the profound influence of the answering word that it anticipates.

The word in living conversation is directly, blatantly, oriented toward a future answer-word: it provokes an answer, anticipates it and structures itself in the answer's direction. Forming itself in an atmosphere of the already spoken, the word is at the same time determined by that which has not yet been said but which is needed and in fact anticipated by the answering word. Such is the situation in any living dialogue.

All rhetorical forms, monologic in their compositional structure, are oriented toward the listener and his answer. This orientation toward the listener is usually considered the basic constitutive feature of rhetorical discourse.[4] It is highly significant for rhetoric that this relationship toward the concrete listener, taking him into account, is a relationship that enters into the very internal construction of rhetorical discourse. This orientation toward an answer is open, blatant and concrete.

This open orientation toward the listener and his answer in everyday dialogue and in rhetorical forms has attracted the attention of linguists. But even where this has been the case, linguists have by and large gotten no further than the compositional forms by which the listener is taken into account; they have not sought influence springing from more profound meaning and style. They have taken into consideration only those aspects of style determined by demands for comprehensibility and clarity—that is, precisely those aspects that are deprived of any internal dialogism, that take the listener for a person who passively understands but not for one who actively answers and reacts.

The listener and his response are regularly taken into account when it comes to everyday dialogue and rhetoric, but every other sort of discourse as well is oriented toward an understanding that is "responsive"—although this orientation is not particularized in an independent act and is not compositionally marked. Responsive understanding is a fundamental force, one that participates in the formulation of discourse, and it is moreover an *active* understanding, one that discourse senses as resistance or support enriching the discourse.

Linguistics and the philosophy of language acknowledge only a passive understanding of discourse, and moreover this takes place by and large on the level of common language, that is, it is an understanding of an utterance's *neutral signification* and not its *actual meaning*.

The linguistic significance of a given utterance is understood against the background of language, while its actual meaning is understood against the background of other concrete utterances on the same theme, a background made up of contradictory opinions, points of view and value judgments—that is, precisely that background that, as we see, complicates the path of any word toward its object. Only now this contradictory environment of alien words is present to the speaker not in the object, but rather in the consciousness of the listener, as his apperceptive background, pregnant with responses and objections. And every utterance is oriented toward this apperceptive background of understanding, which is not a linguistic background but rather one composed of specific objects and emotional expressions. There occurs a new encounter

---

[4]Cf. V. Vinogradov's book *On Artistic Prose,* the chapter "Rhetoric and Poetics," pp. 75ff., where definitions taken from the older rhetorics are introduced.

between the utterance and an alien word, which makes itself felt as a new and unique influence on its style.

A passive understanding of linguistic meaning is no understanding at all, it is only the abstract aspect of meaning. But even a more concrete *passive* understanding of the meaning of the utterance, an understanding of the speaker's intention insofar as that understanding remains purely passive, purely receptive, contributes nothing new to the word under consideration, only mirroring it, seeking, at its most ambitious, merely the full reproduction of that which is already given in the word—even such an understanding never goes beyond the boundaries of the word's context and in no way enriches the word. Therefore, insofar as the speaker operates with such a passive understanding, nothing new can be introduced into his discourse; there can be no new aspects in his discourse relating to concrete objects and emotional expressions. Indeed the purely negative demands, such as could only emerge from a passive understanding (for instance, a need for greater clarity, more persuasiveness, more vividness and so forth), leave the speaker in his own personal context, within his own boundaries; such negative demands are completely immanent in the speaker's own discourse and do not go beyond his semantic or expressive self-sufficiency.

In the actual life of speech, every concrete act of understanding is active: it assimilates the word to be understood into its own conceptual system filled with specific objects and emotional expressions, and is indissolubly merged with the response, with a motivated agreement or disagreement. To some extent, primacy belongs to the response, as the activating principle: it creates the ground for understanding, it prepares the ground for an active and engaged understanding. Understanding comes to fruition only in the response. Understanding and response are dialectically merged and mutually condition each other; one is impossible without the other.

Thus an active understanding, one that assimilates the word under consideration into a new conceptual system, that of the one striving to understand, establishes a series of complex interrelationships, consonances and dissonances with the word and enriches it with new elements. It is precisely such an understanding that the speaker counts on. Therefore his orientation toward the listener is an orientation toward a specific conceptual horizon, toward the specific world of the listener; it introduces totally new elements into his discourse; it is in this way, after all, that various different points of view, conceptual horizons, systems for providing expressive accents, various social "languages" come to interact with one another. The speaker strives to get a reading on his own word, and on his own conceptual system that determines this word, within the alien conceptual system of the understanding receiver; he enters into dialogical relationships with certain aspects of this system. The speaker breaks through the alien conceptual horizon of the listener, constructs his own utterance on alien territory, against his, the listener's, apperceptive background.

This new form of internal dialogism of the word is different from that form determined by an encounter with an alien word within the object itself: here it is not the object that serves as the arena for the encounter, but rather the subjective belief system of the listener. Thus this dialogism bears a more subjective, psychological and (frequently) random character, sometimes crassly accommodating, sometimes provocatively polemical. Very often, especially in the rhetorical forms, this orientation toward the listener and the related internal dialogism of the word may simply overshadow the object: the strong point of any concrete listener becomes a self-sufficient focus of attention, and one that interferes with the word's creative work on its referent.

Although they differ in their essentials and give rise to varying stylistic effects in discourse, the dialogic relationship toward an alien word within the object and the relationship toward an alien word in the anticipated answer of the listener can, nevertheless, be very tightly interwoven with each other, becoming almost indistinguishable during stylistic analysis.

---

1 What reasons does Bakhtin give to support his belief that a new discipline needs to be established based on the belief that words gain their true meaning through interaction within an environment and that consequently dialogue is the most important defining feature of language? How can this "dialogic" orientation be seen (1) in a single language, (2) among "social languages" such as slang, (3) inside a single national language, and (4) within a culture that uses different national languages (para. 1)?

2 What does Bakhtin mean by "internal dialogism" (para. 17)? For example, why, according to Bakhtin, must the study of dialogue always be rooted in the complex expectations of another person's answer? What kinds of dynamic interrelationships connect the speaker's utterances to those of others? In what sense do we live in a world of others' words?

3 How does Bakhtin's approach differ from traditional studies of language that view dialogue only as a compositional form in the organization of speech? Why does Bakhtin believe that a word is never just a word, that the true meaning of a word can only be discovered through dialogue, and that the living word is always contextual (para. 23–25)? How are the emotional meanings of words dependent on the person's emotional state when they came into contact with the word and the connotations and overtones that have been associated with that word in the past?

4 Bakhtin invents a number of technical terms (heteroglossia) and redefines some existing words (dialogic) to convey his ideas. How do these terms function at different points in his essay to express Bakhtin's innovative philosophy of language? What unique meanings do they have? (Glossary: *Definition, Technical Language.*)

5 One way Bakhtin develops his essay is by comparing and contrasting the monologic understanding of language with his own dialogic conception. What specifics does Bakhtin provide to show why he regards one as superior to the other? (Glossary: *Comparison and Contrast.*)

6 Write a dialogue in which you converse with someone who is no longer in your life, using the opportunity to get in touch with your true feelings toward this person. Project what the other person is saying in your dialogue.

The Social Basis of Talk

Ronald Wardhaugh

◆ RONALD WARDHAUGH is the director of the Center for Language and Language Behavior at the University of Toronto, and professor of linguistics. His publications include *The Contexts of Language* (1976), *Introduction to Linguistics* (1977), and *How Conversation Works* (1985), from which the following article is taken.

What determines why we feel completely at ease in talking to one person and utterly uncomfortable in talking with another? Or, to put it another way, what unspoken expectations come into play that result in our sense of comfort or discomfort in any particular conversation? Wardhaugh not only identifies a particular repertoire of skills that successful conversationalists possess, but, more important, explains why communications break down. He, like Bakhtin, emphasizes the social dimension of language and locates the cause of the discomfort we experience in some dialogues as a fundamental lack of trust, which makes a free flow of information difficult, if not impossible.

TO CONSIDER Have you ever had a conversation with someone you did not trust? How did the form of the conversation differ from conversations you have had with people you do trust?

Our concern is with talk and the types of language used in talk. The major emphasis will be on conversation, the most generalized form of talk. We will also be concerned with both speakers and listeners, since talk is, as we shall see, essentially a cooperative undertaking. We will not be concerned with how language is used for private thought nor with speculations and theories about the nature of language itself. These topics we can safely leave to the appropriate experts who, we can be sure, have lots of ideas to challenge many of the beliefs we are likely to hold on such matters. The focus of our concern will be what happens when two or more people exchange words for some reason. Why does one person say one thing and the other reply as he or she does?

Talk is usually a social activity and therefore a public activity. It involves you with others, and each time you are involved with another person you must consider him or her. You must be aware of that person's feelings about what is hap-

---

pening, and you have some right to require him or her to do the same for you, to be aware of you and your feelings. In this sense talk is a reciprocal undertaking. Involvement in conversation therefore requires the two (or various) parties to be conscious of each other's needs, particularly the need not to be offended. Public life is possible only when the opportunities for being seriously offended are reduced to near zero. If the risks in an activity are great, you may be wise to refrain from that activity unless the potential gains are correspon-dingly great or you have no alternative. As we shall see, conversation is an activity which makes use of many devices in order to reduce the risks to participants. Consequently, skilled conversationalists rarely get 'hurt'.

There remains for most of us, however, a certain element of risk in any conversation. You may be hurt or you may inflict hurt in that one of the participants can emerge from the conversation diminished in some way. While it is unlikely that you insulted someone or you yourself were insulted, many lesser hurts are possible. You may have criticized another or have been criticized yourself; you may have incurred an obligation that you did not seek or made a suggestion that another could not refuse; someone may have complimented you, thereby requiring you not only to acknowledge acceptance of that compliment but to live up to it; you may have skirted a topic which others expected you to confront, you may have offered an excuse or an apology but be left with the feeling that it was not necessarily accepted completely—someone's sincerity may therefore be suspect. During a conversation some subtle change in relationships between the parties is likely to have occurred; many conversations result in the participants having definite, residual feelings about them: of pleasure, displeasure, ease, frustration, anger, alarm, satisfaction, and so on. We are not loath to judge conversations in such terms. When we do so, we are in an important sense evaluating the risks we took, counting our gains and losses as a result of taking them, and adding everything up on our mental score cards. That we do such things is apparent from the comments we sometimes make following conversations or reporting on them to others, comments such as *He was pretty short with her, You should have heard her go on about it, Why didn't you speak up?, She shouldn't have spoken to me like that, He just grunted, never said a word,* or that sure sign that a relationship is in trouble: *You're not listening; you never listen!*

Indeed, if all participants in a conversation are to feel happy with it, each must feel that he or she got out of it what was sought. If you wish to appear as a 'sensitive' participant in a conversation, you will therefore try to make sure that all the participants get to share in the various aspects of the conversation that will make it 'successful': in selecting the topics that will be talked about; in having adequate and timely opportunities to speak; in feeling at ease in saying what needs to be said; in achieving a sense of orderliness and adequacy about what is going on and doing this as one of a group of two or more; and so on. None of these characteristics can be prescribed in advance—unless the conversation is a very formal one, for example, a meeting of some kind—so it is necessary for you at all times to be aware of just what exactly is happening in any conversation in which you participate. You must be aware of both what has gone before and what may come next, as well as where you seem to be at the moment. You must be aware that a complicated array of possibilities exists and that each choice must necessarily preclude others. You must exhibit a certain sensitivity if you are to avoid some choices so that no one may feel arbitrarily cut off either from the topic or from other participants. Your goal must be to see that everyone leaves the conversation satisfied.

What we can infer from all this is that if you want to be a successful conversationalist you must command a wide variety of skills. You must have a well developed feeling about what you can (or cannot) say and when you can (or cannot) speak. You must know how to use words to do things and also exactly what words you can use in certain circumstances. And you must be able to supplement and reinforce what you choose to say with other appropriate behaviours: your movements, gestures, posture, gaze, and so on. You must also attune yourself to how others employ these same skills. This is a considerable task for anyone—or *everyone,* as it turns out—to perform, so it is not surprising that individuals vary widely in their ability to be successful in conversation. You can bungle your way through or you can be witty, urbane, and always sure to say the right thing. And some can even exploit the ability they have for ends that are entirely selfish.

The actual requirements will vary from group to group and culture to culture. Some situations may require considerable amounts of silence and others considerable amounts of talk. Others may be partly defined by who gets to talk and in what order, for not everyone necessarily has a right to speak: contrast a state ceremonial with a Quaker meeting. And once speaking has begun, it has to stay within the bounds of the occasion: you do not deliver a lecture at a cocktail party; you do not tell a dirty joke while conveying bad news; and you do not (any longer in many places now) make sexist or racist remarks in public and hope to win or keep public office. In this broad sense linguistic behaviour may be described as appropriate or not, and it is this sense of appropriateness that is the subject of studies by those who work in a discipline known as the ethnography of speaking: the study of who speaks to whom, when, how, and to what ends.

Certain basic conditions seem to prevail in all conversation, and many of the details of individual conversations are best understood as attempts that speakers (and listeners) make to meet these conditions. Above all, conversation is a social activity and, as such, it shares characteristics of all social activities. These characteristics we usually take for granted so that it is only their absence we notice. When there is some kind of breakdown in society, we notice the absence of principles, conventions, laws, rules, and so on, which guided or controlled behaviour in better times. Or, alternatively, we become aware of these same principles only when we have too readily accepted certain things as 'normal' and then find out that we have been deceived, as when someone has tricked or 'conned' us by pretending to do one thing (apparently quite normal) but actually doing another. We may not feel quite as bewildered as Rosencrantz and Guildenstern in Tom Stoppard's play of the same name, but we will recognize their predicament.

Conversation, like daily living, requires you to exhibit a considerable trust in others. Life would be extremely difficult, perhaps even impossible, without such trust. It is this trust that allows you to put money in a bank in the expectation that you will get it back on demand, to cross the street at a busy intersection controlled by either lights or a policeman, to eat food prepared by others, to plan for the future, and so on. But there is also the more general trust we have in the evidence of our senses, in the recurrence of both natural and other events, and in the essential unchanging and possibly unchangeable nature of the world and of the majority of its inhabitants. Trust in other people is the cornerstone of social living: to survive we must believe that people do not change much, if at all, from day to day and from encounter to encounter, and also that the vast majority do not set out deliberately to deceive or harm us. Indeed, we must believe them to be benevolent rather than malevolent. Without such trust in others and in what they do and say we could not get very far in coping with the world in which we find ourselves. So far as conversation is concerned, we would have little or no shared ground on which to build, and communication would become next to impossible. States of enmity and war or 'not speaking' are good examples of the kinds of conditions that exist when trust is broken. However, it is important to realize that even in such cases there is almost never a complete breakdown, since the antagonists usually continue to observe certain rules and decencies. Not everything becomes 'fair', which in such a case could mean only that absolutely anything might be possible, a situation therefore in which no rules of any kind would apply, an example of 'savagery' in its mythical, pathological form.

We cannot survive without putting trust in others, but it must be a trust tempered with a certain amount of caution. We cannot insist on viewing the world with wide-eyed innocence and hope we will never be disappointed. If you want to survive and minimize the hurts you will experience, you must employ a little bit of common sense too. You must exercise certain powers of judgement and you must make sound decisions constantly. For example, in any encounter with another person, you must try to work out exactly what is going on. That requires you to exhibit characteristics for which terms like 'intelligence' and 'sensitivity' are often used: you must judge the actual words you hear in relation to the possible intentions of the speaker, in order to come up with a decision as to what the speaker really means. In abstract, theoretical terms, the possible permutations of meaning are immense. Fortunately, in reality, most of those possibilities are extremely unlikely. You can rule them out, and you must do so—otherwise you could never decide anything at all: you could never be in any way sure about anything anyone said to you. But that ruling-out is not done haphazardly. Certain basic principles that prevail in most conversations help you to narrow down the possibilities to a manageable set: mutual trust, the sincerity of participants, the validity of everyday appearances, and 'common sense'. A certain scepticism may obtain in our views of life and of human motivation, but it must have 'healthy' limits. We cannot question and doubt everything or suspect every motive and still insist that we be regarded as normal people. We must seriously restrict such questioning, doubt, and suspicion; they are indicators, or markers, of very special kinds of conversation—interviews, psychiatric consultations, seminars, investigations—and such special activities must be clearly 'framed' in some way to indicate their special character. In order to participate in a conversation, you must be a willing party to a certain worldview. In that respect conversation is a collusive activity. You may have reservations about certain matters, but unless you are prepared to meet others on common ground and ignore differences which can only be divisive there is little hope that any kind of meaningful communication will occur.

Ethnomethodologists—those who study common-sense knowledge and reasoning as they pertain to social organisation—tell us that we are all parties to an agreement to inhabit a world in which things are what they appear to be and people do not in general go scratching beneath the surface of appearances. Scientists may do that, but that is the hallmark of the *scientific* enterprise. Living is largely a collusive activity, one in which you find yourself united with me because we both use our common sense and our goodwill to blind ourselves to things that do not seem to be important: we do not ask tough questions of each other; we do not seek rigid proofs; we do accept contradictions and uncertainty; and we do prefer to go along with others in most circumstances. That is how ordinary life is lived and must be lived.

Because conversation necessarily has a social basis, we must try to meet each other on common ground. For example, there is a general unspoken agreement among people that what we actually inhabit is a consistent, even mundane, world. It is essentially a world of the common-place and the things in it do not change much, if at all. These 'things' are also what they appear to be; they are not something else. Consequently, we tend to be amused when a 'petrol station' really turns out to be a fast-food restaurant or one of James Bond's cars turns into a submarine and another into an aeroplane. Magicians exploit this kind of amusement. But if such situations and such trickery happened continually we would undoubtedly find them stressful, or, alternatively, we would be forced to recast our image of fast-food outlets, automobiles, and trickery. That world too is one of simple causation: it is a recurrent world in which day follows night and night follows day, and so on. We see ourselves and others as consistent objects within that world; we believe we behave consistently and we tend to grant the same consistency to others.

We also tend to accept what we are told, taking any words spoken to us at close to face value unless we appear to have some very good reason for doing otherwise. For example, we seek only occasional clarification of remarks made to us. We are prepared to tolerate a remarkable amount of unclarity and imprecision in what we are told. We hold our peace and trust that everything will eventually work itself out to our satisfaction. So when we listen to interchanges that do involve considerable questioning and commenting, we know we are observing conversations of a special kind: for example, interrogations, psychiatric interviews, exchanges between teachers and students, and so on. If you suddenly let flow a stream of questions during what is otherwise just an ordinary conversation, you may effectively stop, or at least change, what is happening. You may well be perceived to be trying to turn something commonplace into an investigation and to be violating the basic condition of trust between participants. If I do not believe what you are telling me, I can challenge your truthfulness or I can start probing your account with questions. In either case you are likely to react in much the same way. You will become 'defensive', for your trust in what we were doing *together* will be weakened as you find yourself under attack. I will have violated the normal unspoken agreement that I will believe what you say because in return you will believe what I say. For, after all, are not both of us reasonable, sincere, and honest individuals? Some people regard defensive behaviour as 'bad' behaviour or evidence of some kind of guilt; it need be neither, being just a normal reaction to unwarranted offensive behaviour from others.

Each party in a social encounter has a certain amount of 'face' to maintain; many of the things that happen are concerned with maintaining appearances. I do not want to attack you in any way nor do I want you to attack me. We are, in a sense, parties to an agreement each to accept the other as the other wishes to appear. We may even go further and try to support a particular appearance the other proposes for himself or herself. If you want to act in a manner which I find somewhat peculiar, I may have very great difficulty in 'calling' you on what you are doing. It is much more likely that I will go along with your performance and keep my doubts to myself. After all, you may have a good motive unknown to me for your behaviour, so my initial reaction is likely to be to go along with what you are doing, to help you maintain the 'face' you are presenting, rather than to propose some kind of change in your behaviour. Those individuals who go around trying to 'un-face' others, as it were, may find themselves unwelcome, even to each other, being constantly in violation of this norm that 'good' social behaviour is based on mutual trust in appearances.

It is not surprising, therefore, that people rather infrequently resort to such expressions as *Who do you think you are?*, *Why do you speak to me like that?*, and *What gives you the right to tell me what to do?* Such remarks are quite definitely confrontational, but they do not confront the other person's right to speak. Rather, what they confront is the precise role the other has chosen to adopt, therefore the 'face' he has chosen for himself. In similar vein, one of the difficulties we might experience in saying *No* to a request made of us may well arise from the feeling that to do so is to offer an affront to the other's face. The extreme of request-type face is, of course, that adopted by the beggar who sits head bowed and silent before a container of some kind or with hand outstretched and eyes averted so as not to affront the faces of passers-by or further diminish his or her own when refused.

Conversation proceeds on the basis that the participants are reasonable people who can be expected to deal decently with one another. There must be a kind of reasonableness, a sort of 'commonsenseness', in the actual choice of the words and expressions we employ. There must also be a certain rightness in the quantity as well as the quality of those words. You have to say enough to do the job that must be done: not too little must be said nor, on the other hand, too much. Too little and someone will feel deprived of information; too much and someone will feel either imposed upon or the unwilling beneficiary of a performance rather than of a genuine instance of communication. Unreasonable language may also produce obscurity or even rouse someone to challenge what has been said. It may create problems which the participants can solve only when they have re-established the basic preconditions of trust that are necessary if anything positive is to be accomplished.

You must assume, too, that most others with whom you come into contact can deal adequately with the world, just as adequately as you believe you yourself deal with it. You do not readily question another's ability to state simple facts, or to ask and give directions, or to add new information to old. When you ask another person for directions, you expect that he or she will employ a scheme for giving the directions that will be adequate for the occasion. For example, if you have asked for a description of the interior of a house, you expect to get that description according to an acceptable pattern of spatial organization. You also expect certain kinds of information and not other kinds and to get information that is adequate for the purpose you have in mind, if you have made that purpose clear in some way. And that expectation is generally fulfilled. 'Basic' information is fairly easily accessible, but we should notice how difficult it is quite often to gain certain further kinds of information—or to supply that information if we are asked for it. A lot of 'information' that we actually have access to never becomes part of that body of information we rely on for ordinary living and routine communication with others. Police officers, for example, have to be specially trained to observe certain kinds of details that are, indeed, accessible to the general public. But what they observe and report is very different from what we, commonplace actors in a commonplace world, observe and are therefore able to report. We actually see the same things but we do not observe and record them in the same way; there is really no need to do so, for we know that everyday life does not usually require that intensity of observation. The events in our everyday world are necessarily mundane: life would quickly become unbearable if it were not so ordered and predictable and consequently so unworthy of close and continuing attention.

Even those who are scientifically trained do not usually carry over the scientific attitude into every aspect of life. Adequate functioning requires some disjunctions between the world of science and the world of everyday existence. One parent was reminded of this fact when one winter morning she said to her six-year-old son *Ah, the sun's finally rising!* only to have him offer her the sharp rebuke But, *mummy, the sun doesn't rise: the earth goes round the sun!* Whereas she had separated the two, the scientific and the ordinary, he had learned his basic facts about the solar system from his parents, and had not. It was not surprising that his teacher in school found him both precocious *and* disruptive!

Our sense of adequacy can show itself in many other ways. We all have some sense of what adequate and appropriate behaviour is in particular circumstances. We may actually refuse to do certain things because we know that we lack the requisite skills and we do not want to make fools of ourselves. What is in a way surprising is how adequate we feel in general, not how inadequate. We also know the bounds of our adequacy. If you consider the kinds of things you know that allow you not only to survive in society but sometimes even to flourish, they quickly add up to a formidable list. For example, you know how to behave in a doctor's or dentist's waiting room, in a queue, on a crowded bus or tube train, with a bank teller, in the company of a close friend of either the same or opposite sex, and possibly with a traffic policeman. You know in conversation in such circumstances what topics are suitable, how much you can or must reveal or, alternatively, hide, and what is likely to be quite inappropriate or even taboo. You also know when it is appropriate to speak and when it would be wise to be silent. These skills you must have if you are not to appear ill mannered, out of place, or social deficient in some way. And most of us have them. Actually, many of the skills you must display will have become highly ritualized, so that you no longer have to think about what you are doing. To use one limited domain as an example, you know how to occupy space among strangers and deal with them, and you are aware of the need to avoid potentially offensive remarks, of the importance of 'safe' topics, and of the care you must take to accept and treat others as you want them to accept and treat you. The ability to appear adequate and normal is one of your most precious possessions, but one which you must also grant to others. Inadequacy and abnormality are inherently judgements about social behaviour and clearly indicate some kind of failure in that behaviour.

'Adequacy' and 'normality' are, of course, culture-laden concepts. What is adequate and normal among one group of people may be entirely inappropriate among certain other groups. Those who have travelled in different parts of the world can readily attest to this fact. But many such differences are these days often readily observable on one's own doorstep. Many cities and towns now draw their populations from a variety of cultural and linguistic groups with rather different views of what is 'proper'. Consequently, it is not surprising that linguistic and behavioural differences have become a concern of many who live in such communities, and that the schools have on numerous occasions become the battlegrounds for the disputants.

1 What social expectations, values, and rituals of conversation determine the "rules of the road" that come into play when people engage in discourse?

2 Why is trust such an important emotional factor in permitting the free flow of conversation?

3 What social factors come into play that determine how much about oneself one is willing to reveal in conversation—or, conversely, how much one expects others to reveal about themselves? How do these expectations and others, such as the amount of talking that is appropriate, vary from culture to culture and over time? For example, what topics discussed in everyday American conversations would have been considered taboo as recently as the 1950s? In the cartoon on page 172, how does Jules Feiffer reverse the expectations one would have for each of the two characters from their given time periods?

4 How important is the use of colloquial expressions (for example, "he was pretty short with her" in para. 3) in illustrating Wardhaugh's thesis? Where might he have used additional colloquial interchanges to support his points? (Glossary: *Colloquial Expressions*.)

From *FEIFFER: Jules Feiffer's America from Eisenhower to Reagan,* by Jules Feiffer, edited by Steven Heller, copyright © 1982 by Jules Feiffer. Reprinted by permission of Alfred A. Knopf, Inc.

5 Wardhaugh illustrates his discussion of the important principles governing conversation with a number of specific examples. Which did you find particularly effective? What different kinds of examples can you indentify—i.e., hypothetical or speculative examples to dramatize a key point, generalized examples that typically could happen to any of us at one time or another? (Glossary: *Examples*.)

6 Describe a situation in which two people are exchanging opinions about an issue about which they both have strong views (for example, does ESP exist, are sororities and fraternities worthwhile, should tax money be used to subsidize tobacco growers, are affirmative action programs worthwhile, is it moral to keep animals in zoos, should gays and lesbians have the right to marry and adopt children, should prostitution be decriminalized, should insurance companies be allowed to use genetic screening to set premiums, should public schools be allowed to distribute condoms, etc.). What do they say to each other?

Verbal Dueling

Peter Farb

◆ PETER FARB was a naturalist, linguist, and anthropologist who wrote about natural human sciences in his many books. He was a consultant to the Smithsonian Institution from 1966 to 1971. His many publications include *Human Kind* (1978) and *Word Play: What Happens When People Talk* (1973), in which the following essay first appeared.

Farb looks into the intricate choreography that comprises the social ritual we call conversation. Whereas Wardhaugh delved into the social rules that are relied upon unconsciously to keep conversations going, Farb discusses the range of verbal and nonverbal signals that determine whose turn it is to speak, and whether the dialogue moves back and forth in a way that makes both partici-pants feel comfortable. Conversations over the telephone pose an even greater mystery, since we are deprived of nonverbal cues such as shifts in gaze and pos-ture that might signal whose turn it is to speak. Farb discusses the strategies tele-phone conversations involve (such as the strange rule that the person answering the call speaks first although the caller is the one with something to say) to com-pensate for the lack of face-to-face contact.

TO CONSIDER When was the last time you observed someone trying to exert dominance in the guise of exchanging information during a seemingly casual conversation?

Most speakers unconsciously duel even during seemingly casual conver-sations, as can often be observed at social gatherings where they show less concern for exchanging information with other guests than for asserting their own dominance. Their verbal dueling often employs very subtle weapons like mumbling, a hostile act which defeats the listener's desire to under-stand what the speaker claims he is trying to say (but is really not saying because he is mumbling!). Or the verbal dueler may keep talking after someone has passed out of hearing range—which is often an aggressive challenge to the lis-tener to return and acknowledge the dominance of the speaker.

Whenever two people who know each other approach, a duel immediately takes place over who will speak first. The role of the first speaker is almost always determined by cues from eye contact, facial expressions, and gestures rather than

---

from words. And once he has spoken, the conventions of probably all communities decree that the participants will speak in a rhythm that alternates rapidly from one to the other. Although it might appear to an observer of such a conversation that one speaker starts to talk as soon as the other stops, that is not the case. Careful study of recordings of conversations shows that only about one exchange in four takes place without a definite pause between the conclusion of one speaker's utterance and the beginning of the next speaker's. In most cases, an interval of mutual silence is required to transform a speaker into a listener and a listener into a speaker.

A key feature of any conversation is that only one speaker holds the floor at a time, and that while he does so he suppresses, apparently by the mere sound of his voice as well as some visual cues, any simultaneous speech by the other participant. The absence of simultaneous speech appears to be a universal feature of all languages, which may be due to the limited ability of the human nervous system to process information. The neurophysical make-up of our species seems to prevent us from both imparting our own information and decoding someone else's at the same time.

Dialogue, then, is the basic form of human speech—and monologue, in which one speaker is silent for a very long time, exists only in special cases such as theatrical performances, prayers, and ceremonial speeches. The monologue, rather than being simpler than the dialogue, actually is a very complex structure which is unknown in many speech communities. The linguist who visits an exotic people to study its language learns quickly that he is not offering freedom of expression when he asks someone to tell his life's story. In fact, by asking the native speaker to deliver a monologue, the well-intentioned linguist has deprived him of an essential freedom, the security of being able to speak within the structured framework of a dialogue.

The speaker who initiates a dialogue can select a gambit out of a large number of possible utterances. Whichever utterance he chooses, he will convey fundamental assumptions about his speech community and its conventions, his place in this community, and the rights he possesses and the obligations he owes to its other members. The truly amazing thing is that such far-reaching relationships can be established so promptly and by the utterance of so few words. If we disregard antisocial openings such as *Hey, jerk!* all conversations are opened in one of six ways:

1. A request for information, services, or goods. Examples are: *What time is it? Do you have a match? Please pass the sugar.*

2. A request for a social response. *What a slow bus this is! It sure is raining hard.*

3. An offer of information. *Did you hear about the robbery last night? You seem to be lost.*

4. An emotional expression of anger, pain, joy, which often is a strategy to solicit a comment by a listener. *Ouch! Whoopee! Look at this!*

5. Stereotyped statements, such as greetings, apologies, thanks, and so on. *Hello. I'm sorry. Thanks a lot.*

6. A substitute statement to avoid a conversation about a subject the speaker anticipates the listener will broach. An example would be a water-cooler meeting between a boss and a subordinate; the boss antic-ipates conversation about a raise, so he hurriedly speaks first and uses an avoidance opener: *The traffic sure was heavy this morning.*

Once A has opened a conversation in any of these six ways, he can anticipate a stock reply by B—after which A has the option to make another statement and thus launch a conversation with an ABAB pattern or to break off the conversa-tion. But sometimes the opening utterance can lead to a completely unexpected reply. Witness this example from Jewish folklore of a conversation on the train to Lublin, Poland. A young man chose the first of the six conversation openers and asked a merchant, "Can you tell me the time?"

The merchant looked at him and replied: "Go to hell!"

"What? Why, what's the matter with you! I ask you a civil question in a properly civil way, and you give me such an outrageous answer! What's the idea?"

The merchant looked at him, sighed wearily, and said, "Very well. Sit down and I'll tell you. You ask me a question. I have to give an answer, no? You start a conversation with me—about the weather, politics, business. One thing leads to another. It turns out you're a Jew—I'm a Jew, I live in Lublin—you're a stranger. Out of hospitality, I ask you to my home for din-ner. You meet my daughter. She's a beautiful girl—you're a handsome young man. So you go out together a few times—and you fall in love. Finally you come to ask for my daughter's hand in marriage. So why go to all that trouble? Let me tell you right now, young man, I won't let my daughter marry anyone who doesn't even own a watch!"

The humor in this story hinges, of course, upon our unconscious knowledge of the ABAB pattern in conversations. The merchant made an unconventional reply to a stereotyped conversation opener—and he so well understood the ABAB sequence that he was able to anticipate the entire conversation carried to its ultimate conclusion.

The irreducible minimum for any conversation is two participants. And to reduce the conversation to its barest essentials, the two participants would have to be out of sight of each other, in that way eliminating the interference of facial expressions, gestures, posture, attire, and so on. A telephone conversation pro-vides exactly such a situation. Because of the absence in a telephone conversa-tion of the physical cues that determine the first speaker, a convention has arisen that the person who answers the phone is the one to speak first. So uncon-sciously do people accept this convention that even the obscene caller follows it. He may be a psychopath and a violator of society's rules, but nevertheless he will tend to obey at least this convention and not usually unleash his obscenities until he hears a female speak into the phone.

It is a strange rule that designates the person answering the call to speak first. After all, the caller is the one who possesses all the information: he knows his own identity, the identity of the person whose number he is calling, and what he wishes to convey by the call. The person on the answering end could decide to violate the convention by picking up the receiver and remaining silent. In that case, the caller would probably utter a hesitant Hello? as if checking whether or not the phone was working. The person on the answering end would now possess at least some information: a clue to the identification of the caller's voice. Such a strategy, though, violates accepted behavior for the use of the telephone; it irritates the caller and sometimes it prevents a conversation altogether because the caller may simply hang up.

A good reason does exist why the person being called should speak first. The ringing of the telephone can actually be regarded as the first utterance of A, the caller, which represents a direct summons for B to reply to. Some people so unconsciously regard the ringing as an utterance that they hesitate to pick up the phone in the middle of a ring. Instead, they wait until the moment of silence between rings, much as if they did not want to interrupt a human speaker. B replies to the summons of A's ring with *Hello* or *Doctor Smith's office* or some such statement. No matter how B phrases his first utterance, it has the character of a question that implies a request for information about the caller. And whenever anyone makes such a request, he infers an obligation to respond after the information is supplied.

Once these opening AB statements (A's summoning ring of the phone and B's answer) have been made, the stage is set to generate a conversation. A is now obliged to reply to B by supplying information—such as *Hello, this is Joe* or *I'd like to make an appointment with Doctor Smith.* B has already implied an obligation to speak again after receiving some information; he now does so, since he could not very well insult Joe by hanging up after hearing his name or turn down a patient who wants to make an appointment with Doctor Smith. B might say *Hello, Joe, how are you?* or *What time would you like to see Doctor Smith?*—but, whatever the utterance, B has spoken a second time, asked for additional information, and concluded the process of launching a telephone conversation by rounding out the ABAB sequence.

The course that the conversation takes after A's summoning ring and the three subsequent utterances is partly determined by the paralanguage of those utterances. Both speakers will necessarily express attitudes by their tone of voice: friendliness, sincerity, annoyance, haste, expectation, and so on. The tone of B's initial *Hello,* for example, will inform A whether B is rushed or whether he has time to chat. If B does sound rushed, A may simply hang up without identifying himself. Or he might respond in a conciliatory tone that conveys how sorry he is to bother B. Now it is B's turn to reply, and his tone of voice will influence whether or not the conversation will be launched. He might reply in a tone that indicates *Well, I am rushed, but I'm happy to speak anyway,* in which case the conversation proceeds. Or his tone may indicate that the caller should try again later, in which case the conversation ends abruptly.

The simple ringing of a telephone, followed by three very brief utterances, has enabled two people to interact verbally. Each has committed himself, either by placing the call or by answering the phone, to a willingness to talk at this time; each has produced in the other and assumed in himself the obligation to make inquiries and to reply to them; each has tacitly recognized the existence of the ABAB sequence and waits his turn to speak. So obligatory is the relationship established on the phone that most people find it very difficult to break the sequence, even with a stranger. An obvious example is the clerk in the store who interrupts the customer he has been waiting on to answer the phone. Common courtesy demands that the clerk ask the caller to wait while he finishes with the customer, who took the trouble to come to the store in person. But the clerk, like most people, finds it very difficult to extricate himself from the obligations of the ABAB sequence once it is launched. He supplies the information requested by the caller while the customer is forced to wait.

1 What set of assumptions about the objectives each party tries to achieve underlies Farb's theory about conversations? Explain what Farb means by his statement "most speakers unconsciously duel even during seemingly casual conversations" (para. 1). Evaluate his assumptions about the implicit confrontational nature of conversations. How plausible do you find this assertion in light of his analysis?

2 In what respects are the six permissible opening conversational gambits and stock replies (para. 5) similar to patterns one encounters in such games as chess? What role do these patterns play in guiding the flow of conversation? How does the example of the conversation on the train (para. 6) illustrate the extent to which we rely on expected conversational scenarios and how humor can be created by violating these predictable scenarios?

3 According to Farb, how do the patterns that govern face-to-face discourse become modified in conversations held on the telephone? For example, why do people wait for the moment of silence between rings to pick up the phone (para. 9)? Do you prefer talking to someone in person or on the telephone, all things being equal?

4 How important is the use of commonplace (for example, "what time is it?" in para. 5) and colloquial expressions (for example, "hey, jerk!" in para. 5) in illustrating Farb's thesis? Where might he have used additional examples of what people say in everyday conversations to support his points? (Glossary: *Colloquial Expressions, Examples.*)

5 How does Farb use the introduction to motivate his audience to consider the significance of the process? Would you agree this was an accurate characterization? Why or why not? What kinds of details make it possible for the reader to visualize what Farb is explaining? What minor stages or details does he omit in his description of the major stages in this process? What transitional words and phrases provide the reader with a clear sense of the sequence involved? (Glossary: *Introduction, Process Analysis.*)

6 In comic strips, what conventions govern which of the characters speaks first? Is it always the same and why? Can you think of other languages where these conventions would not apply, and why?

Analyze the use of these conventions in the following Dilbert cartoon in terms of which characters are shown and who speaks first, second, and third.

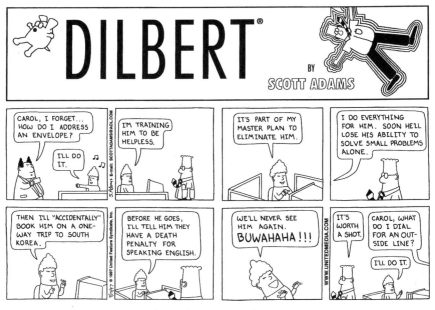

Dilbert, reprinted by permission of United Features Syndicate, Inc.

Like, Uptalk?   *James Gorman*

◆ JAMES GORMAN teaches journalism at New York University. This article first appeared in the *New York Times,* August 1993.

Patterns of American speech are changing in an interesting way. The new way of talking called "uptalk" turns statements into questions by ending sentences with rising intonations. This phenomenon first originated among teenagers and has been increasingly adopted by other segments of the population. In this article, Gorman speculates, somewhat ruefully, about the origins of "uptalk" and the disconcerting changes it has produced in speech patterns across the country. For example, a surgeon might say, "So, first I'll open up your chest?

> **TO CONSIDER**   How much of the impact of what people say is due to *how* they say it as distinct from *what* they say?

I used to speak in a regular voice. I was able to assert, demand, question. Then I started teaching. At a university? And my students had this rising intonation thing? It was particularly noticeable on telephone messages. "Hello? Professor Gorman? This is Albert? From feature writing?"

I had no idea that a change in the "intonation contour" of a sentence, as linguists put it, could be as contagious as the common cold. But before long I noticed a Jekyll-and-Hyde transformation in my own speech. I first heard it when I myself was leaving a message. "This is Jim Gorman? I'm doing an article on Klingon? The language? From 'Star Trek'?" I realized then that I was unwittingly, unwillingly speaking uptalk.

I was, like, appalled?

Rising intonations at the end of a sentence or phrase are not new. In many languages, a "phrase final rise" indicates a question. Some Irish, English, and Southern American dialects use rises all the time. Their use at the end of a declarative statement may date back in America to the seventeenth century.

Nonetheless, we are seeing, well, hearing, something different. Uptalk, under various names, has been noted on *The New York Times* Op-Ed page and on National Public Radio. Cynthia McLemore, a University of Pennsylvania linguist who knows as much about uptalk as anyone, says the frequency and repetition of rises mark a new phenomenon. And although uptalk has been most common among teen-agers, in particular young women, it seems to be spreading. Says McLemore, "What's going on now in America looks like a dialect shift." In other words, what is happening may be a basic change in the way Americans talk.

Nobody knows exactly where uptalk came from. It might have come from California, from Valley Girl talk. It may be an upper-middle-class thing, probably starting with adolescents. But everybody has an idea about what uptalk means. Some twentysomethings say uptalk is part of their attitude: cool, ironic, uncommitted.

I myself was convinced that uptalk was tentative, testing, oversensitive; not feminine so much as wimpy, detumescent. Imagine how it would sound in certain cocksure, authoritative occupations, like police work:

You're under arrest? You have some rights?
Or surgery:
So, first I'll open up your chest?

I also thought how some of the great dead white males of the much maligned canon might sound, reintoned:

It was really dark? Like, on the deep? The face of the deep?
Or:
Hi, I'm Ishmael? I'll be your narrator?
Or:
A horse? A horse? My kingdom for a horse?

My speculations have some support; there are linguists who see uptalk as being about uncertainty and deference to the listener. But McLemore scoffs at these ideas. People tend to hear what they want to hear, she says. One can, for instance, take a speech pattern common among women and link it to a stereo-type of women. (Uncertain? Deferential?)

10   Deborah Tannen—a linguist at Georgetown, who, with her book "You Just Don't Understand: Women and Men in Conversation," may have overtaken Noam Chomsky and become the best-known linguist in America—contends that broad theorizing about uptalk is downright foolish. Speech patterns are contagious, she says, and they spread the way fads do. "There's a fundamental human impulse to imitate what we hear," she says. "Teen-agers talk this way because other teen-agers talk this way and they want to sound like their peers."

11   That doesn't mean rises have no function. They can be used as a signal that "more is coming," says Mark Aronoff of the State University of New York at Stony Brook. An adolescent might be signaling "I have more to say; don't inter-rupt me." McLemore says an early study of telephone conversation suggested that rises may be used as a probe of sorts, to see if the hearer is getting what you are saying.

12   A friend of mine (of no formal linguistic expertise) likes this latter interpre-tation. He insists that the spread of uptalk indicates the lack of shared knowledge in our society. Our society, he contends, has become so fragmented that no one knows anymore whether another person will have a clue as to what he's saying. We need to test the hearer's level of understanding.

13   *Like, suppose I want to talk about Sabicas? Or Charles Barkley? Or nitric oxide? The molecule of the year? For 1992?*

14   By using the questioning tone, I'm trying to see if my conversational part-ner knows anything at all about flamenco guitar, professional basketball, or neu-rochemistry.

15   McLemore studied intonation in one very particular context. She observed uses of intonation in a Texas sorority, where uptalk was not at all about uncer-tainty or deference. It was used most commonly by the leaders, the senior offi-cers. Uptalk was a kind of accent, or tag, to highlight new information for lis-teners: "We're having a bake sale? On the west mall? On Sunday?" When saying something like "Everyone should know that your dues should be in," they used a falling intonation at the end of the sentence.

16   The sorority members' own interpretation of uptalk was that it was a way of being inclusive. McLemore's conclusions are somewhat similar. She says the rises are used to connect phrases, and to connect the speaker to the listener, as a means of "getting the other person involved."

17   Since McLemore did her study, people are constantly calling to her atten-tion other uses of uptalk. It seems to be a common speech pattern in Toronto, where, she says, a radio show called "Ask the Pastors" displays uptalk in spades. She also found that on another radio show the mayor of Austin, Texas, used rises to mark items in a list. Asked to explain why he should maintain bike paths, he said things like: Austin has a good climate? It's good for bike riding? McLemore also observed a second-grade teacher who used rises freely for commands and statements. "Jason? Back to your chair ? Thank you?"

I confess to ambivalence about uptalk. When I use it, I judge it to mark a   18
character flaw. On the other hand, there are some ritual utterances that could
clearly benefit from a change in pitch contour.

Mea culpa? Mea culpa? Mea maxima culpa?
Or, to reflect the true state of matrimony in our society:
I do?

I do not, however, want the speech pattern to spread to airplane pilots. I   19
don't want to hear: *This is Captain McCormick? Your pilot? We'll be flying to
Denver? Our cruising altitude will be, like, 30,000 feet?*

McLemore, however, says it seems possible that we will be hearing such an   20
intonation among pilots in the future. After all, it looks as if pilots are getting
younger every year. Once commercial airline pilots start using uptalk,
McLemore notes, it will mean that a full-blown dialect shift has occurred.
Uptalk won't be uptalk anymore. It will be, like, American English?

---

1 What factors contribute to Gorman's dislike of the phenomenon of "uptalk"? What
is he trying to show by inventing "uptalk" versions of typical statements made by doctors, pilots, and police officers, or by changing passages from works of great literature into their "uptalk" versions?

2 Although Gorman characterizes users of "uptalk" as insecure, he presents other possible reasons why people would use it. Which of these reasons appears most valid
to you? What might the effect of this new style of speech be on the traditionally dif-
ferentiated speech functions of (a) assertions, (b) demands, and (c) questions?

3 Monitor your own conversations for a period of time and observe the number of
times you and other people use "uptalk." In what circumstances do people seem to
use "uptalk" more? Do certain personality types use it more than others? Do you find
it to be as widespread as Gorman thinks it is? In your opinion, is it still marginal and
regional or has it become part of mainstream American English?

4 How successful is Gorman in making it possible for you to hear what "uptalk" sounds
like, how it is created, and why it would be so disconcerting under certain circumstances? For example, consider the phrase "This is Captain McCormick? Your pilot?
We'll be flying to Denver? Our cruising altitude will be, like, 30,000 feet?" in para.
19. (Glossary: *Accent, Phonetics.*)

5 How does Gorman's use of his own experiences add a dimension of self-mockery to
his essay? (Glossary: *Satire, Humor.*)

6 What examples of "uptalk" can you discover in your own speech or in that of other
people? Under what circumstances do you find you use "uptalk"? Select a serious
passage in a traditional essay or story and transform it using "uptalk." How would
you characterize the result?

Gurdjieff Remembered   *Fritz Peters*

◆ FRITZ PETERS (born in 1916) first came into contact with the Russian philosopher George Gurdjieff in Fontainebleau (outside Paris) where he attended the Institute for the Harmonious Development of Man that Gurdjieff had established. Peters studied there between 1924 and 1929 and described Gurdjieff's unusual educational methods in two books, *Boyhood with Gurdjieff* (1964) and *Gurdjieff Remembered* (1965), from which the following is drawn.

We can infer something about the unusual nature of Peters's relationship with George Gurdjieff when we realize his revered and esteemed mentor wished to learn "every four-letter word plus every obscene phrase" his protégé knew, for the express purpose of manipulating the behavior of a socially elite group of people who were going to be his guests for dinner that evening. The ease with which these guests fell into Gurdjieff's trap, and the resulting object lesson about human nature and the power that obscene language possessed to instigate an orgy, provided an invaluable lesson for Peters.

> **TO CONSIDER**   What is your attitude toward the use of "obscenities"?

1   After seeing Mr. Gurdjieff in Chicago in 1932, there was an interval of about two years during which I did not see him again. I had moved to New York in the fall of 1933, and one Saturday afternoon when I came home from work my landlord told me that a very strange man, with a heavy, foreign accent had come to see me and wanted me to get in touch with him. The landlord, however, had not been able to understand him, did not know his name, and only knew that whoever he was, he was living at the Henry Hudson Hotel in New York. I thought of Gurdjieff at once, although it was difficult for me to believe that he had gone to the trouble of finding my address and then coming to search for me in person. I went to the hotel immediately and, as I had expected, found him there.

2   When I got to his apartment in the hotel, he told me that he had tried to find me earlier in the day, but that now it was too late and that he had no further need of—or use for—me. There was no affection in his greeting and he merely looked bored and very tired. In spite of this, and because I was glad to see him and worried about his great weariness, I did not leave but reminded him

that he had once told me that "it was never too late to make reparations in life", and that while I was sorry not to have been home earlier, there was surely something I could do now that I had arrived.

He looked at me with a tired smile and said that perhaps there was something I could do. He led me into the kitchen, indicated an enormous pile of dirty dishes and said they needed to be washed; he then pointed to another equally enormous pile of vegetables and said they needed to be prepared for a dinner he was going to give that evening. After showing these to me, he asked me if I had the time to help him.

When I had assured him that I did, he told me to wash the dishes first and then prepare the vegetables. Before leaving the kitchen, to rest, he said that he hoped he would be able to count on me to finish both jobs—otherwise he would not be able to rest properly. I told him not to worry and went to work on the dishes. He watched me for a few minutes and then said that several people had promised to help him that day but that there were no members of the New York group who were able to keep their promises. I told him that he had better rest while he had the opportunity and not waste his time talking to me, and he laughed and left the kitchen.

I was finished with my work when he returned and he was very pleased. He then began to cook the evening meal and told me to set the table for fifteen people, adding that some very important people—important for his work—were coming to dinner and that when the food was in the oven he would need me to help him by giving him an English lesson as it was essential that he talk to these people in a certain way—in a language that they would understand correctly.

When we had finished our work, he sat down at the table, told me to sit next to him and then began asking me questions about the English language. It turned out that he wanted to learn, before the guests arrived, all the words for the various parts and functions of the body "that were not in the dictionary". We spent perhaps two hours repeating every four-letter word that I knew, plus every obscene phrase I could think of. By about seven o'clock he felt that he was reasonably proficient with our "slang" vocabulary which he, apparently, needed for his dinner. Inevitably, I began to wonder what sort of people would be coming to dinner. At the conclusion of this "lesson" he told me that it was for that lesson that he had been trying to find me, because I was the first person who, some years before in Chicago, had given him the real flavour and meaning of the words "phony" and "leery"; it seems that these words, in the interim, had become very useful in his conversations with his American students. "These very good words," he said, "raw . . . like your America."

When the guests did arrive, they turned out to be a group of well-dressed, well-mannered New Yorkers, and, since Gurdjieff had gone to "prepare" himself for dinner, I greeted them and, according to his precise instructions, served them drinks.

He did not appear until most of them had been there for about half an hour, and when he greeted them, he was very apologetic for the delay and extremely effusive about how beautiful the ladies looked and how much they were all honoring him by consenting to be the guests of a poor, humble man like himself. I was actually embarrassed by what seemed to me a very crude form of flattery and by his presentation of himself as an unworthy and very obsequious host. But, to my surprise, it seemed to work. By the time they were seated at the dinner table, all the guests were in a very mellow mood (they had had only one drink so it was not due to liquor) and they began, in a somewhat jocular and superior way, to ask him questions about his work and his reasons for coming to America. The general tone of the questions was bored—many of the people present were reporters or journalists—and they behaved as if they were carrying out an assignment to interview some crank. I could already see them making mental notes and could imagine the sort of "funny" interview or feature story they might write. After some questioning by this group, I noticed that Gurdjieff's voice changed in tone, and as I watched him he gave me a sudden, sly wink.

8   He then proceeded to tell them that since they were all very superior people that they of course knew—since a simple person like himself knew it, then obviously they did—that humanity in general was in a very sad state and could only be considered as having degenerated into real waste matter, or to use a term that was familiar to all of them, pure "shit". That this transformation of humankind into something worthless was especially apparent in America—which was why he had come there to observe it. He went on to say that the main cause of this sad state of affairs was that people—especially Americans—were never motivated by intelligence or good feelings, but only by the needs—usually dirty—of their genital organs, using, of course (as he talked) only the four-letter words which he had practised with me earlier. He indicated one very well-dressed, handsome woman, complimented her on her coiffure, her dress, her perfume, etc., and then said that while she, of course, might not want everyone to know her motives or her desires, he and she could be honest with each other—that her reasons for turning herself out so elaborately were because she had a strong sexual urge (as he put it "wish to fuck") for some particular person and was so tormented by it that she was using every means and every wile she could think of in order to get that person into a bed with her. He said that her urge was particularly, especially strong because she had a very fertile imagination and could already picture herself performing various sexual acts with this man—"such as, how you say in English? 'Sixty-nine'?"—so that, aided by her imagination, she was now at the point where she would do *anything* to achieve her aim. While the company was somewhat startled with this dissertation (not to say "titillated"), before anyone had time to react, he began a description of his own sexual abilities and of his highly imaginative mind, and described himself as capable of sustained sexual acts of incredible variety—such as even the lady in question would not be able to imagine.

9   He then launched into a detailed description of the sexual habits of various races and nations, during the course of which he pointed out that while the French had a world-wide reputation for amorous prowess, it would be well for the people present to make a note of the fact that those highly civilized French used such words as "Mama" and "Mimi" to describe some of their unnatural and perverted sexual practices. He added, however, that in all justice to the French they were, in reality, very moral people and sexually misunderstood and misrepresented.

The guests had all been drinking heavily during dinner—good old Arma-   10
gnac as always—and after about two hours of unadulterated four-letter word
conversation, their behaviour became completely uninhibited. Whether they
had all come to believe and accept that they had been invited to an orgy, or for
whatever reasons, an orgy—or the beginning of one—was the result. Gurdjieff
egged them on by giving them elaborate descriptions of the male and female
organs, and of some imaginative uses for them, and finally most of the guests
were physically entangled in groups in various rooms of the apartment, and in
various states of undress. The handsome lady had manœuvred herself into a
small bar with Gurdjieff and was busily making "passes" of a rather inventive
nature, at him.

As for me, I was cornered in the kitchen by an overblown, attractive lady   11
who told me that she was outraged that Gurdjieff should use such words in my
presence—I did not look more than about seventeen. I explained, quite honestly, that I had taught them all to him—or at least most of them, and she found
this suddenly hilarious and promptly made a pass at me. I backed away and told
her that, unfortunately, I had to do the dishes. Rebuffed, she glared at me, called
me various dirty names and said that the only reason I had turned her down was
because I was "that dirty old man's little faggot", and only wanted him to
"screw" me. I was somewhat startled at this, but remembered Gurdjieff's reputation for sexual depravity and made no response.

While the other guests were still hard at it, Gurdjieff suddenly disentangled   12
himself from the lady and told them all, in loud, stentorian tones, that they had
already confirmed his observations of the decadence of the Americans and that
they need no longer demonstrate for him. He pointed at various individuals,
mocked their behaviour and then told them that if they were, thanks to him,
now partly conscious of what sort of people they really were, it was an important lesson for them. He said that he deserved to be paid for this lesson and that
he would gladly accept cheques and cash from them as they left the apartment.
I was not particularly surprised, knowing him and having watched the performance of the evening, to find that he had collected *several thousand dollars*. I was
even less surprised when one man told me—as it were, "man to man"—that
Gurdjieff, posing as a philosopher, had the best ideas about sex, and the safest
"cover" for his orgies, of anyone he had ever known.

When everyone had left, I finished washing the dishes, and to my surprise   13
Gurdjieff came into the kitchen to dry them and put them away. He asked me
how I had enjoyed the evening and I said, youthfully and righteously, that I was
disgusted. I also told him about my encounter with the lady in the kitchen and
her description of my relationship with him. He shrugged his shoulders and said
that in such cases the facts were what constituted the truth and that I should
never consider or worry about opinions. Then he laughed and gave me a pierc-
ing look. "Is fine feeling you have—this disgust," he said. "But now is necessary
ask yourself one question. With who you disgusted?"

When I was ready to leave the apartment, he stopped me and referred again   14
to my experience with the lady. "Such lady have in self many homosexual tendencies, one reason she pick on you—young-looking boy, seem almost like girl
to her. Not worry about this thing she say to you. Gossip about sex only give

reputation for sexiness in your country, so not important, maybe even feather in hat, as you say. Some day you will learn much more about sex, but this you can learn by self not from me."

1 What language-related preparations does Mr. Gurdjieff make for his dinner party? How does he draw upon what he has learned from Peters to (a) manipulate his guests to produce a tangible benefit for himself and (b) teach his protégé, Fritz, a lesson about human nature?

2 What lesson does Peters learn about himself and other people from Gurdjieff's experiment manipulating language and social propriety? What do you think it was that Gurdjieff wanted Peters to learn and how did this lesson depend upon the unique set of circumstances Gurdjieff created?

3 How do you feel about what Gurdjieff did? Do you think he was justified? How do you think you would have reacted if you were a guest at this dinner party? What is Gurdjieff really asking at the end of the evening when he says "Is fine feeling you have—this disgust. But now is necessary ask yourself one question. With who you disgusted?" (para. 13).

4 What role does language deemed improper play in the interchange between Peters and George Gurdjieff and his guests? What does obscene or taboo language communicate that polite and acceptable language cannot accomplish (para. 8, 11)? In your opinion, why does this language affect the guests in ways that Gurdjieff predicted? (Glossary: *Taboo Language.*)

5 What is the narrative point or main idea of Peters's account? Express it in your own words. What conflicts make the essay suspenseful? Where does Peters use dialogue to create an aura of immediacy? (Glossary: *Dialogue, Narration.*)

6 Describe a belief that you once held that you no longer hold because of the influence of another person. Create a character sketch of this person, describe the role he/she played, and reproduce the important conversations that were involved.

What's Wrong With TV?: Talk Shows   *Tom Shachtman*

◆ TOM SHACHTMAN has written several works of fiction and nonfiction and has taught writing at New York University and Harvard's Extension School.

Tom Shachtman, "Transforming the News" in "What's Wrong with TV?: Talk Shows," from *The Inarticulate Society: Eloquence and Culture in America*. Copyright © 1995 by Tom Shachtman. Reprinted with the permission of The Free Press, a division of Simon & Schuster.

In the following selection, drawn from his latest book, *The Inarticulate Society* (1996), Shachtman discusses the impact of the pervasive illiteracy now characteristic of television talk shows.

One troubling harbinger of the direction that public eloquence has taken in America can be gleaned from what Shachtman perceives to be the dumbing-down or debasement of language heard on television talk shows, which are tuned into by over 80 million people each day. The ability to have and express complex thoughts has degenerated, in Shachtman's view, to mindless drivel characterized by a diminished vocabulary, misused terms, and language geared to the lowest common denominator of the viewing public. In short, television talk shows are leading America to become an inarticulate society.

TO CONSIDER   How bad does a TV talk show have to be before you change the channel? What do you consider unacceptable?

O n an Oprah Winfrey broadcast, when a young doctor confessed that he   1
was something of a romantic, he reportedly received 40,000 letters
from women wishing to share his life. While not every talk program can
generate that amount of attention, collectively talk shows have an enormous
audience, as many as 80 million viewers daily, and as the doctor's story makes
clear, it is an audience that pays close attention to what is being said on the programs. To learn more about how language is being modeled for us on talk
shows, on November 9, 1993, I spent the day watching and listening to snippets of eight mainstream syndicated talk shows.

At nine in the morning in New York, while NBC and some other channels   2
carry game shows and cartoons, and while Mr. Rogers holds forth on public
television, there are three talk shows in head-to-head competition: Jane Whitney
on CBS, Montel Williams on the Fox network, and Regis Philbin and Kathie Lee
Gifford on ABC.

Jane Whitney features a man whose problem is that he has two girlfriends.   3
Tina and Jim are the guests in the first segment. She is angry about the situation,
while he seems as contented as the cat who swallowed the cream. We later learn
that Jim called the program and offered to appear with his two girlfriends, ostensibly to resolve their predicament. Jane Whitney's questioning demonstrates that
she knows the terms "psychobabble," "avoiding commitment," "relationship,"
and "monogamous," but most of her queries are monosyllabic: "Some people,
like, sleep with only one person at a time."

Jim's two lovers have never met. Now, to applause, the second young   4
woman emerges from behind a curtain, and then, under Jane's questioning, the
two comment on how they are and are not alike.

JANE: Do you feel you have anything in common with her?
SECOND: Him.
TINA: How do you know he loves you? He loves me!
JANE: You're playing, like, seniority here. Like, bookends.

5   Montel Williams's guests are six couples made up of older women and younger men. Each woman introduces her young man, using such terms as "hunk," "sex appeal," and "perfect specimen of humanity," and making sure to announce his birth date, for the men are a decade or two younger than the women. The couples behave as though they are in the first flushes of affairs. We learn that the Montel Williams show arranged and taped a party at which these people were first introduced to one another, in exchange for promises to appear on the program. The basic subject of the program is sex. Queried by the host, one young man speaks of "not having to work for it" and another confides about older women, "they tell you what they want," which prompts an admission from one that "we want a little pleasure for ourselves." Titles over the screen inform us the "JOHN/Likes women of all ages" and "NICK/Loves older women." The snickering quotient of the program is high. At the transition to commercials, footage of the mixer party is followed by a snippet from tomorrow's show, "Two sisters, one man. . . .You'd be surprised at how often this happens." At least one set of sisters are twins. During a later segment of the broadcast, a ponytailed male therapist comments on the couples, using such phrases as "comfort . . . not expected to last . . . emotional ties are suspended." The therapist is then questioned by the panel, which induces Montel to tell about his own experiences with older women. A billboard asks us at home, "Are You a Mom Who Wishes Her Son Would Stop Dating Tramps?" Those who can answer "yes" are to call the show.

6   "Born to Be Unfaithful," Jane Whitney's next program, will feature people who have been unfaithful and are the offspring of unfaithful parents. The subject after that is "Mothers who allow their teenage daughters to have sex in the house"; on videotape, one such mother says she prefers her daughter and the daughter's boyfriend to have sex at home "where I know that they're safe."

7   Barbara Walters visits Regis and Kathie Lee to impart backstage chatter about the celebrities she has interviewed for her latest special, to be broadcast that evening. In a clip, Barbara tries to learn from Julia Roberts whether the movie star thinks her husband of a few months is ugly or just differently handsome. Julia opts for handsome. In the studio Barbara and Kathie Lee brush cheeks and make hand motions to convey that they must phone one another for a lunch date very soon.

8   Fred Rogers visits a pretzel bakery. In an apron and baker's hat, he observes the various processes of the assembly line and kneads some dough with his own hands. His conversation with the bakers, aimed at an audience of preschool children, employs almost as large a vocabulary as that of the nine o'clock talk shows.

9   Not yet ready to make conclusions from such a small sample, later that day I watch segments of five more talk shows: Joan Rivers on CBS and, on NBC, Jerry Springer, Maury Povich, Sally Jessy Raphael, and Phil Donahue.

10   "How going back to the trauma of birth will help you clear up present problems" is the way Joan Rivers touts the subject of her program, but before discussing that she chats with a gossip columnist about the recent birth of Marla Maples's child, in which "aroma therapy" was used, and welcomes a pair of married guests to talk about "past-life therapy." The couple maintains that they were

actually married in a previous life. The wife says that through reliving and understanding an incident in Roman times, she has been cured:

GUEST: All that anger drained away. . . . .My heart got tender. I got compassionate.

JOAN: All this in one session?

. . .Then we are finally introduced to a female "prenatal psychologist." To investigate "early traumas . . . impressed on the psyche," this woman helps patients to go back to the moment of birth, even to the moment of conception. She has brought along some patients, whom Joan Rivers introduces: "My next guests have all been reborn, not through religion." These guests include another ponytailed male psychologist, who has been rescued by regression therapy from suicidal impulses, and a mother-and-daughter pair, similarly rescued from allergies. We shortly see a videotape of a volunteer who has gone through the therapy backstage. After the tape is shown, the volunteer comes onto the set and comments on reliving the attempt to get out of the birth canal: "I was engaged in some sort of battle." 11

From Boston, Jerry Springer features several trios, each consisting of a grandmother, her teenage daughter, and the daughter's infant. The infants have been born out of wedlock, one to a girl who became pregnant at twelve, the others to girls who were thirteen and fourteen. The teenagers had all considered abortion but had decided against it. Jerry asks about birth control. . . . A new grandmother allows that in retrospect she does "feel guilty" at not having given her daughter birth control instruction. "At thirteen, I didn't think she was going to be—you know—actively having sex with her boyfriend," who was nineteen; "I was in denial." Jerry Springer nods, and in general his treatment of an important subject, the epidemic of teenage pregnancies, is evenhanded. He questions the women sympathetically and with dignity, although he never refers to them by their names but says "Mom" and "Grandmom." He asks a woman in the latter category if the sensation of becoming a grandmother could have been a proud one, given the circumstances. She says, "I don't know; it's like, I was in the delivery room with her, and it's like—'Memories.'" Audience members express their belief that the father should be arraigned on charges of statutory rape, but the new mothers and grandmothers all agree that would not help anyone . . . 12

Maury Povich has gone to Texas for "Return to Waco: Answers in the Ashes." In front of an audience of former cult members and Waco residents, Povich questions Mark Breault, who left the Branch Davidians in 1989; Breault's complaints to the authorities have been blamed by some survivors for instigating the raids . . . 13

The government's lead pathologist then summarizes his team's findings about the thirty-two people who died in the bunker. In the most literate language I have heard all day, language that is compassionate, direct, and precise, he details the manner and cause of death: So many had gunshot wounds, so 14 many died of asphyxiation; a gunshot wound in the mouth may have been self-inflicted, but a wound in the back of the head almost certainly was not. His findings, being made public for the first time, devastate the people in the audience and on the set whose relatives died in that bunker—as we at home are forced to learn because the cameras focus on their faces so that we become privy to their emotions. While the pathologist tells the story, Maury Povich approaches one panel member whose face fills the screen and asks, "Is this what you think, Stan, happened to your family?"

15   "Could your sex life use a pick-me-up?"asks the announcer of the Phil Donahue show. Then voice and tape display aphrodisiacs, love potions, and an acupuncturist at work, and a panelist comments that "I'm getting turned on just by watching."

16   That, of course, is just what was intended.

17   Sally Jessy Raphael's program on November 9, 1993, deals with two 1986 cyanide poisoning deaths in the Seattle area, for which the wife of one of the victims was convicted and imprisoned. Of all the programs of this day, it is the worst exemplar in terms of use of language. First, Sally encapsulates the story for us in emotional kindergarten language: "Some family members say Stella was railroaded. 'She's innocent. Poor Stella.' Some say her daughter Cynthia was really the mastermind behind the deaths." A journalist has written a book about the case. He has corralled the guest panelists, but during the course of the program he must frequently interpret and augment what these guests say, for the guests prove remarkably unable to present their thoughts coherently or even clothed in words that aptly convey their meaning.

STELLA'S NIECE: I didn't think that—there wasn't enough problems that would institute her to kill my uncle . . .

STELLA'S FRIEND: She was somebody that would've taken a gun and shot him point-blank, instead of being sneaky and committed murder in the way that she was convicted.

18   When one guest is entirely unable to convey her meaning, Sally is forced to correct her in order that the audience can understand the story:

FORMER HOUSEMATE: She used me as a scapegoat.
SALLY: As a screen.
AUDIENCE MEMBER: Maybe Cynthia was child-abused.

19   As with my student's use of "emitted" for "admitted," these poor grammatical, vocabulary and word usages are evidence of the sort of misperception of language that can only come from learning language in a secondarily oral way. Pop psychology terms aside, the discourse of the moderators, the guests, the experts, and most of the studio audience members of all these programs mixes grade-school vocabulary and grammar with a leavening of naughty language. Granted, there is no pretense of trying to be articulate, but neither are there

many accidental instances of felicitous phrasing. Vocabulary levels are depressingly low, more in line with the spoken-word corpus than might be presumed, since parts of the programs are scripted, and since the guests and stars of these programs are not speaking in private but in rather public circumstances, in front of viewing audiences numbered in the tens of millions.

Talk show language has become almost completely detached from the literate base of English. It is as though the program-makers have concluded that literate English has nothing to do with the emotive, real-life concerns of human beings, and therefore cannot be used to describe or analyze them. As a result, talk shows exist in the realm of vocabularies limited to the few hundred most commonly used words in the spoken language, augmented by a few terms pirated from the sublanguage of therapy. To talk of "Mothers who allow their teenage daughters to have sex in the house," or to inquire "Are You a Mom Who Wishes Her Son Would Stop Dating Tramps?" is to speak down to the audience, not even to address the audience on its own level. These lines employ a vocabulary not much beyond that of a nine- or ten-year-old; the facts show that the daytime viewing audience is chronologically older and better educated than that. . . . But the programming elites seem to have nothing but contempt for their audiences composed of average Americans—for "the people we fly over," as one executive called them. Rather, the programmers embrace the fuzzy McLuhanesque belief that a world dominated by new electronic media will wholeheartedly share tribal emotions.

Walter Ong asserts that the culture of secondary orality may mean a return to the primacy of the unconscious for those within it.[1] That culture's gestation period is being shortened by the practices of today's news programs and talk shows, which encourage the audience to acquire information principally through images, and through a lexicon that mimics the oral rather than the literate language. The limited vocabulary, constrained syntax, unknowing or deliberate misuses of language, affectation of minor wit, constant reference to base emotions, and chronic citation of pop cultural icons in attempts to bond with the audience—these characteristic elements of news and talk programs constitute an enfeebled discourse.

The antidote is well known, since most of the people who create news programs and talk shows are themselves literate and fully capable of using the literate-based language. That antidote is to use the power of words to haul these programs back up to a literate level they once attained. Purveyors of talk shows currently reject such a goal as not commensurate with their objective of gaining the largest audience. However, there is no evidence of which I am aware that demonstrates any inverse relationship between the shows' popularity and the vocabulary and articulateness levels of talk show hosts and hostesses (and that of their carefully screened guests). Precisely the opposite may be true: Articulate behavior is part of the hosts' and hostesses' attractiveness. Phil Donahue and

[1]Walter J. Ong, *Rhetoric, Romance and Technology*, 1971.

Oprah Winfrey are articulate as well as charismatic people. Rush Limbaugh's ability to deflate liberal icons and to create telling puns—"femi-nazis" for strident feminists—have attracted him a wide following. All three, and many others among the talk-show stars, possess good vocabularies, but they have yet to employ them to best use. All too often, they reach for the simple instead of using their tremendous abilities to make complicated matters exciting and understandable. Given these stars' large talents and capacities to enthrall, audiences would undoubtedly follow them up the scale of literacy as gladly (and in just as large numbers) as they have followed them down the scale.

23   As for news broadcasts, the transformation could be even simpler. News broadcasts need to take a pledge to not only convey information but to set aside time in the broadcast to have that information illuminated by the minds and vocabularies of the reporters. Permit reporters once again to do the tasks of synthesis and analysis of information, as well as the job of being on the spot to collect it. Utilize television's fabulous educative ability. Employ vocabularies that may once in a while send an audience member scurrying to a dictionary—or, better yet, set a goal of encouraging the audience to incorporate interesting words into their own vocabularies. During the Gulf War, millions of Americans learned a new word when Peter Jennings of ABC News spoke of oil as a "fungible" commodity, which he explained meant that a unit of it from one source was essentially the same as a unit of it from another source. Network news divisions could improve the articulateness levels of their viewers by raising the vocabulary and sentence-structure levels of their own broadcasts and by taking the pledge to use "fungible" and other such marvelous if unfamiliar words when they are clearly appropriate. How about one new word a day? Such a practice would be unlikely to provoke viewers to turn away from their favorite newscasters and to the competition.

24   We need for our broadcasters once again to champion and employ the power of words as well as the power of images. This is not only in the public interest, but in their own. Informative broadcasting relies, in the end, on an audience that places some premium on the value of ideas. If its discourse is increasingly impoverished, then the audience will retreat from information-based programs into the wholly pictorial realm of video games and interactive fictional programming, where the audience has the illusion of deciding what happens. Then there will be no more market for television news or talk shows. What the informative shows are doing by embracing images and diminished language is the equivalent of a restaurant slowly poisoning all of its customers.

---

1   Based on his sampling of one average day's TV talk shows, Shachtman finds that the use of language on these shows is part of a pervasive deterioration in the quality of American culture. Specifically, what examples of diminished language does he discover in what the talk show guests say and in how the producers and hosts of these shows present the themes of the shows? By contrast, what is different about the way language was used in the news coverage of the FBI's raid in Waco, Texas (para. 14)?

2 In Shachtman's view, what factors are responsible for the deterioration of language on television and why do the producers of talk shows purposely set out to reduce the language used on these shows to the lowest common denominator? In your opinion, is Shachtman correct in believing that people would still want to watch talk shows if the quality of the language was raised in the way he recommends? Why do you think these talk shows are so popular? What function do they serve in our society?

3 What is Walter Ong's theory of "secondary orality" (para. 21)? How does it seek to explain why talk show producers have made the calculated decision to lower the quality of the language used on their shows?

4 Shachtman's style changes a good deal when he moves from describing the language used on TV talk shows to his own analysis and recommendations (para. 19). How does his use of language differ from the language used on TV talk shows? Be specific in terms of vocabulary, syntax, sentence length, complexity of the ideas expressed, etc. (Glossary: *Style*.)

5 Implicit in Shachtman's analysis is an explanation of causes and effects as to why TV talk shows are deteriorating in terms of the language used on them. What are the causes and what are the effects? How does he organize his essay using this rhetorical pattern (see Glossary: *Cause and Effect*)?

6 Conduct your own analysis of TV talk shows based on an average day's fare. In what ways are these shows by and large better or worse, in your opinion, than Shachtman says? Pay attention to specific language in terms of vocabulary, sentence structure, deliberate misuse, grammatical errors, and emotionally stirring phrases. Does the language used on these shows constitute an "enfeebled discourse," as Shachtman claims (para. 21)?

What We Talk About When We Talk About Love   *Raymond Carver*

◆ RAYMOND CARVER (1938–1988) was raised in a logging town in Oregon. He attended Humboldt State College (B.A. 1963) and the University of Iowa, where he studied creative writing. In the 1970s he published stories in the *New Yorker, Esquire,* and the *Atlantic Monthly. Will You Please Be Quiet, Please?* (1976), his first collection of short stories, was nominated for the National Book Award. His later collections include *What We Talk About When We Talk About Love* (1981), in which the following story first appeared, *Cathedral* (1983), and *Where I'm Calling From* (1988). The appeal of Carver's fiction stems from his unique gift for creating dialogue in which what is unsaid is as important as what is said, a characteristic we can observe in this story.

In the following story, two couples are seated around a kitchen table drinking gin. Initially, the emphasis of the story is on Mel and his second wife, Terri. Each of the important aspects of conversation covered in this chapter can be observed in this story, from the different meanings each of the four characters has about love to the creation or violation of trust, enacted as the story progresses. The language and details Mel chooses to use in his story about an elderly couple represents the paradox of his own emotions. Mel, who believes in a traditional definition of love, comes to the painful realization that his love may not be as pure an absolute as he would like it to be. As all four friends delve into the buried connections to former loves, the spirit of the convivial get-together gives way to one of sober thought and anxiety. The attitudes toward love of each of the four participants are directly connected to the language in which they describe what love means to them. This story's nuances of meaning are conveyed through the characters' dialogue and behavior as they discover the instability and complex nature of what had been a taken-for-granted part of the emotional fabric of their lives.

> **TO CONSIDER**   To what extent would having been married and then divorced change your view of what love meant if you then remarried?

My friend Mel McGinnis was talking. Mel McGinnis is a cardiologist, and sometimes that gives him the right.

The four of us were sitting around his kitchen table drinking gin. Sunlight filled the kitchen from the big window behind the sink. There were Mel and me and his second wife, Teresa—Terri, we called her—and my wife, Laura. We lived in Albuquerque then. But we were all from somewhere else.

There was an ice bucket on the table. The gin and the tonic water kept going around, and we somehow got on the subject of love. Mel thought real love was nothing less than spiritual love. He said he'd spent five years in a seminary before quitting to go to medical school. He said he still looked back on those years in the seminary as the most important years in his life.

Terri said the man she lived with before she lived with Mel loved her so much he tried to kill her. Then Terri said, "He beat me up one night. He dragged me around the living room by my ankles. He kept saying, 'I love you, I love you, you bitch.' He went on dragging me around the living room. My head kept knocking on things." Terri looked around the table. "What do you do with love like that?"

She was a bone-thin woman with a pretty face, dark eyes, and brown hair   5
that hung down her back. She liked necklaces made of turquoise, and long pendant earrings.

"My God, don't be silly. That's not love, and you know it," Mel said. "I don't know what you'd call it, but I sure know you wouldn't call it love."

"Say what you want to, but I know it was," Terri said. "It may sound crazy to you, but it's true just the same. People are different, Mel. Sure, sometimes he may have acted crazy. Okay. But he loved me. In his own way maybe, but he loved me. There was love there, Mel. Don't say there wasn't."

Mel let out his breath. He held his glass and turned to Laura and me. "The man threatened to kill me," Mel said. He finished his drink and reached for the gin bottle. "Terri's a romantic. Terri's of the kick-me-so-I'll-know-you-love-me school. Terri, hon, don't look that way." Mel reached across the table and touched Terri's cheek with his fingers. He grinned at her.

"Now he wants to make up," Terri said.

"Make up what?" Mel said. "What is there to make up? I know what I know.   10
That's all."

"How'd we get started on this subject, anyway?" Terri said. She raised her glass and drank from it. "Mel always has love on his mind," she said. "Don't you, honey?" She smiled, and I thought that was the last of it.

"I just wouldn't call Ed's behavior love. That's all I'm saying, honey," Mel said. "What about you guys?" Mel said to Laura and me. "Does that sound like love to you?"

"I'm the wrong person to ask," I said. "I didn't even know the man. I've only heard his name mentioned in passing. I wouldn't know. You'd have to know the particulars. But I think what you're saying is that love is an absolute."

Mel said, "The kind of love I'm talking about is. The kind of love I'm talking about, you don't try to kill people."

Laura said, "I don't know anything about Ed, or anything about the situa-   15
tion. But who can judge anyone else's situation?"

I touched the back of Laura's hand. She gave me a quick smile. I picked up Laura's hand. It was warm, the nails polished, perfectly manicured. I encircled the broad wrist with my fingers, and I held her.

"When I left, he drank rat poison," Terri said. She clasped her arms with her hands. "They took him to the hospital in Santa Fe. That's where we lived then, about ten miles out. They saved his life. But his gums went crazy from it. I mean they pulled away from his teeth. After that, his teeth stood out like fangs. My God," Terri said. She waited a minute, then let go of her arms and picked up her glass.

"What people won't do!" Laura said.

"He's out of the action now," Mel said. "He's dead."

20   Mel handed me the saucer of limes. I took a section, squeezed it over my
drink, and stirred the ice cubes with my finger.

"It gets worse," Terri said. "He shot himself in the mouth, But he bungled
that too. Poor Ed," she said. Terri shook her head.

"Poor Ed nothing," Mel said. "He was dangerous."

Mel was forty-five years old. He was tall and rangy with curly soft hair. His
face and arms were brown from the tennis he played. When he was sober, his
gestures, all his movements, were precise, very careful.

"He did love me though, Mel. Grant me that," Terri said. "That's all I'm
asking. He didn't love me the way you love me. I'm not saying that. But he loved
me. You can grant me that, can't you?"

25   "What do you mean, he bungled it?" I said.

Laura leaned forward with her glass. She put her elbows on the table and
held her glass in both hands. She glanced from Mel to Terri and waited with a
look of bewilderment on her open face, as if amazed that such things happened
to people you were friendly with.

"How'd he bungle it when he killed himself?" I said.

"I'll tell you what happened," Mel said. "He took this twenty-two pistol
he'd bought to threaten Terri and me with. Oh, I'm serious, the man was always
threatening. You should have seen the way we lived in those days. Like fugitives.
I even bought a gun myself. Can you believe it? A guy like me? But I did. I
bought one for self-defense and carried it in the glove compartment. Sometimes
I'd have to leave the apartment in the middle of the night. To go to the hospital, you know? Terri and I weren't married then, and my first wife had the house
and kids, the dog, everything, and Terri and I were living in this apartment here.
Sometimes, as I say, I'd get a call in the middle of the night and have to go in to
the hospital at two or three in the morning. It'd be dark out there in the park-
ing lot, and I'd break into a sweat before I could even get to my car. I never knew
if he was going to come up out of the shrubbery or from behind a car and start
shooting. I mean, the man was crazy. He was capable of wiring a bomb, anything. He used to call my service at all hours and say he needed to talk to the
doctor, and when I'd return the call, he'd say, 'Son of a bitch, your days are
numbered.' Little things like that. It was scary, I'm telling you."

"I still feel sorry for him," Terri said.

30   "It sounds like a nightmare," Laura said. "But what exactly happened after
he shot himself?"

Laura is a legal secretary. We'd met in a professional capacity. Before we
knew it, it was a courtship. She's thirty-five, three years younger than I am. In
addition to being in love, we like each other and enjoy one another's company.
She's easy to be with.

"What happened?" Laura said.

Mel said, "He shot himself in the mouth in his room. Someone heard the
shot and told the manager. They came in with a passkey, saw what had happened,
and called an ambulance. I happened to be there when they brought him in,

alive but past recall. The man lived for three days. His head swelled up to twice the size of a normal head. I'd never seen anything like it, and I hope I never do again. Terri wanted to go in and sit with him when she found out about it. We had a fight over it. I didn't think she should see him like that. I didn't think she should see him, and I still don't."

"Who won the fight?" Laura said.

"I was in the room with him when he died," Terri said. "He never came up   35 out of it. But I sat with him. He didn't have anyone else."

"He was dangerous," Mel said. "If you call that love, you can have it."

"It was love," Terri said. "Sure, it's abnormal in most people's eyes. But he was willing to die for it. He did die for it."

"I sure as hell wouldn't call it love," Mel said. "I mean, no one knows what he did it for. I've seen a lot of suicides, and I couldn't say anyone ever knew what they did it for."

Mel put his hands behind his neck and tilted his chair back. "I'm not interested in that kind of love," he said. "If that's love, you can have it."

Terri said, "We were afraid. Mel even made a will out and wrote to his   40 brother in California who used to be a Green Beret. Mel told him who to look for if something happened to him."

Terri drank from her glass. She said, "But Mel's right—we lived like fugitives. We were afraid. Mel was, weren't you, honey? I even called the police at one point, but they were no help. They said they couldn't do anything until Ed actually did something. Isn't that a laugh?" Terri said.

She poured the last of the gin into her glass and waggled the bottle. Mel got up from the table and went to the cupboard. He took down another bottle.

"Well, Nick and I know what love is," Laura said. "For us, I mean," Laura said. She bumped my knee with her knee. "You're supposed to say something now," Laura said, and turned her smile on me.

For an answer, I took Laura's hand and raised it to my lips. I made a big production out of kissing her hand. Everyone was amused.

"We're lucky," I said.   45

"You guys," Terri said. "Stop that now. You're making me sick. You're still on the honeymoon, for God's sake. You're still gaga, for crying out loud. Just wait. How long have you been together now? How long has it been? A year? Longer than a year?"

"Going on a year and a half," Laura said, flushed and smiling.

"Oh, now," Terri said. "Wait awhile."

She held her drink and gazed at Laura.

"I'm only kidding," Terri said.   50

Mel opened the gin and went around the table with the bottle.

"Here, you guys," he said. "Let's have a toast. I want to propose a toast. A toast to love. To true love," Mel said."

We touched glasses.

"To love," we said.

55   Outside in the backyard, one of the dogs began to bark. The leaves of the aspen that leaned past the window ticked against the glass. The afternoon sun was like a presence in this room, the spacious light of ease and generosity. We could have been anywhere, somewhere enchanted. We raised our glasses again and grinned at each other like children who had agreed on something forbidden.

"I'll tell you what real love is," Mel said. "I mean, I'll give you a good example. And then you can draw your own conclusions." He poured more gin into his glass. He added an ice cube and a silver of lime. We waited and sipped our drinks. Laura and I touched knees again. I put a hand on her warm thigh and left it there.

"What do any of us really know about love?" Mel said. "It seems to me we're just beginners at love. We say we love each other and we do, I don't doubt it. I love Terri and Terri loves me, and you guys love each other too. You know the kind of love I'm talking about now. Physical love, that impulse that drives you to someone special, as well as love of the other person's being, his or her essence, as it were. Carnal love and, well, call it sentimental love, the day-to-day caring about the other person. But sometimes I have a hard time accounting for the fact that I must have loved my first wife too. But I did, I know I did. So I suppose I am like Terri in that regard. Terri and Ed." He thought about it and then he went on. "There was a time when I thought I loved my first wife more than life itself. But now I hate her guts. I do. How do you explain that? What happened to that love? What happened to it, is what I'd like to know. I wish someone could tell me. Then there's Ed. Okay, we're back to Ed. He loves Terri so much he tries to kill her and he winds up killing himself." Mel stopped talking and swallowed from his glass. "You guys have been together eighteen months and you love each other. It shows all over you. You glow with it. But you both loved other people before you met each other. You've both been married before, just like us. And you probably loved other people before that too, even. Terri and I have been together five years, been married for four. And the terrible thing, the terrible thing is, but the good thing too, the saving grace, you might say, is that if something happened to one of us—excuse me for saying this—but if something happened to one of us tomorrow, I think the other one, the other person, would grieve for a while, you know, but then the surviving party would go out and love again, have someone else soon enough. All this, all of this love we're talking about, it would just be a memory. Maybe not even a memory. Am I wrong? Am I way off base? Because I want you to set me straight if you think I'm wrong. I want to know. I mean I don't know anything, and I'm the first one to admit it."

"Mel, for God's sake," Terri said. She reached out and took hold of his wrist. "Are you getting drunk? Honey? Are you drunk?"

"Honey, I'm just talking," Mel said. "All right? I don't have to be drunk to say what I think. I mean, we're all just talking, right?" Mel said. He fixed his eyes on her.

60   "Sweetie, I'm not criticizing," Terri said.

She picked up her glass.

"I'm not on call today," Mel said. "Let me remind you of that. I am not on call," he said.

"Mel, we love you," Laura said.

Mel looked at Laura, He looked at her as if he could not place her, as if she was not the woman she was.

"Love you too, Laura," Mel said. "And you, Nick, love you too. You know   65
something?" Mel said. "You guys are our pals," Mel said.

He picked up his glass.

Mel said, "I was going to tell you about something. I mean, I was going to prove a point. You see, this happened a few months ago, but it's still going on right now, and it ought to make us feel ashamed when we talk like we know what we're talking about when we talk about love."

"Come on now," Terri said. "Don't talk like you're drunk if you're not drunk."

"Just shut up for once in your life," Mel said very quietly. "Will you do me a favor and do that for a minute? So as I was saying, there's this old couple who had this car wreck out on the interstate. A kid hit them and they were all torn to shit and nobody was giving them much chance to pull through."

Terri looked at us and then back at Mel. She seemed anxious, or maybe   70
that's too strong a word.

Mel was handing the bottle around the table.

"I was on call that night," Mel said. "It was May or maybe it was June. Terri and I had just sat down to dinner when the hospital called. There'd been this thing out on the interstate. Drunk kid, teenager, plowed his dad's pickup into this camper with this old couple in it. They were up in their mid-seventies, that couple. The kid—eighteen, nineteen, something—he was DOA. Taken the steering wheel through his sternum. The old couple, they were alive, you understand. I mean, just barely. But they had everything. Multiple fractures, internal injuries, hemorrhaging, contusions, lacerations, the works, and they each of them had themselves concussions. They were in a bad way, believe me. And, of course, their age was two strikes against them. I'd say she was worse off than he was. Ruptured spleen along with everything else. Both kneecaps broken. But they'd been wearing their seatbelts and, God knows, that's what saved them for the time being."

"Folks, this is an advertisement for the National Safety Council," Terri said. "This is your spokesman, Dr. Melvin R. McGinnis, talking." Terri laughed. "Mel," she said, "sometimes you're just too much. But I love you, hon," she said.

"Honey, I love you," Mel said.

He leaned across the table. Terri met him halfway. They kissed.   75

"Terri's right," Mel said as he settled himself again. "Get those seat-belts on. But seriously, they were in some shape, those oldsters. By the time I got down there, the kid was dead, as I said. He was off in a corner, laid out on a gurney. I took one look at the old couple and told the ER nurse to get me a neurologist and an orthopedic man and a couple of surgeons down there right away."

He drank from his glass. "I'll try to keep this short," he said. "So we took the two of them up to the OR and worked like fuck on them most of the night. They had these incredible reserves, those two. You see that once in a while. So we did everything that could be done, and toward morning we're giving them a fifty-fifty chance, maybe less than that for her. So here they are, still alive the next morning. So, okay, we move them into the ICU, which is where they both kept plugging away at it for two weeks, hitting it better and better on all the scopes. So we transfer them out to their own room."

Mel stopped talking. "Here," he said, "let's drink this cheapo gin the hell up. Then we're going to dinner, right? Terri and I know a new place. That's where we'll go, to this new place we know about. But we're not going until we finish up this cut-rate, lousy gin."

Terri said, "We haven't actually eaten there yet. But it looks good. From the outside, you know."

80   "I like food," Mel said. "If I had it to do all over again, I'd be a chef, you know? Right, Terri?" Mel said.

He laughed. He fingered the ice in his glass.

"Terri knows," he said. "Terri can tell you. But let me say this. If I could come back again in a different life, a different time and all, you know what? I'd like to come back as a knight. You were pretty safe wearing all that armor. It was all right being a knight until gunpowder and muskets and pistols came along."

"Mel would like to ride a horse and carry a lance," Terri said.

"Carry a woman's scarf with you everywhere," Laura said.

85   "Or just a woman," Mel said.

"Shame on you," Laura said.

Terri said, "Suppose you came back as a serf. The serfs didn't have it so good in those days," Terri said.

"The serfs never had it good," Mel said. "But I guess even the knights were vessels to someone. Isn't that the way it worked? But then everyone is always a vessel to someone. Isn't that right, Terri? But what I liked about knights, besides their ladies, was that they had that suit of armor, you know, and they couldn't get hurt very easy. No cars in those days, you know? No drunk teenagers to tear into your ass."

"Vassals," Terri said

90   "What?" Mel said.

"Vassals," Terri said. "They were called vassals, not vessels."

"Vassals, vessels," Mel said, "what the fuck's the difference? You knew what I meant anyway. All right," Mel said. "So I'm not educated. I learned my stuff. I'm a heart surgeon, sure, but I'm just a mechanic. I go in and I fuck around and I fix things. Shit," Mel said.

"Modesty doesn't become you," Terri said.

"He's just a humble sawbones," I said. "But sometimes they suffocated in all that armor, Mel. They'd even have heart attacks if it got too hot and they were too tired and worn out. I read somewhere that they'd fall off their horses and not be able to get up because they were too tired to stand with all that armor on them. They got trampled by their own horses sometimes."

"That's terrible," Mel said. "That's a terrible thing, Nicky. I guess they'd just lay there and wait until somebody came along and made a shish kebab out of them."

"Some other vessel," Terri said.

"That's right," Mel said. "Some vassal would come along and spear the bastard in the name of love. Or whatever the fuck it was they fought over in those days."

"Same things we fight over these days," Terri said.

Laura said, "Nothing's changed."

The color was still high in Laura's cheeks. Her eyes were bright. She brought her glass to her lips.

Mel poured himself another drink. He looked at the label closely as if studying a long row of numbers. Then he slowly put the bottle down on the table and slowly reached for the tonic water.

"What about the old couple?" Laura said. "You didn't finish that story you started."

Laura was having a hard time lighting her cigarette. Her matches kept going out.

The sunshine inside the room was different now, changing, getting thinner. But the leaves outside the window were still shimmering, and I stared at the pattern they made on the panes and on the Formica counter. They weren't the same patterns, of course.

"What about the old couple?" I said.

"Older but wiser," Terri said.

Mel stared at her.

Terri said, "Go on with your story, hon. I was only kidding. Then what happened?"

"Terri, sometimes," Mel said.

"Please, Mel," Terri said. "Don't always be so serious, sweetie. Can't you take a joke?"

"Where's the joke?" Mel said.

He held his glass and gazed steadily at his wife.

"What happened?" Laura said.

Mel fastened his eyes on Laura. He said, "Laura, if I didn't have Terri and if I didn't love her so much, and if Nick wasn't my best friend, I'd fall in love with you. I'd carry you off, honey," he said.

"Tell your story," Terri said. "Then we'll go to that new place, okay?"

"Okay," Mel said. "Where was I?" he said. He stared at the table and then he began again.

"I dropped in to see each of them every day, sometimes twice a day if I was up doing other calls anyway. Casts and bandages, head to foot, the both of them. You know, you've seen it in the movies. That's just the way they looked, just like in the movies. Little eye-holes and nose-holes and mouth-holes. And she had to have her legs slung up on top of it. Well, the husband was very depressed for the longest while. Even after he found out that his wife was going to pull through, he was still very depressed. Not about the accident, though. I mean, the accident was one thing, but it wasn't everything. I'd get up to his mouth-hole, you know, and he'd say no, it wasn't the accident exactly but it was because he couldn't see her through his eye-holes. He said that was what was making him feel so bad. Can you imagine? I'm telling you, the man's heart was breaking because he couldn't turn his goddamn head and *see* his god-damn wife."

Mel looked around the table and shook his head at what he was going to say.

"I mean, it was killing the old fart just because he couldn't *look* at the fucking woman."

120   We all looked at Mel.

"Do you see what I'm saying?" he said.

Maybe we were a little drunk by then. I know it was hard keeping things in focus. The light was draining out of the room, going back through the window where it had come from. Yet nobody made a move to get up from the table to turn on the overhead light.

"Listen," Mel said. "Let's finish this fucking gin. There's about enough left here for one shooter all around. Then let's go eat. Let's go to the new place."

"He's depressed," Terri said. "Mel, why don't you take a pill?"

125   Mel shook his head. "I've taken everything there is."

"We all need a pill now and then," I said.

"Some people are born needing them," Terri said.

She was using her finger to rub at something on the table. Then she stopped rubbing.

"I think I want to call my kids," Mel said. "Is that all right with everybody? I'll call my kids," he said.

130   Terri said, "What if Marjorie answers the phone? You guys, you've heard us on the subject of Marjorie? Honey, you know you don't want to talk to Mar-jorie. It'll make you feel even worse."

"I don't want to talk to Marjorie," Mel said. "But I want to talk to my kids."

"There isn't a day goes by that Mel doesn't say he wishes she'd get married again. Or else die," Terri said. "For one thing," Terri said, "she's bankrupting us. Mel says it's just to spite him that she won't get married again. She has a boyfriend who lives with her and the kids, so Mel is supporting the boyfriend too."

"She's allergic to bees," Mel said. "If I'm not praying she'll get married again, I'm praying she'll get herself stung to death by a swarm of fucking bees."

"Shame on you," Laura said.

"Bzzzzzzz," Mel said, turning his fingers into bees and buzzing them at   135
Terri's throat. Then he let his hands drop all the way to his sides.

"She's vicious," Mel said. "Sometimes I think I'll go up there dressed like a
beekeeper. You know, that hat that's like a helmet with the plate that comes
down over your face, the big gloves, and the padded coat? I'll knock on the door
and let loose a hive of bees in the house. But first I'd make sure the kids were
out, of course."

He crossed one leg over the other. It seemed to take him a lot of time to do
it. Then he put both feet on the floor and leaned forward, elbows on the table,
his chin cupped in his hands.

"Maybe I won't call the kids, after all. Maybe it isn't such a hot idea. Maybe
we'll just go eat. How does that sound?"

"Sounds fine to me," I said. "Eat or not eat. Or keep drinking. I could head
right on out into the sunset."

"What does that mean, honey?" Laura said.   140

"It just means what I said," I said. "It means I could just keep going. That's
all it means."

"I could eat something myself," Laura said. "I don't think I've ever been so
hungry in my life. Is there something to nibble on?"

"I'll put out some cheese and crackers," Terri said.

But Terri just sat there. She did not get up to get anything.

Mel turned his glass over. He spilled it out on the table.   145

"Gin's gone," Mel said.

Terri said, "Now what?"

I could hear my heart beating. I could hear everyone's heart. I could hear
the human noise we sat there making, not one of us moving, not even when the
room went dark.

---

1   What can you gauge about Mel's social class from the way he speaks? How is it different from the way Terri, Laura, and Nick speak? Why, for example, is it significant that Terri corrects him when he confuses the words "vassals" and "vessels" (para. 90)? How do differences in social class and who has power in the conversation at various times affect the way people speak? Does this change over the course of the story? In what way?

2   What different views of what love is emerge over the course of the story? How does the anecdote related by Terri about her ex-lover and Mel's story about the elderly couple he treated in the hospital illustrate what they each mean by the term "love"?

3   There are a number of subtle shifts in allegiance that take place over the course of the story. What verbal and nonverbal cues indicate that: (a) Terri gets scared when Mel gets angry at her for bringing up her ex-lover, (b) Nick and Laura—who initially congratulate themselves about the mutual trust they have, especially when compared

with Mel and Terri—go their separate ways after Laura responds to Mel's flirtation, (c) Nick takes Mel as his model.

In your view, what unverbalized message is communicated by the ominous silence at the end of the story?

4 How do the following three images associated with Mel symbolize important things about his view of love: his desire to be a medieval knight in full armor astride a horse (para. 85), his description of the old couple in their head-to-foot casts (para. 115), and his fantasy about showing up at his ex-wife's house in a beekeeper's outfit (para. 135)? (Glossary: *Characterization, Fiction, Symbol.*)

5 Where in Carver's story does he develop the meanings of the term "love" by incorporating rhetorical approaches into his narrative? For example, where does he use exemplification to show some typical instances of "love," comparison and contrast to show what it is like or unlike, cause and effect to show what leads to love or what the consequences of love are, division and classification to show what different forms love can take, etc.? (Glossary: *Cause and Effect, Classification/Division, Comparison and Contrast, Definition.*)

6 What range of particular techniques does Raymond Carver use (including synonym, example, negation, stipulation) to define "love"? Where in the story are these strategies used and which in your view are the most effective?

◆ CONNECTIONS: CAN WE TALK?

Mikhail Bakhtin, "The Dialogic Imagination"

1. How does Raymond Carver's story illustrate the kind of complex echoing of preceding conversations that go on all the time in ways that Bakhtin has identified?
2. To what extent does the conversation reported by Linda Stasi in "Your First Date" (Ch. 5) lend itself to a Bakhtinian analysis of conflicting agendas during a dialogue?

Ronald Wardhaugh, "The Social Basis of Talk"

1. What unspoken assumptions and normal rituals of conversation described by Wardhaugh does Raymond Carver utilize—in order to violate them in his story?
2. How would the assumptions underlying Wardhaugh's analysis of the social basis of talk have to be modified based on Deborah Tannen's research into the different environments in which men and women are socialized (see "Sex, Lies, and Conversation," Ch. 5)?

Peter Farb, "Verbal Dueling"

1. Analyze the patterns of conversation in Raymond Carver's story using the assumption that "verbal dueling" is taking place as Farb describes it.
2. Drawing on Farb's analysis of the principles of "verbal dueling," analyze the conversations Paula Span reports in her article "Women and Computers: Is There Equity in Cyberspace?" (Ch. 11). How have assertions of dominance and the use of conversational gambits been modified by electronic communication?

James Gorman, "Like, Uptalk?"

1. Can you discover "uptalk" (that is, ending declarative sentences with question marks) as discussed by Gorman in Raymond Carver's short story? What function does it serve?
2. Analyze "uptalk" in light of Robin Lakoff's "Language and Woman's Place" (Ch. 5). What similarities can you discover between "uptalk" and the language women use?

Fritz Peters, "Gurdjieff Remembered"

1. Compare the uses of obscene language in Peters's account and in Raymond Carver's story. In what way does obscenity serve different purposes in each work?
2. To what extent do sexism and gender stereotyping, as described by Alleen Pace Nilsen (see "Sexism in English: A 1990s Update," Ch. 8) play a role in Peters's account?

Tom Shachtman, "What's Wrong with TV?: Talk Shows"

1. Both obscenity, as incorporated in Peters's account, and the abuses of language described by Shachtman are commonly perceived as kinds of degraded discourse, yet they differ in fundamental ways. How do they differ and why do they produce such different reactions?
2. What insight do Shachtman, Neil Postman, and Steve Powers (see "How to Watch TV News," Ch. 10) provide into the extent to which talk shows and nightly newscasts are carefully contrived spectacles? How have information and entertainment now become indistinguishable from each other?

Raymond Carver, "What We Talk About When We Talk About Love"

1. Analyze Carver's story using the ritual of turn-taking behavior discussed by Peter Farb.
2. How are the issues of dominance and gender enacted in Carver's story connected to Robin Lakoff's discussion in "Language and Woman's Place" (Ch. 5)?

◆ WRITING ASSIGNMENTS FOR CHAPTER 4

1. Tone is a vital element in the audience's perception of the author. (Glossary: *Tone, Audience.*)

    When we try to identify and analyze the tone of a work, we are seeking to hear the "voice" of the author in order to understand how he or she intended the work to be perceived. Tone indicates the author's attitude toward both the subject and the audience. Tone is a projection of the writer's self.

    Tone is produced by the combined effect of word choice, sentence structure, and the writer's success in adapting her or his particular "voice" to suit the subject, the audience, and the occasion. (Glossary: *Diction.*)

    Select an essay by Wardhaugh, Farb, Gorman, Peters, or Shachtman and try to identify and analyze the tone of the work—that is, the voice of the author. For what audience would the style and tone be appropriate, given the subject matter of the essay and the approach the author takes? What impression of the author does the essay create? Try to be specific in your analysis and point to choices of words, sentence structure, etc. Alternatively, you might consider the work of a writer whose style is unique or someone you know who speaks in a distinct manner. Using the above criteria as well as considerations of sentence variety, slang, usage, vocabulary, and diction, analyze their style and characterize the distinct voice you hear from the way they write or speak. Perform the same analysis on one or more pieces of writing you have done, perhaps in different contexts. What different voices do you project in letters to friends, term papers, essays for courses at school, job applications? How would you characterize your different voices used in these different contexts?

2. Writing a dialogue is another invention strategy useful in discovering what is at stake in the issue. You invent a drama in which you discuss the issue from both sides, playing yourself as well as a devil's advocate to represent different viewpoints fairly. This technique depends on your ability to create an imaginary dialogue where you take both sides.

    To construct the dialogue, simply begin by making an assertion that expresses your view on any aspect of the issue. Then swing around and put yourself in the position of someone with an opposing viewpoint. Next, put down what you would reply as yourself. Then challenge that view by putting yourself in the frame of mind of your opponent, who views the issue from a totally different angle or perspective. The technique is an old one, used by Socrates (as reported by Plato in the *Dialogues*) to challenge people to discover whether they had good reasons for supporting their beliefs. Being cross-examined forces you to look critically at assumptions you might take for granted and pressures you to come up with reasons to support your views. Any reason able to survive objections raised by an opponent would qualify as a sound reason with which to support your belief.

You will know you are on the right track when the dialogue assumes a momentum of its own. It is important to avoid getting bogged down. If you get stuck, ask yourself a question, taking the part of the other person. You might use any of the following starters

a. I wish I could talk my (brother, sister, boyfriend, girlfriend, teacher, mother, father, etc.) into . . .

b. The last argument I had with someone was about . . .

c. Current rules at my college require . . .; I believe they should be changed in the following way . . .

d. My pet peeve regarding the use of language is . . . (for example, clothing that has slogans, logos, designer names, etc., or people who use one adjective such as "incredible" or "unbelievable" to refer to everything from a good hamburger to an attack by space aliens).

3. One of the most useful attempts to study the factors that block communication was made by the prominent psychologist Carl R. Rogers. Rogers believes that people tend to identify with their positions on issues and are not able to separate themselves from their opinions. This automatic preference for one's own opinions makes it impossible to allow oneself to even consider another point of view.

To get beyond these limitations, Rogers recommends the following exercise:

The next time you get into an argument with your wife, or your friend, or with a small group of friends, just stop the discussion for a moment and for an experiment, institute this rule. "Each person can speak up for himself only *after* he has first restated the ideas and feelings of the previous speaker accurately, and to that speaker's satisfaction." You see what this would mean. It would simply mean that before presenting your own point of view it would be necessary for you to really achieve the other speaker's frame of reference—to understand his thoughts and feelings so well that you could summarize them for him. . . . Once you have been able to see the other's point of view, your own comments will have to be drastically revised. You will also find the emotion going out of the discussion, the differences being reduced, and those differences which remain being of a rational and understandable sort.

This intriguing method of introducing some psychological perspective makes it more likely that the writer will be able to define the issue at the center of the argument in terms that reflect the values and beliefs of the audience. That is, by being able to summarize impartially an opponent's viewpoint on an issue, in language that the opponent would consider a fair restatement of the issue, the writer immeasurably increases the chances of reaching a middle ground. As Rogers observes:

> Real communication occurs and this evaluative tendency is avoided when we listen with understanding. What does that mean? It means *to see the expressed idea and attitude from the other person's point of view, to sense how it feels to him, to achieve his frame of reference in regard to the thing he is talking about.*

Write a dialogue in which you converse with someone who is no longer in your life, using the opportunity to get in touch with your true feelings toward this person. Project what the other person is saying in your dialogue.

4. How do people use jokes in conversations? Do men and women use humor differently, and who laughs at what? Draw on conversations you have engaged in or overheard to illustrate your discussion.

5. Some ads for programs to increase your vocabulary make extravagant claims about the positive consequences of enlarging one's vocabulary. Have you ever felt restrained by the size of your vocabulary? How do you think your life would change, if at all, if you had a larger vocabulary?

6. A particular kind of tone encountered in many forms of writing is called irony. Writers adopt this rhetorical strategy to express a discrepancy between opposites, between the ideal and the real, between the literal and the implied, and, most often, between the way things are and the way the writer thinks things ought to be. (Glossary: *Irony.*)

   Sometimes it is difficult to pick up the fact that not everything a writer says is intended to be taken literally. Authors will occasionally say the opposite of what they mean to catch the attention of the reader. Often the first response to an ironic statement or idea is "Can the writer really be serious?" If that is your response, look for clues meant to signal you that the writer means the opposite of what is being said.

   Which of the authors in this chapter would you consider ironic? What signals or clues tell you this?

7. Are there new styles of speech in addition to "uptalk" (identified by Gorman) and those parodied in the cartoon that follows? What are they and how are they used?

"OF THE NEARLY 1000 TEENAGERS POLLED, 48% SAID, 'TOTALLY,' 35% SAID, 'WHATEVER,' WHILE ONLY 17% SAID, 'WELL, DUH!'"

Copyright © 1997. Reprinted courtesy of Bunny Hoest and *Parade Magazine.*

8. Definition is the method of clarifying the meaning of words that are vague or ambiguous. Writers can use a variety of strategies either singly or in combination for defining terms.

One of the simplest methods of defining words is to cite a synonym—that is, another word that has the same meaning. Thus, a writer who wanted to convey the meaning of *feast* might cite a synonym such as *banquet.* By the same token, a writer who wished to communicate the meaning of *labyrinth* could use the synonym *maze.* This method is efficient and workable but cannot always be used because many words have no exact synonyms.

For a more useful way of defining terms, we need to look at the method first discussed by Aristotle in the *Topica* (one of his treatises on logic), still in use today to define terms in dictionaries.

This method, sometimes called analytical definition, puts the thing to be defined into a *genus* or general class and then gives the *differentiae,* or distinguishing features, that differentiate the subject being defined from all other things in its class with which it might be confused.

Another useful strategy for defining a term is to specify what it is not. For example, Paul Theroux in *The Old Patagonian Express* (1979) provides this definition by negation of a *good flight:*

You define a good flight by negatives: you didn't get hijacked, you didn't crash, you didn't throw up, you weren't late, you weren't nauseated by the food so you are grateful.

A negative definition does not release the writer from the responsibility of providing a positive definition of the term, but definition by negation is often a helpful first step in clearing away false assumptions.

In everyday life, arguments on a whole range of issues are really arguments about how terms ought to be defined. There are several reasons why a writer should clarify the basic nature of key terms on which an argument depends. First of all, as a practical matter, the audience must understand what the writer means by certain unfamiliar terms crucial to the argument before they can even begin seriously considering the writer's thesis or the evidence brought forward to support the claim. The writer must define ambiguous terms that might be mistaken to mean something other than what he or she intended. Otherwise, audiences may bring their own assumptions, preconceptions, and associations to the meaning of the terms in question.

Good examples are an essential part of effective writing. Nowhere is this more true than when a writer wishes to define an abstract term. Well-chosen examples are especially useful in clarifying the meaning of a term because they provide readers with a context in which to understand it. For instance, St. Paul (in I Corinthians, ch. 13) in his definition of the spiritual dimensions of love uses a range of examples, both real and hypothetical, along with synonyms and figurative language, to define a heightened state of being:

> And now I will show you the best way of all. I may speak in tongues of men or of angels, but if I am without love, I am a sounding gong or a clanging cymbal. I may have the gift of prophecy, and know every hidden truth; I may have faith strong enough to move mountains; but if I have no love, I am nothing. I may dole out all I possess, or even give my body to be burnt, but if I have no love, I am none the better. Love is patient; love is kind and envies no one. Love is never boastful, nor conceited, nor rude; never selfish, not quick to take offence. Love keeps no score of wrongs; does not gloat over other men's sins, but delights in the truth. There is nothing love cannot face; there is no limit to its faith, its hope, and its endurance. Love will never come to an end. Are these prophets? their work will be over. Are there tongues of ecstasy? they will cease. Is there knowledge? it will vanish away; for our knowledge and our prophecy alike are partial, and the partial vanishes when wholeness comes. When I was a child my speech, my outlook, and my thoughts were all childish. When I grew up, I had finished with childish things. Now we see only puzzling reflections in a mirror, but then we shall see face to face. My knowledge now is partial; then it will be whole, like God's knowledge of me. In a word, there are three things that last for ever: faith, hope, and love; but the greatest of them all is love.

Modern readers might recognize this as a current translation from the New English Bible. In the past, the translation of this same passage in the King James Version of the Bible renders the same word (*agape* in Greek) as *charity*. Without Paul's powerful examples, it would be difficult to see what he means by *love*. The examples broaden the range of associations and make the meaning of the term resonate through specific cases. Paul's definition of love suggests a spiritual depth and richness that goes far beyond what most people normally associate with the term.

Write an essay in which you draw on any of the above methods to define a term of your own choosing (for example, the overused prefix "cyber" from the Greek *kybernan*, "to steer" or "govern," in any of its hybrid manifestations).

A man's command of the language is
most important. Next to kissing, it's the
most exciting form of communication
mankind has evolved.

—Oren Arnold

"I assume, then, that you regard yourself as omniscient.
If I am wrong, correct me!"

Communication Between the Sexes

The authors in this chapter examine how men and women use language to achieve different, often conflicting objectives. The use of language to establish and confirm one's identity within a group is a clear way in which we identify ourselves. Why language should serve a different purpose for men and women to the point where neither sex understands what the other is saying begins, according to Robin Lakoff's pioneering study "Language and Woman's Place," in childhood. Lakoff shows how boys and girls learn to speak in entirely different ways as part of the process by which they are educated and socialized. Not surprisingly, the radically different agendas language is intended to serve for men and women result in entirely different styles of communication whose consequent misunderstandings are examined by Deborah Tannen in "Sex, Lies, and Conversation." The consequences of men and women using language to achieve entirely different goals becomes especially apparent when we look at the special language of courtship. This specialized form of communication between the sexes is rife with misrepresentations and misinterpretations. In the personal ads we place in newspapers and magazines to attract members of the opposite sex (discussed by Lance Morrow in "Advertisements for Oneself"), in the guidelines for what women should say and more pointedly not say to get husbands (Sherrie Schneider and Ellen Fein, "Rule 19: Don't Open Up Too Fast"), and in the unspoken reservations of Linda Stasi ("Your First Date"), the gulf between men's and women's use of language and the way things appear and the way they really are is enormous.

Perhaps the most pernicious consequence of the way men and women misinterpret each other is how this misperception leads to rigidified stereotyped misrepresentations of both genders. Jane Tompkins, in "Women and the Language of Men," reveals how the social roles into which men and women were cast in frontier society legitimized these stereotyped gender roles as a result of hostility toward language that embodied the "decadent" East. The flip side of the coin—that is, the use of language to discriminate against men—is thoroughly explored by Eugene R. August in "Real Men Don't, or Anti-Male Bias in English." August asserts that anti-male prejudice in language is as pervasive, albeit unrecognized, as the use of language to demean women. Each of the essays in this chapter attests to the enormous power language has in validating who we are as men and women and warns us against becoming prisoners of the stereotypes we sanction through the language we use.

Language and Woman's Place

Robin Lakoff

◆ ROBIN TOLMACH LAKOFF is a professor of linguistics at the University of California at Berkeley. Her pioneering studies of language, gender, and power include *Face Value: The Politics of Beauty* (1984, with Raquel Scherr), *Talking Power: The Politics of Language* (1990), and the groundbreaking *Language and Woman's Place* (1975), from which the following selection is taken.

Although it won't come as much of a surprise to learn that little girls are expected to be more polite than boys, what is unexpected, according to Lakoff, is the extent to which women's language acts to keep women from being taken seriously as adults. Lakoff's pioneering research showed that the different ways in which boys and girls are socialized and the very different expectations for each sex are reflected in their typical speech patterns. The resulting impression of hesitancy in women's language—as though the speaker were waiting confirmation—tends to undercut confidence in the speaker's ability. These styles of deference by women and assertion by men lead, in Lakoff's view, to lifelong inequitites between the sexes.

TO CONSIDER   When you were growing up, were you ever told that different styles of speech were expected from girls as opposed to boys?

If a little girl 'talks rough' like a boy, she will normally be ostracized, scolded, or made fun of. In this way society, in the form of a child's parents and friends, keeps her in line, in her place. This socializing process is, in most of its aspects, harmless and often necessary, but in this particular instance—the teaching of special linguistic uses to little girls—it raises serious problems, though the teachers may well be unaware of this. If the little girl learns her lesson well, she is not rewarded with unquestioned acceptance on the part of society; rather, the acquisition of this special style of speech will later be an excuse others use to keep her in a demeaning position, to refuse to take her seriously as a human being. Because of the way she speaks, the little girl—now grown to womanhood—will be accused of being unable to speak precisely or to express herself forcefully.

I am sure that the preceding paragraph contains an oversimplified description of the language-learning process in American society. Rather than saying that little boys and little girls, from the very start, learn two different ways of speaking, I think, from observation and reports by others, that the process is more complicated. Since the mother and other women are the dominant influences in the lives of most children under the age of 5, probably both boys and girls first learn 'women's language' as their first language. (I am told that in Japanese, children of both sexes use the particles proper for women until the age of 5 or so; then the little boy starts to be ridiculed if he uses them, and so soon learns to desist.) As they grow older, boys especially go through a stage of rough talk, as described by Spock and others; this is probably discouraged in little girls more strongly than in little boys, in whom parents may often find it more amusing than shocking. By the time children are 10 or so, and split up into same-sex peer groups, the two languages are already present, according to my recollections and observations. But it seems that what has happened is that the boys have unlearned their original form of expression and adopted new forms of expression, while the girls retain their old ways of speech. (One wonders whether this is related in any way to the often-noticed fact that little boys innovate, in their play, much more than little girls.) The ultimate result is the same, of course, whatever the interpretation.

So a girl is damned if she does, damned if she doesn't. If she refuses to talk like a lady, she is ridiculed and subjected to criticism as unfeminine; if she does learn, she is ridiculed as unable to think clearly, unable to take part in a serious discussion: in some sense, as less than fully human. These two choices which a woman has—to be less than a woman or less than a person—are highly painful.

An objection may be raised here that I am overstating the case against women's language, since most women who get as far as college learn to switch from women's to neutral language under appropriate situations (in class, talking to professors, at job interviews, and such). But I think this objection overlooks a number of problems. First, if a girl must learn two dialects, she becomes in effect a bilingual. Like many bilinguals, she may never really be master of either language, though her command of both is adequate enough for most purposes, she may never feel really comfortable using either, and never be certain that she is using the right one in the right place to the right person. Shifting from one language to another requires special awareness to the nuances of social situations, special alertness to possible disapproval. It may be that the extra energy that must be (subconsciously or otherwise) expended in this game is energy sapped from more creative work, and hinders women from expressing themselves as well, as fully, or as freely as they might otherwise. Thus, if a girl knows that a professor will be receptive to comments that sound scholarly, objective, unemotional, she will of course be tempted to use neutral language in class or in conference. But if she knows that, as a man, he will respond more approvingly to her at other levels if she uses women's language, and sounds frilly and feminine, won't she be confused as well as sorely tempted in two directions at once? It is often noticed that women participate less in class discussion than men—perhaps this linguistic indecisiveness is one reason why. (Incidentally, I don't find this true in my classes.)

It will be found that the overall effect of 'women's language'—meaning both language restricted in use to women and language descriptive of women alone—is this: it submerges a woman's personal identity, by denying her the means of expressing herself strongly, on the one hand, and encouraging expressions that suggest triviality in subject matter and uncertainty about it; and, when a woman is being discussed, by treating her as an object—sexual or otherwise—but never a serious person with individual views. Of course, other forms of behaviour in this society have the same purpose; but the phenomena seem especially clear linguistically.

The ultimate effect of these discrepancies is that women are systematically denied access to power, on the grounds that they are not capable of holding it as demonstrated by their linguistic behaviour along with other aspects of their behaviour; and the irony here is that women are made to feel that they deserve such treatment, because of inadequacies in their own intelligence and/or education. But in fact it is precisely because women have learned their lessons so well that they later suffer such discrimination. (This situation is of course true to some extent for all disadvantaged groups: white males of Anglo-Saxon descent set the standards and seem to expect other groups to be respectful of them but not to adopt them—they are to 'keep in their place'.)

TALKING LIKE A LADY

'Women's language' shows up in all levels of the grammar of English. We find differences in the choice and frequency of lexical items; in the situations in which certain syntactic rules are performed; in intonational and other supersegmental patterns. As an example of lexical differences, imagine a man and a woman both looking at the same wall, painted a pinkish shade of purple. The woman may say (1):

(1) The wall is mauve,

with no one consequently forming any special impression of her as a result of the words alone; but if the man should say (1), one might well conclude he was imitating a woman sarcastically, or was a homosexual, or an interior decorator. Women, then, make far more precise discriminations in naming colours than do men; words like *beige, ecru, aquamarine, lavender,* and so on are unremarkable in a woman's active vocabulary, but absent from that of most men. I have seen a man helpless with suppressed laughter at a discussion between two other people as to whether a book jacket was to be described as 'lavender' or 'mauve'. Men find such discussion amusing because they consider such a question trivial, irrelevant to the real world.

We might ask why fine discrimination of colour is relevant for women, but not for men. A clue is contained in the way many men in our society view other 'unworldly' topics, such as high culture and the church, as outside the world of men's work, relegated to women and men whose masculinity is not unquestionable. Men tend to relegate to women things that are not of concern to them, or do not involve their egos. Among these are problems of fine colour discrimination. We might rephrase this point by saying that since women are not expected to make decisions on important matters, such as what kind of job to hold, they are relegated the non-crucial decisions as a sop. Deciding whether to name a colour 'lavender' or 'mauve' is one such sop.

If it is agreed that this lexical disparity reflects a social inequity in the position of women, one may ask how to remedy it. Obviously, no one could seriously recommend legislating against the use of the terms 'mauve' and 'lavender' by women, or forcing men to learn to use them. All we can do is give women the opportunity to participate in the real decisions of life.

Aside from specific lexical items like colour names, we find differences between the speech of women and that of men in the use of particles that grammarians often describe as 'meaningless'. There may be no referent for them, but they are far from meaningless: they define the social context of an utterance, indicate the relationship the speaker feels between himself and his addressee, between himself and what he is talking about.

As an experiment, one might present native speakers of standard American English with pairs of sentences, identical syntactically and in terms of referential lexical items, and differing merely in the choice of 'meaningless' particle, and ask them which was spoken by a man, which a woman. Consider:

(2) *a* Oh dear, you've put the peanut butter in the refrigerator again.

  b Shit, you've put the peanut butter in the refrigerator again.

It is safe to predict that people would classify the first sentence as part of 'women's language', the second as 'men's language'. It is true that many self-respecting women are becoming able to use sentences like (2)*b* publicly without flinching, but this is a relatively recent development, and while perhaps the majority of Middle America might condone the use of *b* for men, they would still disapprove of its use by women. (It is of interest, by the way, to note that men's language is increasingly being used by women, but women's language is not being adopted by men, apart from those who reject the American masculine image (for example, homosexuals). This is analogous to the fact that men's jobs are being sought by women, but few men are rushing to become housewives or secretaries. The language of the favoured group, the group that holds the power, along with its non-linguistic behaviour, is generally adopted by the other group, not vice versa. In any event, it is a truism to state that the 'stronger' expletives are reserved for men, and the 'weaker' ones for women.)

Now we may ask what we mean by 'stronger' and 'weaker' expletives. (If these particles were indeed meaningless, none would be stronger than any other.) The difference between using 'shit' (or 'damn', or one of many others) as opposed to 'oh dear', or 'goodness', or 'oh fudge' lies in how forcefully one says how one feels—perhaps, one might say, choice of particle is a function of how strongly one allows oneself to feel about something, so that the strength of an emotion conveyed in a sentence corresponds to the strength of the particle. Hence in a really serious situation, the use of 'trivializing' (that is, 'women's') particles constitutes a joke, or at any rate is highly inappropriate. (In conformity with current linguistic practice, throughout this work an (*) will be used to mark a sentence that is inappropriate in some sense, either because it is syntactically deviant or used in the wrong social context.)

(3) *a* *Oh fudge, my hair is on fire.

    b *Dear me, did he kidnap the baby?

As children, women are encouraged to be 'little ladies'. Little ladies don't scream as vociferously as little boys, and they are chastised more severely for throwing tantrums or showing temper: 'high spirits' are expected and therefore tolerated in little boys; docility and resignation are the corresponding traits expected of little girls. Now, we tend to excuse a show of temper by a man where we would not excuse an identical tirade from a woman: women are allowed to fuss and complain, but only a man can bellow in rage. It is sometimes claimed that there is a biological basis for this behaviour difference, though I don't believe conclusive evidence exists that the early differences in behaviour that have been observed are not the result of very different treatment of babies of the two sexes from the beginning; but surely the use of different particles by men and women is a learned trait, merely mirroring non-linguistic differences again, and again pointing out an inequity that exists between the treatment of men, and society's expectations of them, and the treatment of women. Allowing men stronger means of expression than are open to women further reinforces men's position of strength in the real world: for surely we listen with more attention the more strongly and forcefully someone expresses opinions, and a speaker unable—for whatever reason—to be forceful in stating his views is much less likely to be taken seriously. Ability to use strong particles like 'shit' and 'hell' is, of course, only incidental to the inequity that exists rather than its cause. But once again, apparently accidental linguistic usage suggests that women are denied equality partially for linguistic reasons, and that an examination of language points up precisely an area in which inequity exists. Further, if someone is allowed to show emotions, and consequently does, others may well be able to view him as a real individual in his own right, as they could not if he never showed emotion. Here again, then, the behaviour a woman learns as 'correct' prevents her from being taken seriously as an individual, and further is considered 'correct' and necessary for a woman precisely because society does *not* consider her seriously as an individual.

Similar sorts of disparities exist elsewhere in the vocabulary. There is, for instance, a group of adjectives which have, besides their specific and literal meanings, another use, that of indicating the speaker's approbation or admiration for something. Some of these adjectives are neutral as to sex of speaker: either men or women may use them. But another set seems, in its figurative use, to be largely confined to women's speech. Representative lists of both types are below:

Neutral	*Women only*
great	adorable
terrific	charming
cool	sweet
neat	lovely
	divine

As with the colour words and swear words already discussed, for a man to stray into the 'women's' column is apt to be damaging to his reputation, though here a woman may freely use the neutral words. But it should not be inferred from this that a woman's use of the 'women's' words is without its risks. Where a woman has a choice between the neutral words and the women's words, as a man has not, she may be suggesting very different things about her own personality and her view of the subject-matter by her choice of words of the first set or words of the second.

(4) *a* What a terrific idea!
　　b What a divine idea!

It seems to me that *a* might be used under any appropriate conditions by a female speaker. But *b* is more restricted. Probably it is used appropriately (even by the sort of speaker for whom it was normal) only in case the speaker feels the idea referred to to be essentially frivolous, trivial, or unimportant to the world at large—only an amusement for the speaker herself. Consider, then, a woman advertising executive at an advertising conference. However feminine an advertising executive she is, she is much more likely to express her approval with (4)*a* than with *b*, which might cause raised eyebrows, and the reaction: 'That's what we get for putting a woman in charge of this company.'

On the other hand, suppose a friend suggests to the same woman that she should dye her French poodles to match her cigarette lighter. In this case, the suggestion really concerns only her, and the impression she will make on people. In this case, she may use b, from the 'women's language'. So the choice is not really free: words restricted to 'women's language' suggest that concepts to which they are applied are not relevant to the real world of (male) influence and power.

One may ask whether there really are no analogous terms that are available to men—terms that denote approval of the trivial, the personal; that express approbation in terms of one's own personal emotional reaction, rather than by gauging the likely general reaction. There does in fact seem to be one such word: it is the hippie invention 'groovy', which seems to have most of the connotations that separate 'lovely' and 'divine' from 'great' and 'terrific' excepting only that it does not mark the speaker as feminine or effeminate.

(5) *a* What a terrific steel mill!
    b *What a lovely steel mill! (male speaking)
    c What a groovy steel mill!

I think it is significant that this word was introduced by the hippies, and, when used seriously rather than sarcastically, used principally by people who have accepted the hippies' values. Principal among these is the denial of the Protestant work ethic: to a hippie, something can be worth thinking about even if it isn't influential in the power structure, or money-making. Hippies are separated from the activities of the real world just as women are—though in the former case it is due to a decision on their parts, while this is not uncontroversially true in the case of women. For both these groups, it is possible to express approval of things in a personal way—though one does so at the risk of losing one's credibility with members of the power structure. It is also true, according to some speakers, that upper-class British men may use the words listed in the 'women's' column, as well as the specific colour words and others we have categorized as specifically feminine, without raising doubts as to their masculinity among other speakers of the same dialect. (This is not true for lower-class Britons, however.) The reason may be that commitment to the work ethic need not necessarily be displayed: one may be or appear to be a gentleman of leisure, interested in various pursuits, but not involved in mundane (business or political) affairs, in such a culture, without incurring disgrace. This is rather analogous to the position of a woman in American middle-class society, so we should not be surprised if these special lexical items are usable by both groups. This fact points indeed to a more general conclusion. These words aren't, basically, 'feminine'; rather, they signal 'uninvolved', or 'out of power'. Any group in a society to which these labels are applicable may presumably use these words; they are often considered 'feminine', 'unmasculine', because women are the 'uninvolved', 'out of power' group *par excellence*.

Another group that has, ostensibly at least, taken itself out of the search for power and money is that of academic men. They are frequently viewed by other groups as analogous in some ways to women—they don't really work, they are supported in their frivolous pursuits by others, what they do doesn't really count in the real world, and so on. The suburban home finds its counterpart in the ivory tower: one is supposedly shielded from harsh realities in both. Therefore it is not too surprising that many academic men (especially those who emulate British norms) may violate many of these sacrosanct rules I have just laid down: they often use 'women's language'. Among themselves, this does not occasion ridicule. But to a truck driver, a professor saying 'What a lovely hat!' is undoubtedly laughable, all the more so as it reinforces his stereotype of professors as effete snobs.

When we leave the lexicon and venture into syntax, we find that syntactically too women's speech is peculiar. To my knowledge, there is no syntactic rule in English that only women may use. But there is at least one rule that a woman will use in more conversational situations than a man. (This fact indicates, of course, that the applicability of syntactic rules is governed partly by social context—the positions in society of the speaker and addressee, with respect to each other, and the impression one seeks to make on the other.) This is the rule of tag-question formation.[1]

A tag, in its usage as well as its syntactic shape (in English) is midway between an outright statement and a yes-no question: it is less assertive than the former, but more confident than the latter. Therefore it is usable under certain contextual situations: not those in which a statement would be appropriate, nor those in which a yes—no question is generally used, but in situations intermediate between these.

One makes a statement when one has confidence in his knowledge and is pretty certain that his statement will be believed; one asks a question when one lacks knowledge on some point and has reason to believe that this gap can and will be remedied by an answer by the addressee. A tag question, being intermediate between these, is used when the speaker is stating a claim, but lacks full confidence in the truth of that claim. So if I say

(6) Is John here?

I will probably not be surprised if my respondent answers 'no'; but if I say

(7) John is here, isn't he?

instead, chances are I am already biased in favour of a positive answer, wanting only confirmation by the addressee. I still want a response from him, as I do with a yes-no question; but I have enough knowledge (or think I have) to predict that response, much as with a declarative statement. A tag question, then, might be thought of as a declarative statement without the assumption that the statement is to be believed by the addressee: one has an out, as with a question. A tag gives the addressee leeway, not forcing him to go along with the views of the speaker.

There are situations in which a tag is legitimate, in fact the only legitimate sentence form. So, for example, if I have seen something only indistinctly, and have reason to believe my addressee had a better view, I can say:

(8) I had my glasses off. He was out at third, wasn't he?

Sometimes we find a tag question used in cases in which the speaker knows as well as the addressee what the answer must be, and doesn't need confirmation. One such situation is when the speaker is making 'small talk', trying to elicit conversation from the addressee;

(9) Sure is hot here, isn't it?

In discussing personal feelings or opinions, only the speaker normally has any way of knowing the correct answer. Strictly speaking, questioning one's own opinions is futile. Sentences like (10) are usually ridiculous.

(10) *I have a headache, don't I?

But similar cases do, apparently, exist, in which it is the speaker's opinions, rather than perceptions, for which corroboration is sought, as in (11):

(11) The way prices are rising is horrendous, isn't it?

While there are of course other possible interpretations of a sentence like this, one possibility is that the speaker has a particular answer in mind—'yes' or 'no'—but is reluctant to state it baldly. It is my impression, though I do not have precise statistical evidence, that this sort of tag question is much more apt to be used by women than by men. If this is indeed true, why is it true?

These sentence types provide a means whereby a speaker can avoid committing himself, and thereby avoid coming into conflict with the addressee. The problem is that, by so doing, a speaker may also give the impression of not being really sure of himself, of looking to the addressee for confirmation, even of having no views of his own. This last criticism is, of course, one often levelled at women. One wonders how much of it reflects a use of language that has been imposed on women from their earliest years.

Related to this special use of a syntactic rule is a widespread difference perceptible in women's intonational patterns.[2] There is a peculiar sentence intonation pattern, found in English as far as I know only among women, which has the form of a declarative answer to a question, and is used as such, but has the rising inflection typical of a yes-no question, as well as being especially hesitant. The effect is as though one were seeking confirmation, though at the same time the speaker may be the only one who has the requisite information.

(12) *a* When will dinner be ready?
     b Oh . . . around six o'clock . . . ?

It is as though *b* were saying, 'Six o'clock, if that's OK with you, if you agree.' *a* is put in the position of having to provide confirmation, and *b* sounds unsure. Here we find unwillingness to assert an opinion carried to an extreme. One likely consequence is that these sorts of speech patterns are taken to reflect something real about character and play a part in not taking a woman seriously or trusting her with any real responsibilities, since 'she can't make up her mind' and 'isn't sure of herself'. And here again we see that people form judgements about other people on the basis of superficial linguistic behaviour that may have nothing to do with inner character, but has been imposed upon the speaker, on pain of worse punishment than not being taken seriously.

Such features are probably part of the general fact that women's speech sounds much more 'polite' than men's. One aspect of politeness is as we have just described: leaving a decision open, not imposing your mind, or views, or claims on anyone else. Thus a tag question is a kind of polite statement, in that it does not force agreement or belief on the addressee. A request may be in the same sense a polite command, in that it does not overtly require obedience, but rather suggests something be done as a favour to the speaker. An overt order (as in an imperative) expresses the (often impolite) assumption of the speaker's superior position to the addressee, carrying with it the right to enforce compliance, whereas with a request the decision on the face of it is left up to the addressee. (The same is true of suggestions: here, the implication is not that the addressee is in danger if he does not comply—merely that he will be glad if he does. Once again, the decision is up to the addressee, and a suggestion therefore is politer than an order.) The more particles in a sentence that reinforce the notion that it is a request, rather than an order, the politer the result. The sentences of 13 illustrate these points: (13)*a* is a direct order, *b* and *c* simple requests, and *d* and *e* compound requests.[3]

(13) *a* Close the door.
    b Please close the door.
    c Will you close the door?
    d Will you please close the door?
    e Won't you close the door?

Let me first explain why *e* has been classified as a compound request. (A sentence like *Won't you please close the door* would then count as a doubly compound request.) A sentence like (13)*c* is close in sense to 'Are you willing to close the door?' According to the normal rules of polite conversation, to agree that you are willing is to agree to do the thing asked of you. Hence this apparent enquiry functions as a request, leaving the decision up to the willingness of the addressee. Phrasing it as a positive question makes the (implicit) assumption that a 'yes' answer will be forthcoming. Sentence (13)*d* is more polite than *b* or *c* because it combines them: *please* indicating that to accede will be to do something for the speaker, and *will you*, as noted, suggesting that the addressee has the final decision. If, now, the question is phrased with a negative, as in (13)*e*, the speaker seems to suggest the stronger likelihood of a negative response from the addressee. Since the assumption is then that the addressee is that much freer to refuse, (13)*e* acts as a more polite request than (13)*c* or *d*: *c* and *d* put the burden of refusal on the addressee, as e does not.

Given these facts, one can see the connection between tag questions and tag orders and other requests. In all these cases, the speaker is not committed as with a simple declarative or affirmative. And the more one compounds a request, the more characteristic it is of women's speech, the less of men's. A sentence that begins *Won't you please* (without special emphasis on *please*) seems to me at least to have a distinctly unmasculine sound. Little girls are indeed taught to talk like little ladies, in that their speech is in many ways more polite than that of boys or men, and the reason for this is that politeness involves an absence of a strong statement, and women's speech is devised to prevent the expression of strong statements.

NOTES

1. Within the lexicon itself, there seems to be a parallel phenomenon to tag-question usage, which I refrain from discussing in the body of the text because the facts are controversial and I do not understand them fully. The intensive *so,* used where purists would insist upon an absolute superlative, heavily stressed, seems more characteristic of women's language than of men's, though it is found in the latter, particularly in the speech of male academics. Consider, for instance, the following sentences:

a   I feel *so* unhappy!

b   That movie made me *so* sick!

Men seem to have the least difficulty using this construction when the sentence is unemotional, or non-subjective—without reference to the speaker himself:

c   That sunset is *so* beautiful!

d   Fred is *so* dumb!

Substituting an equative like *so* for absolute superlatives (like *very, really, utterly*) seems to be a way of backing out of committing oneself strongly to an opinion, rather like tag questions. One might hedge in this way with perfect right in making aesthetic judgements, as in *c*, or intellectual judgements, as in *d*. But it is somewhat odd to hedge in describing one's own mental or emotional state: who, after all, is qualified to contradict one on this? To hedge in this situation is to seek to avoid making any strong statement: a characteristic, as we have noted already and shall note further, of women's speech.

2. For analogues outside of English to these uses of tag questions and special intonation patterns, see my discussion of Japanese particles in 'Language in context', *Language,* 48 (1972), pp. 907–27. It is to be expected that similar cases will be found in many other languages as well. See, for example, M. R. Haas's very interesting discussion of differences between men's and women's speech (mostly involving lexical dissimilarities) in many languages, in D. Hymes (ed.) *Language in Culture and Society* (New York: Harper & Row 1964).

3. For more detailed discussion of these problems, see Lakoff, 'Language in context'.

---

1 According to Lakoff, what are the features of "women's language"? How are women viewed who use this language? What double-bind confronts women who learn to "switch from women's to neutral language under appropriate situations" (para. 4)?

2 How is the way women talk as adults a result of an entirely different socializing process they undergo as children when compared with how boys are brought up?

3 Lakoff's analysis rests on the assumption of a fundamental inequity in power between the sexes. Do your own observations of current male and female speech patterns suggest that things have changed considerably since Lakoff wrote this in 1975? Are standards governing what is considered polite and what is considered direct now different? If so, in what way?

4 How does Lakoff's analysis depend on pointing out significant contrasts between the way men and women speak (for example, "Oh dear, you've put the peanut butter in the refrigerator again" versus "Shit, you've put the peanut butter in the refrigerator again") and the effects of the different connotations in the words each uses ("great" versus "adorable")? (Glossary: *Comparison and Contrast, Connotation, Denotation.*)

5 In Lakoff's analysis of the way men and women use language, which causes are more important than others? That is, which are the primary and which are the secondary? To what extent is her analysis intended to correct a number of commonly held but mistaken views by disclosing what she perceives to be the actual causes and real effects of differences in the ways men and women express themselves? (Glossary: *Cause and Effect.*)

6 Recall some conversations you heard during your childhood and teenage years between your parents regarding how you were to be raised. To what extent did their different perspectives demonstrate the differences between how the sexes perceive problems and communicate?

Sex, Lies, and Conversation

Deborah Tannen

♦ DEBORAH TANNEN currently teaches linguistics at Georgetown University. She has written and edited several scholarly books on the difficulties of communicating across cultural, class, ethnic, and sexual boundaries. She has also presented her research to the general public in such best-selling books as *That's Not What I Meant!* (1986) and *You Just Don't Understand: Women and Men in Conversation* (1990). "Sex, Lies, and Conversation" originally appeared in the *Washington Post* (1990).

After learning from Robin Lakoff how different expectations for girls and boys lead to different patterns of speech, with the resulting inequities in deference and authority and in who speaks and who listens, Tannen's discoveries will seem inevitable. The goal of speech is to bring people together and not to exacerbate what separates them, yet, as Tannen points out, conversations between men and women all too often break down and leave the participants at cross-purposes. Why this is often the case is the subject of Tannen's research. It is not only that men tend to interrupt women more than vice versa, or that men introduce subjects that become topics of conversation more frequently than those suggested by women, or that women work much harder to keep conversations going than do men, but that men and women talk for entirely different reasons: Men use conversation to establish, maintain, and confirm their status; women talk to foster intimacy and closeness. The means each uses flow from these different objectives. Men provide information and joust as though a conversation were a competitive sport, while women use self-revelation to bond with each other. Neither of these objectives has much in common with the other, and it is not surprising, says Tannen, that during conversations men become frustrated and women become bored.

> **TO CONSIDER**   What differences in speech styles define the ways women express themselves as opposed to how men talk? Do men and women talk about different things? Do you notice these differences, especially in conversations when men and women are talking about the same subject?

1   I was addressing a small gathering in a suburban Virginia living room—a women's group that had invited men to join them. Throughout the evening, one man had been particularly talkative, frequently offering ideas and anecdotes, while his wife sat silently beside him on the couch. Toward the end of the evening, I commented that women frequently complain that their husbands don't talk to them. This man quickly concurred. He gestured toward his wife and said, "She's the talker in our family." The room burst into laughter; the man looked puzzled and hurt. "It's true," he explained. "When I come home from work I have nothing to say. If she didn't keep the conversation going, we'd spend the whole evening in silence."

2   This episode crystallizes the irony that although American men tend to talk more than women in public situations, they often talk less at home. And this pattern is wreaking havoc with marriage.

3   The pattern was observed by political scientist Andrew Hacker in the late '70s. Sociologist Catherine Kohler Riessman reports in her new book *Divorce Talk* that most of the women she interviewed—but only a few of the men—gave lack of communication as the reason for their divorces. Given the current divorce rate of nearly 50 percent, that amounts to millions of cases in the United States every year—a virtual epidemic of failed conversation.

In my own research, complaints from women about their husbands most 4
often focused not on tangible inequities such as having given up the chance for
a career to accompany a husband to his, or doing far more than their share of
daily life-support work like cleaning, cooking, social arrangements and errands.
Instead, they focused on communication: "He doesn't listen to me," "He
doesn't talk to me." I found, as Hacker observed years before, that most wives
want their husbands to be, first and foremost, conversational partners, but few
husbands share this expectation of their wives.

In short, the image that best represents the current crisis is the stereotypical 5
cartoon scene of a man sitting at the breakfast table with a newspaper held up in
front of his face, while a woman glares at the back of it, wanting to talk.

LINGUISTIC BATTLE OF THE SEXES

How can women and men have such different impressions of communication in 6
marriage? Why the widespread imbalance in their interests and expectations?

In the April issue of *American Psychologist,* Stanford University's Eleanor 7
Maccoby reports the results of her own and others' research showing that children's development is most influenced by the social structure of peer interactions. Boys and girls tend to play with children of their own gender, and their
sex-separate groups have different organizational structures and interactive
norms.

I believe these systematic differences in childhood socialization make talk 8
between women and men like cross-cultural communication, heir to all the
attraction and pitfalls of that enticing but difficult enterprise. My research on
men's and women's conversations uncovered patterns similar to those described
for children's groups.

For women, as for girls, intimacy is the fabric of relationships, and talk is the 9
thread from which it is woven. Little girls create and maintain friendships by
exchanging secrets; similarly, women regard conversation as the cornerstone of
friendship. So a woman expects her husband to be a new and improved version
of a best friend. What is important is not the individual subjects that are discussed but the sense of closeness, of a life shared, that emerges when people tell
their thoughts, feelings, and impressions.

Bonds between boys can be as intense as girls', but they are based less on 10
talking, more on doing things together. Since they don't assume talk is the
cement that binds a relationship, men don't know what kind of talk women
want, and they don't miss it when it isn't there.

Boys' groups are larger, more inclusive, and more hierarchical, so boys must 11
struggle to avoid the subordinate position in the group. This may play a role in
women's complaints that men don't listen to them. Some men really don't like
to listen, because being the listener makes them feel one-down, like a child listening to adults or an employee to a boss.

But often when women tell men, "You aren't listening," and the men 12
protest, "I am," the men are right. The impression of not listening results from

misalignments in the mechanics of conversation. The misalignment begins as soon as a man and a woman take physical positions. This became clear when I studied videotapes made by psychologist Bruce Dorval of children and adults talking to their same-sex best friends. I found that at every age, the girls and women faced each other directly, their eyes anchored on each other's faces. At every age, the boys and men sat at angles to each other and looked elsewhere in the room, periodically glancing at each other. They were obviously attuned to each other, often mirroring each other's movements. But the tendency of men to face away can give women the impression they aren't listening even when they are. A young woman in college was frustrated: Whenever she told her boyfriend she wanted to talk to him, he would lie down on the floor, close his eyes, and put his arm over his face. This signaled to her, "He's taking a nap." But he insisted he was listening extra hard. Normally, he looks around the room, so he is easily distracted. Lying down and covering his eyes helped him concentrate on what she was saying.

13   Analogous to the physical alignment that women and men take in conversation is their topical alignment. The girls in my study tended to talk at length about one topic, but the boys tended to jump from topic to topic. The second-grade girls exchanged stories about people they knew. The second-grade boys teased, told jokes, noticed things in the room and talked about finding games to play. The sixth-grade girls talked about problems with a mutual friend. The sixth-grade boys talked about 55 different topics, none of which extended over more than a few turns.

LISTENING TO BODY LANGUAGE

14   Switching topics is another habit that gives women the impression men aren't listening, especially if they switch to a topic about themselves. But the evidence of the 10th-grade boys in my study indicates otherwise. The 10th-grade boys sprawled across their chairs with bodies parallel and eyes straight ahead, rarely looking at each other. They looked as if they were riding in a car, staring out the windshield. But they were talking about their feelings. One boy was upset because a girl had told him he had a drinking problem, and the other was feeling alienated from all his friends.

15   Now, when a girl told a friend about a problem, the friend responded by asking probing questions and expressing agreement and understanding. But the boys dismissed each other's problems. Todd assured Richard that his drinking was "no big problem" because "sometimes you're funny when you're off your butt." And when Todd said he felt left out, Richard responded, "Why should you? You know more people than me."

16   Women perceive such responses as belittling and unsupportive. But the boys seemed satisfied with them. Whereas women reassure each other by implying, "You shouldn't feel bad because I've had similar experiences," men do so by implying, "You shouldn't feel bad because your problems aren't so bad."

17   There are even simpler reasons for women's impression that men don't listen. Linguist Lynette Hirschman found that women make more listener-noise,

such as "mhm," "uhuh," and "yeah," to show "I'm with you." Men, she found, more often give silent attention. Women who expect a stream of listener-noise interpret silent attention as no attention at all.

Women's conversational habits are as frustrating to men as men's are to women. Men who expect silent attention interpret a stream of listener-noise as overreaction or impatience. Also, when women talk to each other in a close, comfortable setting, they often overlap, finish each other's sentences and anticipate what the other is about to say. This practice, which I call "participatory listenership," is often perceived by men as interruption, intrusion and lack of attention. [18]

A parallel difference caused a man to complain about his wife, "She just wants to talk about her own point of view. If I show her another view, she gets mad at me." When most women talk to each other, they assume a conversationalist's job is to express agreement and support. But many men see their conversational duty as pointing out the other side of an argument. This is heard as disloyalty by women, and refusal to offer the requisite support. It is not that women don't want to see other points of view, but that they prefer them phrased as suggestions and inquiries rather than as direct challenges. [19]

In his book *Fighting for Life,* Walter Ong points out that men use "agonistic" or warlike, oppositional formats to do almost anything; thus discussion becomes debate, and conversation a competitive sport. In contrast, women see conversation as a ritual means of establishing rapport. If Jane tells a problem and June says she has a similar one, they walk away feeling closer to each other. But this attempt at establishing rapport can backfire when used with men. Men take too literally women's ritual "troubles talk," just as women mistake men's ritual challenges for real attack. [20]

THE SOUNDS OF SILENCE

These differences begin to clarify why women and men have such different expectations about communication in marriage. For women, talk creates intimacy. Marriage is an orgy of closeness: you can tell your feelings and thoughts, and still be loved. Their greatest fear is being pushed away. But men live in a hierarchical world, where talk maintains independence and status. They are on guard to protect themselves from being put down and pushed around. [21]

This explains the paradox of the talkative man who said of his silent wife, "She's the talker." In the public setting of a guest lecture, he felt challenged to show his intelligence and display his understanding of the lecture. But at home, where he has nothing to prove and no one to defend against, he is free to remain silent. For his wife, being home means she is free from the worry that something she says might offend someone, or spark disagreement, or appear to be showing off; at home she is free to talk. [22]

The communication problems that endanger marriage can't be fixed by mechanical engineering. They require a new conceptual framework about the role of talk in human relationships. Many of the psychological explanations that have become second nature may not be helpful, because they tend to blame [23] either women (for not being assertive enough) or men (for not being in touch with their feelings). A sociolinguistic approach by which male-female conversation is seen as cross-cultural communication allows us to understand the problem and forge solutions without blaming either party.

24   Once the problem is understood, improvement comes naturally, as it did to the young woman and her boyfriend who seemed to go to sleep when she wanted to talk. Previously, she had accused him of not listening, and he had refused to change his behavior, since that would be admitting fault. But then she learned about and explained to him the differences in women's and men's habitual ways of aligning themselves in conversation. The next time she told him she wanted to talk, he began, as usual, by lying down and covering his eyes. When the familiar negative reaction bubbled up, she reassured herself that he really was listening. But then he sat up and looked at her. Thrilled, she asked why. He said, "You like me to look at you when we talk, so I'll try to do it." Once he saw their differences as cross-cultural rather than right and wrong, he independently altered his behavior.

25   Women who feel abandoned and deprived when their husbands won't listen to or report daily news may be happy to discover their husbands trying to adapt once they understand the place of small talk in women's relationships. But if their husbands don't adapt, the women may still be comforted that for men, this is not a failure of intimacy. Accepting the difference, the wives may look to their friends or family for that kind of talk. And husbands who can't provide it shouldn't feel their wives have made unreasonable demands. Some couples will still decide to divorce, but at least their decisions will be based on realistic expectations.

26   In these times of resurgent ethnic conflicts, the world desperately needs cross-cultural understanding. Like charity, successful cross-cultural communication should begin at home.

---

1 What significant differences in male and female communication behaviors (verbal and nonverbal) does Tannen perceive? Why does she refer to this sense of mutual bafflement as "cross-cultural" (para. 8, 23, 26)? In what sense do men and women actually live in different cultures in the way they relate to each other?

2 What examples does Tannen offer to back up her belief that men and women can communicate with each more effectively when both understand that males and females have different objectives when they communicate?

3 How are Tannen's suggestions designed to remedy the "misaligned" (para. 12) aspects of miscommunication between men and women? Given that men and women have such different emotional needs and expectations, would Tannen's suggestions work? Why or why not?

4 In your opinion, what is Tannen's purpose in writing this essay and how do the extended examples she presents about two specific couples further serve this purpose? (Glossary: Examples, Purpose.)

5 Tannen provides many brief examples to contrast male and female patterns of communication. Which compare/contrast method of organization does she use in her

selection? Why might she have chosen this method? (Glossary: *Comparison and Contrast*.)

6 Choose someone from the opposite sex that you know who has a very different perspective from you on a particular subject and compose an account in the first person and try to see the world from this person's viewpoint.

Women and the Language of Men

Jane Tompkins

◆ JANE TOMPKINS is currently professor of English at Duke University. She received a nomination for the Pulitzer Prize in 1992 for *West of Everything: The Inner Life of Westerns,* from which the following selection is taken.

Why are the heroes in Westerns invariably tight-lipped and laconic? In these films and novels, why are women, Easterners, salesmen, and politicians loquacious and ineffectual? Why, in short, is the Western as a genre hostile to language in general and the language of women in particular? Tompkins reveals that Westerns are constructed around a set of oppositions that equate silence with integrity, action, independence, strength, potency, and an acceptance of reality. Talking, by contrast, is equated with the parlor, illusion, weakness, dependency, dishonesty, ineffectuality, bragging, and insincerity. Tompkins adds a cultural, social, and historical dimension to the analyses of childhood socialization that Robin Lakoff presents and the conversational cross-purposes between men and women examined by Deborah Tannen.

TO CONSIDER Do you tend to view people who talk a lot as more trustworthy than those who do not? Why or why not?

Fear of losing his identity drives a man west, where the harsh conditions of life force his manhood into being. Into this do-or-die, all-or-nothing world we step when we read this passage from Louis L'Amour's novel *Radigan* (1958), where a woman about to be attacked by a gunman experiences a moment of truth:

> She had never felt like this before, but right now she was backed up against death with all the nonsense and the fancy words trimmed away. The hide of

the truth was peeled back to expose the bare, quivering raw flesh of itself, and there was no nonsense about it. She had been taught the way a lady should live, and how a lady should act, and it was all good and right and true . . . but out here on the mesa top with a man hunting her to put her back on the grass it was no longer the same . . . There are times in life when the fancy words and pretty actions don't count for much, when it's blood and death and a cold wind blowing and a gun in the hand and you know suddenly you're just an animal with guts and blood that wants to live, love and mate, and die in your own good time. (144–45)

L'Amour lays it on the line. Faced with death, we learn the truth about life. And the truth is that human nature is animal. When your back is to the wall you find out that what you want most is not to save your eternal soul—if it exists— but to live, in the body. For truth is flesh, raw and quivering, with the hide peeled back. All else is nonsense. The passage proposes a set of oppositions fundamental to the way the Western thinks about the world. There are two choices: either you can remain in a world of illusions, by which is understood religion, culture, and class distinctions, a world of fancy words and pretty actions, of "manners for the parlor and the ball room, and . . . womanly tricks for courting"; or you can face life as it really is—blood, death, a cold wind blowing, and a gun in the hand. These are the classic oppositions from which all Westerns derive their meaning: parlor versus mesa, East versus West, woman versus man, illusion versus truth, words versus things. It is the last of these oppositions I want to focus on now because it stands for all the rest.

But first a warning. What is most characteristic of these oppositions is that as soon as you put pressure on them they break down. Each time one element of a pair is driven into a corner, it changes shape and frequently turns into its opposite. It's as if the genre's determination to have a world of absolute dichotomies ensures that interpenetration and transmutation will occur. For instance, when Burt Lancaster, playing Wyatt Earp in *Gunfight at the OK Corral*, declares toward the beginning of the movie, "I've never needed anybody in my life and I sure don't need Doc Holliday," the vehemence of his claim to autonomy virtually guarantees that it will be undermined. And sure enough, by the time the showdown arrives you can hardly tell him and Kirk Douglas (playing Doc) apart: they dress alike, walk alike, talk alike, and finally they fight side by side as brothers. Two who started out as opposites—gambler versus sheriff, drunken failure versus respected citizen, rake versus prude—have become indistinguishable.

Westerns strive to depict a world of clear alternatives—independence versus connection, anarchy versus law, town versus desert—but they are just as compulsively driven to destroying these opposites and making them contain each other.

So it is with language. Westerns distrust language. Time and again they set up situations whose message is that words are weak and misleading, only actions count; words are immaterial, only objects are real. But the next thing you know, someone is using language brilliantly, delivering an epigram so pithy and dense it might as well be a solid thing. In fact, Westerns go in for their own special brand of the bon mot, seasoned with skepticism and fried to a turn. The product—chewy and tough—is recognizable anywhere:

Cow's nothin' but a heap o' trouble tied up in a leather bag.

The Cowboys, 1972

A human rides a horse until he's dead and then goes on foot. An Indian rides him another 20 miles and then eats him.

The Searchers, 1956

A Texan is nothin' but a human man way out on a limb.

The Searchers

Kansas is all right for men and dogs but it's pretty hard on women and horses.

The Santa Fe Trail, 1940

God gets off at Leavenworth, and Cyrus Holliday drives you from there to the devil.

The Santa Fe Trail

There ain't no Sundays west of Omaha

The Cowboys

This is hard country, double hard.

Will Penny, 1968

When you boil it all down, what does a man really need? Just a smoke and a cup of coffee.

Johnny Guitar, 1954

In the end you end up dyin' all alone on a dirty street. And for what? For nothin'.

High Noon, 1952

You can't serve papers on a rat, baby sister. You gotta kill 'em or let 'em be.

True Grit, 1969

He wasn't a good man, he wasn't a bad man, but Lord, he was a *man*.

The Ballad of Cable Hogue, 1969

Some things a man has to do, so he does 'em.

Winchester '73, 1950

Only a man who carries a gun ever needs one.

Angel and the Bad Man, 1947

Mr. Grimes: "God, dear God."

Yaqui Joe: "He won't help you."

100 Rifles, 1969

You haven't gotten tough, you've just gotten miserable.

Cowboy, 1958

The sayings all have one thing in common: they bring you down. Like the wisdom L'Amour offers his female protagonist out on the mesa top, these gritty pieces of advice challenge romantic notions. Don't call on God; he's not there. Think you're tough? You're just miserable. What do you die for? Nothin'. The sayings puncture big ideas and self-congratulation; delivered with perfect timing, they land like stones from a slingshot and make a satisfying thunk.

For the Western is at heart antilanguage. Doing, not talking, is what it values. And this preference is connected to its politics, as a line from L'Amour suggests: "A man can . . . write fine words, or he can do something to hold himself in the hearts of the people" (*Treasure Mountain,* 1972). "Fine words" are contrasted not accidentally with "the hearts of the people." For the men who are the Western's heroes don't have the large vocabularies an expensive education can buy. They don't have time to read that many books. Westerns distrust language in part because language tends to be wielded most skillfully by people who possess a certain kind of power: class privilege, political clout, financial strength. Consequently, the entire enterprise is based on a paradox. In order to exist, the Western has to use words or visual images, but these images are precisely what it fears. As a medium, the Western has to pretend that it doesn't exist at all, its words and pictures, just a window on the truth, not really there.

So the Western's preferred parlance ideally consists of abrupt commands: "Turn the wagon. Tie 'em up short. Get up on the seat" (*Red River*); "Take my horse. Good swimmer. Get it done, boy" (*Rio Grande,* 1950). Or epigrammatic sayings of a strikingly aggressive sort: "There's only one thing you gotta know. Get it out fast and put it away slow" (*Man Without a Star*); "When you pull a gun, kill a man" (*My Darling Clementine*). For the really strong man, language is a snare; it blunts his purpose and diminishes his strength. When Joey asks Shane if he knows how to use a rifle, Shane answers, and we can barely hear him, "Little bit." The understatement and the clipping off of the indefinite article are typical of the minimalist language Western heroes speak, a desperate shorthand, comic, really, in its attempt to communicate without using words.

Westerns are full of contrasts between people who spout words and people who act. At the beginning of Sam Peckinpah's *The Wild Bunch* a temperance leader harangues his pious audience; in the next scene a violent bank robbery makes a shambles of their procession through town. The pattern of talk canceled by action always delivers the same message: language is false or at best ineffectual; only actions are real. When heroes talk, it is action: their laconic put-downs cut people off at the knees. Westerns treat salesmen and politicians, people whose business is language, with contempt. Braggarts are dead men as soon as they appear. When "Stonewall" Tory, in *Shane,* brags that he can face the Riker gang any day, you know he's going to get shot; it's Shane, the man who clips out words between clenched teeth, who will take out the hired gunman.

The Western's attack on language is wholesale and unrelenting, as if language were somehow tainted in its very being. When John Wayne, in John Ford's *The Searchers,* rudely tells an older woman who is taking more than a single sentence to say something, "I'd be obliged, ma'am if you would get to the point," he expresses the genre's impatience with words as a way of dealing with the world. For while the woman is speaking, Indians are carrying a prisoner off. Such a small incident, once you unpack it, encapsulates the Western's attitude toward a whole range of issues:

1. Chasing Indians—that is, engaging in aggressive physical action—is doing something, while talking about the situation is not.

2. The reflection and negotiation that language requires are gratuitous, even pernicious.

3. The hero doesn't need to think or talk; he just *knows*. Being the hero, he is in a state of grace with respect to the truth.

In a world of bodies true action must have a physical form. And so the capacity for true knowledge must be based in physical experience. John Wayne playing Ethan Edwards in *The Searchers* has that experience and knows what is right because, having arrived home after fighting in the Civil War, he better than anyone else realizes that life is "blood and death and a cold wind blowing and a gun in the hand." In such a world, language constitutes an inferior kind of reality, and the farther one stays away from it the better.

Language is gratuitous at best; at worst it is deceptive. It takes the place of things, screens them from view, creates a shadow world where anything can be made to look like anything else. The reason no one in the Glenn Ford movie *Cowboy* can remember the proper words for burying a man is that there aren't any. It is precisely words that cannot express the truth about things. The articulation of a creed in the Western is a sign not of conviction but of insincerity. The distaste with which John Wayne says, "The Lord giveth, the Lord taketh away," as he buries a man in *Red River,* not only challenges the authority of the Christian God but also expresses disgust at all the trappings of belief: liturgies, litanies, forms, representations, all of which are betrayals of reality itself.

The features I am describing here, using the abstract language the Western shuns, are dramatically present in a movie called *Dakota Incident* (1956), whose plot turns in part on the bootlessness of words and, secondarily, on the perniciousness of money (another system of representation the Western scorns). Near the beginning, a windbag senator, about to depart on the stage from a miserable town called Christian Flats, pontificates to a crowd that has gathered to watch a fight, "There's no problem that can't be solved at a conference table," adding, "Believe me, gentlemen, I know whereof I speak." The next minute, two gunfights break out on Main Street; in one of them the hero shoots and kills his own brother.

The theme of loquacity confounded by violence, declared at the outset, replays itself at the end when the main characters have been trapped by some Indians in a dry creek bed. The senator has been defending the Indians throughout, saying that they're misunderstood, have a relationship with the land, and take from the small end of the horn of plenty. Finally, when he and the others are about to die of thirst, he goes out to parley with the Indians. He makes a long and rather moving speech about peace and understanding, and they shoot him; he dies clawing at the arrow in his chest.

In case we hadn't already gotten the point about the ineffectuality of language, we get it now. But no sooner is the point made than the movie does an about-face. The other characters start saying that the senator died for what he believed, that he was wrong about the Indians "but true to himself." They say that perhaps his words "fell on barren ground: the Indians and us." And the story ends on a note of peaceful cooperation between whites and Indians (after the attacking Indians have been wiped out), with talk about words of friendship falling on fertile ground.

Language is specifically linked in this movie to a belief in peace and cooperation as a way of solving conflicts. And though it's made clear from the start that only wimps and fools believe negotiation is the way to deal with enemies (the movie was made in 1956 during the Cold War), that position is abandoned as soon as "our side" wins. *Dakota Incident* is not the only Western to express this ambivalent attitude toward language and the peace and harmony associated with it. Such ambivalence is typical, but it is always resolved in the end. Language gets its day in court, and then it is condemned.

When John Wayne's young protégé in *The Searchers,* for example, returns to his sweetheart after seven years, he's surprised to learn that she hasn't been aware of his affection. "But I always loved you," he protests. "I thought you knew that without me havin' to say it." For a moment here, John Ford seems to be making fun of the idea that you can communicate without language, gently ridiculing the young man's assumption that somehow his feelings would be known although he had never articulated them. But his silence is vindicated ultimately when the girl he loves, who was about to marry another man, decides to stick with him. The cowboy hero's taciturnity, like his awkward manners around women and inability to dance, is only superficially a flaw; actually, it's proof of his manhood and trueheartedness. In Westerns silence, sexual potency, and integrity go together.

Again, in *My Darling Clementine* Ford seems to make an exception to the interdiction against language. When Victor Mature, playing Doc Holliday, delivers the "To be or not to be" speech from *Hamlet,* taking over from the drunken actor who has forgotten his lines, we are treated to a moment of verbal enchantment. The beauty and power of the poetry are recognized even by the hero, Wyatt Earp (played by Henry Fonda), who appreciates Shakespeare and delivers a long soliloquy himself over the grave of his brother. But when the old actor who has been performing locally leaves town, he tricks the desk clerk into accepting his signature on a bill in place of money. The actor, like the language he is identified with, is a lovable old fraud, wonderfully colorful and entertaining, but not, finally, to be trusted.

The position represented by language, always associated with women, religion, and culture, is allowed to appear in Westerns and is accorded a certain plausibility and value. It functions as a critique of force and, even more important, as a symbol of the peace, harmony, and civilization that force is invoked in order to preserve. But in the end, that position is deliberately proven wrong—massively, totally, and unequivocally—with pounding hooves, thundering guns, blood and death. Because the genre is in revolt against a Victorian culture where the ability to manipulate language confers power, the Western equates power with "not-language." And not-language it equates with being male.

In his book *Phallic Critiques* (1984) Peter Schwenger has identified a style of writing he calls "the language of men," a language that belongs to what he terms the School of Virility, starting with Jack London and continuing through Ernest Hemingway to Norman Mailer and beyond. Infused with colloquialism, slang, choppy rhythms, "bitten-off fragments," and diction that marks the writer as "tough," this language is pitted against itself as language, and devoted to maintaining, in Schwenger's terminology, "masculine reserve."

Drawing on Octavio Paz's definition of the *macho* as a "hermetic being, closed up in himself" ("women are inferior beings because, in submitting, they open themselves up"), Schwenger shows the connections these authors make among speaking, feeling, and feminization. "It is by talking," he writes, "that one opens up to another person and becomes vulnerable. It is by putting words to an emotion that it becomes feminized. As long as the emotion itself is restrained, held back, it hardly matters what the emotion itself is; it will retain a male integrity." Thus, "not talking is a demonstration of masculine control over emotion" (43–45).

Control is the key word here. Not speaking demonstrates control not only over feelings but over one's physical boundaries as well. The male, by remaining "hermetic," "closed up," maintains the integrity of the boundary that divides him from the world. (It is fitting that in the Western the ultimate loss of that control takes place when one man puts holes in another man's body.) To speak is literally to open the body to penetration by opening an orifice; it is also to mingle the body's substance with the substance of what is outside it. Finally, it suggests a certain incompleteness, a need to be in relation. Speech relates the person who is speaking to other people (as opposed to things); it requires acknowledging their existence and, by extension, their parity. If "to become a man," as Schwenger says, "must be finally to attain the solidity and self-containment of an object," "an object that is self-contained does not have to open itself up in words." But it is not so much the vulnerability or loss of dominance that speech implies that makes it dangerous as the reminder of the speaker's own interiority.

The interdiction masculinity imposes on speech arises from the desire for complete objectivization. And this means being conscious of nothing, not knowing that one has a self. To be a man is not only to be monolithic, silent, mysterious, impenetrable as a desert butte, it is to *be* the desert butte. By becoming a solid object, not only is a man relieved of the burden of relatedness and responsiveness to others, he is relieved of consciousness itself, which is to say, primarily, consciousness of self.

At this point, we come upon the intersection between the Western's rejection of language and its emphasis on landscape. Not fissured by self-consciousness, nature is what the hero aspires to emulate: perfect being-in-itself. This is why John Wayne was impatient with the woman who took longer than a sentence to speak her mind. As the human incarnation of nature, he neither speaks nor listens. He is monumentality in motion, propelling himself forward by instinct, no more talkable to than a river or an avalanche, and just as good company.

WOMAN   That's a pretty dog.
MAN   (No response)

WOMAN   Well, it's got a pretty coat.
MAN   (Silence)

The foregoing account of the Western's hostility to language refers to a mode of behavior—masculine behavior for the most part—that has left an indelible mark on the experience of practically every person who has lived in this country in the twentieth century. I mean the linguistic behavior of men toward women, particularly in domestic situations.

> He finds it very difficult to talk about his personal feelings, and intimidates me into not talking either. He also finds it very difficult to accept my affection. . . . I become angry that his need to be unemotional is more important than my need to have an outward show of love. Why do I always have to be the one that is understanding? (18)

> When I was married, it was devastatingly lonely—I wanted to die—it was just so awful being in love with someone who . . . never talked to me or consulted me. . . . (23)

> My husband grew up in a very non-emotional family and it took a long time for me to make him understand that it's a good thing to let people (especially the ones you love) know how you feel (18).

> The relationship did not fill my deepest needs for closeness, that's why I'm no longer in it. I did share every part of myself with him but it was never mutual. (19)

> The loneliness comes from knowing you can't contact another person's feelings or actions, no matter how hard you try. (23)

> If I could change one thing—it would be to get him to be more expressive of his emotions, his wants, needs. I most criticize him for not telling me what he wants or how he feels. He denies he feels things when his non-verbals indicate he does feel them. (21)

The quotations come from Shere Hite's *Women and Love: A Cultural Revolution in Progress* (1987). I quote them here because I want to make clear that the Western's hatred of language is not a philosophical matter only; it has codified and sanctioned the way several generations of men have behaved verbally toward women in American society. Young boys sitting in the Saturday afternoon darkness could not ride horses or shoot guns, but they could talk. Or rather, they could learn how to keep silent. The Western man's silence functions as a script for behavior; it expresses and authorizes a power relation that reaches into the furthest corners of domestic and social life. The impassivity of male silence suggests the inadequacy of female verbalization, establishes male superiority, and silences the one who would engage in conversation. Hite comments:

> We usually don't want to see . . . non-communication or distancing types of behavior as expressing attitudes of inequality or superiority, as signs of a man

not wanting to fraternize (sororize?) with someone of lower status. This is too painful. And yet, many men seem to be asserting superiority by their silences and testy conversational style with women. Thus, not talking to a woman on an equal level can be a way for a man to dominate a relationship. . . . (25)

For a man to speak of his inner feelings not only admits parity with the person he is talking to, but it jeopardizes his status as potent being, for talk dissipates presence, takes away the mystery of an ineffable self which silence preserves. Silence establishes dominance at the same time as it protects the silent one from inspection and possible criticism by offering nothing for the interlocutor to grab hold of. The effect, as in the dialogue about the dog quoted above, is to force the speaker into an ineffectual flow of language which tries to justify itself, achieve significance, make an impression by additions which only diminish the speaker's force with every word.

When Matthew Garth returns to his hotel room at the end of *Red River,* he acts the part of silent conqueror to perfection. The heroine, who has been waiting for him, warns him that his enemy is on the way to town. The film has her babble nervously about how she came to be there, how she found out about the danger, how there's no way he can escape, no way to stop his enemy, nothing anyone can do, nothing she can do. As he looks down at her, not hearing a thing she says, her words spill out uncontrollable, until finally she says, "Stop me, Matt, stop me." He puts his hand over her mouth, then kisses her. The fade-out that immediately follows suggests that the heroine, whose name is Tess Millay, is getting laid.

The scene invites diametrically opposed interpretations. From one point of view, what happens is exactly right: the desire these characters feel for each other yearns for physical expression. Nonverbal communication, in this case sex, is entirely appropriate. But the scene gets to this point at the woman's expense.

Tess is the same character who, earlier in the film, had been shot by an arrow and had it removed without batting an eyelash, had seduced the young man with her arm in a sling, and had refused a proposition from his enemy. In this scene she is totally undercut. As her useless verbiage pours out, she falls apart before our eyes, a helpless creature who has completely lost control of herself and has to beg a man to stop her.

When I feel insecure, I need to talk about things a lot. It sometimes worries me that I say the same things over and over. (19)

I can be an emotional drain on my husband if I really open up. (19)

Hite notes that women feel ashamed of their need to talk, blaming themselves and making excuses for the silence of men. "My husband grew up in a very non-emotional family." The heroine of *Red River* cares so much about the hero that her words pour out in a flood of solicitude. But instead of seeing this as a sign of love, the film makes her anxiety look ridiculous and even forces *her* to interpret it this way.

Tess Millay's abject surrender to the hero's superiority at the end of *Red*

River is a supreme example of woman's introjection of the male attitude toward her. She sees herself as he sees her, silly, blathering on about manly business that is none of her concern, and beneath it all really asking for sex. The camera and the audience identify with the hero, while the heroine dissolves into a caricature of herself. Sex joins here with blood and death and a cold wind blowing as the only true reality, extinguishing the authority of women and their words.

Someone might argue that all the Western is doing here is making a case for nonverbal communication. If that were true, so much the better. But, at least when it comes to the relations between men and women, the Western doesn't aim to communicate at all. The message, in the case of Tess Millay, as in the case of women in Westerns generally, is that there's nothing *to* them. They may seem strong and resilient, fiery and resourceful at first, but when push comes to shove, as it always does, they crumble. Even Marian, Joe Starret's wife in *Shane,* one of the few women in Western films who, we are made to feel, is also substantial as a person, dissolves into an ineffectual harangue at the end, unsuccessfully pleading with her man not to go into town to get shot. When the crunch comes, women shatter into words.

A classic moment of female defeat appears in Owen Wister's *The Virginian,* which set the pattern for the Western in the twentieth century. In the following passage, Molly, the heroine, is vanquished by the particular form of male silence that her cowboy lover practices. The Virginian has just passed his mortal enemy on the road with drawn pistol and without a word. But when Molly tries to get him to talk about it and "ventures a step inside the border of his reticence," he turns her away:

> She looked at him, and knew that she must step outside his reticence again. By love and her surrender to him their positions had been exchanged. . . . She was no longer his half-indulgent, half-scornful superior. Her better birth and schooling that had once been weapons to keep him at a distance, to bring her off victorious in their encounters, had given way before the onset of the natural man himself. She knew her cow-boy lover, with all that he lacked, to be more than ever she could be, with all that she had. He was her worshipper still, but her master, too. Therefore now, against the baffling smile he gave her, she felt powerless. (256)

Wister makes explicit the connection between the Virginian's mastery over Molly and his reticence, his conversational droit du seigneur. Like L'Amour, Wister sees the relationship between men and women as a version of the East-West, parlor-mesa, word-deed opposition. Molly is identified by her ties to the East, her class background, her education, but most of all by her involvement in language. Words are her work and her pleasure and the source of her power. She teaches them in school and keeps company with them in books, but they cannot protect her from "the onset of the natural man himself." The man's sheer physical presence is stronger than language, and so words are finally the sign of Molly's and all women's inferiority.

This is what lies behind the strange explanation the Virginian offers Molly of his relationship to the villain, Trampas. He says that he and Trampas just lie in wait for each other, hating each other in silence, always ready to draw. Then he tells a story about a women's temperance meeting he once overheard while staying at a hotel. "Oh, heavens. Well, I couldn't change my room and the hotel man, he apologized to me next mawnin'. Said it didn't surprise him the husbands drank some" (259). Then, reverting to himself and Trampas, the Virginian remarks, "We were not a bit like a temperance meetin' " (259).

The temperance ladies talk and talk; that is *all* they do. It never comes to shooting. Meanwhile, they drive their husbands crazy with their cackle. Drive them to drink, which dulls the feelings men can't talk about. So the Virginian and Trampas (the enemy he passes on the road) hardly exchange a word. They cannot communicate; therefore, they will kill each other someday. Their silence signals their seriousness, their dignity and reality, and the inevitability of their conflict. Silence is a sign of mastery, and goes along with a gun in the hand. They would rather die than settle the argument by talking to each other.

Why does the Western harbor such animus against women's words? Why should it be so extreme and unforgiving? Is it because, being the weaker sex physically, women must use words as their chief weapon, and so, if men are to conquer, the gun of women's language must be emptied? Or is it because, having forsworn the solace of language, men cannot stand to see women avail themselves of it because it reminds them of their own unverbalized feelings? Hite remarks:

> It could be argued that, if men are silent, they are not trying to dominate women; rather, they are trapped in their own silence (and their own pain), unable to talk or communicate about feelings, since this is such forbidden behavior for them. (25)

If Hite has guessed correctly, men's silence in Westerns is the counterpart of women's silence; that is, it is the silence of an interior self who has stopped trying to speak and has no corresponding self to talk to. Its voice is rarely heard, since it represents the very form of interior consciousness the genre wishes to stamp out. But it does burst out occasionally. In *The Virginian* it speaks in the form of a song, roared out by the rebellious cowhands who are getting drunk in a caboose on their way back to the ranch where the Virginian is taking them. They sing:

> "I'm wild and woolly, and full of fleas;
> I'm hard to curry above the knees;
> I'm a she-wolf from Bitter Creek, and It's my night to ho-o-wl—"

The wolf bitch inside men, what would it sound like if they ever let it out? What would it say? The silence of this inner voice, its muteness, keeps the woman's voice, its counterpart, from being heard. It is replaced by the narrative of the gunfight, the range war, the holdup, the chase. By the desert. The Western itself is the language of men, what they do vicariously, instead of speaking.

I used to keep a photograph of the young John Wayne posted on my bulletin board. He has on a cowboy hat, and he is even then developing a little of that inimitable cowboy squint so beloved of millions. But he has not yet gotten the cowboy face, the leathery wall of noncommunication written over by wrinkles, speaking pain and hardship and the refusal to give in to them, speaking the determination to tough it out against all odds, speaking the willingness to be cruel in return for cruelty, and letting you know, beyond all shadow of a doubt, who's boss.

The other expression, the expression of the young John Wayne, is tender, and more than a little wistful; it is delicate and incredibly sensitive. Pure and sweet; shy, really, and demure.

Where is she, this young girl that used to inhabit John Wayne's body along with the Duke? I think of the antiwar song from the sixties, "Where have all the young girls gone?" and the answer comes back, "Gone to young men every one," and the young men in the song are gone to battle and the soldiers to the graveyard. How far is it from the death of the young girl in John Wayne's face to the outbreak of war? How far is it from the suppression of language to the showdown on Main Street? In *The Virginian* Wister suggests that the silence that reigns between the hero and the villain guarantees that one will kill the other someday. And still he ridicules women's language.

The Western hero's silence symbolizes a massive suppression of the inner life. And my sense is that this determined shutting down of emotions, this cutting of the self off from contact with the interior well of feeling, exacts its price in the end. Its equivalent: the force of the bullets that spew forth from the guns in little orgasms of uncontained murderousness. Its trophy: the bodies in the dust. Its victory: the silence of graves. Its epitaph: that redundant sign that keeps on appearing in *Gunfight at the OK Corral*—BOOT HILL GRAVEYARD TOMBSTONE.

Why does the Western hate women's language? I argued earlier that the Western turned against organized religion and the whole women's culture of the nineteenth century and all the sermons and novels that went with them; the rejection took place in the name of purity, of a truth belied by all these trappings, something that could not be stated. But perhaps the words the Western hates stand as well for inner confusion. A welter of thoughts and feelings, a condition of mental turmoil that is just as hateful as the more obvious external constraints of economics, politics, and class distinctions. Women, like language, remind men of their own interiority; women's talk evokes a whole network of familial and social relationships and their corollaries in the emotional circuitry. What men are fleeing in Westerns is not only the cluttered Victorian interior but also the domestic dramas that go on in that setting, which the quotations from Shere Hite recall. The gesture of sweeping the board clear may be intended to clear away the reminders of emotional entanglements that cannot be dealt with or faced. Men would rather die than talk, because talking might bring up their own unprocessed pain or risk a dam burst that would undo the front of imperturbable superiority. It may be the Western hero flees into the desert seeking there what Gretel Ehrlich has called "the solace of open spaces," a place whose physical magnificence and emptiness are the promise of an inward strength and quietude. "Where seldom is heard a discouraging word, and the skies are not cloudy all day."

1 What reasons does Tompkins give to explain the antipathy the Western displays toward language in general and women's language in particular, as evident in John Wayne's comment "I'd be obliged, ma'am, if you would get to the point" (para. 11)? What values associated with women do Westerns as a genre reject?

2 Tompkins cites evidence from a wide variety of sources including novels, dialogue from many Westerns, and academic studies to support her thesis, yet makes clear that for her a classic example is an encounter described in Owen Wister's novel *The Virginian* (para. 31). What features are evident in this that illustrate her claim so persuasively?

3 To what extent is contemporary American life determined by a contrast between people who spout words and people who act? Why, in Tompkins's view, has laconic, clipped speech come to be equated with virtue while loquacious speech is associated with salesmen, politicians, and lawyers, and is viewed with contempt? Who are the contemporary equivalents of the Western hero?

4 How important is the use of colloquial expressions (for example, "there ain't no Sundays west of Omaha") in illustrating Tompkins's thesis? (Glossary: *Colloquial Expressions.*)

5 From your own experience in watching Westerns, do you think Tompkins's characterization of male and female communication styles is accurate? To what extent did Tompkins's comparison and contrast of verbal cues of men and women clarify her thesis? (Glossary: *Comparison and Contrast.*)

6 Have you ever had a job traditionally associated with the opposite sex? Did you find it to be a pleasant or unpleasant experience? Did you encounter any form of sexual stereotyping? Report any relevant conversations that took place on this job.

Real Men Don't, or Anti-Male Bias in English   *Eugene R. August*

◆ EUGENE R. AUGUST teaches linguistics at the University of Dayton in Ohio. He is widely recognized as a pioneer in the emerging field of Men's

Eugene R. August, "Real Men Don't, or Anti-Male Bias in English," from *The University of Dayton Review*. Copyright 1986–87 by *The University of Dayton Review*. Reprinted with permission from Eugene R. August.

Studies. He is the author of *Men's Studies: A Selected and Annotated Interdisciplinary Bibliography* (1985).

Selections by Robin Lakoff, Deborah Tannen, and Jane Tompkins all emphasize how language can be used to victimize women in one way or another. Yet, for Eugene R. August, sexist language cuts both ways and can be used to dehumanize and stereotype men as well. August documents the largely unsuspected extent to which anti-male prejudices make men objects of discrimination. For example, the terms used to label social outcasts (nerd, clod, klutz, dummy, dork, jerk, dweeb, geek, etc.) are applied almost exclusively to males.

> **TO CONSIDER**   Has the political correctness movement led people to assume that men are not the victims of sexist language to the extent women are?

D espite numerous studies of sex bias in language during the past fifteen years, only rarely has anti-male bias been examined. In part, this neglect occurs because many of these studies have been based upon assumptions which are questionable at best and which at worst exhibit their own form of sex bias. Whether explicitly or implicitly, many of these studies reduce human history to a tale of male oppressors and female victims or rebels. In this view of things, all societies become *patriarchal societies,* a familiar term used to suggest that for centuries males have conspired to exploit and demean females. Accordingly, it is alleged in many of these studies that men control language and that they use it to define women and women's roles as inferior.

Despite the popularity of such a view, it has received scant support from leading social scientists, including one of the giants of modern anthropology, Margaret Mead. Anticipating current ideology. Mead in *Male and Female* firmly rejected the notion of a "male conspiracy to keep women in their place," arguing instead that

> the historical trend that listed women among the abused minorities . . . lingers on to obscure the issue and gives apparent point to the contention that this is a man-made world in which women have always been abused and must always fight for their rights.
>
>   It takes considerable effort on the part of both men and women to reorient ourselves to thinking—when we think basically—that this is a world not made by men alone, in which women are unwilling and helpless dupes and fools or else powerful schemers hiding their power under their ruffled petticoats but a world made by mankind for human beings of both sexes. (298, 299–300)

The model described by Mead and other social scientists shows a world in which women and men have lived together throughout history in a symbiotic relationship often mutually agreeing upon the definition of gender roles and the distribution of various powers and duties.

More importantly for the subject of bias in speech and writing, women—as well as men—have shaped language. As Walter J. Ong reminds us,

> Women talk and think as much as men do, and with few exceptions we all . . . learn to talk and think in the first instance largely from women, usually and predominantly our mothers. Our first tongue is called our "mother tongue" in English and in many other languages. . . . There are no father tongues. . . . (36)

Feminists like Dorothy Dinnerstein agree: "There seems no reason to doubt that the baby-tending sex contributed at least equally with the history-making one to the most fundamental of all human inventions: language" (22). Because gender roles and language are shaped by society in general—that is, by both men and women—anti-male bias in language is as possible as anti-female bias.

To say this, however, is emphatically not to blame women alone, or even primarily, for anti-male usage. If guilt must be assigned, it would have to be placed upon sexist people, both male and female, who use language to manipulate gender role behavior and to create negative social attitudes towards males. But often it is difficult to point a finger of blame: except where prejudiced gender stereotypes are deliberately fostered, most people evidently use sex-biased terminology without clearly understanding its import. In the long run, it is wiser to concentrate not on fixing blame, but on heightening public awareness of anti-male language and on discouraging its use. In particular, teachers and writers need to become aware of and to question language which denigrates or stereotypes males.

In modern English, three kinds of anti-male usage are evident: first, gender-exclusive language which omits males from certain kinds of consideration; second, gender-restrictive language which attempts to restrict males to an accepted gender role, some aspects of which may be outmoded, burdensome, or destructive: and third, negative stereotypes of males which are insulting, dehumanizing, and potentially dangerous.

Although gender-exclusive language which excludes females has often been studied, few students of language have noted usage which excludes males. Those academics, for example, who have protested *alumnus* and *alumni* as gender-exclusive terms to describe a university's male and female graduates have failed to notice that, by the same logic, *alma mater* (nourishing mother) is an equally gender-exclusive term to describe the university itself. Those who have protested *man* and *mankind* as generic terms have not begun to question *mammal* as a term of biological classification, but by categorizing animals according to the female's ability to suckle the young through her mammary glands, *mammal* clearly omits the male of the species. Consequently, it is as suspect as generic *man*.

In general, gender-exclusive usage in English excludes males as parents and as victims. Until recently, the equating of *mother* with *parent* in the social sciences was notorious: a major sociological study published in 1958 with the title. *The Changing American Parent* was based upon interviews with 582 mothers and no fathers (Roman and Haddad 87). Although no longer prevalent in the social sciences, the interchangeability of *mother* and *parent* is still common, except for *noncustodial parent* which is almost always a synonym for *father.* A recent ad for *Parents* magazine begins: "To be the best mother you can be, you want practical, reliable answers to the questions a mother must face." Despite the large number of men now seen pushing shopping carts, advertisers still insist that "Choosy mothers choose Jif" and "My Mom's a Butternut Mom." Frequently, children are regarded as belonging solely to the mother, as in phrases like *women and their children.* The idea of the mother as primary parent can be glimpsed in such expressions as *mother tongue, mother wit, mother lode, mother of invention,* and *mothering* as a synonym for *parenting.*

The male as victim is ignored in such familiar expressions as *innocent women and children.* In June 1985, when President Reagan rejected a bombing strike to counter terrorist activities, newspapers reported that the decision had been made to prevent "the deaths of many innocent women and children in strife-torn Lebanon" (Glass). Presumably, strife-torn Lebanon contained no innocent men. Likewise, *rape victim* means females only, an assumption made explicit in the opening sentences of this newspaper article on rape: "Crime knows no gender. Yet, there is one offense that only women are prey to: rape" (Mougey). The thousands of males raped annually, in addition to the sexual assaults regularly inflicted upon males in prison, are here entirely overlooked. (That these males have been victimized mostly by other males does not disqualify them as victims of sexual violence, as some people assume.) Similarly, the term *wife and child abuse* conceals the existence of an estimated 282,000 husbands who are battered annually (O'Reilly et al. 23). According to many expressions in English, males are not parents and they are never victimized.

Unlike gender-exclusive language, gender-restrictive language is usually applied to males only, often to keep them within the confines of a socially prescribed gender role. When considering gender-restrictive language, one must keep in mind that—as Ruth E. Hartley has pointed out—the masculine gender role is enforced earlier and more harshly than the feminine role is (235). In addition, because the boy is often raised primarily by females in the virtual absence of close adult males, his grasp of what is required of him to *be a man* is often unsure. Likewise, prescriptions for male behavior are usually given in the negative, leading to the "Real Men Don't" syndrome, a process which further confuses the boy. Such circumstances leave many males extremely vulnerable to language which questions their sense of masculinity.

Furthermore, during the past twenty years an increasing number of men and women have been arguing that aspects of our society's masculine gender role are emotionally constrictive, unnecessarily stressful, and potentially lethal. Rejecting "the myth of masculine privilege," psychologist Herb Goldberg reports in *The Hazards of Being Male* that "every critical statistic in the area of [early death], disease, suicide, crime, accidents, childhood emotional disorders, alcoholism, and drug addiction shows a disproportionately higher male rate" (5). But changes in the masculine role are so disturbing to so many people that the male who attempts to break out of familiar gender patterns often finds himself facing hostile opposition which can be readily and powerfully expressed in a formidable array of sex-biased terms.

To see how the process works, let us begin early in the male life cycle. A boy quickly learns that, while it is usually acceptable for girls to be *tomboys,* God forbid that he should be a *sissy.* In *Sexual Signatures: On Being a Man or a Woman* John Money and Patricia Tucker note:

> The current feminine stereotype in our culture is flexible enough to let a girl behave "boyishly" if she wants to without bringing her femininity into question, but any boy who exhibits "girlish" behavior is promptly suspected of being queer. There isn't even a word corresponding to "tomboy" to describe such a boy. "Sissy" perhaps comes closest, or "artistic" and "sensitive," but unlike "tomboy," such terms are burdened with unfavorable connotations. (72)

Lacking a favorable or even neutral term to describe the boy who is quiet, gentle, and emotional, the English language has long had a rich vocabulary to insult and ridicule such boys—*mama's boy, mollycoddle, milksop, muff, twit, softy, cream-puff, pantywaist, weenie, Miss Nancy,* and so on. Although sometimes used playfully, the currently popular *wimp* can be used to insult males from childhood right into adulthood.

Discussion of words like *sissy* as insults have been often one-sided: most commentators are content to argue that the female, not the male, is being insulted by such usage. "The implicit sexism" in such terms, writes one commentator, "disparages the woman, not the man" (Sorrels 87). Although the female is being slurred indirectly by these terms, a moment's reflection will show that the primary force of the insult is being directed against the male, specifically the male who cannot differentiate himself from the feminine. Ong argues in *Fighting for Life* that most societies place heavy pressure on males to differentiate themselves from females because the prevailing environment of human society is feminine (70–71). In English-speaking societies, terms like *sissy* and *weak sister,* which have been used by both females and males, are usually perceived not as insults to females but as ridicule of males who have allegedly failed to differentiate themselves from the feminine.

Being *all boy* carries penalties, however: for one thing, it means being less lovable. As the nursery rhyme tells children, little girls are made of "sugar and spice and all that's nice," while little boys are made of "frogs and snails and puppy-dogs' tails." Or, as an American version of the rhyme puts it:

Girls are dandy,
Made of candy—
That's what little girls are made of.
Boys are rotten,
Made of cotton—
That's what little boys are made of.

(Baring-Gould 176n116)

When not enjoined to *be all boy,* our young lad will be urged to *be a big boy, be a brave soldier,* and (the ultimate appeal) *be a man.* These expressions almost invariably mean that the boy is about to suffer something painful or humiliating. The variant—*take it like a man*—provides the clue. As Paul Theroux defines it, *be a man* means: "Be stupid, be unfeeling, obedient and soldierly, and stop thinking."

Following our boy further into the life cycle, we discover that in school he will find himself in a cruel bind: girls his age will be biologically and socially more mature than he is, at least until around age eighteen. Until then, any ineptness in his social role will be castigated by a host of terms which are reserved almost entirely for males. "For all practical purposes," John Gordon remarks, "the word 'turkey' (or whatever the equivalent is now) can be translated as 'a boy spurned by influential girls'" (141). The equivalent of *turkey* are many: *jerk, nerd, clod, klutz, schmuck, dummy, goon, dark, square, dweeb, jackass, meathead, geek, zero, reject, goofball, drip,* and numerous others, including many obscene terms. Recently, a Michigan high school decided to do away with a scheduled "Nerd Day" after a fourteen-year-old male student, who apparently had been so harassed as a nerd by other students, committed suicide ("'Nerd' day"). In this case, the ability of language to devastate the emotionally vulnerable young male is powerfully and pathetically dramatized.

As our boy grows, he faces threats and taunts if he does not take risks or endure pain to prove his manhood. Coward, for example, is a word applied almost exclusively to males in our society, as are its numerous variants—*chicken, chicken-shit, yellow, yellow-bellied, lily-livered, weak-kneed, spineless, squirrelly, fraidy cat, gutless wonder, weakling, butterfly, jellyfish,* and so on. If our young man walks away from a stupid quarrel or prefers to settle differences more rationally than with a swift jab to the jaw, the English language is richly supplied with these and other expressions to call his masculinity into question.

Chief among the other expressions that question masculinity is a lengthy list of homophobic terms such as *queer, pansy, fag, faggot, queen, queeny, pervert, bugger, deviant, fairy, tinkerbell, puss, priss, flamer, feller, sweet, precious, fruit, sodomite,* and numerous others, many obscene. For many people, *gay* is an all-purpose word of ridicule and condemnation. Once again, although homosexuals are being insulted by these terms, the primary target is more often the heterosexual male who fails or refuses to live up to someone else's idea of masculinity. In "Homophobia Among Men" Gregory Lehne explains, "Homophobia is used as a technique of social control . . . to enforce the norms of male sex-role behavior. . . . [H]omosexuality is not the real threat, the real threat is change in the male sex-role" (77).

Nowhere is this threat more apparent than in challenges to our society's male-only military obligation. When a young man and a young woman reach the age of eighteen, both may register to vote; only the young man is required by law to register for military service. For the next decade at least, he must stand ready to be called into military service and even into combat duty in wars, "police actions," "peace-keeping missions," and "rescue missions," often initiated by legally dubious means. Should he resist this obligation, he may be called a *draft dodger, deserter, peacenik, traitor, shirker, slacker, malingerer,* and similar terms. Should he declare himself a conscientious objector, he may be labeled a *conchy* or any of the variants of *coward.*

In his relationships with women, he will find that the age of equality has not yet arrived. Usually, he will be expected to take the initiative, do the driving, pick up the tab, and in general show a deferential respect for women that is a left-over from the chivalric code. Should he behave in an *ungentlemanly* fashion, a host of words—which are applied almost always to males alone—can be used to tell him so: *louse, rat, creep, sleaze, scum, stain, worm, fink, heel, stinker, animal, savage, bounder, cad, wolf, gigolo, womanizer, Don Juan, pig, rotter, boor,* and so on.

In sexual matters he will usually be expected to take the initiative and to *perform.* If he does not, he will be labeled *impotent.* This word, writes Goldberg, "is clearly sexist because it implies a standard of acceptable masculine sexual performance that makes a man abnormal if he can't live up to it" (*New Male* 248). Metaphorically, *impotent* can be used to demean any male whose efforts in any area are deemed unacceptable. Even if our young man succeeds at his sexual performance, the sex manuals are ready to warn him that if he reaches orgasm before a specified time he is guilty of *premature ejaculation.*

When our young man marries, he will be required by law and social custom to support his wife and children. Should he not succeed as breadwinner or should he relax in his efforts, the language offers numerous terms to revile him: *loser, dead-beat, bum, freeloader, leech, parasite, goldbrick, sponge, mooch, ne'er-do-well, good for nothing,* and so on. If women in our society have been regarded as sex objects, men have been regarded as success objects, that is, judged by their ability to provide a standard of living. The title of a recent book—*How to Marry a Winner*—reveals immediately that the intended audience is female (Collier).

When he becomes a father, our young man will discover that he is a second-class parent, as the traditional interchangeability of *mother* and *parent* indicates. The law has been particularly obtuse in recognizing fathers as parents, as evidenced by the awarding of child custody to mothers in ninety percent of divorce cases. In 1975 a father's petition for custody of his four-year-old son was denied because, as the family court judge said, "Fathers don't make good mothers" (qtd. in Levine 21). The judge apparently never considered whether *fathers* make good *parents.*

And so it goes throughout our young man's life: if he deviates from society's gender role norm, he will be penalized and he will hear about it.

The final form of anti-male bias to be considered here is negative stereotyping. Sometimes this stereotyping is indirectly embedded in the language, sometimes it resides in people's assumptions about males and shapes their response to seemingly neutral words, and sometimes it is overtly created for political reasons. It is one thing to say that some aspects of the traditional masculine gender role are limiting and hurtful; it is quite another to gratuitously suspect males in general of being criminal and evil or to denounce them in wholesale fashion as oppressors, exploiters, and rapists. In *The New Male* Goldberg writes, "Men may very well be the last remaining subgroup in our society that can be blatantly, negatively and vilely stereotyped with little objection or resistance" (103). As our language demonstrates, such sexist stereotyping, whether unintentional or deliberate, is not only familiar but fashionable.

In English, crime and evil are usually attributed to the male. As an experiment I have compiled lists of nouns which I read to my composition students, asking them to check whether the words suggest "primarily females," "primarily males," or "could be either." Nearly all the words for law-breakers suggest males rather than females to most students. These words include *murderer, swindler, crook, criminal, burglar, thief, gangster, mobster, hood, hitman, killer, pickpocket, mugger,* and *terrorist.* Accounting for this phenomenon is not always easy. *Hitman* may obviously suggest "primarily males," and the *-er* in *murderer* may do the same, especially if it reminds students of the word's feminine form, *murderess.* Likewise, students may be aware that most murders are committed by males. Other words—like *criminal* and *thief*—are more clearly gender-neutral in form, and it is less clear why they should be so closely linked with "primarily males." Although the dynamics of the association may be unclear, English usage somehow conveys a subtle suggestion that males are to be regarded as guilty in matters of law-breaking.

This hint of male guilt extends to a term like *suspect.* When the person's gender is unknown, the suspect is usually presumed to be a male. For example, even before a definite suspect had been identified, the perpetrator of the 1980–1981 Atlanta child murders was popularly known as *The Man.* When a male and female are suspected of a crime, the male is usually presumed the guilty party. In a recent murder case, when two suspects—Debra Brown and Alton Coleman— were apprehended, police discovered *Brown's* fingerprint in a victim's car and interpreted this as evidence of *Coleman's* guilt. As the Associated Press reported:

> Authorities say for the first time they have evidence linking Alton Coleman with the death of an Indianapolis man.
>   A fingerprint found in the car of Eugene Scott has been identified as that of Debra Brown. Coleman's traveling companion . . ." ("Police").

Nowhere does the article suggest that Brown's fingerprint found in the victim's car linked Brown with the death: the male suspect was presumed the guilty party, while the female was only a "traveling companion." Even after Brown had been convicted of two murders, the Associated Press was still describing her as "the accused accomplice of convicted killer Alton Coleman" ("Indiana").

In some cases, this presumption of male guilt extends to crimes in which males are not the principal offenders. As noted earlier, a term like *wife and child abuse* ignores battered husbands, but it does more: it suggests that males alone abuse children. In reality most child abuse is committed by mothers (Straus, Gelles, Steinmetz 71). Despite this fact, a 1978 study of child abuse bears the title *Sins of the Fathers* (Inglis).

The term *rape* creates special problems. While the majority of rapes are committed by males and the number of female rape victims outdistances the number of male rape victims, it is widely assumed—as evidenced by the newspaper article cited above—that rape is a crime committed only by males in which only females are victims. Consequently, the word *rape* is often used as a brush to tar all males. In *Against Our Will* Susan Brownmiller writes: "From prehistoric times to the present, I believe, rape . . . is nothing more or less than a conscious process of intimidation by which *all men* keep *all women* in a state of fear" (15: italics in original). Making the point explicitly. Marilyn French states, "All men are rapists and that's all they are" (qtd. in Jennes 33). Given this kind of smear tactic, *rape* can be used metaphorically to indict males alone and to exonerate females, as in this sentence: "The rape of nature—and the ecological disaster it presages—is part and parcel of a dominating masculinity gone out of control" (Hoch 137). The statement neatly blames males alone even when the damage to the environment has been caused in part by females like Anne Gorsuch Burford and Rita Lavelle.

Not only crimes but vices of all sorts have been typically attributed to males. As Muriel R. Schulz points out, "The synonyms for *inebriate* . . . seem to be coded primarily 'male': for example, *boozer, drunkard, tippler, toper, swiller, tosspol, guzzler, barfly, drunk, lush, boozehound, souse, tank, stew, rummy,* and *bum*" (126). Likewise, someone may be *drunk as a lord* but never *drunk as a lady.*

Sex bias or sexism itself is widely held to be a male-only fault. When *sexism* is defined as "contempt for women"—as if there were no such thing as contempt for men—the definition of *sexism* is itself sexist (Bardwick 34).

Part of the reason for this masculinization of evil may be that in the Western world the source of evil has long been depicted in male terms. In the Bible the Evil One is consistently referred to as *he,* whether the reference is to the serpent in the Garden of Eden, Satan as Adversary in Job, Lucifer and Beelzebub in the gospels, Jesus' tempter in the desert, or the dragon in Revelations. *Beelzebub,* incidentally, is often translated as *lord of the flies,* a term designating the demon as masculine. So masculine is the word *devil* that the female prefix is needed, as in *she-devil,* to make a feminine noun of it. The masculinization of evil is so unconsciously accepted that writers often attest to it even while attempting to deny it, as in this passage:

> From the very beginning, the Judeo-Christian tradition has linked women and evil. When second-century theologians struggled to explain the Devil's origins, they surmised that Satan and his various devils had once been angels. (Gerzon 224)

If the Judeo-Christian tradition has linked women and evil so closely, why is the writer using the masculine pronoun *his* to refer to Satan, the source of evil according to that tradition? Critics of sex-bias in religious language seldom notice or mention its masculinization of evil: of those objecting to *God the Father as sexist,* no one—to my knowledge—has suggested that designating Satan as the *Father of Lies* is equally sexist. Few theologians talk about Satan and her legions.

The tendency to blame nearly everything on men has climaxed in recent times with the popularity of such terms as *patriarchy, patriarchal society,* and *male-dominated society.* More political than descriptive, these terms are rapidly becoming meaningless, used as all-purpose smear words to conjure up images of male oppressors and female victims. They are a linguistic sleight of hand which obscures the point that, as Mead has observed (299–300), societies are largely created by both sexes for both sexes. By using a swift reference to *patriarchal structures* or *patriarchal attitudes,* a writer can absolve females of all blame for society's flaws while fixing the onus solely on males. The give-away of this ploy can be detected when *patriarchy* and its related terms are never used in a positive or neutral context, but are always used to assign blame to males alone.

Wholesale denunciations of males as oppressors, exploiters, Nazis, and slave-drivers have become all too familiar during the past fifteen years. Too often the academic community, rather than opposing this sexism, has been encouraging it. All too many scholars and teachers have hopped on the male-bashing bandwagon to disseminate what John Gordon calls "the myth of the monstrous male." With increasing frequency, this academically fashionable sexism can also be heard echoing from our students. "A white upper-middle-class straight male should seriously consider another college," declares a midwestern college student in *The New York Times Selective Guide to Colleges.* "You [the white male] are the bane of the world. . . . Ten generations of social ills can and will be strapped upon your shoulders" (qtd. in Fiske 12). It would be comforting to dismiss this student's compound of misinformation, sexism, racism, and self-righteousness as an extreme example, but similar yahooisms go unchallenged almost everywhere in modern academia.

Surely it is time for men and women of good will to reject and protest such bigotry. For teachers and writers, the first task is to recognize and condemn forms of anti-male bias in language, whether they are used to exclude males from equal consideration with females, to reinforce restrictive aspects of the masculine gender role, or to stereotype males callously. For whether males are told that *fathers don't make good mothers,* that *real men don't cry,* or that *all men are rapists,* the results are potentially dangerous: like any other group, males can be subtly shaped into what society keeps telling them they are. In *Why Men Are the Way They Are* Warren Farrell puts the matter succinctly: "The more we make men the enemy, the more they will have to behave like the enemy" (357).

WORKS CITED

Bardwick, Judith. *In Transition: How Feminism, Sexual Liberation, and the Search for Self-Fulfillment Have Altered Our Lives.* New York: Holt, 1979.

Baring-Gould, William S., and Ceil Baring-Gould. *The Annotated Mother Goose: Nursery Rhymes Old and New, Arranged and Explained.* New York: Clarkson N. Potter, 1962.

Brownmiller, Susan. *Against Our Will: Men, Women and Rape.* New York: Simon, 1975.

Collier, Phyllis K. *How to Marry a Winner.* Englewood Cliffs, NJ: Prentice, 1982.

Dinnerstein, Dorothy. *The Mermaid and the Minotaur: Sexual Arrangements and Human Malaise.* New York: Harper, 1976.

Farrell, Warren. *The Myth of Male Power: Why Men Are the Disposable Sex.* New York: Simon, 1993.

———. *Why Men Are the Way They Are: The Male-Female Dynamic.* New York: McGraw-Hill, 1986.

Fiske, Edward B. *The New York Times Selective Guide to Colleges.* New York: New York Times Books, 1982.

Gerzon, Mark. *A Choice of Heroes: The Changing Faces of American Manhood.* Boston: Houghton, 1982.

Goldberg, Herb. *The Hazards of Being Male: Surviving the Myth of Masculine Privilege.* Rev. ed. New York: NAL, 1987.

———. *The New Male: From Self-Destruction to Self-Care.* New York: NAL, 1980.

Gordon, John. *The Myth of the Monstrous Male, and Other Feminist Fables.* New York: Playboy P, 1982.

Hartley, Ruth E. "Sex-Role Pressures and the Socialization of the Male Child." *The Forty-Nine Percent Majority: The Male Sex Role.* Eds. Deborah S. David and Robert Brannon. Reading, MA: Addison-Wesley, 1976. 235–44.

"Indiana jury finds Brown guilty of murder, molesting." *Dayton Daily News* 18 May 1986: 7A.

Inglis, Ruth. *Sins of the Fathers: A Study of the Physical and Emotional Abuse of Children.* New York: St. Martin's, 1978.

Jennes, Gail, "All Men Are Rapists." *People* 20 Feb. 1978: 33–4.

Lehne, Gregory K. "Homophobia Among Men." *The Forty-Nine Percent Majority: The Male Sex Role.* Eds. Deborah S. David and Robert Brannon. Reading, MA: Addison-Wesley, 1976. 66–88.

Levine, James A. *Who Will Raise the Children? New Options for Fathers (and Mothers).* Philadelphia: Lippincott, 1976.

Mead, Margaret. *Male and Female: A Study of the Sexes in a Changing World.* New York: Morrow, 1949, 1967.

Money, John, and Patricia Tucker. *Sexual Signatures: On Being a Man or a Woman.* Boston: Little, 1975.

Moore, Robert, and Douglas Gillette. *King Warrior Magician Lover: Rediscovering the Archetypes of the Mature Masculine.* New York: HarperCollins, 1990.

Mougey, Kate. "Rape: An act of confiscation." *Kettering-Oakwood [OH] Times* 4 Feb. 1981: 1b.

" 'Nerd' day gets a boot after suicide." *Dayton Daily News* 24 Jan. 1986: 38.

Ong, Walter J. *Fighting for Life: Contest, Sexuality, and Consciousness.* Ithaca, NY: Cornell UP, 1981.

O'Reilly, Jane, et al. "Wife-Beating: The Silent Crime." *Time* 5 Sept. 1983: 23–4, 26.

"Police; Print links Coleman, death." *Dayton Daily News* 31 Aug. 1984: 26.

Sarrel, Philip M., and William H. Masters. "Sexual Molestation of Men by Women." *Archives of Sexual Behavior* 11 (1982): 117–31.

Schulz, Muriel R. "Is the English Language Anybody's Enemy?" *Speaking of Words: A Language Reader.* Eds. James MacKillop and Donna Woolfolk Cross. 3rd ed. New York: Holt, 1986. 125–27.

Sommers, Christina Hoff. *Who Stole Feminism? How Women Have Betrayed Women.* New York: Simon, 1994.

Sorrels, Bobbye D. *The Nonsexist Communicator: Solving the Problems of Gender and Awkwardness in Modern English.* Englewood Cliffs, NJ: Prentice, 1983.

Spender, Dale. *Man Made Language.* London: Routledge, 1980.

Straus, Murray A., Richard J. Gelles, and Suzanne K. Steinmetz. *Behind Closed Doors: Violence in the American Family.* Garden City, New York: Doubleday, 1981.

Struckman-Johnson, Cindy. "Forced Sex on Dates: It Happens to Men, Too," *Journal of Sex Research* 24 (1988): 234–41.

Theroux, Paul. "The Male Myth." *New York Times Magazine* 27 Nov. 1983: 116.

1 Why, according to August, has the study of anti-male bias in language been neglected in favor of the examination of terms used to exploit and demean women? What three forms of anti-male bias in language does August identify?

2 Assess August's finding of anti-male bias in the following: the use of the term rape as "a brush to tar all males" (para. 14), the words applied to social outcasts (para. 20), the view that "if women in our society have been regarded as sex objects, men have been regarded as success objects" (para. 19).

3 How does August use the Bible to explain the prevalence of anit-male bias in language? Do you agree with August that the language used to describe male homosexuality is more denigrating than the language used to describe female homosexuality? Discuss August's view that "crime and evil are usually attributable to the male" (para. 30). How does recognizing this phenomenon suggest that it is important to reassess the roles of men and women in our society without language stereotypes?

4 How does the overview of anti-male usage August identifies in paragraph 7 ("in modern English, three kinds of anti-male language are evident . . . gender-exclusive usage, gender-restrictive language, and negative stereotypes of males") serve to organize his essay? What examples are especially effective in illustrating and clarifying these categories? (Glossary: *Examples, Organization.*)

5 August illustrates his thesis with a number of examples. Why is this rhetorical strategy particularly appropriate for his subject? Were his examples relevant, interesting, representative, and specific? (Glossary: *Examples*).

6 In your opinion, does the use of the word "guy(s)" to address women imply an anti-female bias (even if used by women to address other women)? Why or why not?

Advertisements for Oneself

Lance Morrow

◆ LANCE MORROW is a regular contributor to *Time* magazine, where he has been on the staff for over thirty years. His essays for the magazine have earned him a National Magazine Award in 1981 and have been collected in *Fishing in the Tiber* (1988), in which the following selection first appeared. Among his other published works are *The Chief: A Memoir of Fathers and Sons* (1985) and *America: A Rediscovery* (1987).

Almost everyone has read personal ads in the classified sections of newspapers and magazines that are intended to solicit replies that can lead to relationships. You may have even placed or answered such an ad. The language of these ads, the emotional appeals involved, and the way in which people try to package themselves are the subjects of Morrow's essay. They are, in essence, a specialized form of communication between the sexes and are so popular and commonplace as to suggest they are not necessarily the recourse of those desperate to meet someone. The language used in these ads is different from the usual interchanges between men and women, since it is formulated with a particular audience in mind and is designed to present the writer in the most engaging way possible. The ads are forms of self-promotion, and are, as Morrow says, "small rhapsodies of self-celebration."

TO CONSIDER What set of circumstances might lead you to put a personal ad in a newspaper or magazine? What would the ad say?

It is an odd and compact art form, and somewhat unnatural. A person feels quite uncomfortable composing a little song of himself for the classifieds. The personal ad is like haiku of self-celebration, a brief solo played on one's own horn. Someone else should be saying these things. It is for others to pile up the extravagant adjectives ("sensitive, warm, witty, vibrant, successful, handsome, accomplished, incredibly beautiful, cerebral, and sultry") while we stand demurely by. But someone has to do it. One competes for attention. One must advertise. One must chum the waters and bait the hook, and go trolling for love and laughter, for caring and sharing, for long walks and quiet talks, for Bach and brie. Nonsmokers only. Photo a must. 1

There are poetic conventions and clichés and codes in composing a personal ad. One specifies DWF (divorced white female), SBM (single black male), GWM (gay white male) and so on, to describe marital status, race, sex. Readers should understand the euphemisms. "Zaftig" or "Rubenesque," for example, usually means fat. "Unpretentious" is liable to mean boring. "Sensuous" means the party likes sex. 2

Sometimes the ads are quirkily self-conscious. "Ahem," began one suitor in the *New York Review of Books*. "Decent, softspoken sort, sanely silly, philosophish, seeks similar." Then he started to hit his stride: "Central Jersey DM WASP professional, 38, 6'2", slow hands, student of movies and Marx, gnosis and news, craves womanish companionship. . . ." 3

The sociology of personals has changed in recent years. One reason that people still feel uncomfortable with the form is that during the sixties and early 4 seventies personal ads had a slightly sleazy connotation. They showed up in the back of underground newspapers and sex magazines, the little billboards through which wife swappers and odd sexual specialists communicated. In the past several years, however, personal ads have become a popular and reputable way of shopping for new relationships. The *Chicago Tribune* publishes them. So does the conservative *National Review,* although a note from the publisher advises, "*NR* extends maximum freedom in this column, but *NR*'s maximum freedom may be another man's straitjacket. *NR* reserves the right to reject any copy deemed unsuitable." *National Review* would likely have turned down a West Coast entreaty: "Kinky Boy Scout seeks Kinky Girl Scout to practice knots. Your rope or mine?" *National Review*'s personals are notably chaste, but so are those in most other magazines. The emphasis is on "traditional values," on "long-term relationships" and "nest building." The sexual revolution has cooled down to a domestic room temperature. The raciest item might call for a woman with "Dolly Parton-like figure." One ad in Los Angeles stated: "Branflake patent holder tired of money and what it can buy seeks intellectual stimulation from big-bosomed brunette. Photo please." The *Village Voice* rejected the language of a man who wanted a woman with a "big ass." A few days later the man returned with an ad saying he sought a "callipygian" woman.

5   Every week *New York* magazine publishes five or six pages of personals. The *New York Review of Books* publishes column after column of some of the most entertaining personals. Many of them are suffused with a soft-focus romanticism. Firelight plays over the fantasy. Everyone seems amazingly successful. The columns are populated by Ph.D.s. Sometimes one encounters a millionaire. Occasionally a satirical wit breaks the monotony: "I am DWM, wino, no teeth, smell bad, age 40—look 75. Live in good cardboard box in low-traffic alley. You are under 25, tall, sophisticated, beautiful, talented, financially secure, and want more out of life. Come fly with me."

6   Humor helps, especially in a form that usually gives off a flat glare of one-dimensional optimism. It is hard not to like the "well read, well shaped, well disposed widow, early sixties, not half bad in the dusk with the light behind me." She sought a "companionable, educated, professional man of wit and taste," and she probably deserved him. Her self-effacement is fairly rare in personals. The ads tend sometimes to be a little nervous and needing, and anxiously hyperbolic. Their rhetoric tends to get overheated and may produce unintended effects. A man's hair stands on end a bit when he encounters "Alarmingly articulate, incorrigibly witty, overeducated, but extremely attractive NYC woman." A female reader of *New York* magazine might enjoy a chuckling little shudder at this: "I am here! A caring, knowing, daffy, real, tough, vulnerable, and handsome brown-eyed psychoanalyst." One conjures up the patient on the couch and a Freudian in the shape of Daffy Duck shouting: "You're desPICable!"

7   The struggle in composing one's ad is to be distinctive and relentlessly self-confident. What woman could resist the "rugged rascal with masculine determined sensual viewpoint"? An ad should not overreach, however, like the woman who began: "WANTED: One Greek god of refined caliber."

Not all the ads are jaunty or dewy-eyed. One begins: "Have herpes?" Some   8
are improbably specialized: "Fishing Jewish woman over 50 seeks single man to
share delights of angling." Or: "Literate snorkeler . . . have room in my life for
one warm, secure, funny man."

Anyone composing a personal ad faces an inherent credibility problem.   9
While we are accustomed to the self-promotions of politicians, say, we sense
something bizarre when ordinary people erupt in small rhapsodies of self-celebration that are occasioned by loneliness and longing. One is haunted by almost
piteous cries that come with post-office-box number attached: "Is there anyone
out there? Anyone out there for me?"

Composing an ad with oneself as the product is an interesting psychologi-   10
cal exercise, and probably good training in self-assertion. Truth will endure a little decorative writing, perhaps. The personals are a form of courtship that is
more efficient, and easier on the liver, than sitting in bars night after night, hoping for a lucky encounter. Yet one feels sometimes a slightly disturbed and forlorn vibration in those columns of chirpy pleading. It is inorganic courtship.
There is something severed, a lost connection. One may harbor a buried resentment that there are not parents and aunts and churches and cotillions to arrange
the meetings in more seemly style.

That, of course, may be mere sentimentalism. Whatever works. Loneliness   11
is the Great Satan. Jane Austen, who knew everything about courtship, would
have understood the personals columns perfectly. Her novel *Emma,* in fact,
begins, "Emma Woodhouse, handsome, happy, clever, and rich, with a comfortable home and happy disposition." The line might go right into the *New
York Review of Books.*

---

1 Because personal ads are so short, what stylistic strategies are necessary to communicate a lot of information in a few words? Within this framework, what qualities
   become important in using language effectively to convey personality?

2 What different kinds of personal ads does Morrow identify and what needs underlie each category? Do you agree with Morrow's view that "one sometimes feels a
   slightly disturbed and forlorn vibration in those columns of chirpy pleading" (para.
   10)?

3 Try your hand at composing a personal ad for yourself and/or for a modest friend.
   What aspects of personality would the ad emphasize? Would your ad fall into any
   of the categories Morrow identifies? If so, which one? You might consider switching
   ads among class members and then trying to guess who wrote which.

4 Why are the connotations of words particularly important in personal ads? Discuss
   some examples in terms of the signals that are being sent? (Glossary: *Connotation,
   Denotation*).

5 Which of Morrow's examples did you find especially well suited to illustrate how
   people choose to market themselves in personal ads? (Glossary: *Examples.*)

6 Would you ever consider allowing your parents to arrange a marriage for you? If so, why would this be more advantageous than finding someone for yourself? If not, what would be the disadvantages? If your parents wrote an ad for you, what would it say? How would it differ from a personal ad you composed?

Rule #19
Don't Open Up Too Fast

*Sherrie Schneider
and Ellen Fein*

◆ ELLEN FEIN graduated from New York University, is married with two children, and lives on Long Island. Sherrie Schneider, a magazine writer, is married and lives in New Jersey. The following is drawn from *The Rules* (1995). *The Rules II* is a sequel published in 1997.

The "Rules" represents a radical reassessment, or perhaps a return, to a more traditional code governing communication between the sexes. What Schneider and Fein are recommending, after all, is a stylized conversational "dance" in which women are encouraged to withhold potentially damaging, embarrassing, or socially unacceptable information about themselves from men they go out with. Although at first glance their advice might appear manipulative and dishonest, the millions of copies sold of the authors' two books suggest that they are meeting a genuine need in our society in reformulating courtship customs between men and women. It is of, of course, ironic that Schneider and Fein's books, which are based on the withholding of information, are on the same best-seller list with Deborah Tannen's book, which recommends that men and women confide in each other more completely.

TO CONSIDER   If you had to hear some constructive advice on conducting a romantic relationship, who would you rather receive this advice from, a parent or a book?

D ating is not therapy. There are many ways to kill a relationship. Getting heavy and examining everything is certainly one of them. Conditioned by therapy and self-help books to tell all, women tend to overdo it on first dates, bringing up past relationships, their hurts and fears, their alcohol or

---

drug problem—all in an attempt to bond with this new man. This is deadly and boring. Be intelligent but light, interesting yet mysterious. That's why we have suggested not opening up too fast. (See also *Rule #9: How to Act on Dates 1, 2, and 3.*) The first date should be short, so you don't say too much. Remember, the person who talks the most has the most to lose.

By the end of the first date, he should know just a few facts, such as your name, your profession, how many siblings you have, where you went to college, where you grew up, and your favorite restaurants. By the end of the first date, he should not know your dating history. Don't reprimand him for picking you up thirty minutes late and then tell him you were afraid he would never show up, that you felt abandoned, and explain that "abandonment" is one of your issues in therapy. Don't tell him that his behavior reminds you of your ex-boyfriend who was also never on time. Even if this is true, don't tell him. Don't worry. By doing *The Rules,* you will automatically attract a loving, attentive husband who will be around so much that you won't have time to think about your abandonment issues!

If you have a burning desire to tell him a secret, *The Rules* credo is "Haste makes waste." It's always better to wait before telling someone something that you might feel ashamed or nervous about. Wait at least a couple of months. Better yet, wait until after he says "I love you." Unless he loves you, it's none of his business anyway!

Too many women tell intimate details of their lives far too soon. This is not only unwise, but also it doesn't work. No man wants to be the recipient of a therapy session upon first meeting you. No man wants to hear how wrong or messed up your life has been before he *really* loves you.

You are not on this date to get sympathy but to have a nice evening and get him to call you again. Remember *Rule #9*—that the first three dates are about being light and charming, like a summer breeze. Men must always remember you as mysterious on the first three dates. Their initial impression tends to go a long way. If and when things get serious, you can casually tell him about your difficult childhood and some of your fears. Even then, tell him in an easy, short, simple way. Don't be dramatic about your past. Don't go into long details. Don't be burdensome.

Let's say you are a recovering alcoholic. He takes you out for a drink on your first date and to dinner on the second. He notices you only ordered club soda both times. He is about to order a bottle of wine and wants to know if you'll join him. Don't say, "No, I *never* drink. I hit a terrible bottom with drugs and alcohol two years ago and now I'm sober in AA." Just say, "No, thanks," and smile. After a couple of months when he's madly in love with you and you feel that he would not judge you for your drinking problem, you can tell him something like, "I used to drink a lot in college. It really made me sick. Now I'm in AA and I don't drink anymore. I feel better." Then smile and go on to other, more pleasant conversation. If he loves you, he will not make you feel bad. He won't argue with you or try to encourage you to "just have one." He might even start drinking less himself to make you feel better. He might even say that he's proud of your sobriety and discipline.

If you've had a serious illness and you're embarrassed about obvious scars from your surgery, wait until you're about to be intimate with him and then casually mention, as you take your clothes off in the dark, that you had an illness. If he loves you, he will kiss and caress you. Don't bring up the illness in a serious, heart-to-heart talk on your first date. Remember, especially in the beginning, don't be too intense about anything or lay all your cards on the table. In general, the less tragic you are about your life circumstances, the more sympathy you will probably get. Ask for sympathy and you never get it.

If you don't know how to hold on to a dollar, don't balance your checkbook, have an answering machine filled with calls from bill collectors leaving threatening messages, don't tell him what a mess you are with finances and that you got it from your father who once gambled away your college tuition. Now you might feel that we are asking you to act casually about your problems, but the fact is, you are bad with money and he will soon see that. But does he really have to know about the creditors and your canceled credit cards? No, all he has to know is that money is not your strong suit.

We are not suggesting that you hide or lie about bad things in your life, just that you not burden him with all the gory details too soon. Does he really have to know that your last boyfriend dropped you for your best friend? Can't you just say, if he asks, that your last relationship "just didn't work out"?

He should always feel that he's in love with the girl of his dreams, not someone damaged. If you *feel* damaged (many of us do in some way), read *Rule#1* again and again. Remember, you are a creature unlike any other! It's when and how you tell him your darkest secrets, not the secrets themselves, that matter.

By the time you are engaged, he should know *all* that really matters about you and your family and your past. *The Rules* are truthful and spiritual in nature. It is morally wrong to accept an engagement ring without revealing whatever truths about yourself you need to share. Tell him these things in a calm, non-dramatic manner and don't, as some women do, surprise him with these skeletons after you're married. That's not the time to tell him that you were previously married or never finished college. It's not fair to him and not good for a *Rules* marriage.

---

1 Do you agree with the authors' assessment that dating is "not therapy" and that "opening up too fast" may kill a relationship before it gets started? Why or why not? In your opinion, are first impressions indeed as powerful as Schneider and Fein seem to believe?

2 What types of inappropriate revelations do they cite as examples to illustrate their thesis? Are these examples purposely skewed to support their thesis? In your opinion, do men already do what the authors recommend women start doing?

3 Do you agree with Schneider and Fein's assessment? Do you find their rules accurate, manipulative, necessary—or all three? In your opinion, why did their books *The Rules* (1995) and *The Rules II* (1997) hold such profound appeal for the millions who purchased them? Do you find it ironic that books based on the premise that women should withhold information about themselves are on the same best-seller lists with works by Deborah Tannen and others who espouse complete openness between men and women?

4 How would you characterize the voice that you hear in this piece ("Dating is not therapy," "Don't go into long details")? What presumed relationship does this voice have with the audience? (Glossary: *Voice*.)

5 Does this essay by Schneider and Fein present a thesis that clarifies the attitude of the authors toward the process involved? If so, what is it? Is their analysis primarily instructional or informational? Explain. To what extent do the authors try to persuade readers to follow the process they discuss? (Glossary: *Process Analysis*.)

6 Create a list of five to ten things your parents used to say to you and then select one of those "messages" and describe the role it played in creating expectations that have remained with you to this day.

Your First Date   *Linda Stasi*

◆ LINDA STASI is a contemporary American writer whose works include *Simply Beautiful* (1983), *A Field Guide to Impossible Men (1987), Looking Good Is the Best Revenge (1985),* and *Boomer Babes (1998).* She has been a columnist for the *New York Daily News,* and *New York Newsday.* She is currently a columnist for the *Village Voice.*

As Schneider and Fein suggested, what you don't say is frequently more important than what you do say, a point echoed earlier by Ronald Wardhaugh in his identification of trust or lack of it as the single most important feature that determines whether conversations flow along or grind to a halt. What Stasi does is to create a scenario of a first date and make explicit the unexpressed subtext that makes communication between men and women so problematic. These unspoken conversations can certainly be considered as much a part of the communication between men and women as what each speaker actually does say. The resulting transcript of expressed and unexpressed thoughts between the two people is amusing and profoundly ironic.

> **TO CONSIDER**   Why are the unspoken conversations during a date as important as, if not more important than, what is actually said?

SPOTTING AN AWESOMELY UNCOMMITTED MAN

Awesome is likely to be spotted in any place that caters to singles and exceptionally clean people. So you might find him (when he's not at Crazy Eddie's) in a gourmet food shop, Chinese laundry, nouvelle cuisine restaurant, any Hampton except Lionel, Club Med, the cleaning aisle of the supermarket, in the best seat of an obscure classical or sixties rock concert, at the local exotic car dealership.

He wears jeans on the weekends and always has a great pair of sneakers on his feet. He is obsessed by his hair and always has a decent haircut that's never quite right. If he's losing his hair, it is to him the equivalent of having cancer. You are sure to find Monoxidil somewhere in his home, or in his bag if you are away together. He spends a great deal of time gently patting the top of his head in a bizarre manner. It's his way of testing to see if any more hair has come loose in the last three minutes.

He wears glasses and has tried contacts, and he is on a first-name basis with his eye doctor called Larry who's one of his Hampton housemates.

YOUR FIRST DATE

He'll pick you up and take you somewhere nice. He's wearing an all-cotton starched shirt with French cuffs. He smells vaguely of Aramis or some other annoying shaving lotion. He'll drink either single malt Scotch or vodka, and will definitely order the pasta whatever it is. He'll be especially thrilled if they have gnocchi on the menu. Don't even be tempted to ask what gnocchi is.

YOUR FIRST CONVERSATION

HE SAYS: I'd like to be married, have kids, the whole nine yards. I'm getting too old to be a bachelor . . . I'm ready to get married.

HE MEANS: *If* I found someone who looked like Christie Brinkley, took her clothes off as quickly as Debra Winger in a movie, raised children with the skill of Mrs. Cleaver, had the patience of Mother Teresa, and could earn a hundred grand or more in a nice part-time job, I'd marry her in a minute.

YOU SAY: Oh, really?

YOU SHOULD HAVE SAID: If there's anything I don't want to be it's married. Why do I only meet men who want to get married?

HE SAYS: Huh?

HE MEANS: This is a new one for me!

YOU SAY: Is the food good here?

Completely ignoring his lies about wanting to get married makes him totally insane. Every woman he's ever been out with hears the wedding march upon the utterance of these magic words and is sure that he means her, he thinks. (Therefore, if you disregard all his nonsense it will make him—if not mad for you—at least anxious enough to keep calling. Lucky you.)

If the wedding talk hasn't budged you, he will switch tactics to show you that he's a man with *plans*. Plans are his life. He already has plans to take a house in the Hamptons with the same group of survivors that he's housed with for the last five summers. He plans to summer with them this year and next, and by the third summer, he will have accrued enough sick time and vacation time to take a month and a half off, at which he will take a house in Spain with four of his housemates from the Hamptons. He's found out that you can get a cleaning lady in Spain for four dollars a day, including laundry! This may in fact be the most telling part of his whole litany. Because, like it or not, cleaning women mean a great deal to him. Cleanliness and order mean a great deal to him. He is anal to the point of turning it into a religious experience.

His present cleaning lady is the most important woman in his life. She's competent, she's amusing, she's organized, she starches his sheets. He's happy when she's there. She makes no demands and all he has to do is give her a bonus at Christmas. He doesn't even have to make a pretense of going into Gucci's.

He would like, in theory at least, to be married. But in reality he sees no need for it, although he does like to have a steady girlfriend he can see (sleep with) a predictable number of days a week and probably on Saturday night. He would like to have relationships with women that could stay on that basis forever. Why spoil the fun? he thinks. And besides, if you're married, you have to get a station wagon.

Here's the kicker: He may have even been married before. What did she have that you don't have? Him, when he was young enough *not* to know that he didn't want to be married.

WHAT HE LIKES TO DO WITH YOU

- Make love and then roll over so fast you'd think he had ball bearings on his back.
- Go shopping for stereo equipment for his apartment.
- Go to the movies and out for dinner on the weekends.
- Keep your relationship in that gray limbo-land for as long as he's comfortable with it, which could be forever or maybe next week.
- Go for rides with his kids and take them places.

WHAT HE LIKES TO DO WITHOUT YOU

- Attend family functions (his).
- See old girlfriends for dinner and lunch.
- Have dinner with his parents and siblings and *their* spouses or dates.

- Go to his best friend's wedding in another state.
- Escort other women to black tie functions as though you were his mistress and he was secretly keeping you, when as far as you know all you've ever gotten out of him is a Trivial Pursuit game to keep at your house.
- *Make plans.* While you aren't looking, he books a mountain-climbing course for every Sunday for three months, signs on for his share of the summer house, books his Club Med trip.
- Keep all of the above from you until each one is a fait accompli. When you get crazy and scream about being excluded, he'll say, "I thought you wouldn't enjoy it." Or, "I need some space to do my own things once in a while. I don't understand why you don't find things of your own to do. I'm not your social director." Then you'll have a huge fight, and somehow or other *you* end up apologizing.

---

1 What personality features, according to Stasi, define the "awesomely uncommitted man" (para. 1) on a first date?

2 Do the various examples presented by Stasi seem to be exaggerated? How would you characterize her attitude toward the subject? How does this article illustrate how writers can be amusing and still make a point?

3 Why are the prospects for meaningful communication very slight between the "awesomely uncommitted man" and his date? What conversational ploys does he use to create the appearance of wanting a long-term relationship? Create a dialogue between the "awesomely uncommitted man" and a woman following Rule #19 (see Sherrie Schneider and Ellen Fein in this chapter).

4 How are the humorous effects of this essay largely dependent on Stasi's use of irony—that is, the contrast between things as they appear and things as they are? (Glossary: *Irony.*)

5 What transitions does Stasi use to signal the reader that she is weaving back and forth between what is actually said and what is meant in the first date conversation scenario she dramatizes? How is this method of organization well suited to create a sense of irony? (Glossary: *Comparison and Contrast, Transitions, Irony.*)

6 You have brought home a date—not necessarily of the opposite sex—to meet your family. How would they react? Identify the important characteristics of the individuals involved so your readers will understand why each person reacted the way he/she did. Include relevant conversations in your account.

◆ CONNECTIONS: COMMUNICATION BETWEEN THE SEXES

Robin Lakoff, "Language and Woman's Place"

1. To what extent do speech patterns of female deference and male assertion discovered by Lakoff exist in the language and culture of the Old West, as explored by Jane Tompkins?
2. How would Ronald Wardhaugh's findings in "The Social Basis of Talk" (Ch. 4) be modified by Lakoff's discoveries?

Deborah Tannen, "Sex, Lies, and Conversation"

1. In what sense can the difficulties men and women encounter in communicating with each other (as described by Tannen) be seen in the different agendas underlying a conversation, as reported by Stasi? What are the different agendas?
2. How do the differences in childhood socialization between boys and girls, reported by Tannen, reinforce inequalities in communication between men and women as adults, as reported by Alleen Pace Nilsen in "Sexism In English: A 1990s Update" (Ch. 8)?

Jane Tompkins, "Women and the Language of Men"

1. To what extent do the contrasting values of loquacity versus silence, talk versus action, and ineffectuality versus potency underlying the culture of the Old West (as described by Tompkins) resemble the different communication styles of men and women discussed by Deborah Tannen?
2. How have many of the issues of differences in communication styles of men and women explored by Tompkins resurfaced on the Internet, as discussed by Paula Span in "Women and Computers: Is There Equity in Cyberspace?" (Ch. 11)?

Eugene R. August, "Real Men Don't, or Anti-Male Bias in English"

1. How does August's study of anti-male bias in English provide a necessary counterbalance to Jane Tompkins's analysis? What assumptions about what it is to be male underlie both accounts?
2. To what extent is an anti-male bias of the kind August describes present in Julia Penelope's "The Glamour of Grammar" (Ch. 7)?

Lance Morrow, "Advertisements for Oneself"

1. How do both Morrow's and Linda Stasi's essays rely on the assumption that men and women, whether in personal ads or on first dates, present themselves as being very different from the way they really are?
2. In what way do personal ads use the traditional rhetorical appeals of *logos, pathos,* and *ethos* used to sell products as discussed by Stuart Hirschberg in "The Rhetoric of Advertising" (Ch. 9)?

Sherrie Schneider and Ellen Fein, "Rule #19: Don't Open Up Too Fast"

1. Discuss the irony of two books appearing on the *New York Times* best-seller list at the same time, one—Deborah Tannen's—promoting more honest communication between men and women and the other—by Schneider and Fein—advising the opposite.
2. In what sense might Schneider and Fein's advice be seen as a specific practical application of Ronald Wardhaugh's discussion in "The Social Basis of Talk" (Ch. 4) about knowing what to reveal and what not to reveal during conversations?

Linda Stasi, "Your First Date"

1. How does Stasi's essay reveal a man operating much as Sherrie Schneider and Ellen Fein advise women to operate?
2. How does Ronald Wardhaugh's analysis in "The Social Basis of Talk" (Ch. 4) of the key factors governing conversations operate in Stasi's discussion?

◆ WRITING ASSIGNMENTS FOR CHAPTER 5

1. Have you ever been romantically involved with someone of the same sex, or someone from a different racial, religious, or cultural background? What kinds of pressures were you subjected to from parents, relatives, friends, and society that made communicating even more difficult aside from the gender-related problems discussed in this chapter? What was the outcome of this relationship?
2. What unique difficulties in communication arise for new spouses, children, and stepchildren as a result of second marriages? Discuss any relevant experiences you may have had.
3. What actions or reactions are reliable indicators that a person is in love? Do men react differently from women, for the most part, when in love? Describe a relevant incident and include the conversations involved.
4. Compose a letter (that is not intended to be sent) to someone of the opposite sex expressing feelings that you would not feel comfortable expressing in a face-to-face conversation.
5. What memorable lines have you heard used to "break the ice"?
6. What common labels for men and women rely on metaphors associated with food, pets, or plants? (For example, cupcake, honeybun, turkey, rat.) What attitudes do these labels promote?
7. Analyze the following two ads according to any of the authors in this chapter.

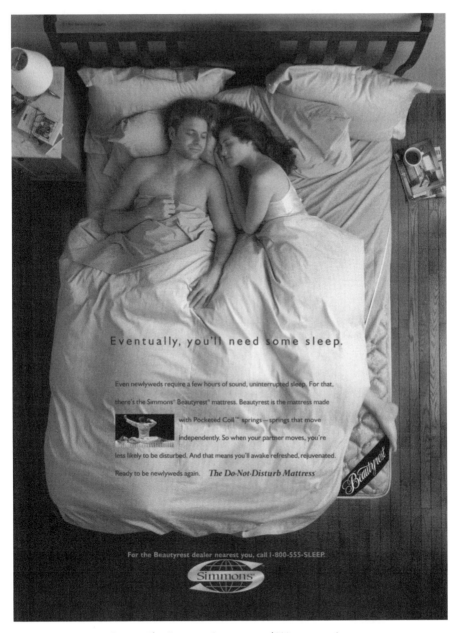

Source: The Simmons Company and Westwayne, Inc.

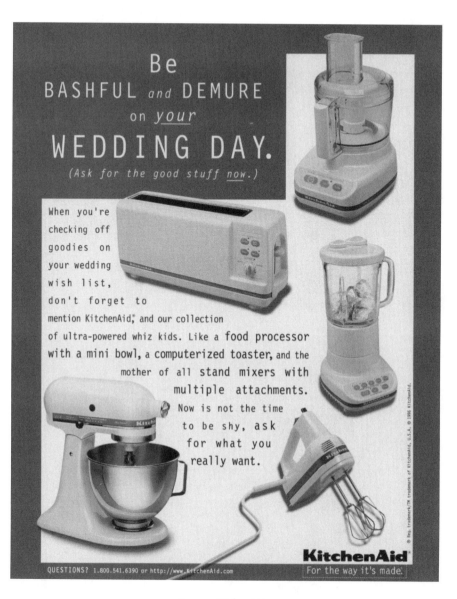

Source: KitchenAid.

8. Take the following quiz and score your answer. Did your interpretations of the questions and answers match those of the editors of this magazine (*Ym*, Oct. 1996)? What other examples of guy talk can you think of?

DO YOU SPEAK GUY TALK?

1. "Were you at the game this weekend?" means:
   - ❏ **a.** I wonder if you like football.
   - ❏ **b.** Did you happen to see the awesome catch I made?
   - ❏ **c.** I want to know what you like to do on weekends, since I'm thinking about asking you out.

2. You invite him over for dinner and he asks, "Is your sister going to be there?" What he means is:
   - ❏ **a.** Are we going to be alone?
   - ❏ **b.** I'm psyched to meet the rest of your family.
   - ❏ **c.** I have a serious crush on your sister.

3. Which of the following does NOT mean "Do you want to make out with me?"
   - ❏ **a.** Wanna take a walk?
   - ❏ **b.** Can I borrow your math home-work?
   - ❏ **c.** My parents will be going out of town for the weekend.

4. Your guy bud has a car, so you ask if he would mind picking you up at the train station. He says, "No problem." What he means is:
   - ❏ **a.** Ask me again right before you need it done, and I'll do it if I have time.
   - ❏ **b.** I don't see any reason why not.
   - ❏ **c.** I promise I'll be there—you can totally count on me.

5. "Are you gonna eat that?" means:
   - ❏ **a.** Can I eat that?
   - ❏ **b.** I can't believe you're gonna eat all that.
   - ❏ **c.** You're taking too long to finish eating.

6. "You're a really great person" means:
   - ❏ **a.** I like you as more than a friend.
   - ❏ **b.** I'm sorry, but I'm really just not attracted to you.
   - ❏ **c.** I'm glad we're such good friends.

7. "I'll talk to you later" means:
   - ❏ **a.** I like you, and I'll definitely be calling you tonight.
   - ❏ **b.** I'll probably see you around, sometime, maybe.
   - ❏ **c.** I hope you'll call me later.

8. Match the following questions with their real meanings:

    a.   Did you do something to your hair?
    b.   What did you do to your hair?
    c.   You got a haircut?
    1.   I've never had a romantic thought about you.
    2.   I never thought you were cute before, but now I do.
    3.   I used to think you were cute, but not anymore.

your score

1. a) 1 b) 2 c)0
2. a) 1 b) 0 c) 2
3. a) 1 b) 2 c) 0
4. a) 2 b) 1 c) 0
5. a) 2 b) 0 c) 1
6. a) 0 b) 2 c) 1
7. a) 1 b) 2 c) 0

Give yourself one point for each correct answer:
8. a) 2 b) 3 c) 1

0–6 points
missing the message
Remember when your guy bud wondered out loud whether you were the type who liked to go to stupid school dances to hang out and make fun of everyone's clothes? News flash: he was trying to ask you to the prom! You're so oblivious to the way guys try to connect that you could be letting key cues about his feelings pass you by. But what's even more potentially humiliating is that you may be reading way too much into his random friendly comments. Brush up on your guy-speak, girl!

7–12 points
learning the lingo
You may never solve all the mysteries of guy-girl interaction, but you have cracked the basic code. You can usually tell by what a guy says whether it's like, love, or lust. Plus, you're savvy enough to know when and if his comments mean he's playing hard to get-or if he's truly out of reach. Most important, you realize that the things that fly out of a guy's mouth sometimes don't mean what they sound like to us, because boys have their own unique (and often clueless) ways of expressing themselves. If you continue to keep your ears open, you should be able to avoid any major communication breakdowns.

13–17 points

talking the talk

Scary! You speak Guy like a, well, guy, decoding their grunts and mumbles with ease. They'll never be able to put anything over on you-or your friends, who are constantly begging you to translate "What did he mean by that?!?" Just beware: if you get much more fluent in studspeak, you might start to blend in with the rest of his buds-and being one of the boys is probably not your ultimate goal.

If you can teach me a new word, I'll walk all the way to China to get it.

—Turkish Proverb

Calvin and Hobbes

ALLO? EEZ THEES DER POOBLIC LAHBRORRY? YAH?

I EM BEEG EEMPORTANT REZEARCHER OOND I REQUIRE EENGLISH VOOLGAR ZYNONYMS FOR DISGUSTINK BODY VUNKTIONS, YAH?

© 1992 Watterson/Distributed by Universal Press Syndicate

by Bill Watterson

ALLO? ALLO?

NO LUCK?

THOSE LIBRARIANS ARE A SHARP BUNCH.

6-11 WATTERSON

Language
Between
Cultures

L anguage is the principal means through which the collective way of life of a people or society, including its economic and political system, rules of behavior, mores and customs, and laws are acquired and passed on from generation to generation. Often the language of a culture is its most apparent feature. What happens when people move from one country to another? They are immediately faced with the challenge of learning an unfamiliar language and deciphering the often concealed logic that governs family organization, religious beliefs, eating habits, courting behavior, and education practices of the new culture? The indispensable key to adjusting to a new society is language. Languages intertwine with cultures in inestimable ways. Because the different language they speak is the most visible sign of their not belonging, immigrants and minorities are subject to hostile judgments that can result in loneliness and disorientation. When people can communicate with each other, they are less likely to be intolerant of cultural differences.

Some immigrants react by making every effort to retain the customs and traditions of their homeland and not be assimilated into American society. At the other extreme, we find people who do everything they can to assimilate. Between these two poles it is more common to find people who attempt to combine traits of the two different cultures so that they can adjust but still not lose their sense of connection to their heritage.

This biculturalism is especially stressful for children of immigrants, as we can see in the accounts by Richard Rodriguez in "Public and Private Language," Sara Min in "Language Lessons," Amy Tan in "The Language of Discretion," and Lydia Minatoya in "Transformation." These accounts make us aware of how the need to establish an American identity through language, values, and attitudes often leads to a conflict at home with parents whose language and customs are at odds with mainstream society. Forming relationships with people whose cultural frame of reference is radically different need not produce "culture shock." Many people feel at ease in combining the traits of two different cultures and make up a new cultural group whose language, like Spanglish, is an amalgam of words and expressions from both Spanish and English. Enrique Fernandez in "Salsa × 2" offers abundant details that document how this process works.

Ironically, many of the same problems individuals face in adjusting to a new culture also confront corporations seeking to market their products abroad, as David A. Ricks amusingly reveals in his essay "What's in a Name?"

Salsa × 2   *Enrique Fernandez*

◆ ENRIQUE FERNANDEZ is a columnist for the *New York Daily News*. Portions of this piece appeared in different form in the *Daily News, New York Newsday,* and the *Village Voice*. The current version was reprinted in *Currents from the Dancing River,* edited by Ray Gonzalez (1994).

The role language plays in acquiring a public identity is complicated when the speaker comes from one cultural and linguistic background and is attempting to communicate using a new language, in a new culture. A current example is resulting amalgam called "Spanglish," a blend of Spanish and English that is heard throughout the United States in cities with large Hispanic-American populations. It is a widely accepted conversational mode that symbolizes, for Fernandez, the increasing influence of Hispanic culture on all features of American life. The most visible aspect of this influence is in the many meanings of the term

As appears in *Currents From the Dancing River*, 1994, Harcourt Brace. Permission by Susan Bergholz Literary Agency.

"salsa," which is not just a sauce but represents an entire attitude toward life conveying passion and nostalgia, honor and loss.

TO CONSIDER   Compare the emotional response you have to hearing Spanish with that produced by hearing English. To what extent is this due to how intertwined language is with music, food, dance, and other aspects of culture?

Salsa music coming out of Puerto Rico. Tito Puente. Gloria Estefan comes out of Miami and she sweeps the country. Los Lobos and Little Joe y La Familia play New York. . . . Bigger than our political accomplishments, which are going to be significant, and our business accomplishments, which are going to be significant, is the cultural dimension. Many changes are going to take place in America over the next fifteen years, but one of the most dramatic is what I have called the Hispanization of the United States. The country will have a sense that there is something new here in the culture. And it's going to be very pervasive. It's going to be in Seattle, in Minneapolis, in Chicago, in Indianapolis, in Cleveland, in Boston, as much as in Miami or Houston. . . . The first phase is going to be sensory awareness: enjoyment. Music, literature, architecture, women's clothing, food . . . Already, the New York Times tells me, salsas have superseded ketchup as the favorite condiment on American foods, and nachos are more popular at the Chicago Cubs baseball stadium than hot dogs. . . .

—HENRY CISNEROS IN AN INTERVIEW
WITH ENRIQUE FERNANDEZ

S alsa + salsa. Salsa × 2. Latin music and Latin food. Culture moves and expands through the same process as demographic growth, through seduction. Hear my music, eat my food, you are mine, you are me. Politics shakes its angry fist, theorists polemicize. Culture keeps on cooking. Culture just happens, and it happens most suavely when it tastes good.

Taste. *Sabor.* Food and music must have it. *Sabor*—flavor—is what Latino life is about. It is the quality of our difference. The flavor of salsa, both the spicy dance and the spicy dip for tortilla chips. The flavor of passion, the flavor of an everyday life that is not life if it is not highly spiked with pleasure. Highly. Every day.

"Why does your mother cook with such little seasoning?" asks Miami salsa star Hansel in his hit song "Americana Americana," a song lamenting the differences between a Latino boy and an Anglo girl. *¡Qué rico!* is the phrase most heard in Spanish-language food commercials. It's also the words most heard in Spanish-language beds. *¡Ay, qué rico!* Salsa means "sauce" and *mutatis mutandi* it means saucy Latin music. At first it was a purely commercial term of no musical significance, invented by record labels intent on marketing the dance grooves that had evolved from the Cuban mambo and taken root among New York's Puerto Rican community in the 1940s and 1950s, the era of the mambo kings. By the seventies, when this Latin dance music really came into its own, African-American music was called not by a specific beat or genre but by an ineffable quality: soul. Eager to cash in on a marketable, simple word, the Latin labels came up with a somewhat more concrete metaphor. If black music had soul, Latin music had . . . sauce! . . . salsa!

In the eighties, another Latin music genre with a culinary metaphor for a name invaded New York: merengue, from the Dominican Republic, brought in by a massive immigration that would only get larger. In Spanish the word meant "meringue," and it was an appropriate term for a groove that was frothy, rich, and, as anything from the Caribbean, filled your veins with sugar energy. It wasn't new or exclusively Dominican; one finds merengues in the folk music of other Latin American countries, though they sound quite different. But Dominican merengue is the only one internationally popular for dancing, one of the Latin classics like the Cuban rhumba, mambo, and cha-cha. As far back as my childhood I could remember merengues that swept the Latin American hit parades. Particularly one superhit titled "El negrito del batey," with lyrics like "I like to dance sideways/dance good and tight/with a very yummy Negress."

I have deliberately translated the lyrics as literally as possible to underscore certain cultural attitudes. One is a casualness toward race. The word *negrito* in the title means something like "little black boy." Words like *negrito* and *negrita* are used among some Latinos with the same nonchalance as "nigger" in the street talk of African Americans. Except that it lacks the ugly violence of American racial language; in fact, *negro, negra,* the gentler diminituves *negrito* and *negrita,* and the humorously sexy augmentatives *negrón* and *negrona* are common terms of endearment in the Spanish Caribbean, used by black and white folk alike to address loved ones of either race.

But what about the "*negra bien sabrosa,*" the yummy Negress the singer wants to dance the sideways step of the merengue, holding her good and tight? We have entered that curious chamber of the Latin house: the bedroom/kitchen, where sex and food fuse in an insouciant synaesthesia. *Comer,* "to eat," is the verb of choice in some Spanish-speaking countries for sexual intercourse; not oral sex, as in colloquial English, just sex. *Quiero comerte,* I want to eat (fuck) you—you're good enough to eat—you're a *negra bien sabrosa*—your body is flavorful—I want to taste you and in our love the senses run into one another—your mouth—my mouth—your sex—my sex—our flavors—¡Ay, qué rico!

A Dominican lady, twice burned in the fires of matrimony, told me recently that if she had known years ago what she knows now, the first thing she would have asked a man is "Do you like *plátanos*?" A man who doesn't like *plátanos,* she has learned the hard way, is quirky and untrustworthy. One who does is a regular guy. Not perfect, but regular. A Latino mensch.

To love *plátanos* is to be a good old boy, since they are the quintessential *criollo* food. When a Spaniard goes native in the Caribbean, he is said to be *aplatanado*—all plantained up. Though *plátanos* is another name for bananas, we're talking plantains, bananas' tougher, bigger cousins, always served cooked and seldom for dessert. Plantains can be a full main course when stuffed with a spicy ground-beef *picadillo* mixture. Or they can be chopped into Caribbean stews, along with cassava, peppers, and corn. Mashed with vegetables and meats, they are shaped into the tamalelike dish Puerto Ricans call *pasteles* and South Americans *huayacas*. They can be sliced paper-thin and fried like potato chips.

Treasonous as it may sound to my compatriots—and to my Dominican lady friend—I have never loved ripe *plátanos*. My mother's cooking was more Spanish than *criollo* and my taste buds are not sufficiently *aplatanado*. The cloying sweetness of fried ripe plantains insinuates itself on my tongue like a corruption. Still, most Cubans die for that taste. To experience the difference between Spanish and *criollo* food, try a basic *tortilla españaola*, an austere dish of eggs, potatoes, onions, olive oil, and salt. Then sample a *tortilla de plátanos,* which uses ripe plantains instead of potatoes. Can you just taste how all that Spanish austerity is seduced by the *plátanos*?

Latin food, Latin music. I walk the full length of Miami's massive Latino street party, Calle Ocho, named after the center strip of Little Havana, S.W. 8th Street. As I emerge my ears are ringing with clanging cowbells, slapped drums, rasping gourds, blaring trumpets, and the aggressively nasal come-ons of feisty *soneros.* My skin is covered with a thick layer of garlic-scented pork fat from hundreds of steaming Cuban sandwiches. I am so saturated in *sabor* that I need to switch on the Evian-water-flavored jazz-fusion station on the car radio in order to detox.

But I go back for more. The nearest Latino restaurant to my midtown Manhattan office is almost a mile away. There are days when I just have to walk it. On a visit to San Antonio I can't resist ordering a side bowl of *menudo* to my breakfast of *huevos con carne seca*. More flour tortillas, señora, please. And when a conjunto accordion begins to moan, I just want to feel this way forever. Virgen de Guadalupe, if I must die in your Amerindian soil instead of fanned by my Afro-Caribbean breezes, let it be like this, among frijoles and chiles, *acordeones y cervezas.*

Cross the threshold of Latin music and food and everything changes. Your heart expands, your soul relaxes, if you're not careful you'll break down and cry. What is styled, camera-ready has no place here. Artifice is blatantly artificial. Sexuality is lurid as hell. And if anything is revved up it's moist sentimentality and Hotspur machismo, not cool attitude.

Twenty-five million Latinos in the U.S., probably more. By the year 2010, more Latinos than African Americans. Latino Cassandras predict that Latinos will become the country's underclass, peons to our aging, glutted, conceited generations of Anglo baby boomers. Latino Pollyannas predict the Hispanization of the U.S. More likely, the future will be dialectical. There will be some of both the bleak and the joyful. There will be serious trials. Where African Americans provoke powerful emotions in the Anglo-American soul, deep fears and deep guilts, Latinos provoke mere disdain. Like pests. Like something that shouldn't be there in the first place. Already, Latinos are at the bottom of any social problem one can think of: the most destitute homeless, the least-cared-for aged, the most-troubled war veterans, the highest school dropout rate, not to mention Latino casualties in the gang and drug wars that ravage our cities.

Among the findings of the Latino National Political Survey, a study of our political attitudes undertaken by important Latino researchers, is the lack of identification with labels like *Latino* and *Hispanic,* with each group preferring designations like *Cuban, Puerto Rican,* and *Mexican-American,* or *mexicano.* The implication is that we don't bond with each other; we are assimilating. We are not Latinos; we are almost Americans. What could unite a light-skinned Cuban settled in a deluxe condo in Miami's Key Biscayne and a dark-skinned Puerto Rican living in the projects of the south Bronx?

Yet we have in common a Caribbean variant of Spanish. A nostalgia for the very same landscape and climate. A shared history of nationalist struggle against Spain and against Uncle Sam. Practically the same food (except the Puerto Rican love of cilantro and the Cuban preference for black beans over *gandules*). The same body language. The same music. The mix of Spain and Africa (unless one subscribes, as far too many people of all races do, to fascist notions of ethnicity, one must conclude that all Cubans and all Puerto Ricans are, culturally, mulatto).

No two Latino groups could be more different or more at odds with one another than Mexicans and Cuban Americans: Chicanos forged their political identity in a revolutionary civil rights struggle based on a dispossession by Anglo-American foes. Cuban Americans forged their political identity in a struggle against revolutionaries that led them to the warm embrace of Anglo Americans when they were dispossessed by leftist ideologues who think and talk suspiciously like Chicano activists. Chicanos and Cuban Americans compete fiercely in the business and political arenas; in the arts and academia, they are, at best, distant. Some Chicanos hate Cuban Americans, and vice versa.

Yet they share a language lost or beleaguered. A Roman Catholic background infused with and deconstructed by non-European belief systems. A Spanish sense of formality and, most important, honor. An ease with the realm of the passions. A common vocabulary of pop culture dating from the day when Cuban music invaded Mexico and Mexican film invaded Cuba. The geographical proximity of both home countries that has always made travel and exchange frequent and common. A baroque sensibility.

Ah, but how do you translate loss, nostalgia, honor, passion, never mind the flash of pop culture or the twists of the baroque into the discourse of social science? What is the language of your tenderness, your wrath, your lusts—Spanish or English? What is the language of your dreams? What do you feel like or want to be, *americano or latinoamericano?* When a Mexican says *pinche gringo,* do you identify with the speaker or the object of the speech? What is your desire? My questionnaire to Latinos would ask not "What are your attitudes?" but "Where lie your passions?"

Unlike African Americans, Latinos do not share a visible sign of bonding, and because our presence in this country is both ancestral (we were here earlier) and recent (we just crossed the border), we are not a cohesive group. But I believe we are seeking—we will seek—each other. A common culture binds us.

Those who fear the emergence of one more bothersome and populous minority must feel reassured by our apparent disunity. I am here to tell you that you should not rest easy. We are not about to dissolve into manageable microminorities. Our currents run deep.

So what is the Hispanic heritage, or at least that part of what we inherited from Spain, that we should be proud of? Here is my list of what's Hispanic worth celebrating.

1. HONOR. If anyone wants to understand what makes Hispanics tick, they should go read Spanish seventeenth-century honor plays—or catch them at the Spanish Repertory Theater on East Twenty-seventh Street in New York.

In the Spanish worldview, honor is a human being's essence. Without it, you're not even human. You're nothing. Only the honorable deserve to have rights, never mind privileges. In our society, where everyone is clamoring for their rights, it might make sense to demand honor in return.

2. FORMALITY. The word *formal* is downright negative in modern American society: "Oh, he's so formal." Not so in the Spanish-speaking world.

First of all, it has nothing to do with wearing black tie. It means that you live up to your word—that honor again—and do what must be done.

To *accomplish* in modern English means to excel in order to fulfill your personal ambitions, while *cumplir* in Spanish means to excel in fulfilling your obligations to others. In Spanish, no one wants to be *informal,* or be around anyone who is. [← how do they combine?]

3. HEART. I never understood all that New Age blarney about "getting in touch with your feelings." To be unfeeling has always been an aberration in the Spanish-speaking world: typically, Spaniards attribute it to their archenemies, the English.

Of course you feel. Of course your heart breaks. This, however, does not mean you loosen up your formality and disregard the demands of honor. On the contrary, the great tragedy of being alive is that one must do the right thing and feel, to the hilt, the pain that inevitably follows.

4. HUNGER FOR THE EARTH. Death is the big no-no in American life, the big nuisance. In traditional Spanish life, death has been a faithful companion. From Spain's bullfights to Mexico's laughing skulls. Hispanic culture not only accepts but celebrates death, even plays with it. In southern Spain, wrote the poet García Lorca, some people never are as alive as the day they are carried out of their houses dead.

Morbid we are, but never depressed. One reason Hispanic humor is so difficult to translate into English is because it's nearly always black humor, cruel and terrible. However, if you swing with it, it's very funny: We're all gonna die someday, so why take it seriously?

Hispanic tastes are deliciously morbid. Centuries before New York downtowners imposed their fashion on the world, King Philip I made it *de rigueur* to wear all black, not only at the Spanish court but at all the great courts of Europe, where Spanish black was aped.

And Hispanic food: the passion for reconstituted food—brought back to life—like beans and salt cod, and for ham and sausages and cheeses dried into a state of voluptuous mummification. And music: The pained wail of flamenco or the woeful songs of Spain's Celtic north. In Spanish culture, death is rich with life.

5. *LOVE*. Spanish is a loving tongue, as the old cowboy song says. That making love is better in Spanish is such a cultural stereotype that one should rush to deny it. Instead, one is likely to rush to try it.

Certainly those of us who live bilingually will tell you that Spanish love songs release feelings that are hard to express in English. I've interviewed both Gloria Estefan and Linda Ronstadt on why they sing in Spanish when they're big pop stars in English and, well, they just gotta do it.

So, let's let this be our finest Hispanic heritage: A language unabashed in lovemaking. We don't have a patent on it. We got it from Spain and, like all languages, it's there for the taking, for the talking, for the singing, for the loving. It's yours, *mi amor, mi corazón*.

"Which language comes most naturally to you?" a Latin American writer asked me not long ago. "Spanish or English?" "Neither and both," I replied. "My natural language is Spanglish." The writer, who was fairly fluent in English, urged me to try some Spanglish on him. I couldn't. He was not a Spanglish speaker. Only with another like myself could I speak this yet uncodified tongue. With Spaniards and Latin Americans I use, not without some strain, a curiously formal Spanish of uncertain origin. But with my fellow Hispanics here in the entrails of the monster, I can relax into our *nuevo* creole.

Like all languages, Spanglish comes in many different flavors and shapes. Tex-Mex and East Harlem variants sound nothing like each other. You don't use the same Spanglish to sell dope uptown as to discuss metalinguistics at Yale. But Spanglish, like Don Juan, has made it in the humblest cabins and the loftiest palaces, east and west, all around the town, the country, even the world. How does it work? How do two languages fuse?

The most obvious mix is in vocabulary. English and Spanish words are juxtaposed. In a business transaction you could ask *¿donde está el* invoice? That new person you met was *bien* nice. Or you can take an English word and add a Spanish suffix, as in *coolear,* Spanglish for *to cool out,* or, my fave, *hanguear* for "to hang out," whence comes the word *hangueadores,* the people you find in clubs night after night. That's not all. You can start a sentence in one language, switch to the other one, then back again, and so on. And that's *el* Spanglish, man, a language *que es bien* nice if you know how to *usarlo, ¿comprendes?*

But why *usarlo* at all when you've got *dos* languages *que son perfectamente* fine *para expresar* what you mean? Well, you might not have the words in one language. No sooner does an immigrant arrive on these shores than the media begins its bombardment. So, *¿cómo se dice* Brillo pad, Dolby sound, Miller Lite *en español?* The answer is *no se dice en español,* you say it in English. There are Spanish words that have perfect equivalents in English but lack the emotional ring, to a Hispanic American, of the words we learned at home from *la familia.* Or we may use the Spanish words because of their power of identification, a way of drawing others like ourselves into a circle and keeping out whoever doesn't share this bilingualism. This works in two ways. Interjecting Spanish words in an

English discourse proclaims one's Latin-ness; interjecting English into Spanish proclaims one's hipness.

I'm making it sound like everyone is highly conscious of the language they use, when, in fact, we open our mouths and words come out. We barely know what we're saying until we've said it. If we, speakers of Spanglish, paid attention to our discourse we might notice, to our horror, that when we switch from one language to another we're switching worldviews, attitudes, personalities. Schizophrenia? On the contrary, Spanglish is an emotional safety valve for the strain of straddling two different, often antagonistic cultures. I believe the switch comes when the pressure of one language reaches a critical level and it's necessary to seek the shelter of the other worldview.

Some years ago, the brilliantly written bilingual sitcom *Que Pasa USA?* explored these cultural and linguistic turns within a three-generation Cuban-American family. The grandparents spoke Spanish and knew only a handful of English words. The kids spoke English and could muster only a few phrases in Spanish. And the parents switched constantly back and forth, mixing the two. The funniest bits in the show came when the oldest or the youngest generation made comments in their main language that the other end of the generational spectrum could not understand. These outbursts were pure comic relief. Relief from the pressure of being too Latin in an American world or too American in a Latin family. This show, which still stands as the best TV presentation of U.S. Hispanics, was written in Spanglish, a clever, fresh, deliberate Spanglish. Though it touched bilingual Hispanics in a particular way, it could be appreciated by anyone. And it proved that Spanglish was a viable language.

Not everyone finds this phenomenon charming, however. The reaction against bilingual education reflects a fear among Anglo-Americans that their linguistic heritage is being eroded. And that's nothing compared to the concerns that English-Spanish fusion has raised on the other side of the Atlantic. Spaniards, who have seen their language gradually submit to the English invasion provoked by Spain's entry into the modern world in the last few decades, are now raising a cry of alarm as the computer revolution threatens to deform the shape of their beautifully archaic tongue. Technotalk is rampant in Spain and there's a lively debate over what to do about it.

Some of the smartest Spanish writers on the subject have pointed out something that should be obvious if one knows linguistics but can be easily overlooked. Language, as the semioticians explain it, works along two axes of signification, two ways of meaning—vocabulary and syntax. A U.S. Latino and a Spanish technocrat will mix Spanish and English words, but, most significantly, they will also arrange the words of one language using the syntax of the other. In the case of Spain's mother tongue, the new technology has meant that the lovely curves of Spanish syntax are being replaced by the sharp-edged word order of English. The result is an awkward Castilian that would make the great writers of the Spanish Baroque spring from their graves, sword in hand, to punish the offenders.

But if this is true for anglicized Castilian, it must also be the case for our homegrown Spanglish. I know so from my own experience. I can tell a U.S. Hispanic from a Latin American by the former's awkward syntax in Spanish, an *English* syntax. My own Spanish is the same, though thanks to the good fortune of higher education and a lifetime of reading Spanish literature, I compensate by adding rococo flourishes to my *español*. It works the other way too, as my editors well know. I bend and twist English in unnatural ways. Editing my copy requires a hot iron and a firm hand. Editing as conk job.

Therefore, if the massive Hispanic immigration has some influence on the American language, this will be more than just Spanish words entering English, like the *hoosegow, calaboose,* and *desperado* of the Old West. Look for exuberant shapes missing from the Queen's English since the Elizabethan era. Look for hyperbatons, redundancies, excess. Look for the death of economy, pithiness, terseness. Look for rhetoric. Look for a new language that will sound like a *concierto barroco.* Look for too much. More *es más.*

Those spices . . . that beat. Latino culture beckons. It promises to fill the sensory vacuum of Anglo America. The frightening nothingness inherited from Puritan England and northern Europe. In an American novel a black character pressed by a white lover to explain how white folk smell answers that what's unpleasant about them is that they don't smell. No-funk. Likewise, when Latinos are pressed to explain what they find lacking in American food and American sexual attractions, the answer is *no tiene sabor.* No-*sabor. Horror vacuii.* Come fill me.

How does *sabor*/seduction work? In that gorgeous morality play, John Ford's *The Searchers,* the John Wayne character relentlessly pursues his kidnapped niece in hope of catching up with her and her Indian abductors before she comes of age, before she can be tainted by miscegenation, before she becomes a mother of a *mestizo,* a mother of an *hijo de la chingada.* After a good long time his search is more of a reflex than an obsession. And somewhere in *la frontera,* the searcher relaxes. His clothes are loose, his drink is Mexican, his body language Latino. Of course, it is at the very precise moment of his *mestizaje*-through-assimilation that he finds his niece: ripe *y bien chingada.* But it's too late for righteousness. The Puritan knight who began the search has yielded to the seduction of the Other. Is the Other. As was the Duke himself, that Latinophile, tequila head, *mestiza* lover. The searcher has found himself.

---

1 In what way does the term "salsa" express a complex range of attitudes about Latin music (para. 3–4), food (para. 6–9), sex (para. 6), race (para. 11), dancing (para. 3–4), and other frames of reference for the Latino community?

2 How does "salsa" function as a bridge that connects otherwise very different Latino groups, like Mexicans and Cuban-Americans? Why is the question of what language you use to express yourself such an important one for Fernandez? How does "Spanglish" permit the expression of a hybrid mentality that fuses aspects of Latino culture (humor, passions, dreams) and mainstream American culture in a new way?

3 In your own words, explain what Fernandez means by each of the five important Hispanic character traits: honor, formality, heart, hunger for the earth (that is, death),

and love. Why are they important defining features of a Spanish sensibility that should be brought into American culture, according to Fernandez?

4 Where is Fernandez most successful in showing how completely words and phrases in Spanish have become interwoven with English to produce a unique hybrid called "Spanglish"? (Glossary: *Idiom, Semantics*.)

5 What is this essay's thesis? Locate the sentence(s) in which Fernandez states his main idea. Express the thesis in your own words. How does Fernandez develop his definition of the term "salsa" to reinforce his thesis? Locate some of the contrasts that Fernandez uses to illustrate the various ways in which the term "salsa" is used. How do these contrasts help him build his definition of "salsa"? (Glossary: *Comparison and Contrast, Definition, Thesis*.)

6 Are there terms with which you are familiar that have no exact synonym in English (for example, *guan-xi* [translated loosely as "relationship"] in Chinese, "sympatico" in Spanish, and "prego" in Italian). Select a term you use and define it in a paragraph or two, giving examples of how it is used in different contexts. Try to convey all the nuances and connotations that would be difficult to get across in English.

Public and Private Language

Richard Rodriguez

◆ RICHARD RODRIGUEZ was born in 1944 in San Francisco, where he grew up as a child of Spanish-speaking Mexican-American parents. As this selection from his autobiography *Hunger of Memory* (1982) reveals, Rodriguez received his education in a language that was not spoken in his home. In recent years he has continued his memoirs in a work titled *Days of Obligation: An Argument with My Mexican Father* (1992).

The predicament of someone who is forced to give up the language he has always spoken with his family when he enters grammar school and must learn to speak English has rarely been more poignantly illustrated than in this memoir by Rodriguez. While Rodriguez feels that English is an indispensable part of his public self, we also feel quite keenly his sense of loss at "growing away" from his family because he no longer spoke the language that had connected him to them in childhood.

Supporters of bilingual education today imply that students like me miss a great deal by not being taught in their family's language. What they seem not to recognize is that, as a socially disadvantaged child, I considered Spanish to be a private language. What I needed to learn in school was that I had the right—and the obligation—to speak the public language of *los gringos*.[1] The odd truth is that my first-grade classmates could have become bilingual, in the conventional sense of that word, more easily than I. Had they been taught (as upper-middle-class children are often taught early) a second language like Spanish or French, they could have regarded it simply as that: another public language. In my case such bilingualism could not have been so quickly achieved. What I did not believe was that I could speak a single public language.

Without question, it would have pleased me to hear my teachers address me in Spanish when I entered the classroom. I would have felt much less afraid. I would have trusted them and responded with ease. But I would have delayed— for how long postponed?—having to learn the language of public society. I would have evaded—and for how long could I have afforded to delay?—learning the great lesson of school, that I had a public identity.

Fortunately, my teachers were unsentimental about their responsibility. What they understood was that I needed to speak a public language. So their voices would search me out, asking me questions. Each time I'd hear them, I'd look up in surprise to see a nun's face frowning at me. I'd mumble, not really meaning to answer. The nun would persist, "Richard, stand up. Don't look at the floor. Speak up. Speak to the entire class, not just to me!" but I couldn't believe that the English language was mine to use. (In part, I did not want to believe it.) I continued to mumble. I resisted the teacher's demands. (Did I somehow suspect that once I learned public language my pleasing family life would be changed?) Silent, waiting for the bell to sound, I remained dazed, diffident, afraid.

Because I wrongly imagined that English was intrinsically a public language and Spanish an intrinsically private one, I easily noted the difference between classroom language and the language of home. At school, words were directed to a general audience of listeners. ("Boys and girls.") Words were meaningfully ordered. And the point was not self-expression alone but to make oneself understood by many others. The teacher quizzed: "Boys and girls, why do we use that word in this sentence? Could we think of a better word to use there? Would the sentence change its meaning if the words were differently arranged? And wasn't

---

[1] *los gringos:* Foreigners.

there a better way of saying much the same thing?" (I couldn't say. I wouldn't try to say.)

Three months. Five. Half a year passed. Unsmiling, ever watchful, my teach-   5
ers noted my silence. They began to connect my behavior with the difficult progress my older sister and brother were making. Until one Saturday morning three nuns arrived at the house to talk to our parents. Stiffly, they sat on the blue living room sofa. From the doorway of another room, spying the visitors, I noted the incongruity—the clash of two worlds, the faces and voices of school intruding upon the familiar setting of home. I overheard one voice gently wondering, "Do your children speak only Spanish at home, Mrs. Rodriguez?" While another voice added, "That Richard especially seems so timid and shy."

That Rich-heard!

With great tact the visitors continued, "Is it possible for you and your husband to encourage your children to practice their English when they are home?" Of course, my parents complied. What would they not do for their children's well-being? And how could they have questioned the Church's authority which those women represented? In an instant, they agreed to give up the language (the sounds) that had revealed and accentuated our family's closeness. The moment after the visitors left, the change was observed. "*Ahora,* speak to us *en inglés,*"[2] my father and mother united to tell us.

At first, it seemed a kind of game. After dinner each night, the family gathered to practice "our" English. (It was still then *inglés,* a language foreign to us, so we felt drawn as strangers to it.) Laughing, we would try to define words we could not pronounce. We played with strange English sounds, often overanglicizing our pronunciations. And we filled the smiling gaps of our sentences with familiar Spanish sounds. But that was cheating, somebody shouted. Everyone laughed. In school, meanwhile, like my brother and sister, I was required to attend a daily tutoring session. I needed a full year of special attention. I also needed my teachers to keep my attention from straying in class by calling out, *Rich-heard*—their English voices slowly prying loose my ties to my other name, its three notes, *Ri-car-do.* Most of all I needed to hear my mother and father speak to me in a moment of seriousness in broken—suddenly heartbreaking—English. The scene was inevitable: One Saturday morning I entered the kitchen where my parents were talking in Spanish. I did not realize that they were talking in Spanish however until, at the moment they saw me, I heard their voices change to speak English. Those *gringo* sounds they uttered startled me. Pushed me away. In that moment of trivial misunderstanding and profound insight, I felt my throat twisted by unsounded grief. I turned quickly and left the room. But I had no place to escape to with Spanish. (The spell was broken.) My brother and sisters were speaking English in another part of the house.

Again and again in the days following, increasingly, angry, I was obliged to hear my mother and father: "Speak to us *en inglés.*" (*Speak.*) Only then did I determine to learn classroom English. Weeks after, it happened: One day in school I had my hand raised to volunteer an answer. I spoke out in a loud voice.

---

[2]"*Now,* speak to us *in English.*"

And I did not think it remarkable when the entire class understood. That day, I moved very far from the disadvantaged child I had been only days earlier. The belief, that calming assurance that I belonged in public, had at last taken hold.

10   Shortly after, I stopped hearing the high and loud sounds of *los gringos*. A more and more confident speaker of English, I didn't trouble to listen to *how* strangers sounded, speaking to me. And there simply were too many English-speaking people in my day for me to hear American accents anymore. Conversations quickened. Listening to persons whose voices sounded eccentrically pitched, I usually noted their sounds for an initial few seconds before I concentrated on *what* they were saying. Conversations became content-full. Transparent. Hearing someone's *tone* of voice—angry or questioning or sarcastic or happy or sad—I didn't distinguish it from the words it expressed. Sound and word were thus tightly wedded. At the end of a day, I was often bemused, always relieved, to realize how "silent," though crowded with words, my day in public had been. (This public silence measured and quickened the change in my life.)

language as an mother   At last, seven years old, I came to believe what had been technically true since my birth: I was an American citizen.

But the special feeling of closeness at home was diminished by then. Gone was the desperate, urgent, intense feeling of being at home; rare was the experience of feeling myself individualized by family intimates. We remained a loving family, but one greatly changed. No longer so close; no longer bound tight by the pleasing and troubling knowledge of our public separateness. Neither my older brother nor sister rushed home after school anymore. Nor did I. When I arrived home there would often be neighborhood kids in the house. Or the house would be empty of sounds.

Following the dramatic Americanization of their children, even my parents grew more publicly confident. Especially my mother. She learned the names of all the people on our block. And she decided we needed to have a telephone installed in the house. My father continued to use the word *gringo*. But it was no longer charged with the old bitterness or distrust. (Stripped of any emotional content, the word simply became a name for those Americans not of Hispanic descent.) Hearing him, sometimes, I wasn't sure if he was pronouncing the Spanish word *gringo* or saying gringo in English.

Matching the silence I started hearing in public was a new quiet at home. The family's quiet was partly due to the fact that, as we children learned more and more English, we shared fewer and fewer words with our parents. Sentences needed to be spoken slowly when a child addressed his mother or father. (Often the parent wouldn't understand.) The child would need to repeat himself. (Still the parent misunderstood.) The young voice, frustrated, would end up saying, "Never mind"—the subject was closed. Dinners would be noisy with the clinking of knives and forks against dishes. My mother would smile softly between her remarks; my father at the other end of the table would chew and at his food, while he stared over the heads of his children.

15   My *mother!* My *father!* After English became my primary language, I no longer knew what words to use in addressing my parents. The old Spanish words (those tender accents of sound) I had used earlier—*mamá* and *papá*—I couldn't use anymore. They would have been too painful reminders of how much had

changed in my life. On the other hand, the words I heard neighborhood kids call *their* parents seemed equally unsatisfactory. *Mother* and *Father; Ma, Papa, Pa, Dad, Pop* (how I hated the all-American sound of that last word especially)— all these terms I felt were unsuitable, not really terms of address for *my* parents. As a result, I never used them at home. Whenever I'd speak to my parents, I would try to get their attention with eye contact alone. In public conversations, I'd refer to "my parents" or "my mother and father."

My mother and father, for their part, responded differently, as their children spoke to them less and less. She grew restless, seemed troubled and anxious at the scarcity of words exchanged in the house. It was she who would question me about my day when I came home from school. She smiled at the small talk. She pried at the edges of my sentences to get me to say something more. (What?) She'd join conversations she overheard, but her intrusions often stopped her children's talking. By contrast, my father seemed reconciled to the new quiet. Though his English improved somewhat, he retired into silence. At dinner he spoke very little. One night his children and even his wife helplessly giggled at his garbled English pronunciation of the Catholic Grace before Meals. Thereafter he made his wife recite the prayer at the start of each meal, even on formal occasions, when there were guests in the house. Hers became the public voice of the family. On official business, it was she, not my father, one would usually hear on the phone or in stores, talking to strangers. His children grew so accustomed to his silence that, years later, they would speak routinely of his shyness. (My mother would often try to explain: Both his parents died when he was eight. He was raised by an uncle who treated him like little more than a menial servant. He was never encouraged to speak. He grew up alone. A man of few words.) But my father was not shy, I realized, when I'd watch him speaking Spanish with relatives. Using Spanish, he was quickly effusive. Especially when talking with other men, his voice would spark, flicker, flare alive with sounds. In Spanish, he expressed ideas and feelings he rarely revealed in English. With firm Spanish sounds, he conveyed confidence and authority English would never allow him.

The silence at home, however, was finally more than a literal silence. Fewer words passed between parent and child, but more profound was the silence that resulted from my inattention to sounds. At about the time I no longer bothered to listen with care to the sounds of English in public, I grew careless about listening to the sounds family members made when they spoke. Most of the time I heard someone speaking at home and didn't distinguish his sounds from the words people uttered in public. I didn't even pay much attention to my parents' accented and ungrammatical speech. At least not at home. Only when I was with them in public would I grow alert to their accents. Though, even then, their sounds caused me less and less concern. For I was increasingly confident of my own public identity.

Today I hear bilingual educators say that children lose a degree of "individuality" by becoming assimilated into public society. (Bilingual schooling was popularized in the seventies, that decade when middle-class ethnics began to resist the process of assimilation—the American melting pot.) But the bilingualists simplistically scorn the value and necessity of assimilation. They do not seem to realize that there are *two* ways a person is individualized. So they do not realize that while one suffers a diminished sense of *private* individuality by becoming assimilated into public society, such assimilation makes possible the achievement of *public* individuality. *private + public sense of self not mutually exclusive*

1 Why is the distinction between "public" and "private" language such an important one for Rodriguez? Although Rodriguez discusses the increasing tension English brought between his "private" and "public" sense of self, he doesn't explicitly define either term. How do you understand these words in the context of his essay?

2 Rodriguez's first reaction to English is to the way it sounds. But there comes a moment (para. 10) when he focuses less on the sounds and more on what people are actually saying. What is the significance of this transformation in his acquiring English? How did his new fluency in English profoundly alter his relationship with his parents? How did his mother and father react to his new knowledge of English?

3 What does Rodriguez wish supporters of bilingual education would realize about the trade-offs involved in trying to assimilate into mainstream American society? What insight does this essay give you into how changing the language you speak also transforms personal and social relationships?

4 How does the issue of bilingualism (as discussed in the first and last paragraphs) serve to frame Rodriguez's personal account of learning English as a child? In what way do his experiences support his views on this issue? (Glossary: *Bilingual Education*.)

5 Where does Rodriguez provide the background and facts necessary for the average reader to understand what the effects of learning a second language were for him? To what extent does he establish that learning English helped undermine the close relationship he had with his family? (Glossary: *Cause and Effect*.)

6 Do you believe children of immigrants are under extra pressures or obligations to excel as a way of repaying their parents for the sacrifices they made in coming to America?

Language Lessons   *Sarah Min*

◆ SARAH MIN is the administrative coordinator at *Glamour* magazine. The following essay appeared in the "Bridges" section of the magazine in November 1997.

Min's situation is different from that of Richard Rodriguez in that she relinquishes speaking Korean to enable her parents to acquire fluency in English. Whereas Rodriguez's parents wished their son would assimilate into mainstream America, Min's parents wanted to join their daughter in becoming Americans and mastering the language of their new home. As a result, Min grew up speaking no Korean and only after feeling she had lost touch with her cultural heritage did she consciously seek to reacquire the language of her childhood.

TO CONSIDER   Would you consider making the commitment in terms of time and effort in learning a language that would put you in closer contact with your family's cultural heritage?

EVEN THOUGH I could understand only snippets of their conversation, I comprehended enough to know that the manicurists at the nail salon were talking about me.

What a shame! Another Korean who cannot speak the language, the woman filing my fingernails said to her colleague, both of them shaking their heads in disapproval. Her remark hit me, and I stumbled for the right words to defend myself.

The fact is, I traded my own Korean voice to give my parents their English ones: My mom and dad came to this country 27 years ago with an English vocabulary dominated by brand names like Tropicana and Samsonite. But they were determined to master the language of their new home. When I was in grade school, my dad read my English textbooks and asked me to give him the same lessons I had learned that day. On long car trips, my parents spent the confined hours in our Impala station wagon practicing their pronunciation aloud. My brother and I, captive tutors, led them in oral exercises, repeating the difficult distinction between *ear* and *year, war* and *wore.*

As my parents' fluency increased, their use of Korean dwindled. Though they spoke to each other in their native tongue, with my brother and me they used only one language: English. They didn't want us to speak Korean, they said, because they didn't want even a trace of an accent to infect our American-style speech.   *Accents aren't chronic contagious*

Still, I absorbed bits and pieces of Korean, important phrases like "Oh-mo-mo" and "Whey-goo-deh?"—the equivalent of "Oh no!" and "What's your problem?"—subtleties that can't be precisely translated but are understood as readily as "oy vey" or "cool." In private, I'd practice the sound effects—the gasps and clucks that are a part of the Korean language.

In public, though, I was reluctant to speak. My words sounded clunky, choppy, unlike the rhythmic cadences of my mother's voice. Once when I attempted conversation with a Korean-speaking woman in my neighborhood, my efforts were clearly unimpressive: She snickered at my accent and answered me in English. By the time I was in college, I had stopped trying to speak Korean, a decision only I noticed. No one expected me to speak the language anyway.

*lang. can't be seen as
a personal attribute/flaw,
but as societal*

Yet I always felt that a part of me had been silenced. As I got older and moved to a city where I met more Koreans, I began to feel as the women in the nail salon did: That those of us who didn't speak Korean had something to be ashamed of, that we were distancing ourselves from our cultural heritage. Language, after all, involves much more than the ability to communicate. It conveys a desire to understand and participate in a culture, to make it one's own. Could I ever fully understand and appreciate my heritage if I couldn't speak the language of my ancestors?

So I registered for a course in Korean at an adult education school. I expected my classmates to be Americans who were going abroad, but I discovered most of the students had come for the same reason that I had: to find their Korean voices.

To my surprise, I picked up the language quickly. Even though my vocabulary was limited and my grammar was rough, I realized I knew quite a bit, as if the Korean words had been lurking somewhere in a quiet corner of my brain. The teacher taught phrases that sounded familiar and came to me effortlessly; I practiced the new tongue placements and inflections to hide my American accent. The first time I called my parents and said, in flawless Korean, "Hello, we haven't spoken in such a long time," I was 24 years old, but they reacted as proudly as if I were a toddler who had just uttered her first words. And when I walked into a Korean restaurant and casually greeted the waiter, who responded in Korean that I could sit anywhere I liked, I knew he took me for the genuine article.

Now whenever I visit my parents, I ask them to speak Korean with me at least some of the time. Although I'm still struggling, still studying so I can become more fluent, I know enough now that my parents can tell me stories, jokes and proverbs that would otherwise have gotten garbled in the static of translation. Eagerly, I listen, laugh and nod in full understanding.

Being able to speak Korean has some surprising bonuses: In American restaurants, my dad and I figure the tip right in front of the waiter. And among Koreans, knowing the language forges an almost instant camaraderie.

That day at the nail salon, when I finally worked up the courage to respond to the manicurist, I spoke slowly, but confidently: *I understand you and yes, it is shameful that I can only speak a little.*

The young woman polishing my fingernails paused. She looked up at me and smiled, as if she were seeing me for the first time. And, for the first time, I too was seeing a new part of myself: a proud Korean American who could finally hear her own voice.

---

1   What circumstances led Min to trade her "own Korean voice" so that her parents could acquire the ability to speak in English?

2   Why did Min wish to reacquire the ability to speak Korean after so many years? What significance did this have for her?

3   What benefits did Min receive from relearning Korean?

4 How does the impact of Min's account depend on the fact that her experiences are narrated in the first person? How would the effect of this piece change if she had written it in the third person? (Glossary: *Point of View.*)

5 What time signals does Min provide to help the reader follow the sequence of events in her account? State the main point of her narrative in your own words. (Glossary: *Narration.*)

6 Is a second language part of your heritage? What steps have you taken, if any, to maintain some fluency in it? Do you feel about this language as Min did—that it is an integral part of your cultural background? Why or why not?

The Language of Discretion   *Amy Tan*

◆ AMY TAN was born in Oakland, California, in 1952. She studied linguistics and worked with disabled children. Tan's first novel, *The Joy Luck Club* (1989), was widely praised for its depiction of the relationship between Chinese mothers and their American-born daughters. Tan has also written *The Kitchen God's Wife* (1991) and *The Hundred Secret Senses* (1995). "The Language of Discretion" was published in 1990.

The bilingual experience is a perplexing one, especially for children of immigrant parents, as we have seen in essays by Richard Rodriguez and Sarah Min and will see in Lydia Minatoya's reminiscence. But Amy Tan is less concerned with the fact that her parents spoke to her in Chinese while she answered them in English than with the presumption by some linguists that speakers of different languages inhabit different worlds. In particular, Tan objects to the stereotype that because the Chinese language has no words for "yes" and "no," Chinese people are "discreet and modest." Her own experiences refute this misperception and serve as a springboard for her to air her views toward linguistic theories that people's perceptions and behavior are circumscribed by the language they speak.

TO CONSIDER How could knowing two languages prove extremely unsettling in terms of which one to think in, dream in, or talk in, under different circumstances?

A t a recent family dinner in San Francisco, my mother whispered to me: "Sau-sau [Brother's Wife] pretends too hard to be polite! Why bother? In the end, she always takes everything."

My mother thinks like a *waixiao*, an expatriate, temporarily away from China since 1949, no longer patient with ritual courtesies. As if to prove her point, she reached across the table to offer my elderly aunt from Beijing the last scallop from the Happy Family seafood dish.

Sau-sau scowled. "*B'yao, zhen b'yao!*" (I don't want it, really I don't!) she cried, patting her plump stomach.

"Take it! Take it!" scolded my mother in Chinese.

"Full, I'm already full," Sau-sau protested weakly, eyeing the beloved scallop.

"Ai!" exclaimed my mother, completely exasperated. "Nobody else wants it. If you don't take it, it will only rot!"

At this point, Sau-sau sighed, acting as if she were doing my mother a big favor by taking the wretched scrap off her hands.

My mother turned to her brother, a high-ranking communist official who was visiting her in California for the first time: "In America a Chinese person could starve to death. If you say you don't want it, they won't ask you again forever."

My uncle nodded and said he understood fully: Americans take things quickly because they have no time to be polite.

I thought about this misunderstanding again—of social contexts failing in translation—when a friend sent me an article from the *New York Times Magazine* (24 April 1988). The article, on changes in New York's Chinatown, made passing reference to the inherent ambivalence of the Chinese language.

Chinese people are so "discreet and modest," the article stated, there aren't even words for "yes" and "no."

That's not true, I thought, although I can see why an outsider might think that. I continued reading.

If one is Chinese, the article went on to say, "One compromises, one doesn't hazard a loss of face by an overemphatic response."

My throat seized. Why do people keep saying these things? As if we truly were those little dolls sold in Chinatown tourist shops, heads bobbing up and down in complacent agreement to anything said!

I worry about the effect of one-dimensional statements on the unwary and guileless. When they read about this so-called vocabulary deficit, do they also conclude that Chinese people evolved into a mild-mannered lot because the language only allowed them to hobble forth with minced words?

Something enormous is always lost in translation. Something insidious seeps into the gaps, especially when amateur linguists continue to compare, one-for-one, language differences and then put forth notions wide open to misinterpretation: that Chinese people have no direct linguistic means to make decisions, assert or deny, affirm or negate, just say no to drug dealers, or behave properly on the witness stand when told, "Please answer yes or no."

Yet one can argue, with the help of renowned linguists, that the Chinese are indeed up a creek without "yes" and "no." Take any number of variations on the old language-and-reality theory stated years ago by Edward Sapir: "Human beings . . . are very much at the mercy of the particular language which has become the medium for their society. . . . The fact of the matter is that the 'real world' is to a large extent built up on the language habits of the group."[1]

This notion was further bolstered by the famous Sapir-Whorf hypothesis, which roughly states that one's perception of the world and how one functions in it depends a great deal on the language used. As Sapir, Whorf, and new carriers of the banner would have us believe, language shapes our thinking, channels us along certain patterns embedded in words, syntactic structures, and intonation patterns. Language has become the peg and the shelf that enables us to sort out and categorize the world. In English, we see "cats" and "dogs"; what if the language had also specified *glatz*, meaning "animals that leave fur on the sofa," and *glotz*, meaning "animals that leave fur and drool on the sofa"? How would language, the enabler, have changed our perceptions with slight vocabulary variations?

And if this were the case—of language being the master of destined thought—think of the opportunities lost from failure to evolve two little words, *yes* and *no*, the simplest of opposites! Ghenghis Khan could have been sent back to Mongolia. Opium wars might have been averted. The Cultural Revolution could have been sidestepped.

There are still many, from serious linguists to pop psychology cultists, who view language and reality as inextricably tied, one being the consequence of the other. We have traversed the range from the Sapir-Whorf hypothesis to est and neurolinguistic programming, which tell us "you are what you say."

I too have been intrigued by the theories. I can summarize, albeit badly, ages-old empirical evidence: of Eskimos and their infinite ways to say "snow," their ability to *see* the differences in snowflake configurations, thanks to the richness of their vocabulary, while non-Eskimo speakers like myself founder in "snow," "more snow," and "lots more where that came from."

I too have experienced dramatic cognitive awakenings via the word. Once I added "mauve" to my vocabulary I began to see it everywhere. When I learned how to pronounce *prix fixe*, I ate French food at prices better than the easier-to-say *à la carte* choices.

But just how seriously are we supposed to take this?

Sapir said something else about language and reality. It is the part that often gets left behind in the dot-dot-dots of quotes: ". . . No two languages are ever sufficiently similar to be considered as representing the same social reality. The worlds in which different societies live are distinct worlds, not merely the same world with different labels attached."

When I first read this, I thought, Here at last is validity for the dilemmas I felt growing up in a bicultural, bilingual family! As any child of immigrant parents knows, there's a special kind of double bind attached to knowing two lan-

---

[1]Edward Sapir, *Selected Writings*, ed. D. G. Mandelbaum (Berkeley and Los Angeles, 1949).

guages. My parents, for example, spoke to me in both Chinese and English; I spoke back to them in English.

"Amy-ah!" they'd call to me.

"What?" I'd mumble back.

"Do not question us when we call," they scolded me in Chinese. "It is not respectful."

"What do you mean?"

"Ai! Didn't we just tell you not to question?"

To this day, I wonder which parts of my behavior were shaped by Chinese, which by English. I am tempted to think, for example, that if I am of two minds on some matter it is due to the richness of my linguistic experiences, not to any personal tendencies toward wishy-washiness. But which mind says what?

Was it perhaps patience—developed through years of deciphering my mother's fractured English—that had me listening politely while a woman announced over the phone that I had won one of five valuable prizes? Was it respect—pounded in by the Chinese imperative to accept convoluted explanations—that had me agreeing that I might find it worth-while to drive seventy-five miles to view a time-share resort? Could I have been at a loss for words when asked, "Wouldn't you like to win a Hawaiian cruise or perhaps a fabulous Star of India designed exclusively by Carter and Van Arpels?"

And when this same woman called back a week later, this time complaining that I had missed my appointment, obviously it was my type A language that kicked into gear and interrupted her. Certainly, my blunt denial—"Frankly I'm not interested"—was as American as apple pie. And when she said, "But it's in Morgan Hill," and I shouted, "Read my lips. I don't care if it's Timbuktu," you can be sure I said it with the precise intonation expressing both cynicism and disgust.

It's dangerous business, this sorting out of language and behavior. Which one is English? Which is Chinese? The categories manifest themselves: passive and aggressive, tentative and assertive, indirect and direct. And I realize they are just variations of the same theme: that Chinese people are discreet and modest.

Reject them all!

If my reaction is overly strident, it is because I cannot come across as too emphatic. I grew up listening to the same lines over and over again, like so many rote expressions repeated in an English phrasebook. And I too almost came to believe them.

Yet if I consider my upbringing more carefully, I find there was nothing discreet about the Chinese language I grew up with. My parents made everything abundantly clear. Nothing wishy-washy in their demands, no compromises accepted: "Of course you will become a famous neurosurgeon," they told me. "And yes, a concert pianist on the side."

In fact, now that I remember, it seems that the more emphatic outbursts always spilled over into Chinese: "Not that way! You must wash rice so not a single grain spills out."

I do not believe that my parents—both immigrants from mainland China—are an exception to the modest-and-discreet rule. I have only to look at the number of Chinese engineering students skewing minority ratios at Berkeley, MIT, and Yale. Certainly they were not raised by passive mothers and fathers who said, "It is up to you, my daughter. Writer, welfare recipient, masseuse, or molecular engineer—you decide."

And my American mind says, See, those engineering students weren't able to say no to their parents' demands. But then my Chinese mind remembers: Ah, but those parents all wanted their sons and daughters to be *pre-med*.

Having listened to both Chinese and English, I also tend to be suspicious of any comparisons between the two languages. Typically, one language—that of the person doing the comparing—is often used as the standard, the benchmark for a logical form of expression. And so the language being compared is always in danger of being judged deficient or superfluous, simplistic or unnecessarily complex, melodious or cacophonous. English speakers point out that Chinese is extremely difficult because it relies on variations in tone barely discernible to the human ear. By the same token, Chinese speakers tell me English is extremely difficult because it is inconsistent, a language of too many broken rules, of Mickey Mice and Donald Ducks.

Even more dangerous to my mind is the temptation to compare both language and behavior *in translation*. To listen to my mother speak English, one might think she has no concept of past or future tense, that she doesn't see the difference between singular and plural, that she is gender blind because she calls my husband "she." If one were not careful, one might also generalize that, based on the way my mother talks, all Chinese people take a circumlocutory route to get to the point. It is, in fact, my mother's idiosyncratic behavior to ramble a bit.

Sapir was right about differences between two languages and their realities. I can illustrate why word-for-word translation is not enough to translate meaning and intent. I once received a letter from China which I read to non-Chinese speaking friends. The letter, originally written in Chinese, had been translated by my brother-in law in Beijing. One portion described the time when my uncle at age ten discovered his widowed mother (my grandmother) had remarried—as a number three concubine, the ultimate disgrace for an honorable family. The translated version of my uncle's letter read in part:

> In 1925, I met my mother in Shanghai. When she came to me, I didn't have greeting to her as if seeing nothing. She pull me to a corner secretly and asked me why didn't have greeting to her. I couldn't control myself and cried, "Ma! Why did you leave us? People told me: one day you ate a bean-cake yourself. Your sister in-law found it and sweared at you, called your names. So . . . is it true?" She clasped my hand and answered immediately, "It's not true, don't say what like this." After this time, there was a few chance to meet her.

"What!" cried my friends. "Was eating a beancake so terrible?"

Of course not. The beancake was simply a euphemism; a ten-year-old boy did not dare question his mother on something as shocking as concubinage. Eating a beancake was his equivalent for committing this selfish act, something inconsiderate of all family members, hence, my grandmother's despairing response to what seemed like a ludicrous charge of gluttony. And sure enough, she was banished from the family, and my uncle saw her only a few times before her death.

While the above may fuel people's argument that Chinese is indeed a language of extreme discretion, it does not mean that Chinese people speak in secrets and riddles. The contexts are fully understood. It is only to those on the *outside* that the language seems cryptic, the behavior inscrutable.

I am, evidently, one of the outsiders. My nephew in Shanghai, who recently started taking English lessons, has been writing me letters in English. I had told him I was a fiction writer, and so in one letter he wrote, "Congratulate to you on your writing. Perhaps one day I should like to read it." I took it in the same vein as "Perhaps one day we can get together for lunch." I sent back a cheery note. A month went by and another letter arrived from Shanghai. "Last one perhaps I hadn't writing distinctly," he said. "In the future, you'll send a copy of your works for me."

I try to explain to my English-speaking friends that Chinese language use is more *strategic* in manner, whereas English tends to be more direct; an American business executive may say, "Let's make a deal," and the Chinese manager may reply, "Is your son interested in learning about your widget business?" Each to his or her own purpose, each with his or her own linguistic path. But I hesitate to add more to the pile of generalizations, because no matter how many examples I provide and explain, I fear that it appears defensive and only reinforces the image: that Chinese people are "discreet and modest"—and it takes an American to explain what they really mean.

Why am I complaining? The description seems harmless enough (after all, the *New York Times Magazine* writer did not say "slippery and evasive"). It is precisely the bland, easy acceptability of the phrase that worries me.

I worry that the dominant society may see Chinese people from a limited—and limiting—perspective. I worry that seemingly benign stereotypes may be part of the reason there are few Chinese in top management positions, in mainstream political roles. I worry about the power of language: that if one says anything enough times—in *any* language—it might become true.

Could this be why Chinese friends of my parents' generation are willing to accept the generalization?

"Why are you complaining?" one of them said to me. "If people think we are modest and polite, let them think that. Wouldn't Americans be pleased to admit they are thought of as polite?"

And I do believe anyone would take the description as a compliment—at first. But after a while, it annoys, as if the only things that people heard one say were phatic remarks: "I'm so pleased to meet you. I've heard many wonderful things about you. For me? You shouldn't have!"

These remarks are not representative of new ideas, honest emotions, or considered thought. They are what is said from the polite distance of social contexts: of greetings, farewells, wedding thank-you notes, convenient excuses, and the like.

It makes me wonder though. How many anthropologists, how many sociologists, how many travel journalists have documented so-called "natural interactions" in foreign lands, all observed with spiral notebook in hand? How many other cases are there of the long-lost primitive tribe, people who turned out to be sophisticated enough to put on the stone-age show that ethnologists had come to see?

And how many tourists fresh off the bus have wandered into Chinatown expecting the self-effacing shopkeeper to admit under duress that the goods are not worth the price asked? I have witnessed it.

"I don't know," the tourist said to the shopkeeper, a Cantonese woman in her fifties. "It doesn't look genuine to me. I'll give you three dollars."

"You don't like my price, go somewhere else," said the shopkeeper.

"You are not a nice person," cried the shocked tourist, "not a nice person at all!"

"Who say I have to be nice," snapped the shopkeeper.

"So how does one say 'yes' and 'no' in Chinese?" ask my friends a bit warily.

And here I do agree in part with the *New York Times Magazine* article. There is no one word for "yes" or "no"—but not out of necessity to be discreet. If anything, I would say the Chinese equivalent of answering "yes" or "no" is dis*crete,* that is, specific to what is asked.

Ask a Chinese person if he or she has eaten, and he or she might say *chrle* (eaten already) or perhaps *meiyou* (have not).

Ask, "So you had insurance at the time of the accident?" and the response would be *dwei* (correct) or *meiyou* (did not have).

Ask, "Have you stopped beating your wife?" and the answer refers directly to the proposition being asserted or denied: stopped already, still have not, never beat, have no wife.

What could be clearer?

As for those who are still wondering how to translate the language of discretion, I offer this personal example.

My aunt and uncle were about to return to Beijing after a three-month visit to the United States. On their last night I announced I wanted to take them out to dinner.

"Are you hungry?" I asked in Chinese.

"Not hungry," said my uncle promptly, the same response he once gave me ten minutes before he suffered a low-blood-sugar attack.

"Not too hungry," said my aunt. "Perhaps you're hungry?"

"A little," I admitted.

"We can eat, we can eat," they both consented.

"What kind of food?" I asked.

"Oh, doesn't matter. Anything will do. Nothing fancy, just some simple food is fine."

"Do you like Japanese food? We haven't had that yet," I suggested.

They looked at each other.

"We can eat it," said my uncle bravely, this survivor of the Long March.

"We have eaten it before," added my aunt. "Raw fish."

"Oh, you don't like it?" I said. "Don't be polite. We can go somewhere else."

"We are not being polite. We can eat it," my aunt insisted.

So I drove them to Japantown and we walked past several restaurants featuring colorful plastic displays of sushi.

"Not this one, not this one either," I continued to say, as if searching for a Japanese restaurant similar to the last. "Here it is," I finally said, turning into a restaurant famous for its Chinese fish dishes from Shandong.

"Oh, Chinese food!" cried my aunt, obviously relieved.

My uncle patted my arm. "You think Chinese."

"It's your last night here in America," I said. "So don't be polite. Act like an American."

And that night we ate a banquet.

---

1 How does the opening episode dramatize the "special kind of double bind attached to knowing two languages" (para. 13) that Tan experienced as a child of immigrant parents? What conventional positive stereotype about the Chinese does Tan dispute? How did this stereotype get started?

2 What is the Sapir-Whorf Hypothesis? How have Tan's experiences led her to accept or reject this concept?

3 How are the terms "discreet" and "discrete" related to each other in Tan's essay? Which of the examples cited by Tan—of how people's interpretations of events are affected by different cultural contexts—seem particularly effective to you?

4 How seriously does Tan take the Sapir-Whorf Hypothesis, which states, as she says, that "one's perception of the world and how one functions in it depends a great deal on the language used"? Does she believe, for example, that the lack of words for "yes" and "no" in Chinese make Chinese people discreet and modest? (Glossary: *Examples, Sapir-Whorf Hypothesis.*)

5 What principle of classification/division does Tan use to sequence the varieties of "Englishes" she discusses? How does this classification help her develop her thesis? (Glossary: *Classification/Division.*)

6 Have you ever been the object of a cross-cultural misperception? What cues, behavior, or customs did others misperceive about you? What steps, if any, did you take to rectify the misperception?

Transformation   *Lydia Minatoya*

◆ LYDIA MINATOYA was born in 1950 in Albany, New York, into one of the few Japanese families in that community. In 1981, she received a Ph.D. in psychology from the University of Maryland. Between 1983 and 1985 she traveled extensively throughout Asia, including Japan, China, and Nepal. She received the 1991 P.E.N./Jerard Fund Award and a grant from the Seattle Arts Commission for *Talking to High Monks in the Snow* (1992), in which "Transformation" first appeared. This memoir of her journey toward self-discovery is based on her childhood, graduate school study, her career as a university professor, and her travels in Asia.

The decision as to what to name a child is ordinarily a process to which much thought is given, and which has lifelong consequences. When this decision is compounded by the fact that the parents are immigrants who wish to give their child an American name, we get some idea of what was at stake for Minatoya's parents in deciding what to name her. Little did her parents know that her name would be yet another reminder of her isolation at school in Albany, New York. Lydia first took the same route as her older sister, Misa, by becoming the "teacher's pet," but soon reached a crucial turning point.

> **TO CONSIDER** Do you like your given name? How has it affected your life? Would you have chosen another name for yourself if you could have?

Perhaps it begins with my naming. During her pregnancy, my mother was   1
reading Dr. Spock. "Children need to belong," he cautioned. "An unusual name can make them the subject of ridicule." My father frowned when he heard this. He stole a worried glance at my sister. Burdened by her Japanese name, Misa played unsuspectingly on the kitchen floor.

The Japanese know full well the dangers of conspicuousness. "The nail that   2
sticks out gets pounded down," cautions an old maxim. In America, Relocation was all the proof they needed.

And so it was, with great earnestness, my parents searched for a conven-   3
tional name. They wanted me to have the full true promise of America.

4   "I will ask my colleague Froilan," said my father. "He is the smartest man I know."

5   "And he has poetic soul," said my mother, who cared about such things.

6   In due course, Father consulted Froilan. He gave Froilan his conditions for suitability.

7   "First, if possible, the full name should be alliterative," said my father. "Like Misa Minatoya." He closed his eyes and sang my sister's name. "Second, if not an alliteration, at least the name should have assonantal rhyme."

8   "Like Misa Minatoya?" said Froilan with a teasing grin.

9   "Exactly," my father intoned. He gave an emphatic nod. "Finally, most importantly, the name must be readily recognizable as conventional." He peered at Froilan with hope. "Do you have any suggestions or ideas?"

10   Froilan, whose own American child was named Ricardito, thought a while.

11   "We already have selected the name for a boy," offered my Father. "Eugene."

12   "Eugene?" wondered Froilan. "But it meets none of your conditions!"

13   "Eugene is a special case," said my father, "after Eugene, Oregon, and Eugene O'Neill. The beauty of the Pacific Northwest, the power of a great writer."

14   "I see," said Froilan, who did not but who realized that this naming business would be more complex than he had anticipated. "How about Maria?"

15   "Too common," said my father. "We want a *conventional* name, not a common one."

16   "Hmmm," said Froilan, wondering what the distinction was. He thought some more and then brightened. "Lydia!" he declared. He rhymed the name with media. "Lydia for *la bonita infanta!*"

17   And so I received my uncommon conventional name. It really did not provide the camouflage my parents had anticipated. I remained unalterably alien. For Dr. Spock had been addressing *American* families, and in those days, everyone knew all real American families were white.

18   Call it denial, but many Japanese Americans never quite understood that the promise of America was not truly meant for them. They lived in horse stalls at the Santa Anita racetrack and said the Pledge of Allegiance daily. They rode to Relocation Camps under armed guard, labeled with numbered tags, and sang "The Star-Spangled Banner." They lived in deserts or swamps, ludicrously imprisoned—where would they run if they ever escaped—and formed garden clubs, and yearbook staffs, and citizen town meetings. They even elected beauty queens.

19   My mother practiced her okoto and was featured in a recital. She taught classes in fashion design and her students mounted a show. Into exile she had carried an okoto and a sewing machine. They were her past and her future. She believed in Art and Technology.

20   My mother's camp was the third most populous city in the entire state of Wyoming. Across the barren lands, behind barbed wire, bloomed these little oases of democracy. The older generation bore the humiliation with pride. "*Kodomo no táme ni,*" they said. For the sake of the children. They thought that

if their dignity was great, then their children would be spared. Call it valor. Call it bathos. Perhaps it was closer to slapstick: a sweet and bitter lunacy.

Call it adaptive behavior. Coming from a land swept by savage typhoons, 21 ravaged by earthquakes and volcanoes, the Japanese have evolved a view of the world: a cooperative, stoic, almost magical way of thinking. Get along, work hard, and never quite see the things that can bring you pain. Against the tyranny of nature, of feudal lords, of wartime hysteria, the charm works equally well.

And so my parents gave me an American name and hoped that I could pass. 22 They nourished me with the American dream: Opportunity, Will, Transformation.

When I was four and my sister was eight, Misa regularly used me as a comic 23 foil. She would bring her playmates home from school and query me as I sat amidst the milk bottles on the front steps.

"What do you want to be when you grow up?" she would say. She would 24 nudge her audience into attentiveness.

"A mother kitty cat!" I would enthuse. Our cat had just delivered her first 25 litter of kittens and I was enchanted by the rasping tongue and soft mewings of motherhood.

"And what makes you think you can become a cat?" Misa would prompt, 26 gesturing to her howling friends—wait for this; it gets better yet.

"This is America," I stoutly would declare. "I can grow up to be anything I 27 want!"

My faith was unshakable. I believed. Opportunity. Will. Transformation. 28

When we lived in Albany, I always was the teachers' pet. "So tiny, so pre- 29 cocious, so prettily dressed!" They thought I was a living doll and this was fine with me.

My father knew that the effusive praise would die. He had been through this 30 with my sister. After five years of being a perfect darling, Misa had reached the age where students were tracked by ability. Then, the anger started. Misa had tested into the advanced track. It was impossible, the community declared. Misa was forbidden entry into advanced classes as long as there were white children being placed below her. In her defense, before an angry rabble, my father made a presentation to the Board of Education.

But I was too young to know of this. I knew only that my teachers praised 31 and petted me. They took me to other classes as an example. "Watch now, as Lydia demonstrates attentive behavior," they would croon as I was led to an empty desk at the head of the class. I had a routine. I would sit carefully, spreading my petticoated skirt neatly beneath me. I would pull my chair close to the desk, crossing my swinging legs at my snowy white anklets. I would fold my hands carefully on the desk before me and stare pensively at the blackboard.

This routine won me few friends. The sixth-grade boys threw rocks at me. 32 They danced around me in a tight circle, pulling at the corners of their eyes. "Ching Chong Chinaman," they chanted. But teachers loved me. When I was in first grade, a third-grade teacher went weeping to the principal. She begged to have me skipped. She was leaving to get married and wanted her turn with the dolly.

33   When we moved, the greatest shock was the knowledge that I had lost my charm. From the first, my teacher failed to notice me. But to me, it did not matter. I was in love. I watched her moods, her needs, her small vanities. I was determined to ingratiate.

34   Miss Hempstead was a shimmering vision with a small upturned nose and eyes that were kewpie doll blue. Slender as a sylph, she tripped around the classroom, all saucy in her high-heeled shoes. Whenever I looked at Miss Hempstead, I pitied the Albany teachers whom, formerly, I had adored. Poor old Miss Rosenberg. With a shiver of distaste, I recalled her loose fleshy arms, her mottled hands, the scent of lavender as she crushed me to her heavy breasts.

35   Miss Hempstead had a pet of her own. Her name was Linda Sherlock. I watched Linda closely and plotted Miss Hempstead's courtship. The key was the piano. Miss Hempstead played the piano. She fancied herself a musical star. She sang songs from Broadway revues and shaped her students' reactions. "Getting to know you," she would sing. We would smile at her in a staged manner and position ourselves obediently at her feet.

36   Miss Hempstead was famous for her ability to soothe. Each day at rest time, she played the piano and sang soporific songs. Linda Sherlock was the only child who succumbed. Routinely, Linda's head would bend and nod until she crumpled gracefully onto her folded arms. A tousled strand of blonde hair would fall across her forehead. Miss Hempstead would end her song, would gently lower the keyboard cover. She would turn toward the restive eyes of the class. "Isn't she sweetness itself!" Miss Hempstead would declare. It made me want to vomit.

37   I was growing weary. My studiousness, my attentiveness, my fastidious grooming and pert poise: all were failing me. I changed my tactics. I became a problem. Miss Hempstead sent me home with nasty notes in sealed envelopes: Lydia is a slow child, a noisy child, her presence is disruptive. My mother looked at me with surprise, "*Nani desu ka?* Are you having problems with your teacher?" But I was tenacious. I pushed harder and harder, firmly caught in the obsessive need of the scorned.

38   One day I snapped. As Miss Hempstead began to sing her wretched lullabies, my head dropped to the desk with a powerful CRACK! It lolled there, briefly, then rolled toward the edge with a momentum that sent my entire body catapulting to the floor. Miss Hempstead's spine stretched slightly, like a cat that senses danger. Otherwise, she paid no heed. The linoleum floor was smooth and cool. It emitted a faint pleasant odor: a mixture of chalk dust and wax.

39   I began to snore heavily. The class sat electrified, There would be no drowsing today. The music went on and on. Finally, one boy could not stand it. "Miss Hempstead," he probed plaintively, "Lydia has fallen asleep on the floor!" Miss Hempstead did not turn. Her playing grew slightly strident but she did not falter.

I lay on the floor through rest time. I lay on the floor through math drill. I 40
lay on the floor while my classmates scraped around me, pushing their sturdy little wooden desks into the configuration for reading circle. It was not until penmanship practice that I finally stretched and stirred. I rose like Sleeping Beauty and slipped back to my seat. I smiled enigmatically. A spell had been broken. I never again had a crush on a teacher.

───────────────────────

1 From the perspective of her Japanese parents, what underlying cultural assumptions should determine the choice of a name for a child born in America? What insight does the account of Japanese internment camps during World War II provide into the pressures Minatoya's parents experienced when deciding what to name her?

2 How does the author's attitude toward her name differ from those of her parents in terms of how having the American name "Lydia" would permit her to fully assimilate into American society?

3 How does Lydia's "transformation" involve liberating herself from the role into which she had been cast at school?

4 What associations and qualities play an important role for Minatoya's parents in choosing her name? What insight does this give you into the field of study called Onomastics? (Glossary: *Onomastics*.)

5 Is Minatoya's narrative a straightforward chronological account or does she use flashbacks to give readers a glimpse of crucial events? What means does she use to keep her narrative point of view and verb tenses consistent? What conflict does the narrator experience? How does Minatoya create tension about the conflict the narrator experiences? (Glossary: *Narration*.)

6 Minatoya's parents attached great importance to what names they were going to give their children. There are trends in names just as in anything else. What names are fashionable nowadays? (Several generations ago, Pearl, Bertha, Mabel, Ethel, Agnes, and Clara were popular. More recently, Amber, Megan, Brittany, Heather, and Tiffany have been in vogue.)

What's in a Name?   *David A. Ricks*

◆ DAVID A. RICKS was born in 1942 in Washington, D.C. and earned his Ph.D. in business administration from Indiana University in 1970. Ricks has taught at Ohio State University (1970–1981), and is currently a professor of international business and director of the Ph.D. program in international business at the University of South Carolina. He is also editor-in-chief of the *Journal of International Business Studies,* and authored or coauthored six books and more than thirty articles on various aspects of international business strategies, including *International Dimensions of Corporate Finance* (1978) and *Big Business Blunders; Mistakes in Multinational Marketing* (1983). He has appeared on the *Today Show,* testified before Congress, and has been recognized as an authority in this area by publications such as the *Wall Street Journal, Business Week,* and *Forbes.* "What's in a Name?," originally published as Chapter Three of *Big Business Blunders,* underscores the importance of test marketing product or company names to avoid unintended humorous, offensive, or even obscene connotations when these names are translated into other languages.

Imagine the recriminations that would ensue in corporate boardrooms when it was discovered that the name given to one of their products had unintended vulgar, humorous, offensive, or obscene connotations when translated into the language of the country in which the product was being marketed. David A. Ricks discusses a number of these marketing blunders as a cautionary tale for business executives.

> **TO CONSIDER**   Have you ever made a purchase because of the name of the item only to discover it was not what you expected it to be?

Shakespeare once queried, "What's in a name?" A number of business people, after a bit of international marketing, might appropriately respond, "More than you might think." Many companies have discovered that even something as seemingly innocuous as a name can prove insulting and embarrassing. Both product and company names can fall prey to such troubles.

PRODUCT NAMES

Product names often take on various unintended and hidden meanings. The experience of a major soapmaker serves as a classic example. When this company was considering a name for a new soap powder to be marketed internationally, it wisely ran a translation test of the proposed soap name in 50 major languages. In English and most of the major European languages, the name meant "dainty." In other tongues, however, the soap name did not translate so appropriately. In Gaelic, it became "song," in Flemish it meant "aloof," and it said "horse" in the language of one African tribe. In Persia, the name was translated as "hazy" or "dimwitted," and to the Koreans, the name sounded like a person out of his mind. Finally, in all of the Slavic languages, the name was considered obscene and offensive. Naturally, the proposed name was hastily abandoned. This experience, though, demonstrates the importance of a name and how carefully it should be considered prior to the introduction of the product.

Unusual Problems

Today, more and more firms are seeking assistance in hopes of avoiding costly and embarrassing mistakes. Even the largest and most sophisticated firms are not immune to the difficulties of product-name interpretation. For example, when the Coca-Cola Company was planning its strategy for marketing in China in the 1920s, it wanted to introduce its product with the English pronunciation of "Coca-Cola." A translator developed a group of Chinese characters which, when pronounced, sounded like the product name. These characters were placed on the cola bottles and marketed. Was it any wonder that sales levels were low? The characters actually translated to mean "a wax-flattened mare" or "bite the wax tadpole." Since the product was new, sound was unimportant to the consumers; meaning was vital.[1] Today Coca-Cola is again marketing its cola in China. The new characters used on the bottle translate to "happiness in the mouth." From its first marketing attempts, Coca-Cola learned a valuable lesson in international marketing.

General Motors was faced with a similar problem. It was troubled by the lack of enthusiasm among the Puerto Rican auto dealers for its recently introduced Chevrolet "Nova." The name "Nova" meant "star" when literally translated. However, when spoken, it sounded like "no va" which, in Spanish, means "it doesn't go." This obviously did little to increase consumer confidence in the new vehicle. To remedy the situation, General Motors changed the automobile name to "Caribe" and sales increased.

Other car manufacturers have also experienced comparable situations. In fact, problems with the names used in international automobile promotions

---

[1]By reporting this incident in some of its annual reports, Coca-Cola has even laughed at itself.

seem to be frequent events. For example, difficulties arose during the translation of the name of the American car "Randan." Apparently this name was interpreted by the Japanese to mean "idiot." The American Motors Corporation's "Matador" name usually conjures up images of virility and strength, but in Puerto Rico it means "killer"—not a favorable connotation in a place with a high traffic fatality rate.

Ford encountered translation problems with some of its cars as well. It introduced a low cost truck, the "Fiera," into some of the less-developed countries. Unfortunately the name meant "ugly old woman" in Spanish. Needless to say, this name did not encourage sales. Ford also experienced slow sales when it introduced a top-of-the-line automobile, the "Comet," in Mexico under the name "Caliente." The puzzlingly low sales levels were finally understood when Ford discovered that "caliente" is slang for a streetwalker. Additional headaches were reportedly experienced when Ford's "Pinto" was briefly introduced in Brazil under its English name. The name was speedily changed to "Corcel" (which means "horse" in Portuguese) after Ford discovered that the Portuguese slang translation of "pinto" is "a small male appendage."

The naming of a new automobile model to be marketed in Germany by Rolls Royce was a difficult undertaking. The company felt that the English name "Silver Mist" was very appealing but discovered that the name would undoubtedly not capture the German market as hoped. In German, the translated meaning of "mist" is actually "excrement," and the Germans could not possibly have found such a name appealing. Unfortunately, the Sunbeam Corporation did not learn of this particular translation problem in time and attempted to enter the German market advertising its new mist-producing hair curling iron, the "Mist-Stick." As should have been expected, the Germans had no interest in a "dung" or "manure" wand.

Firms occasionally try to enter the foreign market promoting a product bearing an untranslated name. Sometimes this tactic works, but other times it does not work as well as expected. At least one global firm can attest to this. The company consistently marketed one of its pieces of equipment under the name "Grab Bucket." To its chagrin, the firm learned that in Germany it was actually advertising the sale of cemetery plot flowers. In German, the word *grab* is interpreted as *grave,* and *bucket* is pronounced like *bouquet.* So because of these linguistic anomalies, the company did not appear to be selling what it thought at all.

Many companies have suffered similar pitfalls. A U.S. company was taken by surprise when it introduced its product in Latin America and learned that the name of the product meant "jackass oil" in Spanish. Another well-intentioned firm sold shampoo in Brazil under the name "Evitol." Little did it realize that it was claiming to be selling a "dandruff contraceptive." A manufacturing company sold its machines in the Soviet Union under the name "Bardak"—a word which signifies a brothel in Russian. An American product failed to capture the Swedish market; the product name translated to "enema," which the product was not. A Finnish brewery introduced two new beverages in the United States— "Koff" beer and "Stiff" beer. Is it any wonder that sales were sluggish? Another name, unappealing to Americans, can be found on the package of a delicious chocolate and fruit product sold in a German or European deli. The chocolate concoction has the undesirable English name "Zit!"

The reported troubles of an American company that markets Pet milk serves as one more example. This firm reportedly experienced difficulties introducing its product in French-speaking areas. It seems that the word *Pet* in French means, among other things, "to break wind." And had Colgate-Palmolive attempted to gain market entry with its Cue toothpaste in French-speaking regions, it too would have encountered comparable problems. *Cue* is a pornographic word in French.[2] An American woman will long remember her international experience with Coca-Cola. She was dispensing sample tasters of Fresca soda pop when she unintentionally elicited a great deal of laughter from passersby. She only later realized the cause when she discovered that in Mexican slang the word *Fresca* means *lesbian.*

Close examination of foreign markets and language differences are necessary and should be required before a product's domestically successful name is introduced abroad. Unfortunately, this simple warning is sometimes neglected in a company's enthusiasm to plunge into overseas marketing operations.

Manufacturers often assume that products which have enjoyed domestic success will naturally receive the same reception overseas. However, this is not always the case as the following examples demonstrate. Princess Housewares, Inc., a large U.S. appliance manufacturer, introduced a line of electric housewares in the German market. The company's brand name, well known and highly regarded in the United States, was relatively unknown in Germany. Its name, though, which had a definite American sound, turned out to be a real drawback as the German consumers disliked the American association.[3] Similarly, in the early 1960s General Mills spent over $1.4 million advertising its Betty Crocker cake mixes in an effort to gain entry into the British market. The costly promotion, though, did not achieve the expected positive r esults either. Although research revealed that the product itself was quite acceptable, the British just could not identify with the exotic names given to the cake mixes.[4]

Name adaptations sometimes prove to be winners; other times they do not. The Johnson Wax Company successfully introduced its product "Pledge" in Germany under the name of "Pronto," but problems arose when the product entered the market in the Netherlands as "Pliz." In Dutch, the pronunciation of "Pliz" sounds like "Piss." Understandably, it was rather difficult for the customer of the conventional Dutch grocery store to ask for the product.

Sometimes the required change in the product name is a rather simple one.

---

[2]It should be noted, however, that reports citing problems with the name "Cue" have been denied by the company.

[3]For a more complete discussion of this problem, see Robert D. Buzzell, "Can You Standardize Multinational, Marketing?" *Harvard Business Review,* November–December 1968, pp. 102–13.

[4]Although the October 1, 1963 issue of *Forbes* reported this case in the article "General Mills: the General and Betty Crocker," pp. 20–24, General Mills now denies the report.

Wrigley for example, merely altered the spelling of its "Spearmint" chewing gum to "Spearmint" to aid in the German pronunciation of the flavor. "Maxwell House" proved slightly more difficult. The name was changed to "Maxwell Kaffee" in Germany, "Legal" in France, and "Monky" in Spain.

As evidenced, firms have blundered by changing product names and by failing to alter names. This is not to say, however, that one is "damned if you do and damned if you don't." Adequate name assessments prior to market introduction can reduce potential name blunders.

More Obscene Meanings

Inappropriate product names sometimes prove to be quite humorous, but in a number of cases, the names have actually borne fairly obscene implications and connotations. A few illustrations of this type of blunder are cited below.

Bird's Eye considered itself quite fortunate when it discovered that a proposed name for one of its fishfood products was inappropriate. Wisely, the company decided against the name when it uncovered that the name translated to "genitals." Not all firms have been so lucky. A well-known oil company was caught in an embarrassing situation when it learned of the "indecent" name it had chosen for its products. The company established operations in Indonesia and manufactured machinery displaying the name "Nonox." One can imagine the firm's discomfort when it was informed that "Nonox" sounded similar to the Javanese slang word *Nonok* which is comparable to the American idiom for female "private parts."

Obviously the employees who proposed the name "Joni" for a new facial cream which was to be marketed in India had never read the erotic Indian classic *Kama Sutra*. If they had, they would surely have known that the Hindu word *joni* represents the most intimate areas of the female body.

The example of a vitamin product introduced in South America serves as a final illustration of how product names can unintentionally become obscenities. In this case, a company introduced its vitamins as "Fundavit" and boasted that they satisfied the fundamental vitamin requirements. The name had to be modified when the firm learned that "fundola" in Spanish stands for the rear end of an attractive young female.

Other Offensive Names

As illustrated, certain product name choices can create embarrassing situations for companies when the names are interpreted as indecencies. On occasion, a company chooses a name which, although not obscene, turns out to be in poor taste and offensive to certain groups of people. One example is the name "Black Nikka" chosen for a brand of Japanese whiskey sold in the United States and found to be demeaning by some black Americans. Also consider the bold experiment in international marketing that brought together the state-controlled tobacco monopolies of five countries (France, Italy, Portugal, Austria, and

Japan) to launch a major promotion of a new brand of cigarettes, "Champagne." This venture proved to be an embarrassment to the French government, and the case wound up in the international law courts with the French champagne producers in a fury. These producers claimed that the use of "Champagne" as a brand name "is deplorable, and the connection with health hazards may permanently damage our image."[5]

Yves St. Laurent drew some unwanted criticism when it named a new fragrance "Opium." Even though the advertising campaign was voted the best for 1978 by the Fragrance Foundation, it created a storm of protest. In general, it was simply viewed as poor judgment to name a fragrance after an illegal drug. The original French slogan "Pour celles qui s'adonnet á Yves St. Laurent" ("For those who are addicted to Yves St. Laurent") only tended to reinforce the resented "connections" and connotations. The Chinese also considered the use of the name "Opium" to be a racial slur. Public pressure eventually forced the company to discontinue the sales promotion in some places.[6] Therefore, it can not be stressed too strongly: Names must be chosen carefully.

COMPANY NAMES

Product names are not the only ones which can generate company blunders. If a firm name is misinterpreted or incorrectly translated, it too can cause the same types of humorous, obscene, offensive, or unexpected situations. A number of examples are described in the following paragraphs.

A private Egyptian airline, Misair, proved to be rather unpopular with the French nationals. Could the fact that the name, when pronounced, meant "misery" in French have contributed to the airline's plight? Another airline trying to gain acceptance in Australia only complicated matters when it chose the firm name "EMU." The emu is an Australian bird which is incapable of flying. But EMU was not the only company to run into snags while conducting business in Australia. The AMF Corporation was forced to change its name. Why? Because AMF is the official designation for the Australian military forces. Similarly, Sears was forbidden to use its unchanged name in Spain. The company commanded respect and had developed a good reputation there, but since the Castillian Spanish pronunciation of Sears sounded much like "Seat" (the name of Spain's largest car manufacturer), Seat forced Sears to incorporate the name "Roebuck" on all of its products.

When Esso realized that its name phonetically meant "stalled car," it under-

[5]For further details, see Carolyn Pfaff, "Champagne Cigs Cause Headache," *Advertising Age,* March 30, 1981, p. 2.

[6]Background information is provided by Pat Sloan in "Fragrance under Fire: Opium Ads Go Up in Smoke," *Advertising Age,* June 4, 1979, p. 1.

stood why it had had difficulties in the Japanese market. And was it any wonder that Ford ran into unexpected low sales levels in Spain? Apparently its cars were not popular with certain groups; some of the locals were interpreting the name "Ford" to mean "Fabrica Ordinaria Reparaciones Diaviamente" (translation: "ordinarily, make repairs daily"). The Vicks Company, however, was more fortunate. It discovered that in German "Vicks" sounds like the most crude slang equivalent of intercourse and was able to change its name to an acceptable "Wicks."

As a final illustration, consider the trade magazine which promoted giftware and launched a worldwide circulation effort. The magazine used the word *gift* in its title and as part of its name. When it was later revealed that *gift* is the German word for *poison*, a red-faced publishing executive supposedly retorted that the Germans should simply find a new word for poison!

Of course not all companies have been forced to change names. In fact, some of them have traveled quite well. Kodak may be the most famous example. A research team deliberately "developed" this name after carefully searching for a word which was pronounceable everywhere but had no specific meaning anywhere. Exxon is another such name which was reportedly accepted only after a lengthy and expensive computer-assisted search.

———————

1 Why should a close examination of language differences be required before a product's domestically successful name is introduced abroad?

2 What are some of the most striking examples of the unanticipated effects (ranging from the harmless and amusing to the insulting, obscene, and costly) when product names are introduced without advance market research into foreign markets? What are the advantages of computer-created names that have no specific meaning but are pronounceable everywhere throughout the world?

3 What product names have produced controversies in recent times? For example, in 1997, Nike had to recall millions of pairs of sneakers because the logo for the shoes—intended to depict flames—was almost identical to the Arabic script for the name "Allah"—which, on a shoe, might led to the perception that the wearer (or Nike) was blasphemously trampling the name of God under foot.

4 What point is Ricks making about the factors that should play an important part in choosing product names? How does the humor of his essay depend on irony—that is, on the contrast between what was intended and what actually occurred, and the idiomatic meaning of the product names in their original languages—for example, "fundavit" in paragraph 19? (Glossary: *Connotation, Denotation, Idiom, Irony, Onomastics.*)

5 Evaluate Ricks's use of a number of examples to illustrate different kinds of marketing blunders. Do his examples support his thesis and illustrate the consequences of lack of cross-cultural meanings of product names? (Glossary: *Examples.*)

6 In your opinion, why do many product names appear to be misspelled ("lite" for light, "tastee freez," for tasty freeze, etc.)?

◆ CONNECTIONS: LANGUAGE BETWEEN CULTURES

Enrique Fernandez, "Salsa × 2"

1. What sort of a shift in societal attitude toward Hispanic language and culture is implied when you compare Richard Rodriguez's account written in the 1970s and Fernandez's essay written in the 1990s?
2. How does Fernandez's discussion on the evolution of the term "salsa" relate to Martha Barnette's account in "Ladyfingers & Nun's Tummies" (Ch. 7)?

Richard Rodriguez, "Public and Private Language"

1. Compare the experiences of Rodriguez with those of Amy Tan as the children of immigrant parents. How are their experiences similar and how are they different?
2. How did Rodriguez's experiences in learning English change him into a different kind of person in ways that Barbara Mellix also experienced? (See "From Outside, In," Ch. 7.)

Sarah Min, "Language Lessons"

1. Compare the consequences, both positive and negative, for Richard Rodriguez and Min in learning English as children of immigrant parents.
2. How did the relearning of Korean entail a shift in psychological perspective for Min that was opposite to the one described by Barbara Mellix in "From Outside, In" when she learned standard English (Ch. 7)?

Amy Tan, "The Language of Discretion"

1. How do the experiences of Tan and of Lydia Minatoya illustrate the kinds of pressures to which children of immigrants are subjected?
2. Compare Tan's essay with Barbara Mellix's account in "From Outside, In" (Ch. 7) to discover the ways in which immigrants, and African-Americans who speak black English, are stereotyped by mainstream culture because of their inability to speak standard English.

Lydia Minatoya, "Transformation"

1. Why do the parents of Minatoya and Richard Rodriguez attach such importance to the Americanization of their children? How do they seek to accomplish this?

2. What different cultural perspectives are in evidence in Minatoya's essay and Itabari Njeri's "What's in a Name?" (Ch. 7)?

David A. Ricks, "What's in a Name?"

1. How does Enrique Fernandez's account underscore the importance of advance research for companies that plan to market products using "Spanglish" in order to avoid blunders of the kind Ricks describes?
2. Compare the advertising strategies used to market products in other countries with those employed in the United States, drawing on Stuart Hirschberg's discussion in "The Rhetoric of Advertising" (Ch. 9).

◆ WRITING ASSIGNMENTS FOR CHAPTER 6

1. If you have older relatives who are not from the United States, interview them to discover how customs they encountered when they were growing up differed from current practices in America. Topics you might discuss include dating, courtship, marriage, child-rearing, cures for illnesses, food preparation, and celebrations. Write an essay describing your findings that incorporates selected excerpts from your conversations.
2. Have you ever constructed a family tree? Describe the method you used to interview family members and to corroborate details. What was the most interesting thing you learned?
3. Is there any custom or cultural practice you wish to make a case for or against (for example, the circumcision of girls in some cultures)? Write an essay providing evidence and reasons to support your views and respond to objections from those holding the opposite views.
4. Have you ever had to overcome psychological, physical, or social barriers to maintain a romantic relationship with someone from another culture? Describe your experiences.
5. Have you ever been invited by someone from another cultural background to witness or participate in a ceremony or ritual that was important to him or her? Describe your experiences.
6. What factors explain the trend of women keeping their maiden names after marriage? How do you feel about this practice?
7. What are some of the names you would consider for your child? What factors would influence your choice? (In some traditions, for example, children are named after either living or dead relatives.) Research your choices in a baby name book and discover the origin of each name and its meaning. (Glossary: *Onomastics.*)
8. Bilingual education programs have been a subject of controversy since they were introduced. How do you feel about these programs?
9. It is characteristic for Native Americans to have descriptive names with unique associations. If you had a name that functioned symbolically, what would it be?

10. How have your own experiences in learning a second language given you insight into the problems faced by immigrants who come to America and try to learn English?
11. A referendum to make English the official language of California has been approved. Should a constitutional amendment be introduced to make English the official language of the United States? Why or why not?
12. If you live in a family where you are the only one who speaks English, what problems have arisen because of your role as translator?

You know that even forms of speech can
change Within a thousand years, and
words we know Were useful once, seem
to us wondrous strange Foolish or
forced—and yet men spoke them so.

—Geoffrey Chaucer

Many Englishes

Who decides what standard English should be? What forces come into play that determine which idioms and dialects are perceived as correct and legitimate and which others are perceived as having a corrupting effect on the imagined purity of the English language? The essays in this chapter clearly demonstrate that language serves other purposes besides enabling us to communicate with one another. Most notably, it establishes boundaries between social groups in which the members speak different languages or dialects. It is also ironic that the imposition of one group's language or dialect upon another has often been a means by which one group has asserted its dominance over another. In "Something About English," Paul Roberts offers a brief survey of how the English language evolved as a result of both historical events and the influence of invaders. When we realize that standard English (spoken by nearly 400 million people) began as a dialect of an obscure Germanic tribe that invaded England in A.D. 600, we gain an appreciation of how accident and circumstance over time can produce what later is perceived as "normal."

Moreover, when we factor in the arbitrary and capricious decisions made by male scholars in imperfectly grafting an evolving English tongue on Latin grammatical forms (as Julia Penelope does in "The Glamour of Grammar"), we can appreciate even more the constructed nature of "standard English." Against this background of how historic forces have shaped and reshaped standard English, we can get a new perspective on the status of black English in the United States. This issue is addressed by Barbara Mellix in "From Outside, In" where she describes the difficulties and challenges she faced in making the shift from black English to standard English. This connection between language and the underlying social issues becomes the issue in Itabari Njeri's decision to adopt an African name (in "What's in a Name?") as a way of resisting the dominant white culture's influence. The choice of a name for Njeri establishes her identity within a distinct ethnic and racial group.

Lewis Carroll's charming "Jabberwocky" is a classic nonsense poem that dramatizes how new words are coined in the ever-evolving process by which language develops. Martha Barnette (in an excerpt from "Ladyfingers & Nun's Tummies") provides further insight into the irrepressible vitality of new words and slang. Barnette takes us on a linguistic and culinary excursion as she examines the unsuspected cultural and historical origins behind the names of foods.

A wonderful window into the heart of the linguistic vortex where new words are formed is Anthony Burgess's *A Clockwork Orange,* one of the most influential creative works of the twentieth century. Burgess takes delight in transforming bad grammar, slang, and neologisms into literature. Lastly, John Agard's poem "Listen mr oxford don" dramatizes the relationship between dialect and social acceptability and makes the point that political rather than linguistic forces determine what is considered proper English.

Something About English   *Paul Roberts*

◆ PAUL ROBERTS (1917–67) was a linguist, teacher, and writer. After teaching at San Jose State and Cornell University, he became director of language at the Center of American Studies in Rome. His published works include *Understanding Grammar* (1954), *Patterns of English* (1956), and *Understanding English* (1958), from which "Something About English" is taken.

The impact of historical events on the evolution of the English language is an amazing story covering 1400 years—a story that Roberts recounts in a concise and accessible way. From its beginnings in several Anglo-Saxon dialects to its current status as the standard language spoken by almost 400 million people around the world, English has been shaped by historical events at every stage in its evolution. It is perhaps this immense flexibility that makes English capable of adapting to the times. To get some idea of how much in flux the English language is, you need only to project past experiences into the future. Return several hundred years and English sounds quaint and archaic, yet understandable. Keep going back to Chaucer's time (1343–1400) and with some help you can understand what the words mean. Now imagine yourself as far in the future as Chaucer wrote in the past and you will realize that the English language you are familiar with will have changed so much that you would need a special course to understand it, just as we study medieval literature now. Then, the presumption that there exists a "standard English" for all time can be seen for the foolish notion that it is.

TO CONSIDER   Are there words that you use frequently that you know have come into English from other languages? What are they?

HISTORICAL BACKGROUNDS

No understanding of the English language can be very satisfactory without a notion of the history of the language. But we shall have to make do with just a notion. The history of English is long and complicated, and we can only hit the high spots.

The history of our language begins a little after A.D. 600. Everything before that is pre-history, which means that we can guess at it but can't prove much. For a thousand years or so before the birth of Christ our linguistic ancestors were savages wandering through the forests of northern Europe. Their language was a part of the Germanic branch of the Indo-European family.

At the time of the Roman Empire—say, from the beginning of the Christian Era to around A.D. 400—the speakers of what was to become English were scattered along the northern coast of Europe. They spoke a dialect of Low German. More exactly, they spoke several different dialects, since they were several different tribes. The names given to the tribes who got to England are *Angles, Saxons,* and *Jutes.* For convenience, we can refer to them all as Anglo-Saxons.

Their first contact with civilization was a rather thin acquaintance with the Roman Empire on whose borders they lived. Probably some of the Anglo-Saxons wandered into the Empire occasionally, and certainly Roman merchants and traders traveled among the tribes. At any rate, this period saw the first of our many borrowings from Latin. Such words as *kettle, wine, cheese, butter, cheap, plum, gem, bishop, church* were borrowed at this time. They show something of the relationship of the Anglo-Saxons with the Romans. The Anglo-Saxons were learning, getting their first taste of civilization.

They still had a long way to go, however, and their first step was to help smash the civilization they were learning from. In the fourth century the Roman power weakened badly. While the Goths were pounding away at the Romans in the Mediterranean countries, their relatives, the Anglo-Saxons, began to attack Britain.

The Romans had been the ruling power in Britain since A.D. 43. They had subjugated the Celts whom they found living there and had succeeded in setting up a Roman administration. The Roman influence did not extend to the outlying parts of the British Isles. In Scotland, Wales, and Ireland the Celts remained free and wild, and they made periodic forays against the Romans in England. Among other defense measures, the Romans built the famous Roman Wall to ward off the tribes in the north.

Even in England the Roman power was thin. Latin did not become the language of the country as it did in Gaul and Spain. The mass of people continued to speak Celtic, with Latin and the Roman civilization it contained in use as a top dressing.

In the fourth century, troubles multiplied for the Romans in Britain. Not only did the untamed tribes of Scotland and Wales grow more and more restive, but the Anglo-Saxons began to make pirate raids on the eastern coast. Furthermore, there was growing difficulty everywhere in the Empire, and the legions in Britain were siphoned off to fight elsewhere. Finally, in A.D. 410, the last Roman ruler in England, bent on becoming emperor, left the islands and took the last of the legions with him. The Celts were left in possession of Britain but almost defenseless against the impending Anglo-Saxon attack.

Not much is surely known about the arrival of the Anglo-Saxons in England. According to the best early source, the eighth-century historian Bede, the Jutes came in 449 in response to a plea from the Celtic king, Vortigern, who wanted their help against the Picts attacking from the north. The Jutes subdued the Picts but then quarreled and fought with Vortigern, and, with reinforcements from the Continent, settled permanently in Kent. Somewhat later the Angles established themselves in eastern England and the Saxons in the south and west. Bede's account is plausible enough, and these were probably the main lines of the invasion.

We do know, however, that the Angles, Saxons, and Jutes were a long time securing themselves in England. Fighting went on for as long as a hundred years before the Celts in England were all killed, driven into Wales, or reduced to slavery. This is the period of King Arthur, who was not entirely mythological. He was a Romanized Celt, a general, though probably not a king. He had some success against the Anglo-Saxons, but it was only temporary. By 550 or so the Anglo-Saxons were firmly established. English was in England.

OLD ENGLISH

All this is pre-history, so far as the language is concerned. We have no record of the English language until after 600, when the Anglo-Saxons were converted to Christianity and learned the Latin alphabet. The conversion began, to be precise, in the year 597 and was accomplished within thirty or forty years. The conversion was a great advance for the Anglo-Saxons, not only because of the spiritual benefits but because it reëstablished contact with what remained of Roman civilization. This civilization didn't amount to much in the year 600, but it was certainly superior to anything in England up to that time.

It is customary to divide the history of the English language into three periods: Old English, Middle English, and Modern English. Old English runs from the earliest records—i.e., seventh century—to about 1100; Middle English from 1100 to 1450 or 1500; Modern English from 1500 to the present day. Sometimes Modern English is further divided into Early Modern, 1500–1700, and Late Modern, 1700 to the present.

When England came into history, it was divided into several more or less autonomous kingdoms, some of which at times exercised a certain amount of control over the others. In the century after the conversion the most advanced kingdom was Northumbria, the area between the Humber River and the Scottish border. By A.D. 700 the Northumbrians had developed a respectable civilization, the finest in Europe. It is sometimes called the Northumbrian Renaissance, and it was the first of the several renaissances through which Europe struggled upward out of the ruins of the Roman Empire. It was in this period that the best of the Old English literature was written, including the epic poem *Beowulf.*

In the eighth century, Northumbrian power declined, and the center of influence moved southward to Mercia, the kingdom of the Midlands. A century later the center shifted again, and Wessex, the country of the West Saxons, became the leading power. The most famous king of the West Saxons was Alfred the Great, who reigned in the second half of the ninth century, dying in 901. He was famous not only as a military man and administrator but also as a champion of learning. He founded and supported schools and translated or caused to be translated many books from Latin into English. At this time also much of the Northumbrian literature of two centuries earlier was copied in West Saxon. Indeed, the great bulk of Old English writing which has come down to us is in the West Saxon dialect of 900 or later.

In the military sphere, Alfred's great accomplishment was his successful opposition to the viking invasions. In the ninth and tenth centuries, the Norsemen emerged in their ships from their homelands in Denmark and the Scandinavian peninsula. They traveled far and attacked and plundered at will and almost with impunity. They ravaged Italy and Greece, settled in France, Russia, and Ireland, colonized Iceland and Greenland, and discovered America several centuries before Columbus. Nor did they overlook England.

After many years of hit-and-run raids, the Norsemen landed an army on the east coast of England in the year 866. There was nothing much to oppose them except the Wessex power led by Alfred. The long struggle ended in 877 with a treaty by which a line was drawn roughly from the northwest of England to the southeast. On the eastern side of the line Norse rule was to prevail. This was called the Danelaw. The western side was to be governed by Wessex.

The linguistic result of all this was a considerable injection of Norse into the English language. Norse was at this time not so different from English as Norwegian or Danish is now. Probably speakers of English could understand, more or less, the language of the newcomers who had moved into eastern England. At any rate, there was considerable interchange and word borrowing. Examples of Norse words in the English language are *sky, give, law, egg, outlaw, leg, ugly, scant, sly, crawl, scowl, take, thrust*. There are hundreds more. We have even borrowed some pronouns from Norse—*they, their,* and *them*. These words were borrowed first by the eastern and northern dialects and then in the course of hundreds of years made their way into English generally.

It is supposed also—indeed, it must be true—that the Norsemen influenced the sound structure and the grammar of English. But this is hard to demonstrate in detail.

A SPECIMEN OF OLD ENGLISH

We may now have an example of Old English. The favorite illustration is the Lord's Prayer, since it needs no translation. This has come to us in several different versions. Here is one:

> Fæder ure þu ðe eart on heofonum si þin nama gehalgod. Tobecume þin rice. Gewurðe þin willa on eorðan swa swa on heofonum. Urne gedæghwamlican hlaf syle us to dæg. And forgyf us ure gyltas swa swa we forgyfaþ urum gyltendum. And ne gelæd þu us on costnunge ac alys us of yfele. Soðlice.

Some of the differences between this and Modern English are merely differences in orthography. For instance, the sign æ is what Old English writers used for a vowel sound like that in modern *hat* or *and*. The *th* sounds or modern *thin* or *then* are represented in Old English by þ or ð. But of course there are many differences in sound too. *Ure* is the ancestor of modern *our*, but the first vowel was like that in *too* or *ooze*. *Hlaf* is modern *loaf;* we have dropped the h sound and changed the vowel, which in *hlaf* was pronounced something like the vowel in *father*. Old English had some sounds which we do not have. The sound represented by y does not occur in Modern English. If you pronounce the vowel in *bit* with your lips rounded, you may approach it.

In grammar, Old English was much more highly inflected than Modern English is. That is, there were more case endings for nouns, more person and number endings for verbs, a more complicated pronoun system, various endings for adjectives, and so on. Old English nouns had four cases—nominative, genitive, dative, accusative. Adjectives had five—all these and an instrumental case besides. Present-day English has only two cases for nouns—common case and possessive case. Adjectives now have no case system at all. On the other hand, we now use a more rigid word order and more structure words (prepositions, auxiliaries, and the like) to express relationships than Old English did.

Some of this grammar we can see in the Lord's Prayer. *Heofonum,* for instance, is a dative plural; the nominative singular was *heofon*. *Urne* is an accusative singular; the nominative is *ure*. In *urum gyltendum* both words are dative plural. *Forgyfaþ* is the third person plural form of the verb. Word order is different: "urne gedæghwamlican hlaf syle us" in place of "Give us our daily bread." And so on.

In vocabulary Old English is quite different from Modern English. Most of the Old English words are what we may call native English: that is, words which have not been borrowed from other languages but which have been a part of English ever since English was a part of Indo-European. Old English did certainly contain borrowed words. We have seen that many borrowings were coming in from Norse. Rather large numbers had been borrowed from Latin, too. Some of these were taken while the Anglo-Saxons were still on the Continent (*cheese, butter, bishop, kettle*, etc.); a larger number came into English after the Conversion (*angel, candle, priest, martyr, radish, oyster, purple, school, spend*, etc.). But the great majority of Old English words were native English.

Now, on the contrary, the majority of words in English are borrowed, taken mostly from Latin and French. Of the words in *The American College Dictionary* only about 14 percent are native. Most of these, to be sure, are common, high-frequency words—*the, of, I, and, because, man, mother, road*, etc.; of the thousand most common words in English, some 62 percent are native English. Even so, the modern vocabulary is very much Latinized and Frenchified. The Old English vocabulary was not.

MIDDLE ENGLISH

Sometime between the years 1000 and 1200 various important changes took place in the structure of English, and Old English became Middle English. The political event which facilitated these changes was the Norman Conquest. The Normans, as the name shows, came originally from Scandinavia. In the early tenth century they established themselves in northern France, adopted the French language, and developed a vigorous kingdom and a very passable civilization. In the year 1066, led by Duke William, they crossed the Channel and made themselves masters of England. For the next several hundred years, England was ruled by kings whose first language was French.

One might wonder why, after the Norman Conquest, French did not become the national language, replacing English entirely. The reason is that the Conquest was not a national migration, as the earlier Anglo-Saxon invasion had been. Great numbers of Normans came to England, but they came as rulers and landlords. French became the language of the court, the language of the nobility, the language of polite society, the language of literature. But it did not replace English as the language of the people. There must always have been hundreds of towns and villages in which French was never heard except when visitors of high station passed through. *[handwritten margin note: econ. Classes w/in same country - Separated by lang.]*

But English, though it survived as the national language, was profoundly changed after the Norman Conquest. Some of the changes—in sound structure and grammar—would no doubt have taken place whether there had been a Conquest or not. Even before 1066 the case system of English nouns and adjectives was becoming simplified; people came to rely more on word order and prepositions than on inflectional endings to communicate their meanings. The process was speeded up by sound changes which caused many of the endings to sound alike. But no doubt the Conquest facilitated the change. German, which didn't experience a Norman Conquest, is today rather highly inflected compared to its cousin English.

But it is in vocabulary that the effects of the Conquest are most obvious. French ceased, after a hundred years or so, to be the native language of very many people in England, but it continued—and continues still—to be a zealously cultivated second language, the mirror of elegance and civilization. When one spoke English, one introduced not only French ideas and French things but also their French names. This was not only easy but socially useful. To pepper one's conversation with French expressions was to show that one was well-bred, elegant, *au courant*. The last sentence shows that the process is not yet dead. By using *au courant* instead of, say, *abreast of things,* the writer indicates that he is no dull clod who knows only English but an elegant person aware of how things are done in *le haut monde.*

Thus French words came into English, all sorts of them. There were words to do with government: *parliament, majesty, treaty, alliance, tax, government;* church words: *parson, sermon, baptism, incense, crucifix, religion;* words for foods: *veal, beef, mutton, bacon, jelly, peach, lemon, cream, biscuit;* colors: *blue, scarlet, vermilion;* household words: *curtain, chair, lamp, towel, blanket, parlor;* play words: *dance, chess, music, leisure, conversation;* literary words: *story, romance, poet, literary;* learned words: *study, logic, grammar, noun, surgeon, anatomy, stomach;* just ordinary words of all sorts: *nice, second, very, age, bucket, gentle, final, fault, flower, cry, count, sure, move, surprise, plain.*

All these and thousands more poured into the English vocabulary between 1100 and 1500, until at the end of that time many people must have had more French words than English at their command. This is not to say that English became French. English remained English in sound structure and in grammar, though these also felt the ripples of French influence. The very heart of the vocabulary, too, remained English. Most of the high-frequency words—the pronouns, the prepositions, the conjunctions, the auxiliaries, as well as a great many ordinary nouns and verbs and adjectives—were not replaced by borrowings.

Middle English, then, was still a Germanic language, but it differed from Old English in many ways. The sound system and the grammar changed a good deal. Speakers made less use of case systems and other inflectional devices and relied more on word order and structure words to express their meanings. This is often said to be a simplification, but it isn't really. Languages don't become simpler; they merely exchange one kind of complexity for another. Modern English is not a simple language, as any foreign speaker who tries to learn it will hasten to tell you.

For us Middle English is simpler than Old English just because it is closer to Modern English. It takes three or four months at least to learn to read Old English prose and more than that for poetry. But a week of good study should put one in touch with the Middle English poet Chaucer. Indeed, you may be able to make some sense of Chaucer straight off, though you would need instruction in pronunciation to make it sound like poetry. Here is a famous passage from the *General Prologue to the Canterbury Tales,* fourteenth century:

Ther was also a nonne, a Prioresse,
That of hir smyling was ful symple and coy,

Hir gretteste oath was but by Seinte Loy,
And she was cleped Madame Eglentyne.
Ful wel she song the service dyvyne,
Entuned in hir nose ful semely.
And Frenshe she spak ful faire and fetisly,
After the scole of Stratford-atte-Bowe,
For Frenshe of Parys was to hir unknowe.

EARLY MODERN ENGLISH

Sometime between 1400 and 1600 English underwent a couple of sound changes which made the language of Shakespeare quite different from that of Chaucer. Incidentally, these changes contributed much to the chaos in which English spelling now finds itself.

One change was the elimination of a vowel sound in certain unstressed positions at the end of words. For instance, the words *name, stone, wine, dance* were pronounced as two syllables by Chaucer but as just one by Shakespeare. The e in these words became, as we say, "silent." But it wasn't silent for Chaucer; it represented a vowel sound. So also the words *laughed, seemed, stored* would have been pronounced by Chaucer as two-syllable words. The change was an important one because it affected thousands of words and gave a different aspect to the whole language.

The other change is what is called the Great Vowel Shift. This was a systematic shifting of half a dozen vowels and diphthongs in stressed syllables. For instance, the word *name* had in Middle English a vowel something like that in the modern word *father; wine* had the vowel of modern *mean; he* was pronounced something like modern *hey; mouse* sounded like *moose; moon* had the vowel of *moan.* Again the shift was thoroughgoing and affected all the words in which these vowel sounds occurred. Since we still keep the Middle English system of spelling these words, the differences between Modern English and Middle English are often more real than apparent.

The vowel shift has meant also that we have come to use an entirely different set of symbols for representing vowel sounds than is used by writers of such languages as French, Italian, or Spanish, in which no such vowel shift occurred. If you come across a strange word—say, *bine*—in an English book, you will pronounce it according to the English system, with the vowel of *wine* or *dine.* But if you read *bine* in a French, Italian, or Spanish book, you will pronounce it with the vowel of *mean* or *seen.*

These two changes, then, produced the basic differences between Middle English and Modern English. But there were several other developments that had an effect upon the language. One was the invention of printing, an invention introduced into England by William Caxton in the year 1475. Where before books had been rare and costly, they suddenly became cheap and common. More and more people learned to read and write. This was the first of many advances in communication which have worked to unify languages and to arrest the development of dialect differences, though of course printing affects writing principally rather than speech. Among other things it hastened the standardization of spelling.

The period of Early Modern English—that is, the sixteenth and seventeenth centuries—was also the period of the English Renaissance, when people developed, on the one hand, a keen interest in the past and, on the other, a more daring and imaginative view of the future. New ideas multiplied, and new ideas meant new language. Englishmen had grown accustomed to borrowing words from French as a result of the Norman Conquest; now they borrowed from Latin and Greek. As we have seen, English had been raiding Latin from Old English times and before, but now the floodgates really opened, and thousands of words from the classical languages poured in. *Pedestrian, bonus, anatomy, contradict, climax, dictionary, benefit, multiply, exist, paragraph, initiate, scene, inspire* are random examples. Probably the average educated American today has more words from French in his vocabulary than from native English sources, and more from Latin than from French.

The greatest writer of the Early Modern English period is of course Shakespeare, and the best-known book is the King James Version of the Bible, published in 1611. The Bible (if not Shakespeare) has made many features of Early Modern English perfectly familiar to many people down to present times, even though we do not use these features in present-day speech and writing. For instance, the old pronouns *thou* and *thee* have dropped out of use now, together with their verb forms, but they are still familiar to us in prayer and in Biblical quotation: "Whither thou goest, I will go." Such forms as *hath* and *doth* have been replaced by *has* and *does;* "Goes he hence tonight?" would now be "Is he going away tonight?"; Shakespeare's "Fie on't, sirrah" would be "Nuts to that, Mac." Still, all these expressions linger with us because of the power of the works in which they occur.

It is not always realized, however, that considerable sound changes have taken place between Early Modern English and the English of the present day. Shakespearian actors putting on a play speak the words, properly enough, in their modern pronunciation. But it is very doubtful that this pronunciation would be understood at all by Shakespeare. In Shakespeare's time, the word *reason* was pronounced like modern *raisin; face* had the sound of modern *glass;* the l in *would, should, palm* was pronounced. In these points and a great many others the English language has moved a long way from what it was in 1600.

RECENT DEVELOPMENTS

The history of English since 1700 is filled with many movements and counter-movements, of which we can notice only a couple. One of these is the vigorous attempt made in the eighteenth century, and the rather half-hearted attempts made since, to regulate and control the English language. Many people of the eighteenth century, not understanding very well the forces which govern language, proposed to polish and prune and restrict English, which they felt was proliferating too wildly. There was much talk of an academy which would rule on what people could and could not say and write. The academy never came into being, but the eighteenth century did succeed in establishing certain attitudes which, though they haven't had much effect on the development of the language itself, have certainly changed the native speaker's feeling about the language.

In part a product of the wish to fix and establish the language was the development of the dictionary. The first English dictionary was published in 1603; it was a list of 2500 words briefly defined. Many others were published with gradual improvements until Samuel Johnson published his *English Dictionary* in 1755. This, steadily revised, dominated the field in England for nearly a hundred years. Meanwhile in America, Noah Webster published his dictionary in 1828, and before long dictionary publishing was a big business in this country. The last century has seen the publication of one great dictionary: the twelve-volume *Oxford English Dictionary,* compiled in the course of seventy-five years through the labors of many scholars. We have also, of course, numerous commercial dictionaries which are as good as the public wants them to be if not, indeed, rather better.

Another product of the eighteenth century was the invention of "English grammar." As English came to replace Latin as the language of scholarship it was felt that one should also be able to control and dissect it, parse and analyze it, as one could Latin. What happened in practice was that the grammatical description that applied to Latin was removed and superimposed on English. This was silly, because English is an entirely different kind of language, with its own forms and signals and ways of producing meaning. Nevertheless, English grammars on the Latin model were worked out and taught in the schools. In many schools they are still being taught. This activity is not often popular with school children, but it is sometimes an interesting and instructive exercise in logic. The principal harm in it is that it has tended to keep people from being interested in English and has obscured the real features of English structure.

But probably the most important force on the development of English in the modern period has been the tremendous expansion of English-speaking peoples. In 1500 English was a minor language, spoken by a few people on a small island. Now it is perhaps the greatest language of the world, spoken natively by over a quarter of a billion people and as a second language by many millions more. When we speak of English now, we must specify whether we mean American English, British English, Australian English, Indian English, or what, since the differences are considerable. The American cannot go to England or the Englishman to America confident that he will always understand and be understood. The Alabaman in Iowa or the Iowan in Alabama shows himself a foreigner every time he speaks. It is only because communication has become fast and easy that English in this period of its expansion has not broken into a dozen mutually unintelligible languages.

---

1 What historical events in England catalyzed the evolution of the English language? How did the following four factors play a crucial role in promoting cross-cultural contacts that brought new words into the English language: (a) trade and commerce, (b) religion, (c) invasions and territorial conquests, and (d) the invention of the printing press in 1475 (para. 37)?

2 To this day, French words that were brought into English by the Norman conquest, (para. 25–30) have possessed an aura of refinement and elitism. What are some of these French words (for example, "chic")? In what areas of life were they applicable, and still are today?

3 How did the linguistic phenomenon known as the Great Vowel Shift (para. 33–36) change the way thousands of words were pronounced and depicted in symbols?

4 How does Roberts organize his essay to reveal the connection between historical events and the development of English? Which of his examples seems to be especially persuasive in demonstrating this connection? How might elements in Roberts's discussion—such as his use of the words "savages" (para. 2) and "untamed tribes" (para. 8)—seem dated or politically incorrect? (Glossary: *Biased Language, Organization, Semantics.*)

5 What time signals does Roberts use to make sure that his narrative is easy to follow? Does he answer the reporter's five questions—what happened, when did it happen, where did it happen, who was involved, and why did it happen? Give some examples. (Glossary: *Narration.*)

6 As a research project, trace the evolution or history of any term. (If it is a traditional term, you might wish to consult the *Oxford English Dictionary* in either its twelve-volume form or its condensed two-volume edition.) Your analysis should give illustrations of the use of the term from its original appearance to the present (for example, the evolution of the term "ware," meaning your "wares or goods or merchandise," as in yren ware—iron ware—in the 1400s, to hardware after the 1500s, to software in the early 1960s, to shareware, with its moral obligation to send some money to the developer if you wish, versus freeware in the 1990s).

Can you discover any terms that reflect the interaction of two or more cultures, as in the following example?

> I've been wondering about this for years: September, October, November and December are the ninth, 10th, 11th and 12th months. Why? Shouldn't they be the seventh, eighth, ninth and 10th months, as their names suggest?   —Christina Smith, San Antonio, Tex.*

> It's because our English names for the months have Latin origins, and the early Romans began their year in March. (Not a bad idea! Think of all that bad weather you could avoid.)

---

* Star Ledger 7/13/97 Marilyn vos Savant *Parade Magazine*, Page 8

The Glamour of Grammar *Julia Penelope*

◆ JULIA PENELOPE has been a visiting professor at the University of Massachusetts in Amherst. Her writings include *Speaking Freely: Unlearning the Lies of the Father's Tongues* (1990), from which the following selection is taken. She is editor of *Out of the Closet: Lesbians Speak* (1994).

Penelope covers some of the same terrain as Paul Roberts does, but from a decidedly different perspective that gives us additional insight into the forces that are responsible for defining what correct grammar is. Penelope reveals how decisions made by male scholars in positions of power distorted an evolving English dialect to fit the prescribed mold of Latin grammatical forms and, in the process, left some conspicuous gaps. For those who think grammar reflects language, it may come as something of a shock to realize that what we know intuitively about English, reflected in our usage, fails to square with some of the grammatical rules for tense dictated by, as Penelope sees it, "patriarchal grammars."

> **TO CONSIDER** What kind of experiences did you have in learning the rules of English grammar? Do you feel it was a worthwhile experience?

In a man's world, language belongs to men. There are two interconnected histories that attest to male control of the development of the English language: the history of the language itself over nearly 2,000 years and the history of **prescriptive grammars** that set forth the "*rights*" and "*wrongs*" of English usage. Men have managed changes in the language and legislated its rules, both structural and social. Prescriptive grammarians established, in some cases, made up rules in order to maintain English in a pure, ideal state in which it never existed. The rules men have contrived to preserve the illusory purity of English are set forth in numerous **grammar** books from the seventeenth century to the present. From those early grammars and their Latin sources the distortions and misinformation imposed on the language have been passed on to us as "fact.". . . Until the Norman Invasion in 1066, Latin was the most important language, the language in which affairs of state were conducted; since, with only exceptional instances, men controlled the institutions that governed people's lives, most of the women who did learn Latin were nuns.

from Scandinavia

Because Latin was the language of intellectual privilege for so long, the only grammars that existed were Latin grammars. Grammars, understood as text-books in which some uses of language are held up as correct and others condemned as wrong, ignorant, or illiterate, come into existence only when some powerful group of speakers decides to screen those who would acquire privilege. In the seventh and eighth centuries, both Bede and Alcuin produced Latin grammars, and, around 1000, Aelfric wrote one of the first grammars of Latin directed at English-speaking students. R. H. Robins, in fact, suggests that, because Aelfric thought his grammar "would be equally suitable as an introduction to (Old) English, . . . it may be taken as setting the seal on several centuries of Latin-inspired English grammar" (70–71). Monks (church clerics) devoted their lives and eyesight to painstakingly transcribing scriptures, word by word, and a few selected (and edited) secular texts such as the OE epic *Beowulf.* Reading and writing were simply not available to common folk who had neither the time nor the need for either. They spoke the language of the poor, Old English. As a result, no grammarians felt compelled to record the language or to make up rules governing its use. For several centuries, English (or anglo-saxon) was the language of the peasants, who chatted and carried on the activities of their lives uninterrupted by grammatical "dos" and "don'ts" and never had to take spelling tests.

Histories of writing generally attribute the movement to standardize languages, **prescriptivism,** to the European invention of printing[1] from movable type by Johann Gutenberg (1400?–1468?) (Baugh, 240–41; Robins, 112–13), postulating that the widespread availability of numerous printed materials *required* standardized spellings and grammars, lest dialectal differences interfere with the intelligibility and interpretation of the printed language. In 1476, William Caxton introduced the printing process into England (Baugh, 240–41). Printed materials, ranging from pamphlets to huge folios, were now within the reach of many men, and those new readers increasingly demanded a standard, uniform language. The spellings that represented dialectal pronunciations must have made identifying some words difficult and tedious. As R. H. Robins observed, "The invention of printing made standardized spellings more important, and, in turning attention to the relation between writing and pronunciation aroused interest, since then perennial, in the problem of spelling reform" (1967, 112–13).

The relationship between the spelling of an English word and its pronunciation has always been problematic and, at times, downright fanciful. In the fourteenth century, for example, *femelle,* from Latin *femella* ('little woman'), borrowed into English from Norman French, had been "standardized" to *female,* by analogy to the word *male.* This "standardization" simultaneously fixed the spelling of *female* **and** made the word look as though it were derived from *male.* (In fact, the two words are not etymologically related.) Here, as in other areas, men's certainty of their innate superiority to women elevated the ridiculous to the status of "fact," and misogyny, masquerading as standardization and "correctness," fabricated an etymology to justify a whimsical spelling.

The demand for identifying the "correct" spelling of words opened the way for the first "grammars" of English, which began to appear during the seventeenth century. At first, they were hardly more than lists of "difficult" latinate words (Baugh, 279–80), but the errors and distortions still taught in public schools were gradually introduced by self-styled grammarians for whom the analysis of English was a diverting avocation. Baugh, always a restrained scholar, said of those early grammarians: "Most of these books were the work of men with no special qualifications for the thing they attempted to do" (331).

Grammarians, like other writers, need an audience and a market. The audience in this case consisted of those who had the leisure and the money that literacy requires: upper-class, aristocratic men. The illiterate, most women and poor men, incapable of reading or writing, had no use for the rules of linguistic etiquette. Prior to this, dialect differences apparently hadn't impeded communication; only some men, and fewer women, were allowed the luxury of education and with it, reading and writing. There wasn't much to read, after all, aside from the bible, and reading that required a knowledge of Hebrew and Greek, as well as Latin. As Chaucer's dialect (East Mercian) grew in importance, men felt that it had to be made "respectable," particularly in its written representation. The accessibility of printed materials, combined with other social changes—the recently acquired respectability of the English language, the rise of the middle class, and nationalism—created a market for the Latin-based grammars written in the early modern period and the standardizations they advocated. International rivalries and nationalism determined that the language had to be protected from "bastardization," so several generations of self-elected "experts" set themselves the task of establishing the rules that would perpetuate their ideas about linguistic purity. From the beginning, grammars of English were written **by** men for a predominantly male audience.

The tradition of English grammar began with descriptions that were inherently inaccurate and distorting (they could not be otherwise), and its confused development has left a legacy that school boards and publishers are unwilling to discard. They have too much money invested in error. That prescriptive grammar has managed to sustain its credibility for so long testifies to the efficacy of persistence and repetition. The modern "back to the basics" movement is only the most recent voice of this pernicious legacy from the past.

The reverence for things classical typical of the renaissance[2] permanently distorted our ideas of what English is or might have been like. As Robins observed: "Men started with the framework handed down from the late Latin grammarians and suggested by Aelfric as suitable for Old English as well as for Latin" (119). That the Early ModE Latin-based grammars purported to describe and elucidate had changed significantly during the eight centuries separating it from OE failed to deter most of those early English grammarians. As a result, in spite of occasional protests, Latin-based grammars and their inadequacies became the standard texts for describing English by the nineteenth century, and their influence has continued, without disruption, through this century.

With notable exceptions such as the *Grammatica Linguae Anglicanae* (1653) by John Wallis and William Loughton's *Practical Grammar of the English Tongue* (1734), early grammars of English generally began with the eight "parts of speech." The idea of dividing the vocabulary of a language into "parts" of speech originated with Greek grammarians, Dionysius Thrax (C. 100 B.C.) and Apollonius Dyscolus (Alexandria, second century A.D.; Robins, 30), and were applied by the Roman grammarian Priscian (C. 500 A.D.) to Latin (Robins, 54). In his sixteenth-century Latin grammar, W. Lily took those "parts of speech" from classical Latin grammars and imposed them on English structures without the benefit of critical thought (Robins, 110).

There was a struggle, though, and some challenged the imposition of Latin and Greek categories onto the structure of English. Loughton, for example, decried those who "attempted to force our Language (contrary to its Nature) to the Method and Rules of the Latin Grammar," and refused to use terms borrowed from Latin grammars, such as *noun, verb, adjective* (Baugh, 330).[3] Unfortunately, the voices of dissenters like Loughton and Wallis were submerged by the appeal of English grammars based on Latin, and classical imitators like Lily triumphed.

The grammatical tradition derived from Latin and Greek generated much confusion and introduced numerous idiocies to the study of English. Those early grammars imposed upon the language and its speakers "rules" that had little to do with the structure of English, borrowed, often without qualification or modification, from grammars of the classical languages.[4] English was forced to "fit" into the categories established first for Greek and then Latin, according to the individual grammarian's notions of linguistic "logic." Some grammarians couldn't figure out what to call the English class of articles (or determiners), a(n) and the, because they weren't in Priscian's Latin grammar (Latin didn't have articles). When Bullokar (*Bref grammar for English,* 1586) classified English words according to the Latin system of categories, he mentioned the articles only as "identifying adjuncts" of nouns. Others, like Ben Jonson's *The English grammar* (1640), did assign them to a distinct class (Robins, 119–20). The rule forbidding us to "split" our infinitives, *to* + verb (*to eat, to dream*), was introduced because one cannot "split" infinitives in Greek or Latin. It's an impossibility. In English, it's not only possible, but often necessary to neatly split one's infinitives. We "split" infinitives in English because we can.

Rather than list and describe every one of the linguistic inaccuracies perpetrated by the imposition of Latin rules onto the English language, a discussion that concentrates on one area of grammar will better demonstrate the lack of fit between language and grammar fostered by linguistic prescriptivism. Of the subjects that suggest themselves, the description of tense in English—how many there are, and how the tense of a verb specifies the time of an act in the "real world"—specifically with reference to the function of the English model verbs, exemplifies how far removed from linguistic reality the prescriptive grammars of patriarchy are.

If we examine the rules for tense formulated by prescriptive grammarians and compare them to what we know intuitively about English (reflected in our usage), the more puzzling the longevity of those rules becomes. Consider, for example, the claim that English has three tenses: present, past, and future. A glance at the ways tense is marked in English suggests that this assertion, borrowed from Latin grammars, is suspect. First, we add to or change verbs in identifiable ways only for the present and past tenses in English. We indicate the present with the suffix -s, but only in the third person singular (*sits, eats, drinks*), so that it is more accurate to say that no ending is added to the verb for the present tense (except in the third person singular), while the past is marked by the suffix *-ed* and various vowel changes in the so-called irregular verbs (*drink > drank, sing > sang*). The "future" tense, however, is said to be marked by two modal verbs, *shall* in the first persons singular and plural (*I shall, we shall*) and *will* in the second and third persons (*you will, they will*). The future "tense" of the prescriptive grammarians is signalled by two modals that are separate words from the main verb, which suggests that what is traditionally called the "future" in English is something other than tense, a more complicated feature of the language altogether.

If we stop to think about it, we realize that every modal (the so-called helping verbs) refers to some future, hypothetical action, not just *shall* and *will,* and the discrepancy between what we know and what we've been taught about tense in English becomes clearer. You may recall being told that *shall* is the "correct" form of the future "tense" for first person subjects and that *will* is to be used only with the second and third persons. According to this rule, saying "I will" is "ungrammatical," even though we say it all the time. In fact, we aren't violating English structure; it is the prescriptive rule that is in violation. Prior to 1622, no English grammar mentioned a distinction between *shall* and *will,* because there wasn't one. It wasn't until 1653 that Wallis stated the "rule" still taught in schools in his *Grammatica Anglicanae* (Baugh, 337). This particular prescription was given its final formulation, the one still included in contemporary textbooks, by William Ward in his *Grammar of the English Language* (1765), although Ward's rules didn't gain currency until Lindley Murray copied them in his 1795 grammar.

In order to grasp the inaccuracy of prescriptive descriptions of tense, consider the "past" forms of *will* and *shall.* (I'll return to the problems of describing the so-called future shortly.) Used in either a declarative sentence or a question, both *would* and *should* stipulate that the action of the verb occurs in some hypothetical future beyond the present context of the utterance in which they appear.

   1.1   a   I *would* go to a movie.
          b. *Would* I go to a movie?
   1.2. a.   I *should* go to a movie.
          b. *Should* I go to a movie?

In the statements, 1.1.a. and 1.2.a., *would* and *should* both indicate that the act of going to a movie isn't likely to happen, but they differ in the degree of control the speaker implies with respect to the event. *Would* indicates that external factors will affect the speaker's decision; *should* suggests that internal or external pressure is compelling a decision one way or the other. In questions, however, these modals are contrastive: *would* repeats a previously asked question as if to clarify or confirm the speaker's understanding of it; *should* requests that someone other than the speaker offer pros and cons about a possible decision.

In spite of differences in meaning, other modal verbs have the same temporal range as *will/would* and *shall/should,* placing the verb's action in a time to come after the utterance in which they occur. *Can/could, may/might, must,* and the semi-modals, *ought to* (in ME the past form of *owe*), *want to, have to, got to,* and *need to,* indicate that the action of the verb with which they are used is cast in the future, as the following examples illustrate.

1.3   a. I *will*
       b. I *would*
       c. I *shall*
       d. I *should*
       e. I *can*
       f. I *could*   } eat pizza for supper.
       g. I *may*
       h. I *might*
       i. I *must*
       j. I *ought to*

The modal and semi-modal verbs all point to an unspecified future time beyond the time of the utterance in which they occur. (From this point on, the semi-modals will be spelled *oughta, hafta, wanta, gotta,* and *needta* to represent the way speakers pronounce them in rapid speech.)[5]

The meaning differences observable among the modals in 1.3 have nothing to do with "tense" or "time," and do not affect the use of these verbs to indicate futurity. Note that I have limited the "subject" of all the example sentences to "I" to show that *will, shall, can, may* (so-called present tense forms), and *would, might,* and *could* (the "past" forms) all indicate that the first person speaker has control (volition) over the action designated by the verb (in [1.1] and [1.2] *go*, in [1.3] *eat*). *Should, must,* and *oughta* are ambiguous with respect to control.[6] The four modals differ in the way they signal the probability that the event will occur. *Will, shall,* and *must* tell us that there is a 99% likelihood (barring unforeseen circumstances) that the speaker is going to eat pizza, whereas *can, may, would, should, could, might,* and *oughta* indicate probability determined by factors known only to the speaker. Adding explanatory clauses will illustrate this conditionality in *can, may,* and *could:*

1.4   a. I *can* eat pizza   { when I leave work / if I want to / till the cows come home }.

       b. I *may* eat pizza   { when I leave work / if I want to / till the cows come home }.

       c. I *could* eat pizza   { when I leave work / if I want to / till the cows come home }.

Each modal specifies the strength either of the speaker's volition or the external pressure to act, and a range of probability that the action described by a verb will occur.[7] In English, modals like *must, should, oughta,* and *hafta* are ambiguous with respect to whether the impulse to act originates with the agent of the verb or external factors. When someone says, "I *must/hafta* eat pizza tonight," only additional information tells us whether the modal of obligation is used because of the speaker's desire or some external pressure. With *must* and *hafta*, perhaps the speaker's craving for pizza is so intense that nothing else will satisfy her at the time, or pizza could be the only thing available to her on that particular evening. Likewise, *should* and *oughta* are moot regarding the source of the articulated necessity to eat pizza. If someone says "I *should/oughta* eat pizza tonight," the determining factor might be that the speaker knows that pizza is the best thing for her to eat (internal) or that a friend she's having dinner with expects to eat pizza (external) and will be angry if her expectations aren't met.

Two of the semi-modals excluded from prescriptive grammars of English exemplify the semantic contrast of internal volition versus external pressure to act: *wanta* and *needta*. *Wanta* signifies the speaker's **desire** to do something, and is not ambiguous; whatever the specific action is, the speaker indicates that she wishes to do it. *Needta,* in contrast, is ambiguous with respect to whether the speaker is indicating internal will or external pressure to act. Unless she makes clear to us that the origins of the hypothetical act are internally or externally motivated, we have no way of identifying the impulse's source for ourselves. We may *wanta* win a trip to New Orleans, but there is no internal or external necessity that we *must, should,* or *oughta* do so. We may *needta* buy groceries, but the source of our expressed urgency can be internal or external. Whether **we say we want** or **need** to perform some act, the modals indicate only the **likelihood** that we will act.

Wanta and *needta* represent the semantic tension between individual control and external pressure to act. Each of the English modals can be imagined as occupying some semantic location along two axes: AGENT ABILITY (the degree of control the individual has over whether an act will or won't occur) versus FORCE OF CONTINGENCY (the extent of control held by external events or individuals) and DEGREE OF PROBABILITY. The perceived relationship between the speaker's will to act and the extent to which contingencies will affect the probability that an act will occur determine which modal verb we choose. I've diagrammed the positions of the modals with respect to these two axes in Figure 7.2: DEGREE OF PROBABILITY (0% to 100%) is the horizontal axis; AGENT ABILITY (internal) versus FORCE OF CONTINGENCY (external control) is the vertical axis.

My diagram represents the underlying semantic parameters that determine our choice of a modal verb as speakers, and how, as listeners, we interpret their use. The modals provide us with ways of hedging our bets. If we look at the four modals at the extremes of Figure 7.2, *oughta, must, wanta,* and *will/shall,* and their placement with respect to the horizontal and vertical axes, AGENT ABILITY (Internal)~FORCE OF CONTINGENCY (External) and DEGREE OF PROBABILITY, our reasons for choosing one rather than another is clearly a function of the degree of commitment or obligation combined with other variables—explicit or implicit—when we speak.

Oughta and *must* are at the top of the diagram because both indicate that external factors weigh greatly in determining whether an action will or will not occur. They differ in meaning because *must* means that the action will probably

Degree of Probability

AGENT ABILITY—FORCE OF CONTINGENCY

0%	50%	100%
oughta		must
should		hafta
would	needta	gotta
may/might		
could	—	gonna
wanta	can	will/shall

occur because it's obligatory, whereas *oughta* implies that the speaker acknowledges the pressure to perform the action but may, in fact, not do it. *Oughta* and *must* contrast in meaning with *wanta* and *will/shall,* respectively, in terms of the speaker's control or desire to act. *Wanta* indicates that the speaker would like to carry out the act but may not, while *oughta* suggests that the speaker isn't personally committed to acting but feels obliged to. *Must* and *will/shall* contrast in the same way, but differ in the probability they describe. If I were betting on the likelihood that a speaker would act, I'd bet on someone who said *will, shall,* or *must. Oughta, wanta,* and *may/might, could, would, needta,* and *should* as well, are deliberate **hedges** that speakers use to give themselves latitude with respect to acting.

The modal *can* is different from the other modals. It is the most "neutral" verb within the parameters represented in Figure 7.2. Speakers use *can* when they have the ability to act in some conceivable future, but won't specify the likelihood of acting. Being able to do something, saying, "I *can* do that," doesn't mean that one will, yet the assertion of capability can be interpreted as placing the probability somewhere above 0% but far below 100%.

Other speakers may find that their own interpretations differ from my own. Other factors determine how we interpret English modals, especially our intonation and whether we use a modal in its full form or contracted, for example, *will/'ll, could, would/'d. Would* and *could* become indistinguishable in their contracted forms, for example, "I'd've" is ambiguous as to whether it was the speaker's ability or desire to do something. (Note that *must* cannot be contracted.) Certainly, our interpretations are affected by whether the modal occurs in a statement or a question, and the person (first, second, third) who appears as the **agent.** For a speaker to say to another individual, "You *wanta* diet," as a direct assertion clearly violates the boundaries of the addressee's volition, and constitutes verbal aggression, unless the accompanying intonation pattern indicates that the utterance is intended as a question, in which case it can be interpreted as a statement of disbelief or a request for confirmation.[8] Using *will* or *must* in a statement with a second or third person agent constitutes a claim of authority, either as having the power to control someone else's behavior or certainty based on prior knowledge or information outside of the immediate context. If I say, "You will eat pizza tonight" or "You'll eat pizza tonight," I'm either informing my hearer that she has no choice in the matter or I'm making a prediction. "She *will* eat pizza tonight" implies that the speaker has the power to make her eat pizza, whereas "She'*ll* eat pizza tonight" sounds more like a prediction. The contracted form of the modal may imply less power on the part of the speaker, but again, intonation indicates the extent to which the speaker is asserting control over a third party.

The preceding discussion illustrates the complexities of the modal system in English and the inadequacies of patriarchal descriptions of how we signal "future" time. The prescriptive grammarians thought that English "ought to" have a "future tense" only because Latin and Greek did. Since English specifies future time semantically, no grammar that imitates classical models is adequate. Isolating *shall* and *will* as the "future tense" doesn't begin to describe the subtleties of modal verbs, and this discussion suggests that the alleged one-to-one correlation between the tense (present, past, future) of a verb and time (in the world) will not withstand scrutiny. None of the "past tense" forms of the modals has anything to do with time prior to an utterance; each one refers to some time to come after the utterance in question.[9]

Yet, English teachers persist in telling us that the "present" tense is used to describe "present time," and we memorize the rules they force on us even though we know that what is called the "present tense" is actually used in a continuative sense to describe behaviors that are habitual and engaged in consistently over time, for example, "I **eat** cereal," "She **looks** for trouble." We consent to perpetuating this lie, but we actually use what is called the "progressive **aspect**" (*be* + Verb-*ing*) when we describe an activity occurring in the present, for example, "I am **eating** cereal," "She is **looking** for trouble." The progressive aspect, not the present tense, marks an action as taking place **at this moment.** The present tense, in fact, is rarely used, with the exceptions of stage directions ("Crowd **exits** right") and the examples contrived for grammar books.

My brief histories of the English language and the Latin-based grammars written to fix its usage illustrate how thoroughly men have controlled not only specific elements of the development of English structure but the way we understand its structure as well. Patriarchal grammars justify descriptions of language as men would have it. Male ideas about English (and language in general), passed from generation to generation as "The Rules," when examined critically, turn out to be as dubious as the "received wisdom" about women we hear every day. The longevity of both false descriptions (of English, of women) is no accident, of course, because men perceive language and women as unruly objects they must tame and control.

NOTES

1. The Chinese had discovered how to make paper in the first century A.D. and invented the process of block printing in the tenth (Robins, 111).

2. It wasn't until the nineteenth century that male scholars applied the term *renaissance* to the period, but it stuck.

3. In spite of the lack of congruence between the terminology of Greek and Latin grammars and the English language, I will, with some exceptions discussed later in the book, use the terms that most of my readers are familiar with. If those words are often imprecise, I hope that a majority will still be able to follow my discussions.

4. Discussions of the history of the grammatical tradition in English and its classical sources are common in linguistics texts. Here, I've relied on Albert C. Baugh's *A History of the English Language* (New York: Appleton-Century-Crofts, 1963) and R. H. Robins, *A Short History of Linguistics* (London: Longmans, Green and Co., 1967). There is also an informative article by Karl W. Dykema, "Where Our Grammar Came From," *College English* April 1961: 455–65. In *Grammar* (London: Penguin Books, 1971), Frank Palmer discusses how the categories and terminology of prescriptive grammars have influenced twentieth-century linguistics, esp. 13–20 and 41–106.

5. Vowel reduction (see en. 1) in final syllables has probably led to the notion among native speakers that *would've* is a contracted form of *would of*, rather than *would have*, an interpretation of the contraction that prescriptive grammarians have condemned (unsuccessfully) since the eighteenth century.

6. In the case of *gotta*, what may appear to be a spelling eccentricity on my part is a necessary way of distinguishing two different senses of got to. *Gotta* functions as a modal, e.g., "I *gotta* leave now," and its pronunciation contrasts with *got to* [gat'tu], as in "I got to go to the movies tonight," which some may find still ambiguous. Both *get to* and *got to* imply that permission was required for an event to occur and that it was granted. The external agency granting permission is seldom explicit.

7. I'm indebted to Lowell Bouma for sharing his analysis of the Modern German modal system, with which my analysis of the Modern English modals began (unpublished paper delivered to the Linguistic Society of America, December, 1968). Because the two systems are dissimilar, in particular the ambiguity with respect to internal agency versus external pressure of the English modals, I've reworked his description of German to represent the English system: For a fuller treatment of the English modals from a linguistic point of view, see F. R. Palmer, *Modality and the English Modals* (London: Longman, 1979).

8. In *The Road to Gandolfo* (Bantam Books, 1982, 272), Robert Ludlum uses *will* as an imperative with the form of a question, and his narrator comments on how it should be interpreted: "'*Will* you keep quiet!' The Hawk did not ask a question."

9. The cover of *TV Guide* (April 18–22, 1988), however, used *may* in what is clearly intended to indicate present, or, perhaps, continuous time: "What You *May* Not Be Noticing About TV News—and Should."

---

1 From Penelope's perspective, why is it important to correct the perception that "language belongs to men" (para. 1)? How has this control been exercised in terms of how words are spelled and pronounced, and what rules should govern English grammar?

2 Why is it important to understand the inequities in access to power that existed for men and women in the past as well as the role played by Latin and Greek grammar in order to understand the patchwork quilt of nonsensical rules that are still in use today?

3 How does Penelope's analysis of the use of modal verbs in the future tense illustrate the confused classification scheme considered correct under English grammar rules? How does this analysis support her view that "men have managed changes in the language and legislated its rules, both structural and social" (para. 1)?

4 How does Penelope's essay shed light on the ongoing argument between those scholars who study language as it is used in contrast to grammarians who dictate rules of what language should be? Does her own account suffer from biased language, and, if so, does it detract from the quality of her analysis? Explain. (Glossary: *Biased Language, Grammar, Descriptivism, Prescriptivism.*)

5 In your own words, summarize Penelope's argument. How would the effect of Penelope's essay have changed if she had taken measures to take opposing views into account? (Glossary: *Argument* and *Tone.*)

6 How do the experiences of the French-speaking people in Quebec, the Basques, the Welsh, and those who speak Gaelic in Ireland demonstrate the relevance of political and cultural agendas on questions of linguistic acceptability? Select one of these groups, or any other, and report on how language and dialect are intertwined with issues of identity, history, and power. In what sense is language "a political instrument and manifestation of power" (in the words of James Baldwin)?

Jabberwocky   *Lewis Carroll*

◆ LEWIS CARROLL is the pseudonym of Charles Lutwidge Dodgson. He is the author of the well-known series of stories beginning with *Alice in Wonderland* (1865). He was a regular member of the teaching faculty at Christ Church at Oxford University, where he served as a teacher in mathematics and logic. He wrote his famous poem "Jabberwocky" in 1855, intending it as a scholar's jest, an attempt to parody Anglo-Saxon poetry. Alice encounters this poem in mirror writing. In it, Carroll synthesizes words to describe the inhabitants of the Looking-Glass world. It offers an unusual perspective on the way new words come into the language.

Have you ever unintentionally combined two words into one to produce an entirely novel combination (for example, rambunctious and supercilious to make "superumptious")? If so, you have duplicated the unusual method, used by Carroll, whereby the meanings of words are suggested by how they sound.

> **TO CONSIDER**   What nonsense rhymes do you know or can you make up?

'Twas brillig, and the slithy toves
    Did gyre and gimble in the wabe:
All mimsy were the borogoves,
    And the mome raths outgrabe.

"Beware the Jabberwock, my son!
    The jaws that bite, the claws that catch!
Beware the Jubjub bird, and shun
    The frumious Bandersnatch!"

He took his vorpal sword in hand;
    Long time the manxome foe he sought—
So rested he by the Tumtum tree
    And stood awhile in thought.

And, as in uffish thought he stood,
    The Jabberwock, with eyes of flame.
Came whiffling through the tulgey wood,
    And burbled as it came!

One, two! One, two! And through and through
    The vorpal blade went snicker-snack!
He left it dead, and with its head
    He went galumphing back.

"And hast thou slain the Jabberwock?
    Come to my arms, my beamish boy!
O frabjous day! Callooh, Callay!"
    He chortled in his joy.

'Twas brillig, and the slithy toves
    Did gyre and gimble in the wabe:
All mimsy were the borogoves,
    And the mome raths outgrabe.

Explaining the Meaning of Jabberwocky   *Lewis Carroll*

"You seem very clever at explaining words, Sir," said Alice. "Would you kindly tell me the meaning of the poem called 'Jabberwocky'?"

"Let's hear it," said Humpty Dumpty. "I can explain all the poems that ever were invented—and a good many that haven't been invented just yet."

This sounded very hopeful, so Alice repeated the first verse:

> "*'Twas brillig, and the slithy toves*
>   *Did gyre and gimble in the wabe;*
> *All mimsy were the borogoves,*
>   *And the mome raths outgrabe.*"

"That's enough to begin with," Humpty Dumpty interrupted; "there are plenty of hard words there. '*Brillig*' means four o'clock in the afternoon—the time when you begin *broiling* things for dinner."

"That'll do very well," said Alice; "and '*slithy*'?"

"Well, '*slithy*' means 'lithe and slimy.' 'Lithe' is the same as 'active.' You see it's like a portmanteau—there are two meanings packed up into one word."

"I see it now," Alice remarked thoughtfully; "and what are '*toves*'?"

"Well, '*toves*' are something like badgers, they're something like lizards, and they're something like corkscrews."

"They must be very curious-looking creatures."

"They are that," said Humpty Dumpty; "also they make their nests under sun-dials; also they live on cheese."

"And what's to '*gyre*' and to '*gimble*'?"

"To '*gyre*' is to go round and round like a gyroscope. To '*gimble*' is to make holes like a gimlet."

"And '*the wabe*' is the grass-plot round a sun-dial, I suppose?" said Alice, surprised at her own ingenuity.

"Of course it is. It's called '*wabe*,' you know, because it goes a long way before it and a long way behind it—"

"And a long way beyond it on each side," Alice added.

"Exactly so. Well, then, '*mimsy*' is 'flimsy and miserable' (there's another portmanteau for you). And a '*borogove*' is a thin, shabby-looking bird with its feathers sticking out all round—something like a live mop."

"And then '*mome raths*'?" said Alice. "I'm afraid I'm giving you a great deal of trouble."

"Well, a '*rath*' is a sort of green pig; but '*mome*' I'm not certain about. I think it's short for 'from home'—meaning that they'd lost their way, you know."

"And what does '*outgrabe*' mean?"

"Well, '*outgribing*' is something between bellowing and whistling, with a kind of sneeze in the middle; however, you'll hear it done, maybe, down in the wood yonder, and when you've once heard it you'll be *quite* content. Who's been repeating all that hard stuff to you?"

"I read it in a book," said Alice.

---

1 What features of this encounter between Alice and Humpty Dumpty play with the idea that we tend to understand what words mean based on how they sound? How do the sounds of specific words (for example, "slithy" or "mimsy") suggest the process by which they have been created? Is this what Carroll means by "a portmanteau," which in Great Britain is a "case or bag to carry clothing in while traveling, usually in the form of a leather trunk or suitcase that opens into two halves"? If you wish, try to make up some of your own "portmanteau" words whose sounds and meanings are drawn from two different words and create an entirely new word. For example "posalutely" is a combination of "absolutely" and "positively."

2 What root words does Carroll draw upon in creating entirely new words that still bear a trace of the original root word's meaning?

3 Keeping in mind that Carroll, who was himself a member of the faculty at Oxford University, wrote this as a spoof of Anglo-Saxon poetry, how are these transformations a source of humor in "Jabberwocky"? Speculate on the meaning of the title as it relates to Carroll's purpose.

4 What insight does Carroll provide into the process by which words are invented and the connotations that they are perceived to possess? (Glossary: *Coinage, Connotation, Denotation.*)

5 In this whimsical spoof, Lewis Carroll, who was a philologist, employs a number of different strategies to "clarify" the meaning of the term "Jabberwocky." Where does he employ synonyms, offer a pseudo etymology of the term, define by negation, or use any traditional rhetorical pattern to clarify what "Jabberwocky" means? (Glossary: *Definition.*)

6 What neologisms—that is, new compounds—are you aware of (such as "bitnik" by analogy with "beatnick" to describe one who logs onto cyberspace using a coin-operated terminal in a coffee house, or "digerati" by analogy with "literati" to describe the computer intellectual elite)? Describe them and speculate on the principles of word formation involved in producing these terms.

From Outside, In   *Barbara Mellix*

◆ BARBARA MELLIX teaches composition and fiction writing at the University of Pittsburgh, where she earned her M.F.A. in creative writing in 1986. Her first published short story appeared in the Summer 1987 issue of the *Pennsylvania Review.* "From outside, In" first appeared in the *Georgia Review,* Summer 1987.

Black English (which has also come to be known as Ebonics) was the language in which Mellix primarily communicated as a child, except during special occasions such as visits by out-of-town relatives or whites in her community, when she spoke standard English. Her situation was not atypical, since many African Americans communicate in both black and standard English depending upon

Barbara Mellix, "From Outside, In" originally appeared in *The Georgia Review,* Volume XLI, No. 2 (Summer 1987). Copyright © 1987 by the University of Georgia, copyright © 1987 by Barbara Mellix. Reprinted by permission of Barbara Mellix and *The Georgia Review.*

the situation. Mellix's experience is unusual in that she consciously set out to master the complexities of standard English. She enrolled in a college composition class and progressively acquired a mastery of English that most of us would envy. She discovered that simply more than learning another language, she was becoming a different person in the process, and came to perceive herself and the world in a different way.

TO CONSIDER   Do you speak a dialect or use slang or a jargon that you feel connects you to your community?

Two years ago, when I started writing this paper, trying to bring order out of chaos, my ten-year-old daughter was suffering from an acute attack of boredom. She drifted in and out of the room complaining that she had nothing to do, no one to "be with" because none of her friends were at home. Patiently I explained that I was working on something special and needed peace and quiet, and I suggested that she paint, read, or work with her computer. None of these interested her. Finally, she pulled up a chair to my desk and watched me, now and then heaving long, loud sighs. After two or three minutes (nine or ten sights), I lost my patience. "Looka here, Allie," I said, "you too old for this kinda carryin' on. I done told you this is important. You wronger than dirt to be in here haggin' me like this and you know it. Now git on outta here and leave me off before I put my foot all the way down."

I was at home, alone with my family, and my daughter understood that this way of speaking was appropriate in that context. She knew, as a matter of fact, that it was almost inevitable; when I get angry at home, I speak some of my finest, most cherished black English. Had I been speaking to my daughter in this manner in certain other environments, she would have been shocked and probably worried that I had taken leave of my sense of propriety.

Like my children, I grew up speaking what I considered two distinctly different languages—black English and standard English (or as I thought of them then, the ordinary everyday speech of "country" coloreds and "proper" English)—and in the process of acquiring these languages, I developed an understanding of when, where, and how to use them. But unlike my children, I grew up in a world that was primarily black. My friends, neighbors, minister, teachers—almost everybody I associated with every day—were black. And we spoke to one another in our own special language: *That sho is a pretty dress you got on. If she don' soon leave me off I'm gon tell her head a mess. I was so mad I could'a pissed a blue nail. He all the time trying to low-rate somebody. Ain't that just about the nastiest thing you ever set ears on?*

Then there were the "others," the "proper" blacks, transplanted relatives and one-time friends who came home from the city for weddings, funerals, and vacations. And the whites. To these we spoke standard English. "Ain't?" my mother would yell at me when I used the term in the presence of "others." "You *know* better than that." And I would hang my head in shame and say the "proper" word.

I remember one summer sitting in my grandmother's house in Greeleyville, South Carolina, when it was full of the chatter of city relatives who were home on vacation. My parents sat quietly, only now and then volunteering a comment or answering a question. My mother's face took on a strained expression when she spoke. I could see that she was being careful to say just the right words in just the right way. Her voice sounded thick, muffled. And when she finished speaking, she would lapse into silence, her proper smile on her face. My father was more articulate, more aggressive. He spoke quickly, his words sharp and clear. But he held his proud head higher, a signal that he, too, was uncomfortable. My sisters and brothers and I stared at our aunts, uncles, and cousins, speaking only when prompted. Even then, we hesitated, formed our sentences in our minds, then spoke softly, shyly.

My parents looked small and anxious during those occasions, and I waited impatiently for our leave-taking when we would mock our relatives the moment we were out of their hearing. "Reeely," we would say to one another, flexing our wrists and rolling our eyes, "how dooo you stan' this heat? Chile, it just too hy*ooo*-mid for words." Our relatives had made us feel "country," and this was our way of regaining pride in ourselves while getting a little revenge in the bargain. The words bubbled in our throats and rolled across our tongues, a balming.

As a child I felt this same doubleness in uptown Greeleyville where the whites lived. "Ain't that a pretty dress you're wearing!" Toby, the town policeman, said to me one day when I was fifteen. "Thank you very much," I replied, my voice barely audible in my own ears. The words felt wrong in my mouth, rigid, foreign. It was not that I had never spoken that phrase before—it was common in black English, too—but I was extremely conscious that this was an occasion for proper English. I had taken out my English and put it on as I did my church clothes, and I felt as if I were wearing my Sunday best in the middle of the week. It did not matter that Toby had not spoken grammatically correct English. He was white and could speak as he wished. I had something to prove. Toby did not.

Speaking standard English to whites was our way of demonstrating that we knew their language and could use it. Speaking it to standard-English-speaking blacks was our way of showing them that we, as well as they, could "put on airs." But when we spoke standard English, we acknowledged (to ourselves and to others—but primarily to ourselves) that our customary way of speaking was inferior. We felt foolish, embarrassed, somehow diminished because we were ashamed to be our real selves. We were reserved, shy in the presence of those who owned and/or spoke *the* language.

My parents never set aside time to drill us in standard English. Their forms of instruction were less formal. When my father was feeling particularly expansive, he would regale us with tales of his exploits in the outside world. In almost flawless English, complete with dialogue and flavored with gestures and embellishment, he told us about his attempt to get a haircut at a white barbershop; his refusal to acknowledge one of the town merchants until the man addressed him as "Mister"; the time he refused to step off the sidewalk uptown to let some whites pass; his airplane trip to New York City (to visit a sick relative) during which the stewardesses and porters—recognizing that he was a "gentleman"—addressed him as "Sir." I did not realize then—nor, I think, did my father—that he was teaching us, among other things, standard English and the <u>relationship between language and power.</u>

My mother's approach was different. Often, when one of us said, "I'm gon wash off my feet," she would say, "And what will you walk on if you wash them off?" Everyone would laugh at the victim of my mother's "proper" mood. But it was different when one of us children was in a proper mood. "You think you are so superior," I said to my oldest sister one day when we were arguing and she was winning. "Superior!" my sister mocked. "You mean I'm acting 'big-gidy'?" My sisters and brothers sniggered, then joined in teasing me. Finally, my mother said, "Leave your sister alone. There's nothing wrong with using proper English." There was a half-smile on her face. I had gotten "uppity," had "put on airs" for no good reason. I was at home, alone with the family, and I hadn't been prompted by one of my mother's proper moods. But there was also a proud light in my mother's eyes; her children were learning English very well.

Not until years later, as a college student, did I begin to understand our ambivalence toward English, our scorn of it, our need to master it, to own and be owned by it—an ambivalence that extended to the public-school classroom. In our school, where there were no whites, my teachers taught standard English but used black English to do it. When my grammar-school teachers wanted us to write, for example, they usually said something like, "I want y'all to write five sentences that make a statement. Anybody git done before the rest can color." It was probably almost those exact words that led me to write these sentences in 1953 when I was in the second grade:

The white clouds are pretty.
There are only 15 people in our room.
We will go to gym.
We have a new poster.
We may go out doors.

Second grade came after "Little First" and "Big First," so by then I knew the implied rules that accompanied all writing assignments. Writing was an occasion for proper English. I was not to write in the way we spoke to one another: The white clouds pretty; There ain't but 15 people in our room; We going to gym; We got a new poster; We can go out in the yard. Rather I was to use the language of "other": clouds *are,* there *are,* we *will,* we *have,* we *may.*

My sentences were short, rigid, perfunctory, like the letters my mother wrote to relatives:

Dear Papa,

How are you? How is Mattie? Fine I hope. We are fine. We will come to see you Sunday. Cousin Ned will give us a ride.

Love,
Daughter

The language was not ours. It was something from outside us, something we used for special occasions.

But my coloring on the other side of that second-grade paper is different. I drew three hearts and a sun. The sun has a smiling face that radiates and envelops everything it touches. And although the sun and its world are enclosed in a circle, the colors I used—red, blue, green, purple, orange, yellow, black—indicate that I was less restricted with drawing and coloring than I was with writing standard English. My valentines were not just red. My sun was not just a yellow ball in the sky.

By the time I reached the twelfth grade, speaking and writing standard English had taken on new importance. Each year, about half of the newly graduated seniors of our school moved to large cities—particularly in the North—to live with relatives and find work. Our English teacher constantly corrected our grammar: "Not 'ain't,' but 'isn't.'" We seldom wrote papers, and even those few were usually plot summaries of short stories. When our teacher returned the papers, she usually lectured on the importance of using standard English: "I *am;* you *are;* he, she, or it *is,*" she would *say,* writing on the chalkboard as she spoke. "How you gon git a job talking about 'I is,' or 'I isn't' or 'I ain't'?"

In Pittsburgh, where I moved after graduation, I watched my aunt and uncle—who had always spoken standard English when in Greeleyville—switch from black English to standard English to a mixture of the two, according to where they were or who they were with. At home and with certain close relatives, friends, and neighbors, they spoke black English. With those less close, they spoke a mixture. In public and with strangers, they generally spoke standard English.

In time, I learned to speak standard English with ease and to switch smoothly from black to standard or a mixture, and back again. But no matter where I was, no matter what the situation or occasion, I continued to write as I had in school:

> Dear Mommie,
>
> How are you? How is everybody else? Fine I hope. I am fine. So are Aunt and Uncle. Tell everyone I said hello. I will write again soon.
>
> Love,
> Barbara

At work, at a health insurance company, I learned to write letters to customers. I studied form letters and letters written by co-workers, memorizing the phrases and the ways in which they were used. I dictated:

> Thank you for your letter of January 5. We have made the changes in your coverage you requested. Your new premium will be $150 every three months. We are pleased to have been of service to you.

In a sense, I was proud of the letters I wrote for the company: they were proof of my ability to survive in the city, the outside world—an indication of my growing mastery of English. But they also indicate that writing was still mechanical for me, something that didn't require much thought.

Reading also became a more significant part of my life during those early years in Pittsburgh. I had always liked reading, but now I devoted more and more of my spare time to it. I read romances, mysteries, popular novels. Looking back, I realize that the books I liked best were simple, unambiguous: good versus bad and right versus wrong with right rewarded and wrong punished, mysteries unraveled and all set right in the end. It was how I remembered life in Greeleyville.

Of course I was romanticizing. Life in Greeleyville had not been so very uncomplicated. Back there I had been—first as a child, then as a young woman with limited experience in the outside world—living in a relatively closed-in society. But there were implicit and explicit principles that guided our way of life and shaped our relationships with one another and the people outside—principles that a newcomer would find elusive and baffling. In Pittsburgh, I had matured, become more experienced: I had worked at three different jobs, associated with a wider range of people, married, had children. This new environment with different prescripts for living required that I speak standard English much of the time, and slowly, imperceptibly, I had ceased seeing a sharp distinction between myself and "others." Reading romances and mysteries, characterized by dichotomy, was a way of shying away from change, from the person I was becoming.

[handwritten marginalia: language as constant reminder of outsider status]

But that other part of me—that part which took great pride in my ability to hold a job writing business letters—was increasingly drawn to the new developments in my life and the attending possibilities, opportunities for even greater change. If I could write letters for a nationally known business, could I not also do something better, more challenging, more important? Could I not, perhaps, go to college and become a school teacher? For years, afraid and a little embarrassed, I did no more than imagine this different me, this possible me. But sixteen years after coming north, when my youngest daughter entered kindergarten, I found myself unable—or unwilling—to resist the lure of possibility. I enrolled in my first college course: Basic Writing, at the University of Pittsburgh.

For the first time in my life, I was required to write extensively about myself. Using the most formal English at my command, I wrote these sentences near the beginning of the term:

> One of my duties as a homemaker is simply picking up after others. A day seldom passes that I don't search for a mislaid toy, book, or gym shoe, etc. I change the Ty-D-Bol, fight "ring around the collar," and keep our laundry smelling "April fresh." Occasionally, I settle arguments between my children and suggest things to do when they're bored. Taking telephone messages for my oldest daughter is my newest (and sometimes most aggravating) chore. Hanging the toilet paper roll is my most insignificant.

My concern was to use "appropriate" language, to sound as if I belonged in a college classroom. But I felt separate from the language—as if it did not and could not belong to me. I couldn't think and feel genuinely in that language, couldn't make it express what I thought and felt about being a housewife. A part of me resented, among other things, being judged by such things as the appearance of my family's laundry and toilet bowl, but in that language I could only imagine and write about a conventional housewife.

For the most part, the remainder of the term was a period of adjustment, a time of trying to find my bearings as a student in a college composition class, to learn to shut out my black English whenever I composed, and to prevent it from creeping into my formulations; a time for trying to grasp the language of the classroom and reproduce it in my prose; for trying to talk about myself in that language, reach others through it. Each experience of writing was like standing naked and revealing my imperfection, my "otherness." And each new assignment was another chance to make myself over in language, reshape myself, make myself "better" in my rapidly changing image of a student in a college composition class.

But writing became increasingly unmanageable as the term progressed, and by the end of the semester, my sentences sounded like this:

> My excitement was soon dampened, however, by what seemed like a small voice in the back of my head saying that I should be careful with my long awaited opportunity. I felt frustrated and this seemed to make it difficult to concentrate.

There is a poverty of language in these sentences. By this point, I knew that the clichéd language of my Housewife essay was unacceptable, and I generally recognized trite expressions. At the same time, I hadn't yet mastered the language of the classroom, hadn't yet come to see it as belonging to me. Most notable is the lifelessness of the prose, the apparent absence of a person behind the words. I wanted those sentences—and the rest of the essay—to convey the anguish of yearning to, at once, become something more and yet remain the same. I had the sensation of being split in two, part of me going into a future the other part didn't believe possible. As that person, the student writer at that moment, I was essentially mute. I could not—in the process of composing—use the language of the old me, yet I couldn't imagine myself in the language of "others."

I found this particularly discouraging because at midsemester I had been writing in a much different way. Note the language of this introduction to an essay I had written then, near the middle of the term:

> Pain is a constant companion to the people in "Footwork." Their jobs are physically damaging. Employers are insensitive to their feelings and in many cases add to their problems. The general public wounds them further by treating them with disgrace because of what they do for a living. Although the workers are as diverse as they are similar, there is a definite link between them. They suffer a great deal of abuse.

The voice here is stronger, more confident, appropriating terms like "physically damaging," "wounds them further," "insensitive," "diverse"—terms I couldn't have imagined using when writing about my own experience—and shaping them into sentences like, "Although the workers are as diverse as they are similar, there is a definite link between them." And there is the sense of a personality behind the prose, someone who sympathizes with the workers: "The general public wounds them further by treating them with disgrace because of what they do for a living."

What caused these differences? I was, I believed, explaining other people's thoughts and feelings, and I was free to move about in the language of "others" so long as I was speaking of others. I was unaware that I was transforming into my best classroom language my own thoughts and feelings about people whose experiences and ways of speaking were in many ways similar to mine.

The following year, unable to turn back or to let go of what had become something of an obsession with language (and hoping to catch and hold the sense of control that had eluded me in Basic Writing), I enrolled in a research writing course. I spent most of the term learning how to prepare for and write a research paper. I chose sex education as my subject and spent hours in libraries, searching for information, reading, taking notes. Then (not without messiness and often-demoralizing frustration) I organized my information into categories, wrote a thesis statement, and composed my paper—a series of paraphrases and quotations spaced between carefully constructed transitions. The process and results felt artificial, but as I would later come to realize I was passing through a necessary stage. My sentences sounded like this:

> This reserve becomes understandable with examination of who the abusers are. In an overwhelming number of cases, they are people the victims know and trust. Family members, relatives, neighbors and close family friends commit seventy-five percent of all reported sex crimes against children, and parents, parent substitutes and relatives are the offenders in thirty to eighty percent of all reported cases. While assault by strangers does occur, it is less common, and is usually a single episode. But abuse by family members, relatives and acquaintances may continue for an extended period of time. In cases of incest, for example children are abused repeatedly for an average of eight years. In such cases, "the use of physical force is rarely necessary because of the child's trusting, dependent relationship with the offender. The child's cooperation is often facilitated by the adult's position of dominance, an offer of material goods, a threat of physical violence, or a misrepresentation of moral standards."

The completed paper gave me a sense of profound satisfaction, and I read it often after my professor returned it. I know now that what I was pleased with was the language I used and the professional voice it helped me maintain. "Use better words," my teacher had snapped at me one day after reading the notes I'd begun accumulating from my research, and slowly I began taking on the language of my sources. In my next set of notes, I used the word "vacillating"; my professor applauded. And by the time I composed the final draft, I felt at ease with terms like "overwhelming number of cases," "single episode," and "reserve," and I shaped them into sentences similar to those of my "expert" sources.

If I were writing the paper today, I would of course do some things differently. Rather than open with an anecdote—as my teacher suggested—I would begin simply with a quotation that caught my interest as I was researching my paper (and which I scribbled, without its source, in the margin of my notebook): "Truth does not do so much good in the world as the semblance of truth does evil." The quotation felt right because it captured what was for me the central idea of my essay—an idea that emerged gradually during the making of my paper—and expressed it in a way I would like to have said it. The anecdote, a hypothetical situation I invented to conform to the information in the paper, felt forced and insincere because it represented—to a great degree—my teacher's understanding of the essay, *her* idea of what in it was most significant. Improving upon my previous experiences with writing, I was beginning to think and feel in the language I used, to find my own voices in it, to sense that how one speaks influences how one means. But I was not yet secure enough, comfortable enough with the language to trust my intuition.

Now that I know that to seek knowledge, freedom, and autonomy means always to be in the concentrated process of becoming—always to be venturing into new territory, feeling one's way at first, then getting one's balance, negotiating, accommodating, discovering one's self in ways that previously defined "others"—I sometimes get tired. And I ask myself why I keep on participating in this highbrow form of violence, this slamming against perplexity. But there is no real futility in the question, no hint of that part of the old me who stood outside standard English, hugging to herself a disabling mistrust of a language she thought could not represent a person with her history and experience. Rather, the question represents a person who feels the consequence of her education, the weight of her possibilities as a teacher and writer and human being, a voice in society. And I would not change that person, would not give back the good burden that accompanies my growing expertise, my increasing power to shape myself in language and share that self with "others."

"To speak," says Frantz Fanon, "means to be in a position to use a certain syntax, to grasp the morphology of this or that language, but it means above all to assume a culture, to support the weight of a civilization."* To write means to do the same, but in a more profound sense. However, Fanon also says that to achieve mastery means to "get" in a position of power, to "grasp," to "assume." This, I have learned—both as a student and subsequently as a teacher—can involve tremendous emotional and psychological conflict for those attempting to master academic discourse. Although as a beginning student writer I had a fairly good grasp of ordinary spoken English and was proficient at what Labov calls "code-switching" (and what John Baugh in *Black Street Speech* terms "style shifting"), when I came face to face with the demands of academic writing, I grew increasingly self-conscious, constantly aware of my status as a black and a speaker of one of the many black English vernaculars—a traditional outsider. For the first time, I experienced my sense of doubleness as something menacing, a

---

Black Skin, White Masks (1952; rpt. New York: Grove Press, 1967), pp. 17–18.

built-in enemy. Whenever I turned inward for salvation, the balm so available during my childhood, I found instead this new fragmentation which spoke to me in many voices. It was the voice of my desire to prosper, but at the same time it spoke of what I had relinquished and could not regain: a safe way of being, a state of powerlessness which exempted me from responsibility for who I was and might be. And it accused me of betrayal, of turning away from blackness. To recover balance, I had to take on the language of the academy, the language of "others." And to do that, I had to learn to imagine myself a part of the culture of that language, and therefore someone free to manage that language, to take liberties with it. Writing and rewriting, practicing, experimenting, I came to comprehend more fully the generative power of language. I discovered—with the help of some especially sensitive teachers—that through writing one can continually bring new selves into being, each with new responsibilities and difficulties, but also with new possibilities. Remarkable power, indeed. I write and continually give birth to myself.

---

1 What prompted Mellix to go from a situation where black English was the language of her community and standard English was only used for formal occasions to apply herself to gain mastery of a language that seemed so foreign to her as a child? How does the title refer to this transformation?

2 What evidence is there that Mellix had to come to terms with her ambivalence over betraying her black culture? In what sense has her mastery of English forced her to sacrifice a part of herself she can never regain? What has she gained instead and how is it connected to the language she now uses? What part does writing play in this process of discovering her new self?

3 Have you ever used English in a way that gave you glimpses of what it would be like to use it at this higher level all the time? Would you be willing to put in the effort to master English at this level? Why or why not?

4 What function does Mellix's inclusion of the letters and notes she wrote in standard English as a child serve in explaining her decision to enroll in a basic writing course as the first step in attempting to master standard English? (For example, "Dear Mommy, How are you? How is everybody else? Fine I hope . . .")? How does the new form in which she learned to express herself reflect changes in her personality and relationship to mainstream society? (Glossary: *Black English, Standard English*.)

5 What specific sensory details about people, places, and events does Mellix use to make her narrative immediate, vigorous, and lively? Does she make sure that each paragraph or group of paragaphs has its own clear focus? Where does she use time signals to make sure her narrative is easy to follow? Most important, what conflict or internal dilemma does her narrative dramatize? (Glossary: *Narration*.)

6 What factors explain the prestige and power of "standard English"? What does this phrase mean to you? Write an essay in which you explore your understanding of what "standard English" means and the function it serves in business, communication, and other areas as a global language.

What's in a Name?   *Itabari Njeri*

◆ ITABARI NJERI is an arts critic, essayist, and reporter whose memoir *Every Goodbye Ain't Gone* (1990), an eloquent testimony to the African-American experience, won the American Book Award. From 1986 to 1992, she was a staff writer for the *Los Angeles Times Magazine,* where the following essay first appeared. Her most recent book is *The Last Plantation* (1995).

Njeri's decision to renounce her given name and adopt one of African origin is a political statement based on her desire to escape from the last vestiges of slavery. To not do so, according to Njeri, would be to tacitly accept a "slave name" with all of its objectionable associations. The strong personal influence of this name change and the frequency with which she has had to defend her choice have made her aware, as few of us ever are, of the extent to which who we are is bound up with what we are called.

> **TO CONSIDER**   Does your name label you in some way or influence the way people think about you? What are the advantages or disadvantages of your name?

1   The decade was about to end when I started my first newspaper job. The seventies might have been the disco generation for some, but it was a continuation of the Black Power, post–civil rights era for me. Of course in some parts of America it was still the pre-civil rights era. And that was the part of America I wanted to explore. As a good reporter I needed a sense of the whole country, not just the provincial Northeast Corridor in which I was raised.

2   I headed for Greenville ("Pearl of the Piedmont"), South Carolina.

3   "*Wheeere,*" some people snarled, their nostrils twitching, their mouths twisted so their top lips went slightly to the right, the bottom ones way down and to the left, "did you get *that* name from?"

4   Itabiddy, Etabeedy. Etabeeree. Eat a berry. Mata Hari. Theda Bara. And one secretary in the office of the Greenville Urban League told her employer: "It's Ms. Idi Amin."

5   Then, and now, there are a whole bunch of people who greet me with: "Hi, Ita." They think "Bari" is my last name. Even when they don't, they still want to call me "Ita." When I tell them my first name is Itabari, they say, "Well, what do people call you for short?"

"They don't call me anything for short," I say. "The name is Itabari."   6

Sophisticated white people, upon hearing my name, approach me as would   7
a cultural anthropologist finding a piece of exotica right in his own living room.
This happens a lot, still, at cocktail parties.

"Oh, what an unusual and beautiful name. Where are you from?"   8

"Brooklyn," I say. I can see the disappointment in their eyes. Just another   9
home-grown Negro.

Then there are other white people who, having heard my decidedly north-   10
eastern accent, will simply say, "What a lovely name," and smile knowingly, indicating that they saw Roots and understand.

Then there are others, black and white, who for different reasons take me   11
through this number:

"What's your *real* name?"   12

"Itabari Njeri is my real, legal name," I explain.   13

"Okay, what's your original name?" they ask, often with eyes rolling, exas-   14
peration in their voices.

After Malcolm X, Muhammad Ali, Kareem Abdul-Jabbar, Ntozake Shange,   15
and Kunta Kinte, who, I ask, should be exasperated by this question-and-answer
game?

Nevertheless, I explain, "Because of slavery, black people in the Western   16
world don't usually know their original names. What you really want to know is
what my slave name was."

Now this is where things get tense. Four hundred years of bitter history, cul-   17
ture, and politics between blacks and whites in America is evoked by this one
term, "slave name."

Some white people wince when they hear the phrase, pained and embar-   18
rassed by this reminder of their ancestors' inhumanity. Further, they quickly
scrutinize me and conclude that mine was a post-Emancipation Proclamation
birth. "You were never a slave."

I used to be reluctant to tell people my slave name unless I surmised that   19
they wouldn't impose their cultural values on me and refuse to use my African
name. I don't care anymore. When I changed my name, I changed my life, and
I've been Itabari for more years now than I was Jill. Nonetheless, people will say:
"Well, that's your *real* name, you were born in America and that's what I am
going to call you." My mother tried a variation of this on me when I legalized
my traditional African name. I respectfully made it clear to her that I would not
tolerate it. Her behavior, and subsequently her attitude, changed.

But many black folks remain just as skeptical of my name as my mother was.   20

"You're one of those black people who changed their name, huh," they are   21
likely to begin. "Well, I still got the old slave master's Irish name," said one man
named O'Hare at a party. This man's defensive tone was a reaction to what I call
the "blacker than thou" syndrome perpetrated by many black nationalists in the
sixties and seventies. Those who reclaimed their African names made blacks who
didn't do the same thing feel like Uncle Toms.

These so-called Uncle Toms couldn't figure out why they should use an   22
African name when they didn't know a thing about Africa. Besides, many of

them were proud of their names, no matter how they had come by them. And it should be noted that after the Emancipation Proclamation in 1863, four million black people changed their names, adopting surnames such as Freeman, Freedman, and Liberty. They eagerly gave up names that slave masters had imposed upon them as a way of identifying their human chattel.

23   Besides names that indicated their newly won freedom, blacks chose common English names such as Jones, Scott, and Johnson. English was their language. America was their home, and they wanted names that would allow them to assimilate as easily as possible.

24   Of course, many of our European surnames belong to us by birth-right. We are the legal as well as "illegitimate" heirs to the names Jefferson, Franklin, Washington, et al., and in my own family, Lord.

25   Still, I consider most of these names to be by-products of slavery, if not actual slave names. Had we not been enslaved, we would not have been cut off from our culture, lost our indigenous languages, and been compelled to use European names.

26   The loss of our African culture is a tragic fact of history, and the conflict it poses is a profound one that has divided blacks many times since Emancipation: do we accept the loss and assimilate totally or do we try to reclaim our culture and synthesize it with our present reality?

27   A new generation of black people in America is reexamining the issues raised by the cultural nationalists and Pan-Africanists of the sixties and seventies: what are the cultural images that appropriately convey the "new" black aesthetic in literature and art?

28   The young Afro-American novelist Trey Ellis has asserted that the "New Black Aesthetic shamelessly borrows and reassembles across both race and class lines." It is not afraid to embrace the full implications of our hundreds of years in the New World. We are a new people who need not be tied to externally imposed or self-inflicted cultural parochialism. Had I understood that as a teenager, I might still be singing today.

29   Even the fundamental issue of identity and nomenclature, raised by Baraka and others twenty years ago, is back on the agenda: are we to call ourselves blacks or African-Americans?

30   In reality, it's an old debate. "Only with the founding of the American Colonization Society in 1816 did blacks recoil from using the term African in referring to themselves and their institutions," the noted historian and author Sterling Stuckey pointed out in an interview with me. They feared that using the term "African" would fuel white efforts to send them back to Africa. But they felt no white person had the right to send them back when they had slaved to build America.

31   Many black institutions retained their African identification, most notably the African Methodist Episcopal Church. Changes in black self-identification in America have come in cycles, usually reflecting the larger dynamics of domestic and international politics.

32   The period after World War II, said Stuckey, "culminating in the Cold War years of Roy Wilkins's leadership of the NAACP," was a time of "frenzied inte-

grationism." And there was "no respectable black leader on the scene evincing any sort of interest in Africa—neither the NAACP or the Urban League."

This, he said, "was an example of historical discontinuity, the likes of which   33
we, as a people, had not seen before." Prior to that, for more than a century and a half, black leaders were Pan-Africanists, including Frederick Douglass. "He recognized," said Stuckey, "that Africa was important and that somehow one had to redeem the motherland in order to be genuinely respected in the New World."

The Reverend Jesse Jackson has, of course, placed on the national agenda   34
the importance of blacks in America restoring their cultural, historical, and political links with Africa.

But what does it really mean to be called an African-American?   35

"Black" can be viewed as a more encompassing term, referring to all people   36
of African descent. "Afro-American" and "African-American" refer to a specific ethnic group. I use the terms interchangeably, depending on the context and the point I want to emphasize.

But I wonder: as the twenty-first century breathes down our necks—prod-   37
ding us to wake up to the expanding mélange of ethnic groups immigrating in record numbers to the United States, inevitably intermarrying, and to realize the eventual reshaping of the nation's political imperatives in a newly multicultural society—will the term "African-American" be as much of a racial and cultural obfuscation as the term "black"? In other words, will we be the only people, in a society moving toward cultural pluralism, viewed to have no history and no culture? Will we just be a color with a new name: African-American?

Or will the term be—as I think it should—an ethnic label describing people   38
with a shared culture who descended from Africans, were transformed in (as well as transformed) America, and are genetically intertwined with myriad other groups in the United States?

Such a definition reflects the historical reality and distances us from the falla-   39
cious, unscientific concept of separate races when there is only one: *Homo sapiens*.

But to comprehend what should be an obvious definition requires knowl-   40
edge and a willingness to accept history.

When James Baldwin wrote *Nobody knows My Name,* the title was a   41
metaphor—at the deepest level of the collective African-American psyche—for the blighting of black history and culture before the nadir of slavery and since.

The eradication or distortion of our place in world history and culture is   42
most obvious in the popular media. Liz Taylor—and, for an earlier generation, Claudette Colbert—still represent what Cleopatra—a woman of color in a multiethnic society, dominated at various times by blacks—looks like.

And in American homes, thanks to reruns and cable, a new generation of   43
black kids grow up believing that a simpleton shouting "Dy-no-mite!" is a genuine reflection of Afro-American culture, rather than a white Hollywood writer's stereotype.

More recently, *Coming to America,* starring Eddie Murphy as an African   44
prince seeking a bride in the United States, depicted traditional African dancers in what amounted to a Las Vegas stage show, totally distorting the nature and beauty of real African dance. But with every burlesque-style pelvic thrust on the

screen, I saw blacks in the audience burst into applause. They think that's African culture, too.

45   And what do Africans know of us, since blacks don't control the organs of communication that disseminate information about us?

46   "No!" screamed the mother of a Kenyan man when he announced his engagement to an African-American woman who was a friend of mine. The mother said marry a European, marry a white American. But please, not one of those low-down, ignorant, drug-dealing, murderous black people she had seen in American movies. Ultimately, the mother prevailed.

47   In Tanzania, the travel agent looked at me indignantly. "Njeri, that's Kikuyu. What are you doing with an African name?" he demanded.

48   I'd been in Dar es Salaam about a month and had learned that Africans assess in a glance the ethnic origins of the people they meet.

49   Without a greeting, strangers on the street in Tanzania's capital would comment, "Oh, you're an Afro-American or West Indian."

50   "Both."

51   "I knew it," they'd respond, sometimes politely, sometimes not.

52   Or, people I got to know while in Africa would mention, "I know another half-caste like you." Then they would call in the "mixed-race" person and say, "Please meet Itabari Njeri." The darker-complected African, presumably of unmixed ancestry, would then smile and stare at us like we were animals in the zoo.

53   Of course, this "half-caste" (which I suppose is a term preferable to "mulatto," which I hate, and which every person who understands its derogatory meaning—"mule"—should never use) was usually the product of a mixed marriage, not generations of ethnic intermingling. And it was clear from most "half-castes" I met that they did not like being compared to so mongrelized and stigmatized a group as Afro-Americans.

54   I had minored in African studies in college, worked for years with Africans in the United States, and had no romantic illusions as to how I would be received in the motherland. I wasn't going back to find my roots. The only thing that shocked me in Tanzania was being called, with great disdain, a "white woman" by an African waiter. Even if the rest of the world didn't follow the practice, I then assumed everyone understood that any known or perceptible degree of African ancestry made one "black" in America by law and social custom.

55   But I was pleasantly surprised by the telephone call I received two minutes after I walked into my Dar es Salaam hotel room. It was the hotel operator. "Sister, welcome to Tanzania. . . . Please tell everyone in Harlem hello for us." The year was 1978, and people in Tanzania were wearing half-foot-high platform shoes and dancing to James Brown wherever I went.

56   Shortly before I left, I stood on a hill surrounded by a field of endless flowers in Arusha, near the border of Tanzania and Kenya. A toothless woman with a wide smile, a staff in her hand, and two young girls at her side, came toward me on a winding path. I spoke to her in fractured Swahili and she to me in broken English.

57   "I know you," she said smiling. "Wa-Negro." "Wa" is a prefix in Bantu languages meaning people. "You are from the lost tribe," she told me. "Welcome," she said, touching me, then walked down a hill that lay in the shadow of Mount Kilimanjaro.

I never told her my name, but when I told other Africans, they'd say: 58
"*Emmmm* Itabari. Too long. How about I just call you Ita.*"*

━━━━━━━━━━━━━━━

1 The variety of reactions Njeri's name elicits prompts her to make the case explaining why she changed her name to an African one. What were these reactions and how would this explain why she would want to justify her decision? Why was it ironic she met with the same responses in Tanzania as she did in Greenville, South Carolina?

2 Evaluate Njeri's contention that the continued use of English language names such as Jones, Scott, and Johnson perpetuates a legacy of slavery, whereas adoption of African names would allow African-Americans to have their own identity?

3 Would you ever consider changing your name? If so, what would it be and what would it say about you that your present given name does not?

4 What negative connotations did Njeri's given name have for her? By contrast, what positive associations does she have with her African name, Itabari? (Glossary: *Connotation, Denotation, Onomastics*.)

5 How does Njeri use her essay to answer the question of why she chose to change her name? Trace the chain of questions and answers, or causes and effects, that Njeri uses to reveal the complex causes for her decision. (Glossary: *Cause and Effect*.)

6 Describe the circumstances underlying the choice of your name. Do you like your given name or do you prefer to be called by a nickname you chose or others gave you?

Ladyfingers & Nun's Tummies

Martha Barnette

◆ MARTHA BARNETTE did graduate work in classical languages at the University of Kentucky. She was a reporter for the *Washington Post* and is now a contributing editor at *Allure* magazine. Barnette is the author of *A Garden of Words* (1992) and *Ladyfingers & Nun's Tummies* (1997), from which the following excerpt is taken.

Unsuspected revelations about the true origins of such common foods as Welsh rarebit (or rabbit), plum pudding (which contains no plums), and Buffalo wings (which are not, of course, wings of buffalos) await readers of Barnette's enter-

Martha Barnette, "Words That Intentionally Mislead," from *Ladyfingers Nun's Tummies*. Copyright © 1997 by Martha Barnette. Reprinted by permission of Times Books, a division of Random House, Inc.

taining and informative exploration of the derivation of unlikely food names. On the other hand, words that have nothing to do with food, even though they sound as if they do—such as "big cheese" and "chowderhead"—are examples of how slang enters the English language.

> **TO CONSIDER**   Which of your favorite foods has a locale as part of its name (for example, Buffalo wings)?

WORDS THAT INTENTIONALLY MISLEAD

Like a last-minute addition of spice to make an unappealing dish more palatable, many food names apparently reflect a deliberate effort to cover up their true identities. *Welsh rabbit,* for example, is a meatless dish that can be as simple as melted cheese on toast or as complex as a sauce of cheese, butter, cayenne pepper, salt, and ale over buttered toast. The term for this cheap, filling meal has been around since at least the early eighteenth century. Another name for the same dish sounds even more exotic: *Welsh rarebit.* Similarly, *English monkey* is a mixture of bread crumbs, milk, butter, and cheese poured over crackers and garnished with tomatoes.

The plentiful supply of codfish off the northern Atlantic coast prompted New Englanders to apply the name *Cape Cod turkey* to their inexpensive meals of baked fish. And a century or two ago, New York's Hudson River so abounded with sturgeon that upstate dwellers called their exceedingly cheap fare *Albany beef.* (Sturgeon caviar was so plentiful that tavern owners regularly offered it as a free snack with drinks.)

Other food names sound even more wistful. American cowboys who endured countless meals of beans, beans, and more beans, jokingly tried to add a little linguistic seasoning to the monotony by christening them *Arizona strawberries, prairie strawberries,* or *Mexican strawberries.* Then there's *Liberty cabbage,* a patriotic attempt during World War I to do away with the vegetable's German name, *sauerkraut.* Like so many other attempts to reform everyday language by decree, the effort failed miserably.

And what discussion of food-name euphemisms would be complete without a mention of *Rocky Mountain oysters?* Testicles from a bull, lamb, or pig are also called *calf fries, prairie oysters, Spanish kidneys,* and simply *mountain oysters.* The organs, which can be fried, sautéed, braised, or poached, aren't on many Americans' Top Ten Appetizers list, even if they are considered a delicacy in France and Italy. (Perhaps this isn't surprising given this country's puritanical streak, which once prompted its more prudish citizens to substitute the phrases *a cow's father, a gentleman cow, a male cow, a Jonathan,* and simply *a cow creature* for the word *bull.*) The name *prairie oyster,* by the way, also applies to a cocktail made from an unbroken egg yolk, Worcestershire and Tabasco sauces, malt vinegar, salt, and pepper and traditionally offered by bartenders as a cure for hiccups. Then again, maybe merely eyeing a glass of such a mixture is enough to scare the hiccups out of anyone.

A few other foods have names that aren't intentionally misleading but are confusing nevertheless. An *egg cream,* that New York City favorite whose frothy head and rich consistency suggest it contains both eggs and cream, actually contains neither. First concocted around the turn of the century, when eggs were relatively expensive, an egg cream is made from chocolate syrup, ice-cold milk, and a jet of seltzer water. *Buttermilk,* likewise, contains no butter; it's simply the sour liquid that remains after the butterfat has been removed by churning.

Plum pudding is another misnomer. This dish usually contains bread crumbs, suet, raisins, currants and other fruits, eggs, spices, and sometimes brandy—in other words, just about everything but plums. As early as A.D. 725, our ancestors used the word *plum* or its variants to designate the familiar fleshy fruit, but from at least the seventeenth century, this word also denoted raisins or currants used in cooking, raisins being a good substitute if dried plums were unavailable. This interchangeable sense is clear in one late-eighteenth-century writer's wry observation that "Children, to whom you give a pill wrapped up in a raisin, will suck the plum and spit out the medicine." The spotted texture of plum pudding, in any case, inspired several terms, including *plum pudding mahogany,* a type of wood with a mottled finish, and *plum pudding dog,* a name that now applies, fittingly, to the pup otherwise known as a Dalmatian.

Finally, *Buffalo wings* exist nowhere in nature, of course. They're simply chicken wings, deep-fried and served with hot sauce and a blue-cheese dressing. They were invented in 1964 at the Anchor Bar in Buffalo, New York, by owner Teressa Bellissimo, who found herself simultaneously facing the problems of an oversupply of chicken wings and the need to come up with a snack for her son and his visiting friends. In 1977, according to *The Dictionary of American Food and Drink,* the city of Buffalo honored the accomplishment by proudly declaring July 29 "Chicken Wing Day."

FOOD WORDS THAT AREN'T WHAT THEY SEEM

Just as gastronomic names sometimes fail to reflect a food's true origins or nature, many everyday words *seem* as though they have something to do with food, when in fact they do not. And often, these too are the results of mistranslations and misunderstandings.

There's nothing particularly orderly, for example, about a pie shell containing a jumble of sliced apples, sugar, and spices. But the expression *apple-pie order* denotes something that is "primly, properly in order." The reason may be that this sweet phrase is a corruption of French *nappes pliées,* which means "folded linen." Supporting this hypothesis is the fact that the old practice of "short-sheeting" a bed—folding its linens in half so that a would-be sleeper's legs won't fit into it—has long been known as making an *apple-pie bed.* (One nineteenth-century magazine writer described the results of such a practical joke: "He . . . began to fancy that the bed was too small for him, when . . . little Oxtowne . . . told him . . . 'it was only an apple-pie.'") Many lexicographers suspect the British borrowed the French phrase to describe such a bed, then transformed it into the more familiar-sounding *apple-pie bed* by the same type of misdivision that led to *bumble pie* and *orange.* It certainly seems reasonable that, in a similar fashion, the phrase *nappes pliées* could give rise to *apple-pie order,* also suggesting the idea of efficiency as crisp and clean as neatly folded linens. (No word, however, on whether the practice of short-sheeting beds was also borrowed from the French—or if the British had been playing such practical jokes for years on their own.)

The term *big cheese,* meaning "an important person," does not refer to something from the dairy case but comes from the Persian and Urdu word *chīz,* which simply means "thing." Similarly, the expression *Cheese it!,* meaning "Look out!" or "Stop what you're doing and flee," may be simply an alteration of a similar imperative, "Cease it!," according to *Partridge's Concise Dictionary of Slang and Unconventional English.*

And while we're on the subject, it's worth noting that the term *green cheese* refers not to its color but to the fact that it's fresh and not yet thoroughly dried. The notion of the moon being made of such cheese apparently stems from an old expression suggesting that someone is so gullible that he or she would believe such a thing. Bishop John Wilkins mentioned such folk in 1638: "You may as soon perswade some Country Peasants, that the Moon is made of Green-Cheese (as we say) as that 'tis bigger than his Cart-Wheel." (Bishop Wilkins, incidentally, deserves a special place in the hearts of serious language lovers for his earnest efforts to develop a logical and universal language based on categories and subcategories—a page of which resembles a salmagundi of English, Arabic, Hindi, and modern-day computer emoticons. Unfortunately, his artificial language was so spectacularly complicated that it didn't get very far. Still, Wilkins's painstaking attempts to describe the pronunciation of various words continue to prove especially helpful to scholars attempting to reconstruct the sound of English in the years following the death of William Shakespeare.)

Many more words aren't what they seem. For example, even though chili peppers are a hot item these days, the word *chiliast* doesn't indicate someone who's fond of them, nor is a *chiliasm* the ecstatic result of biting into one. Actually, these are words we can expect to hear more of in the near future. A descendant of the Greek word *khilioi,* or "thousand," the word *chiliad* denotes both "a group containing a thousand elements" and the thousand years otherwise known as a "millennium." *Chiliasm* refers to the belief that Jesus will return to earth and reign for a thousand years. A *chiliast* is someone who believes in chiliasm. Similarly, a *chiliagon* refers to what must be a mind-boggling image—a geometric figure containing a thousand angles—while *chiliarchy* suggests the equally mind-boggling idea of "government by a thousand rulers."

Similarly, a *chowderhead* isn't a thick-soup enthusiast; it's someone who once might have been called a *jolterhead* or *jolthead.* These English slang terms, which are obscure in origin, apparently once referred to a large, thick, clumsy-looking head, then later came to refer less to the head's outer appearance than to its supposedly paltry contents. In 1605, Ben Jonson was apparently thinking of the earlier sense when he wrote, "Your red saucy cap, that seemes (to me) / Nayl'd to your iolthead." Some three and a quarter centuries later, F. Scott Fitzgerald used the latter sense when telling a correspondent, "I do not destinate to signify that you were a wiseacre, witling, dizzard, chowderhead." (Speaking of chowder and food words that aren't what they seem, the name *littleneck clams* doesn't refer to these creatures' anatomy. Originally, these small clams came from either Little Neck Bay on New York's Long Island or from Little Neck Bay, Ipswich, Massachusetts, although no one knows which for sure.)

---

1   Which of the revelations concerning the true origins and nature of different names for foods were surprising to you?

2   What insight did Barnette's account give you into how cross-cultural linguistic mis-understandings led to expressions that seemed to have something to do with food, but in fact do not?

3   What common names of foods do not fully reflect their origins or true nature, as in this passage from Thackeray's *Vanity Fair?*

> "Try a chili with it, Miss Sharp," said Joseph, really interested. "A chili," said Rebecca, gasping. "Oh yes!" She thought a chili was something cool, as its name imported, and was served with some. "How fresh and green they look," she said, and put one in her mouth. It was hotter than the curry; flesh and blood could bear it no longer. She laid down her fork "Water, for Heaven's sake, water!" she cried.
> —WILLIAM MAKEPEACE THACKERAY, *Vanity Fair* (1848)

How are some foods marketed to sound as if they are something they are not—for example, "kosher bacon," "turkey ham"? You might wish to research terms that sound as if they are associated with food but are not, such as "small fry," "to egg on," "pea jacket." For example, see the letter to Ann Landers below.

> **Dear Ann Landers:** My wife and I laughed so hard we cried when we read your column about those crazy lawsuits. When "Harriet" put down the paper, she said, "I read something in the Memphis Commercial Appeal a few days ago that certainly qualifies for Ann Landers' collection of goofy lawsuits."
>
> It seems a woman has filed suit against a small mom-and-pop pharmacy because she purchased a tube of contraceptive jelly, spread it on a piece of toast and ate it. She then had unprotected sex, believing she was "safe," and became pregnant.
>
> The contraceptive came with instructions, but the woman says the pharmacist should have put a specific warning on the box saying it wasn't effective if eaten. She is asking for a half million dollars, even though she is quoted as saying, "Who has time to sit around reading directions these days, especially when you're sexually aroused?"

4   Which of Barnette's examples are particularly effective in conveying how misunder-standings can arise in relationship to food names or words that seem to have to do with food but do not? (Glossary: *Connotation, Denotation, Examples.*)

5   How is Barnette's essay organized to reveal the actual causes of commonly held mis-taken views as to the origin of traditional food names? How is her essay structured to encourage her readers to look more closely at the origins of these food names in order to gain a more accurate understanding of actual causes and effects? (Glos-sary: *Cause and Effect.*)

6 How does the following discussion of the evolution of the term "hot dog" shed light on the social and cultural forces that contributed to its acceptance?

Perhaps part of the early fun of eating the "hot dog" at Coney Island was the idea of an inversion of eating proper, sanctioned meat. The origin of the name *hot dog* until recently has been shrouded in spurious folklore. Etymologist Gerald L. Cohen, continuing his work with the late Peter Tamony, has pieced together a jigsaw puzzle that is beginning to reveal the true story of *hot dog*. The story is rich in middle and late nineteenth-century urban folklore, some about the fate of city dogs.

The earliest found printed instance of *hot dog* is 1896 where it was used as an adjective for good or superior. By 1900 *hot dog* had printed use for the sandwich, though it probably had such oral use several years earlier. The invention of the hot dog and, so, the slang term *hot dog* has been traditionally but without proof placed at Coney Island. Hot dogs replaced fried clams at Coney Island as the favorite food of the summer weekend refugees from the streaming city streets. *Coney Island* itself was one of the several names for a hot dog, and this name persists today in some parts of the country for an extra-long hot dog. After 1900 or so the hot dog was also called a *Coney-Island red hot, Coney (Island) chicken,* a *New York tube steak,* and other names.

The hot-dog sandwich, like the American hamburger sandwich, is of German ancestry and of the same period and urban culture. In this country, before the sausage was called a hot dog, at least in respectable print, it was a *frankfurter,* "one from Frankfurt." It was also called a *wienerwurst* (i.e., "Vienna sausage"), which was shortened to *wiener* and more slangily to *wienie.* The slang name *hot dog* either originated in, or was greatly influenced by, mid-nineteenth-century urban humor, and it was often very nervous humor, about sausages being made from dogs, cats, horses, and even rats. Cohen shows how a well-publicized dog-meat scandal in New York in 1843 may have been the beginning of the idea. The muckraking Mike Walsh, reporting the scandal, referred to the "spurious dog sandwich." By the 1850s the odious suggestion was widespread, fact mixing with humor and rumor.

German immigrants in New York in the 1860s humorously called smoked frankfurter sausages *hundewurst,* "dog sausage" or *hundchen,* "little dogs," while larger bologna-type sausages were called *pferdewurst,* "horse baloney." Later, small sausages were humorously called *dogs* and *doggies.* Popular culture, too, supported the notion in the late nineteenth century. Cartoons in humor magazines and low theatrical skits had images of butchers stuffing puppies into sausage grinders and strings of sausage links coming out the other end. The German dachshund, because of its round, elongated, sway-backed shape, was irresistibly made to be *the* dog in the hot dog, and graphic and spoken humor made the sausage-dachshund connection, too. In 1914, Charles McCarron, Thomas J. Gray, and Raymond Walker's song title declared "Fido Is a Hot Dog Now."

The true hot dog is not just a sausage. It is a spiced, heated sausage served on a split roll, classically garnished with *rags and paint* (sauerkraut and mustard), a slang complement from its earliest days. New Yorkers probably began to speak of the edible "hot dog" in the 1890s. "We deal here," says Cohen, "with irreverent American humor in its purest form." The allusion was shocking enough that it probably took several more years before someone dared to set *hot dog* in print for public consumption. *Hot dog* was also 1890s slang meaning good, superior, or the best, but this does not seem to be the primary source of the name. At any rate, *hot dog!* became the uniquely American exclamation of delight, perhaps by way of *hot damn,* a euphemism for *goddamn,* further euphemized to *hot dog.* And *hot dog* is the progenitor of other and recent American slang uses of the term with a surprisingly wide variety of referents.

The name *hot dog* for many years remained in disrepute at the beach resort because of its canine connotations. In 1913 the Coney Island Chamber of Commerce passed a resolution banning the use of the name by their member merchants. But the concern had been completely set aside by 1939 when President Franklin Roosevelt and the visiting King and Queen of England sampled the all-American dish. That put the hot dog into ultimate respectability. On July 23, 1939, Coney Island officially observed "Hot Dog Day" to mark the supposed Golden Anniversary of the hot dog and to claim the invention of the sandwich in 1889; the event was presided over by Milton Berle.

An invention associated directly with Coney Island was the sidewalk stand with the built-in cooker from which the dog on a bun was served. For this reason, small lunch counters and wagons with such cookers all across the country came to be called *Coney Islands, hot dogs,* or just *dogs,* and *dog wagons,* recalling *lunch wagons* from the 1890s. A good many dog wagons remained small, wheeled carts that vendors pushed to set up at a good corner of city streets. Photographer Berenice Abbott saw them as a part of New York street life in the 1930s and captured one on film, *Hot Dog Stand,* on April 8, 1936. Similar pushcarts, but now of stainless steel, with a large umbrella are today a familiar sight in the streets of New York and still serve hurried lunch-hour eaters.*

From A Clockwork Orange

Anthony Burgess

◆ ANTHONY BURGESS (1917–1993) was remarkably prolific and an always entertaining writer of biographies, essays, and novels, and was a composer of symphonic music as well. He is known for his surreal darkly comic novels, the best known of which is the futuristic *A Clockwork Orange* (1962), from which the following chapter is taken. His last work was *A Mouthful of Air: Language, Languages . . . Especially English* (1992).

*Adapted from *The City in Slang,* 1993, by Irving Lewis Allen.

This chapter is from the classic novel by Burgess that is widely considered to be a masterpiece of literary invention, and yet the narrator in the story, a violent fifteen year-old delinquent, uses language that would most certainly be judged substandard and unacceptable because of its poor grammar, neologisms, and slang. Burgess, an accomplished linguist and scholar, invented this dialect of English for his protagonist, drawing in the main on Slavic languages—traces of which can be discerned in words such as "devotchka" (attractive female) and "bolshy" (large). In fact, one of the most entertaining aspects of reading *A Clockwork Orange* is trying to guess the English language equivalent of the terms Burgess has invented.

> **TO CONSIDER**   Have you ever used an invented slang or jargon to keep outsiders from knowing what you were talking about?

I COULD not believe, brothers, what I was told. It seemed that I had been in that vonny mesto for near ever and would be there for near ever more. But it had always been a fortnight and now they said the fortnight was near up. They said: 'Tomorrow, little friend, out out out.' And they made with the old thumb like pointing to freedom. And then the white-coated veck who had tolchocked me and who had still brought me my trays of pishcha and like escorted me to my everyday torture said: 'But you still have one real big day in front of you. It's to be your passing-out day.' And he had a leery smeck at that.

I expected this morning that I would be ittying as usual to the sinny mesto in my pyjamas and toofles and over-gown. But no. This morning I was given my shirt and underveshches and my platties of the night and my horrorshow kickboots, all lovely and washed or ironed or' polished. And I was even given my cutthroat britva that I had used in those old happy days for fillying and dratsing. So I gave with the puzzled frown at this as I got dressed, but the white-coated under-veck just like grinned and would govoreet nothing, O my brothers.

I was led quite kindly to the same old mesto, but there were changes there. Curtains had been drawn in front of the sinny screen and the frosted glass under the projection holes was no longer there, it having perhaps been pushed up or folded to the sides like blind or shutters. And where there had been just the noise of coughing kashl kashl kashl and like shadows of lewdies was now a real audience, and in this audience there were litsos I knew. There was the Staja Governor and the holy man, the charlie or charles as he was called, and the Chief Chasso and this very important and well-dressed chelloveck who was the Minister of the Interior or Inferior. All the rest I did not know. Dr Brodsky and Dr Branom were there, though not now white-coated, instead they were dressed as doctors would dress who were big enough to want to dress in the heighth of fashion. Dr Branom just stood, but Dr Brodsky stood and govoreeted in a like learned manner to all the lewdies assembled. When he viddied me coming in he said: 'Aha. At this stage, gentlemen, we introduce the subject himself. He is, as you will perceive, fit and well nourished. He comes straight from a night's sleep and a good breakfast, undrugged, unhypnotized. Tomorrow we send him with confidence out into the world again, as decent a lad as you would meet on a May morning, unvicious, unviolent, if anything—as you will observe—inclined to the kindly word and the helpful act. What a change is here, gentlemen, from the wretched hoodlum the State committed to unprofitable punishment some two years ago, unchanged after two years. Unchanged, do I say? Not quite. Prison taught him the false smile, the rubbed hands of hypocrisy, the fawning greased obsequious leer. Other vices it taught him, as well as confirming him in those he had long practised before. But, gentlemen, enough of words. Actions speak louder than. Action now. Observe, all.'

I was a bit dazed by all this govoreeting and I was trying to grasp in my mind that like all this was about me. Then all the lights went out and then there came on two like spotlights shining from the projection-squares, and one of them was full on Your Humble and Suffering Narrator. And into the other spotlight there walked a bolshy big chelloveck I had never viddied before. He had a lardy like litso and a moustache and like strips of hair pasted over his near-bald gulliver. He was about thirty or forty or fifty, some old age like that, starry. He ittied up to me and the spotlight ittied with him, and soon the two spotlights had made like one big pool. He said to me; very sneery: 'Hello heap of dirt. Pooh, you don't wash much, judging from the horrible smell.' Then, as if he was like dancing, he stamped on my nogas, left, right, then he gave me a finger-nail flick on the nose that hurt like bezoomny and brought the old tears to my glazzies, then he twisted at my left ooko like it was a radio dial. I could slooshy titters and a couple of real horrorshow hawhawhaws coming from like the audience. My nose and nogas and ear-hole stung and pained like benzoomny, so I said:

'What do you do that to me for? I've never done wrong to you, brother.'

'Oh,' this veck said, 'I do this'—flickflicked nose again—'and that'—twisted smarting ear-hole—'and the other'—stamped nasty on right noga—'because I don't care for your horrible type. And if you want to do anything about it, start, start, please do.' Now I knew that I'd have to be real skorry and get my cut-throat britva out before this horrible killing sickness whooshed up and turned the like joy of battle into feeling I was going to snuff it. But, O brothers, as my rooker reached for the britva in my inside carman I got this like picture in my mind's glazzy of this insulting chelloveck howling for mercy with the red red krovvy all streaming out of his rot, and hot after this picture the sickness and dryness and pains were rushing to overtake, and I viddied that I'd have to change the way I felt about this rotten veck very very skorry indeed, so I felt in my carmans for cigarettes or for pretty polly, and, O my brothers, there was not either of these veshches. I said, like all howly and blubbery:

'I'd like to give you a cigarette, brother, but I don't seem to have any.' This veck went:

'Wah wah. Boohoohoo. Cry, baby.' Then he flickflick-flicked with his bolshy horny nail at my nose again, and I could slooshy very loud smecks of like mirth coming from the dark audience. I said, real desperate, trying to be nice to this insulting and hurtful veck to stop the pains and sickness coming up:

'Please let me do something for you, please.' And I felt in my carmans but could find only my cut-throat britva, so I took this out and handed it to him and said: 'Please take this, please. A little present. Please have it.' But he said:

'Keep your stinking bribes to yourself. You can't get round me that way.' And he banged at my rooker and my cut-throat britva fell on the floor. So I said:

'Please, I must do something. Shall I clean your boots? Look, I'll get down and lick them.' And, my brothers, believe it or kiss my sharries, I got down on my knees and pushed my red yahzick out a mile and a half to lick his grahzny vonny boots. But all this veck did was to kick me not too hard on the rot. So then it seemed to me that it would not bring on the sickness and pain if I just gripped his ankles with my rookers tight round them and brought this grahzny bratchny down to the floor. So I did this and he got a real bolshy surprise, coming down crack amid loud laughter from the vonny audience. But viddying him on the floor I could feel the whole horrible feeling coming over me, so I gave him my rooker to lift him up skorry and up he came. Then just as he was going to give me a real nasty and earnest tolchock on the litso Dr Brodsky said:

'All right, that will do very well.' Then this horrible veck sort of bowed and danced off like an actor while the lights came up on me blinking and with my rot square for howling. Dr Brodsky said to the audience: 'Our subject is, you see, impelled towards the good by, paradoxically, being impelled towards evil. The intention to act violently is accompanied by strong feelings of physical distress. To counter these the subject has to switch to a diametrically opposed attitude. Any questions?'

'Choice,' rumbled a rich deep goloss. I viddied it belonged to the prison charlie. 'He has no real choice, has he? Self-interest, fear of physical pain, drove him to that grotesque act of self-abasement. Its insincerity was clearly to be seen. He ceases to be a wrongdoer. He ceases also to be a creature capable of moral choice.'

'These are subtleties,' like smiled Dr Brodsky. 'We are not concerned with motive, with the higher ethics. We are concerned only with cutting down crime—'

'And,' chipped in this bolshy well-dressed Minister, 'with relieving the ghastly congestion in our prisons.'

'Hear hear,' said somebody.

There was a lot of govoreeting and arguing then and I just stood there, brothers, like completely ignored by all these ignorant bratchnies, so I creeched out:

'Me, me, me. How about me? Where do I come into all this? Am I like just some animal or dog?' And that started them off govoreeting real loud and throwing slovos at me. So I creeched louder still, creeching: 'Am I just to be like a clockwork orange?' I didn't know what made me use those slovos, brothers, which just came like without asking into my gulliver. And that shut all those vecks up for some reason for a minoota or two. Then one very thin starry professor type chelloveck stood up, his neck like all cables carrying like power from his gulliver to his plott, and he said:

'You have no cause to grumble, boy. You made your choice and all this is a consequence of your choice. Whatever now ensues is what you yourself have chosen.' And the prison charlie creeched out:

'Oh, if only I could believe that.' And you could viddy the Governor give him a look like meaning that he would not climb so high in like Prison Religion as he thought he would. Then loud arguing started again, and then I could slooshy the slovo Love being thrown around, the prison charles himself creeching as loud as any about Perfect Love Casteth Out Fear and all that cal. And now Dr Brodsky said, smiling all over his litso:

'I am glad, gentlemen, this question of Love has been raised. Now we shall see in action a manner of Love that was thought to be dead with the Middle Ages.' And then the lights went down and the spotlights came on again, one on your poor and suffering Friend and Narrator, and into the other there like rolled or sidled the most lovely young devotchka you could ever hope in all your jeezny, O my brothers, to viddy. That is to say, she had real horrorshow groodies all of which you could like viddy, she having on platties which came down down down off her pletchoes. And her nogas were like Bog in His Heaven, and she walked like to make you groan in your keeshkas, and yet her litso was a sweet smiling young like innocent litso. She came up towards me with the light like it was the like light of heavenly grace and all that cal coming with her, and the first thing that flashed into my gulliver was that I would like to have her right down there on the floor with the old in-out real savage, but skorry as a shot came the sickness, like a like detective that had been watching round a corner and now followed to make his grahzny arrest. And now the von of lovely perfume that came off her made me want to think of starting to like heave in my keeshkas, so I knew I had to think of some new like way of thinking about her before all the pain and thirstiness and horrible sickness come over me real horrorshow and proper. So I creeched out:

'O most beautiful and beauteous of devotchkas, I throw like my heart at your feet for you to like trample all over. If I had a rose I would give it to you. If it was all rainy and cally now on the ground you could have my platties to walk on so as not to cover your dainty nogas with filth and cal.' And as I was saying all this, O my brothers, I could feel the sickness like slinking back. 'Let me,' I creeched out, 'worship you and be like your helper and protector from the wicked like world.' Then I thought of the right slovo and felt better for it, saying: 'Let me be like your true knight,' and down I went again on the old knees, bowing and like scraping.

And then I felt real shooty and dim, it having been like an act again, for this devotchka smiled and bowed to the audience and like danced off, the lights coming up to a bit of applause. And the glazzies of some of these starry vecks in the audience were like popping out at this young devotchka with dirty and like unholy desire, O my brothers.

'He will be your true Christian,' Dr Brodsky was creeching out, 'ready to turn the other cheek, ready to be crucified rather than crucify, sick to the very heart at the thought even of killing a fly.' And that was right, brothers, because when he said that I thought of killing a fly and felt just that tiny bit sick, but I pushed the sickness and pain back by thinking of the fly being fed with bits of sugar and looked after like a bleeding pet and all that cal. 'Reclamation,' he creeched. 'Joy before the Angels of God.'

'The point is,' this Minister of the Inferior was saying real gromky, 'that it works.'

'Oh,' the prison charlie said, like sighing, 'it works all right, God help the lot of us.'

---

1 How would you characterize the personality of the narrator as he describes what has happened to him? What clues alert you to the fact that he has been the subject of an experiment to condition his behavior? What was he like before he was repro-

grammed? How do his reactions when he is presented to the public show the ways in which he has changed? In what way is the newly transformed narrator like "a clockwork orange"?

2 What is Burgess's attitude toward the formerly vicious young protagonist, the doctors who have changed his behavior, and the public officials who are viewing the results? How does the unusual language the narrator uses define him as a person and tell you about his social class and relationship to society? Contrast the way he uses language with the way it is used by his examiners in terms of vocabulary, sentence structure and length, expressions of emotion, grammar, slang, and any other relevant linguistic criteria.

3 Translate the dialect of the main character into more familiar terms that make it possible to understand him. Use clues provided by the context in which the words are used and any associations they evoke (for example, "viddied"for saw). Rewrite any paragraph in this manner. What dialect, slang, or jargon do you and your friends use that would be difficult for others to decipher?

4 What are the distinguishing features of the dialect Burgess invented for his protagonist in such phrases as "Dr. Brodsky stood and govoreeted in a like learned manner to all the lewdies assembled" (para. 4) in contrast to the way the experimenters speak (for example, "He is, as you will perceive, fit and well-nourished," para. 4)? (Glossary: *Coinage, Dialect, Fiction, Protagonist/Antagonist.*)

5 Evaluate Burgess's use of details that advance the narrative point of his story. What conflict does the narrative dramatize? What means does Burgess use to build the tension in his story? Locate two paragraphs in which Burgess's use of words and phrases is especially effective in making you understand the experiences of the narrator. How does Burgess use dialogue to reveal the scientists' attitude toward their human subject? Burgess's story raises the question of whether psychological conditioning in this extreme form is ever justified. In your opinion, should societal needs and values take precedence in this case over the rights of the narrator? (Glossary: *Dialogue, Narration.*)

6 In England, regional accents are often a barrier to career advancement. Is the same true in the United States? Would you consider altering regional pronunciation patterns to get ahead?

Listen mr oxford don   *John Agard*

◆ JOHN AGARD was born in Guyana in 1930. He is a poet, short story writer, journalist, and actor. He has been a frequent contributor to the magazines *Expression* and *Plexis* as well as to Guyana's newspaper the *Sunday*

John Agard, "Listen mr oxford don," from *Mangoes and Bullets* published by Pluto Press copyright 1985. Reprinted by kind permission of John Agard c/o Caroline Sheldon Literary Agency.

Chronicle. His poetry has been collected in *Shoot Me with Flowers* (1985). In the following poem, we hear a voice that reflects the speech patterns and rhythm of reggae and steel-pan music as the speaker launches a witty assault on British linguistic colonialism.

How dialect functions as a class marker in determining what forms of English are judged to be correct and which others should be shunned is treated with considerable wit and humor in this poem by Agard. What makes the speaker's condemnation by the linguistic powers that be all the more ironic is the obvious skill with which the speaker voices his complaints. The intricate patterns of reggae rhyme and rhythm and the sophisticated wordplay ("I bashing future wit present tense") belie the accusations of "assault / on de Oxford dictionary."

> **TO CONSIDER** Do you feel that rap music is a respectable literary form? What is the basis of its appeal?

Me not no Oxford don
me a simple immigrant
from Clapham Common
I didn't graduate
I immigrate   5

But listen Mr Oxford don
I'm a man on de run
and a man on de run
is a dangerous one   10

I ent have no gun
I ent have no knife
but mugging de Queen's English
is the story of my life

I dont need no axe   15
to split/up yu syntax
I dont need no hammer
to mash up yu grammar

I warning you Mr Oxford don
I'm a wanted man
and a wanted man   20
is a dangerous one

Dem accuse me of assault
on de Oxford dictionary
imagin a concise peaceful man like me
dem want me serve time   25
for inciting rhyme to riot

but I tekking it quiet
down here in Clapham Common

I'm not a violent man Mr Oxford don
30   I only armed wit muh human breath
but human breath
is a dangerous weapon

So mek dem send one big word after me
I ent serving no jail sentence
35   I slashing suffix in self-defence
I bashing future wit present tense
and if necessary

I making de Queen's English accessory/to my offence

---

1   What elements in the poem contribute to its tone, humor, and satiric wit? How does the speaker's sophisticated mastery of nonstandard English refute assumptions you might have had about the crime of which he stands accused? To what extent do you associate "voice" with social class or region of the country?

2   How does the poem carry the argument forward through skillfully varied parallel assertions, contrasts, and antitheses?

3   Does this poem trigger any memories of situations other than in an English class in school in which you were judged by the way you used colloquial or nonstandard English? What is the best example of current rap you have heard? You might wish to make up your own rap by writing out a story you know well and telling it to a beat.

4   What norms of standard English, correct grammar, syntax, and usage has the speaker contravened? How does his dialect put him at odds with the powers that be? How do we know that the speaker can use language in a sophisticated, agile, and creative way although he does not express himself in standard English? (Glossary: Dialect, Speaker, Standard English, Syntax, Usage.)

5   In Agard's poem, how does the preposterous nature of the "crime" of which the speaker is accused employ the kind of exaggeration associated with satire? (Glossary: Satire, Humor.)

6   Select an author whose characters speak in a dialect (for example, William Faulkner, Mark Twain, Toni Morrison), and after reading a passage aloud, try to locate the defining features of the dialect that would allow you to classify it (in terms of region, social class, etc.). Evaluate how accurately the author can evoke the sounds of speech on the written page.

◆ CONNECTIONS: MANY ENGLISHES

Paul Roberts, "Something About English"

1. How does Martha Barnette's account provide a glimpse into the recent influences that are adding new words to English in much the same way English developed, according to Roberts?
2. What new influences has the advent of the computer had on the development of the English language, according to David Angell and Brent Heslop in "Return to Sender" (Ch. 11)? In your opinion, how would Roberts view these latest influences?

Julia Penelope, "The Glamour of Grammar"

1. In what respects is Penelope's essay designed to correct misconceptions about the evolution of grammar promulgated by men? In what ways is her approach different from that of Paul Roberts?
2. How does Penelope's analysis add an interesting perspective on what is supposedly objective grammar in ways that reflect Alleen Pace Nilsen's treatment of words in "Sexism in English: A 1990s Update" (Ch. 8)?

Lewis Carroll, "Jabberwocky" and "Explaining the Meaning of Jabberwocky"

1. In what way does Lewis Carroll's poem "Jabberwocky" provide a nonsensical example of the processes by which new words are added to the language, as discussed by Paul Roberts? What are some of these methods?
2. How does Lewis Carroll's poem provide a humorous illustration of the playful and sensuous dimension of language that children discover through babbling, as discussed by Steven Pinker in "Baby Born Talking—Describes Heaven" in Ch. 1?

Barbara Mellix, "From Outside, In"

1. In what way do Mellix's experiences with black English take her in a very different direction from that of Itabari Njeri? What different values are important to each writer?
2. In what sense might Mellix's mastery of standard English enable her to change her position within the culture in ways that are as profound as those discussed by Amy Tan (see "The Language of Discretion," Ch. 6)?

Itabari Njeri, "What's in a Name?"

1. What accounts for Njeri's decision to establish a strong connection with her African roots? In your opinion, would Barbara Mellix ever consider adopting an African name? Why or why not?
2. How does the account by Njeri and Jack Solomon's analysis (see "What's in a Name: The Ideology of Cultural Classification," Ch. 8) show how closely intertwined issues of language and power are in our society?

Martha Barnette, "Ladyfingers & Nun's Tummies"

1. How does Barnette illuminate the process by which new words enter American English in connection with food? Are these essentially the same methods as those discussed by Paul Roberts?
2. To what extent do both Barnette and David Ricks (see "What's In a Name?," Ch. 6) explore how the power of names can mislead through suggestion and inference?

Anthony Burgess, *A Clockwork Orange*

1. How does the author's invention of nonsensical terms that nonetheless communicate meaning resemble the process used by Lewis Carroll in his poem "Jabberwocky"?
2. Drawing on Mikhail Bakhtin (see "The Dialogic Imagination," Ch. 4), discuss how Burgess incorporates different patterns of speech to underscore differences in social class in conversations between the narrator and the scientists.

John Agard, "Listen mr oxford don"

1. What connections can you discover between Agard's defense of West Indian culture, through its distinctive dialect in opposition to British English, and Itabari Njeri's decision to adopt her African name?
2. Compare Agard's poem with James Finn Garner's "Little Red Riding Hood" (Ch. 8) as examples of the use of humor to satirize the language and values, respectively, of colonial British and contemporary American cultures.

◆ WRITING ASSIGNMENTS FOR CHAPTER 7

1. What role does black English play in novels by Toni Morrison, including *The Bluest Eye* (1993), *Song of Solomon* (1977), and *Beloved* (1988)? How would the impact of these works have changed had she substituted standard English for black English?
2. Are there disadvantages to a traditional education for African-American students that an Afrocentric curriculum would correct?
3. What new words are being added to the language because of new advances in science, technology, politics, government, communication, health care, the globalization of cultures, or any other area of modern life (for example, "ethnic cleansing," "transgenic," or "cloning")? You might look through any recent issue of *Time, Newsweek,* the *New York Times,* or the *Los Angeles Times* for words now being commonly used that did not exist in the past.
4. We all use different "Englishes" in different situations. How does the way you speak change according to what circumstances you are in and who you are with (friends, parents, teachers, salespeople, etc.)?
5. In each of the following cases, how were the names celebrities adopted designed to have more positive connotations than their given names? Why might the person have changed his or her name and chosen the stage name?

Frances Gumm	Judy Garland
Marion Morrison	John Wayne
Thomas Mapother	Tom Cruise
Albert Einstein	Albert Brooks
Doris von Kappelhoff	Doris Day
Robert Zimmerman	Bob Dylan
Steveland Judkins Morris	Stevie Wonder
Reginald Kenneth Dwight	Elton John
Annie Mae Bullock	Tina Turner
Richard Starkey	Ringo Starr

6. Each of the following names have been authenticated by John Train in his books *Remarkable Names of Real People* (1977), and *Even More Remarkable Names* (1979). How do you think your life would be affected if you had one of these names?

Herman Sherman Berman	Commissioner of Deeds, Bronx, N.Y.
J. Fido Spot	West Palm Beach, Florida
(Miss) Mignon Hamburger	U. of Wisconsin, Madison, WI.
Peter Beter, Attorney	Washington, D.C.
Solomon Gemorah	Brooklyn, New York
T. Fud Pucker Tucker	Bountiful, Utah
Katz Meow	Hoquiam, Washington
Rosetta Stone	New York City
Shanda Lear	Battle Creek, Michigan
Mrs. Screech, Singing Teacher	Victoria, British Columbia

7. An important kind of language often encountered in specialized fields is jargon. (Glossary: *Jargon.*) Basically, jargon is the specialized language of a trade, field, or profession. It provides a shorthand way of quickly communicating a lot of information. For example, in publishing, horror stories combined with romantic melodrama are called "creepy weepys," and historical romances filled with sex and violence to stimulate sales are known as "bodice rippers." In police work, officers refer to confiscated drug money as "dead presidents."

The word *jargon* comes from the fifteenth-century French term *jargoun* (twittering or gibberish). In its original context, *jargoun* referred to the secret language criminals used to communicate with each other without being understood by the authorities. The impenetrable nature of jargon makes it all too easy for it to be used to disguise the inner workings of a particular trade or profession or to avoid being held accountable.

Part of the function of jargon is to make the ordinary seem extraordinary and to give an air of importance to everyday situations encountered in different fields. For example, Diane Johnson in "Doctor Talk" (*The New*

Republic [1979]) reports that new physicians have been told to use "scientific-sounding euphemisms" in the presence of patients. An alcoholic patient might be told he was suffering from "hyperingestion of ethanol." Not only is the use of specialized terms part of the medical shorthand doctors use in communicating with each other, but such jargon has the added benefit of impressing patients, forestalling counterarguments (how can the patient argue without knowing what the terms mean?), and justifying larger fees.

Lawyers, along with academicians, scientists, and bureaucrats, have their own trade talk that often presents what would normally be easy to grasp in language that mystifies and obscures. For example, in Connecticut the *New Haven Register* (August 9, 1986) reports that the estate of a man who was killed when a barn collapsed on him is bringing a suit against the owners of the barn. The legalese of the suit states that the man's death "destroyed his capacity to carry on life's activities, resulting in loss and damage to his estate." According to the suit, death also "curtailed his earning capacity" and caused him to lose "the joy of life" (cited in *Quarterly Review of Doublespeak* [October 1987]).

In the following excerpt, Dave Barry spoofs the catch phrases that players rely on in interviews with sportswriters. After listening to some radio or television interviews, identify the kinds of phrases that Barry discusses. If you wish, write a dialogue between an interviewer and a sports figure that incorporates some of these phrases. What features does sports jargon display?

So player quotes are critical; the problem is that the players almost never have anything to say. This is not their fault. They shoot the ball; it goes into the basket or it doesn't. What is there to say about this?

But reporters are constantly badgering the players for quotes. In response, the players have developed sports blather. This is a special language consisting of meaningless words and phrases—such as "execute," "focus," "step up," "find a rhythm," "game plan," "mental errors" and "the next level"—that professional athletes can string together in any random order to form quotes, as in: "We made some mental errors, but we found our rhythm and were able to focus on executing our game plan and stepping up to the next level" or "We gamely planned to erroneously focus on stepping up our level of mental rhythm." You think I'm kidding, but professional athletes regularly make statements just as incoherent as these while hordes of reporters religiously record every word.

8. Each of the following examples of jargon is used in a particular subculture. Translate as many as you can into standard English. If you wish, you might provide additional expressions that you use or know about in these or other areas.

Baseball:	bean ball, a free trip
Football:	a bomb, clothesline
Restaurant:	Adam & Eve on a raft, to travel

Television Industry:	meat puppet, crawl
Police Officers:	ate his gun, code 7
Stereophiles:	silver doughnut, tweakophiles
Computers:	bullet proof, mouse droppings
Motorcycle riders:	crotch rocket, skid lid
Body piercing and tattooing:	bodmods, quaker
Architecture:	ranch burger, puff 'n' powder

9. Consider the amount of jargon, acronyms, and abbreviations that you use without being aware of it in a sport you participate in or any hobby you have, or in your intended college major or at a job. What words do you use or have you encountered in any of these areas that would be considered jargon—that is, a specialized language or shorthand way of quickly communicating? Which of these terms would be understandable only to experts in that area?

10. Make up a new name for yourself that has personal meaning and does not rely on conventional spelling or typeface (as did the couple in the following news article and the pop music star formerly known as Prince).

Worst Spelling News*

From Agence France-Presse: An appeals court has ordered a Swedish couple to pay a fine of 5000 kronor ($735) for having named their son "Brfxxccxxmnpcccclllmmnprxvclmnckssqlbbl1116."

The unconventional parents had not given their child a name by the time he was 5 years old, when tax authorities said they would have to give him one.

The couple, who subscribe to the surrealist doctrine of pataphysics, came up with this 43-character string, which they said is pronounced "Albin."

Swedish tax officials rejected this choice, and in April an administrative court in the southwestern Halland region ordered the couple to pay the 5000 kronor fine. The couple said their name was "full of meaning and typographically expressionistic, and we consider it a new artistic creation in the pataphysical tradition in which we believe."

They could have named him zxiiilqrrrqagh—pronounced "Fred."

---

*Parade Magazine, December 29, 1996, page 7.

A language is a dialect that has an army and navy.

—Max Weinreich

Gary Brookins, *Richmond Times Dispatch*, 6/13/97. Used by permission.

The Politics of Everyday Language

anguage clearly has an influence on our beliefs and actions. As the selections in this chapter illustrate, those who have an interest in convincing us to believe something are often quite skillful in using language to persuade. Thus, it follows that the more aware we are of how politicians and other public advocates use language to manipulate our behavior, the less likely it becomes that we can be deceived into acting against our own best interests. The authors in this chapter also examine the ways in which language is used to discriminate against selected groups. This issue is addressed by Jack Solomon in "What's in a Name?: The Ideology of Cultural Classification," an insightful analysis of the hidden agendas underlying supposedly objective classifications involving race, species, and ethnicity.

Articles by Alleen Pace Nilsen ("Sexism in English: A 1990s Update"), Susan Sontag ("AIDS and Its Metaphors), and Frank Nuessel ("Old Age Needs a New Name, But Don't Look for It in Webster's") apply the theory of how stereotyping works against women, those with AIDS, and the elderly. How a person or event is labeled influences our perceptions of what is being described and can prove quite intimidating to the person or group so labeled. Stereotypes are dangerous because they portray people in terms of a single trait, often misrepresenting them in the process, and provide a pretext for those who wish to deny basic human rights to this stigmatized group.

This is what happened to Fan Shen, although in a less extreme form, when he was a student in China who dared to express himself using the prohibited pronoun "I," as he tells us in "The Classroom and the Wider Culture: Identity as a Key to Learning English Composition." In America, one can be just as easily stigmatized because of not being able to read or write, as we learn from Jonathan Kozol in "The Human Cost of an Illiterate Society."

The prospect of changing attitudes by changing language (or reflecting changed attitudes in new terminology) is the subject of an essay by Michiko Kakutani ("The Word Police"). At its core, the debate over "political correctness" must consider both the desire to squelch prejudicial language by any means, on the one hand, and the equally fervent wish on the other to preserve the time-honored principle of free speech, no matter how offensive, hateful, and even damaging such speech may be. There have been excesses on both sides, and James Finn Garner in his updated children's story "Little Red Riding Hood" is quick to satirize the elaborate verbal contortions "political correctness" advocates use to avoid sexist, racist, species, and ageist stereotyping.

What's in a Name? The Ideology of Cultural Classification

Jack Solomon

◆ JACK SOLOMON is a researcher in the field of semiotics, which investigates the hidden messages of environments, objects, and cultural images. He is the author of *The Signs of Our Time* (1988), from which the following article is taken, a coeditor of *California Dreams and Realities* (1995), and the coeditor of *Signs of Life in the U.S.A.* (2nd ed., 1997).

As Solomon points out, the ways we choose to classify things can be made to serve political purposes. Solomon sheds light on the mechanisms by which supposedly neutral descriptive terms can serve an underlying ideology, turn one group against another, and present a stereotyped picture of the world. Politicized language used in this way serves a hidden agenda in ways that have always been characteristic of totalitarian states. It is designed to reduce an entire complex range of meanings to slogans, labels, and epithets that are meant to preclude a full understanding of the issues involved. Solomon's analysis of the mechanism of stereotyping through classification permits us to understand the many different kinds of degradation of thought and language that have become a part of everyday life.

TO CONSIDER   Have you ever been stereotyped or unfairly labeled? Why do you think that people have a need to fit others into categories?

And out of the ground the Lord God formed every beast of the field, and every fowl of the air; and brought them unto Adam to see what he would call them; and whatsoever Adam called every living creature, that was the name thereof.

Gen. 2.19

There's a funny story that anthropologists tell to demonstrate how many different ways the same things can be named and classified, depending on the culture doing the naming. A group of anthropologists were giving a sort of IQ test to a band of aboriginal tribesmen. The purpose of the test (and there really is such a test) is to see how someone will group a collection of twenty different objects drawn from four classes: food, tools, cooking utensils, and clothes. The test predicts that the more intelligent individual will, say, group knives and forks under "cooking utensils" and apples and oranges under "foods."

In this particular test, the tribesmen consistently chose the "less intelligent" classification, however, grouping knives with oranges rather than with forks. After each classification, they would chant together a phrase in their own language that in translation might run, "This is how a wise man would do this." The anthropologists administering the test finally became exasperated and asked the tribesmen "how a damned fool would do it." They immediately regrouped the knives with the forks and the apples with the oranges.

The moral of the story has partly to do with the different ways that various cultures classify the same things and partly with the cultural arrogance that causes one culture—ours—to judge the intelligence of other cultures by its own standards. It happens to be the case that our Western approach to classification is an abstract one; we tend to group things together conceptually rather than concretely. A knife, for instance, is a very concrete object and so is a fork, but an "eating utensil" is a conceptual abstraction, a generalization rather than a thing. Our understanding of the actual knife and fork, in other words, is shaped by a cultural code that groups objects conceptually and abstractly, and we expect all other "intelligent" people to understand such things in the same way.

[handwritten margin note: abstraction as the expected norm]

But can't we look at knives and forks differently? After all, you use a knife, not a fork, to cut an orange, and so there would seem to be a perfectly good—and intelligent—reason for grouping the knife with the orange rather than with the fork. This, in fact, is precisely what the tribesmen in the story did: they classified the objects placed before them by virtue of their concrete relations to each other. A knife, in other words, is concretely related to an orange because it is used for the physical act of cutting. Within the terms of a cultural code constituted by concrete rather than abstract perceptions, it is perfectly reasonable and only simple common sense to group the knife with the orange.

Even the most trivial of classifications can be seen sometimes to conceal a particular point of view. Several years ago, for example, the Reagan administration created something of a flap when it decided to classify tomato ketchup as a "vegetable" in order to save money on school lunch programs. At the time, a feeble attempt was made to defend this reclassification of ketchup from "condiment" to "vegetable" on the grounds that since ketchup is made from tomatoes (which means, of course, that it is really derived from a "fruit," but that's another issue) it could be seen as belonging to one of the four major food groups (which, if you're old enough to remember, were once the seven major food groups: meat, fish, dairy, grains, green vegetables, yellow vegetables, and fruit). This attempt to change a classification was quickly abandoned, however, in the face of protests from parents and jeers from administration critics.

In the ketchup caper, we find the conflict of two political interests. One believes that it is not the role of government to subsidize nutritional programs, and one believes that it is. From the former perspective, it may seem expedient to reclassify ketchup, but the decision to do so is determined by political rather than natural reasons. Conversely, keeping ketchup in its place as a "sauce" can also be seen to be a political decision because there is nothing to prevent us from viewing it as "food." It does have *some* nutritional value. The question is simply where we draw the line, and where that line is drawn will be determined by our interests, not by some "natural" power outside those interests.

In fact, all the most basic distinctions represent some human interest. In the United States, for instance, we presume that there is an obvious difference between the "inside" and the "outside" of a house. "Inside," we take off our coats and turn on the heat. "Outside," we put on "outerwear." It seems to be a perfectly natural distinction. Yet a friend of mine in the People's Republic of China tells me that the Chinese do not make quite the same distinction that we do between the inside and the outside of a house. When the temperature drops, the Chinese simply put on more underclothing rather than turn on the heat. Because outdoor and indoor temperatures are similar, there is no need to make a sharp distinction between indoor and outdoor clothing. Thus, where my friend would take off her overcoat when going indoors, and then shiver until she put it on again to go outside, her hosts were equally comfortable indoors and out. That's not because they wore their overcoats indoors and out, for as far as my friend could see they did not even have overcoats. Instead, the Chinese bundle up in winter underneath the jackets they wear in warmer weather.

The interest served by this lack of a clear distinction between indoors and out is not difficult to find: it conserves fuel in a country where fuel is scarce. But this does not mean that the Chinese can't differ among themselves on how to classify things. My friend also tells me, for instance, that even though it is technically illegal to do so, Chinese peasants strew their un-threshed grain onto roadways in order to benefit from the threshing action that automobile traffic accomplishes for them. What the authorities see as a "road," built solely to bear traffic, the peasants see as a "threshing floor." The interest behind this reclassification of roadways is also easy to spot. There isn't much space to spare for threshing purposes in a typical Chinese village. So a little-used road may be redefined to satisfy a specific need.

Americans also disagree on where to draw the line. Is a one-minute pause in a school classroom a "moment of silence" or a constitutionally forbidden "prayer"? Is an abortion an act of "murder" or an act of "privacy" protected by the Fifth Amendment? Is a fifteen-year-old killer an "adult" or a "juvenile"? Is a nuclear warhead an "offensive weapon" or a "peacekeeper"? In each of these controversies you will find two sides equally certain that their designation is the right one, that they alone have drawn the line strictly according to the "truth." It would be nice if the truth were that easy to find, but in each of these cases the line we draw is only ideologically true.

The interests served by a classification scheme can sometimes be harmlessly personal. I was once told the story of a certain retired Harvard professor who, somewhat against his own more indolent inclinations, had been persuaded by his wife to take up the fashionable hobby of bird-watching. Wishing to avoid the labor of having to distinguish among, and remember the names of, too many species, he drastically simplified the usual scheme by employing only four basic names for the classes of birds he was able (or willing) to recognize. These four classes included "crows," "gulls and robins," "small brown birds," and "other." That simplified things. Crows, gulls, and robins are easy to spot. So are small brown birds. Anything more complicated—say, a scarlet ibis—can be effortlessly tucked away into the class of "other."

But even this harmless approach to classifying animals harbors ideological implications. As long as we are only talking about recreational bird-watchers, there's no problem at all. But if the question of where to draw the line appears in the context of a controversy over environmental protection, it can be quite another matter.

In the mid-1970s, for instance, the Tennessee Valley Authority's plan to build a dam on the Little Tennessee River was halted when it was discovered that the dam would threaten the survival of several local species, including the snail darter and the Anthony's River snail. Proponents of the dam, known as the Tellico project, argued that the snail darter was not an endangered species since there were plenty of closely related darter species scattered throughout the region. Opponents of the dam argued conversely that the snail darter was an irreplaceable component of the biological diversity of the earth and was accordingly covered by the Endangered Species Act of 1973. The differing political interests of each camp were reflected in the way each chose to classify the darter. The pro-dam forces took a more general approach—once you've seen one darter you've seen them all—while the anti-dam forces insisted on detail. The whole issue depended on where you chose to draw the line. The line was finally drawn, and the snail darter was saved.

One reason we disagree so often on where to draw the line is because there are so many different ways to categorize objects and images. Thus, we usually classify them in terms of how they affect and serve our individual or cultural interest. An individual horse, for example, can be classified in quite a number of ways that are not all necessarily biologically based. There's nothing to stop us from seeing a horse as a rather oversized, short-eared donkey—after all, with a little help from a breeder, horses and donkeys can interbreed—but that would drive down the value of horseflesh, which would hardly be in the interest of the horse-breeding industry.

But what about the horse's potential to end up on your dinner plate? We eat cattle, after all, and horses, like cattle, are herbivores, a group of animals generally classed as edible within the terms of our culinary code. This is the way the French draw the line to include the horse in the class of edible meats, and if you were a horsemeat-peddling entrepreneur with an interest in cracking the U.S. market with "le fillet de cheval," you'd want to get Americans to think this way too.

How we choose to classify things may seem to be a trivial matter, but its implications can be deadly. For when one powerful group of people classifies another less powerful group as either inferior or, even worse, not quite human at all, the result can be genocidal. We only need to look at what happened to the American Indians in the nineteenth century, or to European Jewry in the twentieth century to see what the stakes can be in the matter of human classification.

THE SEMIOTICS OF RACE

Before commencing his extermination of European Jewry, Hitler first set his Nazi biologists to work on "proving" the "natural" racial inferiority of the Jews. He then had others come up with a definition of just what constituted a Jew in the first place. To create as large a net as possible, it was decided that anyone with at least one Jewish grandparent was a Jew, regardless of his or her actual religion or parentage. It was one short step from the creation of this taxonomic myth to behaving as if the Jews weren't people at all, turning them effectively into cattle who could be slaughtered at will. It is bloodcurdling to realize that the eventual boiling down of human beings into soap was first sanctioned by ideologically motivated biologists and genealogists who shifted at will the crucial boundary line between the human and the nonhuman.

The point here is not that there is such a thing as an absolute racial classification scheme, which the Nazis perverted. After all, Jewish scholars have themselves struggled for centuries over the definition of a Jew in the Diaspora. In the scheme they have devised, any child whose parents are Jewish is, of course, Jewish, but so too is a child of mixed parentage if his or her mother is Jewish. The child of a Jewish father and non-Jewish mother, however, is not considered Jewish.

Hitler's racial taxonomy was motivated purely by a murderous interest. One might say that the entire code was genocidal in intent. That is not to say there is no interest behind the Jewish manner of self-definition, but the interest here is a peaceful one, motivated by the Jewish desire for cultural survival. Believing that our life essence is contained in our blood, Orthodox rabbis have made a distinction between the male and female role in procreation. The ancient rabbinical teaching reasons that since a fetus is generated in the body of its mother, it must inherit her blood, not the blood of its father. If that blood is Jewish, the child has Jewish blood in its veins. To preserve the blood-identity of the Jewish people, the rabbis have insisted on the maternal descent of the racial essence.

In these cases, we can distinguish between two different classification schemes on the basis of their different motivations. It doesn't matter whether you classify someone as a Jew or not when the issue is considered taxonomically, but when one definition is motivated by a murderous ideology and the other by a desire for survival, it is easy to say which is the morally superior scheme. In fact, we can say that the moral value of a classification can be judged not by its form but by its motivation and by its effects. . . .

Things are subtler in America, but not necessarily less pernicious. In the stories of William Faulkner, you can see just how sensitive the South has been to the classificatory challenges created by racial admixture. For instance, Charles Bon, the hero of Faulkner's novel *Absalom, Absalom!*, has a fair-skinned mistress who is just one-eight Negro—hence, an "octoroon"—but that slim one-eighth is enough to cast her among the slaves. At the end of the novel, we discover that Bon, who is an officer in the Confederate Army, has a trace of "black blood" in his veins as well, which is enough to cause his all-white half-brother to murder him.

Just one drop of Negro blood in America, it seems, is enough to make you "black"—and not only in fiction. My father, who is a physician, has told me a story of how once during World War II he was called in to diagnose the illness of a civilian child who lived near his southern boot camp. The child was blonde, blue-eyed, and, as my father informed his thunderstruck parents, suffering from sickle-cell anemia. "But he can't have *that!*" the child's parents insisted. I'm afraid that I don't know what became of the child, but given the racial situation in the South in the 1940s, it can only have been tragic.

HUMAN OR ANIMAL

We not only draw lines between races, of course, but between species as well, and here, too, cultural interests may be at work. Take the way that the aboriginal Dalabon tribesmen of northern Australia name and classify the flora and fauna of their environment. As traditional hunter-gatherers, the Dalabon must have a keen awareness of their natural surroundings in order to survive. And yet, when we look at their classifications, we may be in for a surprise. For rather than identifying the hundreds of species that a European zoologist or botanist would be able to identify in their territory, the Dalabon give names to only four major groups: *djen* (fish); *du:l* (trees); *guin* (large marsupials); and *ma:n* (which includes small marsupials, lizards, snakes, insects, dogs, and birds). Where we might distinguish "lizards" from "birds," then, the Dalabon see two related animals that can be called by the same name. For those of us trained in the Western scheme of taxonomic classification, which groups animals according to biological and evolutionary traits, the Dalabon taxonomy may look rather "primitive" and "unintelligent."

But it is nothing of the sort. For if you, like the Dalabon, spent your entire life hunting and gathering, you'd be more interested in the number of meals a given animal could provide than in its biological similarity to another species. You'd accordingly be likely to distinguish between small marsupials and large ones too, even though they're biologically related. Similarly, if your interest in fish did not extend beyond their potential for a meal, you wouldn't need to distinguish among their many kinds. All you'd need to know was that fish are found in water, and the Dalabon carefully distinguish between those animals which are found exclusively in water and those which are not.

Seen from a Dalabon perspective, then, a fourfold natural order makes perfect sense because it serves a concrete interest. This leads us to a related question: "What interest is served by *our* way of classifying natural species?" This isn't an easy question to answer, much less to ask, because it ordinarily doesn't occur to us to ask it. The way we classify and name things seems to be the only way that it can be done. Ask a Dalabon tribesman why he calls both dogs and birds by the same name (*ma:n*), and he is likely to respond, "because they are *ma:n*." If he asked us why we call one *ma:n* a "dog" and another a "bird," we are likely to say, "because that *is* a 'dog' and that *is* a 'bird.'"

Only recently in the history of the West has it been possible to ask the semiotic question, "What interests do our classification of natural species serve?" It would have been unintelligible to the founders of Western culture. To answer this question, we must begin, as semiotic analysis often does, by examining history. For the writers of the Bible, the names that Adam gave to the beasts of the field were the only names that could be given. Cows were "cows" and camels were "camels," and that was the end of it.

For the ancient Greeks the situation was somewhat different, but their taxonomic outlook was essentially the same. Aristotle, writing in the fourth century B.C., believed that while various peoples might give different names to things (in the Greek language or in the Persian, for example), these names ultimately referred to the same classes of things. Various peoples may name their world differently, use different signs, but their names all refer to the same reality.

Aristotle's attitude is probably the one most of us hold today. It seems to be only common sense. But as the first of our fundamental semiotic precepts tell us, "common sense" is really "communal sense," the set of concepts shared by a group. For the Western community, for instance, it is only common sense that cows were put on earth for us to eat. But that isn't common sense in India.

Let's look more closely now at the interests behind our Western way of classifying animals. Our first clue as to the nature of this interest comes from the Bible itself, in which the West has encoded its belief that all Creation has been turned over to humanity for its own use. God gives Adam dominion over all the species of the earth, as well as the right to name them. This act of naming symbolizes the control that we have over the earth, for to name a thing, as we have seen, is to define its uses. It is to gain power over it.

The "myth" of Genesis (and I use the term *myth* in its semiotic sense) reflects the interests of a people whose relation to nature was an embattled one. Life on the Mesopotamian plain, where the Semitic "myths" that eventually culminated in the Bible originated, was not easy. Disastrous floods, murderous heat, and wild beasts all threatened the lives of the forefathers of Western culture. Animal rights and environmental considerations had no significance for a people at war with a natural environment that appeared to be at war with them.

The fact that Adam names the species of the earth also symbolizes the ancient Hebrews' sense of separation from their environment. By exercising his power to name every other species, Adam places himself in a special category above them. Adam never names himself, for no one except God stands above him. Adam also never attempts to speak with the animals, as happens so often in what we call "primitive" mythology, because there is simply no dialogue between Adam and the rest of Creation, and little sense of creaturely community. Adam just tells the animals what their names are and accordingly exercises his dominion over them, thus symbolizing the Western belief that animals are just things, soulless objects over which humans have absolute control.

Our Western heritage thus bequeaths to us a sense of a profound division between humanity and the rest of nature. Nature is there to be subdued, to be forced to conform to the needs of human culture. This attitude serves a clear interest that our culture has concealed by "naturalizing" it. To us, it seems only natural to divide up the animate world into the broad classes of "animals" and "humans," with the covert assumption that it is equally "natural" for the one class to dominate the other.

The results of the West's conceptual division between nature and culture are all too apparent today. The massive extinction of species, the pollution of our land, air, and water, the crowding out of other forms of life can all be traced, semiotically speaking, to our own isolation of ourselves from nature.

The current controversy over the linguistic capabilities of such animals as great apes and whales involves a similar set of clashing interests in the question of where to draw the line. From the time of the ancient Greeks, who defined man as the animal with the "logos"—that is, the only animal with a capacity for rational speech—to the present, philosophers have believed that it is our ability to use language that separates us from the lower animals. If it could be proved that at least some animal species share our capacity to use language, then we might be compelled to redraw the line between the human and animal kingdoms. A number of long-term experiments have been conducted accordingly to see whether an animal can be taught a human language, the most famous involving a chimpanzee named Washoe and a gorilla named Koko. But the results of these experiments have been controversial, because the ways they are interpreted reflect the particular interests of the interpreters. . . .

If it could be proved that Koko really can communicate with us, and if, more generally, we really could learn to "talk to the animals," then our ordinary way of treating them would be profoundly shaken. For if animals could talk, they would seem a lot closer to humans than they seem now. What we now call poaching or hunting would then be seen as simply murder—like the way the late naturalist Dian Fossey viewed the poaching of her gorillas or the way the poisoning of your dog would appear to you. Eating your next roast beef dinner might be viewed as an act of cannibalism. And not only our pets but all animals would merit their own proper names.

The interests at stake here are clear. On the one side we find the interests of the beef and poultry industry, or anyone who profits (if only in a culinary way) from the assumption that animals are something less than human beings. On the other side, we find those who believe animals deserve the same rights that we assume are "natural" to human society.

Another example of this division is the raging battle over where the line should be drawn in animal experimentation. On the one side, we find cosmetics firms, drug companies, cigarette manufacturers, medical researchers, universities . . . almost the whole gamut of corporate and institutional America. On the other side, we find such antivivisectionist groups as the People for the Ethical Treatment of Animals, In Defense of Animals, and the Humane Society. The former camp attempts to conceal its economic and professional interests by emphasizing the benefits to humans that accrue from animal research and seeks to draw the line as broadly as possible to include everything from fruit flies to chimpanzees in the class of "experimental animals." The latter camp would like to see the class abolished and bring an end to animal vivisection. Both sides see their position as the more natural and moral, but though it is not easy to judge between them, one can say that the antivivisectionists have less of an economic stake in the outcome of the debate and thus may be said to be less in danger of being motivated by selfish interests. . . .

It's not always necessary for us to be conscious of the motives behind our ways of naming and classifying things. But sometimes our ignorance of the original interests served by our taxonomic schemes can impel us to act in ways that are no longer in our interest at all. At such times, it can be useful indeed to know just how and why we classify things as we do; such knowledge might enable us to think of some other way of perceiving our world.

Here is where semiotics can help us. For it is one of the tasks of semiotics to explore the different ways in which various cultures classify and name things. In this enterprise, semiotics often joins hands with anthropology, seeking to get to the heart of a culture by uncovering the hidden interests or, we might say, the ideologies that cause a culture to classify things as it does.

To look at our organization of the world as a reflection of our interests can help us to change our views when some change becomes necessary. When we know that we are not required to see the world in any particular way, we are free to choose new ways that can better serve our changing interests.

1　What insight does this essay provide into the ideological agendas that underlie questions of abstract classification?

2　How does the first section of Solomon's article provide an overview that frames his subsequent discussions of racial, species, and ethnic classifications? In each case, why is it important to recognize the hidden agendas of the classifiers?

3 How are questions of classification always involved with questions of who has the power to classify? How do the examples of classification Solomon presents provide ample proof that those who have the power to classify can pursue propagandist agendas in each of the cases he examines?

4 How do the values and assumptions on which classifications are based and the corresponding interests and agendas that they serve vary from society to society? What are some conspicuous examples of how this works? What light does this phenomenon shed on ethnocentricity within and between cultures? (Glossary: *Ethnocentricity*.)

5 Before explaining the categories into which cultural classifications can be grouped, Solomon provides a description of how presumably objective classifications can serve hidden cultural and political agendas. How does this prepare his readers to better understand specific applications of this principle? (Glossary: *Classification/Division*.)

6 In a debate on abortion, where would you draw the line between the terms "tissue," "fetus," "embryo," "fertilized egg," and "baby"? Why would such distinctions be important? How are definitions used to control our attitudes and perceptions?

The Classroom and the Wider Culture: Identity as a Key to Learning English Composition

Fan Shen

◆ Originally from the People's Republic of China, Fan Shen is now a professor of English at Rochester Community and Technical College. He has translated three books from English into Chinese and has written many articles for both English and Chinese publications. This essay first appeared in the December 1989 issue of *College Composition and Communication*.

Students whose composition teachers urge them to reduce the number of times they use the pronoun "I" in their essays (or conversely, encourage the use of "I") may be surprised to discover that in some cultures this grammatical choice has profound political connotations. Such was the case for Fan Shen, who as a student growing up in China was taught to always use "we" instead of "I" lest he give the impression of being selfish, individualistic, and bourgeois. This tradition is so strong in the People's Republic of China that Shen attributed his own ideas to authority figures rather than appear to be putting himself above the group. Emigrating to the United States and entering school here required him, as he says, "to imagine looking at a world with my head upside down" and to invent a new "English self" that could use the pronoun "I."

> **TO CONSIDER**   Have your teachers ever commented on your overuse or underuse of the pronoun "I" in your papers? When do you think it is appropriate to use "I" and "me"? When is it not appropriate?

One day in June 1975, when I walked into the aircraft factory where I was working as an electrician, I saw many large-letter posters on the walls and many people parading around the workshops shouting slogans like "Down with the word 'I'!" and "Trust in masses and the Party!" I then remembered that a new political campaign called "Against Individualism" was scheduled to begin that day. Ten years later, I got back my first English composition paper at the University of Nebraska-Lincoln. The professor's first comments were: "Why did you always use 'we' instead of 'I'?" and "Your paper would be stronger if you eliminated some sentences in the passive voice." The *clashes* between my Chinese background and the requirements of English composition had begun. At the center of this mental struggle, which has lasted several years and is still not completely over, is the prolonged, uphill battle to recapture "myself."

In this paper I will try to describe and explore this experience of reconciling my Chinese identity with an English identity dictated by the rules of English composition. I want to show how my cultural background shaped—and shapes—my approaches to my writing in English and how writing in English redefined—and redefines—my *ideological* and *logical* identities. By "ideological identity" I mean the system of values that I acquired (consciously and unconsciously) from my social and cultural background. And by "logical identity" I mean the natural (or Oriental) way I organize and express my thoughts in writing. Both had to be modified or redefined in learning English composition. Becoming aware of the process of redefinition of these different identities is a mode of learning that has helped me in my efforts to write in English, and, I hope, will be of help to teachers of English composition in this country. In presenting my case for this view, I will use examples from both my composition courses and literature courses, for I believe that writing papers for both kinds of courses contributed to the development of my "English identity." Although what I will describe is based on personal experience, many Chinese students whom I talked to said that they had had the same or similar experiences in their initial stages of learning to write in English.

IDENTITY OF THE SELF: IDEOLOGICAL AND CULTURAL

Starting with the first English paper I wrote, I found that learning to compose in English is not an isolated classroom activity, but a social and cultural experience. The rules of English composition encapsulate values that are absent in, or sometimes contradictory to, the values of other societies (in my case, China). Therefore, learning the rules of English composition is, to a certain extent, *learning as political/ideological act* learning the values of Anglo-American society. In writing classes in the United States I found that I had to reprogram my mind, to redefine some of the basic concepts and values that I had about myself, about society, and about the universe, values that had been imprinted and reinforced in my mind by my cultural background, and that had been part of me all my life.

Rule number one in English composition is: Be yourself. (More than one composition instructor has told me, "Just write what *you* think.") The values behind this rule, it seems to me, are based on the principle of protecting and promoting individuality (and private property) in this country. The instruction was probably crystal clear to students raised on these values, but, as a guideline of composition, it was not very clear or useful to me when I first heard it. First of all, the image or meaning that I attached to the word "I" or "myself" was, as I found out, different from that of my English teacher. In China, "I" is always subordinated to "We"—be it the working class, the Party, the country, or some other collective body. Both political pressure and literary tradition require that "I" be somewhat hidden or buried in writings and speeches; presenting the "self" too obviously would give people the impression of being disrespectful of the Communist Party in political writings and boastful in scholarly writings. The word "I" has often been identified with another "bad" word, "individualism," which has become a synonym for selfishness in China. For a long time the words "self" and "individualism" have had negative connotations in my mind, and the negative force of the words naturally extended to the field of literary studies. As a result, even if I had brilliant ideas, the "I" in my papers always had to show some modesty by not competing with or trying to stand above the names of ancient and modern authoritative figures. Appealing to Mao or other Marxist authorities became the required way (as well as the most "forceful" or "persuasive" way) to prove one's point in written discourse. I remember that in China I had even committed what I can call "reversed plagiarism"—here, I suppose it would be called "forgery"—when I was in middle school: willfully attributing some of my thoughts to "experts" when I needed some arguments but could not find a suitable quotation from a literary or political "giant."

Now, in America, I had to learn to accept the words "I" and "self" as some- 5 thing glorious (as Whitman did), or at least something not to be ashamed of or embarrassed about. It was the first and probably biggest step I took into English composition and critical writing. Acting upon my professor's suggestion, I intentionally tried to show my "individuality" and to "glorify" "I" in my papers by using as many "I's" as possible—"I think," "I believe," "I see"—and deliberately cut out quotations from authorities. It was rather painful to hand in such "pompous" (I mean immodest) papers to my instructors. But to an extent it worked. After a while I became more comfortable with only "the shadow of myself." I felt more at ease to put down *my* thoughts without looking over my shoulder to worry about the attitudes of my teachers or the reactions of the Party secretaries, and to speak out as "bluntly" and "immodestly" as my American instructors demanded.

But writing many "I's" was only the beginning of the process of redefining myself. Speaking of redefining myself is, in an important sense, speaking of redefining the word "I." By such a redefinition I mean not only the change in how I envisioned myself, but also the change in how *I* perceived the world. The old "I" used to embody only one set of values, but now it had to embody multiple sets of values. To be truly "myself," which I knew was a key to my success in learning English composition, meant *not to be my Chinese self* at all. That is to say, when I write in English I have to wrestle with and abandon (at least temporarily) the whole system of ideology which previously defined me in myself. I had to forget Marxist doctrines (even though I do not see myself as a Marxist by choice) and the Party lines imprinted in my mind and familiarize myself with a system of capitalist/bourgeois values. I had to put aside an ideology of collectivism and adopt the values of individualism. In composition as well as in literature classes, I had to make a fundamental adjustment: If I used to examine society and literary materials through the microscopes of Marxist dialectical materialism and historical materialism, I now had to learn to look through the microscopes the other way around, i.e., to learn to look at and understand the world from the point of view of "idealism." (I must add here that there are American professors who use a Marxist approach in their teaching.)

The word "idealism," which affects my view of both myself and the universe, is loaded with social connotations, and can serve as a good example of how redefining a key word can be a pivotal part of redefining my ideological identity as a whole.

To me, idealism is the philosophical foundation of the dictum of English composition: "Be yourself." In order to write good English, I knew that I had to be myself, which actually meant not to be my Chinese self. It meant that I had to create an English self and be *that* self. And to be that English self, I felt, I had to understand and accept idealism the way a Westerner does. That is to say, I had to accept the way a Westerner sees himself in relation to the universe and society. On the one hand, I knew a lot about idealism. But on the other hand, I knew nothing about it. I mean I knew a lot about idealism through the propaganda and objections of its opponent, Marxism, but I knew little about it from its own point of view. When I thought of the word "materialism"—which is a major part of Marxism and in China has repeatedly been "shown" to be the absolute truth—there were always positive connotations, and words like "right," "true," etc., flashed in my mind. On the other hand, the word "idealism" always came to me with the dark connotations that surround words like "absurd," "illogical," "wrong," etc. In China "idealism" is depicted as a ferocious and ridiculous enemy of Marxist philosophy. Idealism, as the simplified definition imprinted in my mind had it, is the view that the material world does not exist; that all that exists is the mind and its ideas. It is just the opposite of Marxist dialectical materialism which sees the mind as a product of the material world. It is not too difficult to see that idealism, with its idea that mind is of primary importance, provides a philosophical foundation for the Western emphasis on the value of individual human minds, and hence individual human beings. Therefore, my final acceptance of myself as of primary importance—an importance that overshadowed that of authority figures in English composition—was, I decided, dependent on an acceptance of idealism.

My struggle with idealism came mainly from my efforts to understand and to write about works such as Coleridge's *Biographia Literaria* and Emerson's "Over-Soul." For a long time I was frustrated and puzzled by the idealism expressed by Coleridge and Emerson—given their ideas, such as "I think, therefore I am" (Coleridge obviously borrowed from Descartes) and "the transparent eyeball" (Emerson's view of himself)—because in my mind, drenched as it was in dialectical materialism, there was always a little voice whispering in my ear "You are, therefore you think." I could not see how human consciousness, which is not material, could create apples and trees. My intellectual conscience refused to let me believe that the human mind is the primary world and the material world secondary. Finally, I had to imagine that I was looking at a world with my head upside down. When I imagined that I was in a new body (born with the head upside down) it was easier to forget biases imprinted in my sub-consciousness about idealism, the mind, and my former self. Starting from scratch, the new inverted self—which I called my "English Self" and into which I have transformed myself— could understand and *accept,* with ease, idealism as "the truth" and "himself" (i.e., my English Self) as the "creator" of the world.

Here is how I created my new "English Self," I played a "game" similar to ones played by mental therapists. First I made a list of (simplified) features about writing associated with my old identity (the Chinese Self), both ideological and logical, and then beside the first list I added a column of features about writing associated with my new identity (the English Self). After that I pictured myself getting out of my old identity, the timid, humble, modest Chinese "I," and creeping into my new identity (often in the form of a new skin or a mask), the confident, assertive, and aggressive English "I." The new "Self" helped me to remember and accept the different rules of Chinese and English composition and the values that underpin these rules. In a sense, creating an English Self is a way of reconciling my old cultural values with the new values required by English writing, without losing the former. 10

---

1 How did the new conventions of writing Shen had to learn when he emigrated from China to the United States require him to become aware of and change cultural and political presuppositions?

2 In Shen's experience, what were the important differences between Western and Chinese views of individuality? What contrasting assumptions are inherent in the grammatical and rhetorical stances he was encouraged to adopt in both cultures?

3 Have you been encouraged in writing classes to assert your individuality or conform to a group perspective? Discuss your experiences.

4 In Shen's experiences, the language he is encouraged to use ("I" or "we") conveys what is considered valid by the given society (whether China or the United States). What insight does this give you into ethnocentrism? How do you think being part of American culture influences your use of the pronoun "I"? (Glossary: *Ethnocentricity*.)

5 How does Shen organize his analysis of the differences between the Western and Chinese views of the self using the comparison/contrast format? Does he use a point-by-point or subject-by-subject method of organization? In your opinion, is the method he chooses well suited to his thesis? (Glossary: *Comparison and Contrast*.)

6 What other issues of language related to gender and ethnicity have you encountered in writing classes that might be termed ideological in the sense that they reveal an underlying value system? How would you characterize your own writing style? Do you tend to employ or avoid the first person singular? Under what circumstances would you feel comfortable using "I"?

Sexism in English: A 1990s Update

Alleen Pace Nilsen

◆ ALLEEN PACE NILSEN is currently a professor at Arizona State University, where she specializes in children's literature and the study of sexist language. Her books on language include *Sexism and Language* (1977), *Language Play* (with D. Nilsen, 1983), and *The Language of Humor/The Humor of Language* (with D. Nilsen, 1983). More than twenty years ago, as assistant vice president for academic affairs at ASU, she began a card catalog of sexist language, an interest that she has pursued with results that can be seen in the following article.

The approach Nilsen takes is sociolinguistic—that is, she analyzes how slang, metaphors, definitions, and other usages reveal underlying societal attitudes about what it has meant to be a man or woman in this society over the past twenty-five years. She discovers a great many sexist attitudes toward both males and females and some evidence that recent linguistic reforms have been successful in reducing the use of sexist language.

> **TO CONSIDER** What expressions, metaphors, or slang reflect our society's attitude toward women?

Twenty years ago I embarked on a study of the sexism inherent in American English. I had just returned to Ann Arbor, Michigan, after living for two years (1967–69) in Kabul, Afghanistan, where I had begun to look critically at the role society assigned to women. The Afghan version of the *chaderi* prescribed for Moslem women was particularly confining. Afghan jokes and folklore were blatantly sexist, such as this proverb: "If you see an old man, sit down and take a lesson; if you see an old woman, throw a stone."   1

But it wasn't only the native culture that made me question women's roles, it was also the American community.   2

Most of the American women were like myself—wives and mothers whose husbands were either career diplomats, employees of USAID, or college professors who had been recruited to work on various contract teams. We were suddenly bereft of our traditional roles: some of us became alcoholics, others got very good at bridge, while still others searched desperately for ways to contribute either to our families or to the Afghans. The local economy provided few jobs for women and certainly none for foreigners; we were isolated from former friends and the social goals we had grown up with.   3

When I returned in the fall of 1969 to the University of Michigan in Ann Arbor, I was surprised to find that many other women were also questioning the expectations they had grown up with. In the spring of 1970, a women's conference was announced. I hired a babysitter and attended, but I returned home more troubled than ever. The militancy of these women frightened me. Since I wasn't ready for a revolution, I decided I would have my own feminist movement. I would study the English language and see what it could tell me about sexism. I started reading a desk dictionary and making notecards on every entry that seemed to tell something about male and female. I soon had a dog-eared dictionary, along with a collection of notecards filling two shoe boxes.   4

Ironically, I started reading the dictionary because I wanted to avoid getting involved in social issues, but what happened was that my notecards brought me right back to looking at society. Language and society are as intertwined as a chicken and an egg. The language a culture uses is telltale evidence of the values and beliefs of that culture. And because there is a lag in how fast a language changes—new words can easily be introduced, but it takes a long time for old words and usages to disappear—a careful look at English will reveal the attitudes that our ancestors held and that we as a culture are therefore predisposed to hold. My notecards revealed three main points. Friends have offered the opinion that I didn't need to read the dictionary to learn such obvious facts. Nevertheless, it was interesting to have linguistic evidence of sociological observations.   5

WOMEN ARE SEXY; MEN ARE SUCCESSFUL

First, in American culture a woman is valued for the attractiveness and sexiness of her body, while a man is valued for his physical strength and accomplishments. A woman is sexy. A man is successful.   6

7   A persuasive piece of evidence supporting this view are the eponyms—words that have come from someone's name–found in English. I had a two-and-a-half-inch stack of cards taken from men's names but less than a half-inch stack from women's names, and most of those came from Greek mythology. In the words that came into American English since we separated from Britain, there are many eponyms based on the names of famous American men: *Bartlett pear, boysenberry, diesel engine, Franklin stove, Ferris wheel, Gatling gun, mason jar, sideburns, sousaphone, Schick test,* and *Winchester rifle.* The only common eponyms taken from American women's names are *Alice blue* (after Alice Roosevelt Longworth), *bloomers* (after Amelia Jenks Bloomer), and *Mae West jacket* (after the buxom actress). Two out of the three feminine eponyms relate closely to a woman's physical anatomy, while the masculine eponyms (except for *sideburns* after General Burnsides) have nothing to do with the namesake's body but, instead, honor the man for an accomplishment of some kind.

8   Although in Greek mythology women played a bigger role than they did in the biblical stories of the Judeo-Christian cultures and so the names of goddesses are accepted parts of the language in such place names as Pomona from the goddess of fruit and Athens from Athena and in such common words as *cereal* from Ceres, *psychology* from Psyche, and *arachnoid* from Arachne, the same tendency to think of women in relation to sexuality is seen in the eponyms *aphrodisiac* from Aphrodite, the Greek name for the goddess of love and beauty, and *veneral disease* from Venus, the Roman name for Aphrodite.

9   Another interesting word from Greek mythology is *Amazon.* According to Greek folk etymology, the *a* means "without" as in *atypical* or *amoral,* while *mazon* comes from *mazos* meaning "breast" as still seen in *mastectomy.* In the Greek legend, Amazon women cut off their right breasts so that they could better shoot their bows. Apparently, the storytellers had a feeling that for women to play the active, "masculine" role the Amazons adopted for themselves, they had to trade in part of their femininity.

10   This preoccupation with women's breasts is not limited to ancient stories. As a volunteer for the University of Wisconsin's *Dictionary of American Regional English (DARE),* I read a western trapper's diary from the 1930s. I was to make notes of any unusual usages or language patterns. My most interesting finding was that the trapper referred to a range of mountains as *The Teats,* a metaphor based on the similarity between the shapes of the mountains and women's breasts. Because today we use the French wording, *The Grand Tetons,* the metaphor isn't as obvious, but I wrote to mapmakers and found the following listings: *Nippletop* and *Little Nipple Top* near Mount Marcy in the Adirondacks; *Nipple Mountain* in Archuleta County, Colorado; *Nipple Peak* in Coke County, Texas; *Nipple Butte* in Pennington, South Dakota; *Squaw Peak* in Placer County, California (and many other locations); *Maiden's Peak* and *Squaw Tit* (they're the same mountain) in the Cascade Range in Oregon; *Mary's Nipple* near Salt Lake City, Utah; and *Jane Russell Peaks* near Stark, New Hampshire.

11   Except for the movie star Jane Russell, the women being referred to are anonymous—it's only a sexual part of their body that is mentioned. When topographical features are named after men, it's probably not going to be to draw

attention to a sexual part of their bodies but instead to honor individuals for an accomplishment. For example, no one thinks of a part of the male body when hearing a reference to Pike's Peak, Colorado, or Jackson Hole, Wyoming.

Going back to what I learned from my dictionary cards, I was surprised to realize how many pairs of words we have in which the feminine word has acquired sexual connotations while the masculine word retains a serious businesslike aura. For example, a *callboy* is the person who calls actors when it is time for them to go on stage, but a *callgirl* is a prostitute. Compare *sir* and *madam*. *Sir* is a term of respect, while *madam* has acquired the specialized meaning of a brothel manager. Something similar has happened to *master* and *mistress*. Would you rather have a painting by an *old master* or an *old mistress*?   12

It's because the word *woman* had sexual connotations, as in "She's his woman," that people began avoiding its use, hence such terminology as *ladies' room, lady of the house,* and *girls' school* or *school for young ladies*. Feminists, who ask that people use the term *woman* rather than *girl* or *lady*, are rejecting the idea that *woman* is primarily a sexual term. They have been at least partially successful in that today *woman* is commonly used to communicate gender without intending implications about sexuality.   13

I found two hundred pairs of words with masculine and feminine forms, e.g., *heir-heiress, hero-heroine, steward-stewardess, usher-usherette*. In nearly all such pairs, the masculine word is considered the base, with some kind of a feminine suffix being added. The masculine form is the one from which compounds are made, e.g., from *king-queen* comes *kingdom* but not *queendom*, from *sportsman-sportslady* comes *sportsmanship* but not *sportsladyship*. There is one—and only one—semantic area in which the masculine word is not the base or more powerful word. This is in the area dealing with sex and marriage. When someone refers to a *virgin*, a listener will probably think of a female, unless the speaker specifies *male* or uses a masculine pronoun. The same is true for *prostitute*.   14

In relation to marriage, there is much linguistic evidence showing that weddings are more important to women than to men. A woman cherishes the wedding and is considered a bride for a whole year, but a man is referred to as a groom only on the day of the wedding. The word *bride* appears in *bridal attendant, bridal gown, bridesmaid, bridal shower*, and even *bridegroom*. *Groom* comes from the Middle English *grom*, meaning "man," and in the sense is seldom used outside of the wedding. With most pairs of male/female words, people habitually put the masculine word first, *Mr. and Mrs., his and hers, boys and girls, men and women, kings and queens, brothers and sisters, guys and dolls*, and *host and hostess*, but it is the *bride and groom* who are talked about, not the *groom and bride*.   15

The importance of marriage to a woman is also shown by the fact that when a marriage ends in death, the woman gets the title of *widow*. A man gets the derived title of *widower*. This term is not used in other phrases or contexts, but *widow* is seen in *widowhood, widow's peak*, and *widow's walk*. A *widow* in a card game is an extra hand of cards, while in typesetting it is an extra line of type.   16

How changing cultural ideas bring changes to language is clearly visible in this semantic area. The feminist movement has caused the differences between   17 the sexes to be downplayed, and since I did my dictionary study two decades ago, the word *singles* has largely replaced such sex specific and value-laden terms as *bachelor, old maid, spinster, divorcee, widow,* and *widower.* And in 1970 I wrote that when a man is called *a professional* he is thought to be a doctor or a lawyer, but when people hear a woman referred to as *a professional* they are likely to think of a prostitute. That's not as true today because so many women have become doctors and lawyers that it's no longer incongruous to think of women in those professional roles.

18   Another change that has taken place is in wedding announcements. They used to be sent out from the bride's parents and did not even give the name of the groom's parents. Today, most couples choose to list either all or none of the parents' names. Also it is now much more likely that both the bride and groom's picture will be in the newspaper, while a decade ago only the bride's picture was published on the "Women's" or the "Society" page. Even the traditional wording of the wedding ceremony is being changed. Many officials now pronounce the couple "husband and wife" instead of the old "man and wife," and they ask the bride if she promises "to love, honor, and cherish," instead of "to love, honor, and obey."

WOMEN ARE PASSIVE; MEN ARE ACTIVE

19   The wording of the wedding ceremony also relates to the second point that my cards showed, which is that women are expected to play a passive or weak role while men play an active or strong role. In the traditional ceremony, the official asks, "Who gives the bride away?" and the father answers, "I do." Some fathers answer, "Her mother and I do," but that doesn't solve the problem inherent in the question. The idea that a bride is something to be handed over from one man to another bothers people because it goes back to the days when a man's servants, his children, and his wife were all considered to be his property. They were known by his name because they belonged to him, and he was responsible for their actions and their debts.

20   The grammar used in talking or writing about weddings as well as other sexual relationships shows the expectation of men playing the active role. Men *wed* women while women *become* brides of men. A man *possesses* a woman; he *deflowers* her; he *performs;* he *scores;* he *takes away* her virginity. Although a woman can *seduce* a man, she cannot offer him her virginity. When talking about virginity, the only way to make the woman the actor in the sentence is to say that "She lost her virginity," but people lose things by accident rather than by purposeful actions, and so she's only the grammatical, not the real-life, actor.

21   The reason that women tried to bring the term *Ms.* into the language to replace *Miss* and *Mrs.* relates to this point. Married women resent being identified only under their husband's names. For example, when Susan Glascoe did something newsworthy, she would be identified in the newspaper only as Mrs. John Glascoe. The dictionary cards showed what appeared to be an attitude on the part of the editors that it was almost indecent to let a respectable woman's name march unaccompanied across the pages of a dictionary. Women were listed

with male names whether or not the male contributed to the woman's reason for being in the dictionary or in his own right was as famous as the woman. For example, Charlotte Brontë was identified as Mrs. Arthur B. Nicholls, Amelia Earhart as Mrs. George Palmer Putnam, Helen Hayes as Mrs. Charles MacArthur, Jenny Lind as Mme. Otto Goldschmit, Cornelia Otis Skinner as the daughter of Otis, Harriet Beecher Stowe as the sister of Henry Ward Beecher, and Edith Sitwell as the sister of Osbert and Sacheverell. A very small number of women got into the dictionary without the benefit of a masculine escort. They were rebels and crusaders: temperance leaders Frances Elizabeth Caroline Willard and Carry Nation, women's rights leaders Carrie Chapman Catt and Elizabeth Cady Stanton, birth control educator Margaret Sanger, religious leader Mary Baker Eddy, and slaves Harriet Tubman and Phillis Wheatley.

Etiquette books used to teach that if a woman had *Mrs.* in front of her name, then the husband's name should follow because *Mrs.* is an abbreviated form of *Mistress* and a woman couldn't be a mistress of herself. As with many arguments about "correct" language usage, this isn't very logical because *Miss* is also an abbreviation of *Mistress*. Feminists hoped to simplify matters by introducing *Ms.* as an alternative to both *Mrs.* and *Miss,* but what happened is that *Ms.* largely replaced *Miss,* to become a catch-all business title for women. Many married women still prefer the title *Mrs.,* and some resent being addressed with the term *Ms.* As one frustrated newspaper reporter complained, "Before I can write about a woman, I have to know not only her marital status but also her political philosophy." The result of such complications may contribute to the demise of titles, which are already being ignored by many computer programmers who find it more efficient to simply use names, for example in a business letter: "Dear Joan Garcia," instead of "Dear Mrs. Joan Garcia," "Dear Ms. Garcia," or "Dear Mrs. Louis Garcia." 22

The titles given to royalty provide an example of how males can be disadvantaged by the assumption that they are always to play the more powerful role. In British royalty, when a male holds a title, his wife is automatically given the feminine equivalent. But the reverse is not true. For example, a *count* is a high political officer with a *countess* being his wife. The same is true for a *duke* and a *duchess* and a *king* and a *queen.* But when a female holds the royal title, the man she marries does not automatically acquire the matching title. For example, Queen Elizabeth's husband has the title of *prince* rather than *king,* but if Prince Charles should become king while he is still married to Lady or Princess Diana, she will be known as the queen. The reasoning appears to be that since masculine words are stronger, they are reserved for true heirs and withheld from males coming into the royal family by marriage. If Prince Phillip were called *King Phillip,* it would be much easier for British subjects to forget where the true power lies. 23

The names that people give their children show the hopes and dreams they have for them, and when we look at the differences between male and female names in a culture, we can see the cumulative expectations of that culture. In our culture girls often have names taken from small, aesthetically pleasing items, e.g., *Ruby, Jewel,* and *Pearl. Esther* and *Stella* mean "star," *Ada* means "ornament," and *Vanessa* means "butterfly." Boys are more likely to be given names with 24 meanings of power and strength, e.g., *Neil* means "champion," *Martin* is from Mars, the God of War, *Raymond* means "wise protection," *Harold* means "chief of the army," *Ira* means "vigilant," *Rex* means "king," and *Richard* means "strong king."

25   We see similar differences in food metaphors. Food is a passive substance just sitting there waiting to be eaten. Many people have recognized this and so no longer feel comfortable describing women as "delectable morsels." However, when I was a teenager, it was considered a compliment to refer to a girl (we didn't call anyone a *woman* until she was middle-aged) as a *cute tomato*, a *peach*, a *dish*, a *cookie, honey, sugar*, or *sweetie-pie*. When being affectionate, women will occasionally call a man *honey* or *sweetie*, but in general, food metaphors are used much less often with men than with women. If a man is called a *fruit*, his masculinity is being questioned. But it's perfectly acceptable to use a food metaphor if the food is heavier and more substantive than that used for women. For example pin-up pictures of women have long been known as *cheesecake*, but when Burt Reynolds posed for a nude centerfold the picture was immediately dubbed *beefcake*, c.f., *a hunk of meat*. That such sexual references to men have come into the language is another reflection of how society is beginning to lessen the differences between their attitudes toward men and women.

26   Something similar to the *fruit* metaphor happens with references to plants. We insult a man by calling him a *pansy*, but it wasn't considered particularly insulting to talk about a girl being a *wallflower*, a *clinging vine*, or a *shrinking violent*, or to give girls such names as *Ivy, Rose, Lily, Iris, Daisy, Camellia, Heather*, and *Flora*. A plant metaphor can be used with a man if the plant is big and strong, for example, Andrew Jackson's nickname of *Old Hickory*. Also, the phrases *blooming idiots* and *budding geniuses* can be used with either sex, but notice how they are based on the most active thing a plant can do which is to bloom or bud.

27   Animal metaphors also illustrate the different expectations for males and females. Men are referred to as *studs, bucks*, and *wolves* while women are referred to with such metaphors as *kitten, bunny, beaver, bird, chick*, and *lamb*. In the 1950s we said that boys went *tomcatting*, but today it's just *catting around* and both boys and girls do it. When the term *foxy*, meaning that someone was sexy, first became popular it was used only for girls, but now someone of either sex can be described as *a fox*. Some animal metaphors that are used predominantly with men have negative connotations based on the size and/or strength of the animals, e.g., *beast, bullheaded, jackass, rat, loanshark*, and *vulture*. Negative metaphors used with women are based on smaller animals, e.g., *social butterfly, mousy, catty*, and *vixen*. The feminine terms connote action, but not the same kind of large scale action as with the masculine terms.

WOMEN ARE CONNECTED WITH NEGATIVE CONNOTATIONS; MEN WITH POSITIVE CONNOTATIONS

28   The final point that my notecards illustrated was how many positive connotations are associated with the concept of masculine, while there are either trivial

or negative connotations connected with the corresponding feminine concept. An example from the animal metaphors makes a good illustration. The word *shrew* taken from the name of a small but especially vicious animal was defined in my dictionary as "an ill-tempered scolding woman," but the word *shrewd* taken from the same root was defined as "marked by clever, discerning aware-ness" and was illustrated with the phrase "a shrewd businessman."

Early in life, children are conditioned to the superiority of the masculine   29
role. As child psychologists point out, little girls have much more freedom to experiment with sex roles than do little boys. If a little girl acts like a *tomboy,* most parents have mixed feelings, being at least partially proud. But if their lit-tle boy acts like a *sissy* (derived from *sister*), they call a psychologist. It's perfectly acceptable for a little girl to sleep in the crib that was purchased for her brother, to wear his hand-me-down jeans and shirts, and to ride the bicycle that he has outgrown. But few parents would put a boy baby in a white and gold crib dec-orated with frills and lace, and virtually no parents would have their little boys wear his sister's hand-me-down dresses, nor would they have their son ride a girl's pink bicycle with a flower-bedecked basket. The proper names given to girls and boys show this same attitude. Girls can have "boy" names—*Cris, Craig, Jo, Kelly, Shawn, Teri, Toni,* and *Sam*—but it doesn't work the other way around. A couple of generations ago, *Beverley, Frances, Hazel, Marion,* and *Shirley* were common boys' names. As parents gave these names to more and more girls, they fell into disuse for males, and some older men who have these names prefer to go by their initials or by such abbreviated forms as *Haze* or *Shirl.*

When a little girl is told to *be a lady,* she is being told to sit with her knees   30
together and to be quiet and dainty. But when a little boy is told to *be a man* he is being told to be noble, strong, and virtuous—to have all the qualities that the speaker looks on as desirable. The concept of manliness has such positive con-notations that it used to be a compliment to call someone a *he-man,* to say that he was doubly a man. Today many people are more ambivalent about this term and respond to it much as they do to the word *macho.* But calling someone a *manly man* or *a virile man* is nearly always meant as a compliment. *Virile* comes from the Indo-European *vir* meaning "man," which is also the basis of *virtuous.* Contrast the positive connotations of both *virile* and *virtuous* with the negative connotations of *hysterical.* The Greeks took this latter word from their name for *uterus* (as still seen in *hysterectomy*). They thought that women were the only ones who experienced uncontrolled emotional outbursts, and so the condition must have something to do with a part of the body that only women have.

Differences in the connotations between positive male and negative female   31
connotations can be seen in several pairs of words that differ denotatively only in the matter of sex. *Bachelor* as compared to *spinster* or *old maid* has such pos-itive connotations that women try to adopt them by using the term *bachelor-girl* or *bachelorette. Old maid* is so negative that it's the basis for metaphors: preten-tious and fussy old men are called *old maids,* as are the leftover kernels of unpopped popcorn, and the last card in a popular children's game.

Patron and *matron* (Middle English for *father* and *mother*) have such dif-   32
ferent levels of prestige that women try to borrow the more positive masculine connotations with the word *patroness,* literally "female father." Such a peculiar

term came about because of the high prestige attached to *patron* in such phrases as *a patron of the arts* or *a patron saint Matron* is more apt to be used in talking about a woman in charge of a jail or a public restroom.

33   When men are doing jobs that women often do, we apparently try to pay the men extra by giving them fancy titles, for example, a male cook is more likely to be called a *chef* while a male seamstress will get the title of *tailor*. The armed forces have a special problem in that they recruit under such slogans as "The Marine Corps builds men!" and "Join the Army! Become a Man." Once the recruits are enlisted, they find themselves doing much of the work that has been traditionally thought of as "women's work." The solution to getting the work done and not insulting anyone's masculinity was to change the titles as shown below:

waitress	orderly
nurse	medic or corpsman
secretary	clerk-typist
assistant	adjutant
dishwasher or kitchen helper	KP (kitchen police)

34   Compare *brave* and *squaw*. Early settlers in America truly admired Indian men and hence named them with a word that carried connotations of youth, vigor, and courage. But they used the Algonquin's name for "woman" and over the years it developed almost opposite connotations to those of *brave*. *Wizard* and *witch* contrast almost as much. The masculine *wizard* implies skill and wisdom combined with magic, while the feminine *witch* implies evil intentions combined with magic. Part of the unattractiveness of both *witch* and *squaw* is that they have been used so often to refer to old women, something with which our culture is particularly uncomfortable, just as the Afghans were. Imagine my surprise when I ran across the phrases *grandfatherly advice* and *old wives' tales* and realized that the underlying implication is the same as the Afghan proverb about old men being worth listening to while old women talk only foolishness.

35   Other terms that show how negative we view old women as compared to young women are *old nag* as compared to *filly*, *old crow* or *old bat* as compared to *bird*, and of being *catty* as compared to being *kittenish*. There is no matching set of metaphors for men. The chicken metaphor tells the whole story of a woman's life. In her youth she is a *chick*. Then she marries and begins *feathering her nest*. Soon she begins feeling *cooped up*, so she goes to *hen parties* where she *cackles* with her friends. Then she has her *brood*, begins to *henpeck* her husband, and finally turns into an *old biddy*.

36   I embarked on my study of the dictionary not with the intention of prescribing language change but simply to see what the language would tell me about sexism. Nevertheless I have been both surprised and pleased as I've watched the changes that have occurred over the past two decades. I'm one of those linguists who believes that new language customs will cause a new generation of speakers to grow up with different expectations. This is why I'm happy about people's efforts to use inclusive language, to say *he or she* or *they* when

speaking about individuals whose names they do not know. I'm glad that leading publishers have developed guidelines to help writers use language that is fair to both sexes, and I'm glad that most newspapers and magazines list women by their own names instead of only by their husbands' names and that educated and thoughtful people no longer begin their business letters with "Dear Sir" or "Gentlemen," but instead use a memo form or begin with such salutations as "Dear Colleagues," "Dear Reader," or "Dear Committee Members." I'm also glad that such words as *poetess, authoress, conductress,* and *aviatrix* now sound quaint and old-fashioned and that *chairman* is giving way to *chair or head, mailman* to *mail carrier, clergyman* to *clergy,* and *stewardess* to *flight attendant.* I was also pleased when the National Oceanic and Atmospheric Administration bowed to feminist complaints and in the late 1970s began to alternate men's and women's names for hurricanes. However, I wasn't so pleased to discover that the change did not immediately erase sexist thoughts from everyone's mind, as shown by a headline about Hurricane David in a 1979 New York tabloid, "David Rapes Virgin Islands." More recently a similar metaphor appeared in a headline in the *Arizona Republic* about Hurricane Charlie, "Charlie Quits Carolinas, Flirts with Virginia."

What these incidents show is that sexism is not something existing independently in American English or in the particular dictionary that I happened to read. Rather, it exists in people's minds. Language is like an X ray in providing visible evidence of invisible thoughts. The best thing about people being interested in and discussing sexist language is that as they make conscious decisions about what pronouns they will use, what jokes they will tell or laugh at, how they will write their names, or how they will begin their letters, they are forced to think about the underlying issue of sexism. This is good because as a problem that begins in people's assumptions and expectations, it's a problem that will be solved only when a great many people have given it a great deal of thought. 37

---

1 What circumstances led Nilsen to investigate sexism in the English language? How did her agenda differ from that of the "feminist" movement?

2 In each of the following areas, what social or cultural attitudes does Nilsen discover revealing sexist language: (a) English words derived from the name of a person; (b) geographical names; (c) pairs of words, one masculine and one feminine; (d) words referring to food, plants, animals, and women; (e) names given to male and female infants; (f) the pronoun Ms.; (g) biographical or dictionary listings of famous women; (h) connotations of terms that are masculine and feminine.

3 Has the fundamental cultural dynamic that Nilsen observed—that is, valuing women for physical appearance and men for what they achieve—changed in ways that can be seen in language? To assess the extent to which expectations in gender roles have changed, you might wish to look at the language any general-circulation magazine over the last twenty years has used to refer to men and women.

4 What is the relationship between the personal anecdote with which Nilsen begins her essay (para. 1–5) and her thesis regarding the different connotations of terms associated with masculinity and femininity? (Glossary: *Introduction, Conclusion, Thesis, Sexist Language.*)

5 How does Nilsen use the comparison/contrast method to support her claim that users of English unwittingly glorify maleness and denigrate femaleness? For example, what is the significance of the titles different professions give to a job depending on whether it is performed by a male or a female? (Glossary: *Comparison and Contrast.*)

6 What "women's studies" classes are available at your college? To what extent do the content and methodology of these courses emphasize political issues of power and oppression in ways that have implications for the study of sexist language? For example, what issue does the following cartoon depict?

Source: Mike Peters. Reprinted by permission: Tribune Media Services.

AIDS and Its Metaphors   *Susan Sontag*

◆ SUSAN SONTAG is an influential critic and novelist who has taught English and philosophy at the University of Connecticut, Harvard, Columbia, and Rutgers. She received the National Book Critics Circle Prize in 1978 and is the author of numerous books of critical essays, including *On Photography* (1977) and *AIDS and Its Metaphors* (1988), from which the following selection is taken.

After being diagnosed with cancer in the 1970s, Sontag underwent treatment and was subsequently cured. This experience sparked her interest in how the meanings of various illnesses (syphilis, tuberculosis, leprosy) are socially constructed. The defining features of AIDS at its metaphorical level are the military and medical metaphors that are used to describe its progress. AIDS is conceived of as a modern-day plague that evokes medieval religious attitudes and encourages the public to view its victims as being punished for moral transgressions. Having experienced the isolation of being classified as a pariah because of having cancer (a not unusual fate of cancer victims), Sontag is sensitive to the dehumanizing effect of the stereotyped images through which Americans understand cancer and AIDS.

> **TO CONSIDER**   Does language used to describe people with AIDS create particular impressions that unconsciously manipulate perceptions of them?

1

By metaphor I meant nothing more or less than the earliest and most succinct definition I know, which is Aristotle's, in his *Poetics* (1457b). "Metaphor," Aristotle wrote, "consists in giving the thing a name that belongs to something else." Saying a thing is or is like something-it-is-not is a mental operation as old as philosophy and poetry, and the spawning ground of most kinds of understanding, including scientific understanding, and expressiveness. (To acknowledge which I prefaced the polemic against metaphors of illness I wrote ten years ago with a brief, hectic flourish of metaphor, in mock exorcism of the seductiveness of metaphorical thinking.) Of course, one cannot think without metaphors. But that does not mean there aren't some metaphors we might well abstain from or try to retire. As, of course, all thinking is interpretation. But that does not mean it isn't sometimes correct to be "against" interpretation.

Take, for instance, a tenacious metaphor that has shaped (and obscured the understanding of) so much of the political life of this century, the one that distributes, and polarizes, attitudes and social movements according to their relation to a "left" and a "right." The terms are usually traced back to the French Revolution, to the seating arrangements of the National Assembly in 1789, when republicans and radicals sat to the presiding officer's left and monarchists and conservatives sat to the right. But historical memory alone can't account for the startling longevity of this metaphor. It seems more likely that its persistence in discourse about politics to this day comes from a felt aptness to the modern, secular imagination of metaphors drawn from the body's orientation in space— left and right, top and bottom, forward and backward—for describing social conflict, a metaphoric practice that did add something new to the perennial description of society as a kind of body, a well-disciplined body ruled by a "head." This has been the dominant metaphor for the polity since Plato and

Aristotle, perhaps because of its usefulness in justifying repression. Even more than comparing society to a family, comparing it to a body makes an authoritarian ordering of society seem inevitable, immutable.

Rudolf Virchow, the founder of cellular pathology, furnishes one of the rare scientifically significant examples of the reverse procedure, using political metaphors to talk about the body. In the biological controversies of the 1850s, it was the metaphor of the liberal state that Virchow found useful in advancing his theory of the cell as the fundamental unit of life. However complex their structures, organisms are, first of all, simply "multicellular"—multicitizened, as it were; the body is a "republic" or "unified commonwealth." Among scientist-rhetoricians Virchow was a maverick, not least because of the politics of his metaphors, which, by mid-nineteenth-century standards, are antiauthoritarian. But likening the body to a society, liberal or not, is less common than comparisons to other complex, integrated systems, such as a machine or an economic enterprise.

At the beginning of Western medicine, in Greece, important metaphors for the unity of the body were adapted from the arts. One such metaphor, harmony, was singled out for scorn several centuries later by Lucretius, who argued that it could not do justice to the fact that the body consists of essential and unessential organs, or even to the body's materiality: that is, to death. Here are the closing lines of Lucretius' dismissal of the musical metaphor—the earliest attack I know on metaphoric thinking about illness and health:

> Not all the organs, you must realize,
> Are equally important nor does health
> Depend on all alike, but there are some—
> The seeds of breathing, warm vitality—
> Whereby we are kept alive; when these are gone
> Life leaves our dying members. So, since mind
> And spirit are by nature part of man,
> Let the musicians keep that term brought down
> To them from lofty Helicon—or maybe
> They found it somewhere else, made it apply
> To something hitherto nameless in their craft—
> I speak of *harmony*. Whatever it is,
> Give it back to the musicians.
> —*De Rerum Natura*, III, 124–35 trans. Rolfe Humphries

A history of metaphoric thinking about the body on this potent level of generality would include many images drawn from other arts and technology, notably architecture. Some metaphors are anti-explanatory, like the sermonizing, and poetic, notion enunciated by Saint Paul of the body as a temple. Some have considerable scientific resonance, such as the notion of the body as a factory, an image of the body's functioning under the sign of health, and of the body as a fortress, an image of the body that features catastrophe.

The fortress image has a long prescientific genealogy, with illness itself a metaphor for mortality, for human frailty and vulnerability. John Donne in his great cycle of prose arias on illness, *Devotions upon Emergent Occasions* (1627), written when he thought he was dying, describes illness as an enemy that invades, that lays siege to the body-fortress:

> We study Health, and we deliberate upon our meats, and drink, and ayre, and exercises, and we hew and wee polish every stone, that goes to that building; and so our Health is a long and a regular work; But in a minute a Canon batters all, overthrowes all, demolishes all; a Sicknes unprevented for all our diligence, unsuspected for all our curiositie. . . .

Some parts are more fragile than others: Donne speaks of the brain and the liver being able to endure the siege of an "unnatural" or "rebellious" fever that "will blow up the heart, like a mine, in a minute." In Donne's images, it is the illness that invades. Modern medical thinking could be said to begin when the gross military metaphor becomes specific, which can only happen with the advent of a new kind of scrutiny, represented in Virchow's cellular pathology, and a more precise understanding that illnesses were caused by specific, identifiable, visible (with the aid of a microscope) organisms. It was when the invader was seen not as the illness but as the microorganism that causes the illness that medicine really began to be effective, and the military metaphors took on new credibility and precision. Since then, military metaphors have more and more come to infuse all aspects of the description of the medical situation. Disease is seen as an invasion of alien organisms, to which the body responds by its own military operations, such as the mobilizing of immunological "defenses," and medicine is "aggressive," as in the language of most chemotherapies.

The grosser metaphor survives in public health education, where disease is regularly described as invading the society, and efforts to reduce mortality from a given disease are called a fight, a struggle, a war. Military metaphors became prominent early in the century, in campaigns mounted during World War I to educate people about syphilis, and after the war about tuberculosis. One example, from the campaign against tuberculosis conducted in Italy in the 1920s, is a poster called "*Guerre alle Mosche*" (War against Flies), which illustrates the lethal effects of fly-borne diseases. The flies themselves are shown as enemy aircraft dropping bombs of death on an innocent population. The bombs have inscriptions. One says "*Microbi*," microbes. Another says "*Germi della tisi*," the germs of tuberculosis. Another simply says "*Malattia*," illness. A skeleton clad in a hooded black cloak rides the foremost fly as passenger or pilot. In another poster, "With These Weapons We Will Conquer Tuberculosis," the figure of death is shown pinned to the wall by drawn swords, each of which bears an inscription that names a measure for combating tuberculosis. "Cleanliness" is written on one blade. "Sun" on another. "Air." "Rest." "Proper food." "Hygiene." (Of course, none of these weapons was of any significance. What conquers—that is, cures—tuberculosis is antibiotics, which were not discovered until some twenty years later, in the 1940s.)

Where once it was the physician who waged *bellum contra morbum,* the war against disease, now it's the whole society. Indeed, the transformation of war-making into an occasion for mass ideological mobilization has made the notion of war useful as a metaphor for all sorts of ameliorative campaigns whose goals are cast as the defeat of an "enemy." We have had wars against poverty, now replaced by "the war on drugs," as well as wars against specific diseases, such as cancer. Abuse of the military metaphor may be inevitable in a capitalist society, a society that increasingly restricts the scope and credibility of appeals to ethical principle, in which it is thought foolish not to subject one's actions to the calculus of self-interest and profitability. War-making is one of the few activities that people are not supposed to view "realistically"; that is, with an eye to expense and practical outcome. In all-out war, expenditure is all-out, unprudent—war being defined as an emergency in which no sacrifice is excessive. But the wars against diseases are not just calls for more zeal, and more money to be spent on research. The metaphor implements the way particularly dreaded diseases are envisaged as an alien "other," as enemies are in modern war; and the move from the demonization of the illness to the attribution of fault to the patient is an inevitable one, no matter if patients are thought of as victims. Victims suggest innocence. And innocence, by the inexorable logic that governs all relational terms, suggests guilt.

Military metaphors contribute to the stigmatizing of certain illnesses and, by extension, of those who are ill. It was the discovery of the stigmatization of people who have cancer that led me to write *Illness as Metaphor*.

Twelve years ago, when I became a cancer patient, what particularly enraged me—and distracted me from my own terror and despair at my doctors' gloomy prognosis—was seeing how much the very reputation of this illness added to the suffering of those who have it. Many fellow patients with whom I talked during my initial hospitalizations, like others I was to meet during the subsequent two and a half years that I received chemotherapy as an outpatient in several hospitals here and in France, evinced disgust at their disease and a kind of shame. They seemed to be in the grip of fantasies about their illness by which I was quite unseduced. And it occurred to me that some of these notions were the converse of now thoroughly discredited beliefs about tuberculosis. As tuberculosis had been often regarded sentimentally, as an enhancement of identity, cancer was regarded with irrational revulsion, as a diminution of the self. There were also similar fictions of responsibility and of a characterological predisposition to the illness: cancer is regarded as a disease to which the psychically defeated, the inexpressive, the repressed—especially those who have repressed anger or sexual feelings—are particularly prone, as tuberculosis was regarded throughout the nineteenth and early twentieth centuries (indeed, until it was discovered how to cure it) as a disease apt to strike the hypersensitive, the talented, the passionate.

These parallels—between myths about tuberculosis to which we can all feel superior now, and superstitions about cancer still given credence by many cancer patients and their families—gave me the main strategy of a little book I decided to write about the mystifications surrounding cancer. I didn't think it would be useful—and I wanted to be useful—to tell yet one more story in the first person of how someone learned that she or he had cancer, wept, struggled, was comforted, suffered, took courage . . . though mine was also that story. A narrative, it seemed to me, would be less useful than an idea. For narrative pleasure I would appeal to other writers; and although more examples from literature immediately came to mind for the glamorous disease, tuberculosis, I found the diagnosis of cancer as a disease of those who have not really lived in such books as Tolstoy's "The Death of Ivan Ilyich," Arnold Bennett's *Riceyman Steps,* and Bernanos's *The Diary of a Country Priest.*

And so I wrote my book, wrote it very quickly, spurred by evangelical zeal as well as anxiety about how much time I had left to do any living or writing in. My aim was to alleviate unnecessary suffering—exactly as Nietzsche formulated it, in a passage in *Daybreak* that I came across recently:

> *Thinking about illness!*—To calm the imagination of the invalid, so that at least he should not, as hitherto, have to suffer more from thinking about his illness than from the illness itself—that, I think, would be something! It would be a great deal!

The purpose of my book was to calm the imagination, not to incite it. Not to confer meaning, which is the traditional purpose of literary endeavor, but to deprive something of meaning: to apply that quixotic, highly polemical strategy, "against interpretation," to the real world this time. To the body. My purpose was, above all, practical. For it was my doleful observation, repeated again and again, that the metaphoric trappings that deform the experience of having cancer have very real consequences: they inhibit people from seeking treatment early enough, or from making a greater effort to get competent treatment. The metaphors and myths, I was convinced, kill. (For instance, they make people irrationally fearful of effective measures such as chemotherapy, and foster credence in thoroughly useless remedies such as diets and psychotherapy.) I wanted to offer other people who were ill and those who care for them an instrument to dissolve these metaphors, these inhibitions. I hoped to persuade terrified people who were ill to consult doctors, or to change their incompetent doctors for competent ones, who would give them proper care. To regard cancer as if it were just a disease—a very serious one, but just a disease. Not a curse, not a punishment, not an embarrassment. Without "meaning." And not necessarily a death sentence (one of the mystifications is that cancer = death). *Illness as Metaphor* is not just a polemic, it is an exhortation. I was saying: Get the doctors to tell you the truth; be an informed, active patient; find yourself good treatment, because good treatment does exist (amid the widespread ineptitude). Although *the* remedy does not exist, more than half of all cases can be cured by existing methods of treatment.

In the decade since I wrote *Illness as Metaphor*—and was cured of my own cancer, confounding my doctors' pessimism— attitudes about cancer have evolved. Getting cancer is not quite as much of a stigma, a creator of "spoiled identity" (to use Erving Goffman's expression). The word cancer is uttered more freely, and people are not often described anymore in obituaries as dying of a "very long illness." Although European and Japanese doctors still regularly impart a cancer diagnosis first to the family, and often counsel concealing it from the patient, American doctors have virtually abandoned this policy; indeed, a brutal announcement to the patient is now common. The new candor about cancer is part of the same obligatory candor (or lack of decorum) that brings us diagrams of the rectal-colon or genito-urinary tract ailments of our national leaders on television and on the front pages of newspapers—more and more it is precisely a virtue in our society to speak of what is supposed *not* to be named. The change can also be explained by the doctors' fear of lawsuits in a litigious society. And not least among the reasons that cancer is now treated less phobically, certainly with less secrecy, than a decade ago is that it is no longer the most feared disease. In recent years some of the onus of cancer has been lifted by the emergence of a disease whose charge of stigmatization, whose capacity to create spoiled identity, is far greater. It seems that societies need to have one illness which becomes identified with evil, and attaches blame to its "victims," but it is hard to be obsessed with more than one.

2

Just as one might predict for a disease that is not yet fully understood as well as extremely recalcitrant to treatment, the advent of this terrifying new disease, new at least in its epidemic form, has provided a large-scale occasion for the metaphorizing of illness.

Strictly speaking, AIDS—acquired immune deficiency syndrome—is not the name of an illness at all. It is the name of a medical condition, whose consequences are a spectrum of illnesses. In contrast to syphilis and cancer, which provide prototypes for most of the images and metaphors attached to AIDS, the very definition of AIDS requires the presence of other illnesses, so-called opportunistic infections and malignancies. But though not in *that* sense a single disease, AIDS lends itself to being regarded as one—in part because, unlike cancer and like syphilis, it is thought to have a single cause.

AIDS has a dual metaphoric genealogy. As a microprocess, it is described as cancer is: an invasion. When the focus is transmission of the disease, an older metaphor, reminiscent of syphilis, is invoked: pollution. (One gets it from the blood or sexual fluids of infected people or from contaminated blood products.) But the military metaphors used to describe AIDS have a somewhat different focus from those used in describing cancer. With cancer, the metaphor scants the issue of causality (still a murky topic in cancer research) and picks up at the point at which rogue cells inside the body mutate, eventually moving out from an original site or organ to overrun other organs or systems—a domestic subversion. In the description of AIDS the enemy is what causes the disease, an infectious agent that comes from the outside:

> The invader is tiny, about one sixteen-thousandth the size of the head of a pin. . . . Scouts of the body's immune system, large cells called macrophages, sense the presence of the diminutive foreigner and promptly alert the immune system. It begins to mobilize an array of cells that, among other things, produce antibodies to deal with the threat. Single-mindedly, the AIDS virus ignores many of the blood cells in its path, evades the rapidly advancing defenders and homes in on the master coordinator of the immune system, a helper T cell. . . .

This is the language of political paranoia, with its characteristic distrust of a pluralistic world. A defense system consisting of cells "that, among other things, produce antibodies to deal with the threat" is, predictably, no match for an invader who advances "single-mindedly." And the science-fiction flavor, already present in cancer talk, is even more pungent in accounts of AIDS—this one comes from *Time* magazine in late 1986—with infection described like the high-tech warfare for which we are being prepared (and inured) by the fantasies of our leaders and by video entertainments. In the era of Star Wars and Space Invaders, AIDS has proved an ideally comprehensible illness:

> On the surface of that cell, it finds a receptor into which one of its envelope proteins fits perfectly, like a key into a lock. Docking with the cell, the virus penetrates the cell membrane and is stripped of its protective shell in the process. . . .

Next the invader takes up permanent residence, by a form of alien takeover familiar in science-fiction narratives. The body's own cells *become* the invader. With the help of an enzyme the virus carries with it,

> the naked AIDS virus converts its RNA into . . . DNA, the master molecule of life. The molecule then penetrates the cell nucleus, inserts itself into a chromosome and takes over part of the cellular machinery, directing it to produce more AIDS viruses. Eventually, overcome by its alien product, the cell swells and dies, releasing a flood of new viruses to attack other cells. . . .

As viruses attack other cells, runs the metaphor, so "a host of opportunistic diseases, normally warded off by a healthy immune system, attacks the body," whose integrity and vigor have been sapped by the sheer replication of "alien product" that follows the collapse of its immunological defenses. "Gradually weakened by the onslaught, the AIDS victim dies, sometimes in months, but almost always within a few years of the first symptoms." Those who have not already succumbed are described as "under assault, showing the telltale symptoms of the disease," while millions of others "harbor the virus, vulnerable at any time to a final, all-out attack."

Cancer makes cells proliferate; in AIDS, cells die. Even as this original model of AIDS (the mirror image of leukemia) has been altered, descriptions of how the virus does its work continue to echo the way the illness is perceived as infiltrating the society. "AIDS Virus Found to Hide in Cells, Eluding Detection by Normal Tests" was the headline of a recent front-page story in *The New York Times* announcing the discovery that the virus can "lurk" for years in the macrophages—disrupting their disease-fighting function without killing them, "even when the macrophages are filled almost to bursting with virus," and without producing antibodies, the chemicals the body makes in response to "invading agents" and whose presence has been regarded as an infallible marker of the syndrome.* That the virus isn't lethal for *all* the cells where it takes up residence,

---

*The larger role assigned to the macrophages—"to serve as a reservoir for the AIDS virus because the virus multiplies in them but does not kill them, as it kills T-4 cells"—is said to explain the not uncommon difficulty of finding infected T-4 lymphocytes in patients who have antibodies to the

as is now thought, only increases the illness-foe's reputation for wiliness and invincibility.

What makes the viral assault so terrifying is that contaminatio an, and therefore vulnerability, is understood as permanent. Even if someone infected were never to develop any symptoms—that is, the infection remained, or could by medical intervention be rendered, inactive—the viral enemy would be forever within. In fact, so it is believed, it is just a matter of time before something awakens ("triggers") it, before the appearance of "the telltale symptoms." Like syphilis, known to generations of doctors as "the great masquerader," AIDS is a clinical construction, an inference. It takes its identity from the presence of *some* among a long, and lengthening, roster of symptoms (no one has everything that AIDS could be), symptoms which "mean" that what the patient has is this illness. The construction of the illness rests on the invention not only of AIDS as a clinical entity but of a kind of junior AIDS, called AIDS-related complex (ARC), to which people are assigned if they show "early" and often intermittent symptoms of immunological deficit such as fevers, weight loss, fungal infections, and swollen lymph glands. AIDS is progressive, a disease of time. Once a certain density of symptoms is attained, the course of the illness can be swift, and brings atrocious suffering. Besides the commonest "presenting" illnesses (some hitherto unusual, at least in a fatal form, such as a rare skin cancer and a rare form of pneumonia), a plethora of disabling, disfiguring, and humiliating symptoms make the AIDS patient steadily more infirm, helpless, and unable to control or take care of basic functions and needs.

The sense in which AIDS is a slow disease makes it more like syphilis, which is characterized in terms of "stages," than like cancer. Thinking in terms of "stages" is essential to discourse about AIDS. Syphilis in its most dreaded form is "tertiary syphilis," syphilis in its third stage. What is called AIDS is generally understood as the last of three stages—the first of which is infection with a human immunodeficiency virus (HIV) and early evidence of inroads on the immune system—with a long latency period between infection and the onset of the "telltale" symptoms. (Apparently not as long as syphilis, in which the latency period between secondary and tertiary illness might be decades. But it is worth noting that when syphilis first appeared in epidemic form in Europe at the end of the fifteenth century, it was a rapid disease, of an unexplained virulence that is unknown today, in which death often occurred in the second stage, sometimes within months or a few years.) Cancer *grows* slowly: it is not thought to be, for a long time, latent. (A convincing account of a process in terms of "stages" seems invariably to include the notion of a normative delay or halt in the process, such as is supplied by the notion of latency.) True, a cancer is "staged." This is a principal tool of diagnosis, which means classifying it according to its gravity,

virus and symptoms of AIDS. (It is still assumed that antibodies will develop once the virus spreads to these "key target" cells.) Evidence of presently infected populations of cells has been as puzzlingly limited or uneven as the evidence of infection in the populations of human societies—puzzling, because of the conviction that the disease is everywhere, and must spread. "Doctors have estimated that as few as one in a million T-4 cells are infected, which led some to ask where the virus hides. . . ." Another resonant speculation, reported in the same article (*The New York Times,* June 7, 1988): "Infected macrophages can transmit the virus to other cells, possibly by touching the cells."

determining how "advanced" it is. But it is mostly a spatial notion: that the cancer advances through the body, traveling or migrating along predictable routes. Cancer is first of all a disease of the body's geography, in contrast to syphilis and AIDS, whose definition depends on constructing a temporal sequence of stages.

Syphilis is an affliction that didn't have to run its ghastly full course, to paresis (as it did for Baudelaire and Maupassant and Jules de Goncourt), and could and often did remain at the stage of nuisance, indignity (as it did for Flaubert). The scourge was also a cliché, as Flaubert himself observed. "SYPHILIS. Everybody has it, more or less" reads one entry in the *Dictionary of Accepted Opinions,* his treasury of mid-nineteenth-century platitudes. And syphilis did manage to acquire a darkly positive association in late-nineteenth- and early-twentieth-century Europe, when a link was made between syphilis and heightened ("feverish") mental activity that parallels the connection made since the era of the Romantic writers between pulmonary tuberculosis and heightened emotional activity. As if in honor of all the notable writers and artists who ended their lives in syphilitic witlessness, it came to be believed that the brain lesions of neurosyphilis might actually inspire original thought or art. Thomas Mann, whose fiction is a storehouse of early-twentieth-century disease myths, makes this notion of syphilis as muse central to his *Doctor Faustus,* with its protagonist a great composer whose voluntarily contracted syphilis—the Devil guarantees that the infection will be limited to the central nervous system—confers on him twenty-four years of incandescent creativity. E. M. Cioran recalls how, in Romania in the late 1920s, syphilis-envy figured in his adolescent expectations of literary glory: he would discover that he had contracted syphilis, be rewarded with several hyperproductive years of genius, then collapse into madness. This romanticizing of the dementia characteristic of neurosyphilis was the forerunner of the much more persistent fantasy in this century about mental illness as a source of artistic creativity or spiritual originality. But with AIDS—though dementia is also a common, late symptom—no compensatory mythology has arisen, or seems likely to arise. AIDS, like cancer, does not allow romanticizing or sentimentalizing, perhaps because its association with death is too powerful. In Krzysztof Zanussi's film *Spiral* (1978), the most truthful account I know of anger at dying, the protagonist's illness is never specified; therefore, it *has* to be cancer. For several generations now, the generic idea of death has been a death from cancer, and a cancer death is experienced as a generic defeat. Now the generic rebuke to life and to hope is AIDS.

------

1 In what contexts have metaphors for AIDS become a kind of weapon directed against those who suffer from it?

2 How do Sontag's observations about metaphors she has identified in the French Revolution and in the writings of Virchow and Lucretius provide a framework in which she discusses the metaphors used to characterize illness?

3 How have images from architecture been used to refer to the body? When did metaphors drawing on military origins begin to be used and what explains the persistence of these metaphors as the primary ones used to describe AIDS? For exam-

ple, how do advertisers, in the following ad, draw on the system of metaphors Sontag identifies in marketing Crixivin for those diagnosed as HIV positive?

4 How did the metaphors people used in speaking about diseases in past eras shape public perception? How do the metaphors people use in speaking about AIDS influence thoughts and feelings about this disease (for example, "The invader is tiny, about one sixteen-thousandth the size of a head of a pin")? How do military metaphors, in particular (for example, "onslaught," "attack," "assault"), come to dominate descriptions of the medical situations of those with AIDS? See the ad for Crixivan. (Glossary: *Biased Language, Metaphor.*)

5 Sontag takes an analogical approach to show her readers how different illnesses (syphilis, tuberculosis, AIDS, cancer) have been perceived by the public at different periods in history. Why is this rhetorical strategy indispensable in presenting her thesis as to the way illnesses are projected through various metaphors? (Glossary: *Analogy.*) Where does Sontag use transitions to signal the reader that she is moving from a discussion of one disease to another? How do these verbal cues make it easier for the reader to follow her discussion and pick up similarities and differences? (Glossary: *Transitions.*)

6 As distinct from the common metaphorical perception of AIDS Susan Sontag analyzes, academic disciplines apply unique frameworks in studying AIDS-related phenomena. For example, if the issue were "Can needle exchange programs help slow the spread of AIDS," how would this question be examined by an ethicist, an epidemiologist, a sociologist, and an economist? How does the different language used in each discipline reflect its distinctive approach?

The Word Police   *Michiko Kakutani*

◆ MICHIKO KAKUTANI is a staff writer for the *New York Times,* where this
article first appeared in January 1993.

One consequence of the politicization of everyday language is the excesses of a
movement called political correctness, whose aims are praiseworthy in seeking
to help us become more civil to each other and to eliminate offensive epithets
that stigmatize others. What Kakutani objects to is the way we are required, in
the interests of civility and sensitivity, to eliminate words from our vocabulary
and replace them with pleasing meaningless euphemisms that often are so non-
descriptive and bland as to make communication pointless.

TO CONSIDER   Has the English language been diminished by the
political correctness movement?

---

1   This month's inaugural festivities, with their celebration, in Maya
Angelou's words, of "humankind"—"the Asian, the Hispanic, the Jew/
The African, the Native American, the Sioux,/The Catholic, the Muslim,
the French, the Greek/The Irish, the Rabbi, the Priest, the Sheik,/The Gay, the
Straight, the Preacher,/The privileged, the homeless, the Teacher"—constituted
a kind of official embrace of multiculturalism and a new politics of inclusion.

2   The mood of political correctness, however, has already made firm inroads
into popular culture. Washington boasts a store called Politically Correct that
sells pro-whale, anti-meat, ban-the-bomb T-shirts, bumper stickers and buttons,
as well as a local cable television show called "Politically Correct Cooking" that
features interviews in the kitchen with representatives from groups like People
for the Ethical Treatment of Animals.

3   The Coppertone suntan lotion people are planning to give their longtime
cover girl, Little Miss (Ms?) Coppertone, a male equivalent, Little Mr. Coppertone. And even Superman (Super-person?) is rumored to be returning this
spring, reincarnated as four ethnically diverse clones: an African-American, an
Asian, a Caucasian and a Latino.

4   Nowhere is this P.C. mood more striking than in the increasingly noisy
debate over language that has moved from university campuses to the country
at large—a development that both underscores Americans' puritanical zeal for
reform and their unwavering faith in the talismanic power of words.

5   Certainly no decent person can quarrel with the underlying impulse behind
political correctness: a vision of a more just, inclusive society in which racism,

---

sexism and prejudice of all sorts have been erased. But the methods and fervor of the self-appointed language police can lead to a rigid orthodoxy—and unintentional self-parody—opening the movement to the scorn of conservative opponents and the mockery of cartoonists and late-night television hosts.

It's hard to imagine women earning points for political correctness by saying "ovarimony" instead of "testimony"—as one participant at the recent Modern Language Association convention was overheard to suggest. It's equally hard to imagine people wanting to flaunt their lack of prejudice by giving up such words and phrases as "bull market," "kaiser roll," "Lazy Susan," and "charley horse."   6

Several books on bias-free language have already appeared, and the 1991 edition of the Random House Webster's College Dictionary boasts an appendix titled "Avoiding Sexist Language." The dictionary also includes such linguistic mutations as "womyn" (women, "used as an alternative spelling to avoid the suggestion of sexism perceived in the sequence m-e-n") and "waitron" (a gender-blind term for waiter or waitress).   7

Many of these dictionaries and guides not only warn the reader against offensive racial and sexual slurs, but also try to establish and enforce a whole new set of usage rules. Take, for instance, "The Bias-Free Word Finder, a Dictionary of Nondiscriminatory Language" by Rosalie Maggio (Beacon Press)—a volume often indistinguishable, in its meticulous solemnity, from the tongue-in-cheek "Official Politically Correct Dictionary and Handbook" put out last year by Henry Beard and Christopher Cerf (Villard Books). Ms. Maggio's book supplies the reader intent on using kinder, gentler language with writing guidelines as well as a detailed listing of more than 5,000 "biased words and phrases."   8

Whom are these guidelines for? Somehow one has a tough time picturing them replacing "Fowler's Modern English Usage" in the classroom, or being adopted by the average man (sorry, individual) in the street.   9

The "pseudogeneric 'he,'" we learn from Ms. Maggio, is to be avoided like the plague, as is the use of the word "man" to refer to humanity. "Fellow," "king," "lord" and "master" are bad because they're "male-oriented words," and "king," "lord" and "master" are especially bad because they're also "hierarchical, dominator society terms." The politically correct lion becomes the "monarch of the jungle," new-age children play "someone on the top of the heap," and the "Mona Lisa" goes down in history as Leonardo's "acme of perfection."   10

As for the word "black," Ms. Maggio says it should be excised from terms with a negative spin: she recommends substituting words like "mouse" for "black eye," "ostracize" for "blackball," "payola" for "blackmail" and "outcast" for "black sheep." Clearly, some of these substitutions work better than others: somehow the "sinister humor" of Kurt Vonnegut or "Saturday Night Live" doesn't quite make it; nor does the "denouncing" of the Hollywood 10.   11

For the dedicated user of politically correct language, all these rules can make for some messy moral dilemmas. Whereas "battered wife" is a gender-biased term, the gender-free term "battered spouse," Ms. Maggio notes, incorrectly implies "that men and women are equally battered."   12

On one hand, say Francine Wattman Frank and Paula A. Treichler in their book "Language, Gender, and Professional Writing" (Modern Language Association), "he or she" is an appropriate construction for talking about an individ-   13 ual (like a jockey, say) who belongs to a profession that's predominantly male—it's a way of emphasizing "that such occupations are not barred to women or that women's concerns need to be kept in mind." On the other hand, they add, using masculine pronouns rhetorically can underscore ongoing male dominance in those fields, implying the need for change.

14   And what about the speech codes adopted by some universities in recent years? Although they were designed to prohibit students from uttering sexist and racist slurs, they would extend, by logic, to blacks who want to use the word "nigger" to strip the term of its racist connotations, or homosexuals who want to use the word "queer" to reclaim it from bigots.

15   In her book, Ms. Maggio recommends applying bias-free usage retroactively: she suggests paraphrasing politically incorrect quotations, or replacing "the sexist words or phrases with ellipsis dots and/or bracketed substitutes," or using "sic" "to show that the sexist words come from the original quotation and to call attention to the fact that they are incorrect."

16   Which leads the skeptical reader of "The Bias-Free Word Finder" to wonder whether "All the King's Men" should be retitled "All the Ruler's People"; "Pet Semetary," "Animal Companion Graves"; "Birdman of Alcatraz," "Bird-person of Alcatraz," and "The Iceman Cometh," "The Ice Route Driver Cometh"?

17   Will making such changes remove the prejudice in people's minds? Should we really spend time trying to come up with non-male-based alternatives to "Midas touch," "Achilles' heel," and "Montezuma's revenge"? Will tossing out Santa Claus—whom Ms. Maggio accuses of reinforcing "the cultural male-as-norm system"—in favor of Belfana, his Italian female alter ego, truly help banish sexism? Can the avoidance of "violent expressions and metaphors" like "kill two birds with one stone," "sock it to 'em" or "kick an idea around" actually promote a more harmonious world?

18   The point isn't that the excesses of the word police are comical. The point is that their intolerance (in the name of tolerance) has disturbing implications. In the first place, getting upset by phrases like "bullish on America" or "the City of Brotherly Love" tends to distract attention from the real problems of prejudice and injustice that exist in society at large, turning them into mere questions of semantics. Indeed, the emphasis currently put on politically correct usage has uncanny parallels with the academic movement of deconstruction—a method of textual analysis that focuses on language and linguistic pyrotechnics—which has become firmly established on university campuses.

19   In both cases, attention is focused on surfaces, on words and metaphors; in both cases, signs and symbols are accorded more importance than content. Hence, the attempt by some radical advocates to remove "The Adventures of Huckleberry Finn" from curriculums on the grounds that Twain's use of the word "nigger" makes the book a racist text—never mind the fact that this American classic (written in 1884) depicts the spiritual kinship achieved between a white boy and a runaway slave, never mind the fact that the "nigger" Jim emerges as the novel's most honorable, decent character.

20   Ironically enough, the P.C. movement's obsession with language is accompanied by a strange Orwellian willingness to warp the meaning of words by plac-

ing them under a high-powered ideological lens. For instance, the "Dictionary of Cautionary Words and Phrases"—a pamphlet issued by the University of Missouri's Multicultural Management Program to help turn "today's journalists into tomorrow's multicultural newsroom managers"—warns that using the word "articulate" to describe members of a minority group can suggest the opposite, "that 'those people' are not considered well educated, articulate and the like."

The pamphlet patronizes minority groups, by cautioning the reader against using the words "lazy" and "burly" to describe any member of such groups; and it issues a similar warning against using words like "gorgeous" and "petite" to describe women.   21

As euphemism proliferates with the rise of political correctness, there is a spread of the sort of sloppy, abstract language that Orwell said is "designed to make lies sound truthful and murder respectable, and to give an appearance of solidity to pure wind." "Fat" becomes "big boned" or "differently sized"; "stupid" becomes "exceptional"; "stoned" becomes "chemically inconvenienced."   22

Wait a minute here! Aren't such phrases eerily reminiscent of the euphemisms coined by the Government during Vietnam and Watergate? Remember how the military used to speak of "pacification," or how President Richard M. Nixon's press secretary, Ronald L. Ziegler, tried to get away with calling a lie an "inoperative statement"?   23

Calling the homeless "the underhoused" doesn't give them a place to live; calling the poor "the economically marginalized" doesn't help them pay the bills. Rather, by playing down their plight, such language might even make it easier to shrug off the seriousness of their situation.   24

Instead of allowing free discussion and debate to occur, many gung-ho advocates of politically correct language seem to think that simple suppression of a word or concept will magically make the problem disappear. In the "Bias-Free Word Finder," Ms. Maggio entreats the reader not to perpetuate the negative stereotype of Eve. "Be extremely cautious in referring to the biblical Eve," she writes; "this story has profoundly contributed to negative attitudes toward women throughout history, largely because of misogynistic and patriarchal interpretations that labeled her evil, inferior, and seductive."   25

The story of Bluebeard, the rake (whoops!—the libertine) who killed his seven wives, she says, is also to be avoided, as is the biblical story of Jezebel. Of Jesus Christ, Ms. Maggio writes: "There have been few individuals in history as completely androgynous as Christ, and it does his message a disservice to overinsist on his maleness." She doesn't give the reader any hints on how this might be accomplished; presumably, one is supposed to avoid describing him as the Son of God.   26

Of course the P.C. police aren't the only ones who want to proscribe what people should say or give them guidelines for how they may use an idea; Jesse Helms and his supporters are up to exactly the same thing when they propose to patrol the boundaries of the permissible in art. In each case, the would-be censor aspires to suppress what he or she finds distasteful—all, of course, in the name of the public good.   27

28   In the case of the politically correct, the prohibition of certain words, phrases and ideas is advanced in the cause of building a brave new world free of racism and hate, but this vision of harmony clashes with the very ideals of diversity and inclusion that the multi-cultural movement holds dear, and it's purchased at the cost of freedom of expression and freedom of speech.

29   In fact, the utopian world envisioned by the language police would be bought at the expense of the ideals of individualism and democracy articulated in "The Gettysburg Address": "Fourscore and seven years ago our fathers brought forth on this continent a new nation, conceived in liberty and dedicated to the proposition that all men are created equal."

30   Of course, the P.C. police have already found Lincoln's words hopelessly "phallocentric." No doubt they would rewrite the passage: "Fourscore and seven years ago our foremothers and forefathers brought forth on this continent a new nation, formulated with liberty, and dedicated to the proposition that all humankind is created equal."

———

1 Why is Kakutani concerned that specific revisions or substitutions of words made in the spirit of political correctness are not-so-subtle acquiescences to coercion? Why, in her view, are many of these recommended substitutions not only incorrect, but misleading and a corruption of language? What does the title of her essay mean?

2 According to Kakutani, what is wrong with the assumption that making the kinds of changes politically correct advocates recommend—such as avoiding "king" and "master," substituting acceptable euphemisms such as "chemically inconvenienced" for "stoned" and "exceptional" for "stupid"—will remove prejudice? Should politically correct changes be applied retroactively (para. 15)? Why or why not?

3 What experiences have you had in revising your own writing to avoid politically incorrect terms? Were you able to find acceptable substitutions?

4 What point is Kakutani making by asking the rhetorical question in paragraph 9 ("Whom are these guidelines for")? How is this part of her overall rhetorical strategy of calling into question the value and relevance of the political correctness movement? How does her title express her attitude? (Glossary: *Attitude, Connotation, Denotation, Rhetorical Question.*)

5 Where does Kakutani point out problems with the opposition's viewpoint in terms of the quality of the evidence offered or the logic used? Does this analysis strengthen her own argument and prepare readers to be more receptive to her opinions? (Glossary: *Argument.*)

6 Should local, state and national maps be revised to eliminate place name's such as "Little Squaw," "Intercourse," and "Dago Hill," for being offensive? Why or why not?

Old Age Needs a New Name: But Don't Look For it in Webster's

Frank Nuessel

◆ FRANK NUESSEL was born in 1943 and received his Ph.D. from the University of Illinois, Urbana-Champaign in 1973. Since 1982, Nuessel has been professor of Spanish and linguistics at the University of Louisville. He edited *Linguistic Approaches to the Romance Lexicon* (1978) and is the author of a number of studies on general linguistics, phonology, and morphology, including "An Annotated, Critical Bibliography of Generative-based Grammatical Analyses of Spanish: Syntax and Semantics," *Bilingual Review* (1979). In "Old Age Needs a New Name: But Don't Look For it in Webster's," which first appeared in *Aging* (1984), Nuessel discloses how society's current view of old people reveals a systematic pattern of discrimination as damaging as sexism or racism.

How are older people depicted in newspaper stories, on local television news, and in the movies? To what extent does the language used to characterize the elderly encourage discrimination toward them? These are the questions that Nuessel addresses in his essay exploring current cultural attitudes.

> **TO CONSIDER**   Are you aware of any terms, endearing or otherwise, that you use to refer to your older relatives or the elderly in general? What are the emotional connotations of these terms?

The phenomenon of ageism has existed far longer than the term refers to this practice. This new word was first coined in 1967 by Robert N. Butler, former director of the National Institute on Aging. Butler (1975:12) specified that ageism "can be seen as a process of systematic stereotyping of and discrimination against people because they are old, just as racism and sexism accomplish this with skin color and gender. Old people are characterized as senile, rigid in thought and manner, old-fashioned in morality and skills. . . . Ageism allows the younger generations to see old people as different from themselves; thus they subtly cease to identify with their elders as human beings."

Frank Neussel, "Old Age Needs a New Name: But Don't Look For It in Webster's," from *Aging*, Aug/Sept., 1984. Reprinted with permission from Lippincott-Raven Publishers and *Aging* magazine.

Evidence for the acceptance of this concept may be found in the fact that an entry for this term now exists in *The American Heritage Dictionary of the English Language* (1979:24) which defines ageism as "discrimination based on age, especially discrimination against middle-aged and elderly people."

Ageism is a doubly harmful form of prejudice. First, it lumps together and sets apart a significant and heterogeneous group of people within our society. Second, this misperception leads to a negative self-image on the part of the elderly. Brubaker and Powers (1976:442) have observed that "the character of the stereotype of old age . . . is at issue because it affects not only the manner in which younger persons perceive and interact with aged individuals but also influences the self-definitions and behavior of older persons."

EUPHEMISMS AND LOADED WORDS

There are a number of words commonly used to refer to older people, but the determination of an appropriate designation for this sector of our society continues to be problematic.

Louis Harris and Associates conducted a poll (Ward, 1979:165) for the National Council on the Aging in order to determine an acceptable label for elders. Disagreement, however, over the proper and correct designation continues. *Senior citizen,* preferred by one-third and liked by one-half of the respondents in the Harris survey, was proclaimed a euphemism by the Usage panel of *The American Heritage Dictionary of the English Language* and was acceptable to only 47 percent of that jury. In fact, Fischer (1978:94) has observed that ". . . praise words invented for old people . . . such as *senior citizen* are often laden with a heavy freight of sarcasm." One term which is seemingly devoid of the pejorative connotations that some of the Harris survey participants attached to other expressions (*senior citizen, retired person, mature American, older American, golden ager, old-timer, old man / old woman*) is the word *elder* which is rapidly emerging as the semantically neutral and preferred name for this group.

The dictionary offers few positive adjectives for alluding to elders. Examples of such favorable age-specific words are rare, e.g., *mature, mellow, sage, venerable,* and *veteran.* Even the adjective *mature* is quickly being transformed into a euphemism, i.e., a substitution of an agreeable or pleasant-sounding word for one which conjures up unpleasant and unappealing images. In addition, the descriptive adjectives *aged* and *old* normally only carry positive implications if these qualities refer to inanimate objects such as cheese, wood, brandy, or lace. The overwhelming majority of words and phrases for elders are unfavorable and prejudicial (Nuessel, 1982). In this regard, the extensive, pejorative, and ageist vocabulary of the English language constitutes a verbal record of this society's fear of getting old.

Ageist language belongs to two separate realms. One group of expressions specifically denotes elders. The other segment comprises words with connotations, or intensional significance, associated exclusively with elders.

Ageist language is often doubly pernicious because many of the words denigrate individuals on the basis of both age and gender (Matthews, 1979; Sontag, 1972). For example, *beldam* (e), *biddy, crone, granny, grimalkin, hag, harridan* and *witch* all denote elder females with undesirable physical features or objectionable behavior. In the same vein, another set of ageist expressions is marked for the male sex. Such nouns as *codger, coot,* and *geezer,* depict elder males in an unflattering way by ascribing aberrant behavior to them.

When appended to any of a number of terms that designate people with bad habits, personality quirks, and other displeasing traits (*crank, fogy, fool, fossil, fuddy-duddy, grump, miser,* and *reprobate*), the adjective *old* (a word encumbered with almost completely negative implications) creates a set of hybrid noun phrases that truly demean and defame our elders. In the future, it is conceivable that the word *old* may undergo a semantic shift to an entirely positive concept through public education and activities. Such a phenomenon occurred in the 1960's when the term *black* acquired the sense of cultural pride and awareness for another oppressed minority.

Many of the adjectives frequently assigned to elders are predominantly negative. In general, they assign unpleasant physical (*infirm, doddering, decrepit*), behavioral (*cantankerous, cranky*), and mental (*senile, foolish, rambling*) characteristics to a group of people who are as diverse in personality, intellect and health status as any other segment of our society.

Unfortunately, the childhood refrain, "sticks and stones may break my bones but words will never hurt me," is not true. In fact, language can be a very potent and harmful instrument, because stereotypic vocabulary has the power to shape people's concepts of reality. The public often comes to believe the preconceptions that are the basis of stereotypes and thus fails to differentiate individual uniqueness.

Dehumanization is the net effect of employing prejudicial language of any kind. Such depersonalization facilitates abuse and mistreatment of vulnerable minorities (especially elders) by a systematic devaluation of their dignity and worth. This form of disenfranchisement facilitates their subjugation because it enables elders to be segregated into urban ghettos, nursing homes, and other modern warehouses for presumed undesirables. In this regard Bosmajian (1974:6) has observed that ". . . names, words and language . . . can also be used to dehumanize human beings and to 'justify' their suppression and even their extermination." The use of euphemistic labels to describe nursing homes and retirement villages (*Tendercare, Crystal Pines, Forest Villa, Leisure World, Sunset Lodge* etc.) eases the public's guilt and remorse over accepting the isolation of elders. To ignore the awesome power of linguistic labeling is to contribute to the continued mistreatment of the elderly.

AGEISM IN DRAMATIC SCRIPTS

Written language (dramatic literature, film and television scripts, commercial advertising copy) is the common source of the portrayal of elders in movies, television, videocassettes, cartoons and radio. Scripts frequently include, in parentheses, stage directions and character descriptions, such as physical qualities and personality traits. Intonation, stress, rhythm of voices as well as gestures are generally designated by adverbial phrases (*feebly, weakly, in a deteriorated condition, in a senile state*) or by highly specific verbal expressions (*teeter, dodder, mumble, mutter, drool*). The selection of such stereotypic phraseology intensifies ageist images in a particularly malicious fashion. Often, however, the mere use of such adjectives as *old, elderly,* and *aged* is sufficient to cause actors and actresses to perform a role according to certain prevailing social preconceptions about elders—so powerful are the presuppositions entailed in these words.

ELIMINATING THE DISTORTIONS

We are beginning to see some efforts to correct ageism in films, radio and TV. The Gray Panthers, for example, have developed the Media Watch Observer's Report form in response to the problem of misrepresentation of elders in mass communications. The approach, a response to offenses already committed, has an important educational function if the distortions reported are properly publicized (letters to the editor, local news coverage, etc.)

More important, however, is the elimination of these distortions prior to their public dissemination. Two publications designed to prevent ageist portrayal of older people now exist. The first is *Truth About Aging: Guidelines for Accurate Communications,* by Mary E. Spencer, a 1984 publication of the American Association of Retired Persons. Copies of this pamphlet are available for AARP, 1909 K Street, Washington, D.C. 20049.

The second publication, *Media Guidelines for Sexuality and Aging,* by Carol Jean Wisnieski, Susan Leigh Star and Christiane Herrmann, is available free from Carol Jean Wisnieski, 348 Diamond Street, San Francisco, California 94114. This two-page set of guidlines has been reproduced in Richard H. Davis', *Television and The Aging Audience,* which was published by The University of Southern California Press, in 1980 (pp. 83 and 84).

Continual vigilance will be necessary if ageism is to be reduced significantly, if not eradicated, from our language and literature. One positive step has already begun in this regard. The newly established national intergenerational organization, Understanding Aging, Incorporated (Center for Understanding Aging, Conant Schools, Acton, MA 01720), has recently established an award for authors who portray elders in a realistic and nonstereotypic fashion.

As previously suggested in this article, the scarcity of positive words in the English language referring to old age is probably merely a reflection of society's fear of growing old. Perhaps Americans will have to come to better terms with the last stage of life before words will come into common usage that truly describe the attributes of our older population. But since it may take a while for Americans to get over their love affair with youth, there are steps we can take in the meantime to begin to eradicate ageism. One of these steps involves making the public more aware of the damaging effects of ageist language.

REFERENCES

Bosmajian, Haig. 1975. *The Languages of Oppression*. Washington, D.C.: Public Affairs Press.

Brubaker, Timothy, and Edward Powers. 1976. "The Stereotypes of Old: A Review and Alternative Approach." *Journal of Gerontology* 31,441–447.

Butler, Robert N. 1969. "Age-ism: Another Form of Bigotry." *The Gerontologist* 9,243–246.

Butler, Robert N. 1975. *Why Survive? Being Old In America*. New York: Harper and Row.

Fischer, David Hackett. 1978. *Growing Old in America*. Expanded ed. Oxford: Oxford University Press.

Matthews, Sarah, 1979. *The Social World of Old Women: Management of Self-identity*. Sage Library of Social Research (Vol. 78). Beverly Hills, CA: Sage Publications.

Morris, William (Ed.). 1979. *The American Heritage Dictionary of the English Language*. Boston, MA: Houghton Mifflin Company.

Nuessel, Frank. 1982. "The Language of Ageism." *The Gerontologist* 22, 273–276.

Sontag, Susan. 1972. "The Double Standard of Aging." *The Saturday Review* (September 23),29–38.

Ward, Russell, 1979. *The Aging Experience: An Introduction to Social Gerontology*. New York: J. P. Lippincott Company.

1 How does Nuessel document the phenomenon of ageism—that is, the stereotyping of older people in pejorative terms and phrases? How have words used to describe the elderly acquired negative connotations as society's fear of growing old increases?

2 How does Nuessel's analysis demonstrate that negative labeling, whether based on sex, age, race, or religion, paves the way for discounting a particular group and ignoring its members' civil rights?

3 What evidence drawn from monitoring films, television, and commercials does Nuessel offer to document the stereotyped depiction of older people as a reflection of the prevailing societal attitude? Analyze the following paragraph from P. J. O'Rourke's article denouncing Social Security ("Graft for the Millions: Social Security") and identify pejorative, ageist phrases or terms; revise them to be more neutral and bias-free. How do these substitutions affect the impact of the passage as a whole?

The senior citizen lobby seems to be approaching this frightful proportion. I mean what's with these old people? Where'd they come from? All of a sudden there are geezers and duffers and biddies and fusspots every place you look. Not a highway in the nation is safe from Florida-bound codgers swaying lane to lane at 52 mph in their Cruise Master motor homes with novelty license plates bolted to the front: "Retired—No Job—No Phone—No Excuse for Living." Every Sun Belt Plane Flight has its aisles jammed [to] impassibility, with blue-rinse wide-loads and their carry-on cat boxes. Fogies crowd shopping centers in mall-walking packs and swamp the ten-items-or-less supermarket check out lanes with case-lot purchases of Campbells soup for one. Turn on the television, and the ads are all for bran, PeptoBismol, hemorrhoid medications and high-fiber this and that. *Sic transit* the Pepsi generation. Everyone in commercials is over seventy and has something wrong with his butt.

4 How do the connotations of words used to describe the elderly (for example, "crone," "hag," "geezer") project a series of negative stereotypes that have damaging consequences? (Glossary: *Biased Language, Connotation, Denotation.*)

5 Summarize Nuessel's argument. In your own words, what is at stake in the issue? What means does Nuessel use to document sources that are not common knowledge or a matter of historical record? Why is such a range of evidence required in this kind of argument? (Glossary: *Argument.*)

6 Do the words used to characterize old women have more pejorative connotations than those used to describe old men? If so, why do you think this is the case?

The Human Cost Of An Illiterate Society
Jonathan Kozol

in the business world, you also pay a price if you are illiterate
English - illiterate

◆ JONATHAN KOZOL was born in Boston in 1936 and graduated from Harvard in 1958. He was a Rhodes scholar at Oxford University and has taught at numerous colleges, including Yale. His many books on education and literacy include *Death at an Early Age* (1967), *Illiterate America* (1985), from which the following selection is taken, *Rachel and Her Children* (1988), and *Savage Inequalities* (1991).

In varying ways, the writers in this chapter—especially Solomon, Nilsen, Sontag, Kakutani, and Nuessel—show how language that serves a political agenda poses a danger for a democratic society. But, as Kozol points out, there is another danger to our society connected to language: the prospect that increasingly smaller numbers of people will be able to read well enough to be informed voters. After all, those who are illiterate find it nearly impossible to function in our society on even the most basic level (to know what products to buy, to pay bills, to adhere to leases, to meet insurance obligations, etc.). Kozol points out that as of 1985 in certain cities, almost 40 percent of the adult population was functionally illiterate with more than 60 million people nationally (and this number is increasing dramatically). Kozol's article is a wake-up call for those who are reluctant to believe that illiteracy of this magnitude exists in our society.

TO CONSIDER   What would your typical day be like if you could not read or write? Record all your activities and describe how each would be different because of your illiteracy.

PRECAUTIONS, READ BEFORE USING.

Poison: Contains sodium hydroxide (caustic soda-lye).

Corrosive: Causes severe eye and skin damage, may cause blindness.

Harmful or fatal if swallowed.

If swallowed, give large quantities of milk or water.

Do not induce vomiting.

Important: Keep water out of can at all times to prevent contents from
   violently erupting . . .

— warning on a can of Drano

Questions of literacy, in Socrates' belief, must at length be judged as matters of morality. Socrates could not have had in mind the moral compromise peculiar to a nation like our own. Some of our Founding Fathers did, however, have this question in their minds. One of the wisest of those Founding Fathers (one who may not have been most compassionate but surely was more prescient than some of his peers) recognized the special dangers that illiteracy would pose to basic equity in the political construction that he helped to shape.

"A people who mean to be their own governors," James Madison wrote, "must arm themselves with the power knowledge gives. A popular government without popular information or the means of acquiring it, is but a prologue to a farce or a tragedy, or perhaps both."

Tragedy looms larger than farce in the United States today. Illiterate citizens seldom vote. Those who do are forced to cast a vote of questionable worth. They cannot make informed decisions based on serious print information. Sometimes they can be alerted to their interests by aggressive voter education. More frequently, they vote for a face, a smile, or a style, not for a mind or character or body of beliefs. *true democracy can't come w/o education*

The number of illiterate adults exceeds by 16 million the entire vote cast for the winner in the 1980 presidential contest. If even one third of all illiterates could vote, and read enough and do sufficient math to vote in their self-interest, Ronald Reagan would not likely have been chosen president. There is, of course, no way to know for sure. We do know this: Democracy is a mendacious term when used by those who are prepared to countenance the forced exclusion of one third of our electorate. So long as 60 million people are denied significant participation, the government is neither of nor for, nor by, the people. It is a government, at best, of those two thirds whose wealth, skin color, or parental privilege allows them opportunity to profit from the provocation and instruction of the written word.

5   The undermining of democracy in the United States is one "expense" that sensitive Americans can easily deplore because it represents a contradiction that endangers citizens of all political positions. The human price is not so obvious at first.

6   Since I first immersed myself within this work I have often had the following dream: I find that I am in a railroad station or a large department store within a city that is utterly unknown to me and where I cannot understand the printed words. None of the signs or symbols is familiar. Everything looks strange: like mirror writing of some kind. Gradually I understand that I am in the Soviet Union. All the letters on the walls around me are Cyrillic. I look for my pocket dictionary but I find that it has been mislaid. Where have I left it? Then I recall that I forgot to bring it with me when I packed my bags in Boston. I struggle to remember the name of my hotel. I try to ask somebody for directions. One person stops and looks at me in a peculiar way. I lose the nerve to ask. At last I reach into my wallet for an ID card. The card is missing. Have I lost it? Then I remember that my card was confiscated for some reason, many years before. Around this point, I wake up in a panic.

7   This panic is not so different from the misery that millions of adult illiterates experience each day within the course of their routine existence in the U.S.A.

8   Illiterates cannot read the menu in a restaurant.

9   They cannot read the cost of items on the menu in the *window* of the restaurant before they enter.

10   Illiterates cannot read the letters that their children bring home from their teachers. They cannot study school department circulars that tell them of the courses that their children must be taking if they hope to pass the SAT exams. They cannot help with homework. They cannot write a letter to the teacher. They are afraid to visit in the classroom. They do not want to humiliate their child or themselves.

11   Illiterates cannot read instructions on a bottle of prescription medicine. They cannot find out when a medicine is past the year of safe consumption; nor can they read of allergenic risks, warnings to diabetics, or the potential sedative effect of certain kinds of nonprescription pills. They cannot observe preventive health care admonitions. They cannot read about "the seven warning signs of cancer" or the indications of blood-sugar fluctuations or the risks of eating certain foods that aggravate the likelihood of cardiac arrest.

12   Illiterates live, in more than literal ways, an uninsured existence. They cannot understand the written details on a health insurance form. They cannot read the waivers that they sign preceding surgical procedures. Several women I have known in Boston have entered a slum hospital with the intention of obtaining a

tubal ligation and have emerged a few days later after having been subjected to a hysterectomy. Unaware of their rights, incognizant of jargon, intimidated by the unfamiliar air of fear and atmosphere of ether that so many of us find oppressive in the confines even of the most attractive and expensive medical facilities, they have signed their names to documents they could not read and which nobody, in the hectic situation that prevails so often in those overcrowded hospitals that serve the urban poor, had even bothered to explain.

Childbirth might seem to be the last inalienable right of any female citizen   13
within a civilized society. Illiterate mothers, as we shall see, already have been cheated of the power to protect their progeny against the likelihood of demolition in deficient public schools and, as a result, against the <u>verbal servitude</u> within which they themselves exist. Surgical denial of the right to bear that child in the first place represents an ultimate denial, an unspeakable metaphor, a final darkness that denies even the twilight gleamings of our own humanity. What greater violation of our biological, our biblical, our spiritual humanity could possibly exist than that which takes place nightly, perhaps hourly these days, within such overburdened and benighted institutions as the Boston City Hospital? Illiteracy has many costs; few are so irreversible as this.

Even the roof above one's head, the gas or other fuel for heating that pro-   14
tects the residents of northern city slums against the threat of illness in the winter months become uncertain guarantees. Illiterates cannot read the lease that they must sign to live in an apartment which, too often, they cannot afford. They cannot manage check accounts and therefore seldom pay for anything by mail. Hours and entire days of difficult travel (and the cost of bus or other public transit) must be added to the real cost of whatever they consume. Loss of interest on the check accounts they do not have, and could not manage if they did, must be regarded as another of the excess costs paid by the citizen who is excluded from the common instruments of commerce in a numerate society.

"I couldn't understand the bills," a woman in Washington, D.C., reports,   15
"and then I couldn't write the checks to pay them. We signed things we didn't know what they were."

Illiterates cannot read the notices that they receive from welfare offices or   16
from the IRS. They must depend on word-of-mouth instruction from the welfare worker—or from other persons whom they have good reason to mistrust. They do not know what rights they have, what deadlines and requirements they face, what options they might choose to exercise. They are half-citizens. Their rights exist in print but not in fact.

Illiterates cannot look up numbers in a telephone directory. Even if they can   17
find the names of friends, few possess the sorting skills to make use of the yellow pages; categories are bewildering and trade names are beyond decoding capabilities for millions of nonreaders. Even the emergency numbers listed on the first page of the phone book—"Ambulance," "Police," and "Fire"—are too frequently beyond the recognition of nonreaders.

Many illiterates cannot read the admonition on a pack of cigarettes. Neither   18
the Surgeon General's warning nor its reproduction on the package can alert them to the risks. Although most people learn by word of mouth that smoking

is related to a number of grave physical disorders, they do not get the chance to read the detailed stories which can document this danger with the vividness that turns concern into determination to resist. They can see the handsome cowboy or the slim Virginia lady lighting up a filter cigarette; they cannot heed the words that tell them that this product is (not "may be") dangerous to their health. Sixty million men and women are condemned to be the unalerted, high-risk candidates for cancer.

19   Illiterates do not buy "no-name" products in the supermarkets. They must depend on photographs or the familiar logos that are printed on the packages of brand-name groceries. The poorest people, therefore, are denied the benefits of the least costly products.

20   Illiterates depend almost entirely upon label recognition. Many labels, however, are not easy to distinguish. Dozens of different kinds of Campbell's soup appear identical to the nonreader. The purchaser who cannot read and does not dare to ask for help, out of the fear of being stigmatized (a fear which is unfortunately realistic), frequently comes home with something which she never wanted and her family never tasted.

21   Illiterates cannot read instructions on a pack of frozen food. Packages sometimes provide an illustration to explain the cooking preparations; but illustrations are of little help to someone who must "boil water, drop the food—*within* its plastic wrapper—in the boiling water, wait for it to simmer, instantly remove."

22   Even when labels are seemingly clear, they may be easily mistaken. A woman in Detroit brought home a gallon of Crisco for her children's dinner. She thought that she had bought the chicken that was pictured on the label. She had enough Crisco now to last a year—but no more money to go back and buy the food for dinner.

23   Recipes provided on the packages of certain staples sometimes tempt a semiliterate person to prepare a meal her children have not tasted. The longing to vary the uniform and often starchy content of low-budget meals provided to the family that relies on food stamps commonly leads to ruinous results. Scarce funds have been wasted and the food must be thrown out. The same applies to distribution of food-surplus produce in emergency conditions. Government inducements to poor people to "explore the ways" by which to make a tasty meal from tasteless noodles, surplus cheese, and powdered milk are useless to nonreaders. Intended as benevolent advice, such recommendations mock reality and foster deeper feelings of resentment and of inability to cope. (Those, on the other hand, who cautiously refrain from "innovative" recipes in preparation of their children's meals must suffer the opprobrium of "laziness," "lack of imagination. . . .")

24   Illiterates cannot travel freely. When they attempt to do so, they encounter risks that few of us can dream of. They cannot read traffic signs and, while they often learn to recognize and to decipher symbols, they cannot manage street names which they haven't seen before. The same is true for bus and subway stops. While ingenuity can sometimes help a man or woman to discern directions from familiar landmarks, buildings, cemeteries, churches, and the like, most illiterates are virtually immobilized. They seldom wander past the streets and neighborhoods they know. Geographical paralysis becomes a bitter metaphor for their

entire existence. They are immobilized in almost every sense we can imagine. They can't move up. They can't move out. They cannot see beyond. Illiterates may take an oral test for drivers' permits in most sections of America. It is a questionable concession. Where will they go? How will they get there? How will they get home? Could it be that some of us might like it better if they stayed where they belong?

Travel is only one of many instances of circumscribed existence. Choice, in   25
almost all its facets, is diminished in the life of an illiterate adult. Even the printed TV schedule, which provides most people with the luxury of preselection, does not belong within the arsenal of options in illiterate existence. One consequence is that the viewer watches only what appears at moments when he happens to have time to turn the switch. Another consequence, a lot more common, is that the TV set remains in operation night and day. Whatever the program offered at the hour when he walks into the room will be the nutriment that he accepts and swallows. Thus, to passivity, is added frequency—indeed, almost uninterrupted continuity. Freedom to select is no more possible here than in the choice of home or surgery of food.

"You don't choose," said one illiterate woman. "You take your wishes from   26
somebody else." Whether in perusal of a menu, selection of highways, purchase of groceries, or determination of affordable enjoyment, illiterate Americans must trust somebody else: a friend, a relative, a stranger on the street, a grocery clerk, a TV copywriter.

"All of our mail we get, it's hard for her to read. Settin' down and writing a   27
letter, she can't do it. Like if we get a bill . . . we take it over to my sister-in-law . . . My sister-in-law reads it."

Billing agencies harass poor people for the payment of the bills for purchases   28
that might have taken place six months before. Utility companies offer an agreement for a staggered payment schedule on a bill past due. "You have to trust them," one man said. Precisely for this reason, you end up by trusting no one and suspecting everyone of possible deceit. A submerged sense of distrust becomes the corollary to a constant need to trust. "They are cheating me . . . I have been tricked . . . I do not know . . ."

Not knowing: This is a familiar theme. Not knowing the right word for the   29
right thing at the right time is one form of subjugation. Not knowing the world that lies concealed behind those words is a more terrifying feeling. The longitude and latitude of one's existence are beyond all easy apprehension. Even the hard, cold stars within the firmament above one's head begin to mock the possibilities for self-location. Where am I? Where did I come from? Where will I go?

"I've lost a lot of jobs," one man explains. "Today, even if you're a janitor,   30
there's still reading and writing . . . They leave a note saying, 'Go to room so-and-so . . .' You can't do it. You can't read it. You don't know."

"The hardest thing about it is that I've been places where I didn't know   31
where I was. You don't know where you are . . . You're lost."

"Like I said: I have two kids. What do I do if one of my kids starts choking?   32
I go running to the phone . . . I can't look up the hospital phone number. That's if we're at home. Out on the street, I can't read the sign. I get to a pay phone. 'Okay, tell us where you are. We'll send an ambulance.' I look at the street sign.

Right there, I can't tell you what it says. I'd have to spell it out, letter for letter. By that time, one of my kids would be dead . . . These are the kinds of fears you go with, every single day . . ."

33   "Reading directions, I suffer with. I work with chemicals . . . That's scary to begin with . . ."

34   "You sit down. They throw the menu in front of you. Where do you go from there? Nine times out of ten you say, 'Go ahead. Pick out something for the both of us.' I've eaten some weird things, let me tell you!"

35   Menus. Chemicals. A child choking while his mother searches for a word she does not know to find assistance that will come too late. Another mother speaks about the inability to help her kids to read: "I can't read to them. Of course that's leaving them out of something they should have. Oh, it matters. You *believe* it matters! I ordered all these books. The kids belong to a book club. Donny wanted me to read a book to him. I told Donny: 'I can't read,' He said: 'Mommy, you sit down. I'll read it to you.' I tried it one day, reading from the pictures. Donny looked at me. He said, 'Mommy, that's not right.' He's only five. He knew I couldn't read . . .' "

36   A landlord tells a woman that her lease allows him to evict her if her baby cries and causes inconvenience to her neighbors. The consequence of challenging his words conveys a danger which appears, unlikely as it seems, even more alarming than the danger of eviction. Once she admits that she can't read, in the desire to maneuver for the time in which to call a friend, she will have defined herself in terms of an explicit impotence that she cannot endure. Capitulation in this case is preferable to self-humiliation. Resisting the definition of oneself in terms of what one cannot do, what others take for granted, represents a need so great that other imperatives (even one so urgent as the need to keep one's home in winter's cold) evaporate and fall away in face of fear. Even the loss of home and shelter, in this case, is not so terrifying as the loss of self.

37   "I come out of school. I was sixteen. They had their meetings. The directors meet. They said that I was wasting their school paper. I was wasting pencils . . ."

38   Another illiterate, looking back, believes she was not worthy of her teacher's time. She believes that it was wrong of her to take up space within her school. She believes that it was right to leave in order that somebody more deserving could receive her place.

39   Children choke. Their mother chokes another way: on more than chicken bones.

40   People eat what others order, know what others tell them, struggle not to see themselves as they believe the world perceives them. A man in California speaks about his own loss of identity, of self-location, definition:

41   "I stood at the bottom of the ramp. My car had broke down on the freeway. There was a phone. I asked for the police. They was nice. They said to tell them where I was. I looked up at the signs. There was one that I had seen before. I read it to them: ONE WAY STREET. They thought it was a joke. I told them I couldn't read. There was other signs above the ramp. They told me to try. I looked around for somebody to help. All the cars was going by real fast. I couldn't make them understand that I was lost. The cop was nice. He told me:

'Try once more.' I did my best. I couldn't read. I only knew the sign above my head. The cop was trying to be nice. He knew that I was trapped. 'I can't send out a car to you if you can't tell me where you are.' I felt afraid. I nearly cried. I'm forty-eight years old. I only said: 'I'm on a one-way street . . .' "

The legal problems and the courtroom complications that confront illiter-   42
ate adults have been discussed above. The anguish that may underlie such matters was brought home to me this year while I was working on this book. I have spoken, in the introduction, of a sudden phone call from one of my former students, now in prison for a criminal offense. Stephen is not a boy today. He is twenty-eight years old. He called to ask me to assist him in his trial, which comes up next fall. He will be on trial for murder. He has just knifed and killed a man who first enticed him to his home, then cheated him, and then insulted him— as "an illiterate subhuman."

Stephen now faces twenty years to life. Stephen's mother was illiterate. His   43
grandparents were illiterate as well. What parental curse did not destroy was killed off finally by the schools. Silent violence is repaid with interest. It will cost us $25,000 yearly to maintain this broken soul in prison. But what is the price that has been paid by Stephen's victim? What is the price that will be paid by Stephen?

Perhaps we might slow down a moment here and look at the realities   44
described above. This is the nation that we live in. This is a society that most of us did not create but which our President and other leaders have been willing to sustain by virtue of malign neglect. Do we possess the character and courage to address a problem which so many nations, poorer than our own, have found it natural to correct?

The answers to these questions represent a reasonable test of our belief in   45
the democracy to which we have been asked in public school to swear allegiance.

---

1 What is Kozol's purpose in writing this essay? How would you characterize his attitude toward the subject?

2 Kozol says that an illiterate person leads a "circumscribed existence" (para. 25). Which of his examples, real or hypothetical, best illustrates the kinds of limitations that beset an illiterate person and limit his or her ability to function in everyday life? How do these examples dramatize the costs of illiteracy in personal rather than statistical terms?

3 Why would an illiterate society be more likely to become less democratic? How does Kozol use the views of Socrates and Madison (para. 1–2) to support his thesis?

4 Kozol introduces his essay with a specific example that dramatizes the dangers of illiteracy. He concludes his essay with a stirring appeal to eliminate illiteracy lest it destroy democracy. What organizational strategy and rhetorical techniques does he use in making such a generalization seem credible? (Glossary: *Introduction, Conclusion, Organization*.)

5 Kozol provides a number of examples to illustrate the everyday consequences of illiteracy. Why is this rhetorical method well suited to illustrate his thesis? What different kinds of examples does he use (i.e., hypothetical or speculative, typical case histories, extended examples)? (Glossary: *Examples*.)

6 Recall a conversation you heard recently where a person's pronunciation, grammar, or vocabulary provided clear indicators about his or her background and social class. What criteria did you use in your evaluation? Has the reverse process ever happened to you when you were judged because of the way you speak? Describe one such incident (which can be positive or negative).

Little Red Riding Hood   *James Finn Garner*

◆ JAMES FINN GARNER'S satires have appeared in the *Chicago Tribune Magazine* and he is a regularly heard performer on Chicago public radio. His hilarious send-ups include *Politically Correct Bedtime Stories* (1994), from which the following spoof is taken, *Politically Correct Holiday Stories* (1995), and *Apocalypse Wow* (1997).

The more advocates of political correctness lose their sense of humor, the more we appreciate a satiric story of the kind Garner contrives. Garner neatly caricatures the nonsensical coinage of elaborately contorted terms designed to avoid political incorrectness ("optically challenged" for "nearsighted," "log-fuel technician" for "woodchopper"). Admittedly, extremists on this issue are an easy target, but Garner's point using the vehicle of the classic children's story "Little Red Riding Hood" is worth making: Our desire to be politically correct, when taken to extremes, is not only ridiculous but diminishes the richness of the English language and compromises our ability to think for ourselves.

> **TO CONSIDER** In your view, have the excesses of "political correctness" become so much a joke that they have undercut the legitimacy of the movement?

1   There once was a young person named Red Riding Hood who lived with her mother on the edge of a large wood. One day her mother asked her to take a basket of fresh fruit and mineral water to her grandmother's house—not because this was womyn's work, mind you, but because the deed was generous and helped engender a feeling of community. Furthermore, her grandmother was *not sick*, but rather was in full physical and mental health and was fully capable of taking care of herself as a mature adult.

So Red Riding Hood set off with her basket through the woods. Many peo-   2
ple believed that the forest was a foreboding and dangerous place and never set
foot in it. Red Riding Hood, however, was confident enough in her own budding sexuality that such obvious Freudian imagery did not intimidate her.

On the way to Grandma's house, Red Riding Hood was accosted by a wolf,   3
who asked her what was in her basket. She replied, "Some healthful snacks for my
grandmother, who is certainly capable of taking care of herself as a mature adult."

The wolf said, "You know, my dear, it isn't safe for a little girl to walk   4
through these woods alone."

Red Riding Hood said, "I find your sexist remark offensive in the extreme,   5
but I will ignore it because of your traditional status as an outcast from society,
the stress of which has caused you to develop your own, entirely valid, worldview. Now, if you'll excuse me, I must be on my way."

Red Riding Hood walked on along the main path. But, because his status   6
outside society had freed him from slavish adherence to linear, Western-style
thought, the wolf knew a quicker route to Grandma's house. He burst into the
house and ate Grandma, an entirely valid course of action for a carnivore such as
himself. Then, unhampered by rigid, traditionalist notions of what was masculine or feminine, he put on Grandma's nightclothes and crawled into bed.

Red Riding Hood entered the cottage and said, "Grandma, I have brought   7
you some fat-free, sodium-free snacks to salute you in your role of a wise and
nurturing matriarch."

From the bed, the wolf said softly, "Come closer, child, so that I might see   8
you."

Red Riding Hood said, "Oh, I forgot you are as optically challenged as a   9
bat. Grandma, what big eyes you have!"

"They have seen much, and forgiven much, my dear."   10

"Grandma, what a big nose you have—only relatively, of course, and cer-   11
tainly attractive in its own way."

"It has smelled much, and forgiven much, my dear."   12

"Grandma, what big teeth you have!"   13

The wolf said, "I am happy with *who* I am and *what* I am," and leaped out   14
of bed. He grabbed Red Riding Hood in his claws, intent on devouring her. Red
Riding Hood screamed, not out of alarm at the wolf's apparent tendency toward
cross-dressing, but because of his willful invasion of her personal space.

Her screams were heard by a passing woodchopper-person (or log-fuel tech-   15
nician, as he preferred to be called). When he burst into the cottage, he saw the
melee and tried to intervene. But as he raised his ax, Red Riding Hood and the
wolf both stopped.

"And just what do you think you're doing?" asked Red Riding Hood.   16

The woodchopper-person blinked and tried to answer, but no words came   17
to him.

"Bursting in here like a Neanderthal, trusting your weapon to do your   18
thinking for you!" she exclaimed. "Sexist! Speciesist! How dare you assume that
womyn and wolves can't solve their own problems without a man's help!"

When she heard Red Riding Hood's impassioned speech, Grandma jumped   19
out of the wolf's mouth, seized the woodchopper-person's ax, and cut his head

off. After this ordeal, Red Riding Hood, Grandma, and the wolf felt a certain commonality of purpose. They decided to set up an alternative household based on mutual respect and cooperation, and they lived together in the woods happily ever after.

---

1 How does the humor of Garner's updated version of this fairy tale depend on his use of elaborate verbal contortions and gender-neutral terms for words and phrases that might be found objectionable?

2 How does Garner's revision depend on applying modern-day sensitivities to words whose ethnic, sexual, racial, or social bias existed before these views became objectionable? Why is it more politically correct to refer to grandma as "optically challenged" (para. 9) rather than "blind as a bat"?

3 Do you think the desire to revise language to avoid subtle or overt stereotyping is worthwhile? Has the attempt to avoid sexual, racist, ageist, and species stereotyping reached the ridiculous extreme satirized by Garner (for example, spelling "woman" so the word "man" does not appear, para. 1)? You might try making up your own bias-free version of your favorite fairy tale or animal fable and share it with your classmates.

4 What might Garner be suggesting by omitting "little" from "Red Riding Hood" when she is introduced as a character? At what other points in the story do characters display or fail to display linguistic sensitivity? (Glossary: *Biased Language.*)

5 How does Garner use exaggeration to puncture the pretentions of those who aspire to be politically correct? (Glossary: *Satire, Humor.*)

6 Satire is an enduring form of argument that uses parody, irony, and caricature to poke fun at a subject, idea, or person. (Glossary: *Satire.*) The satirist frequently creates a "mask" or *persona* that is very different from the author's real voice in order to shock the audience into a new awareness about an established institution or custom. Enduring satirical works include Aristophanes' *The Birds,* Samuel Johnson's *Rasselas,* Voltaire's *Candide,* Swift's *Gulliver's Travels,* Mark Twain's *A Connecticut Yankee in King Arthur's Court,* and Joseph Heller's *Catch-22.* These works assail folly, greed, corruption, pride, self-righteous complacency, hypocrisy, and other permanent targets of the satirists' pen.

One clear signal the author is being ironic is a noticeable disparity between the tone and the subject. (Glossary: *Irony, Tone.*) For example, in Jonathan Swift's "A Modest Proposal" (1729), the tone in which the narrator speaks is reasonable, matter-of-fact, and totally at odds with his recommendation that Ireland solve its overpopulation problem by encouraging poor people to sell their babies as food to the wealthy:

I shall now therefore humbly propose my own thoughts, which I hope will not be liable to the least objection.

I have been assured by a very knowing American of my acquaintance in London, that a young healthy child well nursed is at a year old a most delicious, nourishing, and wholesome food, whether stewed, roasted, baked, or boiled, and I make no doubt that it will equally serve in a fricassee, or a ragout.

I do therefore humbly offer it to public consideration, that of the hundred and twenty thousand children already computed, twenty thousand may be reserved for breed, whereof only one fourth part to be males, which is more than we allow to sheep, black-cattle, or swine, and my reason is that these children are seldom the fruits of marriage, a circumstance not much regarded by our savages, therefore one male will be sufficient to serve four females. That the remaining hundred thousand may at a year old be offered in sale to the persons of quality, and fortune, through the kingdom, always advising the mother to let them suck plentifully in the last month, so as to render them plump, and fat for a good table. A child will make two dishes at an entertainment for friends, and when the family dines alone, the fore or hind quarter will make a reasonable dish, and seasoned with a little pepper or salt will be very good boiled on the fourth day, especially in winter.

I have reckoned upon a medium [average], that a child just born will weight 12 pounds, and in a solar year if tolerably nursed increaseth to 28 pounds.

I grant this food will be somewhat dear, and therefore very proper for landlords, who, as they have already devoured most of the parents, seem to have the best title to the children.

You may have noticed the practical, down-to-earth, and understated voice with which the narrator enumerates the financial and culinary advantages of his proposed "solution." The discrepancy between his matter-of-fact tone and the outrageous content is a clear signal that the writer means the exact opposite of what is being said. If you missed Swift's signals, you might even think he was being serious!

Take any traditional text such as one of Aesop's fables or another children's story ("Snow White and the Seven Dwarfs," "Jack and the Beanstalk," "Cinderella," "Hansel and Gretel," etc.) or a section of the Old Testament and transform it in ways that correspond to those used by James Finn Garner.

◆ CONNECTIONS: THE POLITICS OF EVERYDAY LANGUAGE

Jack Solomon, "What's in a Name? the Ideology of Cultural Classification"

1. Drawing on Solomon's analysis of how supposedly objective classifications can serve hidden agendas, discuss Frank Nuessel's essay on the public perceptions of those classified as being elderly.

2. How did the perception of Jews in Nazi Germany (as discussed by Solomon) pave the way for Hitler's manipulation of the public, as described by Aldous Huxley in "Propaganda Under a Dictatorship" (Ch. 10)?

Fan Shen, " The Classroom and the Wider Culture: Identity as a Key to Learning English Composition"

1. How do the political and cultural agendas of Chinese and Western composition classes (as discussed by Shen) reveal a form of what is politically correct in different cultures in ways that are similar to those satirized by James Finn Garner in "Little Red Riding Hood"?
2. How can the use of "I" instead of "we" as discussed by Shen be considered the "dancing of an attitude" of the kind described by Kenneth Burke in "Symbolic Action" (Ch. 3)?

Alleen Pace Nilsen, "Sexism in English: A 1990s Update"

1. In what way do some of the sexist terms Alleen Pace Nilsen discusses exemplify the kind of stereotyping Jack Solomon analyzes?
2. Drawing on George Lakoff's analysis of cognitive systems underlying metaphors (see "Anger" Ch. 3), analyze one system of related expressions for either men or women in Nilsen's article to discover the hidden metaphors.

Susan Sontag, "AIDS and Its Metaphors"

1. In what sense are the metaphors that shape public perception of illnesses in the past and AIDS in the present, according to Sontag, an example of how a classification can serve a political agenda, as discussed by Jack Solomon?
2. How does Sontag extend the kind of analysis George Lakoff proposed in his essay "Anger" (Ch. 3) into the physical basis of metaphor to study the public perception of AIDS?

Michiko Kakutani, "The Word Police"

1. Compare the approaches taken by Kakutani and James Finn Garner in criticizing and satirizing the extremes to which advocates of politically correct language sometimes go.
2. Compare Kakutani's spoof of the politically correct version of the opening to the Gettysburg Address with Gilbert Highet's analysis, "The Gettysburg Address," in Ch. 10.

Frank Nuessel, "Old Age Needs a New Name, But Don't Look for It in Webster's"

1. Compare the phenomenon of ageism with that of sexism as described by Alleen Pace Nilsen. What similarities can you discover in the means by which each operates?
2. Drawing on Naomi Wolf's essay "The Beauty Myth" (Ch. 9), analyze how advertising contains implicit ageist stereotyping in marketing products.

Jonathan Kozol, "The Human Cost of an Illiterate Society"

1. In what way is the perception of those who are illiterate as damaging as ageism, as discussed by Nuessel?
2. Evaluate the kind of political consequences for a country when a large number of its adults watch television talk shows that promote illiteracy (see Tom Shachtman "What's Wrong with TV?: Talk Shows," Ch. 4).

James Finn Garner, "Little Red Riding Hood"

1. Which of the objectionable words, phrases, and attitudes criticized by Alleen Pace Nilsen does Garner render in a more politically correct form?
2. In what sense might Garner's fable be perceived as a spoof of the kind of feminist perspective exemplified by Julia Penelope in "The Glamour of Grammar" (Ch. 7)?

◆ WRITING ASSIGNMENTS FOR CHAPTER 8

1. How a person or event is labeled influences the readers' or listeners' perception of what is being described. Labels can be damaging because they classify people in ways that stereotype or stigmatize. The label creates a stereotyped picture that portrays the person only in terms of a single trait. Perhaps the most dangerous thing about stereotypes is that they create a mind-set that makes it impossible to accept people as they really are. Stereotypes distort our perceptions and make it impossible to acknowledge experiences that conflict with the stereotype. Research shows that if your expectations about members of an entire group are shaped by a stereotyped view, you are more likely to disregard contradictory evidence in order to avoid giving up the stereotype.

   Labels act as filters to screen out everything that does not confirm the stereotype. (Glossary: *Stereotype*.) For example, let's say you were asked to complete any of the following statements:

Southerners are . . .   Texans are . . .

Rock stars are . . .   Easterners are . . .

Hairdressers are . . .   Football players are . . .

Each completed statement reveals one of your attitudes or beliefs. If you were then asked to write down whatever experiences you have had that justify or explain this attitude, you might discover that your ideas are based much more on portrayals and labels conveyed by the media than on your own personal experiences. In a short essay discuss how stereotyping works with any of the groups above.

2. Ageist stereotypes—that is, the negative labels used to refer to old age—are as destructive as racist or sexist language. Referring to elderly women as *biddy* or *hag* or to elderly men as *codger, coot, geezer,* or *fogey* fosters a conception of the elderly as senile, incapable of learning new things, and antiquated. These labels promote a notion of the elderly that makes it difficult for the young and middle-aged to identify with them as human beings.

Keep a log of television programs that you watch for a few days. To what extent do prime-time programs stereotype the elderly?

3. What would you suggest as a more accurate descriptive term to define the age group described here? How would you correct the stereotype?

So what does it mean to be a part of "Generation X?" What should we expect as our generation grows older? More importantly, why must we and other generations be labeled and what does it mean to us (if anything)? This phenomenon was given birth by Douglas Coupland with the release of his 1990 novel *Generation* X. From it we have adopted such buzzwords as McJob— "a low-pay, low-prestige, low-dignity, low-benefit, no-future job in the service sector"—and developed an annoyingly new way of defining the twenty something generation. Once this novel of catch phrases and semi-truisms took off, those in the media and, subsequently the advertising and business worlds began selectively programming its campaigns for a generation commonly thought of as pessimistic, cynical, and apathetic. (Dan Roberts, Jr., "The Labelling of a Generation," *Inside BEAT,* September 15, 1994.)

4. Are the defining attributes of the term *African American* (when compared with previous terms, e.g., colored, Negro, black, Afro-American) more meaningful than prior ones?

5. Where do you draw the line in the issue discussed in the following extract? How does where you draw the line distinguish between and define *tissue, fetus,* and *baby*?

Our ritual and religious practices underscore the fact that we make distinctions among fetuses. If a woman took the bloody matter—indistinguishable from a heavy period—of an early miscarriage and insisted upon putting it in a tiny coffin and marking its grave, we would have serious concerns about her mental health. By the same token, we would feel squeamish about flushing a seven month-old fetus down the toilet—something we would quite normally do with an early miscarriage. There are no prayers for the matter of a miscarriage, nor do we feel there should be. Even a Catholic priest would not baptize the issue of an early miscarriage. (Mary Gordon, "A Moral Choice," *Atlantic,* April 1990.)

6. In what way has a widely used term changed its meanings or shifted its connotations in recent times (for example, Palestinian homeland, safe sex,)?

7. What, in your opinion, should constitute protected areas of speech? For example, should the right to free expression permit newspapers to report the names of rape victims? Why or why not?

8. Emotionally charged language is a principal means by which language affects perceptions. Basically, emotive language is designed to elicit certain feelings in an audience. To see how this works, formulate three short descriptions using neutral, negative, or positive adjectives for the postal service, the National Rifle Association, Greenpeace, the American Civil Liberties Union, the John Birch Society, the National Organization for Women, or any other defined association or organization. How were the connotations of the words you used intended to influence perceptions of this group?

9. How are differences in social class suggested by the different connotation of the words "cuisine," "food," and "eats"?

10. How are differences in social class suggested by the phrases that people use to describe the same activity: (a) trying to get a *job,* (b) looking for *work,* (c) seeking *employment,* (d) finding a *position?*

11. *Euphemism* comes from Greek ("to speak well of" or "to use words of good omen"). Originally these words were used to placate the gods. (Glossary: *Euphemism.*) Euphemistic language is used to smooth things over, present activities in a more favorable light, and make things seem better than they are. More commonly, euphemisms are used to avoid taboo subjects. For example, in ancient Greece, baby boys were encouraged to call their genitals their "kokko," their "laloo," or their "lizard." Roman nannies taught little girls to call their genitals their "piggy." In the nineteenth century, Victorians used a wide range of euphemisms to avoid explicit references to sex, birth, and bodily functions. Trousers were called "unmentionables," sexual organs became "private parts," and the birth of a baby became the arrival of "the little stranger" or "the patter of tiny feet."

A principal subject of euphemisms is death, whose implacable reality has been skirted by such phrases as the following: to go to a better place, just reward, with God, cash in one's chips, to pop off, to croak, cross over, go to the hereafter, join one's ancestors, meet the grim reaper, go to the last roundup, bite the dust, pass out of the picture, slip away. In fact, the systematic use of language to mask the reality of death has been the subject of satiric novels like Evelyn Waugh's *The Loved One* (1948) and exposés like Jessica Mitford's *The American Way of Death* (1963).

How are the connotations of key terms designed to present things in a better light in the following excerpt from Jessica Mitford's "Mortuary Solaces"?

Jones is now ready for casketing (this is the present participle of the verb "to casket"). In this operation his right shoulder should be depressed slightly "to turn the body a bit to the right and soften the appearance of lying flat on the back." Positioning the hands is a matter of importance and special rubber positioning blocks may be used. The hands should be cupped for a more life like, relaxed appearance. Proper placement of the body requires a delicate sense of balance. It should lie as high as possible in the casket, yet not so high that the lid, when lowered, will hit the nose. On the other hand, we are cautioned, placing the body too low "creates the impression that the body is in a box." Jones is next wheeled into the appointed slumber room where a few last touches may be added—his favorite pipe placed in his hand or, if he was a great reader, a book propped into position. (In the case of little Master Jones a Teddy bear may be clutched.) (Jessica Mitford, "Mortuary Solaces," from *The American Way of Death*, 1963.)

What additional terms not mentioned by Mitford illustrate the way euphemisms work? Consider, for example, "floral tributes" instead of flowers, "grief therapists" instead of morticians, "memorial service" instead of funeral. What new terms have replaced grave, the body that is buried, the hearse, cemetery? You might wish to make up some of your own euphemisms for any of these terms.

12. How does the following cartoon illustrate the use of euphemisms? what underlying political agenda is at work?

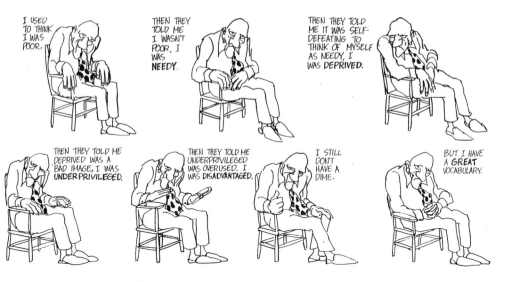

From *FEIFFER: Jules Feiffer's America from Eisenhower to Reagan,* by Jules Feiffer, edited by Steven Heller, copyright © 1982 by Jules Feiffer. Reprinted by permission of Alfred A. Knopf, Inc.

9

Advertising is the greatest art form of the
20th century

— Marshall McLuhan

"Advertise! Advertise! That's always been your answer to everything."

The Rhetoric
of Advertising

A dvertising has long been a favorite topic with students of language, since careful reading of ads and their accompanying texts can provide an invaluable seminar on the manipulative uses of language. The authors in this chapter approach advertising from a wide range of perspectives. The first three selections take a broad view of how the ideologies, objectives, and techniques of advertising have evolved. Bill Bryson in "The Hard Sell: Advertising in America" describes how the marketing campaigns of American advertising developed over the past century. Bryson is especially adept at pointing out how advertising has tapped into fundamental social values of American culture to shape a consumer ideology. Although the techniques and ploys used in advertising have changed very little from its inception, the ingenuity advertisers display in adapting these basic techniques is truly amazing, a point made by Stuart Hirschberg in "The Rhetoric of Advertising."

John Berger's discussion in "Ways of Seeing" of the motives, intents, and methods of advertising can trigger critical thinking in a rather different way. It asks us to place ourselves in the position of the advertisers and understand what they hope to achieve by creating vignettes and scenarios that invest products in the present with values from the past. Advertising appropriates these values and uses them to lend authority to the publicity campaigns that are the most visible signs of what for Berger is our consumer culture, whose ultimate mythology is that you are what you buy.

In the selection by Naomi Wolf ("The Beauty Myth"), we discover how advertisers have manufactured and exploited what has become a fundamental tenet of American culture: that unless a woman's appearance conforms to standards of beauty promulgated by advertisers, she can expect none of the good life accessible to women who are judged to be "beautiful." What is bizarre is that contemporary standards of feminine beauty now have created an ideal that can be attained only through eating disorders such as anorexia and bulimia. Consider what recent Calvin Klein ads that feature supermodel Kate Moss in scenes that evoke abuse, heroin addiction, and decadence say about our culture. Jean Kilbourne, in her article "Beauty and the Beast of Advertising," makes the point that advertising has taken a disturbing turn in its increasing sexualization of very young girls. In "Sprayed and Neutered," Susan Irvine discusses a counter-trend in recent advertising designed to market perfume. She believes that advertisers have become wary of using blatant sexuality to market fragrances and have turned instead to more discreet, chaste ad campaigns that market innocence, wholesomeness, and self-sufficiency. This chapter also includes a portfolio of ads for class discussion and analysis.

The Hard Sell: Advertising in America   *Bill Bryson*

◆ BILL BRYSON is an American journalist who lives in England and writes for *National Geographic.* He has also written for the *New York Times, Granta, Esquire,* and *GQ* (*Gentleman's Quarterly*). His books include the widely praised *The Mother Tongue* (1990) and *Made in America: An Informal History of the English Language in the United States* (1994), in which this chapter originally appeared. His latest book is *A Walk in the Woods* (1998).

We are surrounded by ads in our daily lives; by one estimate, we see nearly 38,000 commercials on television within a year, not to mention ads in magazines, newspapers, and on the radio. Yet surprisingly few of us know anything about their origin or early history, even though advertising as we know it has only been around for a hundred years. Bryson reveals how from the onset advertisers have been less interested in the product than in the image they can create to sell it. The story of the Eastman Kodak camera serves to introduce us to the way products are marketed and the techniques and strategies that have transformed advertising into a multibillion-dollar industry. The marketing of products (many of which are nearly identical) largely depends on creating a distinctive image that consumers will buy along with the product—we are encouraged to define ourselves through what we buy.

> **TO CONSIDER**   Have you ever bought something because of the advertising for this product? What was the item and what was the ad? Why do you think this particular ad worked on you? Did the product or service fulfill the ad's promise?

I n 1885, a young man named George Eastman formed the Eastman Dry   1
Plate and Film Company in Rochester, New York. It was rather a bold thinking to do. Aged just thirty-one, Eastman was a junior clerk in a bank on a comfortable but modest salary of $15 a week. He had no background in business. But he was passionately devoted to photography and had become increasingly gripped with the conviction that anyone who could develop a simple, untechnical camera, as opposed to the cumbersome, outsized, fussily complex contrivances then on the market, stood to make a fortune.

Eastman worked tirelessly for three years to perfect his invention, support-   2
ing himself in the meantime by making dry plates for commercial photographers, and in June 1888 produced a camera that was positively dazzling in its simplicity: a plain black box just six and a half inches long by three and a quarter inches wide, with a button on the side and a key for advancing the film. Eastman called his device the *Detective Camera*. Detectives were all the thing—Sherlock Holmes was just taking off with American readers—and the name implied that it was so small and simple that it could be used unnoticed, as a detective might.

The camera had no viewfinder and no way of focusing. The *photographer* or   3
photographist (it took a while for the first word to become the established one) simply held the camera in front of him, pressed a button on the side, and hoped for the best. Each roll took a hundred pictures. When the roll was fully exposed, the anxious owner sent the entire camera to Rochester for developing. Eventually he received the camera back, freshly loaded with film, and—assuming all had gone well—one hundred small circular pictures, two and a half inches in diameter.

Often all didn't go well. The film Eastman used at first was made of paper,   4
which tore easily and had to be carefully stripped of its emulsion before the exposures could be developed. It wasn't until the invention of celluloid roll film by a sixty-five-year-old Episcopal minister named Hannibal Goodwin in Newark, New Jersey—this truly was the age of the amateur inventor—that amateur photography became a reliable undertaking. Goodwin didn't call his invention *film* but *photographic pellicule*, and, as was usual, spent years fighting costly legal battles with Eastman without ever securing the recognition or financial payoff he deserved—though eventually, years after Goodwin's death, Eastman was ordered to pay $5 million to the company that inherited the patent.

In September 1888, Eastman changed the name of the camera to *Kodak*—   5
an odd choice, since it was meaningless, and in 1888 no one gave meaningless

names to products, especially successful products. Since British patent applications at the time demanded a full explanation of trade and brand names, we know how Eastman arrived at his inspired name. He crisply summarized his reasoning in his patent application: "First. It is short. Second. It is not capable of mispronunciation. Third. It does not resemble anything in the art and cannot be associated with anything in the art except the Kodak." For years later the whole enterprise was renamed the Eastman Kodak Company.

6   Despite the considerable expense involved—a Kodak camera sold for $25, and each roll of film cost $10, including developing—by 1895, over 100,000 Kodaks had been sold and Eastman was a seriously wealthy man. A lifelong bachelor, he lived with his mother in a thirty-seven-room mansion with twelve bathrooms. Soon people everywhere were talking about snapshots, originally a British shooting term for a hastily executed shot. Its photographic sense was coined by the English astronomer Sir John Herschel, who also gave the world the terms *positive* and *negative* in their photographic senses.

7   From the outset, Eastman developed three crucial strategies that have been the hallmarks of virtually every successful consumer goods company since. First, he went for the mass market, reasoning that it was better to make a little money each from a lot of people rather than a lot of money from a few. He also showed a tireless, obsessive dedication to making his products better and cheaper. In the 1890s, such an approach was widely perceived as insane. If you had a successful product you milked it for all it was worth. If competitors came along with something better, you bought them out or tried to squash them with lengthy patent fights or other bullying tactics. What you certainly did not do was create new products that made you existing lines obsolescent. Eastman did. Throughout the late 1890s, Kodak introduced a series of increasingly cheaper, niftier cameras—the Bull's Eye model of 1896, which cost just $12, and the famous slimline Folding Pocket Kodak of 1898, before finally in 1900 producing his eureka model: the little box Brownie, priced at just $1 and with film at 15 cents a reel (though with only six exposures per reel.)

8   Above all, what set Eastman apart was the breathtaking lavishness of his advertising. In 1899 alone, he spent $750,000, an unheard of sum, on advertising. Moreover, it was *good* advertising: crisp, catchy, reassuringly trustworthy. "You press the button—we do the rest" ran the company's first slogan, thus making a virtue of its shortcomings. Never mind that you couldn't load or unload the film yourself. Kodak would do it for you. In 1905, it followed with another classic slogan: "If It Isn't an Eastman, It Isn't a Kodak."

9   Kodak's success did not escape other businessmen, who also began to see virtue in the idea of steady product refinement and improvement. AT&T and Westinghouse, among others, set up research laboratories with the idea of creating a stream of new products, even at the risk of displacing old ones. Above all, everyone everywhere began to advertise.

10   Advertising was already a well established phenomenon by the turn of the twentieth century. Newspapers had begun carrying ads as far back as the early 1700s, and magazines soon followed. (Benjamin Franklin has the distinction of having run the first magazine ad, seeking the whereabouts of a runaway slave, in

1741.) By 1850, the country had its first *advertising agency,* the American Newspaper Advertising Agency, though its function was to buy advertising space rather than come up with creative campaigns. The first advertising agency in the modern sense was N. W. Ayer & Sons of Philadelphia, established in 1869. To *advertise* originally carried the sense of to broadcast or disseminate news. Thus a nineteenth-century newspaper that called itself the *Advertiser* meant that it had lots of news, not lots of ads. By the early 1800s the term had been stretched to accommodate the idea of spreading the news of the availability of certain goods or services. A newspaper notice that read "Jos. Parker, Hatter" was essentially announcing that if anyone was in the market for hats, Jos. Parker had them. In the sense of persuading members of the public to acquire items they might not otherwise think of buying—items they didn't know they needed—advertising is a phenomenon of the modern age.

By the 1890s, advertising was appearing everywhere in newspapers and   11
magazines, on *billboards* (an Americanism dating from 1850), on the sides of buildings, on passing streetcars, on paper bags, even on match-books, which were invented in 1892 and were being extensively used as an advertising medium within three years.

Very early on, advertisers discovered the importance of a good slogan. Many   12
of our more venerable slogans are older than you might think. Ivory Soap's "99 44/100 percent pure" dates from 1879. Schlitz has been calling itself "the beer that made Milwaukee famous" since 1895, and Heinz's "57 varieties" followed a year later. Morton Salt's "When it rains, it pours" dates from 1911, the American Florist Association's "Say it with flowers" was first used in 1912, and the "good to the last drop" of Maxwell House coffee, named for the Maxwell House Hotel in Nashville, where it was first served, has been with us since 1907. (The slogan is said to have originated with Teddy Roosevelt, who pronounced the coffee "good to the last drop," prompting one wit to ask, "So what's wrong with the last drop?")

Sometimes slogans took a little working on. Coca-Cola described itself as   13
"the drink that makes a pause refreshing" before realizing, in 1929, that "the pause that refreshes" was rather more succinct and memorable. A slogan could make all the difference to a product's success. After advertising its soap as an efficacious way of dealing with "conspicuous nose pores," Woodbury's Facial Soap came up with the slogan "The skin you love to touch" and won the hearts of millions. The great thing about a slogan was that it didn't have to be accurate to be effective. Heinz never actually had exactly "57 varieties" of anything. The catchparase arose simply because H.J. Heinz, the company's founder, decided he liked the sound of the number. Undeterred by considerations of varity, he had the slogan slapped on every one of the products he produced, already in 1896 far more than fifty-seven. For a time the company tried to arrange its products into fifty-seven arbitrary clusters, but in 1969 it gave up the ruse altogether and abandoned the slogan.

Early in the 1900s, advertisers discovered another perennial feature of mar-   14
keting—the *giveaway,* as it was called almost from the start. Consumers soon became acquainted with the irresistibly tempting notion that if they bought a

particular product they could expect a reward—the chance to receive a prize, a free book (almost always ostensibly dedicated to the general improvement of one's well-being but invariably a thinly disguised plug for the manufacturer's range of products), a free sample, or a rebate in the form of a shiny dime, or be otherwise endowed with some gratifying bagatelle. Typical of the genre was a turn-of-the-century tome called *The Vital Question Cook Book*, which was promoted as an aid to livelier meals, but which proved upon receipt to contain 112 pages of recipes all involving the use of Shredded Wheat. Many of these had a certain air of desperation about them, notably the "Shredded Wheat Biscuit Jellied Apple Sandwich" and the "Creamed Spinach on Shredded Wheat Biscuit Toast." Almost all involved nothing more than spooning some everyday food on a piece of shredded wheat and giving it an inflated name. Nonetheless the company distributed no fewer than four million copies of *The Vital Question Cook Book* to eager consumers.

15   The great breakthrough in twentieth-century advertising, however, came with the identification and exploitation of the American consumer's Achilles' heel: anxiety. One of the first to master the form was King Gillette, inventor of the first safety razor and one of the most relentless advertisers of the early 1900s. Most of the early ads featured Gillette himself, who with his fussy toothbrush mustache and well-oiled hair looked more like a caricature of a Parisian waiter than a captain of industry. After starting with a few jaunty words about the ease and convenience of the safety razor—"Compact? Rather!"—he plunged the reader into the heart of the matter: "When you use my razor you are exempt from the dangers that men often encounter who allow their faces to come in contact with brush, soap, and barbershop accessories used on other people."

16   Here was an entirely new approach to selling goods. Gillette's ads were in effect telling you that not only did there exist a product that you never previously suspected you needed, but if you *didn't* use it you would very possibly attract a crop of facial diseases you never knew existed. The combination proved irresistible. Though the Gillette razor retailed for a hefty $5—half the average workingman's weekly pay—it sold by the millions, and King Gillette became a very wealthy man. (Though only for a time, alas. Like many others of his era, he grew obsessed with the idea of the perfectibility of mankind and expended so much of his energies writing books of convoluted philosophy with titles like *The Human Drift* that he eventually lost control of his company and most of his fortune.)

17   By the 1920s, advertisers had so refined the art that a consumer could scarcely pick up a magazine without being bombarded with unsettling questions: "Do You Make These Mistakes in English?"; "Will Your Hair Stand Close Inspection?"; "When Your Guests Are Gone—Are You Sorry You Ever Invited Them?" (because, that is, you lack social polish); "Did Nature fail to put roses in your cheeks?"; "Will There be a Victrola in Your Home This Christmas?"*

---

*The most famous 1920s ad of them all didn't pose a question, but it did play on the reader's anxiety: "They Laughed When I Sat Down, but When I Started to Play . . ." It was originated by the U.S. School of Music in 1925.

The 1920s truly were the Age of Anxiety. One ad pictured a former golf champion, "now only a wistful onlooker," whose career had gone sour because he had neglected his teeth. Scott Tissues mounted a campaign showing a forlorn-looking businessman sitting on a park bench beneath the bold caption "A Serious Business Handicap—These Troubles That Come from Harsh Toilet Tissue." Below the picture the text explained: "65% of all men and women over 40 are suffering from some form of rectal trouble, estimates a prominent specialist connected with one of New York's largest hospitals. 'And one of the contributing causes,' he states, 'is inferior toilet tissue.'" There was almost nothing that one couldn't become uneasy about. One ad even asked: "Can You Buy a Radio Safely?" Distressed bowels were the most frequent target. The makers of Sal Hepatica warned: "We rush to meetings, we dash to parties. We are on the go all day long. We exercise too little, and we eat too much. And, in consequence, we impair our bodily functions—often we retain food within us too long. And when that occurs, poisons are set up—*Auto-Intoxication begins.*"

In addition to the dread of auto-intoxication, the American consumer faced a gauntlet of other newly minted maladies—*pyorrhea, halitosis* (coined as a medical term in 1874, but popularized by Listerine beginning in 1922 with the slogan "Even your best friend won't tell you"), *athlete's foot* (a term invented by the makers of Absorbine Jr. in 1928), *dead cuticles, scabby toes, iron-poor blood, vitamin deficiency* (*vitamins* had been coined in 1912, but the word didn't enter the general vocabulary until the 1920s, when advertisers realized it sounded worryingly scientific), *fallen stomach, tobacco breath,* and *psoriasis,* though Americans would have to wait until the next decade for the scientific identification of the gravest of personal disorders—*body odor,* a term invented in 1933 by the makers of Lifebuoy soap and so terrifying in its social consequences that it was soon abbreviated to a whispered *B.O.* [18]

The white-coated technicians of American laboratories had not only identified these new conditions, but—miraculously, it seemed—simultaneously come up with cures for them. Among the products that were invented or rose to greatness in this busy, neurotic decade were *Cutex* (for those deceased cuticles), *Vick's VapoRub, Geritol, Serutan* ("Natures spelled backwards," as the voiceover always said with somewhat bewildering reassurance, as if spelling a product's name backward conferred some medicinal benefit), *Noxzema* (for which read: "knocks eczema"), *Preparation H, Murine* eyedrops, and *Dr. Scholl's Foot Aids.*** It truly was an age of miracles—one in which you could even cure a smoker's cough by smoking, so long as it was Old Golds you smoked, because, as the slogan proudly if somewhat untruthfully boasted, they contained "Not a cough in a carload." (As late as 1953, L&M cigarettes were advertised as "just what the doctor ordered!") [19]

By 1927, advertising was a $1.5-billion-a-year industry in the United States, and advertising people were held in such awe that they were asked not only to [20]

**And yes there really was a Dr. Scholl. His name was William Scholl, he was a real doctor, genuinely dedicated to the well-being of feet, and they are still very proud of him in his hometown of La Porte, Indiana.

mastermind campaigns but even to name the products. An ad man named Henry N. McKinney, for instance, named *Keds* shoes, *Karo* syrup, *Meadow Gold* butter, and *Uneeda Biscuits*.

21   Product names tended to cluster around certain sounds. Breakfast cereals often ended in *-ies* (*Wheaties, Rice Krispies, Frosties*); washing powders and detergents tended to be gravely monosyllabic (*Lux, Fab, Tide, Duz*). It is often possible to tell the era of a product's development by its termination. Thus products dating from the 1920s and early 1930s often ended in *-ex* (*Pyrex, Cutex, Kleenex, Windex*), while those ending in *-master* (*Mixmaster, Toastmaster*) generally betray a late-1930s or early-1940s genesis. The development of *Glo-Coat* floor wax in 1932 also heralded the beginning of American business's strange and long-standing infatuation with illiterate spellings, a trend that continued with *ReaLemon* juice in 1935, *Reddi-Wip* whipped cream in 1947, and many hundreds of others since, from *Tastee-Freez* drive-ins to *Toys я Us*, along with countless others with a *Kwik, E-Z,* or U (as in *While-U-Wait*) embedded in their titles. The late 1940s saw the birth of a brief vogue for endings in *-matic,* so that car manufacturers offered vehicles with *Seat-O-Matic* levers and *Cruise-O-Matic* transmissions, and even fitted sheets came with *Ezy-Matic* corners. Some companies became associated with certain types of names. Du Pont, for instance, had a special fondness for words ending in *-on*. The practice began with *nylon*—a name that was concocted out of thin air and owes nothing to its chemical properties—and was followed with *Rayon, Dacron, Orlon,* and *Teflon,* among many others. In recent years the company has moved on to what might be called its *Star Trek* phase with such compounds as *Tyvek, Kevlar, Sontara, Condura, Nomex,* and *Zemorain*.

22   Such names have more than passing importance to their owners. If American business has given us a large dose of anxiety in its ceaseless quest for a healthier *bottom line* (a term dating from the 1930s, though not part of mainstream English until the 1970s), we may draw some comfort from the thought that business has suffered a great deal of collective anxiety over protecting the names of its products.

23   A certain cruel paradox prevails in the matter of preserving brand names. Every business naturally wants to create a product that will dominate its market. But if that product so dominates the market that the brand name becomes indistinguishable in the public mind from the product itself—when people begin to ask for a *thermos* rather than a "Thermos brand vacuum flask"—then the term has become generic and the owner faces the loss of its trademark protection. That is why advertisements and labels so often carry faintly paranoid-sounding lines like "Tabasco is the registered trademark for the brand of pepper sauce made by McIlhenny Co." and why companies like Coca-Cola suffer palpitations when they see a passage like this (from John Steinbeck's *The Wayward Bus*):

> "Got any coke?" another character asked.
> "No," said the proprietor. "Few bottles of Pepsi-Cola. Haven't had any coke for a month. . . . It's the same stuff. You can't tell them apart."

24   An understandable measure of confusion exists concerning the distinction between patents and trademarks and between trademarks and trade names. A

patent protects the name of the product and its method of manufacture for seventeen years. Thus from 1895 to 1912, no one but the Shredded Wheat Company could make shredded wheat. But because patents require manufacturers to divulge the secrets of their products—and thus make them available to rivals to copy when the patent runs out—companies sometimes choose not to seek their protection. *Coca-Cola*, for one, has never been patented. A *trademark* is effectively the name of a product, its *brand name*. A *trade name* is the name of the manufacturer. So *Ford* is a trade name, *Taurus* a trademark. Trademarks apply not just to names, but also to logos, drawings, and other symbols and depictions. The MGM lion, for instance, is a trademark. Unlike patents, trademark protection goes on forever, or at least as long as the manufacturer can protect it.

For a long time, it was felt that this permanence gave the holder an unfair 25 advantage. In consequence, America did not enact its first trademark law until 1870, almost a century after Britain, and then it was declared unconstitutional by the Supreme Court. Lasting trademark protection did not begin for American companies until 1881. Today, more than a million trademarks have been issued in the United States and the number is rising by about thirty thousand a year.

A good trademark is almost incalculably valuable. Invincible-seeming brand 26 names do occasionally falter and fade. *Pepsodent, Rinso, Chase & Sanborn, Sal Hepatica, Vitalis, Brylcreem,* and *Burma-Shave* all once stood on the commanding heights of consumer recognition but are now defunct or have sunk to the status of what the trade calls "ghost brands"—products that are still produced but little promoted and largely forgotten. For the most part, however, once a product establishes a dominant position in a market, it is exceedingly difficult to depose it. In nineteen of twenty-two product categories, the company that owned the leading American brand in 1925 still has it today—*Nabisco* in cookies, *Kellogg's* in breakfast cereals, *Kodak* in film, *Sherwin Williams* in paint, *Del Monte* in canned fruit, *Wrigley's* in chewing gum, *Singer* in sewing machines, *Ivory* in soap, *Campbell's* in soup, *Gillette* in razors. Few really successful brand names of today were not just as familiar to your grandparents or even great-grandparents, and a well-established brand name has a sort of self-perpetuating power. As *The Economist* has noted: "In the category of food blenders, consumers were still ranking General Electric second twenty years after the company had stopped making them."

An established brand name is so valuable that only about 5 percent of the 27 sixteen thousand or so new products introduced in America each year bear all-new brand names. The others are variants on an existing product—*Tide with Bleach, Tropicana Twister Light Fruit Juices,* and so on. Among some types of product a certain glut is evident. At last count there were 220 types of branded breakfast cereal in America. In 1993, according to an international business survey, the world's most valuable brand was *Marlboro*, with a value estimated at $40 billion, slightly ahead of *Coca-Cola*. Among the other top ten brands were *Intel, Kellogg's, Budweiser, Pepsi, Gillette,* and *Pampers. Nescafe* and *Bacardi* were the only foreign brands to make the top ten, underlining American dominance.

Huge amounts of effort go into choosing brand names. General Foods 28 reviewed 2,800 names before deciding on *Dreamwhip*. (To put this in proportion, try to think of just ten names for an artificial whipped cream.) Ford considered more than twenty thousand possible car names before finally settling on *Edsel* (which proves that such care doesn't always pay), and Standard Oil a similar number of names before it opted for *Exxon*. Sometimes, however, the most successful names are the result of a moment's whimsy. *Betty Crocker* came in a flash to an executive of the Washburn Crosby Company (later absorbed by General Mills), who chose *Betty* because he thought it sounded wholesome and sincere and *Crocker* in memory of a beloved fellow executive who had recently died. At first the name was used only to sign letters responding to customers' requests for advice or information, but by the 1950s, Betty Crocker's smiling, confident face was appearing on more than fifty types of food product, and her loyal followers could buy her recipe books and even visit her "kitchen" at the General Foods headquarters.

29   Great efforts also go into finding out why people buy the brands they do. Advertisers and market researchers bandy about terms like *conjoint analysis technique, personal drive patterns, Gaussian distributions, fractals,* and other such arcana in their quest to winnow out every subliminal quirk in our buying habits. They know, for instance, that 40 percent of all people who move to a new address will also change their brand of toothpaste, that the average supermarket shopper makes fourteen impulse decisions in each visit, that 62 percent of shoppers will pay a premium for mayonnaise even when they think a cheaper brand is just as good, but that only 24 percent will show the same largely irrational loyalty to frozen vegetables.

30   To preserve a brand name involves a certain fussy attention to linguistic and orthographic details. To begin with, the name is normally expected to be treated not as a noun but as a proper adjective—that is, the name should be followed by an explanation of what it does: *Kleenex facial tissues, Q-Tip cotton swabs, Jello-O brand gelatin desert, Sanka brand decaffeinated coffee.* Some types of products—notably cars—are granted an exemption, which explains why General Motors does not have to advertise *Cadillac self-propelled automobiles* or the like. In all cases, the name may not explicitly describe the product's function, though it may hint at what it does. Thus *Coppertone* is acceptable; *Coppertan* would not be.

31   The situation is more than a little bizarre. Having done all they can to make their products household words, manufacturers must then in their advertisements do all in their power to imply that they aren't. Before trademark law was clarified, advertisers positively encouraged the public to treat their products as generics. Kodak invited consumers to "Kodak as you go," turning the brand name into a dangerously ambiguous verb. It would never do that now. The American Thermos Product Company went so far as to boast, "Thermos is a household word," to its considerable cost. Donald F. Duncan, Inc., the original manufacturer of the *Yo-Yo,* lost its trademark protection partly because it was amazingly casual about capitalization in its own promotional literature. "In case you don't know what a yo-yo is . . ." one of its advertisements went, suggesting that in commercial terms Duncan didn't. Duncan also made the elemental error of declaring, "If it Isn't a Duncan, It Isn't a Yo-Yo," which on the face of it would seem a reasonable claim, but was in fact held by the courts to be inviting

the reader to consider the product generic. Kodak had long since stopped saying "If it isn't an Eastman, it isn't a Kodak."

Because of the confusion, and occasional lack of fastidiousness on the part   32
of their owners, many dozens of products have lost their trademark protection, among them *aspirin, linoleum, yo-yo, thermos, cellophane, milk of magnesia, mimeograph, lanolin, celluloid, dry ice, escalator, shredded wheat, kerosene,* and *zipper.* All were once proudly capitalized and worth a fortune.

On July 1, 1941, the New York television station WNBT-TV interrupted its   33
normal viewing to show, without comment, a Bulova watch ticking. For sixty seconds the watch ticked away mysteriously, then the picture faded and normal programming resumed. It wasn't much, but it was the first television *commercial.*

Both the word and the idea were already well established. The first com-   34
mercial—the term was used from the very beginning—had been broadcast by radio station WEAF in New York on August 28, 1922. It lasted for either ten or fifteen minutes, depending on which source you credit. Commercial radio was not an immediate hit. In its first two months, WEAF sold only $550 worth of airtime. But by the mid-1920s, sponsors were not only flocking to buy airtime but naming their programs after their products—*The Lucky Strike Hour, The A&P Gypsies, The Lux Radio Theater,* and so on. Such was the obsequiousness of the radio networks that by the early 1930s, many were allowing the sponsors to take complete artistic and production control of the programs. Many of the most popular shows were actually written by the advertising agencies, and the agencies naturally seldom missed an opportunity to work a favorable mention of the sponsor's products into the scripts.

With the rise of television in the 1950s, the practices of the radio era were   35
effortlessly transferred to the new medium. Advertisers inserted their names into the program title—*Texaco Star Theater, Gillette Cavalcade of Sports, Chesterfield Sound-Off Time, The U.S. Steel Hour, Kraft Television Theater, The Chevy Show, The Alcoa Hour, The Ford Star Revue, Dick Clark's Beechnut Show,* and the arresting hybrid *The Lux-Schlitz Playhouse,* which seemed to suggest a cozy symbiosis between soapflakes and beer. The commercial dominance of program titles reached a kind of hysterical peak with a program officially called *Your Kaiser Dealer Presents Kaiser-Frazer "Adventures in Mystery" Starring Betty Furness in "Byline."* Sponsors didn't write the programs any longer, but they did impose a firm control on the contents, most notoriously during a 1959 *Playhouse 90* broadcast of *Judgment at Nuremberg,* when the sponsor, the American Gas Association, managed to have all references to gas ovens and the gasing of Jews removed from the script.

Where commercial products of the late 1940s had scientific-sounding   36
names, those of the 1950s relied increasingly on secret ingredients. Gleem toothpaste contained a mysterious piece of alchemy called *GL-70.** There was

---

*For purposes of research, I wrote to Procter & Gamble, Gleem's manufacturer, asking what GL-70 was, but the public relations department evidently thought it eccentric of me to wonder what I had been putting in my mouth all through childhood and declined to reply.

never the slightest hint of what GL-70 was, but it would, according to the advertising, not only rout odor-causing bacteria but "wipe out their enzymes!"

37   A kind of creeping illiteracy invaded advertising, too, to the dismay of many. When Winston began advertising its cigarettes with the slogan "Winston tastes good like a cigarette should," nationally syndicated columnists like Sydney J. Harris wrote anguished essays on what the world was coming to—every educated person knew it should be "as a cigarette should"—but the die was cast. By 1958, Ford was advertising that you could "travel smooth" in a Thunderbird Sunliner and the maker of Ace Combs was urging buyers to "comb it handsome"—a trend that continues today with "pantihose that fits you real comfortable" and other grammatical manglings too numerous and dispiriting to dwell on.

38   We may smile at the advertising ruses of the 1920s—frightening people with the threat of "fallen stomach" and "scabby toes"—but in fact such creative manipulation still goes on, albeit at a slightly more sophisticated level. *The New York Times Magazine* reported in 1990 how an advertising copywriter had been told to come up with some impressive labels for a putative hand cream. She invented the arresting and healthful-sounding term *oxygenating moisturizers* and wrote accompanying copy with references to "tiny bubbles of oxygen that release moisture into your skin." This done, the advertising was turned over to the company's research and development department, which was instructed to come up with a product that matched the copy.

39   If we fall for such commercial manipulation, we have no one to blame but ourselves. When Kentucky Fried Chicken introduced "Extra Crispy" chicken to sell alongside its "Original" chicken, and sold it at the same price, sales were disappointing. But when its advertising agency persuaded it to promote "Extra Crispy" as a premium brand and to put the price up, sales soared. Much the same sort of verbal hypnosis was put to work for the benefit of the fur industry. Dyed muskrat makes a perfectly good fur, for those who enjoy cladding themselves in dead animals, but the name clearly lacks stylishness. The solution was to change the name to *Hudson seal*. Never mind that the material contained not a strand of seal fur. It sounded good, and sales skyrocketed.

40   Truth has seldom been a particularly visible feature of American advertising. In the early 1970s, Chevrolet ran a series of ads for the Chevelle boasting that the car had "109 advantages to keep it from becoming old before its time." When looked into, it turned out that these 109 vaunted features included such items as rearview mirrors, backup lights, balanced wheels, and many other components that were considered pretty well basic to any car. Never mind; sales soared. At about the same time, Ford, not to be outdone, introduced a "limited edition" Mercury Monarch at $250 below the normal list price. It achieved this, it turned out, by taking $250 worth of equipment off the standard Monarch.

41   And has all this deviousness led to a tightening of the rules concerning what is allowable in advertising? Hardly. In 1986, as William Lutz relates in *Doublespeak*, the insurance company John Hancock launched an ad campaign in which "real people in real situations" discussed their financial predicaments with remarkable candor. When a journalist asked to speak to these real people, a company spokesman conceded that they were actors and "in that sense they are not real people."

During the 1982 presidential campaign, the Republican National Committee ran a television advertisement praising President Reagan for providing cost-of-living pay increases to federal workers "in spite of those sticks-in-the-mud who tried to keep him from doing what we elected him to do." When it was pointed out that the increases had in fact been mandated by law since 1975 and that Reagan had in any case three times tried to block them, a Republican official responded: "Since when is a commercial supposed to be accurate?" Quite.   42

In linguistic terms, perhaps the most interesting challenge facing advertisers today is that of selling products in an increasingly multicultural society. Spanish is a particular problem, not just because it is spoken over such a widely scattered area but also because it is spoken in so many different forms. Brown sugar is *azucar negra* in New York, *azucar prieta* in Miami, *azucar morena* in much of Texas, and *azucar pardo* pretty much everywhere else—and that's just one word. Much the same bewildering multiplicity applies to many others. In consequence, embarrassments are all but inevitable.   43

In mainstream Spanish, *bichos* means *insects,* but in Puerto Rico it means *testicles,* so when a pesticide maker promised to bring death to the *bichos,* Puerto Rican consumers were at least bemused, if not alarmed. Much the same happened when a maker of bread referred to its product as *un bollo de pan* and discovered that to Spanish-speaking Miamians of Cuban extraction that means a woman's private parts. And when Perdue Chickens translated its slogan "It takes a tough man to make a tender chicken" into Spanish, it came out as the slightly less macho "It takes a sexually excited man to make a chick sensual."   44

Never mind. Sales soared.   45

---

1 Why does the story of George Eastman symbolize the methods advertisers use to market their products? How have Eastman's pioneering strategies come to define what advertisers do to market their products? What function did the name Kodak serve as a precedent for the way American companies still name their products?

2 What is the difference between a trademark and a brand name? Why is it important for companies that their trademarks *do not* become household words? Have any current trademarks become synonymous with a generic product or service (as, for example, "Kleenex" did for tissue and "Xerox" did for photocopying)?

3 Bryson is alarmed by a tendency toward "creeping illiteracy" (para. 37) in both the spelling of recent product names and the advertising copy used to describe them. Analyze at least two ads that use unconventional spelling, incomplete sentences, and grammatical errors to sell their wares (for example, Kool-Aid, Cheez-Its). What other aspects of product naming does Bryson find manipulative or deceptive?

4 What purpose does Bryson's discussion of George Eastman serve at the beginning of the essay (para. 1–8)? (Glossary: *Introduction, Conclusion.*)

5 Bryson offers a number of specific examples of changing practices in American advertising. Why is this rhetorical strategy especially apt for his discussion? Which examples did you find especially interesting? Where does he use an extended example to clarify his thesis? (Glossary: *Examples.*)

6 What slogans for products or services in recent advertising campaigns strike you as effective, and why? What aspect of the product or service does the slogan emphasize and promote?

Ways of Seeing *John Berger*

◆ JOHN BERGER, who is known primarily as an author of art criticism and fiction, is also a poet, essayist, translater, playwright, screenwriter, painter (his work has been exhibited in galleries in London), and teacher of drawing, and he has served as an art critic for the *New Statesman* and the *Sunday Times.* A prolific author, he has written nine novels and fourteen works of nonfiction including *Ways of Seeing* (1972), which was composed in association with a television series created for the BBC and is essentially an argument against the dehumanizing process of consumerism that Berger, as a Marxist, sees as a defining feature of contemporary Western culture. It is from this book that the following chapter is drawn.

Just as Bill Bryson showed how creating a unique image for a product has from the first been an indispensable feature of advertising, Berger demonstrates how many of the distinctive qualities of a particular advertising campaign are, in reality, borrowed from traditional art and sculpture from the past. Berger analyzes, from a Marxist perspective, the values that underlie ads and argues that advertising's fundamental ideology is the way it commodifies values by suggesting that middle-class consumers can share, through the purchase of an item, the lifestyles of the rich. How ads do this is by instilling envy and the feeling that life has value only insofar as we are able to purchase things.

> **TO CONSIDER** What have you bought whose purpose, either consciously or unconsciously, was to make people envy you? How important was this feeling of being enviable in your decision to buy this product?

I n the cities in which we live, all of us see hundreds of publicity images every day of our lives. No other kind of image confronts us so frequently.

In no other form of society in history has there been such a concentration of images, such a density of visual messages.

One may remember or forget these messages but briefly one takes them in, and for a moment they stimulate the imagination by way of either memory or expectation. The publicity image belongs to the moment. We see it as we turn a page, as we turn a corner, as a vehicle passes us. Or we see it on a television screen whilst waiting for the commercial break to end. Publicity images also belong to the moment in the sense that they must be continually renewed and made up-to-date. Yet they never speak of the present. Often they refer to the past and always they speak of the future.

We are now so accustomed to being addressed by these images that we scarcely notice their total impact. A person may notice a particular image or place of information because it corresponds to some particular interest he has. But we accept the total system of publicity images as we accept an element of climate. For example, the fact that these images belong to the moment but speak of the future produces a strange effect which has become so familiar that we scarcely notice it. Usually it is *we* who pass the image—walking, travelling, turning a page; on the tv screen it is somewhat different but even then we are theoretically the active agent—we can look away, turn down the sound, make some coffee. Yet despite this, one has the impression that publicity images are continually passing us, like express trains on their way to some distant terminus. We are static; they are dynamic—until the newspaper is thrown away, the television programme continues or the poster is posted over.

Publicity is usually explained and justified as a competitive medium which ultimately benefits the public (the consumer) and the most efficient manufacturers—and thus the national economy. It is closely related to certain ideas about freedom: freedom of choice for the purchaser: freedom of enterprise for the manufacturer. The great hoardings and the publicity neons of the cities of capitalism are the immediate visible sign of 'The Free World'.

For many in Eastern Europe such images in the West sum up what they in the East lack. Publicity, it is thought, offers a free choice.

It is true that in publicity one brand of manufacture, one firm, competes with another; but it is also true that every publicity image confirms and enhances every other. Publicity is not merely an assembly of competing messages: it is a language in itself which is always being used to make the same general proposal. Within publicity, choices are offered between this cream and that cream, that car and this car, but publicity as a system only makes a single proposal.

It proposes to each of us that we transform ourselves, or our lives, by buying something more.

This more, it proposes, will make us in some way richer—even though we will be poorer by having spent our money.

Publicity persuades us of such a transformation by showing us people who have apparently been transformed and are, as a result, enviable. The state of being envied is what constitutes glamour. And publicity is the process of manufacturing glamour.

It is important here not to confuse publicity with the pleasure or benefits to be enjoyed from the things it advertises. Publicity is effective precisely because it feeds upon the real. Clothes, food, cars, cosmetics, baths, sunshine are real things to be enjoyed in themselves. Publicity begins by working on a natural appetite for pleasure. But it cannot offer the real object of pleasure and there is no convincing substitute for a pleasure in that pleasure's own terms. The more convincingly publicity conveys the pleasure of bathing in a warm, distant sea, the more the spectator-buyer will become aware that he is hundreds of miles away from that sea and the more remote the chance of bathing in it will seem to him. This is why publicity can never really afford to be about the product or opportunity it is proposing to the buyer who is not yet enjoying it. Publicity is never a celebration of a pleasure-in-itself. Publicity is always about the future buyer. It offers him an image of himself made glamorous by the product or opportunity it is trying to sell. The image then makes him envious of himself as he might be. Yet what makes this self-which-he-might-be enviable? The envy of others. Publicity is about social relations, not objects. Its promise is not of pleasure, but of happiness: happiness as judged from the outside by others. The happiness of being envied is glamour.

Being envied is a solitary form of reassurance. It depends precisely upon not sharing your experience with those who envy you. You are observed with interest but you do not observe with interest—if you do, you will become less enviable. In this respect the envied are like bureaucrats; the more impersonal they are, the greater the illusion (for themselves and for others) of their power. The power of the glamorous resides in their supposed happiness: the power of the bureaucrat in his supposed authority. It is this which explains the absent, unfocused look of so many glamour images. They look out *over* the looks of envy which sustain them.

The spectator-buyer is meant to envy herself as she will become if she buys the product. She is meant to imagine herself transformed by the product into an object of envy for others, an envy which will then justify her loving herself. One could put this another way: the publicity image steals her love of herself as she is, and offers it back to her for the price of the product.

Does the language of publicity have anything in common with that of oil painting which, until the invention of the camera, dominated the European way of seeing during four centuries?

It is one of those questions which simply needs to be asked for the answer to become clear. There is a direct continuity. Only interests of cultural prestige have obscured it. At the same time, despite the continuity, there is a profound difference which it is no less important to examine.

There are many direct references in publicity to works of art from the past. Sometimes a whole image is a frank pastiche of a well-known painting.

Publicity images often use sculptures or paintings to lend allure or authority to their own message. Framed oil paintings often hang in shop windows as part of their display.

Any work of art 'quoted' by publicity serves two purposes. Art is a sign of affluence; it belongs to the good life; it is part of the furnishing which the world gives to the rich and the beautiful.

But a work of art also suggests a cultural authority, a form of dignity, even of wisdom, which is superior to any vulgar material interest; an oil painting belongs to the cultural heritage; it is a reminder of what it means to be a culti-vated European. And so the quoted work of art (and this is why it is so useful to publicity) says two almost contradictory things at the same time: it denotes wealth and spirituality: it implies that the purchase being proposed is both a lux-ury and a cultural value. Publicity has in fact understood the tradition of the oil painting more thoroughly than most art historians. It has grasped the implica-tions of the relationship between the work of art and its spectator-owner and with these it tries to persuade and flatter the spectator-buyer.

The continuity, however, between oil painting and publicity goes far deeper than the 'quoting' of specific paintings. Publicity relies to a very large extent on the language of oil painting. It speaks in the same voice about the same things. Sometimes the visual correspondences are so close that it is possible to play a game of 'Snap'—putting almost identical images or details of images side by side. It is not, however, just at the level of exact pictorial correspondence that the continuity is important: it is at the level of the sets of signs used.

Compare the images of publicity and paintings in this book, or take a pic-ture magazine, or walk down a smart shopping street looking at the window dis-plays, and then turn over the pages of an illustrated museum catalogue, and notice how similarly messages are conveyed by the two media. A systematic study needs to be made of this. Here we can do no more than indicate a few areas where the similarity of the devices and aims is particularly striking.

The gestures of models (mannequins) and mythological figures.

The romantic use of nature (leaves, trees, water) to create a place where innocence can be refound.

The exotic and nostalgic attraction of the Mediterranean.

The poses taken up to denote stereotypes of women: serene mother (madonna), free-wheeling secretary (actress, king's mistress), perfect hostess (spectator-owner's wife), sex-object (Venus, nymph surprised), etc.

The special sexual emphasis given to women's legs.

The materials particularly used to indicate luxury: engraved metal, furs, pol-ished leather, etc.

The gestures and embraces of lovers, arranged frontally for the benefit of the spectator.

The sea, offering a new life.

The physical stance of men conveying wealth and virility.

The treatment of distance by perspective-offering mystery.

The equation of drinking and success.

The man as knight (horseman) become motorist.

Why does publicity depend so heavily upon the visual language of oil paint-ing?

Publicity is the culture of the consumer society. It propagates through images that society's belief in itself. There are several reasons why these images use the language of oil painting.

Oil painting, before it was anything else was a celebration of private property. As an art-form it derived from the principle that *you are what you have.*

It is a mistake to think of publicity supplanting the visual art of post-Renaissance Europe; it is the last moribund form of that art.

Is it Italian tile? Or a real Armstrong floor?

Come and play footsy with Armstrong

Publicity is, in essence, nostalgic. It has to sell the past to the future. It cannot itself supply the standards of its own claims. And so all its references to quality are bound to be retrospective and traditional. It would lack both confidence and credibility if it used a strictly contemporary language.

Publicity needs to turn to its own advantage the traditional education of the average spectator-buyer. What he has learnt at school of history, mythology, poetry can be used in the manufacturing of glamour. Cigars can be sold in the name of a King, underwear in connection with the Sphinx, a new car by reference to the status of a country house.

In the language of oil painting these vague historical or poetic or moral references are always present. The fact that they are imprecise and ultimately meaningless is an advantage: they should not be understandable, they should merely be reminiscent of cultural lessons half-learnt. Publicity makes all history mythical, but to do so effectively it needs a visual language with historical dimensions.

Lastly, a technical development made it easy to translate the language of oil painting into publicity clichés. This was the invention, about fifteen years ago, of cheap colour photography. Such photography can reproduce the colour and texture and tangibility of objects as only oil paint had been able to do before. Colour photography is to the spectator-buyer what oil paint was to the spectator-owner. Both media use similar, highly tactile means to play upon the spectator's sense of acquiring the *real* thing which the image shows. In both cases his feeling that he can almost touch what is in the image reminds him how he might or does possess the real thing.

Yet, despite this continuity of language, the function of publicity is very different from that of the oil painting. The spectator-buyer stands in a very different relation to the world from the spectator-owner.

The oil painting showed what its owner was already enjoying among his possessions and his way of life. It consolidated his own sense of his own value. It enhanced his view of himself as he already was. It began with facts, the facts of his life. The paintings embellished the interior in which he actually lived.

The purpose of publicity is to make the spectator marginally dissatisfied with his present way of life. Not with the way of life of society, but with his own within it. It suggests that if he buys what it is offering, his life will become better. It offers him an improved alternative to what he is.

The oil painting was addressed to those who made money out of the market. Publicity is addressed to those who constitute the market, to the spectator-buyer who is also the consumer-producer from whom profits are made twice over as worker and then as buyer. The only places relatively free of publicity are the quarters of the very rich; their money is theirs to keep.

All publicity works upon anxiety. The sum of everything is money, to get money is to overcome anxiety. Alternatively the anxiety on which publicity plays is the fear that having nothing you will be nothing.

Money is life. Not in the sense that without money you starve. Not in the sense that capital gives one class power over the entire lives of another class. But in the sense that money is the token of, and the key to, every human capacity. The power to spend money is the power to live. According to the legends of publicity, those who lack the power to spend money become literally faceless. Those who have the power become lovable.

Publicity increasingly uses sexuality to sell any product or service. But this sexuality is never free in itself; it is a symbol for something presumed to be larger than it: the good life in which you can buy whatever you want. To be able to buy is the same thing as being sexually desirable; occasionally this is the explicit message of publicity as in the Barclaycard advertisement above [not shown]. Usually it is the implicit message, i.e. If you are able to buy this product you will be lovable. If you cannot buy it, you will be less lovable.

For publicity the present is by definition insufficient. The oil painting was thought of as a permanent record. One of the pleasures a painting gave to its owner was the thought that it would convey the image of his present to the future of his descendants. Thus the oil painting was naturally painted in the present tense. The painter painted what was before him, either in reality or in imagination. The publicity image which is ephemeral uses only the future tense. With this you *will* become desirable. In these surroundings all your relationships *will* become happy and radiant.

Publicity principally addressed to the working class tends to promise a personal transformation through the function of the particular product it is selling (Cinderella); middle-class publicity promises a transformation of relationships through a general atmosphere created by an ensemble of products (The Enchanted Palace).

Publicity speaks in the future tense and yet the achievement of this future is endlessly deferred. How then does publicity remain credible—or credible enough to exert the influence it does? It remains credible because the truthfulness of publicity is judged, not by the real fulfilment of its promises, but by the relevance of its fantasies to those of the spectator-buyer. Its essential application is not to reality but to day-dreams.

To understand this better we must go back to the notion of *glamour*. Glamour is a modern invention. In the heyday of the oil painting it did not exist. Ideas of grace, elegance, authority amounted to something apparently similar but fundamentally different.

Mrs Siddons as seen by Gainsborough[1] is not glamorous, because she is not presented as enviable and therefore happy. She may be seen as wealthy, beautiful, talented, lucky. But her qualities are her own and have been recognized as such. What she is does not entirely depend upon others wanting to be like her. She is not purely the creature of others' envy—which is how, for example, Andy Warhdl presents Marilyn Monroe.[2]

Glamour cannot exist without personal social envy being a common and widespread emotion. The industrial society which has moved towards democracy and then stopped half way is the ideal society for generating such an emotion. The pursuit of individual happiness has been acknowledged as a universal right. Yet the existing social conditions make the individual feel powerless. He lives in the contradiction between what he is and what he would like to be. Either he then becomes fully conscious of the contradiction and its causes, and so joins the political struggle for a full democracy which entails, amongst other things, the overthrow of capitalism; or else he lives, continually subject to an envy which, compounded with his sense of powerlessness, dissolves into recurrent day-dreams.

---

[1] *Mrs. Siddons* by Thomas Gainsborough, 1727–88, National Gallery, London.
[2] *Marilyn Monroe* by Andy Warhol.

It is this which makes it possible to understand why publicity remains credible. The gap between what publicity actually offers and the future it promises, corresponds with the gap between what the spectator-buyer feels himself to be and what he would like to be. The two gaps become one; and instead of the single gap being bridged by action or lived experience, it is filled with glamorous day-dreams.

The process is often reinforced by working conditions. The interminable present of meaningless working hours is 'balanced' by a dreamt future in which imaginary activity replaces the passivity of the moment. In his or her day-dreams the passive worker becomes the active consumer. The working self envies the consuming self.

No two dreams are the same. Some are instantaneous, others prolonged. The dream is always personal to the dreamer. Publicity does not manufacture the dream. All that it does is to propose to each one of us that we are not yet enviable—yet could be.

Publicity has another important social function. The fact that this function has not been planned as a purpose by those who make and use publicity in no way lessens its significance. Publicity turns consumption into a substitute for democracy. The choice of what one eats (or wears or drives) takes the place of significant political choice. Publicity helps to mask and compensate for all that is undemocratic within society. And it also masks what is happening in the rest of the world.

Publicity adds up to a kind of philosophical system. It explains everything in its own terms. It interprets the world.

The entire world becomes a setting for the fulfilment of publicity's promise of the good life. The world smiles at us. It offers itself to us. And because *everywhere* is imagined as offering itself to us, *everywhere* is more or less the same.

Publicity, situated in a future continually deferred, excludes the present and so eliminates all becoming, all development. Experience is impossible within it. All that happens, happens outside it.

The fact that publicity is eventless would be immediately obvious if it did not use a language which makes of tangibility an event in itself. Everything publicity shows is there awaiting acquisition. The act of acquiring has taken the place of all other actions, the sense of having has obliterated all other senses.

Publicity exerts an enormous influence and is a political phenomenon of great importance. But its offer is as narrow as its references are wide. It recognizes nothing except the power to acquire. All other human faculties or needs are made subsidiary to this power. All hopes are gathered together, made homogeneous, simplified, so that they become the intense yet vague, magical yet repeatable promise offered in every purchase. No other kind of hope or satisfaction or pleasure can any longer be envisaged within the culture of capitalism.

Publicity is the life of this culture—in so far as without publicity capitalism could not survive—and at the same time publicity is its dream.

Capitalism survives by forcing the majority, whom it exploits, to define their own interests as narrowly as possible. This was once achieved by extensive deprivation. Today in the developed countries it is being achieved by imposing a false standard of what is and what is not desirable.

1 Berger says that "publicity [that is, advertising] is not merely an assembly of competing messages: it is a language in itself which is always being used to make the same general proposal" (para. 7). What is it that advertising tries to accomplish besides getting us to purchase this or that product?

2 Why do the settings of luxury, wealth, exotic places, romance, and other images in oil paintings play such an important part in getting us to imagine ourselves "transformed by the product into an object of envy for others" (para. 13)? What function does glamour serve in making people dissatisfied with themselves and their lives? How is glamour different from the traditional images of "grace, elegance and authority" found in oil paintings?

3 Implicit in Berger's Marxist critique of capitalism is the belief that advertising "helps to mask and compensate for all that is undemocratic within society." Do you agree with him that "the choice of what one eats (or wears or drives) takes the place of significant political choice"? To which advertising images are you most responsive? Analyze these ads as Berger might see them.

4 How does advertising use the motifs and themes found in traditional oil paintings that display wealth and belong to a cultural heritage to sell modern products? What are people really buying along with the product (floor tile, etc.)? How would you answer Berger's question "Why does publicity [advertising] depend so heavily upon the visual language of oil painting?" (Glossary: Comparison and Contrast.)

5 Evaluate the organizational structure Berger uses in presenting his argument. How does this structure clarify what he sees as the basic issue? What different kinds of sources does he draw upon to clarify his thesis? (Glossary: Argument.)

6 Advertisers spend a considerable amount of time, money, and effort in formulating brand names for their products. In an essay, discuss the connotations of one or several of these names or examine the connotations of brand names for any other product category. For example, in automotive advertising, car names can be designed to manipulate emotions. Cars named Regal, Le Baron, and Grand Marquis appeal to the need for status. Riviera, Capri, Monte Carlo, and Park Avenue are all names of places where the wealthy congregate. Skylark, Mustang, Cougar, Firebird, Thunderbird, and Eagle play upon the need for freedom and adventure. What emotional needs are any of the following car names designed to play upon: Taurus, Seville, Bonneville, Cherokee, Cutlass, Intrepid, Blazer, Lumina, Prelude, Cavalier, Reliant, Explorer, and Sonata? What others can you think of?

The Rhetoric of Advertising

Stuart Hirschberg

◆ STUART HIRSCHBERG currently teaches English at Rutgers University, Newark, and is the author of *At the Top of the Tower: W. B. Yeats's Poetry Explored Through* A Vision (1979) and *Myth in the Poetry of Ted Hughes* (1981). He is the editor and coeditor (with Terry Hirschberg) of over a dozen rhetorics, textbooks, and anthologies, including *One World, Many Cultures* (1998) and *The Millennium Reader* (1997). The following essay is drawn from *Essential Strategies of Argument* (1996).

The range of strategies advertisers use to manipulate consumers' responses, as Hirschberg points out, bears an uncanny similarity to the rhetorical techniques Aristotle first identified as being capable of producing persuasive arguments. That these techniques are so successful in a country that, as Jane Tompkins observed (in Ch. 5), had a deep-seated suspicion of anyone—lawyers, pitchmen, Easterners, etc.—who uses words too glibly is all the more astounding. Hirschberg analyzes a range of contemporary ads and identifies the devices that advertisers use to obfuscate their claims, evade legal accountability, and manipulate the emotions of consumers so that they will yearn to possess the products that falsely promise to fulfill their needs—"needs" that the advertisers have manufactured in the first place. Only a careful analysis of ads can reveal how skillful advertisers are at what they do.

> **TO CONSIDER**   What ads do you most remember? What was there about the images and copy that attracted your attention and stayed in your mind?

Whether ads are presented as sources of information enabling the consumer to make educated choices between products or aim at offering memorable images or witty, thoughtful, or poetic copy, the underlying intent of all advertising is to persuade specific audiences. Seen in this way, ads appear as mini-arguments whose strategies and techniques of persuasion can be analyzed just like a written argument. We can discover which elements are designed to appeal to the audience's emotions (*pathos* according to Aristotle), which elements make their appeal in terms of reasons, evidence, or logic (*logos*), and how the advertiser goes about winning credibility for itself or in terms of the spokesperson employed to speak on behalf of the product (the *ethos* dimension). Like arguments, ads can be effective if they appeal to the needs, values, and beliefs of the audience. Advertisers use a variety of visual and verbal means to encourage their audience to identify with the people in the ads, the experiences the ads depict, and the values the ads promote. Although the verbal and visual elements within an ad are designed to work together, we can study these elements separately. We can look at how the composition of the elements within an ad is intended to function. We can look at the role of language and how it is used to persuade. We can study how objects and settings are used to promote the audience's identification with the products being sold. We can judge ads according to the skill with which they deploy all of these resources while at the same time being critically aware of their intended effects on us.

THE TECHNIQUES OF ADVERTISING

The claim the ad makes is designed to establish the superiority of the product in the minds of the audience and to create a distinctive image for the product, whether it is a brand of cigarettes, a financial service, or a type of gasoline. The single most important technique for creating this image depends on transferring ideas, attributes, or feelings from outside the product onto the product itself. In this way the product comes to represent an obtainable object or service that embodies, represents, or symbolizes a whole range of meanings. This transfer can be achieved in many ways. For example, when Elizabeth Taylor lends her glamour and beauty to the merchandising of a perfume, the consumer is meant to conclude that the perfume must be superior to other perfumes in the way that Elizabeth Taylor embodies beauty, glamour, and sex appeal. The attempt to transfer significance can operate in two ways. It can encourage the audience to discover meanings and to correlate feelings and attributes that the advertiser wishes the product to represent in ways that allow these needs and desires to become attached to specific products. It can also prevent the correlation of thoughts or feelings that might discourage the audience from purchasing a particular product. For example, the first most instinctive response to the thought of smoking a cigarette might be linked with the idea of inhaling hot and dry smoke from what are essentially burning tobacco leaves. Thus, any associations the audience might have with burning leaves, coughing, and dry hot smoke must be short-circuited by supplying them with a whole set of other associations to receive and occupy the perceptual "slot" that might have been triggered by their first reactions. Cigarette advertisers do this in a variety of ways:

> By showing active people in outdoorsy settings they put the thought of emphysema, shortness of breath, or lung disease very far away indeed.
> By showing cigarette packs set against the background of grass glistening with morning dew or bubbling streams or cascading waterfalls, they

subtly guide the audience's response away from what is dry, hot, congested, or burning toward what is open, airy, moist, cool, and clean.

In some brands, menthol flavoring and green and blue colors are intended to promote these associations.

Thus, ads act as do all other kinds of persuasion to intensify correlations that work to the advertiser's advantage and to suppress associations that would lessen the product's appeal.

The kinds of associations audiences are encouraged to perceive reflect a broad range of positive emotional appeals that encourage the audience to find self-esteem through the purchase of a product that by itself offers a way to meet personal and social needs. The particular approach taken in the composition of the ad, the way it is laid out, and the connotations of the advertising copy vary according to the emotional appeal of the ad.

The most common manipulative techniques are designed to make consumers want to consume to satisfy deep-seated human drives. Of course, no one consciously believes that purchasing a particular kind of toothpaste, perfume, lipstick, or automobile will meet real psychological and social needs, but that is exactly how products are sold—through the promise of delivering unattainable satisfactions through tangible purchasable objects or services. In purchasing a certain product, we are offered the chance to create ourselves, our personality, and our relationships through consumption.

EMOTIONAL APPEALS USED IN ADVERTISING

The emotional appeals in ads function exactly the way assumptions about value do in written arguments. They supply the unstated major premise that supplies a rationale to persuade an audience that a particular product will meet one or another of several different kinds of needs. Some ads present the purchase of a product as a means by which consumers can find social acceptance.

These ads address the consumer as "you" ("wouldn't 'you' really father have a Buick?"). The "you" here is plural but is perceived as being individual and personal by someone who has already formed the connection with the product. Ironically, the price of remaining in good standing with this "group" of fellow consumers requires the consumer to purchase an expensive automobile. In this sense, ads give consumers a chance to belong to social groups that have only one thing in common—the purchase of a particular product.

One variation on the emotional need to belong to a designated social group is the appeal to status or "snob appeal." Snob appeal is not new. In 1710, the *Spectator,* a popular newspaper of the time, carried an ad that read:

An incomparable Powder for Cleaning Teeth, which has given great satisfaction to most of the Nobility Gentry in England. (Quoted in W. Duncan Reekie, *Advertising: Its Place in Political and Managerial Economics,* 1974.)

Ads for scotch, expensive cars, boats, jewelry, and watches frequently place their products in upper-class settings or depict them in connection with the fine arts (sculpture, ballet, etc.). The *value warrant* in these ads encourages the consumer to imagine that the purchase of the item will confer qualities associated with the background or activities of this upper-class world onto the consumer.

In other ads the need to belong takes a more subtle form of offering the product as a way to become part of a time in the past the audience might look back to with nostalgia. Grandmotherly figures wearing aprons and holding products that are advertised as being "like Grandma used to make" offer the consumer an imaginary past, a family tradition, or a simpler time looked back to with warmth and sentimentality. For many years, Smucker's preserves featured ads in which the product was an integral part of a scene emanating security and warmth, which the ad invited us to remember as if it were our own past. Ads of this kind are often photographed through filters that present misty sepia-tone images that carefully recreate old-fashioned kitchens with the accompanying appliances, dishes, clothes, and hairstyles. The ads thus supply us with false memories and invite us to insert ourselves into this imaginary past and to remember it as if it were our own. At the furthest extreme, ads employing the appeal to see ourselves as part of a group may try to evoke patriotic feelings so that the prospective consumer will derive the satisfactions of good citizenship and sense of participation in being part of the collective psyche of an entire nation. The point is that people really do have profound needs that advertisers can exploit, but it would be a rare product indeed that could really fulfill such profound needs.

Advertisers use highly sophisticated market research techniques to enable them to define and characterize precisely those people who are most likely to be receptive to ads of particular kinds. The science of demographics is aided and abetted by psychological research that enables advertisers to "target" a precisely designated segment of the general public. For example, manufacturers of various kinds of liquor can rely on studies that inform them that vodka drinkers are most likely to read *Psychology Today* and scotch drinkers the *New Yorker*, while readers of *Time* prefer rum and the audience for *Playboy* has a large number of readers who prefer gin. Once a market segment with defined psychological characteristics has been identified, an individual ad can be crafted for that particular segment and placed in the appropriate publication.

Ads, of course, can elicit responses by attempting to manipulate consumers through negative as well as positive emotional appeals. Helen Woodward, the head copywriter for an ad agency, once offered the following advice for ad writers trying to formulate a new ad for baby food: "Give 'em the figures about the baby death rate—but don't say it flatly . . . if we only had the nerve to put a hearse in the ad, you couldn't keep the women away from the food" (Stuart Ewen, *Captains of Consciousness: Advertising and the Social Roots of Consumer Culture* [1976]). Ads of this kind must first arouse the consumer's anxieties and then offer the product as the solution to the problem that more often than not the ad has created.

For example, an advertisement for Polaroid evokes the fear of not having taken pictures of moments that cannot be re-created and then offers the product as a form of insurance that will prevent this calamity from occurring. Nikon does the same in claiming that "a moment is called a moment because it doesn't last forever. Think of sunsets. A child's surprise. A Labrador's licky kiss. This is precisely why the Nikon N50 has the simple 'Simple' switch on top of the camera."

Ads for products that promise to guarantee their purchasers sex appeal, youth, health, social acceptance, self-esteem, creativity, enlightenment, a happy family life, loving relationships, escape from boredom, vitality, and many other things frequently employ scare tactics to frighten or worry the consumer into purchasing the product to ease his or her fears. These ads must first make the consumer dissatisfied with the self that exists. In this way, they function exactly as do *policy arguments* that recommend solutions to problems with measurably harmful consequences. The difference is that these kinds of ads actually are designed to arouse and then exploit the anxieties related to these problems.

Large industrial conglomerates, whether in oil, chemicals, pharmaceuticals, or agribusiness, frequently use advertising to accomplish different kinds of objectives than simply persuading the consumer to buy a particular product. These companies often seek to persuade the general public that they are not polluting the environment, poisoning the water, or causing environmental havoc in the process of manufacturing their products. The emotional appeal they use is to portray themselves as concerned "corporate citizens," vitally interested in the public good as a whole, and especially in those communities where they conduct their operations. In some cases, the ads present products as if they were directly produced from nature without being subjected to intermediary processing, preservatives, and contaminants, thereby lessening concern that they produce harmful byproducts. For example, Mazola might depict a spigot producing corn oil directly inserted into an ear of corn. A Jeep might appear to have materialized out of thin air on a seemingly inaccessible mountain peak. Companies sensitive to accusations that they are polluting the air and water can mount an advertising campaign designed to prove that they are not simply exploiting the local resources (whether timber, oil, fish, coal) for profits but are genuinely interested in putting something back into the community. The folksy good-neighbor tone of these ads is designed to create a benign image of the company.

THE LANGUAGE OF ADVERTISING

We can see how the creation of a sense of the company's credibility as a concerned citizen corresponds to what Aristotle called the *ethos* dimension. For example, Chevron expresses concern that the light from their oil drilling operations be shielded so that spawning sea turtles won't be unintentionally misdirected and lose their way!

The appeals to logic, statements of reasons, and presentations of evidence in ads correspond to the *logos* dimension of argument. The wording of the claims is particularly important, since it determines whether companies are legally responsible for any claims they make.

Claims in advertising need to be evaluated to discover whether something is asserted that needs to be proved or is implied without actually being stated.

Claims may refer to authoritative-sounding results obtained by supposedly independent laboratories, teams of research scientists, or physicians without ever saying how these surveys were conducted, what statistical methods were used, and who interpreted the results. Ads of this kind may make an impressive-sounding quasi-scientific claim; Ivory Soap used to present itself as "99 and 44/100% pure" without answering "pure" what. Some ads use technical talk and scientific terms to give the impression of a scientific breakthrough. For example, STP claims that it added "an anti-wear agent and viscosity improvers" to your oil. The copy for L. L. Bean claims of one of its jackets that "even in brutal ice winds gusting to 80 knots this remarkable anorak kept team members who wore it warm and comfortable." It would be important to know that the team members referred to are members of the "L. L. Bean test team."

Other claims cannot be substantiated, for example, "we're the Dexter Shoe Company. And for nearly four decades we put a lot of Dexter Maine into every pair of shoes we make."

In an ad for lipstick, Aveda makes the claim that "it's made of rich, earthy lip colours formulated with pure plant pigment from the Uruku tree. Organically grown by indigenous people in the rain forest."

Claims may be deceptive in other ways. Of all the techniques advertisers use to influence what people believe and how they spend their money, none is more basic than the use of so-called *weasel words*. This term was popularized by Theodore Roosevelt in a speech he gave in St. Louis, May 31, 1916, when he commented that notes from the Department of State were filled with weasel words that retract the meaning of the words they are next to just as a weasel sucks the meat out of the egg.

In modern advertising parlance, a weasel word has come to mean any qualifier or comparative that is used to imply a positive quality that cannot be stated as a fact, because it cannot be substantiated. For example, if an ad claims a toothpaste will "help" stop cavities it does not obligate the manufacturer to substantiate this claim. So, too, if a product is advertised as "fighting" germs, the equivocal claim hides the fact that the product may fight and lose.

A recent ad for STP claimed that "no matter what kind of car you drive, STP gas treatment helps remove the water that leads to gas line freeze. And unlike gas line anti-freeze, our unique gas treatment formula works to reduce intake valve deposits and prevent clogged injectors." The key words are "helps" and "works," neither of which obligates STP to be legally accountable to support the claim.

The words *virtually* (as in "virtually spotless") and *up to* or *for as long as* (as in "stops coughs up to eight hours") also remove any legal obligation on the part of the manufacturer to justify the claim.

Other favorite words in the copywriter's repertoire, such as *free* and *new*, are useful in selling everything from cat food to political candidates.

THE ETHICAL DIMENSION OF PERSUASION

As we have seen in our examination of the methods advertisers use to influence consumers, ethical questions are implicit in every act of persuasion. For example, what are we to make of a persuader whose objectives in seeking to influence an audience may be praiseworthy but who consciously makes use of distorted facts or seeks to manipulate an audience by playing on their known attitudes, values, and beliefs. Is success in persuasion the only criterion or should we hold would-be persuaders accountable to some ethical standards of responsibility about the means they use to achieve specific ends? Perhaps the most essential quality in determining whether any act of persuasion is an ethical one depends on the writer maintaining an open dialogue with different perspectives that might be advanced on a particular issue. By contrast, any act of persuasion that intentionally seeks to avoid self-criticism or challenges from competing perspectives will come across as insincere, dogmatic, deceptive, and defensive. The desire to shut down debate or control an audience's capacity to respond to the argument might well be considered unethical. The consequence of this attitude may be observed in the arguer's use of fraudulent evidence, illogical reasoning, emotionally laden irrelevant appeals, simplistic representation of the issue, or the pretense of expertise. Standards to apply when judging the ethical dimension in any act of persuasion require us to consider whether any element of coercion, deception, or manipulation is present. This becomes especially true when we look at the relationship between propaganda as a form of mass persuasion and the rhetorical means used to influence large groups of people.

1 How do modern advertisers make use of the traditional Aristotelian appeals to an audience's emotions (*pathos*), reason (*logos*), or sense of credibility of the advertiser (*ethos*)?

2 Explain in your own words the transfer technique that is at the root of all advertising. What kinds of different ideas and themes can be transferred? Why do advertisers rely on this technique almost exclusively?

3 How does the language of advertising skirt the legal requirement that its words be truthful and objectively verifiable? Analyze the claims in a few magazine, newspaper, television, or radio ads to discover if they are deceptive in any way. That is, do they use "weasel words" that imply something that cannot be substantiated and leave it to the consumer to imagine that the claim is true? In particular, look for words like "helps," "virtually," "up to," "for as long as," and "fights." Write a short analysis in which you point out the difference between what the claim actually states versus what a consumer might believe it states. How does the language used in the ad invite the consumer to supply the unspoken conclusion?

4 How do the terms *ethos, logos,* and *pathos* function as a special vocabulary of rhetorical analysis? Why is it important to understand the meaning of these terms to

grasp how three very different approaches are employed simultaneously by advertisers? (Glossary: *Technical Language*.)

5 Where does Hirschberg provide background about the advertising process readers would find useful before describing it in some depth? What are the main stages in the advertiser's formulation of an effective ad? What happens at each stage? Does Hirschberg provide sufficient detail for you to understand the many steps that go into the process of creating an ad? Explain. What technical terms of advertising does Hirschberg define? (Glossary: *Process Analysis*.)

6 How does the ad copy used by the makers of Trojan Brand Latex Condoms attempt to associate their product with an implicit guarantee of safe sex? How does the use of the word "genius" create a relationship between the potential consumer and the advertiser? What is this relationship, and how does it intensify the message of the ad?

"I didn't use one because I didn't have one with me."

GET REAL

If you don't have a parachute, don't jump, genius.

Helps reduce the risk

In another case, how does the ad for Hamilton watches combine status appeal, nostalgia appeal, and patriotic appeal?

How are each of the following ads designed to create a distinctive image for the company, product, or service being promoted? In each case, what function does the picture serve? What psychological needs or values do the advertisers appeal to? How is the ad copy or language designed to manipulate the emotions of the readers in ways that are positive for the advertisers? In your opinion, is the approach taken by each advertiser in the following ads successful? Why or why not?

Source: Hamilton.

Print advertisement featuring "The Pipeline and the Dancing Bird" provided courtesy of Chevron Corporation.

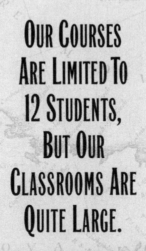

OUR COURSES ARE LIMITED TO 12 STUDENTS, BUT OUR CLASSROOMS ARE QUITE LARGE.

People who've taken our courses say they learned more about themselves in that one week than they had in years. Which isn't too surprising, when you consider that we have incredibly qualified instructors. Limited groups. A challenging curriculum. And whether you backpack, sail, canoe or even dogsled, our classroom settings just can't be beat. So call 1-800-243-8520 and we'll send you a free color catalog today.

A nonprofit, nondiscriminatory organization celebrating over 50 years of excellence in education worldwide.

Outward Bound.
THE ADVENTURE LASTS A LIFETIME.

Source: Outward Bound, created by Ogilvy & Mather.

THERE WILL ALWAYS BE THOSE WHO REFUSE TO SKI MAMMOTH.

Admittedly, with an elevation of 11,053 feet and 3,100 foot vertical, there are those of you who just flat out won't pay us a visit. Guess you probably don't realize we have 150 trails – spread out over 3,500 skiable acres – so there's lots of prime terrain, no matter what your ability. But hey, if you don't want to call 1-800-832-7320 and get the complete story in our free travel planner, far be it for us to insist. We certainly wouldn't want to ruffle anyone's feathers.

MAMMOTH

No other mountain lives up to its name.

Source: Mammoth.

0% Fat. 100% Fun.

Plymouth Breeze $15,330* (Nicely equipped.) Here's a cool treat you won't feel guilty about—Plymouth Breeze. No extra calories, just plenty of room. And it's filled with features  you crave, including standard air. To get a taste of Breeze, see your Plymouth dealer, call 1-800-PLYMOUTH or visit the Web at www.plymouthcars.com.

One clever idea after another. That's Plymouth.

*MSRP includes destination, excludes tax. Brush after every meal. Floss regularly.

Source: Chrysler Corporation and Bozell Worldwide, Inc.

Source: Sherwood America.

Here's the direction. You thought milk was just a kid thing. But the plot thickens and you discover your bones are still growing until you're 35. You're on a mad quest for calcium. AND... ACTION. You open the fridge, you grab the lowfat milk, you drink it. CUT. Not from the carton. TAKE 2. Let's use a glass.

MILK
Where's *your* mustache?

SPIKE LEE ©1996 NATIONAL FLUID MILK PROCESSOR PROMOTION BOARD

Used by permission of the National Milk Processor Promotion Board and Bozell Worldwide, Inc.

From *The Beauty Myth*   *Naomi Wolf*

◆ NAOMI WOLF analyzes cultural practices from a feminist perspective. She has written *Fire with Fire* (1993), *Promiscuities* (1997), and *The Beauty Myth* (1991), from which this selection, which appears as the first chapter, is drawn.

Why do so many women in our society obsess about their appearance, put themselves under the surgeon's knife, and undertake strenuous dieting and exercise regimens? It is precisely at this time in history when educated, affluent, and liberated women should presumably be enjoying the kind of freedom that has never been available to them before. Wolf asserts, however, that women are being tormented by a regressive mythology designed to reenslave them and to negate advances made since the 1970s. For every advance in legal and reproductive rights, employment, and education, there is an offsetting loss of empowerment due to the ascendancy of what Wolf calls "the beauty myth"—the belief that the sole value of a woman lies in her appearance and physical attractiveness.

TO CONSIDER What does the increasing popularity of cosmetic surgery such as liposuction, face-lifts, and breast implants say about our culture? Why is it so important for women, especially, to appear beautiful?

At last, after a long silence, women took to the streets. In the two decades of radical action that followed the rebirth of feminism in the early 1970s, Western women gained legal and reproductive rights, pursued higher education, entered the trades and the professions, and overturned ancient and revered beliefs about their social role. A generation on, do women feel free?

The affluent, educated, liberated women of the First World, who can enjoy freedoms unavailable to any woman ever before, do not feel as free as they want to. And they can no longer restrict to the subconscious their sense that this lack of freedom has something to do with—with apparently frivolous issues, things that really should not matter. Many are ashamed to admit that such trivial concerns—to do with physical appearance, bodies, faces, hair, clothes—matter so much. But in spite of shame, guilt, and denial, more and more women are won-

---

dering if it isn't that they are entirely neurotic and alone but rather that something important is indeed at stake that has to do with the relationship between female liberation and female beauty.

The more legal and material hindrances women have broken through, the more strictly and heavily and cruelly images of female beauty have come to weigh upon us. Many women sense that women's collective progress has stalled; compared with the heady momentum of earlier days, there is a dispiriting climate of confusion, division, cynicism, and above all, exhaustion. After years of much struggle and little recognition, many older women feel burned out; after years of taking its light for granted, many younger women show little interest in touching new fire to the torch.

During the past decade, women breached the power structure; meanwhile, eating disorders rose exponentially and cosmetic surgery became the fastest-growing medical specialty. During the past five years, consumer spending doubled, pornography became the main media category, ahead of legitimate films and records combined, and thirty-three thousand American women told researchers that they would rather lose ten to fifteen pounds than achieve any other goal. More women have more money and power and scope and legal recognition than we have ever had before; but in terms of how we feel about ourselves *physically*, we may actually be worse off than our unliberated grandmothers. Recent research consistently shows that inside the majority of the West's controlled, attractive, successful working women, there is a secret "underlife" poisoning our freedom; infused with notions of beauty, it is a dark vein of self-hatred, physical obsessions, terror of aging, and dread of lost control.

It is no accident that so many potentially powerful women feel this way. We are in the midst of a violent backlash against feminism that uses images of female beauty as a political weapon against women's advancement: the beauty myth. It is the modern version of a social reflex that has been in force since the Industrial Revolution. As women released themselves from the feminine mystique of domesticity, the beauty myth took over its lost ground, expanding as it waned to carry on its work of social control. 5

The contemporary backlash is so violent because the ideology of beauty is the last one remaining of the old feminine ideologies that still has the power to control those women whom second-wave feminism would have otherwise made relatively uncontrollable: It has grown stronger to take over the work of social coercion that myths about motherhood, domesticity, chastity, and passivity no longer can manage. It is seeking right now to undo psychologically and covertly all the good things that feminism did for women materially and overtly.

This counterforce is operating to checkmate the inheritance of feminism on every level in the lives of Western women. Feminism gave us laws against job discrimination based on gender; immediately case law evolved in Britain and the United States that institutionalized job discrimination based on women's appearances. Patriarchal religion declined; new religious dogma, using some of the mind-altering techniques of older cults and sects, arose around age and weight to functionally supplant traditional ritual. Feminists, inspired by Betty Friedan, broke the stranglehold on the women's popular press of advertisers for household products, who were promoting the feminine mystique; at once, the diet and skin care industries became the new cultural censors of women's intellectual space, and because of their pressure, the gaunt, youthful model supplanted the happy housewife as the arbiter of successful womanhood. The sexual revolution promoted the discovery of female sexuality; "beauty pornography"—which for the first time in women's history artificially links a commodified "beauty" directly and explicitly to sexuality—invaded the mainstream to undermine women's new and vulnerable sense of sexual self-worth. Reproductive rights gave Western women control over our own bodies; the weight of fashion models plummeted to 23 percent below that of ordinary women, eating disorders rose exponentially, and a mass neurosis was promoted that used food and weight to strip women of that sense of control. Women insisted on politicizing health; new technologies of invasive, potentially deadly "cosmetic" surgeries developed apace to re-exert old forms of medical control of women.

Every generation since about 1830 has had to fight its version of the beauty myth. "It is very little to me," said the suffragist Lucy Stone in 1855, "to have the right to vote, to own property, etcetera, if I may not keep my body, and its uses, in my absolute right." Eighty years later, after women had won the vote, and the first wave of the organized women's movement had subsided, Virginia Woolf wrote that it would still be decades before women could tell the truth about their bodies. In 1962, Betty Friedan quoted a young woman trapped in the Feminine Mystique: "Lately, I look in the mirror, and I'm so afraid that I'm going to look like my mother." Eight years after that, heralding the cataclysmic second wave of feminism, Germaine Greer described "the Stereotype": "To her belongs all that is beautiful, even the very word beauty itself . . . she is a doll . . . I'm sick of the masquerade." In spite of the great revolution of the second wave, we are not exempt. Now we can look out over ruined barricades: A revolution has come upon us and changed everything in its path, enough time has passed since then for babies to have grown into women, but there still remains a final right not fully claimed.

The beauty myth tells a story: The quality called "beauty" objectively and universally exists. Women must want to embody it and men must want to possess women who embody it. This embodiment is an imperative for women and not for men, which situation is necessary and natural because it is biological, sexual, and evolutionary: Strong men battle for beautiful women, and beautiful women are more reproductively successful. Women's beauty must correlate to their fertility, and since this system is based on sexual selection, it is inevitable and changeless.

10　　None of this is true. "Beauty" is a currency system like the gold standard. Like any economy, it is determined by politics, and in the modern age in the West it is the last, best belief system that keeps male dominance intact. In assigning value to women in a vertical hierarchy according to a culturally imposed physical standard, it is an expression of power relations in which women must unnaturally compete for resources that men have appropriated for themselves.

"Beauty" is not universal or changeless, though the West pretends that all ideals of female beauty stem from one Platonic Ideal Woman; the Maori admire a fat vulva, and the Padung, droopy breasts. Nor is "beauty" a function of evolution: Its ideals change at a pace far more rapid than that of the evolution of species, and Charles Darwin was himself unconvinced by his own explanation that "beauty" resulted from a "sexual selection" that deviated from the rule of natural selection; for women to compete with women through "beauty" is a reversal of the way in which natural selection affects all other mammals. Anthropology has overturned the notion that females must be "beautiful" to be selected to mate: Evelyn Reed, Elaine Morgan, and others have dismissed sociobiological assertions of innate male polygamy and female monogamy. Female higher primates are the sexual initiators; not only do they seek out and enjoy sex with many partners, but "every nonpregnant female takes her turn at being the most desirable of all her troop. And that cycle keeps turning as long as she lives." The inflamed pink sexual organs of primates are often cited by male sociobiologists as analogous to human arrangements relating to female "beauty," when in fact that is a universal, nonhierarchical female primate characteristic.

Nor has the beauty myth always been this way. Though the pairing of the older rich men with young, "beautiful" women is taken to be somehow inevitable, in the matriarchal Goddess religions that dominated the Mediterranean from about 25,000 B.C.E. to about 700 B.C.E, the situation was reversed: "In every culture, the Goddess has many lovers. . . .The clear pattern is of an older woman with a beautiful but expendable youth—Ishtar and Tammuz, Venus and Adonis, Cybele and Attis, Isis and Osiris . . . their only function the service of the divine 'womb.'" Nor is it something only women do and only men watch: Among the Nigerian Wodaabes, the women hold economic power and the tribe is obsessed with male beauty; Wodaabe men spend hours together in elaborate makeup sessions, and compete—provocauvely painted and dressed, with swaying hips and seductive expressions—in beauty contests judged by women. There is no legitimate historical or biological justification for the beauty myth; what it is doing to women today is a result of nothing more exalted than the need of today's power structure, economy, and culture to mount a counteroffensive against women.

If the beauty myth is not based on evolution, sex, gender, aesthetics, or God, on what is it based? It claims to be about intimacy and sex and life, a celebration of women. It is actually composed of emotional distance, politics, finance, and sexual repression. The beauty myth is not about women at all. It is about men's institutions and institutional power.

The qualities that a given period calls beautiful in women are merely symbols of the female behavior that that period considers desirable: *The beauty myth is always actually prescribing behavior and not appearance.* Competition between women has been made part of the myth so that women will be divided from one another. Youth and (until recently) virginity have been "beautiful" in women since they stand for experiential and sexual ignorance. Aging in women is "unbeautiful" since women grow more powerful with time, and since the links between generations of women must always be newly broken: Older women fear young ones, young women fear old, and the beauty myth truncates for all the female life span. Most urgently, women's identity must be premised upon our "beauty" so that we will remain vulnerable to outside approval, carrying the vital sensitive organ of self-esteem exposed to the air.

15   Though there has, of course, been a beauty myth in some form for as long as there has been patriarchy, the beauty myth in its modern form is a fairly recent invention. The myth flourishes when material constraints on women are dangerously loosened. Before the Industrial Revolution, the average woman could not have had the same feelings about "beauty" that modern women do who experience the myth as continual comparison to a mass-disseminated physical ideal. Before the development of technologies of mass production—daguerreotypes, photographs, etc.—an ordinary woman was exposed to few such images outside the Church. Since the family was a productive unit and women's work complemented men's, the value of women who were not aristocrats or prostitutes lay in their work skills, economic shrewdness, physical strength, and fertility. Physical attraction, obviously, played its part; but "beauty" as we understand it was not, for ordinary women, a serious issue in the marriage marketplace. The beauty myth in its modern form gained ground after the upheavals of industrialization, as the work unit of the family was destroyed, and urbanization and the emerging factory system demanded what social engineers of the time termed the "separate sphere" of domesticity, which supported the new labor category of the "breadwinner" who left home for the workplace during the day. The middle class expanded, the standards of living and of literacy rose, the size of families shrank; a new class of literate, idle women developed, on whose submission to enforced domesticity the evolving system of industrial capitalism depended. Most of our assumptions about the way women have always thought about "beauty" date from no earlier than the 1830s, when the cult of domesticity was first consolidated and the beauty index invented.

For the first time new technologies could reproduce—in fashion plates, daguerreotypes, tintypes, and rotogravures—images of how women should look. In the 1840s the first nude photographs of prostitutes were taken; advertisements using images of "beautiful" women first appeared in mid-century. Copies of classical artworks, postcards of society beauties and royal mistresses, Currier and Ives prints, and porcelain figurines flooded the separate sphere to which middle-class women were confined.

Since the Industrial Revolution, middle-class Western women have been controlled by ideals and stereotypes as much as by material constraints. This situation, unique to this group, means that analyses that trace "cultural conspiracies" are uniquely plausible in relation to them. The rise of the beauty myth was just one of several emerging social fictions that masqueraded as natural components of the feminine sphere, the better to enclose those women inside it. Other such fictions arose contemporaneously: a version of childhood that required continual maternal supervision; a concept of female biology that required middle-class women to act out the roles of hysterics and hypochondriacs; a conviction that respectable women were sexually anesthetic; and a definition of women's work that occupied them with repetitive, time-consuming, and painstaking tasks such as needlepoint and lacemaking. All such Victorian inventions as these served a double function—that is, though they were encouraged as a means to expend female energy and intelligence in harmless ways, women often used them to express genuine creativity and passion.

But in spite of middle-class women's creativity with fashion and embroidery and child rearing, and, a century later, with the role of the suburban housewife that devolved from these social fictions, the fictions' main purpose was served: During a century and a half of unprecedented feminist agitation, they effectively counteracted middle-class women's dangerous new leisure, literacy, and relative freedom from material constraints.

Though these time- and mind-consuming fictions about women's natural role adapted themselves to resurface in the postwar Feminine Mystique, when the second wave of the women's movement took apart what women's magazines had portrayed as the "romance," "science," and "adventure" of homemaking and suburban family life, they temporarily failed. The cloying domestic fiction of "togetherness" lost its meaning and middle-class women walked out of their front doors in masses.

So the fictions simply transformed themselves once more: Since the   20
women's movement had successfully taken apart most other necessary fictions of femininity, all the work of social control once spread out over the whole network of these fictions had to be reassigned to the only strand left intact, which action consequently strengthened it a hundred-fold. This reimposed onto liberated women's faces and bodies all the limitations, taboos, and punishments of the repressive laws, religious injunctions and reproductive enslavement that no longer carried sufficient force. Inexhaustible but ephemeral beauty work took over from inexhaustible but ephemeral housework. As the economy, law, religion, sexual mores, education, and culture were forcibly opened up to include women more fairly, a private reality colonized female consciousness. By using ideas about "beauty," it reconstructed an alternative female world with its own laws, economy, religion, sexuality, education, and culture, each element as repressive as any that had gone before.

Since middle-class Western women can best be weakened psychologically now that we are stronger materially, the beauty myth, as it has resurfaced in the last generation, has had to draw on more technological sophistication and reactionary fervor than ever before. The modern arsenal of the myth is a dissemination of millions of images of the current ideal; although this barrage is generally seen as a collective sexual fantasy, there is in fact little that is sexual about it. It is summoned out of political fear on the part of male-dominated institutions threatened by women's freedom, and it exploits female guilt and apprehension about our own liberation—latent fears that we might be going too far. This frantic aggregation of imagery is a collective reactionary hallucination willed into being by both men and women stunned and disoriented by the rapidity with which gender relations have been transformed: a bulwark of reassurance against the flood of change. The mass depiction of the modern woman as a "beauty" is a contradiction: Where modern women are growing, moving, and expressing their individuality, as the myth has it, "beauty" is by definition inert, timeless, and generic. That this hallucination is necessary and deliberate is evident in the way "beauty" so directly contradicts women's real situation.

And the unconscious hallucination grows ever more influential and pervasive because of what is now conscious market manipulation: powerful industries—the $33-billion-a-year diet industry, the $20-billion cosmetics industry, the $300-million cosmetic surgery industry, and the $7-billion pornography industry—have arisen from the capital made out of unconscious anxieties, and are in turn able, through their influence on mass culture, to use, stimulate, and reinforce the hallucination in a rising economic spiral.

This is not a conspiracy theory; it doesn't have to be. Societies tell themselves necessary fictions in the same way that individuals and families do. Henrik Ibsen called them "vital lies," and psychologist Daniel Goleman describes them working the same way on the social level that they do within families: "The collusion is maintained by directing attention away from the fearsome fact, or by repackaging its meaning in an acceptable format." The costs of these social blind spots, he writes, are destructive communal illusions. Possibilities for women have become so open-ended that they threaten to destabilize the institutions on which a male-dominated culture has depended, and a collective panic reaction on the part of both sexes has forced a demand for counter-images.

The resulting hallucination materializes, for women, as something all too real. No longer just an idea, it becomes three-dimensional, incorporating within itself how women live and how they do not live: It becomes the Iron Maiden. The original Iron Maiden was a medieval German instrument of torture, a body-shaped casket painted with the limbs and features of a lovely, smiling young woman. The unlucky victim was slowly enclosed inside her; the lid fell shut to immobilize the victim, who died either of starvation or, less cruelly, of the metal spikes embedded in her interior. The modern hallucination in which women are trapped or trap themselves is similarly rigid, cruel, and euphemistically painted. Contemporary culture directs attention to imagery of the Iron Maiden, while censoring real women's faces and bodies.

25   Why does the social order feel the need to defend itself by evading the fact of real women, our faces and voices and bodies, and reducing the meaning of women to these formulaic and endlessly reproduced "beautiful" images? Though unconscious personal anxieties can be a powerful force in the creation of a vital lie, economic necessity practically guarantees it. An economy that depends on slavery needs to promote images of slaves that "justify" the institution of slavery. Western economics are absolutely dependent now on the continued underpayment of women. An ideology that makes women feel "worth less" was urgently needed to counteract the way feminism had begun to make us feel worth more. This does not require a conspiracy; merely an atmosphere. The contemporary economy depends right now on the representation of women within the beauty myth. Economist John Kenneth Galbraith offers an economic explanation for "the persistence of the view of homemaking as a 'higher calling'": the concept of women as naturally trapped within the Feminine Mystique, he feels, "has been forced on us by popular sociology, by magazines, and by fiction to disguise the fact that woman in her role of consumer has

been essential to the development of our industrial society. . . . Behavior that is essential for economic reasons is transformed into a social virtue." As soon as a woman's primary social value could no longer be defined as the attainment of virtuous domesticity, the beauty myth redefined it as the attainment of virtuous beauty. It did so to substitute both a new consumer imperative and a new justification for economic unfairness in the workplace where the old ones had lost their hold over newly liberated women.

Another hallucination arose to accompany that of the Iron Maiden: The caricature of the Ugly Feminist was resurrected to dog the steps of the women's movement. The caricature is unoriginal; it was coined to ridicule the feminists of the nineteenth century. Lucy Stone herself, whom supporters saw as "a prototype of womanly grace . . . fresh and fair as the morning," was derided by detractors with "the usual report" about Victorian feminists: "a big masculine woman, wearing boots, smoking a cigar, swearing like a trooper." As Betty Friedan put it presciently in 1960, even before the savage revamping of that old caricature: "The unpleasant image of feminists today resembles less the feminists themselves than the image fostered by the interests who so bitterly opposed the vote for women in state after state." Thirty years on, her conclusion is more true than ever: That resurrected caricature, which sought to punish women for their public acts by going after their private sense of self, became the paradigm for new limits placed on aspiring women everywhere. After the success of the women's movement's second wave, the beauty myth was perfected to checkmate power at every level in individual women's lives. The modern neuroses of life in the female body spread to woman after woman at epidemic rates. The myth is undermining—slowly, imperceptibly, without our being aware of the real forces of erosion—the ground women have gained through long, hard, honorable struggle.

The beauty myth of the present is more insidious than any mystique of femininity yet: A century ago, Nora slammed the door of the doll's house; a generation ago, women turned their backs on the consumer heaven of the isolated multi-applianced home; but where women are trapped today, there is no door to slam. The contemporary ravages of the beauty backlash are destroying women physically and depleting us psychologically. If we are to free ourselves from the dead weight that has once again been made out of femaleness, it is not ballots or lobbyists or placards that women will need first; it is a new way to see.

---

1 Explain in your own words what Wolf means by "the beauty myth." In her opinion, how has "the beauty myth" replaced the "feminine myth of domesticity"?

2 Evaluate Wolf's analysis of the hidden forces that compel women to adopt behaviors that "poison" modern women's lives. How credible do you find her analysis to be?

3 To what extent has your own body image been determined by the prevailing myth of feminine beauty described by Wolf? To discover this, make up an inventory of parts of your body with which you are satisfied or dissatisfied and try to locate ads whose implicit value judgments may have shaped your perceptions. Alternatively, you might

wish to investigate whether men have their own version of a "beauty myth." What is the signifance of recent changes in the measurements of the new Barbie doll—not as tall, smaller breasts, wider waist—as compared to the original Barbie?

4 How does Wolf use the "iron maiden" (para. 24) as a kind of equivalent to the predicament in which modern women find themselves? What causal relationships does Wolf see between "the beauty myth" and the advances made by the feminist movement? (Glossary: *Analogy, Cause and Effect.*)

5 In your own words, summarize Wolf's argument. What pattern of organization does she rely on to develop her thesis? Why is this organization especially useful given her thesis? (Glossary: *Argument.*)

6 Examine copies of women's fashion magazines such as *Vogue, Mademoiselle, Cosmopolitan, and Glamour,* and compare the images of female beauty displayed in both the advertising and fashion sections with representations of women's bodies in painting and sculpture from different historical periods in different countries. Alternatively, examine copies of men's magazines such as *M, GQ, Ebony, Esquire, Playboy,* or *Sports Illustrated* to see how ads define what men should be and how they should look.

Beauty and the Beast of Advertising　　*Jean Kilbourne*

◆ JEAN KILBOURNE is an educator and writer who has been a visiting scholar at Wellesley College and has produced a number of films, including *Killing Us Softly: Advertising's Image of Women* (1979), *Calling the Shot* (1982), and *Still Killing Us Softly* (1987). She has done a number of innovative multimedia shows, including *The Naked Truth* (1970), *Under the Influence,* and *You've Come the Wrong Way, Baby: Women and Cigarette Advertising.* She serves on the board of directors for the National Council on Alcoholism. The following article originally appeared in *Media & Values Magazine,* 1990.

Kilbourne's analysis delves into the relationship between advertising, the values it purveys, and its impact on contemporary American society. Her discussion begins where Naomi Wolf's leaves off and shows how "the beauty myth" has seeped into teen and preteen advertising. Kilbourne assails the distorted images that have led an increasing number of young women to develop eating disorders

Jean Kilbourne, "Beauty and the Beast of Advertising," from *Media & Values.* Copyright 1990. Reprinted with permission from *Media & Values* Magazine.

such as anorexia. In this unhealthy climate, the selling of women's bodies as separate parts to be perfected and the marketing of children as sex objects to sell products have become a destructive force in our society.

> **TO CONSIDER** Have you seen any ads recently that offended you because of the way in which they depicted little girls as sex objects to sell products? What does the increasing prevalence of eating disorders such as bulimia and anorexia say about the effect of these ads?

"You're a Halston woman from the very beginning," the advertisement proclaims. The model stares provocatively at the viewer, her long blonde hair waving around her face, her bare chest partially covered by two curved bottles that give the illusion of breasts and a cleavage.

The average American is accustomed to blue-eyed blondes seductively touting a variety of products. In this case, however, the blonde is about five years old.

Advertising is an over $145 billion a year industry and affects all of us throughout our lives. We are each exposed to over 1,500 ads a day, constituting perhaps the most powerful educational force in society. The average adult will spend one and one-half years of his/her life watching television commercials. But the ads sell a great deal more than products. They sell values, images and concepts of success and worth, love and sexuality, popularity and normalcy. They tell us who we are and who we should be. Sometimes they sell addictions.

Advertising's foundation and economic lifeblood is the mass media, and the primary purpose of the mass media is to deliver an audience to advertisers, just as the primary purpose of television programs is to deliver an audience for commercials.

Adolescents are particularly vulnerable, however, because they are new and inexperienced consumers and are the prime targets of many advertisements. They are in the process of learning their values and roles and developing their self-concepts. Most teenagers are sensitive to peer pressure and find it difficult to resist or even question the dominant cultural messages perpetuated and reinforced by the media. Mass communication has made possible a kind of nationally distributed peer pressure that erodes private and individual values and standards.

But what does society, and especially teenagers, learn from the advertising messages that proliferate in the mass media? On the most obvious level they learn the stereotypes. Advertising creates a mythical, WASP-oriented world in which no one is ever ugly, overweight, poor, struggling or disabled either physically or mentally (unless you count the housewives who talk to little men in the toilet bowls). And it is a world in which people talk only about products.

HOUSEWIVES OR SEX OBJECTS

The aspect of advertising most in need of analysis and change is the portrayal of women. Scientific studies and the most casual viewing yield the same conclusion: Women are shown almost exclusively as housewives or sex objects.

The housewife, pathologically obsessed by cleanliness and lemon-fresh scents, debates cleaning products with herself and worries about her husband's "ring around the collar."

The sex object is a mannequin, a shell. Conventional beauty is her only attribute. She has no lines or wrinkles (which would indicate she had the bad taste and poor judgment to grow older), no scars or blemishes—indeed, she has no pores. She is thin, generally tall and long-legged, and, above all, she is young. All "beautiful" women in advertisements (including minority women), regardless of product or audience, conform to this norm. Women are constantly exhorted to emulate this ideal, to feel ashamed and guilty if they fail, and to feel that their desirability and lovability are contingent upon physical perfection.

CREATING ARTIFICIALITY

The image is artificial and can only be achieved artificially (even the "natural look" requires much preparation and expense). Beauty is something that comes from without; more than one million dollars is spent every hour on cosmetics. Desperate to conform to an ideal and impossible standard, many women go to great lengths to manipulate and change their faces and bodies. A woman is conditioned to view her face as a mask and her body as an object, as *things* separate from and more important than her real self, constantly in need of alteration, improvement, and disguise. She is made to feel dissatisfied with the ashamed of herself, whether she tries to achieve "the look" or not. Objectified constantly by others, she learns to objectify herself. (It is interesting to note that one in five college-age women have an eating disorder.)

"When *Glamour* magazine surveyed its readers in 1984, 75 percent felt too heavy and only 15 percent felt just right. Nearly half of those who were actually underweight reported feeling too fat and wanting to diet. Among a sample of college women, 40 percent felt overweight when only 12 percent actually were too heavy," according to Rita Freedman in her book *Beauty Bound*.

There is evidence that this preoccupation with weight begins at ever-earlier ages for women. According to a recent article in *New Age Journal*, "even grade-school girls are succumbing to stick-like-standards of beauty enforced by a relentless parade of wasp-waisted fashion models, movie stars and pop idols." A study by a University of California professor showed that nearly 80 percent of fourth-grade girls in the Bay Area are watching their weight.

A recent *Wall Street Journal* survey of students in four Chicago-area schools found that more than half the fourth-grade girls were dieting and three-quarters felt they were overweight. One student said, "We don't expect boys to be that handsome. We take them as they are." Another added, "But boys expect girls to be perfect and beautiful. And skinny."

Dr. Steven Levenkron, author of *The Best Little Girl in the World,* the story of an anorexic, says his blood pressure soars every time he opens a magazine and finds an ad for women's fashions. "If I had my way," he said, "every one of them would have to carry a line saying, 'Caution: This model may be hazardous to your health.'"

Women are also dismembered in commercials, their bodies separated into parts in need of change or improvement. If a woman has "acceptable" breasts, then she must also be sure that her legs are worth watching, her hips slim, her feet sexy, and that her buttocks look nude under her clothes ("like I'm not wearin' nothin'"). This image is difficult and costly to achieve and impossible to maintain (unless you buy the product)—no one is flawless and everyone ages. Growing older is the great taboo. Women are encouraged to remain little girls ("because innocence is sexier than you think"), to be passive and dependent, never to mature. The contradictory message—"sensual, but not too far from innocence"—places women in a double bind; somehow we are supposed to be both sexy and virginal, experienced and naive, seductive and chaste. The disparagement of maturity is, of course, insulting and frustrating to adult women, and the implication that little girls are seductive is dangerous to real children.

INFLUENCING SEXUAL ATTITUDES

Young people also learn a great deal about sexual attitudes from the media and from advertising in particular. Advertising's approach to sex is pornographic; it reduces people to objects and de-emphasizes human contact and individuality. This reduction of sexuality to a dirty joke and of people to objects is the real obscenity of the culture. Although the sexual sell, overt and subliminal, is at a fevered pitch in most commercials, there is at the same time a notable absence of sex as an important and profound human activity.

There have been some changes in the images of women. Indeed, a "new woman" has emerged in commercials in recent years. She is generally presented as superwoman, who manages to do all the work at home and on the job (with the help of a product, of course, not of her husband or children or friends), or as the liberated woman, who owes her independence and self-esteem to the products she uses. These new images do not represent any real progress but rather create a myth of progress, an illusion that reduces complex sociopolitical problems to mundane personal ones.

Advertising images do not cause these problems, but they contribute to them by creating a climate in which the marketing of women's bodies—the sexual sell and dismemberment, distorted body image ideal and children as sex objects—is seen as acceptable.

This is the real tragedy, that many women internalize these stereotypes and learn their "limitations," thus establishing a self-fulfilling prophecy. If one accepts these mythical and degrading images, to some extent one actualizes them. By remaining unaware of the profound seriousness of the ubiquitous influence, the redundant message and the subliminal impact of advertisements, we ignore one of the most powerful "educational" forces in the culture—one that greatly affects our self-images, our ability to relate to each other, and effectively destroys any awareness and action that might help to change that climate.

1 Why would the particular set of qualities that characterize the female mannequin model be so influential in persuading women to emulate this ideal image? Is the achievement of such an image realistic for most women?

2 How might this explain the increase in eating disorders among young girls and among young women who are "encouraged to remain little girls . . . to be passive and dependent, never to mature" (para. 14)?

3 In which recent ads can you discern the kind of cultural messages described by Kilbourne? What are the subliminal messages in these ads and to what extent do they use distortions of body images to sell products to women? If Kilbourne could change the attitudes of a segment of consumers, who would they be, and what would she hope to achieve?

4 What is Kilbourne's thesis? How does she correlate the images (para. 9) that portray women in ads with the results of surveys and statistics (para. 11–13) as evidence to support her thesis? (Glossary: *Evidence, Thesis.*)

5 How is Kilbourne's analysis designed to probe beyond superficial relationships to reveal the connections between eating disorders such as anorexia in adolescents and the role of advertising? (Glossary: *Cause and Effect.*)

6 What relationship can you discover between the widespread phenomenon of anorexia and bulimia and other eating disorders and the kinds of ads that have become so prevalent? Locate several of these ads and analyze the imagery, emotional appeals, and content to determine the basis of this relationship. For example, why do recent Calvin Klein ads use the model Kate Moss—among others—to suggest that qualities of emaciation, androgyny, stylized decadence, and detachment are now desirable in terms of selling perfume?

Sprayed and Neutered   *Susan Irvine*

◆ SUSAN IRVINE is a freelance writer who received her M.A. in English literature from Wadham College, Oxford University. Her work has been published in the *Sunday Times,* the *Financial Times,* the *Independent,* and the *Sunday Telegraph.* Her book *Perfume* (1995) explores the relationship between perfume, fashion, and the media. Irvine is the five-time winner of the Jasmine Award, given to writers by the fragrance industry. The following essay appeared in the April 1996 issue of *Allure*.

Some preliminary signs indicate that advertisers may have gotten the message that excessive sexualization of the kind discussed by Jean Kilbourne is no longer acceptable. For example, a recent trend uses images of purity, freshness, innocence, spiritual enlightenment, and escape, in contrast to previous ads that depend on overt sexuality in perfume ad campaigns. Irvine discusses the underlying shift in cultural values responsible for this radical change, and speculates as to why innocence is now prized and sexual images are out of style. Could it be that women are liberating themselves from the tyranny of the "beauty myth" discussed by Wolf and are starting to value themselves rather than be slavishly dependent on the approval of others?

> **TO CONSIDER** What is your favorite perfume? What image is created by ads for this perfume? What qualities or feelings do you associate with it?

Let's face it, there is no fragrance that drives men mad. It is fragrance advertising that has always kept women hoping. Sex, after all, sells scent. Come to think of it, sex sells everything from cars to ice cream to Folgers Instant. But fragrance has always flirted with sex a little more outrageously than almost any other product has, because perfume (unlike ice cream) is what women tend to put on before a date.

But that was then. Just recently sex has become a dirty word in perfume marketing. The three major launches of recent months studiously avoided the s word and gave us sex-free scent advertising. Estée Lauder Pleasures is about "feeling good about yourself," says Muriel Gonzalez, Lauder's senior vice president of marketing. The ad shows a woman and some puppies in the great outdoors. Only a pervert could find that sexy.

For Poême, the somewhat more "intellectual" Lancôme launch also ditches sex in favor of some personal downtime. "Perfume now is a way to escape in a positive sense, to let your mind dream," says Sylvie de Champenois, Lancôme's international marketing director of fragrances. The perfume is promoted with love poetry from the elusive French surrealist Paul Eluard. De Champenois says that sex is not the point: "We have chosen a poem that is a declaration of love. Poême is about putting poetry back in your life."

Allure, the new Chanel fragrance, sounds as if it might be sexy. An alluring woman is—at least semantically—an attractive one. But the ads show elegant women alone, dressed for a day at the office or a casual Saturday. "We've chosen images of different women of different ages, colors, types—the message is that women are all individual and Allure crosses age, culture, and race barriers," says Laurie Palma, vice president of marketing, fragrances for Chanel. As concepts go, it may be politically correct. Smoldering it ain't.

"I think we are definitely moving into an era where sex is less important as a marketing tool," says Ann Gottlieb, a fragrance consultant who has helped create the Calvin Klein fragrances—in which, ironically, sex used to be very important. "Middle-class women are disillusioned with men. The sexual part of their lives has gone from being a fantasy to a burden. A man is no longer a given for happiness." Exit the classic fragrance ad of a man in a tux falling for a scent-drenched woman in stilettos. Enter trouble-free images of a woman with a child (Sunflowers) or peacefully alone (Adrienne Vittadini AV).

6   Sex has become dangerous, and in an era of play-it-safe scents that all smell similar—simple and fresh—sex is out of place. Even that old smolderer Opium has a new image and advertising campaign. The ads used to show a smoky-eyed Kate Moss sprawled atop lush cushions in a state of abandon. According to Patricia Turck Paquelier, who oversaw the concept for the upcoming Opium for Men, Rupert Everett and Linda Evangelista are supposed to look like brother and sister in the mirror-image ads for the fragrances. Everett even had his chest waxed for the photo shoot to enhance his sexlessness.

7   The liquid in the bottle, too, is losing carnal undertones. The trend is toward sparkling fruit notes, sheer girly florals, and banal lovelike fragrances with the widespread appeal of a good air freshener. Base notes like vanilla and musk have traditionally been linked with sensuality, and these are the scents that are missing from some of the new fragrances. For instance, Alfred Sung Forever features something called River Rock, which is supposed to smell like a mountain stream.

8   Nature, of course, is perceived to be fresher, purer, and less complicated than real life. Consequently, fragrances are lighter; many new scents, like Ralph Lauren's Polo Sport Women and the ubiquitous CK One, do not even come in the heavier, oilier perfume formula, but only as eau de toilette.

9   The gist of that infamous CK One ad is, not too surprisingly, androgyny. But there are other ways to read it. "Unisex fragrances aren't about gender-bending," says Annette Green, president of the industry's cheer-leader, the Fragrance Foundation. "They're about not really being interested in sex at all. Look at the kids in the CK One ads. In some ads, they're not even touching. They're just a bunch of kids hanging out together." Fragrance, she says, has become more about mood and less about mating.

10   Sylvie de Champenois thinks that, above all, we want to feel clean. "There is a feeling that sex is tainted, the planet is tainted. Women are using scent now as part of a cleansing ritual," she says. (L'Eau d'Issey, for instance, claims to smell close to water itself.) De Champenois suggests we are moving away from sexual scents toward those that not only refresh us, she says a bit philosophically, but "irrigate the soul" as well.

11   Scents that try to be, soulful—Angel, Ghost Myst, Dream, and Far Away—are fast replacing sexual ones. The Gap's Heaven is "the mist from the angel's wing," and Carolina Herrera's Flore is "a world within," according to their ads. Joachim Mensing, a clinical psychologist who does consulting for the fragrance industry, goes so far as to suggest that the whole business is in the grip of "angel fever."

12   Mensing thinks that society's idea of the "ideal woman" has shifted from femme fatale to the classic Christian ideal of the pure woman who redeems the

sinful man. Believe it or not, a redemption scent is on the way. Nina Ricci's L'Air du Temps may have been a classic floral that aimed only to smell good. But not anymore. In a new commercial not yet released, it is worn by a virginal woman who rescues a man from his inner demons with her sisterly embrace. Feminists, obviously, will be wearing something else.

Scent does, of course, have connections with spirituality. The ancient Egyptians used various incenses to induce a peaceful mood in religious gatherings and even to bring devotees to a higher state of consciousness, one supposedly closer to God. 13

"I don't think any fragrance can promise you spiritual enlightenment," Laurie Palma of Chanel says, laughing. In her view, women are not disillusioned with sex or sexy fragrances and in favor of spiritual ones. They are just redefining what sexy means. "We polled women when we were formulating Allure, especially young women. And they said that what was sexy now was a fragrance that smells clean and fresh with warmth to it." Innocence itself is sexy. 14

Innocence is sexy to the young women precisely because they are young— and presumably innocent. And this is the real marketing strategy behind these seemingly sexless new fragrances: They are aimed at the younger section of the market. These women want wholesome, natural, fresh, and light fragrances. No mystery there. 15

Sex, however, isn't dead yet. Just a little tired, perhaps. After a short nap, the frankly seductive fragrance will no doubt soon be bumping and grinding its way into ad campaigns everywhere. 16

---

1 Why have ad campaigns for perfume recently moved away from sexual and sensual images and replaced them with images of innocence, wholesomeness, purity, and self-acceptance?

2 Describe in detail how each of the following perfume ads reveals the current trend: (a) Poême (para. 3), (b) Allure (para. 4), (c) Sunflowers (para. 5), and (d) CKone (para. 9).

3 To what extent does a current ad for perfume exemplify the trend Irvine discusses? Are there qualities about this ad that you would characterize as childlike, naive, and innocent? Does the model project a sense of a search for purity, escape, and simplicity? If so, in what way? Do you find this ad more effective than ones that used sex and the promise of fulfilment in a relationship to sell perfume? Why or why not?

4 What explanation does Irvine offer to clarify the paradox that advertisers have recently adopted an "innocence is sexy" pitch to sell perfume? Do you agree with Irvine's reasons? Why or why not? (Glossary: *Paradox*.)

5 Irvine supports her discussion of recent changes in perfume advertising with a number of examples. Why are these examples needed to underscore her thesis? (Glossary: *Examples*.)

6 Just as advertisers must create distinctive images for perfumes that have no already existing associations, they also fashion images for other products that must be sold by image alone. Examine the ad campaign for another luxury product (such as diamonds) and discuss how the slogans, images, and language in the ad copy are intended to motivate consumers to empathize with the stories depicted in the ad and to imagine how purchasing the product will change their lives.

◆ CONNECTIONS: THE RHETORIC OF ADVERTISING

Bill Bryson, "The Hard Sell: Advertising in America"

1. How does Bryson's analysis of the importance of brand names and the marketing techniques used to advertise them shed light on the significance of recent ads for perfume described by Susan Irvine?
2. Compare Bryson's and David A. Ricks's analyses (see "What's In a Name?," Ch. 6) of the marketing considerations that go into the choice of a brand name according to whether the product will be sold domestically or internationally.

John Berger, "Ways of Seeing"

1. How do the images that manipulate women (as described by Jean Kilbourne) provide a specific application of the general theory of advertising's reliance on envy and glamour, as explored by Berger?
2. What connections can you discover between Susanne K. Langer's discussion of symbolism in "Language and Thought" (Ch. 2) and Berger's analysis of how advertising works?

Stuart Hirschberg, "The Rhetoric of Advertising"

1. How do the manipulative techniques of ads described by Jean Kilbourne employ rhetorical strategies discussed by Hirschberg?
2. How might any of the products identified by David A. Ricks in "What's In a Name?" (Ch. 6) have been marketed using a typical range of advertising techniques discussed by Hirschberg?

Naomi Wolf, From The Beauty Myth

1. How do the consequences of advertising on preteen and adolescent girls, as described by Jean Kilbourne, become more comprehensible in the light of Wolf's analysis of the myth of feminine beauty?
2. What connections can you discover between Wolf's analysis of how the myth of feminine beauty influences the way in which women see themselves and Robin Lakoff's discussion in "Language and Woman's Place" (Ch. 5) of how women should speak?

Jean Kilbourne, "Beauty and the Beast of Advertising"

1. How does Kilbourne's analysis of "scare tactics" targeted at adolescents relate to the theory of emotional appeals discussed by Hirschberg?
2. Discuss the irony that society, on one hand, is so sensitive to sexist language (as described by Alleen Pace Nilsen in "Sexism in English: A 1990s Update," Ch. 8) and, on the other hand, exhorts adolescent girls to internalize and act on these stereotypes (as discussed by Kilbourne).

Susan Irvine, "Sprayed and Neutered"

1. To what extent do new ad campaigns for perfume, as described by Irvine, represent a shift away from "the beauty myth," as analyzed by Naomi Wolf?
2. How do the new ad campaigns for perfume use images in a way that is equivalent to politically correct uses of language discussed by Michiko Kakutani in "The Word Police" (Ch. 8)?

◆ WRITING ASSIGNMENTS FOR CHAPTER 9

1. What is the phenomenon of subliminal advertising? You might wish to read Wilson Bryan Keyes's books *Subliminal Seduction* (1973), *Media Sexploitation* (1976), and *The Clam Plate Orgy* (1980) for analyses of the use of imbedded subliminal messages in a variety of contexts. If relevant, describe an experience you may have had with this phenomenon.
2. If you could appear on the cover of any magazine for an achievement or quality for which you would be celebrated, what would it be and why (for example, *Sports illustrated, Time, Rolling Stone, Ms., WIRED, Gourmet, Business Week*)?
3. Much of the effectiveness of advertising depends on its ability to tap into our hopes and dreams as expressed in sensory details, characters, symbols, images and impressions, and colors. In this respect it is like the "wish fulfillment" characteristic of many of our dreams. Write a short essay in which you describe a recurring or powerful dream using the following technique: (a) write a narrative of the dream, identifying yourself with an important character or symbol, (b) express your experiences in the first person, (c) render an account of the dream complete with details, characters, impressions, observations, and colors, and try to speculate on the message the dream contains, if any. You might wish to give your essay a title that expresses the point of the dream, for example, "Nude in Public." Analyze any ad you have recently come across in terms of the features you encountered in your own dreams.
4. Bumper stickers are a unique form of public advertising. What are some of the more unusual and interesting ones you have seen? What is your opinion of them?

5. What memorable advertising slogans have caught your attention? Choose a few and analyze possible reasons for their success. Think of a few ad campaigns that were not successful and analyze why they were ineffective.

6. In the course of a day, how many ads try to persuade you with impressive sounding quasi-scientific technical talk? Make a list of these and choose a few to analyze for their pseudoappeals to logic.

7. What are your least favorite ads? What about them makes them so objectionable to you? Are there specific cases where you think the ad was designed to be purposely irritating to stand out and capture your attention?

8. Whatever specific emotional route the advertiser takes (appealing to the desire for popularity, good health, financial security, or adventure), an underlying emotional appeal of ads is based on the unspoken assumption that you can change your future for the better. Choose any ad and analyze its pictorial and print components to show how it feeds into this desire.

9. Would you want to go into advertising as a career? Why or why not?

10. What features make advertising like or unlike other specialized uses of language that share common elements? For example, how do ads use language, imagery, and symbolism in ways characteristic of poetry? What features of advertising appear in actual political propaganda (see Aldous Huxley's "Propaganda in a Dictatorship," Ch. 10)?

11. Consider the use of language to advertise and promote food on menus and in ads. Find a particularly extravagant example where the description and name of the food is pure hype in relationship to the actual item. How does the same principle operate in names given to cosmetics, carpeting, etc.?

12. What cues can you identify in any particular ad that would enable you to surmise which socioeconomic group the advertiser was targeting?

13. Write a letter to a company whose product has failed to live up to the expectations created by its advertising. Conversely, you might write a letter of praise because a product fulfilled and even surpassed claims made for it. Keep a copy of your letter and all responses you receive from the company.

14. Is there a product or invention that you wish existed? Describe this product or invention and write an advertising campaign that extols its virtues.

15. What names of products do you find effective in creating a positive set of associations? Analyze a few of these names to discover the qualities they bring to mind.

16. In the last few years, a new form of advertising is the "infomercial." After watching one or several of these, analyze how infomercials use some of the following techniques to capture the audience's attention for a relatively long period of time: hosts who establish rapport with television audiences, testimonials of convinced users, preplanned interviews, known personalities, weasel words ("virtually," "helps," "up to," etc.) that don't obligate the advertiser to support their claims, and the tried and true litany of "new," "fast," and "easy." Do you find infomercials to be more effective than traditional ads? Why or why not?

17. How do advertisers try to achieve a match between the television show and the ads placed to appeal to the audience for that show? What is your favorite

show and how are the ads designed to appeal to the segment of the population that watches it?

18. Locate ads for competing products whose real differences are slight or nonexistent. How do the advertisements for each brand create these imaginary differences and make them seem to exist? Have you ever been "sold" on one brand over another because of the advertising? Describe the ad that "sold" you.

19. The slogan "A Diamond Is Forever" played an indispensable role in the De Beers marketing campaign for over fifty years. What other slogans are you familiar with that you find particularly effective in advertising the product (for example, FTD's "Say it with flowers")?

    How do the De Beers' ads for diamonds suggest that the giving and receiving of diamonds are the supreme expression of love at key moments in life? Keep in mind that De Beers has been refining its "A Diamond Is Forever" campaign for fifty years and has succeeded in making the desire for diamonds something approaching a basic human need—a supreme testament to the power of advertising to transform illusion into reality.

    A diamond is given as:

an engagement ring

a gift to renew an earlier commitment

a birthday gift

an anniversary gift, especially the tenth and twenty-fifth (with its slogan, "This year, tell her you'd marry her all over again")

On what other occasions are diamonds deemed a suitable gift? What values are promoted to motivate the purchase of diamonds for these occasions? How exactly do the advertisers create this archetypal equivalence between the diamond and eternal love?

Man does not live by words alone,
despite the fact that sometimes he has to
eat them.

—Adlai Stevenson

Larson, *In Search of the Far Side* © 1984, Andrews & McNeel, a
Universal Syndicate Company. Used by permission.

The Language of Politics

Entering the political dimension of language is rather like entering the Twilight Zone. With some conspicuous exceptions, nothing is as it seems to be. George Orwell first identified the use of language by politicians to evade reality (he called it "the defense of the indefensible") in his classic essay "Politics and the English Language." Ever attentive to changes in the public mood, some politicians use language filled with calculated evasions designed to avoid taking responsibility for failed policies, pious platitudes intended to stir the emotions, and mind-numbing doubletalk. Orwell's analysis of how politicians manipulate the language to manipulate us is a skillful autopsy of dead political speech.

The misuse of rhetorical techniques to distort and manipulate and the intentional use of slanting, labeling, and emotionally loaded language can be observed in Richard Nixon's "Checker's Speech," as analyzed by Stuart Hirschberg.

Political rhetoric has a more menacing side, as Aldous Huxley makes clear in "Propaganda Under a Dictatorship." The highly charged rhetoric Hitler used to play on fear and hatred is a prime example of the ways in which political language can persuade even while it corrupts. Ultimately, it is the intention with which words are used that determines whether any of the time-tested propaganda techniques pose a genuine threat to the public good.

Political language can be used to inspire as well as to deceive. Instead of appealing to fears and weaknesses, political speeches can appeal to our better natures, give us strength and courage, and move us to become more altruistic in seeking the common good. Classic examples of these kinds of speeches are Lincoln's "Gettysburg Address," whose rhetorical techniques are analyzed by Gilbert Highet, and Martin Luther King. Jr.'s clarion call for racial harmony and equality in "I Have a Dream." It is ironic that in the speeches of Lincoln and King we can observe the same set of persuasive strategies that have been used by those who seek to foment discord.

Just as the language of political rhetoric is expressly intended to transform politics into theater, so television news reports of political events, as Neil Postman and Steve Powers reveal in "How to watch TV News" are staged to provide "bread and circuses" for the masses. The production of an entertaining spectacle, complete with fast-paced images, sound, and music—and, as Postman and powers describe it, a "recreation" of events rather than reporting on the events themselves—has displaced the traditional objective analysis and genuine information most people think of as being the news. We can see how political and theatrical concerns merge in the reporting of the death of Princess Diana. The eulogy delivered by Earl Charles Spencer, her younger brother, on September 6, 1997, achieves a provocative blend of rhetoric and passion in his heartfelt tribute on the occasion of the funeral for his sister. Spencer's speech displays a skillful adaptation of many of the rhetorical techniques (powerful metaphors, emotionally charged language, parallel clauses, conversational style) speakers use to establish a bond with the audience, speak to their concerns and values, and urge them to action.

Politics and the English Language

George Orwell

♦ GEORGE ORWELL is the pen name taken by Eric Blair (1903–1950). In 1936, Orwell went to Spain to cover the Civil War and fight against the Fascists, an experience he described in *Homage to Catalonia* (1938). His distrust of totalitarianism emerged in *Animal Farm* (1945) and in his acclaimed novel *1984* (1949). Five collections of his essays have appeared in print, including *Shooting an Elephant* (1946), in which "Politics and the English Language" first appeared. In this essay, Orwell diagnoses the lin-

George Orwell, "Politics and the English Language," from *Shooting an Elephant and Other Essays.* Copyright © 1946 by Sonia Brownell Orwell and renewed 1974 by Sonia Orwell. Reprinted with permission by Harcourt Brace & Company.

guistic maladies that afflict the English language and attributes them to a deterioration of language and ideas of those in power.

Political rhetoric, Orwell observed, is designed to diminish the public's capacity for thinking clearly about important issues. As such, it is an important component of propaganda, whose primary task, as Aldous Huxley shows later in this chapter, is to suppress the critical faculties of listeners and substitute slogans and catchwords designed to inflame collective passions. The calculated distortion of language to serve a political agenda depends on euphemisms and other circumlocutions that disguise the true intent of the persuader. The use of political rhetoric to evade responsibility is just as true of today's politicians as it was in Orwell's time. Orwell also explored this process in depth in his acclaimed novel *1984,* where constant revisions of the dictionary produced citizens who lacked the words and corresponding thoughts necessary to understand their society. The official language of Oceania in *1984* is Newspeak, which, Orwell writes, "was designed not to extend but to *diminish* the range of thought," an objective that is also pursued by journalists, academics, bureaucrats, and others. The corruption of language Orwell describes encourages people to speak in canned phrases that make critical analysis impossible. To remedy these abuses, Orwell proposes a few straightforward and practical rules that writers can follow.

TO CONSIDER We often use clichés or ready-made phrases without realizing it. Which ones do you use most frequently? Do they seem trite or do they offer an economical means for expressing a complex idea quickly?

Most people who bother with the matter at all would admit that the   1 English language is in a bad way, but it is generally assumed that we cannot by conscious action do anything about it. Our civilization is decadent and our language—so the argument runs—must inevitably share in the general collapse. It follows that any struggle against the abuse of language is a sentimental archaism, like preferring candles to electric light or hansom cabs to aeroplanes. Underneath this lies the half-conscious belief that language is a natural growth and not an instrument which we shape for our own purposes.

Now, it is clear that the decline of a language must ultimately have political   2 and economic causes: it is not due simply to the bad influence of this or that individual writer. But an effect can become a cause, reinforcing the original cause and producing the same effect in an intensified form, and so on indefinitely. A man may take to drink because he feels himself to be a failure, and then fail all the more completely because he drinks. It is rather the same thing that is happening to the English language. It becomes ugly and inaccurate because our thoughts are foolish, but the slovenliness of our language makes it easier for us to have foolish thoughts. The point is that the process is reversible. Modern English, especially written English, is full of bad habits which spread by imitation and which can be avoided if one is willing to take the necessary trouble. If one gets rid of these habits one can think more clearly, and to think clearly is a necessary first step towards political regeneration: so that the fight against bad English is not frivolous and is not the exclusive concern of professional writers. I will come back to this presently, and I hope that by that time the meaning of what I have said here will have become clearer. Meanwhile here are five specimens of the English language as it is now habitually written.

3   These five passages have not been picked out because they are especially bad—I could have quoted far worse if I had chosen—but because they illustrate various of the mental vices from which we now suffer. They are a little below the average, but are fairly representative samples. I number them so that I can refer back to them when necessary:

(1) I am not, indeed, sure whether it is not true to say that the Milton who once seemed not unlike a seventeenth-century Shelley had not become, out of an experience ever more bitter in each year, more alien [*sic*] to the founder of that Jesuit sect which nothing could induce him to tolerate.
                    Professor Harold Laski (Essay in *Freedom of Expression*)

(2) Above all, we cannot play ducks and drakes with a native battery of idioms which prescribes such egregious collocations of vocables as the Basic *put up with* for *tolerate* or *put at a loss* for *bewilder*.
                    Professor Lancelot Hogben (*Interglossa*)

(3) On the one side we have the free personality: by definition it is not neurotic, for it has neither conflict nor dream. Its desires, such as they are, are transparent, for they are just what institutional approval keeps in the forefront of consciousness; another institutional pattern would alter their number and intensity; there is little in them that is natural, irreducible, or culturally dangerous. But *on the other side,* the social bond itself is nothing but the mutual reflection of these self-secure integrities. Recall the definition of love. Is not this the very picture of a small academic? Where is there a place in this hall of mirrors for either personality or fraternity?
                    Essay on psychology in *Politics* (New York)

(4) All the "best people" from the gentlemen's clubs, and all the frantic fascist captains, united in common hatred of Socialism and bestial horror of the rising tide of the mass revolutionary movement, have turned to acts of provocation, to foul incendiarism, to medieval legends of poisoned wells, to legalize their own destruction of proletarian organizations, and rouse the agitated petty-bourgeoisie to chauvinistic fervor on behalf of the fight against the revolutionary way out of the crisis.

                    Communist pamphlet

(5) If a new spirit *is* to be infused into this old country, there is one thorny and contentious reform which must be tackled, and that is the humanization and galvanization of the B.B.C. Timidity here will bespeak canker and atrophy of the soul. The heart of Britain may be sound and of strong beat, for instance, but the British lion's roar at present is like that of Bottom in Shakespeare's *Midsummer Night's Dream*—as gentle as any sucking dove. A virile new Britain cannot continue indefinitely to be traduced in the eyes

or rather ears, of the world by the effete languors of Langham Place, brazenly masquerading as "standard English." When the voice of Britain is heard at nine o'clock, better far and infinitely less ludicrous to hear aitches honestly dropped than the present priggish, inflated, inhibited, school-ma'amish arch braying of blameless bashful mewing maidens

Letter in *Tribune*

Each of these passages has faults of its own, but, quite apart from avoidable ugliness, two qualities are common to all of them. The first is staleness of imagery; the other is lack of precision. The writer either has a meaning and can-not express it, or he inadvertently says something else, or he is almost indiffer-ent as to whether his words mean anything or not. This mixture of vagueness and sheer incompetence is the most marked characteristic of modern English prose, and especially of any kind of political writing. As soon as certain topics are raised, the concrete melts into the abstract and no one seems able to think of turns of speech that are not hackneyed: prose consists less and less of *words* cho-sen for the sake of their meaning, and more and more of *phrases* tacked together like the sections of a prefabricated henhouse. I list below, with notes and exam-ples, various of the tricks by means of which the work of prose-construction is habitually dodged:

DYING METAPHORS. A newly invented metaphor assists thought by evoking a visual image, while on the other hand a metaphor which is tech-nically "dead" (e.g., *iron resolution*) has in effect reverted to being an ordi-nary word and can generally be used without loss of vividness. But in between these two classes there is a huge dump of worn-out metaphors which have lost all evocative power and are merely used because they save people the trouble of inventing phrases for themselves. Examples are: *Ring the changes on, take up the cudgels for, toe the line, ride roughshod over, stand shoulder to shoulder with, play into the hands of, no axe to grind, grist to the mill, fishing in troubled waters, on the order of the day, Achilles' heel, swan song, hotbed.* Many of these are used without knowledge of their meaning (what is a "rift," for instance?), and incompatible metaphors are frequently mixed, a sure sign that the writer is not interested in what he is saying. Some metaphors now current have been twisted out of their original meaning without those who use them even being aware of the fact. For example, *toe the line* is sometimes written *tow the line.* Another example is the *hammer and the anvil,* now always used with the implication that the anvil gets the worst of it. In real life it is always the anvil that breaks the hammer, never the other way about: a writer who stopped to think what he was saying would be aware of this, and would avoid perverting the original phrase.

OPERATORS OR VERBAL FALSE LIMBS. These save the trouble of picking out appropriate verbs and nouns, and at the same time pad each sentence with extra syllables which give it an appearance of symmetry. Characteristic phrases are *render inoperative, militate against, make contact with, be sub-jected to, give rise to, give grounds for, have the effect of, play a leading part (role) in, make itself felt, take effect, exhibit a tendency to, serve the purpose of,* etc., etc. The keynote is the elimination of simple verbs. Instead of being a single word, such as *break, stop, spoil, mend, kill,* a verb becomes a *phrase,* made up of a noun or adjective tacked on to some general-purposes verb such as *prove, serve, form, play, render.* In addition, the passive voice is wherever possible used in preference to the active, and noun constructions are used instead of gerunds (*by examination of* instead of *by examining*). The range of verbs is further cut down by means of the *-ize* and *de-* formations, and the banal statements are given an appearance of profundity by means of the *not un-*formation. Simple conjunctions and prepositions are replaced by such phrases as *with respect to, having regard to, the fact that, by dint of, in view of, in the interests of, on the hypothesis that;* and the ends of sentences are saved from anticlimax by such resounding common-places as *greatly to be desired, cannot be left out of account, a development to be expected in the near future, deserving of serious consideration, brought to a satisfactory conclusion,* and so on and so forth.

7   **PRETENTIOUS DICTION.** Words like *phenomenon, element, individual* (as noun), *objective, categorical, effective, virtual, basic, primary, promote, constitute, exhibit, exploit, utilize, eliminate, liquidate,* are used to dress up simple statements and give an air of scientific impartiality to biased judgments. Adjectives like *epoch-making, epic, historic, unforgettable, triumphant, age-old, inevitable, inexorable, veritable,* are used to dignify the sordid processes of international politics, while writing that aims at glorifying war usually takes on an archaic color, its characteristic words being: *realm, throne, chariot, mailed fist, trident, sword, shield, buckler, banner, jackboot, clarion.* Foreign words and expressions such as *cul de sac, ancien régime, deus ex machina, mutatis mutandis, status quo, gleichschaltung, weltanschauung,* are used to give an air of culture and elegance. Except for the useful abbreviations *i.e., e.g.,* and *etc.,* there is no real need for any of the hundreds of foreign phrases now current in English. Bad writers, and especially scientific, political and sociological writers, are nearly always haunted by the notion that Latin or Greek words are grander than Saxon ones, and unnecessary words like *expedite, ameliorate, predict, extraneous, deracinated, clandestine, subaqueous* and hundreds of others constantly gain ground from their Anglo-Saxon opposite numbers.[1] The jargon peculiar to Marxist writing (*hyena, hangman, cannibal, petty bourgeois, these gentry, lacquey, flunkey, mad dog, White Guard,* etc.) consists largely of words and phrases translated from Russian, German or French; but the normal way of coining a new word is to use a Latin or Greek root with the appropriate affix and, where necessary, the *-ize* formation. It is often easier to make up words of this kind

---

[1]An interesting illustration of this is the way in which the English flower names which were in use till very recently are being ousted by Greek ones, *snapdragon* becoming *antirrhinum, forget-me-not* becoming *myosotis, etc.* It is hard to see any practical reason for this change of fashion: it is probably due to an instinctive turning-away from the more homely word and a vague feeling that the Greek word is scientific.

(*deregionalize, impermissible, extramarital, non-fragmentary* and so forth) than to think up the English words that will cover one's meaning. The result, in general, is an increase in slovenliness and vagueness.

MEANINGLESS WORDS. In certain kinds of writing, particularly in art criticism and literary criticism, it is normal to come across long passages which are almost completely lacking in meaning.[2] Words like *romantic, plastic, values, human, dead, sentimental, natural, vitality,* as used in art criticism, are strictly meaningless, in the sense that they not only do not point to any discoverable object, but are hardly ever expected to do so by the reader. When one critic writes, "The outstanding feature of Mr. X's work is its living quality," while another writes, "The immediately striking thing about Mr. X's work is its peculiar deadness," the reader accepts this as a simple difference of opinion. If words like *black and white* were involved, instead of the jargon words *dead* and *living,* he would see at once that language was being used in an improper way. Many political words are similarly abused. The word *Fascism* has now no meaning except in so far as it signifies "something not desirable." The words *democracy, freedom, patriotic, realistic, justice,* have each of them several different meanings which cannot be reconciled with one another. In the case of a word like *democracy,* not only is there no agreed definition, but the attempt to make one is resisted from all sides. It is almost universally felt that when we call a country democratic we are praising it: consequently the defenders of every kind of regime claim that it is a democracy, and fear that they might have to stop using the word if it were tied down to any one meaning. Words of this kind are often used in a consciously dishonest way. That is, the person who uses them has his own private definition, but allows his hearer to think he means something quite different. Statements like, *Marshal Pétain was a true patriot, The Soviet Press is the freest in the world, The Catholic Church is opposed to persecution,* are almost always made with intent to deceive. Other words used in variable meanings, in most cases more or less dishonestly, are: *class, totalitarian, science, progressive, reactionary, bourgeois, equality.*

8

Now that I have made this catalogue of swindles and perversions, let me give another example of the kind of writing that they lead to. This time it must of its nature be an imaginary one. I am going to translate a passage of good English into modern English of the worst sort. Here is a well-known verse from *Ecclesiastes:*

9

> I returned and saw under the sun, that the race is not to the swift, nor the battle to the strong, neither yet bread to the wise, nor yet riches to men of

---

[2]Example:. "Comfort's catholicity of perception and image, strangely Whitmanesque in range, almost the exact opposite in aesthetic compulsion, continues to evoke that trembling atmospheric accumulative hinting at a cruel, an inexorably serene timelessness. . . . Wrey Gardiner scores by aiming at simple bull's-eyes with precision. Only they are not so simple, and through this contented sadness runs more than the surface bittersweet of resignation." (*Poetry Quarterly*)

understanding, nor yet favour to men of skill; but time and chance happeneth to them all.

10   Here it is in modern English:

Objective consideration of contemporary phenomena compels the conclusion that success or failure in competitive activities exhibits no tendency to be commensurate with innate capacity, but that a considerable element of the unpredictable must invariably be taken into account.

11   This is a parody, but a very gross one. Exhibit (3), above, for instance, contains several patches of the same kind of English. It will be seen that I have not made a full translation. The beginning and ending of the sentence follow the original meaning fairly closely, but in the middle the concrete illustrations—race, battle, bread—dissolve into the vague phrase "success or failure in competitive activities." This had to be so, because no modern writer of the kind I am discussing—no one capable of using phrases like "objective consideration of contemporary phenomena"—would ever tabulate his thoughts in that precise and detailed way. The whole tendency of modern prose is away from concreteness. Now analyse these two sentences a little more closely. The first contains forty-nine words but only sixty syllables, and all its words are those of everyday life. The second contains thirty-eight words of ninety syllables: eighteen of its words are from Latin roots, and one from Greek. The first sentence contains six vivid images, and only one phrase ("time and chance") that could be called vague. The second contains not a single fresh, arresting phrase, and in spite of its ninety syllables it gives only a shortened version of the meaning contained in the first. Yet without a doubt it is the second kind of sentence that is gaining ground in modern English. I do not want to exaggerate. This kind of writing is not yet universal, and outcrops of simplicity will occur here and there in the worst-written page. Still, if you or I were told to write a few lines on the uncertainty of human fortunes, we should probably come much nearer to my imaginary sentence than to the one from *Ecclesiastes*.

12   As I have tried to show, modern writing at its worst does not consist in picking out words for the sake of their meaning and inventing images in order to make the meaning clearer. It consists in gumming together long strips of words which have already been set in order by someone else, and making the results presentable by sheer humbug. The attraction of this way of writing is that it is easy. It is easier—even quicker, once you have the habit—to say *In my opinion it is not an unjustifiable assumption that* than to say *I think*. If you use ready-made phrases, you not only don't have to hunt about for words; you also don't have to bother with the rhythms of your sentences, since these phrases are generally so arranged as to be more or less euphonious. When you are composing in a hurry—when you are dictating to a stenographer, for instance, or making a public speech—it is natural to fall into a pretentious, Latinized style. Tags like *a consideration which we should do well to bear in mind* or *a conclusion to which all of us would readily assent* will save many a sentence from coming down with a

bump. By using stale metaphors, similes and idioms, you save much mental effort, at the cost of leaving your meaning vague, not only for your reader but for yourself. This is the significance of mixed metaphors. The sole aim of a metaphor is to call up a visual image. When these images clash—as in *The Fascist octopus has sung its swan song, the jackboot is thrown into the melting pot*—it can be taken as certain that the writer is not seeing a mental image of the objects he is naming; in other words he is not really thinking. Look again at the examples I gave at the beginning of this essay. Professor Laski (1) uses five negatives in fifty-three words. One of these is superfluous, making nonsense of the whole passage, and in addition there is the slip *alien* for *akin*, making further nonsense, and several avoidable pieces of clumsiness which increase the general vagueness. Professor Hogben (2) plays ducks and drakes with a battery which is able to write prescriptions, and, while disapproving of the everyday phrase *put up with,* is unwilling to look *egregious* up in the dictionary and see what it means; (3), if one takes an uncharitable attitude towards it, is simply meaningless: probably one could work out its intended meaning by reading the whole of the article in which it occurs. In (4), the writer knows more or less what he wants to say, but an accumulation of stale phrases chokes him like tea leaves blocking a sink. In (5), words and meaning have almost parted company. People who write in this manner usually have a general emotional meaning—they dislike one thing and want to express solidarity with another—but they are not interested in the detail of what they are saying. A scrupulous writer, in every sentence that he writes, will ask himself at least four questions, thus: What am I trying to say? What words will express it? What image or idiom will make it clearer? Is this image fresh enough to have an effect? And he will probably ask himself two more: Could I put it more shortly? Have I said anything that is avoidably ugly? But you are not obliged to go to all this trouble. You can shirk it by simply throwing your mind open and letting the ready-made phrases come crowding in. They will construct your sentences for you—even think your thoughts for you, to a certain extent—and at need they will perform the important service of partially concealing your meaning even from yourself. It is at this point that the special connection between politics and the debasement of language becomes clear.

In our time it is broadly true that political writing is bad writing. Where it is not true, it will generally be found that the writer is some kind of rebel, expressing his private opinions and not a "party line." Orthodoxy, of whatever color, seems to demand a lifeless, imitative style. The political dialects to be found in pamphlets, leading articles, manifestos, White Papers and the speeches of under-secretaries do, of course, vary from party to party, but they are all alike in that one almost never finds in them a fresh, vivid, homemade turn of speech. When one watches some tired hack on the platform mechanically repeating the familiar phrases—*bestial atrocities, iron heel, bloodstained tyranny, free peoples of the world, stand shoulder to shoulder*—one often has a curious feeling that one is not watching a live human being but some kind of dummy: a feeling which suddenly becomes stronger at moments when the light catches the speaker's spectacles and turns them into blank discs which seem to have no eyes behind them. And this is not altogether fanciful. A speaker who uses that kind of phraseology has gone some distance towards turning himself into a machine. The appropriate noises are coming out of his larynx, but his brain is not involved as it would be if he were choosing his words for himself. If the speech he is making is one that he is accustomed to make over and over again, he may be almost unconscious of what he is saying, as one is when one utters the responses in church. And this reduced state of consciousness, if not indispensable, is at any rate favorable to political conformity.

14   In our time, political speech and writing are largely the defence of the indefensible. Things like the continuance of British rule in India, the Russian purges and deportations, the dropping of the atom bombs on Japan, can indeed be defended, but only by arguments which are too brutal for most people to face, and which do not square with the professed aims of political parties. Thus political language has to consist largely of euphemism, question-begging and sheer cloudy vagueness. Defenceless villages are bombarded from the air, the inhabitants driven out into the countryside, the cattle machine-gunned, the huts set on fire with incendiary bullets: this is called *pacification*. Millions of peasants are robbed of their farms and sent trudging along the roads with no more than they can carry: this is called *transfer of population* or *rectification of frontiers*. People are imprisoned for years without trial, or shot in the back of the neck or sent to die of scurvy in Arctic lumber camps: this is called *elimination of unreliable elements*. Such phraseology is needed if one wants to name things without calling up mental pictures of them. Consider for instance some comfortable English professor defending Russian totalitarianism. He cannot say outright, "I believe in killing off your opponents when you can get good results by doing so." Probably, therefore, he will say something like this:

> While freely conceding that the Soviet régime exhibits certain features which the humanitarian may be inclined to deplore, we must, I think, agree that a certain curtailment of the right to political opposition is an unavoidable concomitant of transitional periods, and that the rigors which the Russian people have been called upon to undergo have been amply justified in the sphere of concrete achievement.

15   The inflated style is itself a kind of euphemism. A mass of Latin words falls upon the facts like soft snow, blurring the outlines and covering up all the details. The great enemy of clear language is insincerity. When there is a gap between one's real and one's declared aims, one turns as it were instinctively to long words and exhausted idioms, like a cuttlefish squirting out ink. In our age there is no such thing as "keeping out of politics." All issues are political issues, and politics itself is a mass of lies, evasions, folly, hatred and schizophrenia. When the general atmosphere is bad, language must suffer. I should expect to find—this is a guess which I have not sufficient knowledge to verify—that the German, Russian and Italian languages have all deteriorated in the last ten or fifteen years, as a result of dictatorship.

16   But if thought corrupts language, language can also corrupt thought. A bad usage can spread by tradition and imitation, even among people who should and do know better. The debased language that I have been discussing is in some ways very convenient, Phrases like *a not unjustifiable assumption, leaves much to*

be desired, would serve no good purpose, a consideration which we should do well to bear in mind, are a continuous temptation, a packet of aspirins always at one's elbow. Look back through this essay, and for certain you will find that I have again and again committed the very faults I am protesting against. By this morning's post I have received a pamphlet dealing with conditions in Germany. The author tells me that he "felt impelled" to write it. I open it at random, and here is almost the first sentence that I see: "[The Allies] have an opportunity not only of achieving a radical transformation of Germany's social and political structure in such a way as to avoid a nationalistic reaction in Germany itself, but at the same time of laying the foundations of a cooperative and unified Europe." You see, he "feels impelled" to write—feels, presumably, that he was something new to say—and yet his words, like cavalry horses answering the bugle, group themselves automatically into the familiar dreary pattern. The invasion of one's mind by ready-made phrases (*lay the foundations, achieve a radical transformation*) can only be prevented if one is constantly on guard against them, and every such phrase anaesthetizes a portion of one's brain.

I said earlier that the decadence of our language is probably curable. Those who deny this would argue, if they produced an argument at all, that language merely reflects existing social conditions, and that we cannot influence its development by any direct tinkering with words and constructions. So far as the general tone or spirit of a language goes, this may be true, but it is not true in detail. Silly words and expressions have often disappeared, not through any evolutionary process but owing to the conscious action of a minority. Two recent examples were *explore every avenue* and *leave no stone unturned,* which were killed by the jeers of a few journalists. There is a long list of fly-blown metaphors which could similarly be got rid of if enough people would interest themselves in the job; and it should also be possible to laugh the *not un-* formation out of existence,[3] to reduce the amount of Latin and Greek in the average sentence, to drive out foreign phrases and strayed scientific words, and, in general, to make pretentiousness unfashionable. But all these are minor points. The defence of the English language implies more than this, and perhaps it is best to start by saying what it does *not* imply.

To begin with, it has nothing to do with archaism, with the salvaging of obsolete words and turns of speech, or with the setting up of a "standard English" which must never be departed from. On the contrary, it is especially concerned with the scrapping of every word or idiom which has outworn its usefulness. It has nothing to do with correct grammar and syntax, which are of no importance so long as one makes one's meaning clear, or with the avoidance of Americanisms, or with having what is called a "good prose style." On the other hand it is not concerned with fake simplicity and the attempt to make written English colloquial. Nor does it even imply in every case preferring the Saxon word to the Latin one, though it does imply using the fewest and shortest words that will cover one's meaning. What is above all needed is to let the meaning

---

[3]One can cure oneself of the *not un-* formation by memorizing this sentence: *A not unblack dog was chasing a not unsmall rabbit across a not ungreen field.*

choose the word, and not the other way about. In prose, the worst thing one can do with words is to surrender to them. When you think of a concrete object, you think wordlessly, and then, if you want to describe the thing you have been visualizing you probably hunt about till you find the exact words that seem to fit it. When you think of something abstract you are more inclined to use words from the start, and unless you make a conscious effort to prevent it, the existing dialect will come rushing in and do the job for you, at the expense of blurring or even changing your meaning. Probably it is better to put off using words as long as possible and get one's meaning as clear as one can through pictures or sensations. Afterwards one can choose—not simply *accept*—the phrases that will best cover the meaning, and then switch round and decide what impression one's words are likely to make on another person. This last effort of the mind cuts out all stale or mixed images, all prefabricated phrases, needless repetitions, and humbug and vagueness generally. But one can often be in doubt about the effect of a word or a phrase, and one needs rules that one can rely on when instinct fails. I think the following rules will cover most cases:

1. Never use a metaphor, simile, or other figure of speech which you are used to seeing in print.
2. Never use a long word where a short one will do.
3. If it is possible to cut a word out, always cut it out.
4. Never use the passive where you can use the active.
5. Never use a foreign phrase, a scientific word or a jargon word if you can think of an everyday English equivalent.
6. Break any of these rules sooner than say anything outright barbarous.

These rules sound elementary, and so they are, but they demand a deep change of attitude in anyone who has grown used to writing in the style now fashionable. One could keep all of them and still write bad English, but one could not write the kind of stuff that I quoted in those five specimens at the beginning of this article.

19   I have not here been considering the literary use of language, but merely language as an instrument for expressing and not for concealing or preventing thought. Stuart Chase and others have come near to claiming that all abstract words are meaningless, and have used this as a pretext for advocating a kind of political quietism. Since you don't know what Fascism is, how can you struggle against Fascism? One need not swallow such absurdities as this, but one ought to recognize that the present political chaos is connected with the decay of language, and that one can probably bring about some improvement by starting at the verbal end. If you simplify your English, you are freed from the worst follies of orthodoxy. You cannot speak any of the necessary dialects, and when you make a stupid remark its stupidity will be obvious, even to yourself. Political language—and with variations this is true of all political parties, from Conservatives to Anarchists—is designed to make lies sound truthful and murder respectable, and to give an appearance of solidity to pure wind. One cannot change this all in a moment, but one can at least change one's own habits, and from time to time one can even, if one jeers loudly enough, send some worn-out and useless

phrase—some *jack-boot, Achilles' heel, hotbed, melting pot, acid test, veritable inferno* or other lump of verbal refuse—into the dustbin where it belongs.

1 How is the deterioration of the English language identified by Orwell the result of the public's tolerance for the deceptive and confusing language used by politicians, thinkers, and writers? What relationship does Orwell reveal between obfuscated language and ill-conceived ideas? How does each lead to the other in a vicious circle (para. 2)?

2 How do Orwell's five examples of shoddy English exemplify the features of bad writing he condemns? Why would writing with these deficiencies be a consequence of the public's acceptance of clichéd political rhetoric? Why does Orwell condemn euphemisms as a symptom of our growing inability to express ourselves accurately and clearly?

3 To remedy the situation, Orwell recommends certain rules to follow (para. 18) and four important prewriting questions careful writers always ask themselves. How would these suggestions, if they were followed, be capable of correcting the language abuses he discusses? Bring in some editorials on political issues from newspapers or magazines and evaluate them using Orwell's criteria to discover whether the writers use language in a way that is deceptive, misleading, and inaccurate.

4 Orwell believes that the use of shoddy and inaccurate language sets in motion a vicious cycle that makes it increasingly difficult for us to think clearly: we deceive ourselves and deceive others. But, before suggesting means by which the "decadence of language" can be cured, Orwell discusses the forms the corruption of the language can take through clichés, euphemisms, logical fallacies, and other abuses. What is the advantage of organizing his essay in this particular way? If you applied Orwell's own criteria (stated in para. 3–16) to some of the metaphors and similes he himself uses (para. 4–5, 12, 15–16) how would his own prose stand up? (Glossary: *Clichés, Euphemism, Logical Fallacies, Metaphors, Organization, Similes.*)

5 In your own words, state Orwell's position in a way that clarifies what is at stake in his essay. Why does Orwell rely on a problem solution format (i.e., presenting an analysis of linguistic abuses and then suggesting feasible alternatives to remedy these problems) in structuring his argument? What means does Orwell use to document sources he draws on as evidence to support his contention? How does the range of sources he utilizes serve to make his argument more persuasive? (Glossary: *Argument.*)

6 What examples of the kinds of linguistic abuses Orwell discusses (incompatible metaphors, clichés, debased language, ready-made phrases, meaningless labels, etc.) can you identify in current newspapers, editorials, magazines, books, political speeches on televisions, commentaries, or public service advertisements? Collect a sampling and identify instances of language corruption. For example, what ready-made phrases can you add to the following list: street smart, in your dreams, check it out, in your face, the whole nine yards, easy for you to say, it doesn't take a rocket scientist, from the git-go, it works for me, don't give up your day job.

Analyzing the Rhetoric of Nixon's "Checker's Speech"

Stuart Hirschberg

◆ STUART HIRSCHBERG currently teaches English at Rutgers University, Newark, and is the author of *At the Top of the Tower: W. B. Yeats's Poetry Explored Through* A Vision (1979) and *Myth in the Poetry of Ted Hughes* (1981). He is the editor and coeditor (with Terry Hirschberg) of over a dozen rhetorics, textbooks, and anthologies, including *One World, Many Cultures* (3rd ed, 1998) and *The Millennium Reader* (1997). The following essay is drawn from *Strategies of Argument* (1990).

Richard Nixon's "Checker's Speech" is one of the preeminent examples of how a skillful politician can use rhetorical strategies to subvert the objectives of political discourse (which should be to disclose the truth to the public) and manipulate the audience by appealing to their emotions. The subtle forms of coercion Nixon employed hinged on winning points with his audience by managing their emotional responses to the charge that he was guilty of dipping into campaign funds. His speech may be considered an example of political rhetoric in that it is designed to reduce the public's capacity for independent critical analysis and lead them to accept his version of reality. The means by which he accomplished this objective are based on diverting attention from what might prove embarrassing to him while, at the same time, focusing attention on the purported transgressions of his opponents and on his own virtue. The replacement of rational appeals with emotional ones (appeal to pity, *argumentum ad hominem,* scare tactics, and others) shows an underlying contempt for his audience and a keen knowledge of what did, in fact, persuade them.

> **TO CONSIDER** Do you find yourself or have you heard others instinctively diverting attention away from what might prove embarrassing while at the same time focusing attention on something to be proud of?

PROPAGANDA: THE LANGUAGE OF DOUBLESPEAK

Ultimately, it is the intention with which words are used that determines whether any of the techniques already discussed, such as slanting, labeling, and emotionally loaded language, pose a political danger. Of themselves, strategies of persuasion are neither good nor bad, it is the purpose for which they are employed that makes them unethical and offensive. It is for this reason that the techniques of rhetorical persuasion have been decried throughout the ages. Aldous Huxley in "Propaganda Under a Dictatorship" in *Brave New World Revisited* (1958) discussed how the manipulation of language through propaganda techniques in Nazi Germany conditioned thoughts and behavior. Some of the key techniques identified by Huxley included the use of slogans, unqualified assertions, and sweeping generalizations. Huxley notes that Hitler had said "all effective propaganda must be confined to a few bare necessities and then must be expressed in a few stereotyped formulas. . . . Only constant repetition will finally succeed in imprinting an idea upon the memory of a crowd." Hitler knew that any lie can seem to be the truth if it is repeated often enough. Repeated exposure encourages a sense of acceptance and familiarity with the slogan. Hitler's use of propaganda required that all statements be made without qualification.

George Orwell commented frequently on the dangers posed by political propaganda. In his novel *1984* he coined the term *doublespeak* to show how political language could be used to deceive, beg the question, and avoid responsibility.

Doublespeak can take forms that can range from the innocuous, such as Lt. Colonel Oliver North's intention to give "a non-visual slide show," (cited in *Quarterly Review of Doublespeak* [January 1988]) to the deceptive and dangerous, such as the Pentagon's reference to the neutron bomb as "an efficient nuclear weapon that eliminates an enemy with a minimum degree of damage to friendly territory." Or consider a statement by the U.S. Army that "we do not call it 'killing,' we call it 'servicing the target'" (cited in *Quarterly Review of Doublespeak* [January 1988]). In each of these cases language is used against itself to distort and manipulate rather than to communicate.

INTENSIFYING AND DOWNPLAYING: STRATEGIES FOR PERSUASION

One of the most valuable ways of analyzing forms of public persuasion was suggested by Hugh Rank in "Teaching about Public Persuasion: Rationale and a Schema" (1976). Rank won the 1976 *Orwell Award* (presented by the Committee on Public Doublespeak) for his "Intensifying/Downplaying Schema." Rank observed that all acts of public persuasion are variations of what he terms *intensifying* and *downplaying*.

Persuaders use intensifying and downplaying in the following ways: (1) to intensify, focus on, or draw attention to anything that would make their case look good; (2) to intensify, focus on, or draw attention to anything that would make counterclaims or their opponent's arguments look bad; (3) to downplay, dismiss, or divert attention from any weak points that would make their case look bad; and (4) to downplay, dismiss, or divert attention from anything that would make their opponent's case look good.

What is meant by intensifying and downplaying can be seen by comparing the words a country uses to refer to actions of the enemy (by intensifying) with those words it uses to describe its own identical activities (by downplaying):

Intensifying	Downplaying
Bombing	Air support
Spying	Intelligence gathering
Invasion	Pacification
Infiltration	Reinforcement
Retreat	Strategic withdrawal

The calculated manipulation and conditioning of thought and behavior by propaganda experts is now a fact of everyday life. Professional persuaders have an unequal advantage over those whom they seek to influence and persuade. By contrast, the average citizen has never received any training in critically examining the various techniques professional persuaders use.

The three basic techniques of intensification are (1) repetition, (2) association, and (3) composition.

Repetition. Slogans, unqualified assertions, and sweeping generalizations will seem more true if they are constantly repeated. Much of commercial advertising is built on the repetition of slogans, product logos, and brand names. Political campaigns rely on repetition of candidates' names and messages over the airwaves and on posters and bumper stickers.

Association. Intensifying by association is a technique that is also known as virtue (or guilt) by association. This strategy depends on linking an idea, person, or product with something already loved or admired (or hated and despised) by the intended audience. That is, an idea, person, or product, is put into a context that already has an emotional significance for the intended audience. Once market researchers discover needs and values of a target audience, political campaigns and advertising for commercial products can exploit the audience's needs by linking their idea, candidate, or product to values already known to be appealing to the audience. Much of advertising exploits this technique of correlating feelings and emotions with purchasable objects.

Composition. A message gains intensity when it is arranged in a clearly perceivable pattern. Arranging the message can rely on the traditional rhetorical patterns (comparison and contrast, cause and effect, process analysis, classification, analogy, narration, description, and exemplification) as well as inductive or deductive logic or any other distinctive way of grouping elements of the message.

The three basic techniques of downplaying are (1) omission, (2) diversion, and (3) confusion.

Omission. If persuaders wish to downplay or divert attention away from an issue that is felt to be potentially damaging to their purposes, they can use the opposite of each of the intensifying techniques. If repetition is an effective way to intensify, persuaders can downplay by omitting, biasing, or slanting. Omissions can range from euphemisms that downplay serious issues to acts of overt censorship.

Diversion. Just as persuaders intensify by associating, they can downplay by diverting attention through an emphasis on unimportant or unrelated side issues. These tactics include the *red herring, non sequitur, straw man, argumentum ad hominem, argumentum ad populum, argumentum ad misericordiam or appeal to pity, argumentum ad baculum or appeal to force, circular reasoning or begging the question,* and *appeal to ignorance.* All these techniques are used to divert or distract attention from the main issues to peripheral or entirely unrelated issues.

Confusion. Just as a message gains intensity when it is well structured and coherent, so persuaders can downplay by using a variety of techniques designed to obscure or cloud the points at issue. These techniques include the calculated use of faulty logic, including the *fallacy of complex question, false dilemma, false cause, post hoc, slippery slope,* and *faulty analogy.* Downplaying via confusion also results from the use of ambiguous terms or phrases as in the fallacies of *equivocation, amphiboly,* and *accent,* as well as the use of bureaucratese, medicalese, legalese, pentagonese, and all other jargons used to obscure or cloud the real issues.

We should realize that all these strategies of intensifying and downplaying can take place *simultaneously* during any attempt to persuade.

To see how this works in practice, we can apply Rank's "Intensifying/ Downplaying Schema" to one of the most famous cases of public persuasion in this century—Richard Nixon's "Checkers" speech. Before the speech was broadcast on radio and television in Los Angeles, on September 23, 1952, Dwight Eisenhower, an immensely popular Republican presidential candidate, was going to dump Nixon as his running mate because of accusations that Nixon had accepted $18,000 in personal gifts from lobbyists. Nixon appealed for one last chance to go on television and make his case before the American public. After the speech, two million favorable telegrams were received and Nixon stayed on the ticket. This speech accomplished what it set out to do—it neutralized the charges against him and brought about a favorable public image of Nixon. After disclosing his financial assets, Nixon concluded:

> . . . That's what we have and that's what we owe. It isn't very much.
>
> But, Pat and I have the satisfaction that every dime that we've go is honestly ours. I should say this, that Pat doesn't have a mink coat, but she does have a respectable Republican cloth coat.
>
> And I always tell her that she'd look good in anything. One other thing I probably should tell you because if I don't they'll probably be saying this about me too. We did get something, a gift, after the election. A man down in Texas heard Pat on the radio mention the fact that our two youngsters would like to have a dog. And, believe it or not, the day before we left in this campaign trip, we got a message from Union Station in Baltimore saying they had a package for us. We went down to get it. You know what it

was. It was a little cocker spaniel dog in a crate that he sent all the way from Texas. Black and white spotted. And our little girl Tricia the 6 year old, named it "Checkers." And you know, the kids like all kids, love the dog and I just want to say this, right now, that regardless of what they say about it, we're going to keep it.

It isn't easy to come before a nationwide audience and bare your life as I have done. But I want to say some things before I conclude that I think most of you will agree on. Mr. Mitchell, the Chairman of the Democratic National Committee, made the statement that if a man couldn't afford to be in the United States Senate he shouldn't run for the Senate. And, I just want to make my position clear. I don't agree with Mr. Mitchell when he says that only a rich man should serve his government in the U.S. Senate or in the Congress. I don't believe that represents the thinking of the Democratic Party. And, I know that it doesn't represent the thinking of the Republican Party.

I believe that it's fine that a man like Governor Stevenson who inherited a fortune from his father can run for President. But I also feel that it is essential in this country of ours that a man of modest means can also run for President. Because you know, remember Abraham Lincoln, you remember what he said "God must have loved the common people, he made so many of them." And now I am going to suggest some courses of conduct. First of all, you have read in the papers about other funds now, Mr. Stevenson apparently had a couple, one of them in which a group of business people paid and helped to supplement the salaries of state employees. Here is where the money went directly into their pockets. And I think what Mr. Stevenson should do should be to come before the American people as I have, give the names of the people that contributed to that fund, give the names of the people who put this money into their pockets at the same time that they were receiving money from their state government and see what favors, if any, they gave out for that. I don't condemn Mr. Stevenson for what he did, but until the facts are in, there is a doubt that will be raised. And as far as Mr. Sparkman is concerned, I would suggest the same thing. He's had his wife on the payroll. I don't condemn him for that, but I think that he should come before the American people and indicate what outside sources of income he has had. I would suggest that under the circumstances both Mr. Sparkman and Mr. Stevenson should come before the American people as I have and make complete financial statements as to their financial history. And, if they don't, it will be an admission that they have something to hide. And, I think you will agree with me. Because folks, remember, a man that's to be President of the U.S., a man that's to be Vice President of the U.S. must have the confidence of all the people. And, that's why I'm doing what I'm doing and that's why I suggest that Mr. Stevenson and Mr. Sparkmen, since they are under attack, should do what they're doing [sic].

Now, let me say this, I know that this is not the last of the smears. In spite of my explanation tonight, other smears will be made. Others have been made in the past. And the purpose of the smears, I know, is this—to silence me, to make me let up. Well, they just don't know who they're dealing with. I'm going to tell you this. I remember in the dark days of the Hiss case, some of the same columnists, some of the same radio commentators who are attacking me now, and misrepresenting my position, were violently opposing me at the time I was after Alger Hiss. But I continued to fight because I knew I was right and I can say to this great television and radio audience that I have no apologies to the American people for my part in putting Alger Hiss where he is today. And as far as this is concerned, I intend to continue to fight. Why do I feel so deeply, why do I feel that in spite of the smears, the misunderstandings, the necessity for a man to come up here and bare his soul as I have? Why is it necessary for me to continue this fight? I want to tell you why, because you see, I love my country and I think my country is in danger and I think the only man that can save America at this time is the man that's running for President on my ticket, Dwight Eisenhower.

A breakdown of this speech using the intensify/downplay schema might appear as follows:

1. Nixon intensifies positive features in the following lines:
   a. "But, Pat and I have the satisfaction that every dime that we've got is honestly ours."
   b. "Pat doesn't have a mink coat, but she does have a respectable Republican cloth coat." [Virtue by association.]
   c. "And I always tell her that she'd look good in anything."
   d. "It was a little cocker spaniel dog . . . named . . . 'Checkers.' And you know, the kids like all kids, love the dog and I just want to say this, right now, that regardless of what they say about it, we're going to keep it." [Virtue by association; i.e., loves his children who love dogs, wouldn't hurt his children by sending Checkers back, implies opponents would take his children's puppy away; name Checkers has folksy connotation of people playing checkers.]
   e. "a man of modest means can also run for President." [Just plain folks appeal.]
   f. "Because you know, remember Abraham Lincoln, you remember what he said 'God must have loved the common people . . .'" [Virtue by association, plain folks appeal and suggests a link with a respected Republican president.]
   g. "I think the only man that can save America at this time is the man that's running for President on my [sic] ticket, Dwight Eisenhower." [Virtue by association with a person already loved and admired by the voting public; although perhaps a slip of the tongue, note how Nixon, who is the vice-presidential candidate, makes himself as important as the respected and very popular presidential candidate.]
2. Nixon intensifies the points on which his opponents might be vulnerable:
   a. "and I just want to say this, right now, that regardless of what they say about it, we're going to keep it." [Wouldn't hurt his children by sending Checkers back, with the clear implication that his opponents would.]
   b. "I don't agree with Mr. Mitchell when he says that only a rich man should serve his government in the U.S. Senate or in the Congress." [Characterizing himself as poor but honest in contrast to rich elitist Democrats.]
   c. "Mr. Stevenson apparently had a couple [of funds] . . . where the money went directly into their pockets."

    d. I don't condemn Mr. Stevenson for what he did, but until the facts are in, there is a doubt that will be raised. And as far as Mr. Sparkman is concerned, I would suggest the same thing. He's had his wife on the payroll. I don't condemn him for that . . ." [Presented as a search for the truth, Nixon accrues the added benefit of appearing to be nonjudgmental; he raises the issue while at the same time appears to deny he is doing so.]

    e. "I know that this is not the last of the smears. In spite of my explanation tonight, other smears will be made. Others have been made in the past. And the purpose of the smears . . ." [Technique of repetition, characterizing the accusation that prompted this speech as a smear.]

3. Nixon downplays potential weaknesses in his own position:

    a. "It isn't very much." [Diminishes importance of financial holdings; by implication, he would be richer if he had really been accepting money.]

    b. "One other thing I probably should tell you because if I don't they'll probably be saying this about me too." [A classic straw man maneuver since no one had or conceivably would accuse him of accepting a puppy for his little girls as a payoff.]

    c. "Because you know, remember Abraham Lincoln, you remember what he said 'God must have loved the common people . . .'" [Diverting attention with an unrelated *argumentum ad populum.*]

    d. "Mr. Sparkman and Mr. Stevenson should come before the American people as I have and make complete financial statement as to their financial history. And, if they don't, it will be an admission that they have something to hide." [Diverting attention to Stevenson and Sparkman who Nixon characterizes as being under a cloud of guilt.]

    e. "And the purpose of the smears, I know, is this—to silence me, to make me let up. Well, they just don't know who they're dealing with. I'm going to tell you this. I remember in the dark days of the Hiss case, some of the same columnists, some of the same radio commentators who are attacking me now, and misrepresenting my position, were violently opposing me at the time I was after Alger Hiss." [Diversion by attributing a false cause to confuse the issue; diversion by introducing a red herring converts the charge of financial impropriety being made against him into an occasion for characterizing "some" of his accusers as un-American.]

    f. "In spite of the smears, the misunderstandings, the necessity for a man to come up here and bare his soul as I have." [Diversion through appeal to pity, fused with the common man theme.]

    g. "Why is it necessary for me to continue this fight. I want to tell you why, because you see, I love my country and I think my country is in danger . . ." [Scare tactics combined with elevation of his campaign for the vice-presidency into a holy cause to save the country.]

4. Nixon downplays what some might consider to be a point in Stevenson's favor, i.e., a man or woman wealthy at the time he or she took office might be seen as less likely to exploit power for financial gain.

    a. "I believe that it's fine that a man like Governor Stevenson who inherited a fortune from his father can run for President." [In light of his earlier condemnation of Mitchell for implying that "only a rich man should serve his government" this statement is transparently false.]

1 How does Hugh Rank's method for analyzing forms of public persuasion provide real insight into the dynamics of what makes a speech persuasive to the public? In your own words, explain the principles of intensifying and downplaying.

2 Why is it especially important to understand that all four kinds of strategies Rank identifies (two ways of intensifying and two ways of downplaying) usually operate simultaneously in any act of political persuasion? What role do different kinds of logical fallacies play in diverting attention from important issues and purposely sowing confusion?

3 Where does Nixon most skillfully use intensifying and downplaying strategies to manipulate his audience's perceptions? Since a cursory glance through the "Checker's Speech" would seem to raise doubts about Nixon's credibility, how do you account for the indisputable effectiveness of this speech on the voters? (Keep in mind that people only heard the speech and could not analyze the written text.)

4 In what sense can the techniques of downplaying and intensifying be considered a form of doublespeak? Which of Nixon's statements reveal a calculated use of faulty logic to obscure the issue of his dipping into campaign funds and deceive his audience? (Glossary: *Doublespeak, Downplaying/Intensifying, Logical Fallacies*.)

5 Most of Hirschberg's essay is divided into an analysis of the different methods persuaders use to influence audience's perceptions. Are the subdivisions of the "intensifying/downplaying" schema mutually exclusive? Explain. (Glossary: *Classification/Division*.)

6 What examples of doublespeak, intensifying and downplaying, and other linguistic abuses can you identify in the rhetoric of administrators or student leaders on your campus, as reported in the school newspaper?

The Gettysburg Address *Gilbert Highet*

◆ GILBERT HIGHET (1906–1978) was born in Glasgow, Scotland, and educated at the University of Glasgow and Oxford University. From 1937 to 1972 Highet was professor of Greek, Latin, and comparative literature at Columbia University. His many distinguished books include *The Classical Tradition: Greek and Roman Influences on Western Literature* (1949), *The Anatomy of Satire* (1962), and *The Immortal Profession: The Joy of Teaching and Learning* (1976). He was particularly successful in bridging the gap from classicism to popular culture as an editor for the Book of the Month Club, chairman of the editorial board of *Horizon* magazine, and literary critic for *Harper's.* "The Gettysburg Address," from *A Clerk of Oxenford* (1959), shows Highet at his most illuminating in his analysis of the structure, themes, and rhetoric of Lincoln's famous speech.

Moving from the manipulative political rhetoric of Richard Nixon (sometimes referred to as "Tricky Dick") to Abraham "Honest Abe" Lincoln's model of plain speaking eloquence dramatizes the contrast between language used to deceive and language used to inspire. Admittedly, there was a greater public appetite for illuminating debate and oratory in Lincoln's time, and as a senatorial candidate in 1858 Lincoln joined with Stephen Douglas in a series of seven public discussions (that ran over three hours each) to audiences that sometimes exceeded ten thousand to exchange views on the issues of slavery and states' rights. Lincoln's concern for the common good is expressed in images that are brief, clear, to the point, and meaningful. Highet's analysis of the rhetorical techniques Lincoln wove together leads us to a more complete understanding of the thought, diligence, and sophistication that Lincoln brought to this important moment in history. His speech stands as an example of political rhetoric of the highest order.

TO CONSIDER What, in your view, is the importance of the Gettysburg Address (1863) as a speech and political document that would explain why it has been quoted so often and is still remembered after all these years?

Fourscore and seven years ago our fathers brought forth on this continent, a new nation, conceived in Liberty, and dedicated to the proposition that all men are created equal.

Now we are engaged in a great civil war, testing whether that nation or any nation so conceived and so dedicated, can long endure. We are met on a great battle-field of that war. We have come to dedicate a portion of that field, as a final resting place for those who here gave their lives that that nation might live. It is altogether fitting and proper that we should do this.

But, in a larger sense, we can not dedicate—we can not consecrate—we can not hallow—this ground. The brave men, living and dead, who struggled here, have consecrated it, far above our poor power to add or detract. The world will little note, nor long remember, what we say here, but it can never forget what they did here. It is for us the living, rather, to be dedicated here to the unfinished work which they who fought here have thus far so nobly advanced. It is rather for us to be here dedicated to the great task remaining before us—that from these honored dead we take increased devotion to that cause for which they gave the last full measure of devotion—that we here highly resolve that these dead shall not have died in vain—that this nation, under God, shall have a new birth of freedom—

and that government of the people, by the people, for the people, shall not perish from the earth.

Fourscore and seven years ago . . .

These five words stand at the entrance to the best-known monument of American prose, one of the finest utterances in the entire language and surely one of the greatest speeches in all history. Greatness is like granite: it is molded in fire, and it lasts for many centuries.

Fourscore and seven years ago. . . . It is strange to think that President Lincoln was looking back to the 4th of July 1776, and that he and his speech are now further removed from us than he himself was from George Washington and the Declaration of Independence. Fourscore and seven years before the Gettysburg Address, a small group of patriots signed the Declaration. Fourscore and seven years after the Gettysburg Address, it was the year 1950, and that date is already receding rapidly into our troubled, adventurous, and valiant past.

Inadequately prepared and at first scarcely realized in its full importance, the dedication of the graveyard at Gettysburg was one of the supreme moments of American history. The battle itself had been a turning point of the war. On the 4th of July 1863, General Meade repelled Lee's invasion of Pennsylvania. Although he did not follow up his victory, he had broken one of the most formidable aggressive enterprises of the Confederate armies. Losses were heavy on both sides. Thousands of dead were left on the field, and thousands of wounded died in the hot days following the battle. At first, their burial was more or less haphazard; but thoughtful men gradually came to feel that an adequate burying place and memorial were required. These were established by an interstate commission that autumn, and the finest speaker in the North was invited to dedicate them. This was the scholar and statesman Edward Everett of Harvard. He made a good speech—which is still extant: not at all academic, it is full of close strategic analysis and deep historical understanding.

Lincoln was not invited to speak, at first. Although people knew him as an effective debater, they were not sure whether he was capable of making a serious speech on such a solemn occasion. But one of the impressive things about Lincoln's career is that he constantly strove to *grow*. He was anxious to appear on that occasion and to say something worthy of it. (Also, it has been suggested, he was anxious to remove the impression that he did not know how to behave properly—an impression which had been strengthened by a shocking story about his clowning on the battlefield of Antietam the previous year). Therefore when he was invited he took considerable care with his speech. He drafted rather more than half of it in the White House before leaving, finished it in the hotel at Gettysburg the night before the ceremony (not in the train, as sometimes reported). and wrote out a fair copy next morning.

There are many accounts of the day itself, 19 November 1863. There are many descriptions of Lincoln, all showing the same curious blend of grandeur and awkwardness, or lack of dignity, or—it would be best to call it humility. In the procession he rode horseback: a tall lean man in a high plug hat, straddling a short horse, with his feet too near the ground. He arrived before the chief speaker, and had to wait patiently for half an hour or more. His own speech came right at the end of a long and exhausting ceremony, lasted less than three minutes, and made little impression on the audience. In part this was because they were tired, in part because (as eyewitnesses said) he ended almost before they knew he had begun, and in part because he did not speak the Address, but read it, very slowly, in a thin high voice, with a marked Kentucky accent, pronouncing "to" as "toe" and dropping his final R's.

Some people of course were alert enough to be impressed. Everett congratulated him at once. But most of the newspapers paid little attention to the speech, and some sneered at it. The *Patriot and Union* of Harrisburg wrote, "We pass over the silly remarks of the President; for the credit of the nation we are willing . . . that they shall no more be repeated or thought of"; and the London *Times* said, "The ceremony was rendered ludicrous by some of the sallies of that poor President Lincoln," calling his remarks "dull and commonplace." The first commendation of the Address came in a single sentence of the Chicago *Tribune,* and the first discriminating and detailed praise of it appeared in the Springfield *Republican,* the Providence *Journal,* and the Philadelphia *Bulletin.* However, three weeks after the ceremony and then again the following spring, the editor of *Harper's Weekly* published a sincere and thorough eulogy of the Address, and soon it was attaining recognition as a masterpiece.

At the time, Lincoln could not care much about the reception of his words. He was exhausted and ill. In the train back to Washington, he lay down with a wet towel on his head. He had caught smallpox. At that moment he was incubating it, and he was stricken down soon after he reentered the White House. Fortunately it was a mild attack, and it evoked one of his best jokes: he told his visitors, "At last I have something I can give to everybody."

He had more than that to give to everybody. He was a unique person, far greater than most people realize until they read his life with care. The wisdom of his policy, the sources of his statesmanship—these were things too complex to be discussed in a brief essay. But we can say something about the Gettysburg Address as a work of art.

A work of art. Yes: for Lincoln was a literary artist, trained both by others and by himself. The textbooks he used as a boy were full of difficult exercises and skillful devices in formal rhetoric, stressing the qualities he practiced in his own speaking: antithesis, parallelism, and verbal harmony. Then he read and reread many admirable models of thought and expression: the King James Bible, the essays of Bacon, the best plays of Shakespeare. His favorites were *Hamlet, Lear, Macbeth, Richard III,* and *Henry VIII,* which he had read dozens of times. He loved reading aloud, too, and spent hours reading poetry to his friends. (He told his partner Herndon that he preferred getting the sense of any document by reading it aloud.) Therefore his serious speeches are important parts of the long and noble classical tradition of oratory which begins in Greece, runs through Rome to the modern world, and is still capable (if we do not neglect it) of producing masterpieces.

The first proof of this is that the Gettysburg Address is full of quotations—or rather of adaptations—which give it strength. It is partly religious, partly (in the highest sense) political: therefore it is interwoven with memories of the Bible and memories of American history. The first and the last words are Biblical cadences. Normally Lincoln did not say "fourscore" when he meant eighty but on this solemn occasion he recalled the important dates in the Bible—such as the age of Abram when his first son was born to him, and he was "fourscore and six years old."[1] Similarly he did not say there was a chance that democracy might die out: he recalled the somber phrasing of the Book of Job—where Bildad speaks of the destruction of one who shall vanish without a trace, and says that "his branch shall be cut off; his remembrance shall perish from the earth."[2] Then again, the famous description of our State as "government of the people, by the people, for the people" was adumbrated by Daniel Webster in 1830 (he spoke of "the people's government, made for the people, made by the people, and answerable to the people") and then elaborated in 1854 by the abolitionist Theodore Parker (as "government of all the people, by all the people, for all the people"). There is good reason to think that Lincoln took the important phrase "under God" (which he interpolated at the last moment) from Weems, the biographer of Washington; and we know that it had been used at least once by Washington himself.

Analyzing the Address further, we find that it is based on a highly imaginative theme, or group of themes. The subject is—how can we put it so as not to disfigure it?—the subject is the kinship of life and death, that mysterious linkage which we see sometimes as the physical succession of birth and death in our world, sometimes as the contrast, which is perhaps a unity, between death and immortality. The first sentence is concerned with birth:

Our *fathers brought forth a new* nation, *conceived* in liberty.

The final phrase but one expresses the hope that

this nation, under God, shall have a *new birth* of freedom.

And the last phrase of all speaks of continuing life as the triumph over death. Again and again throughout the speech, this mystical contrast and kinship reappear: "those who *gave their lives* that that nation might *live*," "the brave men *living* and *dead*," and so in the central assertion that the dead have already consecrated their own burial place, while "it is for us, the *living*, rather to be dedicated . . . to the great task remaining." The Gettysburg Address is a prose poem; it belongs to the same world as the great elegies, and the adagios of Beethoven. Its structure, however, is that of a skillfully contrived speech. The oratorical pattern is perfectly clear. Lincoln describes the occasion, dedicates the ground, and then draws a larger conclusion by calling on his hearers to dedicate themselves to the preservation of the Union. But within that, we can trace his constant use of at least two important rhetorical devices.

---

[1]Gen. 16.16.
[2]Job 18.16–17.

The first of these is *antithesis:* opposition, contrast. The speech is full of it. Listen:

> The world will little *note*
>   nor long *remember*   what *we say* here
>   but   it can never *forget*   what *they did* here.

And so in nearly every sentence: "brave men, *living* and *dead*"; "to *add* or *detract.*" There is the antithesis of the Founding Fathers and the men of Lincoln's own time:

> Our *fathers brought forth* a new nation . . .
> now *we* are testing whether that nation . . . can *long endure.*

And there is the more terrible antithesis of those who have already died and those who still live to do their duty. Now, antithesis is the figure of contrast and conflict. Lincoln was speaking in the midst of a great civil war.

The other important pattern is different. It is technically called *tricolon*—the division of an idea into three harmonious parts, usually of increasing power. The most famous phrase of the Address is a tricolon:

> government of the people
>   by the people
>   and   for the people

The most solemn sentence is a tricolon:

> we cannot dedicate
> we cannot consecrate
> we cannot hallow this ground.

And above all, the last sentence (which has sometimes been criticized as too complex) is essentially two parallel phrases, with a tricolon growing out of the second and then producing another tricolon: a trunk, three branches, and a cluster of flowers. Lincoln says that it is for his hearers to be dedicated to the great task remaining before them. Then he goes on,

> that from these honored dead

—apparently he means "in such a way that from these honored dead"—

> we take increased devotion to that cause.

Next, he restates this more briefly:

> that we here highly resolve . . .

And now the actual resolution follows, in three parts of growing intensity:

> that these dead shall not have died in vain
> that this nation, under God, shall have a new birth of freedom

and that (one more tricolon)

> government of the people
>   by the people
>   and   or the people
> shall not perish from the earth.

Now, the tricolon is the figure which, through division, emphasizes basic harmony and unity. Lincoln used antithesis because he was speaking to a people at war. He used the tricolon because he was hoping, planning, praying for peace.

No one thinks that when he was drafting the Gettysburg Address, Lincoln deliberately looked up these quotations and consciously chose these particular patterns of thought. No, he chose the theme. From its development and from the emotional tone of the entire occasion, all the rest followed, or grew—by that marvelous process of choice and rejection which is essential to artistic creation. It does not spoil such a work of art to analyze it as closely as we have done; it is altogether fitting and proper that we should do this: for it helps us to penetrate more deeply into the rich meaning of the Gettysburg Address, and it allows us the very rare privilege of watching the workings of a great man's mind.

---

1 Why was the Battle of Gettysburg important enough to warrant a presidential address? What three principles of rhetorical organization did Lincoln utilize in creating the Gettysburg Address?

2 Where does Lincoln draw on the language and rhythms of the Bible to give his speech a sense of solemnity and importance? What evidence does Highet give of Lincoln's care in drafting this speech for this particular occasion?

3 How do the metaphors of birth and death contribute to the strength and eloquence of the Gettysburg Address? What documentary evidence does Highet draw upon to illustrate his assertion that Lincoln soon became aware that he had given a great speech?

4 Lincoln's purpose in giving this address was to reunite a nation shattered by the Civil War and to motivate citizens to begin the Reconstruction. What means did he use in addressing his audience to capture their attention, speak to their concerns, put the moment in a historical framework, and bring the country together? How is Lincoln's style and diction intended to achieve a tone appropriate for the subject, the occasion, and his purpose? (Glossary: *Diction, Style*.)

5 What three principles of rhetorical organization does Highet perceive in "The Gettysburg Address"? How does Highet use this analysis of Lincoln's mastery of rhetorical techniques to suport his thesis? (Glossary: *Classification/Division*.)

6 Analyze any example of what you would consider to be an effective public discourse—such as John F. Kennedy's inaugural address reprinted below—and classify the rhetorical strategies employed.

John F. Kennedy's Inaugural Address (1961)

Vice President Johnson, Mr. Speaker, Mr. Chief Justice, President Eisenhower, Vice President Nixon, President Truman, Reverend Clergy, fellow citizens:

1 We observe today not a victory of party but a celebration of freedom—symbolizing an end as well as a beginning—signifying renewal as well as change. For I have sworn before you and Almighty God the same solemn oath our forebears prescribed nearly a century and three quarters ago.

2 The world is very different now. For man holds in his mortal hands the power to abolish all forms of human poverty and all forms of human life. And yet the same revolutionary beliefs for which our forebears fought are still at issue around the globe—the belief that the rights of man come not from the generosity of the state but from the hand of God.

3 We dare not forget today that we are the heirs of that first revolution. Let the word go forth from this time and place, to friend and foe alike, that the torch has been passed to a new generation of Americans—born in this century, tempered by war, disciplined by a hard and bitter peace, proud of our ancient heritage—and unwilling to witness or permit the slow undoing of those human rights to which this nation has always been committed, and to which we are committed today at home and around the world.

4 Let every nation know, whether it wishes us well or ill, that we shall pay any price, bear any burden, meet any hardship, support any friend, oppose any foe to assure the survival and the success of liberty.

5 This much we pledge—and more.

6 To those old allies whose cultural and spiritual origins we share, we pledge the loyalty of faithful friends. United, there is little we cannot do in a host of cooperative ventures. Divided, there is little we can do—for we dare not meet a powerful challenge at odds and split asunder.

7 To those new states whom we welcome to the ranks of the free, we pledge our word that one form of colonial control shall not have passed away merely to be replaced by a far more iron tyranny. We shall not always expect to find them supporting our view. But we shall always hope to find them strongly supporting their own freedom—and to remember that, in the past, those who foolishly sought power by riding the back of the tiger ended up inside.

8 To those people in the huts and villages of half the globe struggling to break the bonds of mass misery, we pledge our best efforts to help them help themselves, for whatever period is required—not because the communists may be doing it, not because we seek their votes, but because it is right. If a free society cannot help the many who are poor, it cannot save the few who are rich.

9 To our sister republics south of the border, we offer a special pledge—to convert our good words into good deeds—in a new alliance for progress—to assist free men and free governments in casting off the chains of poverty. But this

peaceful revolution of hope cannot become the prey of hostile powers. Let all our neighbors know that we shall join with them to oppose aggression or sub-version anywhere in the Americas. And let every other power know that this Hemisphere intends to remain the master of its own house.

To that world assembly of sovereign states, the United Nations, our last best hope in an age where the instruments of war have far outpaced the instruments of peace, we renew our pledge of support—to prevent it from becoming merely a forum for invective—to strengthen its shield of the new and the weak—and to enlarge the area in which its writ may run.   10

Finally, to those nations who would make themselves our adversary, we offer not a pledge but a request: that both sides begin anew the quest for peace, before the dark powers of destruction unleashed by science engulf all humanity in planned or accidental self-destruction.   11

We dare not tempt them with weakness. For only when our arms are suffi-cient beyond doubt can we be certain beyond doubt that they will never be employed.   12

But neither can two great and powerful groups of nations take comfort from our present course—both sides overburdened by the cost of modern weapons, both rightly alarmed by the steady spread of the deadly atom, yet both racing to alter that uncertain balance of terror that stays the hand of mankind's final war.   13

So let us begin anew—remembering on both sides that civility is not a sign of weakness, and sincerity is always subject to proof. Let us never negotiate out of fear. But let us never fear to negotiate.   14

Let both sides explore what problems unite us instead of belaboring those problems which divide us.   15

Let both sides, for the first time, formulate serious and precise proposals for the inspection and control of arms—and bring the absolute power to destroy other nations under the absolute control of all nations.   16

Let both sides seek to invoke the wonders of science instead of its terrors. Together let us explore the stars, conquer the deserts, eradicate disease, tap the ocean depths and encourage the arts and commerce.   17

Let both sides unite to heed in all corners of the earth the command of Isa-iah—to "undo the heavy burdens . . . (and) let the oppressed go free."   18

And if a beach-head of cooperation may push back the jungle of suspicion, let both sides join in creating a new endeavor, not a new balance of power, but a new world of law, where the strong are just and the weak secure and the peace preserved.   19

All this will not be finished in the first one hundred days. Nor will it be fin-ished in the first one thousand days, nor in the life of this Administration, nor even perhaps in our lifetime on this planet. But let us begin.   20

In your hands, my fellow citizens, more than mine, will rest the final success or failure of our course. Since this country was founded, each generation of Americans has been summoned to give testimony to its national loyalty. The graves of young Americans who answered the call to service surround the globe.   21

Now the trumpet summons us again—not as a call to bear arms, though arms we need—not as a call to battle, though embattled we are—but a call to   22 bear the burden of a long twilight struggle, year in and year out, "rejoicing in hope, patient in tribulation"—a struggle against the common enemies of man: tyranny, poverty, disease and war itself.

23   Can we forge against these enemies a grand and global alliance, North and South, East and West, that can assure a more fruitful life for all mankind? Will you join in that historic effort?

24   In the long history of the world, only a few generations have been granted the role of defending freedom in its hour of maximum danger. I do not shrink from this responsibility—I welcome it. I do not believe that any of us would exchange places with any other people or any other generation. The energy, the faith, the devotion which we bring to this endeavor will light our country and all who serve it—and the glow from that fire can truly light the world.

25   And so, my fellow Americans: ask not what your country can do for you—ask what you can do for your country.

26   My fellow citizens of the world: ask not what America will do for you, but what together we can do for the freedom of man.

27   Finally, whether you are citizens of America or citizens of the world, ask of us here the same high standards of strength and sacrifice which we ask of you. With a good conscience our only sure reward, with history the final judge of our deeds, let us go forth to lead the land we love, asking His blessing and His help, but knowing that here on earth God's work must truly be our own.

Propaganda Under a Dictatorship   *Aldous Huxley*

◆ ALDOUS HUXLEY (1894–1963) was born in Surrey, England, and was educated at Eaton and Balliol College, Oxford. Despite a serious eye disease, Huxley read with the aid of a magnifying glass and graduated from Oxford in 1915 with honors in English literature. After joining the staff of *Atheneum*, a literary magazine, in 1919, he began writing the novels, essays, and short stories that would bring him international fame. His brilliant social satires and wide-ranging essays on architecture, science, music, history, philosophy, and religion explore the relationship between man and society. *Brave New World* (1932) is his best-known satire on how futuristic mass technology will achieve a sinister utopia of scientific breeding and conditioned happiness. In *Ape and Essence* (1948), he explores an alternate future where subhuman survivors of an atomic war scratch for existence. Huxley's other works, including *Eyeless in Gaza* (1936), *After Many a Summer* (1939), *Time Must Have a Stop* (1944), *The Doors of Perception* (1954), *Heaven and Hell* (1956), and *Island* (1962), can be seen as attempts to search in new spiritual directions—through mysticism, mescaline, and parapsychology—as a reaction to the grim future he so devastastingly portrayed. In "Propaganda Under a Dictatorship," from *Brave New World Revisited* (1958), Huxley reveals how the manipulation of language in the propaganda of Nazi Germany conditioned the thoughts and behavior of the masses.

The ways in which the Nazi regime under Hitler and Josef Goebbels sought to distort language to serve its objectives depended to a great extent, as Huxley points out, on creating a slogan mentality that precluded critical thought. Mass rallies, marches, and the new technological apparatus of radios and loudspeakers conditioned the public to think in catchwords and phrases, dogmas, and slogans. Propaganda is the most extreme form of political rhetoric and Huxley identifies its distinguishing features as Hitler practiced it. Hitler sought to eliminate opposing viewpoints, make public debate of issues impossible, and create an incendiary climate of inflamed passions that could be invoked to support any policy.

> **TO CONSIDER**   Is it possible that Hitler and the Nazi regime used propaganda techniques so effectively that the German people were actually brainwashed?

At his trial after the Second World War, Hitler's Minister for Armaments, Albert Speer, delivered a long speech in which, with remarkable acuteness, he described the Nazi tyranny and analyzed its methods. "Hitler's dictatorship," he said, "differed in one fundamental point from all its predecessors in history. It was the first dictatorship in the present period of modern technical development, a dictatorship which made complete use of all technical means for the domination of its won country. Through technical devices like the radio and the loud-speaker, eighty million people were deprived of independent thought. It was thereby possible to subject them to the will of one man. . . . Earlier dictators needed highly qualified assistants even at the lowest level—men who could think and act independently. The totalitarian system in the period of modern technical development can dispense with such men; thanks to modern methods of communication, it is possible to mechanize the lower leadership. As a result of this there has arisen the new type of the uncritical recipient of orders." In the Brave New World of my prophetic fable technology had advanced far beyond the point it had reached in Hitler's day; consequently the recipients of orders were far less critical than their Nazi counterparts, far more obedient to the order-giving elite. Moreover, they had been genetically standarized and postnatally conditioned to perform their subordinate functions, and could therefore be depended upon to behave almost as predictably as machines. As we shall see in a later chapter, this conditioning of "the lower leadership" is already going on under the Communist dictatorships. The Chinese and the Russians are not relying merely on the indirect effects of advancing technology; they are working directly on the psychophysical organisms of their lower leaders, subjecting minds and bodies to a system of ruthless and, from all accounts, highly effective conditioning. "Many a man," said Speer, "has been haunted by the nightmare that one day nations might be dominated by technical means. That nightmare was almost realized in Hitler's totalitarian system." Almost, but not quite. The Nazis did not have time—and perhaps did not have the intelligence and the necessary knowledge—to brainwash and condition their lower leadership. This, it may be, is one of the reasons why they failed.

Since Hitler's day the armory of technical devices at the disposal of the would-be dictator has been considerably enlarged. As well as the radio, the loudspeaker, the moving picture camera and the rotary press, the contemporary propagandist can make use of television to broadcast the image as well as the voice of his client, and can record both image and voice on spools of magnetic tape. Thanks to technological progress, Big Brother can now be almost as omnipresent as God. Nor is it only on the technical front that the hand of the would-be dictator has been strengthened. Since Hitler's day a great deal of work has been carried out in those fields of applied psychology and neurology which are the special province of the propagandist, the indoctrinator and the brainwasher. In the past these specialists in the art of changing people's minds were empiricists. By a method of trial and error they had worked out a number of techniques and procedures, which they used very effectively without, however, knowing precisely why they were effective. Today the art of mind-control is in process of becoming a science. The practitioners of this science know what they are doing and why. They are guided in their work by theories and hypotheses solidly established on a massive foundation of experimental evidence. Thanks to the new insights and the new techniques made possible by these insights, the nightmare that was "all but realized in Hitler's totalitarian system" may soon be completely realizable.

But before we discuss these new insights and techniques let us take a look at the nightmare that so nearly came true in Nazi Germany. What were the methods used by Hitler and Goebbels for "depriving eighty million people of independent thought and subjecting them to the will of one man"? And what was the theory of human nature upon which those terrifyingly successful methods were based? These questions can be answered, for the most part, in Hitler's own words. And what remarkably clear and astute words they are! When he writes about such vast abstractions as Race and History and Providence, Hitler is strictly unreadable. But when he writes about the German masses and the methods he used for dominating and directing them, his style changes. Nonsense gives place to sense, bombast to a hard-boiled and cynical lucidity. In his philosophical lucubrations Hitler was either cloudily day-dreaming or reproducing other people's half-baked notions. In his comments on crowds and propaganda he was writing of things he knew by firsthand experience. In the words of his ablest biographer, Mr. Alan Bullock, "Hitler was the greatest demagogue in history." Those who add, "only a demagogue," fail to appreciate the nature of political power in an age of mass politics. As he himself said, "To be a leader means to be able to move the masses." Hitler's aim was first to move the masses and then, having pried them loose from their traditional loyalties and moralities, to impose upon them (with the hypnotized consent of the majority) a new authoritarian order of his own devising. "Hitler," wrote Hermann Rauschning in 1939, "has a deep respect for the Catholic church and the Jesuit order; not because of their Christian doctrine, but because of the 'machinery' they have elaborated and controlled, their hierarchical system, their extremely clever tactics, their knowledge of human nature and their wise use of human weaknesses in ruling over believers." Ecclesiasticism without Christianity, the discipline of a monastic rule, not for God's sake or in order to achieve personal salvation, but for the sake of the State and for the greater glory and power of the demagogue turned Leader—this was the goal toward which the systematic moving of the masses was to lead.

Let us see what Hitler thought of the masses he moved and how he did the moving. The first principle from which he started was a value judgment: the masses are utterly contemptible. They are incapable of abstract thinking and uninterested in any fact outside the circle of their immediate experience. Their behavior is determined, not by knowledge and reason, but by feelings and unconscious drives. It is in these drives and feelings that "the roots of their positive as well as their negative attitudes are implanted." To be successful a propagandist must learn how to manipulate these instincts and emotions. "The driving force which has brought about the most tremendous revolutions on this earth has never been a body of scientific teaching which has gained power over the masses, but always a devotion which has inspired them, and often a kind of hysteria which has urged them into action. Whoever wishes to win over the masses must know the key that will open the door of their hearts.". . . In post-Freudian jargon, of their unconscious.

Hitler made his strongest appeal to those members of the lower middle classes who had been ruined by the inflation of 1923, and then ruined all over again by the depression of 1929 and the following years. "The masses" of whom he speaks were these bewildered, frustrated and chronically anxious millions. To make them more masslike, more homogeneously subhuman, he assembled them, by the thousands and the tens of thousands, in vast halls and arenas, where individuals could lose their personal identity, even their elementary humanity, and be merged with the crowd. A man or woman makes direct contact with society in two ways: as a member of some familial, professional or religious group, or as a member of a crowd. Groups are capable of being as moral and intelligent as the individuals who form them; a crowd is chaotic, has no purpose of its own and is capable of anything except intelligent action and realistic thinking. Assembled in a crowd, people lose their powers of reasoning and their capacity for moral choice. Their suggestibility is increased to the point where they cease to have any judgment or will of their own. They become very excitable, they lose all sense of individual or collective responsibility, they are subject to sudden accesses of rage, enthusiasm and panic. In a word, a man in a crowd behaves as though he had swallowed a large dose of some powerful intoxicant. He is a victim of what I have called "herd-poisoning." Like alcohol, herd-poison is an active, extraverted drug. The crowd-intoxicated individual escapes from responsibility, intelligence and morality into a kind of frantic, animal mindlessness.

During his long career as an agitator, Hitler had studied the effects of herd-poison and had learned how to exploit them for his own purposes. He had discovered that the orator can appeal to those "hidden forces" which motivate men's actions, much more effectively than can the writer. Reading is a private, not a collective activity. The writer speaks only to individuals, sitting by themselves in a state of normal sobriety. The orator speaks to masses of individuals, already well primed with herd-poison. They are at his mercy and, if he knows his business, he can do what he likes with them. As an orator, Hitler knew his business supremely well. He was able, in his own words, "to follow the lead of the great mass in such a way that from the living emotion to his hearers the apt word which he needed would be suggested to him and in its turn this would go straight to the heart of his hearers." Otto Strasser called him a "loud-speaker, proclaiming the most secret desires, the least admissible instincts, the sufferings and personal revolts of a whole nation." Twenty years before Madison Avenue embarked upon "Motivational Research," Hitler was systematically exploring and exploiting the secret fears and hopes, the cravings, anxieties and frustrations of the German masses. It is by manipulating "hidden forces" that the advertising experts induce us to buy their wares—a toothpaste, a brand of cigarettes, a political candidate. And it is by appealing to the same hidden forces—and to others too dangerous for Madison Avenue to meddle with—that Hitler induced the German masses to buy themselves a Fuehrer, an insane philosophy and the Second World War.

Unlike the masses, intellectuals have a taste for rationality and an interest in facts. Their critical habit of mind makes them resistant to the kind of propaganda that works so well on the majority. Among the masses "instinct is supreme, and from instinct comes faith. . . . While the healthy common folk instinctively close their ranks to form a community of the people" (under a Leader, it goes without saying) "intellectuals run this way and that, like hens in a poultry yard. With them one cannot make history; they cannot be used as elements composing a community." Intellectuals are the kind of people who demand evidence and are shocked by logical inconsistencies and fallacies. They regard over-simplification as the original sin of the mind and have no use for the slogans, the unqualified assertions and sweeping generalizations which are the propagandist's stock in trade. "All effective propaganda," Hitler wrote, "must be confined to a few bare necessities and then must be expressed in a few stereotyped formulas." These stereotyped formulas must be constantly repeated, for "only constant repetition will finally succeed in imprinting an idea upon the memory of a crowd." Philosophy teaches us to feel uncertain about the things that seem to us self-evident. Propaganda, on the other hand, teaches us to accept as self-evident matters about which it would be reasonable to suspend our judgment or to feel doubt. The aim of the demagogue is to create social coherence under his own leadership. But, as Bertrand Russell has pointed out, "systems of dogma without empirical foundations, such as scholasticism, Marxism and fascism, have the advantage of producing a great deal of social coherence among their disciples." The demagogic propagandist must therefore be consistently dogmatic. All his statements are made without qualification. There are no grays in his picture of the world; everything is either diabolically black or celestially white. In Hitler's words, the propagandist should adopt "a systematically one-sided attitude towards every problem that has to be dealt with." He must never admit that he might be wrong or that people with a different point of view might be even partially right. Opponents should not be argued with; they should be attacked, shouted down, or, if they become too much of a nuisance, liquidated. The morally squeamish intellectual may be shocked by this kind of thing. But the masses are always convinced that "right is on the side of the active aggressor."

Such, then, was Hitler's opinion of humanity in the mass. It was a very low opinion. Was it also an incorrect opinion? The tree is known by its fruits, and a theory of human nature which inspired the kind of techniques that proved so horribly effective must contain at least an element of truth. Virtue and intelligence belong to human beings as individuals freely associating with other individuals in small groups. So do sin and stupidity. But the subhuman mindlessness to which the demagogue makes his appeal, the moral imbecility on which he relies when he goads his victims into action, are characteristic not of men and women as individuals, but of men and women in masses. Mindlessness and moral idiocy are not characteristically human attributes; they are symptoms of herd-poisoning. In all the world's higher religions, salvation and enlightenment are for individuals. The kingdom of heaven is within the mind of a person, not within the collective mindlessness of a crowd. Christ promised to be present where two or three are gathered together. He did not say anything about being present where thousands are intoxicating one another with herd-poison. Under the Nazis enormous numbers of people were compelled to spend an enormous amount of time marching in serried ranks from point A to point B and back again to point A. "This keeping of the whole population on the march seemed to be a senseless waste of time and energy. Only much later," adds Hermann Rauschning, "was there revealed in it a subtle intention based on a well-judged adjustment of ends and means. Marching diverts men's thoughts. Marching kills thought. Marching makes an end of individuality. Marching is the indispensable magic stroke performed in order to accustom the people to a mechanical, quasiritualistic activity until it becomes second nature."

From his point of view and at the level where he had chosen to do his dreadful work, Hitler was perfectly correct in his estimate of human nature. To those of us who look at men and women as individuals rather than as members of crowds, or of regimented collectives, he seems hideously wrong. In an age of accelerating over-population, of accelerating over-organization and even more efficient means of mass communication, how can we preserve the integrity and reassert the value of the human individual? This is a question that can still be asked and perhaps effectively answered. A generation from now it may be too late to find an answer and perhaps impossible, in the stifling collective climate of that future time, even to ask the question.

1   What role did the disastrous inflation of 1923 and the depression of 1929 play in setting the stage for Hitler's rise to power? Why were the lower middle classes the most receptive to Hitler's propaganda? How did Hitler act as an amplifier or "loud-speaker" (para. 4) to project the fears and frustrations of the masses? According to Huxley, what was Hitler's opinion of the masses whom he manipulated?

2   How did Hitler use crowd-control techniques to create an environment in which suggestibility was heightened? Why were slogans so effective in conditioning the thoughts and behavior of the masses? How, in Huxley's view, have many of the propaganda techniques used by Hitler been updated and adapted by advertisers in contemporary society?

3   Have you ever found yourself swept up in the emotions of a crowd to the point where you might have lost any sense of personal responsibility or accepted the ideas of slogans heard or chanted without thinking about what they meant? What insights do these experiences give you into the power of effective propaganda techniques?

4   How did the Nazi regime's propaganda effort depend on the now discredited Sapir-Whorf Hypothesis (that what we think depends upon the language we use)? What particular strategies were used to manipulate language and create a public atmosphere conducive to accepting Hitler's distorted views? (Glossary: *Propaganda, Sapir-Whorf Hypothesis.*)

5   How is Huxley's essay organized to explore both the immediate and distant causes of the triumph of propaganda under Hitler's dictatorship? According to Huxley, which causes are immediate and which are remote? (Glossary: *Cause and Effect.*)

6   Aldous Huxley discusses the role slogans played in propaganda. What slogans have you heard on the radio or seen on television, tee shirts, pamphlets, banners, bumper stickers, buttons, etc., that function as propaganda or that are intended to persuade an audience to accept a belief of an organization or social movement?

I Have a Dream   *Martin Luther King, Jr.*

◆ MARTIN LUTHER KING, JR. (1929–1968), a monumental figure in the civil rights movement and a persuasive advocate of nonviolent means for producing social change, was born in Atlanta, Georgia, in 1929. He was ordained as a Baptist minister in his father's church when he was eighteen and went on to earn degrees from Morehouse College (B.A., 1948), Crozer Theological Seminary (B.D., 1951), Chicago Theological Seminary (D.D., 1957), and Boston University (Ph.D., 1955; D.D., 1959). On December 5, 1955, while he was pastor of a church in Montgomery, Alabama, King focused national attention on the predicament of southern blacks by leading a city-wide boycott of the segregated bus system, a boycott that lasted over one year and nearly bankrupted the bus company. He founded the Southern Christian Leadership Conference and adapted techniques of nonviolent protest employed by Gandhi in a series of sit-ins and mass marches, which were instrumental in bringing about the Civil Rights Act of 1964 and the Voting Rights Act of 1965. He was awarded the Nobel Prize for Peace in 1964 in recognition of his great achievements as the leader of the American civil rights movement. Sadly, King's affirmation of the need to meet physical violence with peaceful resistance led to his being jailed more than fourteen times, beaten, stoned, stabbed in the chest, and finally murdered in Memphis, Tennessee, on April 4, 1968. His many distinguished writings include *Stride Towards Freedom: The Montgomery Story* (1958), *Letter from Birmingham Jail*, written in 1963 and published in 1968, *Why We Can't Wait* (1964), *Where Do We Go From Here: Community or Chaos?* (1967), and *The Trumpet of Conscience* (1968). "I Have a Dream" (1963) is the inspiring sermon delivered by King from the steps of the Lincoln Memorial to the nearly 250,000 people who came to Washington, D.C., to commemorate the centennial of Lincoln's Emancipation Proclamation. Additional millions who watched on television were moved by this eloquent, noble, and impassioned plea that America might fulfill its original promise of freedom and equality for all its citizens.

The tradition of public eloquence can be observed in Martin Luther King Jr.'s stirring, perceptive, and incantatory "I Have a Dream" speech. Seldom has the plea that America might fulfill its promise of freedom and equality for all its citizens been stated with such majesty. Aware of his need to reach many different constituencies with this one speech, King draws together references from the Bible and the Emancipation Proclamation, along with ideas of nonviolent protest, in a series of stirring metaphors that allude to ideas held sacred by all.

TO CONSIDER   Why would a speech delivered by Martin Luther King, Jr. (1963), who was not a politician, be considered an example of political rhetoric? What qualities do you expect to find in political speeches? Has any recent speech by a politician lived up to your expectations? Remember that political speeches can be inspiring as well as manipulative.

I am happy to join with you today in what will go down in history as the greatest demonstration for freedom in the history of our nation.

Five score years ago, a great American, in whose symbolic shadow we stand today, signed the Emancipation Proclamation. This momentous decree came as a great beacon light of hope to millions of Negro slaves who had been seared in the flames of withering injustice. It came as a joyous daybreak to end the long night of their captivity. But one hundred years later, the Negro is still not free. One hundred years later, the life of the Negro is still sadly crippled by the manacles of segregation and the chains of discrimination. One hundred years later, the Negro lives on a lonely island of poverty in the midst of a vast ocean of material prosperity. One hundred years later, the Negro is still anguished in the corners of American society and finds himself in exile in his own land. And so we have come here today to dramatize a shameful condition.

In a sense we have come to our nation's capital to cash a check. When the architects of our republic wrote the magnificent words of the Constitution and the Declaration of Independence, they were signing a promissory note to which every American was to fall heir. This note was the promise that all men—yes, Black men as well as white men—would be guaranteed the inalienable rights of life, liberty, and the pursuit of happiness.

It is obvious today that America has defaulted on this promissory note insofar as her citizens of color are concerned. Instead of honoring this sacred obligation, America has given the Negro people a bad check, a check which has come back marked "insufficient funds." But we refuse to believe that the bank of justice is bankrupt. We refuse to believe that there are insufficient funds in the great vaults of opportunity of this nation; and so we have come to cash this check, a check that will give us upon demand the riches of freedom and the security of justice.

We have also come to this hallowed spot to remind America of the fierce urgency of *now*. This is no time to engage in the luxury of cooling off or to take the tranquilizing drug of gradualism. *Now* is the time to make real the promises of democracy. *Now* is the time to rise from the dark and desolate valley of segregation to the sunlit path of racial justice. *Now* is the time to lift our nation from the quicksands of racial injustice to the solid rock of brotherhood. *Now* is the time to make justice a reality for all of God's children.

It would be fatal for the nation to overlook the urgency of the moment. This sweltering summer of the Negro's legitimate discontent will not pass until there is an invigorating autumn of freedom and equality. Nineteen Sixty-three is not an end, but a beginning. And those who hope that the Negro needed to blow off steam and will now be content will have a rude awakening if the nation returns to business as usual. There will be neither rest nor tranquility in America until the Negro is granted his citizenship rights. The whirlwinds of revolt will continue to shake the foundations of our nation until the bright day of justice emerges.

But there is something that I must say to my people who stand on the warm threshhold which leads into the palace of justice. In the process of gaining our rightful place, we must not be guilty of wrongful deeds. Let us not seek to satisfy our thirst for freedom by drinking from the cup of bitterness and hatred. We must forever conduct our struggle on the high plane of dignity and discipline. We must not allow our creative protest to degenerate into physical violence. Again and again we must rise to the majestic heights of meeting physical force with soul force. And the marvelous new militancy which has engulfed the Negro community must not lead us to a distrust of all white people; for many of our white brothers, as evidenced by their presence here today, have come to realize that their destiny is tied up with our destiny, and they have come to realize that their freedom is inextricably bound to our freedom.

We cannot walk alone. And as we walk we must make the pledge that we shall always march ahead. We cannot turn back. There are those who are asking the devotees of civil rights, "When will you be satisfied?" We can never be satisfied as long as the Negro is the victim of the unspeakable horrors of police brutality. We can never be satisfied as long as our bodies, heavy with the fatigue of travel, cannot gain lodging in the motels of the highways and the hotels of the cities. We cannot be satisfied as long as the Negro's basic mobility is from a smaller ghetto to a larger one. We can never be satisfied as long as our children are stripped of their selfhood and robbed of their dignity by signs stating "For Whites Only." We cannot be satisfied as long as the Negro in Mississippi cannot vote and a Negro in New York believes he has nothing for which to vote. No, no, we are not satisfied, and we will not be satisfied until justice rolls down like waters and righteousness like a mighty stream.

I am not unmindful that some of you have come here out of great trials and tribulations. Some of you have come fresh from narrow jail cells. Some of you have come from areas where your quest for freedom left you battered by the storms of persecution and staggered by the winds of police brutality. You have been the veterans of creative suffering. Continue to work with the faith that unearned suffering is redemptive.

Go back to Mississippi, and go back to Alabama. Go back to South Carolina. Go back to Georgia. Go back to Louisiana. Go back to the slums and ghettos of our Northern cities, knowing that somehow this situation can and will be changed. Let us not wallow in the valley of despair.

I say to you today, my friends, even though we face the difficulties of today and tomorrow, I still have a dream. It is a dream deeply rooted in the American dream. I have a dream that one day this nation will rise up and live out the true meaning of its creed: "We hold these truths to be self-evident, that all men are created equal." I have a dream that one day, on the red hills of Georgia, sons of former slaves and the sons of former slave owners will be able to sit down together at the table of brotherhood. I have a dream that one day even the state of Mississippi, a state sweltering with the heat of injustice, sweltering with the heat of oppression, will be transformed into an oasis of freedom and justice. I have a dream that my four little children will one day live in a nation where they will not be judged by the color of their skin, but by the content of their character.

I have a dream today. I have a dream that one day down in Alabama—with its vicious racists, with its governor's lips dripping with the words of interposition and nullification—one day right there in Alabama, little Black boys and Black girls will be able to join hands with little white boys and white girls as sisters and brothers.

I have a dream today. I have a dream that one day every valley shall be exalted and every hill and mountain shall be made low, the rough places will be made plain and the crooked places will be made straight, and the glory of the Lord shall be revealed, and all flesh shall see it together.

This is our hope. This is the faith that I go back to the South with. And with this faith we will be able to hew out of the mountain of despair a stone of hope. With this faith we will be able to transform the jangling discords of our nation into a beautiful symphony of brotherhood. With this faith we will be able to work together, to play together, to struggle together, to go to jail together, to stand up for freedom together, knowing that we will be free one day.

And this will be the day—this will be the day when all of God's children will be able to sing with new meaning.

> My country, 'tis of thee,
> Sweet land of liberty,
>   Of thee I sing;
> Land where my fathers died,
> Land of the Pilgrims' pride,
> From every mountainside
>   Let freedom ring.

And if America is to be a great nation, this must become true.

And so let freedom ring from the prodigious hilltops of New Hampshire. Let freedom ring from the mighty mountains of New York. Let freedom ring from the heightening Alleghenies of Pennsylvania. Let freedom ring from the snowcapped Rockies of Colorado. Let freedom ring from the curvaceous slopes of California.

But not only that. Let freedom ring from Stone Mountain of Georgia. Let freedom ring from Lookout Mountain of Tennessee. Let freedom ring from every hill and molehill of Mississippi. "From every mountainside let freedom ring."

And when this happens—when we allow freedom to ring, when we let it ring from every village and every hamlet, from every state and every city—we will be able to speed up that day when all of God's children, Black men and white men, Jews and Gentiles, Protestants and Catholics, will be able to join hands and sing in the words of the old Negro spiritual: "Free at last! Free at last! Thank God Almighty. We are free at last!"

----

1 What evidence is there that King was trying to reach many different groups of people, each with its own concerns, with this one speech? Where in the speech does King seem to shift his attention from one group to another?

2 How does King use analogies, equating financial obligations with moral responsibilities, to make abstract concepts of freedom and equality more tangible? How does

King use parallelism and figurative language that echo the Bible to enhance the effectiveness of his speech?

3   How does King's allusion to the Emancipation Proclamation adapt his argument for the occasion of a march by over 200,000 persons through Washington, D.C., to the Lincoln Memorial? What importance does King place on the idea of nonviolent protest?

4   How does King's use of the metaphor of "cashing a check" to the "bank of justice" (para. 2, 3) embody the thesis of his speech in a form that his audience can easily grasp? What other figures of speech does King use to connect with his audience in terms of their values and concerns? (Glossary: *Audience, Figurative Language, Metaphor.*)

5   Where in his argument does King seem to address different groups of people in his audience and adapt his message for these different factions? How is the effectiveness of King's argument enhanced by the use of vivid metaphors to take the abstract idea of inalienable rights and put it into concrete terms? What role does figurative language and parallelism play in making King's case more persuasive? (Glossary: *Argument, Audience, Figurative Language, Metaphor, Persuasion.*)

6   Is there any idea or belief so important to you that you would be prepared to undergo imprisonment and/or torture to defend it? Discuss why this idea or belief means so much to you.

Eulogy for a Princess   *Earl Charles Spencer*

◆ EARL CHARLES SPENCER is the younger brother of the late Diana, Princess of Wales, who was killed in a car accident. On September 6. 1997, he delivered a eulogy for his sister at Westminster Abbey. The speech is unusual in its candor. He declared that Diana, although stripped of her title of "Her Royal Highness" because of her divorce from Charles, "needed no royal title." He pledged that he and the rest of the Spencers, Diana's "blood" family, would instill humanistic qualities in her children, William and Harry, that they would be unlikely to receive from the Windsors. He accused the tabloid press of tormenting his sister and pledged to protect his nephews from similar treatment. His speech was met with applause from the multitudes who heard it.

In many respects, Spencer's eulogy is a traditional one and makes use of predictable cadences of parallel phrases to sustain a mood of public grief. Yet the precise and moving way Spencer expresses his thoughts creates a space for meditation and reflection that contrasts with the public turmoil, agitation, and clamor that surrounded his sister's death. He gracefully sums up the essence of Diana's personality while making points that would have particular resonance with the audience in Great Britain. His speech was not cleared in advance by the monarchy, and although some critized him for using this occasion to air grievances against the House of Windsor (perhaps alluding to the fact that they originally came from Germany), Spencer asserts that his sister was "a truly British girl who transcended nationality."

> **TO CONSIDER**   What role did Earl Charles Spencer's speech play in the unfolding drama of the funeral of his sister, Princess Diana? Do you feel it was inappropriate to use the occasion of a public eulogy to air his private grievances against the monarchy?

I stand before you today the representative of a family in grief, in a country in mourning before a world in shock. We are all united not only in our desire to pay our respects to Diana, but rather in our need to do so.

For such was her extraordinary appeal that the tens of millions of people taking part in this service all over the world via television and radio who never actually met her, feel that they, too, lost someone close to them in the early hours of Sunday morning. It is more remarkable tribute to Diana than I can ever hope to offer her today.

Diana was the very essence of compassion, of duty, of style of beauty. All over the world she was a symbol of selfless humanity, a standard-beare for the rights of the truly downtrodden, a truly British girl who transcended nationality someone with a natural nobility who was classless, who proved in the last year that she needed no royal title to continue to generate her particular brand of magic.

Today is our chance to say thank you for the way you brightened our lives, even though God granted you but half a life. We will all feel cheated that you were taken from us so young, and yet we must learn to be grateful that you came along at all.

Only now you are gone do we truly appreciate what we are now without, and we want you to know that life without you is very, very difficult.

We have all despaired at our loss over the past week, and only the strength of the message you gave us through your years of giving has afforded us the strength to move forward.

There is a temptation to rush to canonize your memory. There is no need to do so. You stand tall enough as a human being of unique qualities not to need to be seen as a saint. Indeed, to sanctify your memory would be to miss out on the very core of your being—your wonderfully mischievous sense of humor with the laugh that bent you double, your joy for life transmitted wherever you took your smile and the sparkle in those unforgettable eyes, your boundless energy which you could barely contain.

But your greatest gift was your intuition, and it was a gift you used wisely. This is what underpinned all your wonderful attributes. And if we look to analyze what it was about you that had such a wide appeal, we find it in your instinctive feel for what was really important in all our lives.

Without your God-given sensitivity, we would be immersed in greater ignorance at the anguish of AIDS and HIV sufferers, the plight of the homeless, the isolation of lepers, the random destruction of land mines. Diana explained to me once that it was her innermost feelings of suffering that made it possible for her to connect with her constituency of the rejected.

And here we come to another truth about her. For all the status the glamour, the applause, Diana remained throughout a very insecure person at heart, almost childlike in her desire to do good for others so she could release herself from deep feelings of unworthiness, of which her eating disorders were merely a symptom.

The world sensed this part of her character and cherished her for her vulnerability, whilst admiring her for her honesty. The last time I saw Diana was on July the first, her birthday, in London, when typically she was not taking time to celebrate her special day with friends but was guest of honor at a charity fundraising evening.

She sparkled, of course, but I would rather cherish the days I spent with her in March when she came to visit me and my children in our home in South Africa. I am proud of the fact that apart from when she was on public display meeting President Mandela, we managed to contrive to stop the ever-present paparazzi from getting a single picture of her.

That meant a lot to her.

These are days I will always treasure. It was as if we'd been transported back to our childhood, when we spent such an enormous amount of time together, the two youngest in the family.

Fundamentally she hadn't changed at all from the big sister who mothered me as a baby, fought with me at school and endured those long train journeys between our parents' homes with me at weekends. It is a tribute to her levelheadedness and strength that despite the most bizarre life imaginable after her childhood, she remained intact, true to herself.

There is no doubt that she was looking for a new direction in her life at this time. She talked endlessly of getting away from England, mainly because of the treatment she received at the hands of the newspapers.

I don't think she ever understood why her genuinely good intentions were sneered at by the media, why there appeared to be a permanent quest on their behalf to bring her down. It is baffling. My own, and only, explanation is that genuine goodness is threatening to those at the opposite end of the moral spectrum.

It is a point to remember that of all the ironies about Diana, perhaps the greatest is this: that a girl given the name of the ancient goddess of hunting was, in the end, the most hunted person of the modern age.

She would want us today to pledge ourselves to protecting her beloved boys, William and Harry, from a similar fate. And I do this here, Diana, on your behalf. We will not allow them to suffer the anguish that used regularly to drive you to tearful despair.

Beyond that, on behalf of your mother and sisters, I pledge that we, your blood family, will do all we can to continue the imaginative and loving way in which you were steering these two exceptional young men, so that their souls are not simply immersed by duty and tradition, but can sing openly as you planned.

We fully respect the heritage into which they have both been born, and will always respect and encourage them in their royal role. But we, like you, recognize the need for them to experience as many different aspects of life as possible, to arm them spiritually and emotionally for the years ahead. I know you would have expected nothing less from us.

William and Harry, we all care desperately for you today. We are all chewed up with sadness at the loss of a woman who wasn't even our mother. How great your suffering is, we cannot even imagine.

I would like to end by thanking God for the small mercies he has shown us at this dreadful time; for taking Diana at her most beautiful and radiant and when she had so much joy in her private life.

Above all, we give thanks for the life of a woman I am so proud to be able to call my sister: the unique, the complex, the extraordinary and irreplaceable Diana, whose beauty, both internal and external, will never be extinguished from our minds.

---

1 How does Spencer manage to combine his tribute to his sister with a not so thinly veiled reproach to the monarchy and to the paparazzi for their treatment of Diana? For example, why does he describe his sister as a "truly British girl" who possessed a "natural nobility" or say that Diana was "classless . . . and needed no royal title"? Why does Spencer draw a parallel between his sister and her namesake Diana, who was the Roman goddess of the hunt?

2 How does Spencer seek to strike a balance between respect for the royal heritage of the monarchy while pledging that his nephews, William and Harry, will be raised to know a life beyond the stifling traditions of the palace, as Diana would have wished?

3 What is the overall impression of Diana that Spencer wishes the world to remember? How does Spencer's description of Diana provide an important personal perspective on what the public knew of her?

4 Evaluate the appropriateness of the language Spencer uses in terms of the context, the audience, and what you understand to be the purpose of his speech. Why would specific words and phrases such as "a truly British girl who transcended nationality," "someone with a natural nobility who is classless," and "I pledge that we, your blood family . . ." have particular resonance for his audience in Great Britain? (Glossary: Audience, Diction, Purpose.)

5 Spencer paints a vivid picture of his sister, Princess Diana. What descriptive details does he offer about her? Which details are objective and factual and which are subjective and allow his audience to understand what Spencer considers precious and worth memorializing in his sister? What is the overall dominant impression this eulogy communicates? (Glossary: Description.)

6 Locate coverage in your school newspaper of a recent event of which you have some personal knowledge. Analyze how the event was depicted compared with your own experience. What aspects of the event were intensified or exaggerated and which were downplayed, ignored, suppressed, or overlooked? Write a short essay on how the report differed, if at all, from your own experience and perception and try to determine if these differences reflect an agenda on the part of the reporter, the paper, or the audience for which it was written.

How to Watch TV News   *Neil Postman and Steve Powers*

◆ NEIL POSTMAN is the chairman of the Department of Communication Arts at New York University. He has written nineteen books, including *Amusing Ourselves to Death* (1985) and *Conscientious Objections* (1992). Steve Powers is a journalist in broadcast news who has served as a correspondent for Fox Television News and the ABC Information Radio Network. The following essay is drawn from their book *How to Watch TV News* (1992).

While seemingly in an adversarial relationship with politicians, TV news journalists, according to Postman and Powers, are cocreators of political spectacle in the guise of presenting factual and authoritative news reports. Why this should be so and how the pressure for ratings has transformed the nightly news into a form of entertainment are analyzed by the authors. Formerly, the news was thought to be a service (in the era of the literate anchorman Walter Cronkite) delivered in grammatically correct sentences replete with real information. Now, according to Postman and Powers, news broadcasts depend much more heavily on striking visual images rather than reflective and well-thought-out commentary. News, like politics, has become a form of entertainment that has been distorted by a sensationalistic tabloid mentality, a new form of the Roman "bread and circuses."

> **TO CONSIDER**   Did you ever have the feeling that TV news is a carefully contrived form of entertainment designed to create the illusion of giving you objective information?

1 When a television news show distorts the truth by altering or manufacturing facts (through re-creations), a television viewer is defenseless even if a recreation is properly labeled. Viewers are still vulnerable to misinformation since they will not know (at least in the case of docudramas) what parts are fiction and what parts are not. But the problems of verisimilitude posed by recreations pale to insignificance when compared to the problems viewers face when encountering a straight (no-monkey-business) show. All news shows, in a sense, are re-creations in that what we hear and see on them are attempts to represent actual events, and are not the events themselves. Perhaps, to avoid ambiguity, we might call all news shows "re-presentations" instead of "re-creations." These re-presentations come to us in two forms: language and pictures. The question then arises: what do viewers have to know about language and pictures in order to be properly armed to defend themselves against the seductions of eloquence (to use Bertrand Russell's apt phrase)? . . .

2 [Let us look at] the problem of pictures. It is often said that a picture is worth a thousand words. Maybe so. But it is probably equally true that one word is worth a thousand pictures, at least sometimes—for example, when it comes to understanding the world we live in. Indeed, the whole problem with news on television comes down to this: all the words uttered in an hour of news coverage could be printed on one page of a newspaper. And the world cannot be understood in one page. Of course, there is a compensation: television offers pictures, and the pictures move. Moving pictures are a kind of language in themselves, but the language of pictures differs radically from oral and written language, and the differences are crucial for understanding television news.

3 To begin with, pictures, especially single pictures, speak only in particularities. Their vocabulary is limited to concrete representation. Unlike words and sentences, a picture does not present to us an idea or concept about the world, except as we use language itself to convert the image to idea. By itself, a picture cannot deal with the unseen, the remote, the internal, the abstract. It does not speak of "man," only of a man; not of "tree," only of a tree. You cannot produce an image of "nature," any more than an image of "the sea." You can only show a particular fragment of the here-and-now—a cliff of a certain terrain, in a certain condition of light; a wave at a moment in time, from a particular point of view. And just as "nature" and "the sea" cannot be photographed, such larger abstractions as truth, honor, love, and falsehood cannot be talked about in the lexicon of individual pictures. For "showing of" and "talking about" are two very different kinds of processes: individual pictures give us the world as object; language, the world as idea. There is no such thing in nature as "man" or "tree." The universe offers no such categories or simplifications; only flux and infinite variety. The picture documents and celebrates the particularities of the universe's infinite variety. Language makes them comprehensible.

4 Of course, moving pictures, video with sound, may bridge the gap by juxtaposing images, symbols, sound, and music. Such images can present emotions and rudimentary ideas. They can suggest the panorama of nature and the joys and miseries of humankind.

Picture—smoke pouring from the window, cut to people coughing, an 5
ambulance racing to a hospital, a tombstone in a cemetery.

Picture—jet planes firing rockets, explosions, lines of foreign soldiers sur- 6
rendering, the American flag waving in the wind.

Nonetheless, keep in mind that when terrorists want to prove to the world 7
that their kidnap victims are still alive, they photograph them holding a copy of
a recent newspaper. The dateline on the newspaper provides the proof that the
photograph was taken on or after that date. Without the help of the written
word, film and videotape cannot portray temporal dimensions with any precision. Consider a film clip showing an aircraft carrier at sea. One might be able
to identify the ship as Soviet or American, but there would be no way of telling
where in the world the carrier was, where it was headed, or when the pictures
were taken. It is only through language—words spoken over the pictures or
reproduced in them—that the image of the aircraft carrier takes on specific
meaning.

Still, it is possible to enjoy the image of the carrier for its own sake. One 8
might find the hugeness of the vessel interesting; it signifies military power on
the move. There is a certain drama in watching the planes come in at high speeds
and skid to a stop on the deck. Suppose the ship were burning: that would be
even more interesting. This leads to an important point about the language of
pictures. Moving pictures favor images that change. That is why violence and
dynamic destruction find their way onto television so often. When something is
destroyed violently it is altered in a highly visible way; hence the entrancing
power of fire. Fire gives visual form to the ideas of consumption, disappearance,
death—the thing that burned is actually taken away by fire. It is at this very basic
level that fires make a good subject for television news. Something was here,
now it's gone, and the change is recorded on film.

Earthquakes and typhoons have the same power. Before the viewer's eyes 9
the world is taken apart. If a television viewer has relatives in Mexico City and
an earthquake occurs there, then he or she may take a special interest in the
images of destruction as a report from a specific place and time; that is, one may
look at television pictures for information about an important event. But film of
an earthquake can be interesting even if the viewer cares nothing about the event
itself. Which is only to say, as we noted earlier, that there is another way of participating in the news—as a spectator who desires to be entertained. Actually to
see buildings topple is exciting, no matter where the buildings are. The world
turns to dust before our eyes.

Those who produce television news in America know that their medium 10
favors images that move. That is why they are wary of "talking heads," people
who simply appear in front of a camera and speak. When talking heads appear on
television, there is nothing to record or document, no change in process. In the
cinema the situation is somewhat different. On a movie screen, closeups of a
good actor speaking dramatically can sometimes be interesting to watch. When
Clint Eastwood narrows his eyes and challenges his rival to shoot first, the spectator sees the cool rage of the Eastwood character take visual form, and the nar-

rowing of the eyes is dramatic. But much of the effect of this small movement depends on the size of the movie screen and the darkness of the theater, which make Eastwood and his every action "larger than life."

11   The television screen is smaller than life. It occupies about 15 percent of the viewer's visual field (compared to about 70 percent for the movie screen). It is not set in a darkened theater closed off from the world but in the viewer's ordinary living space. This means that visual changes must be more extreme and more dramatic to be interesting on television. A narrowing of the eyes will not do. A car crash, an earthquake, a burning factory are much better.

12   With these principles in mind, let us examine more closely the structure of a typical newscast, and here we will include in the discussion not only the pictures but all the nonlinguistic symbols that make up a television news show. For example, in America, almost all news shows begin with music, the tone of which suggests important events about to unfold. The music is very important, for it equates the news with various forms of drama and ritual—the opera, for example, or a wedding procession—in which musical themes underscore the meaning of the event. Music takes us immediately into the realm of the symbolic, a world that is not to be taken literally. After all, when events unfold in the real world, they do so without musical accompaniment. More symbolism follows. The sound of teletype machines can be heard in the studio, not because it is impossible to screen this noise out, but because the sound is a kind of music in itself. It tells us that data are pouring in from all corners of the globe, a sensation reinforced by the world map in the background (or clocks noting the time on different continents). The fact is that teletype machines are rarely used in TV news rooms, having been replaced by silent computer terminals. When seen, they have only a symbolic function.

13   Already, then, before a single news item is introduced, a great deal has been communicated. We know that we are in the presence of a symbolic event a form of theater in which the day's events are to be dramatized. This theater takes the entire globe as its subject, although it may look at the world from the perspective of a single nation. A certain tension is present, like the atmosphere in a theater just before the curtain goes up. The tension is represented by the music, the staccato beat of the teletype machines, and often the sight of news workers scurrying around typing reports and answering phones. As a technical matter, it would be no problem to build a set in which the newsroom staff remained off camera, invisible to the viewer, but an important theatrical effect would be lost. By being busy on camera, the workers help communicate urgency about the events at hand, which suggests that situations are changing so rapidly that constant revision of the news is necessary.

14   The staff in the background also helps signal the importance of the person in the center, the anchor, "in command" of both the staff and the news. The anchor plays the role of host. He or she welcomes us to the newscast and welcomes us back from the different locations we visit during the filmed reports.

15   Many features of the newscast help the anchor to establish the impression of control. These are usually equated with production values in broadcasting.

They include such things as graphics that tell the viewer what is being shown, or maps and charts that suddenly appear on the screen and disappear on cue, or the orderly progression from story to story. They also include the absence of gaps, or "dead time," during the broadcast, even the simple fact that the news starts and ends at a certain hour. These common features are thought of as purely technical matters, which a professional crew handles as a matter of course. But they are also symbols of a dominant theme of television news: the imposition of an orderly world—called "the news"—upon the disorderly flow of events.

While the form of a news broadcast emphasizes tidiness and control, its content can best be described as fragmented. Because time is so precious on television, because the nature of the medium favors dynamic visual images, and because the pressures of a commercial structure require the news to hold its audience above all else, there is rarely any attempt to explain issues in depth or place events in their proper context. The news moves nervously from a warehouse fire to a court decision, from a guerrilla war to a World Cup match, the quality of the film most often determining the length of the story. Certain stories show up only because they offer dramatic pictures. Bleachers collapse in South America: hundreds of people are crushed—a perfect television news story, for the cameras can record the face of disaster in all its anguish. Back in Washington, a new budget is approved by Congress. Here there is nothing to photograph because a budget is not a physical event; it is a document full of language and numbers. So the producers of the news will show a photo of the document itself, focusing on the cover where it says "Budget of the United States of America." Or sometimes they will send a camera crew to the government printing plant where copies of the budget are produced. That evening, while the contents of the budget are summarized by a voice-over, the viewer sees stacks of documents being loaded into boxes at the government printing plant. Then a few of the budget's more important provisions will be flashed on the screen in written form, but this is such a time-consuming process—using television as a printed page—that the producers keep it to a minimum. In short, the budget is not televisable, and for that reason its time on the news must be brief. The bleacher collapse will get more time that evening.

While appearing somewhat chaotic, these disparate stories are not just dropped in the news program helter-skelter. The appearance of a scattershot story order is really orchestrated to draw the audience from one story to the next—from one section to the next—through the commercial breaks to the end of the show. The story order is constructed to hold and build the viewership rather than place events in context or explain issues in depth.

Of course, it is a tendency of journalism in general to concentrate on the surface of events rather than underlying conditions; this is as true for the newspaper as it is for the newscast. But several features of television undermine whatever efforts journalists may make to give sense to the world. One is that a television broadcast is a series of events that occur in sequence, and the sequence is the same for all viewers. This is not true for a newspaper page, which displays many items simultaneously, allowing readers to choose the order in which they read them. If newspaper readers want only a summary of the latest tax bill, they can read the headline and the first paragraph of an article, and if they want more, they can keep reading. In a sense, then, everyone reads a different newspaper, for no two readers will read (or ignore) the same items.

19   But all television viewers see the same broadcast. They have no choices. A report is either in the broadcast or out, which means that anything which is of narrow interest is unlikely to be included. As NBC News executive Reuven Frank once explained.

> A newspaper, for example, can easily afford to print an item of conceivable interest to only a fraction of its readers. A television news program must be put together with the assumption that each item will be of some interest to everyone that watches. Every time a newspaper includes a feature which will attract a specialized group it can assume it is adding at least a little bit to its circulation. To the degree a television news program includes an item of this sort . . . it must assume that its audience will diminish.

20   The need to "include everyone," an identifying feature of commercial television in all its forms, prevents journalists from offering lengthy or complex explanations, or from tracing the sequence of events leading up to today's headlines. One of the ironies of political life in modern democracies is that many problems which concern the "general welfare" are of interest only to specialized groups. Arms control, for example, is an issue that literally concerns everyone in the world, and yet the language of arms control and the complexity of the subject are so daunting that only a minority of people can actually follow the issue from week to week and month to month. If it wants to act responsibly, a newspaper can at least make available more information about arms control than most people want. Commercial television cannot afford to do so.

21   But even if commercial television could afford to do so, it wouldn't. The fact that television news is principally made up of moving pictures prevents it from offering lengthy, coherent explanations of events. A television news show reveals the world as a series of unrelated, fragmentary moments. It does not—and cannot be expected to—offer a sense of coherence or meaning. What does this suggest to a TV viewer? That the viewer must come with a prepared mind—information, opinions, a sense of proportion, an articulate value system. To the TV viewer lacking such mental equipment, a news program is only a kind of rousing light show. Here a falling building, there a five-alarm fire, everywhere the world as an object, much without meaning, connections, or continuity.

---

1 In what sense, according to the authors, are TV news programs a form of theater? What devices are used to add a sense of drama and importance to routine news broadcasts?

2 What considerations are responsible for the shaping of news stories and determine the sequence in which they are presented and what is or is not reported?

3 Does the nature of the TV medium make some kinds of stories preferable to others? If so, what are they?

4 How do Postman and Powers feel about TV news shows? Why do they choose the term "theater" (para. 13) to describe news broadcasts? Specifically, what elements of TV news broadcasts are theatrical? (Glossary: *Attitude, Connotation, Denotation.*)

5 The authors explore both the causes and consequences of the current look of TV news programs. Locate places in their essay where they explicitly identify causal relationships and evaluate whether the effects they observe can truly be attributed to the causes they identify? (Glossary: *Cause and Effect.*)

6 In what way does Postman and Powers's analysis clarify the techniques that are at the heart of reporting political news in terms of revealing how conflicts are manufactured, managed, and resolved? That is, how are supposedly objective news accounts the contemporary media equivalent of the "bread and circuses" that were used in ancient Rome to divert and placate the population?

◆ CONNECTIONS: THE LANGUAGE OF POLITICS

George Orwell, "Politics and the English Language"

1. Apply Orwell's analysis of the principles of effective discourse (and his critique of linguistic abuses) to Earl Charles Spencer's speech. What do you conclude?
2. What connections can you discover between Orwell's critique of political language and Sven Birkerts's analysis of the consequences of computers and electronic communications in modern life (see "Into the Electronic Millennium," Ch. 11)?

Stuart Hirschberg, "Analyzing the Rhetoric of Nixon's 'Checkers Speech'"

1. Analyze the rhetoric of Martin Luther King Jr.'s speech, drawing on the analytical framework used by Hirschberg.
2. How do the rhetorical techniques of "intensifying" and "downplaying" discussed by Hirschberg function in everyday conversation, as dramatized by Raymond Carver in "What We Talk About When We Talk About Love" (Ch. 4)?

Gilbert Highet, "The Gettysburg Address"

1. How does Highet's analysis of the Gettysburg Address reveal many of the same qualities that characterize King's speech and all effective public discourse?
2. Analyze the range of logical and emotional appeals in the Gettysburg Address, drawing on the framework outlined by Stuart Hirschberg (see "The Rhetoric of Advertising," Ch. 9).

Aldous Huxley, "Propaganda Under a Dictatorship"

1. What connections can you discover between Huxley's analysis of the propaganda techniques used in Nazi Germany and George Orwell's analysis of the political consequences of corrupt political discourse? How does the degradation of political discourse pave the way for the uses of propaganda that Huxley describes?
2. How, according to Jack Solomon, did racial classification play a crucial role in Nazi propaganda (see "What's in a Name?: The Ideology of Cultural Classification," Ch. 8), which then was promulgated to the masses by methods described by Huxley?

Martin Luther King. Jr., "I Have a Dream"

1. Compare the rhetorical strategies used by King with those of Abraham Lincoln in the Gettysburg Address, as examined by Gilbert Highet.
2. Analyze the metaphors used in King's speech to discover the cognitive systems utilized, as discussed by George Lakoff (see "Anger," Ch. 3).

Earl Charles Spencer, "Eulogy for a Princess"

1. Compare the rhetorical strategies used by Spencer on the occasion of his sister's death with those used by Abraham Lincoln in commemorating soldiers who were killed during the Battle of Gettysburg. How does Spencer politicize the personal? How does Lincoln personalize the political?
2. Drawing on Mikhail Bakhtin's concepts (see "The Dialogic Imagination," Ch. 4), analyze words and phrases in Spencer's speech that illustrate the kind of complex echoing of preceding conversations that Bakhtin describes.

Neil Postman and Steve Powers, "How to Watch TV News"

1. Drawing on Huxley's analysis of propaganda techniques, discuss the extent to which news with a political content might be considered a more subtle form of propaganda designed to elict a sense of awe and powerlessness.
2. Drawing on Oliver Sacks's "The President's Speech" (Ch. 3) analyze the effect of a TV news broadcast first with the sound on and then with the sound off. Did you find that your impressions of what was going on differed when sound did or did not accompany the images? What insight did this give you into the way TV news programs are constructed?

◆ WRITING ASSIGNMENTS FOR CHAPTER 10

1. The ability to create compelling images in picturesque language is an important element in communicating a writer's thoughts, feelings, and experiences. Creating a vivid picture or image in an audience's mind requires writers to use metaphors, similes, and other figures of speech. Imagery works by evoking a vivid picture in the audience's imagination. A simile compares one object or experience to another using *like* or *as*. For example, if you wrote that "on a trip home the train was crowded and the passengers were packed in like sardines," your audience would be expected to understand the idea rather than literally assume you were accompanied by sardines in the train. A metaphor applies a word or phrase to an object it does not literally denote in order to suggest the comparison. Thus, if you looked into the crowded train and yelled, "Hey, you sardines," most people on the train would know what you meant.

   The way a writer chooses to describe something expresses an opinion that is capable of persuading an audience. To be effective, metaphors must look at things in a fresh light to let the reader see a familiar subject in a new way. As George Orwell observed in *Politics and the English Language* (1946), "the sole aim of a metaphor is to call up a visual image." When they are first conceived, metaphors can call up pictures in the mind, but worn-out metaphors lack the power to summon these images.

   In each of the following, how do the writers use figurative language to persuade an audience to accept their point of view? Do they meet Orwell's test?

> In Mexico, an air conditioner is called a politician because it makes a lot of noise but doesn't work very well.
>
> Chen Deighton, *Mexico Set* (1985).

> "Politics is the art of looking for trouble, finding it everywhere, diagnosing it incorrectly, and applying the wrong remedies."
>
> (Groucho Marx)

> "Money is like manure. If you spread it around, it does a lot of good, but if you pile it up in one place it stinks like hell."
>
> (Clint W. Murchison, Texas financier)

> "You can take all the sincerity in Hollywood, place it in the navel of a fruit fly, and still have room enough for three caraway seeds and a producer's heart."
>
> (Fred Allen)

2. Words that through overuse lose their power to evoke concrete images become clichés. A cliché is a trite, timeworn expression or outworn phrase that has become commonplace or lost its freshness.

   Metaphors that are no longer relevant, stereotyped expressions, and overused idioms no longer have the ability to conjure up an image in the hearer's mind. They have been used so often that they become a ready-made way of substituting a phrase to avoid thinking.

a. What clichés can you think of that might have seemed fresh and original when they first occurred? For example, "asleep at the switch."

b. What clichés can you think of that depend on alliteration and rhyming, such as "high and dry," "wishy washy," or "safe and sound"?

c. What clichés can you think of that use two words when one would suffice, such as "null and void," or "ways and means"?

d. What clichés can you think of that are really overused similes, such as "dead as a doornail," "quiet as a mouse," "ugly as sin," "good as gold"?

e. What clichés can you think of that are stale or overused metaphors, such as "like a bat out of hell," "out like a light," "dropping like flies"?

3. Formulate three short descriptions using neutral, negative, or positive adjectives for the National Rifle Association, Greenpeace, the ACLU (American Civil Liberties Union), the National Organization for Women, the Postal Service, or any other defined association or organization.

4. For a research project, read the complete text of Jonathan Swift's "A Modest Proposal" (1729). What clues suggest that Swift creates a narrator (in this case, a reasonable, seemingly well-intentioned bureaucrat) who proposes a drastic solution to Ireland's economic and social problems, and whose "proposal" is meant as a satire?

5. Why is the cartoon reprinted below funny?

Compare several headlines from several newspapers with those of tabloids. How do tabloids use the following attention-getting devices: use of first rather than last names, words with emotionally charged connotations, pseudoquotations, and techniques associated with poetry such as rhyme and alliteration? What other devices can you find? Have "serious" newspapers and TV news programs become dependent on tabloid techniques to boost

Source: Reprinted by permission of Doug Marlette and Creators Syndicate.

their ratings? What current examples can you discover that illustrate   this trend?

6. The rhetoric of President Clinton offers an instructive case study of the "vocabulary of lying." Analyze the following three examples from the transcript of President Clinton's grand jury testimony as reprinted by the *New York Times,* September 22, 1998.

Q: Mr. President, I want to, before I go into a new subject area, briefly go over something you were talking about with Mr. Bittman. The statement of your attorney, Mr. Bennett, at the Paula Jones deposition, "Counsel is fully aware"—it's page 54, line 5—"Counsel is fully aware that Ms. Lewinsky has filed, has an affidavit which they are in possession of saying that there is absolutely no sex of any kind in any manner, shape or form, with President Clinton." That statement is made by your attorney in front of Judge Susan Webber Wright, correct?

A: That's correct.

Q: That statement is a completely false statement. Whether or not Mr. Bennett knew of your relationship with Ms. Lewinsky, the statement that there was "no sex of any kind in any manner, shape or form, with President Clinton," was an utterly false statement. Is that correct?

A: It depends on what the meaning of the word "is" is. If the—if he—if "is" means is and never has been, that is not—that is one thing. If it means there is none, that was a completely true statement. But, as I have testified, and I'd like to testify again, this is—it is somewhat unusual for a client to be asked about his lawyer's statements, instead of the other way around.

Q: Well, the grand jury would like to know, Mr. President, why it is that you think that oral sex performed on you does not fall within the definition of sexual relations as used in your deposition.

A: Because that is—if the deponent is the person who has oral sex performed on him, then the contact is with—not with anything on that list, but with the lips of another person. It seems to be self-evident that that's what it is. And I thought it was curious. Let me remind you, sir, I read this carefully. And I thought about it. I thought about what "contact" meant, thought about what "intent to arouse or gratify" meant. And I had to admit under this definition that I'd actually had sexual relations with Gennifer Flowers.

To err is human. but to really foul things up requires a computer.

> —Anonymous

Dilbert, reprinted by permission of United Features Syndicate, Inc.

Cybertalk

The authors in this chapter explore how computers and electronic communications have changed the English language in ways that are as profound as those produced by the invention of the printing press by Johannes Gutenberg in the mid-1400s. Purists who look nostalgically back to the past may recoil before the onslaught of constantly changing technical slang that besieges us daily—including neologisms such as "newbies" who become "netizens" and observe "netiquette" on the Net. Learning cybertalk is like learning a new language. For example, images don't blend, they "morph." SPAM, the "suspect" canned luncheon meat, now means electronic garbage. Terminology aside (in some respects, it's the most superficial—although the most visible—aspect of the impact of computers on language), consider how documents appear on the web—filled with icons and hypertext links to other sites—when compared with traditional prose. The basic notion of what text is and what writing is has undergone a profound transformation. Important social issues are connected to the presumption that most people will have to be able to use computers in order to work and live in our society. Yet, as LynNell Hancock points out in "The Haves and the Have-Nots," there are already sharply defined race, class, and age lines separating those who have access to this technology and can expect to prosper and those who are shut out.

In "Into the Electronic Millennium," Sven Birkerts raises fundamental questions about the nature of the electronic age of communication to which we are committing ourselves and how it will alter our perceptions of information and experience. Libraries may not become simply museums with computer terminals, but electronically produced documents will have to be stored and retrieved in ways that are completely different from traditional texts, according to Brian Hayes in "The Electronic Palimpsest."

Several authors in this chapter examine how computers are altering what we communicate and how we communicate it. It has become customary to champion the superiority of composing on a computer when compared with the traditional mechanics of writing, and to wax enthusiastic about the democratizing effects of cyberspace—but a few notes of caution are in order. In "How the Web Destroys the Quality of Students' Research Papers," David Rothenberg explores the relationship between how students now write term papers and the accessible cornucopia of sources available on the Net. Rothenberg believes that too many students are being seduced into quick, easy, and superficial treatments of research topics. In "Return to Sender," David Angell and Brent Heslop make the same observation about the increasingly slipshod writing and inadequately thought-out responses that are characteristic of e-mail (while defending its democratizing tendency).

As information and experiences become interchangeable, people may be willing to settle for representations of reality as they live more and more in the world of "virtual reality." The new technology of e-mail, fax machines, and the like might gradually erode the concept of a private self in ways that Amy Bruckman describes in "Christmas Unplugged," an account of how computer technology has come to dominate her life and her relationships with others. It can also open up a whole new world of social contact and community, as described by Paula Span in "Women and Computers: Is There Equity in Cyberspace?". She relates her experience with WELL, a "virtual" meeting ground where intelligent discourse can take place without the verbal harrassment toward women that has become so pervasive in cyberspace.

The amusing short story by Chet Williamson with which the chapter concludes ("The Personal Touch") creates an ingenious scenario of a consumer's loss of privacy to computer-driven mass marketing.

The Haves and the Have-Nots

LynNell Hancock

◆ LYNNELL HANCOCK is an assistant professor of journalism and director of the Prudential Fellowship for Children and the News at Columbia University. A former education editor for *Newsweek,* her expertise is in public education and segregation issues. The following essay first appeared in *Newsweek*, February 27, 1995.

Discussions of the impact of computers tend to focus on such specialized issues as e-mail, chat rooms, and composing and editing techniques, without considering the more basic question of who gets access to this new technology. Hancock points out that advocates tend to overestimate the democratizing effect of the Internet and claim that, as a result, we will become the modern version of the informed participatory public Jefferson envisioned. A more realistic assessment of what is really possible must ask and answer the question of who is going to pay for all this. The poor certainly can't afford computers; minorities to a great extent are cut out of the loop; and many middle-aged and older citizens are not able to use this new technology in productive ways.

TO CONSIDER   Do you think computers are making our society more democratic or more stratified in terms of who has access to the web? What about the poor and the elderly or children in school districts that cannot afford computers?

Aaron Smith is a teenager on the techno track. In America's breathless race to achieve information nirvana, the senior from Issaqua, a middle-class district east of Seattle, has the hardware and hookups to run the route. Aaron and 600 of his fellow students at Liberty High School have their own electronic-mail addresses. They can log on to the Internet every day, joining only about 15 percent of America's schoolchildren who can now forage on their own for documents in European libraries or chat with experts around the world. At home, the 18-year-old e-mails his teachers, when he is not prowling the World Wide Web to track down snowboarding conditions on his favorite Cascade mountain passes. "We have the newest, greatest thing," Aaron says.

On the opposite coast, in Boston's South End, Marilee Colon scoots a mouse along a grimy Apple pad, playing a Kid Pix game on an old black-and-white terminal. It's Wednesday at a neighborhood center, Marilee's only chance to poke around on a computer. Her mom, a secretary at the center, can't afford one in their home. Marilee's public-school classroom doesn't have any either. The 10-year-old from Roxbury depends on the United South End Settlement Center and its less than state-of-the-art Macs and IBMs perched on mismatched desks. Marilee has never heard of the Internet. She is thrilled to double-click on the stick of dynamite and watch her teddy-bear creation fly off the screen. "It's fun blowing it up," says the delicate fifth grader, twisting a brown ponytail around her finger.

Certainly Aaron was born with a stack of statistical advantages over Marilee. He is white and middle class and lives with two working parents who both have higher degrees. Economists say the swift pace of hightech advances will only drive a further wedge between these youngsters. To have an edge in America's job search, it used to be enough to be well educated. Now, say the experts, it's critical to be digital. Employees who are adept at technology "earn roughly 10 to 15 percent higher pay," according to Alan Krueger, chief economist for the U.S. Labor Department. Some argue that this pay gap has less to do with technology than with industries' efforts to streamline their work forces during the recession. . . . Still, nearly every American business from Wall Street to McDonald's requires some computer knowledge. Taco Bell is modeling its cash registers after Nintendo controls, according to Rosabeth Moss Kanter. The "haves." says the Harvard Business School professor, will be able to communicate around the globe. The "have-nots" will be consigned to the "rural backwater of the information society."

Like it or not, America is a land of inequities. And technology, despite its potential to level the social landscape, is not yet blind to race, wealth and age. The richer the family, the more likely it is to own and use a computer, according to 1993 census data. White families are three times as likely as blacks or Hispanics to have computers at home. Seventy-four percent of Americans making more than $75,000 own at least one terminal, but not even one third of all Americans own computers. A small fraction—only about 7 percent—of students' families subscribe to online services that transform the plastic terminal into a telecommunications port.

5   At least in public schools, the computer gap is closing. More than half the students have some kind of computer, even if it's obsolete. But schools with the biggest concentration of poor children have the least equipment, according to Jeanne Hayes of Quality Education Data. Ten years ago schools had one computer for every 125 children, according Hayes. Today that figure is one for 12.

Though the gap is slowly closing, technology is advancing so fast, and at such huge costs, that it's nearly impossible for cash-strapped municipalities to catch up. Seattle is taking bids for one company to wire each ZIP code with fiber optics, so everyone—rich or poor—can hook up to video, audio and other multimedia services. Estimated cost: $500 million. Prosperous Montgomery Country, Md., has an $81 million plan to put every classroom online. Next door, the District of Columbia public schools have the same ambitious plan but less than $1 million in the budget to accomplish it.

New ideas—and demands—for the schools are announced every week. The '90s populist slogan is no longer "A chicken in every pot" but "A computer on every desk." Vice President Al Gore has appealed to the telecommunications industry to cut costs and wire all schools, a task Education Secretary Richard Riley estimates will cost $10 billion. House Speaker Newt Gingrich stumbled into the discussion with a suggestion that every poor family get a laptop from Uncle Sam. Rep. Ed Markey wants a computer sitting on every school desk within 10 years. "The opportunities are enormous," Markey says.

Enormous, yes, but who is going to pay for them? Some successful school projects have relied heavily on the kindness of strangers. In Union City, N.J., school officials renovated the guts of a 100-year-old building five years ago, overhauling the curriculum and wiring every classroom in Christopher Columbus Middle School for high tech. Bell Atlantic provided wiring free and agreed to give each student in last year's seventh-grade class a computer to take home. Even parents, most of whom are South American immigrants, can use their children's computers to e-mail the principal in Spanish. He uses translation software and answers them electronically. The results have shown up in test scores. In a school where 80 percent of the children are poor, reading, math, attendance and writing scores are now the best in the district. "We believe that technology will improve our everyday life," says principal Bob Fazio. "And that other schools will piggyback and learn from us."

Still, for every Christopher Columbus, there are far more schools like Jordan High School in South-Central Los Angeles. Only 30 computers in the school's lab, most of them 12 to 15 years old, are available for Jordan's 2,000 students, many of whom live in the nearby Jordan Downs housing project. "I am teaching these kids on a system that will do them no good in the real world when they get out there," says Robert Doornbos, Jordan's computer-science instructor. "The school system has not made these kids' getting on the Information Highway a priority."

Donkey Kong: Having enough terminals to go around is one problem. But 10 another important question is what the equipment is used for. Not much beyond rote drills and word processing, according to Linda Roberts, a technology consultant for the U.S. Department of Education. A 1992 National Assessment of Educational Progress survey found that most fourth-grade math students were using computers to play games, "like Donkey Kong." By the eighth grade, most math students weren't using them at all.

Many school officials think that access to the Internet could become the most effective equalizer in the educational lives of students. With a modem attached, even most ancient terminals can connect children in rural Mississippi to universities in Asia. A Department of Education report last week found that 35 percent of schools have at least one computer with a modem. But only half the schools let students use it. Apparently administrators and teachers are hogging the Info Highway for themselves.

There is another gap to be considered. Not just between rich and poor, but between the young and the used-to-be-young. Of the 100 million Americans who use computers at home, school or work, nearly 60 percent are 17 or younger, according to the census. Children, for the most part, rule cyberspace, leaving the over-40 set to browse through the almanac.

The gap between the generations may be the most important, says MIT guru Nicholas Negroponte, author of the new book "Being Digital." Adults are the true "digitally homeless, the needy," he says. In other words, adults like Debbie Needleman, 43, an office manager at Wallpaper Warehouse in Natick, Mass., are wary of the digital age. "I really don't mind that the rest of the world passes me by as long as I can still earn a living," she says.

These aging choose-nots become a more serious issue when they are teachers in schools. Even if schools manage to acquire state-of-the-art equipment, there is no guarantee that trained adults will be available to understand them. This is something that tries Aaron Smith's patience. "A lot of my teachers are quite illiterate," says Aaron, the fully equipped Issaqua teenager. "You have to explain it to them real slow to make sure they understand everything." Fast or slow, Marilee Colon, Roxbury's fifth-grade computer lover, would like her chance to understand everything too.

---

1 How do Aaron Smith's experiences with technology as compared with Marilee Colon's dramatize the social inequities between the "haves" and the "have-nots"? How will access to these resources affect the kind of lives each will have? How does this contrast set the stage for Hancock's analysis?

2 Why does "race, wealth, and age" (para. 4) play such an important part in determining who has access to this new technology?

3 Who, in your view, is going to belong to the world of cyberspace in the future? Who should belong and who is going to pay for it? How do these concerns bring into question the fundamental role of the Internet in a democracy?

4 How does the contrast between Aaron Smith and Marilee Colon with which Hancock opens her essay dramatize the issue of unequal access to technology (para. 1–3)? (Glossary: Comparison and Contrast, Introduction, Conclusion.)

5 How does Hancock use the comparison/contrast format to reveal the inequities in access to computers among schoolchildren in the same age group? Which method of comparison does she use and why is it effective in getting her point across? (Glossary: Comparison and Contrast.)

6 How realistic a picture of access to cyberspace do computer magazines present? To what extent are the articles and advertising skewed in such a way as to exclude those groups that Hancock identifies as the "have-nots"?

Into the Electronic Millennium

Sven Birkerts

◆ SVEN BIRKERTS teaches expository writing at Harvard. He is recognized as a thoughtful critic of technology by those who agree with his views and called a neo-Luddite by those who don't. His published works include *An Artificial Wilderness: Essays on Twentieth Century Literature* (1987), which

---

Sven Birkerts, "Into the Electronic Millennium," from *The Gutenberg Elegies: The Fate of Reading in an Electronic Age*. Copyright © 1994 by Sven Birkerts. Reprinted by permission of Faber and Faber Publishers, Inc.

earned the National Book Critics Circle Award, *The Electric Life: Essays on Modern Poetry* (1989), *American Energies, Essays on Fiction* (1992), and *The Gutenberg Elegies: The Fate of Reading in an Electronic Age* (1994), from which the following essay is taken. He is also the author of *Writing Well* (1997) and *Readings* (1999).

Birkerts's harsh critique of the increasing dominance of electronic communications may lead you to inquire what is so dangerous about cyberspace. He believes that how we read and the nature of text itself are undergoing a significant transformation as the page is replaced by the screen. Complex sentences capable of expressing complex thoughts, along with standard spelling and punctuation, will disappear, to be replaced by a kind of written equivalent of spoken language. Vocabularies will shrink, along with literacy, conversation, and informed political debate, and the ideals of an articulate culture will give way to an electronic equivalent of jazzy graphics.

TO CONSIDER How would you feel about walking into a library of the future that did not have any books and only had computer terminals?

Some years ago, a friend and I comanaged a used and rare book shop in Ann Arbor, Michigan. We were often asked to appraise and purchase libraries— by retiring academics, widows, and disgruntled graduate students. One day we took a call from a professor of English at one of the community colleges outside Detroit. When he answered the buzzer I did a double take—he looked to be only a year or two older than we were. "I'm selling everything," he said, leading the way through a large apartment. As he opened the door of his study I felt a nudge from my partner. The room was wall-to-wall books and as neat as a chapel.

The professor had a remarkable collection. It reflected not only the needs of his vocation—he taught nineteenth- and twentieth-century literature—but a book lover's sensibility as well. The shelves were strictly arranged, and the books themselves were in superb condition. When he left the room we set to work inspecting, counting, and estimating. This is always a delicate procedure, for the buyer is at once anxious to avoid insult to the seller and eager to get the goods for the best price. We adopted our usual strategy, working out a lower offer and a more generous fallback price. But there was no need to worry. The professor took our first offer without batting an eye.

As we boxed up the books, we chatted. My partner asked the man if he was moving. "No," he said, "but I am getting out." We both looked up. "Out of the teaching business, I mean. Out of books." He then said that he wanted to show us something. And indeed, as soon as the books were packed and loaded, he led us back through the apartment and down a set of stairs. When we reached the basement, he flicked on the light. There, on a long table, displayed like an exhibit in the Space Museum, was a computer. I didn't know what kind it was then, nor could I tell you now, fifteen years later. But the professor was keen to explain and demonstrate.

4   While he and my partner hunched over the terminal, I roamed to and fro, inspecting the shelves. It was purely a reflex gesture, for they held nothing but thick binders and paperbound manuals. "I'm changing my life," the ex-professor was saying. "This is definitely where it's all going to happen." He told us that he already had several good job offers. And the books? I asked. Why was he selling them all? He paused for a few beats. "The whole profession represents a lot of pain to me," he said. "I don't want to see any of these books again."

5   The scene has stuck with me. It is now a kind of marker in my mental life. That afternoon I got my first serious inkling that all was not well in the world of print and letters. All sorts of corroborations followed. Our professor was by no means an isolated case. Over a period of two years we met with several others like him. New men and new women who had glimpsed the future and had decided to get out while the getting was good. The selling off of books was sometimes done for financial reasons, but the need to burn bridges was usually there as well. It was as if heading to the future also required the destruction of tokens from the past.

6   A change is upon us—nothing could be clearer. The printed word is part of a vestigial order that we are moving away from—by choice and by societal compulsion. I'm not just talking about disaffected academics, either. This shift is happening throughout our culture, away from the patterns and habits of the printed page and toward a new world distinguished by its reliance on electronic communications.

7   This is not, of course, the first such shift in our long history. In Greece, in the time of Socrates, several centuries after Homer, the dominant oral culture was overtaken by the writing technology. And in Europe another epochal transition was effected in the late fifteenth century after Gutenberg invented movable type. In both cases the long-term societal effects were overwhelming, as they will be for us in the years to come.

8   The evidence of the change is all around us, though possibly in the manner of the forest that we cannot see for the trees. The electronic media, while conspicuous in gadgetry, are very nearly invisible in their functioning. They have slipped deeply and irrevocably into our midst, creating sluices and circulating through them. I'm not referring to any one product or function in isolation, such as television or fax machines or the networks that make them possible. I mean the interdependent totality that has arisen from the conjoining of parts— the disk drives hooked to modems, transmissions linked to technologies of reception, recording, duplication, and storage. Numbers and codes and frequencies. Buttons and signals. And this is no longer "the future," except for the poor or the self-consciously atavistic—it is now. . . .

9   To get a sense of the enormity of the change, you must force yourself to imagine—deeply and in nontelevisual terms—what the world was like a hundred, even fifty, years ago. If the feat is too difficult, spend some time with a novel from the period. Read between the lines and reconstruct. Move through the sequence of a character's day and then juxtapose the images and sensations you find with those in the life of the average urban or suburban dweller today.

Inevitably, one of the first realizations is that a communications net, a soft   10
and pliable mesh woven from invisible threads, has fallen over everything. The
so-called natural world, the place we used to live, which served us so long as the
yardstick for all measurements, can now only be perceived through a scrim.
Nature was then; this is now. Trees and rocks have receded. And the great geographical Other, the faraway rest of the world, has been transformed by the pure
possibility of access. The numbers of distance and time no longer mean what
they used to. Every place, once unique, itself, is strangely shot through with
radiations from every other place. "There" was then; "here" is now. . . .

To underscore my point, I have been making it sound as if we were all   11
abruptly walking out of one room and into another, leaving our books to the
moths while we settle ourselves in front of our state-of-the-art terminals. The
truth is that we are living through a period of overlap; one way of being is
pushed athwart another. Antonio Gramsci's often-cited sentence comes
inevitably to mind: "The crisis consists precisely in the fact that the old is dying
and the new cannot be born; in this interregnum a great variety of morbid symptoms appears." The old surely is dying, but I'm not so sure that the new is having any great difficulty being born. As for the morbid symptoms, these we have
in abundance.

The overlap in communications modes, and the ways of living that they are   12
associated with, invites comparison with the transitional epoch in ancient Greek
society, certainly in terms of the relative degree of disturbance. Historian Eric
Havelock designated that period as one of "protoliteracy," of which his fellow
scholar Oswyn Murray has written:

> To him [Havelock] the basic shift from oral to literate culture was a slow
> process; for centuries, despite the existence of writing, Greece remained
> essentially an oral culture. This culture was one which depended heavily on
> the encoding of information in poetic texts, to be learned by rote and to
> provide a cultural encyclopedia of conduct. It was not until the age of Plato
> in the fourth century that the dominance of poetry in an oral culture was
> challenged in the final triumph of literacy.

That challenge came in the form of philosophy, among other things, and   13
poetry has never recovered its cultural primacy. What oral poetry was for the
Greeks, printed books in general are for us. But our historical moment, which
we might call "proto-electronic," will not require a transition period of two centuries. The very essence of electronic transmissions is to surmount impedances
and to hasten transitions. Fifty years, I'm sure, will suffice. As for what the conversion will bring—and *mean*—to us, we might glean a few clues by looking to
some of the "morbid symptoms" of the change. But to understand what these
portend, we need to remark a few of the more obvious ways in which our various technologies condition our senses and sensibilities.

I won't tire my reader with an extended rehash of the differences between   14
the print orientation and that of electronic systems. Media theorists from Marshall McLuhan to Walter Ong to Neil Postman have discoursed upon these at
length. What's more, they are reasonably commonsensical. I therefore will
abbreviate.

15   The order of print is linear, and is bound to logic by the imperatives of syntax. Syntax is the substructure of discourse, a mapping of the ways that the mind makes sense through language. Print communication requires the active engagement of the reader's attention, for reading is fundamentally an act of translation. Symbols are turned into their verbal referents and these are in turn interpreted. The print engagement is essentially private. While it does represent an act of communication, the contents pass from the privacy of the sender to the privacy of the receiver. Print also posits a time axis; the turning of pages, not to mention the vertical descent down the page, is a forward-moving succession, with earlier contents at every point serving as a ground for what follows. Moreover, the printed material is static—it is the reader, not the book, that moves forward. The physical arrangements of print are in accord with our traditional sense of history. Materials are layered; they lend themselves to rereading and to sustained attention. The pace of reading is variable, with progress determined by the reader's focus and comprehension.

16   The electronic order is in most ways opposite. Information and contents do not simply move from one private space to another, but they travel along a network. Engagement is intrinsically public, taking place within a circuit of larger connectedness. The vast resources of the network are always there, potential, even if they do not impinge on the immediate communication. Electronic communication can be passive, as with television watching, or interactive, as with computers. Contents, unless they are printed out (at which point they become part of the static order of print) are felt to be evanescent. They can be changed or deleted with the stroke of a key. With visual media (television, projected graphs, highlighted "bullets") impression and image take precedence over logic and concept, and detail and linear sequentiality are sacrificed. The pace is rapid, driven by jump-cut increments, and the basic movement is laterally associative rather than vertically cumulative. The presentation structures the reception and, in time, the expectation about how information is organized.

17   Further, the visual and nonvisual technology in every way encourages in the user a heightened and ever-changing awareness of the present. It works against historical perception, which must depend on the inimical notions of logic and sequential succession. If the print medium exalts the word, fixing it into permanence, the electronic counterpart reduces it to a signal, a means to an end.

18   Transitions like the one from print to electronic media do not take place without rippling or, more likely, *reweaving* the entire social and cultural web. The tendencies outlined above are already at work. We don't need to look far to find their effects. We can begin with the newspaper headlines and the millennial lamentations sounded in the op-ed pages: that our educational systems are in decline; that our students are less and less able to read and comprehend their required texts, and that their aptitude scores have leveled off well below those of previous generations. Tag-line communication, called "bite-speak" by some, is destroying the last remnants of political discourse; spin doctors and media consultants are our new shamans. As communications empires fight for control of all information outlets, including publishers, the latter have succumbed to the tyranny of the bottom line; they are less and less willing to publish work, however worthy, that will not make a tidy profit. And, on every front, funding for

the arts is being cut while the arts themselves appear to be suffering a deep crisis of relevance. And so on.

Every one of these developments is, of course, overdetermined, but there can be no doubt that they are connected, perhaps profoundly, to the transition that is underway.

Certain other trends bear watching. One could argue, for instance, that the entire movement of postmodernism in the arts is a consequence of this same macroscopic shift. For what is postmodernism at root but an aesthetic that rebukes the idea of an historical time line, as well as previously uncontested assumptions of cultural hierarchy. The postmodern artifact manipulates its stylistic signatures like Lego blocks and makes free with combinations from the formerly sequestered spheres of high and popular art. Its combinatory momentum and relentless referencing of the surrounding culture mirror perfectly the associative dynamics of electronic media.

One might argue likewise, that the virulent debate within academia over the canon and multiculturalism may not be a simple struggle between the entrenched ideologies of white male elites and the forces of formerly disenfranchised gender, racial, and cultural groups. Many of those who would revise the canon (or end it altogether) are trying to outflank the assumption of historical tradition itself. The underlying question, avoided by many, may be not only whether the tradition is relevant, but whether it might not be too taxing a system for students to comprehend. Both the traditionalists and the progressives have valid arguments, and we must certainly have sympathy for those who would try to expose and eradicate the hidden assumptions of bias in the Western tradition. But it also seems clear that this debate could only have taken the form it has in a society that has begun to come loose from its textual moorings. To challenge repression is salutary. To challenge history itself, proclaiming it to be simply an archive of repressions and justifications, is idiotic.*. . .

A collective change of sensibility may already be upon us. We need to take seriously the possibility that the young truly "know no other way," that they are not made of the same stuff that their elders are. In her *Harper's* magazine debate with Neil Postman, Camille Paglia observed:

> Some people have more developed sensoriums than others. I've found that
> most people born before World War II are turned off by the modern media.·

19

20

21

22

---

*The outcry against the modification of the canon can be seen as a plea for old reflexes and routines. And the cry for multicultural representation may be a last-ditch bid for connection to the fading legacy of print. The logic is simple. When a resource is threatened—made scarce—people fight over it. In this case the struggle is over textual power in an increasingly nontextual age. The future of books and reading is what is at stake, and a dim intuition of this drives the contending factions.

As Katha Pollitt argued so shrewdly in her much-cited article in *The Nation:* If we were a nation of readers, there would be no issue. No one would be arguing about whether to put Toni Morrison on the syllabus because her work would be a staple of the reader's regular diet anyway. These lists are suddenly so important because they represent, very often, the only serious works that the student is ever likely to be exposed to. Whoever controls the lists comes out ahead in the struggle for the hearts and minds of the young.

They can't understand how we who were born after the war can read and watch TV at the same time. But we *can*. When I wrote my book, I had earphones on, blasting rock music or Puccini and Brahms. The soap operas—with the sound turned down—flickered on my TV. I'd be talking on the phone at the same time. Baby boomers have a multilayered, multitrack ability to deal with the world.

23   I don't know whether to be impressed or depressed by Paglia's ability to disperse her focus in so many directions. Nor can I say, not having read her book, in what ways her multitrack sensibility has informed her prose. But I'm baffled by what she means when she talks about an ability to "deal with the world." From the context, "dealing" sounds more like a matter of incessantly repositioning the self within a barrage of on-rushing stimuli. . . .

24   My final exhibit—I don't know if it qualifies as a morbid symptom as such—is drawn from a *Washington Post Magazine* essay on the future of the Library of Congress, our national shrine to the printed word. One of the individuals interviewed in the piece is Robert Zich, so-called "special projects czar" of the institution. Zich, too, has seen the future, and he is surprisingly candid with his interlocutor. Before long, Zich maintains, people will be able to get what information they want directly off their terminals. The function of the Library of Congress (and perhaps libraries in general) will change. He envisions his library becoming more like a museum: "Just as you go to the National Gallery to see its Leonardo or go to the Smithsonian to see the Spirit of St. Louis and so on, you will want to go to libraries to see the Gutenberg or the original printing of Shakespeare's plays or to see Lincoln's hand-written version of the Gettysburg Address."

25   Zich is outspoken, voicing what other administrators must be thinking privately. The big research libraries, he says, "and the great national libraries and their buildings will go the way of the railroad stations and the movie palaces of an earlier era which were really vital institutions in their time . . . Somehow folks moved away from that when the technology changed."

26   And books? Zich expresses excitement about Sony's hand-held electronic book, and a miniature encyclopedia coming from Franklin Electronic Publishers. "Slip it in your pocket," he says. "Little keyboard, punch in your words and it will do the full text searching and all the rest of it. Its limitation, of course, is that it's devoted just to that one book." Zich is likewise interested in the possibility of memory cards. What he likes about the Sony product is the portability: one machine, a screen that will display the contents of whatever electronic card you feed it.

27   I cite Zich's views at some length here because he is not some Silicon Valley research and development visionary, but a highly placed executive at what might be called, in a very literal sense, our most conservative public institution. When men like Zich embrace the electronic future, we can be sure it's well on its way.

28   Others might argue that the technologies cited by Zich merely represent a modification in the "form" of reading, and that reading itself will be unaffected, as there is little difference between following words on a pocket screen or a

printed page. Here I have to hold my line. The context cannot but condition the process. Screen and book may exhibit the same string of words, but the assumptions that underlie their significance are entirely different depending on whether we are staring at a book or a circuit-generated text. As the nature of looking—at the natural world, at paintings—changed with the arrival of photography and mechanical reproduction, so will the collective relation to language alter as new modes of dissemination prevail.

Whether all of this sounds dire or merely "different" will depend upon the reader's own values and priorities. I find these portents of change depressing, but also exhilarating—at least to speculate about. On the one hand, I have a great feeling of loss and a fear about what habitations will exist for self and soul in the future. But there is also a quickening, a sense that important things are on the line. As Heraclitus once observed, "The mixture that is not shaken soon stagnates." Well, the mixture is being shaken, no doubt about it. And here are some of the kinds of developments we might watch for as our "proto-electronic" era yields to an all-electronic future:

1. *Language erosion.* There is no question but that the transition from the culture of the book to the culture of electronic communication will radically alter the ways in which we use language on every societal level. The complexity and distinctiveness of spoken and written expression, which are deeply bound to traditions of print literacy, will gradually be replaced by a more telegraphic sort of "plainspeak." Syntactic masonry is already a dying art. Neil Postman and others have already suggested what losses have been incurred by the advent of telegraphy and television—how the complex discourse patterns of the nineteenth century were flattened by the requirements of communication over distances. That tendency runs riot as the layers of mediation thicken. Simple linguistic prefab is now the norm, while ambiguity, paradox, irony, subtlety, and wit are fast disappearing. In their place, the simple "vision thing" and myriad other "things." Verbal intelligence, which has long been viewed as suspect as the act of reading, will come to seem positively conspiratorial. The greater part of any articulate person's energy will be deployed in dumbing-down her discourse.

Language will grow increasingly impoverished through a series of vicious cycles. For, of course, the usages of literature and scholarship are connected in fundamental ways to the general speech of the tribe. We can expect that curricula will be further streamlined, and difficult texts in the humanities will be pruned and glossed. One need only compare a college textbook from twenty years ago to its contemporary version. A poem by Milton, a play by Shakespeare—one can hardly find the text among the explanatory notes nowadays. Fewer and fewer people will be able to contend with the so-called masterworks of literature or ideas. Joyce, Woolf, Soyinka, not to mention the masters who preceded them, will go unread, and the civilizing energies of their prose will circulate aimlessly between closed covers.

2. *Flattening of historical perspectives.* As the circuit supplants the printed page, and as more and more of our communications involve us in network processes—which of their nature plant us in a perpetual present—our perception of history will inevitably alter. Changes in information storage and access are

bound to impinge on our historical memory. The depth of field that is our sense of the past is not only a linguistic construct, but is in some essential way represented by the book and the physical accumulation of books in library spaces. In the contemplation of the single volume, or mass of volumes, we form a picture of time past as a growing deposit of sediment; we capture a sense of its depth and dimensionality. Moreover, we meet the past as much in the presentation of words in books of specific vintage as we do in any isolated fact or statistic. The database, useful as it is, expunges this context, this sense of chronology, and admits us to a weightless order in which all information is equally accessible. . . .

33   3. *The waning of the private self.* We may even now be in the first stages of a process of social collectivization that will over time all but vanquish the ideal of the isolated individual. For some decades now we have been edging away from the perception of private life as something opaque, closed off to the world; we increasingly accept the transparency of a life lived within a set of systems, electronic or otherwise. Our technologies are not bound by season or light—it's always the same time in the circuit. And so long as time is money and money matters, those circuits will keep humming. The doors and walls of our habitations matter less and less—the world sweeps through the wires as it needs to, or as we need it to. The monitor light is always blinking; we are always potentially on-line.

34   I am not suggesting that we are all about to become mindless, soulless robots, or that personality will disappear altogether into an oceanic homogeneity. But certainly the idea of what it means to be a person living a life will be much changed. The figure-ground model, which has always featured a solitary self before a background that is the society of other selves, is romantic in the extreme. It is ever less tenable in the world as it is becoming. There are no more wildernesses, no more lonely homesteads, and, outside of cinema, no more emblems of the exalted individual.

35   The self must change as the nature of subjective space changes. And one of the many incremental transformations of our age has been the slow but steady destruction of subjective space. The physical and psychological distance between individuals has been shrinking for at least a century. In the process, the figure-ground image has begun to blur its boundary distinctions. One day we will conduct our public and private lives within networks so dense, among so many channels of instantaneous information, that it will make almost no sense to speak of the differentiations of subjective individualism.

36   We are already captive in our webs. Our slight solitudes are transected by codes, wires, and pulsations. We punch a number to check in with the answering machine, another to tape a show that we are too busy to watch. The strands of the web grow finer and finer—this is obvious. What is no less obvious is the fact that they will continue to proliferate, gaining in sophistication, merging functions so that one can bank by phone, shop via television, and so on. The natural tendency is toward streamlining: The smart dollar keeps finding ways to shorten the path, double-up the function. We might think in terms of a circuit-board model, picturing ourselves as the contact points. The expansion of electronic options is always at the cost of contractions in the private sphere. We will

soon be navigating with ease among cataracts of organized pulsations, putting out and taking in signals. We will bring our terminals, our modems, and menus further and further into our former privacies; we will implicate ourselves by degrees in the unitary life, and there may come a day when we no longer remember that there was any other life. . . .

Trafficking with tendencies—extrapolating and projecting as I have been doing—must finally remain a kind of gambling. One bets high on the validity of a notion and low on the human capacity for resistance and for unpredictable initiatives. No one can really predict how we will adapt to the transformations taking place all around us. We may discover, too, that language is a hardier thing than I have allowed. It may flourish among the beep and the click and the monitor as readily as it ever did on the printed page. I hope so, for language is the soul's ozone layer and we thin it at our peril.

37

---

1 Birkerts, along with Kirkpatrick Sale, Theodore Rozak, Clifford Stoll, and Chellis Glendinning, has been called a *neo-Luddite*—that is, a modern intellectual who rails against the effects of technology in much the same way as early 19th-century members of a radical agrarian movement in England violently opposed the Industrial Revolution. What features of Birkerts's argument have led to this perception? For example, why does he begin his essay with a story of a professor who sold all his books?

2 What predictions does Birkerts make as to the effects of computers and technology on public discourse, books, libraries, and privacy? Have any of these effects become so noticeable that you have become aware of them? Describe your experiences.

3 In a short essay, discuss Birkerts's vision of the future and your own response to it. You might consider how your relationship to the printed text has changed. What features of a possible electronic future suggest wonderful possibilities—or, conversely, worry you?

4 What part do each of the following rhetorical features play in Birkerts's essay: the opening story about the professor selling his books (para. 1–4), the metaphors in paragraph 10, 33–34 that play on the concept of the web, and the invented term "plainspeak" in paragraph 30? (Glossary: *Definition, Metaphor, Introduction, Conclusion.*)

5 Birkerts believes that the advent of electronic communication has helped undermine traditional concepts of literacy. Do you think his assessment is fair? Why or why not? How widespread are the changes that Birkerts describes? (Glossary: *Cause and Effect.*)

6 The invention of the printing press liberated texts from being the proprietary domain of academia, the Church, and the wealthy. It is a common belief that access to databases, e-mail, the Internet, and other forms of electronic communication will be profoundly democratic. Do these technological advances really destroy elitism or simply transfer it to those with access to computers? For a research project, you might look up what percentage of what groups have access to computers. Are they available to the poor, minorities, the elderly, and less affluent school districts?

Return to Sender

*David Angell
and Brent Heslop*

◆ DAVID ANGELL and BRENT HESLOP have written thirteen books together. Heslop currently teaches at the University of California at Santa Cruz and Angell writes books and articles based on his extensive experience with programming languages and the Internet. Their collaborative works include *The Elements of E-mail Style* (1994) and *Mosaic for Dummies* (1995).

Angell and Heslop's enthusiasm about e-mail is based on the ease with which messages can be dashed off, retrieved, and responded to, and the possibility it offers for expressing comments you might not wish to make in person or on the telephone. They see it as remarkably effective in getting the attention of people who wouldn't ordinarily respond to letters. The authors are mindful that the time-saving function of e-mail is offset by not having control over who reads it, of being besieged by unrequested e-mail, and not knowing how the recipient has responded to your message. They provide a guide to e-mail etiquette and some commonsense recommendations on style to eliminate unintentional misunderstandings, sloppy syntax and grammar, and inadequately thought-out responses.

> **TO CONSIDER** If you do not use e-mail, would you consider doing so? Why or why not? If you do use e-mail, would you consider giving it up? Why or why not? Have you noticed a change in the style of communication with e-mail? When was the last time you wrote a traditional letter?

1 First there were smoke signals. Now there's e-mail. And because there's e-mail, people who haven't picked up a pencil in years are zipping off notes to each other, to presidents, to Russian researchers, to newspaper editors, to National Public Radio. E-mail's creating a renaissance in written correspondence, a revival in post-card-style composition. It may not be poetry, but it's quick, simple, and into and out of your life faster than you can lick a stamp. Clearly, e-mail is a medium whose time has come. As Scott McNealy, CEO of Sun Microsystems Inc., a *Fortune* 500 company, puts it: "You could take out every one of the 300 to 400 computer applications that we run our company on and we could continue. But if you took out our e-mail system, Sun would grind to an immediate halt."

2 That's because in many corporations e-mail is replacing the telephone and even face-to-face conversations as the communications vehicle of choice. Short, simple notes are accepted fare among e-mail users; no salutations, datelines or

return addresses are required. Correspondents respond to e-mail at their leisure, and, because messages can be written down, users avoid the embarrassing verbal rambling so typical of voice-mail messages.

Even better—best of all for some e-mail devotees—almost every e-mail pro- 3 gram has a reply button. Simply click on that button, type your message and send it. Magically, the program will return your reply to the address from which the message originated. In other words, you don't even have to know where to send a reply; the e-mail program tracks it for you.

For all those who hate addressing envelopes, searching for stamps or using 4 interoffice mail, or who carry stamped envelopes around in their pockets for days, e-mail has arrived to help them correspond quickly and effectively. As Internet analyst and author Daniel Dern says, e-mail is "the ultimate convenience."

In business, e-mail has enhanced collaboration by flattening corporate hier- 5 archies, thus enabling employees at all levels to communicate more easily. "For some reason," explains one corporate employee, "most people, regardless of their stature, read and respond to e-mail."

E-mail also has sped up the time it takes to exchange larger files of informa- 6 tion. Many e-mail programs enable users to attach other documents and files to their notes and transmit them in a fraction of the time it would take a courier service or the U.S. postal system to deliver them. Of course, for files to be transferred successfully, the recipient's e-mail program must be able to accept and translate the files. Not all programs can do this.

The speed and ease of e-mail make it simple to abuse. Pounding out an 7 informal note to a friend is one thing, but such informality might not go over well with your boss. "I once zipped off a testy note to my manager before I really had a chance to consider the ramifications of my message," one e-mail user explains. "I would never have been able to say what I said to my boss's face or even over the phone."

Although this man's boss took the note in stride, not all managers will. 8 Thoughtlessness is next to insubordination in many managers' eyes. Savvy e-mail users have learned to pause and reread their notes before sending them.

If e-mail easily seduces users into careless responses, it is even more likely to 9 lure them into improper grammar, inaccurate punctuation, and lapses in politeness. Unfortunately, William Strunk Jr. and E.B. White are no longer available to call attention to the elements of a good writing style. But it's fascinating to envision them perusing someone's e-mail files. Undoubtedly, they would cringe at the all-too-frequent abuses of language in e-mail parlance, such as run-on sentences, misspellings, and dangling participles. But, they might actually be amused by some of its more colorful inventions, like emoticons (see below). Indeed, the elements of e-mail style are evolving slowly. Some of them mirror traditional rules of writing; others have sprung spontaneously from the creative imaginations of early users. The following are some reliable composition and netiquette conventions to help you write e-mail that will be read.

Identify Yourself and Your Purpose. E-mail gets stuffed into mail- 10 boxes like junk mail. And the first thing most owners of those mailboxes do is separate the junk from the important mail. In most e-mail programs, new messages appear according to the name of the person who sent the mail. A subject line also shows up, which explains briefly what the message concerns. The best way to ensure that your message will be opened: Write a subject line that is concise and descriptive.

11   ***Don't Blather.*** Proust wanted to publish *Remembrance of Things Past* without punctuation. His publishers refused. It became and remains one of the great masterpieces of world literature. Remember: With e-mail, you are your own publisher. If you write long, rambling sentences that don't get to the point, no one will read them. They may remember your name, but they will not read what you write. E-mail demands short, coherent sentences and effective punctuation. Use them.

Practice Tone Control. On the whole, a conversational tone is prefer-
12   able to a highly formal one in e-mail writing (more Walt Whitman than Ralph Waldo Emerson). In fact, with the possible exception of international e-mail, an overly formal style may alienate the reader.

13   ***Be Careful With Humor.*** What do ducks do when they fly upside down? They quack up. Now, some people might think that's funny; others will think it's sophomoric, which is why you should watch your step with humor and irony when writing e-mail. Why take the risk of annoying someone with a thoughtless joke or ironic statement that may be misinterpreted? Consider the impact that alienating your correspondent may have on your future exchanges, if there are any.

14   ***DON'T SHOUT!*** Typing your message in uppercase letters is known in the e-mail world as shouting. Some individuals find it easier to type their messages uppercase, but that makes it more difficult for the recipient to read. Readers may well take it personally and probably will respond in kind.

15   ***Beware of Flame Wars.*** Want to open your mail every day and find someone spewing a bunch of illogical profanity at you? If not, watch your step. Don't respond rashly to an irritating e-mail message. Calm down and then respond. Ask yourself, "What would I say to this person face-to-face?" That should put some water on the fire.

16   ***Watch the Column Width.*** Unlike word processing programs, a line ends in many e-mail programs only when you hit Return. Messages with line lengths of more than 80 characters will cause line distortion on receiving monitors that can display only 80 characters. Keep line lengths between 65 and 70 characters.

17   ***Avoid Formatting That Won't Translate.*** Some e-mail programs don't recognize formatted text, such as bold or italic. Use asterisks instead.

18   ***Use the Signature File.*** Most e-mail systems let you add a signatur file at the end of your e-mail message. A signature file acts as a letterhead for your e-mail and may include all sorts of information, such as your full name, your company's name, a postal address, and voice and fax numbers. Some users also include art, logos, or quotations.

Learn the Shortcuts. One curious tradition that distinguishes e-mail [19] from other forms of correspondence is the use of acronyms. It's perfectly OK in e-mail to abbreviate common phrases. Common sense, however, dictates that you don't overuse them. People won't be ROTEL IMHO if you do.

A few of the more popular acronyms follow: [20]

BTW—*By the way*
F2F—*Face to face*
IMHO—*In my humble opinion*
IOW—*In other words*
TIA—*Thanks in advance*
BRB—*Be right back*
WTG—*Way to go*
LOL—*Laughing out loud*
ROTEL—*Rolling on the floor laughing*
SO—*Significant other*
TTFN—*Ta-ta for now*
RTFM—*Read the [expletive deleted] manual*

Punctuate Your Emotion. Emoticons are the equivalent of mail slang. [21] They serve as visual representations of emotional states and are constructed by combining punctuation marks and other non-letter-keys. Accepted usage: Place emotions at the end of a sentence as an additional note, such as adding a ;-) for a wink, or a:-] for a smirk. Here's a sampling of emoticons:

:-) *Happy*
:-(*Sad*
:-o *Shocked or amazed*
:-] *Happy sarcasm or smirk*
X-(*Brain dead*
;-) *Winking*
:-* *Kiss*
:-‖ *Angry*
%-) *Happy confused*
:'-(*Crying*
]];-) *I wish I were Lyle Lovett*

Don't Send Junk Mail. You may get paid back in spades. The ease of [22] replying to an e-mail message makes it easy for recipients of junk mail to return the favor. They may even mail bomb your e-mail box, filling it with a steady stream of inflamed messages.

Remember: Your Boss May be Reading Your E-Mail. If you have a [23] yearning to be Rona Barrett, you'd better practice in the coffee room, not in your e-mail. Amazing as it sounds, the 1986 Electronic Communications Privacy Act states that employers have the right to read and monitor their employees' e-mail. In addition, e-mail is routinely saved in system backups, and these messages can come back to haunt you. The indictment of Gordon Eubanks, CEO of Symantec Corp., who is accused of conspiring to steal another company's trade secrets was based on e-mail messages found in his co-conspirator's e-mail archives.

24   ***Watch Your P's and Q's.*** Like it or not, good grammar and accurate spelling in e-mail messages can influence someone's opinion of you. There's even a cyberword for those who point out other people's grammar and spelling mistakes on the Internet. They're called "nit noids." Typos are inevitable, but it will make your message easier to read if words are spelled correctly and basic grammar rules are followed. No what we've meen?

25   Once you get in the habit of communicating via e-mail, the importance of the preceding suggestions will become self-evident. And if you've yet to join the electronic-mail revolution, just remember that e-mail is primarily a convenience tool, the ultimate Pony Express. It may seem intimidating at first, but eventually you too will ride off into the sunset of dataspace, a better connected and perhaps more articulate correspondent.

1   As Angell and Heslop see it, a realistic assessment of e-mail would have to take into account some of the ways that e-mail differs from sending letters or talking on the telephone or in person. What are some of the important differences (and potential disadvantages) between e-mail and these earlier forms of communication?

2   In the view of the authors, how can e-mail "seduce" (para. 9) users into poor writing and thinking habits? Would you consider e-mail a lazy person's alternative to writing a letter? Why or why not? What are some of the advantages and disadvantages of using the abbreviations known as acronyms and graphic forms of e-mail slang known as emoticons?

3   What effect has e-mail had, according to the authors, in democratizing the communication channels between employees at different levels of authority within corporations? If you have worked in a corporation, have you found e-mail to be more egalitarian than letter writing or telephoning? Discuss your experiences, which can include e-mail communications with teachers at your college.

4   What role do acronyms (for example, TTFN or IMHO) and emoticons (:-), etc.) play in e-mail? (Glossary: *Acronym, E-mail.*)

5   What language do Angell and Heslop employ to express the complexity of the cause-and-effect relationships they are analyzing? Where do they look beyond the obvious and superficial to examine the subject in some depth in terms of possible future and positive consequences of electronic communications? To what extent do they adopt a speculative approach outlining potential consequences of e-mail and its ramifications? (Glossary: *Cause and Effect.*)

6   Is there a single form of electronic communication that has had an overwhelming impact on your life? In a short essay, discuss its role and the changes it has brought,

both wanted and unwanted. (For example, are you more or less inclined to write letters if you have e-mail? Which would you rather use, keeping in mind you can decide not to mail a letter, but once e-mail is sent it cannot be recalled and may be available to be looked at for a long time?)

Women and Computers: *Paula Span*
Is There Equity in Cyberspace?

◆ PAULA SPAN is a journalist who writes for the *Washington Post Magazine*. The following essay describing how she came to navigate her way through cyberspace and overcame obstacles thrown in the path of women seeking access to the computer culture first appeared in the *Washington Post Magazine* (1994).

Cyberspace, according to Span, is a preeminently male realm, since it is mostly men who inhabit it. As children, boys are more likely to be interested in computers than are girls, and as men they tend to become more involved in the whole culture of computers. As Span endeavored to make her way into cyberspace, she discovered a network called WELL that remedied many of the problems she had encountered in other contexts in various chat rooms. WELL was such a positive experience for Span because it allowed her to communicate and socialize with many people. She allows the reader to get a glimpse of these interactions through narratives with her friends on the WELL. Her experiences are especially interesting because she is a good example of someone who did not grow up with computers but nonetheless overcame obstacles, such as insulting sexual innuendos and put-downs.

TO CONSIDER   Is there an intrinsically male bias to the Internet in terms of the way men act and the way women are treated? What kinds of things would have to be done to enable women and men to interact equally in cyberspace in the future? In your opinion, does the anonymity of cyberspace encourage male adults to act in ways they would never do in offices, in person, or on the telephone (i.e. like idiots)?

The love affair between men and computers was something I knew about but didn't really get, until that morning at the local coffee shop. My pal Pam and I were gabbing in the front booth when in walked Michael, a

---

friend and journalist about to take a leave from his newspaper to write a book. His first step, naturally, was to sink a significant chunk of his book advance into a shiny new computer. It was a beauty: worked faster than a speeding locomotive, boasted many megabytes of RAM, brewed cappuccino, etc.

Pam and I exchanged glances. This sounded familiar. She had written several books on an Apple so antediluvian that the company no longer manufactures it, and abandoned it only when it got damaged by clumsy movers. Yet her husband was about to invest in a pricey new CD-ROM rig, making unconvincing noises about how useful their daughter would find it for schoolwork. My own husband, as it happened, was also taking advantage of a new work assignment and plunging computer prices to replace the system he'd purchased just two years before, though his new machine wasn't as powerful as Michael's. ("Mike could fly to Chicago with that thing," he would later remark, wistfully.)

More speed. Better performance. With names like Quadra and Performa, computers even sound like cars these days. (Quick, is it a fastback or a sedan?) The women I know, who all primarily use these things for work, don't give them two seconds' thought unless they encounter some problem. On the other hand, a lot of the men I know ogle weird software in the MacWarehouse catalogue and always seem to require some new $200 gizmo that quacks.

"It's a guy thing," Pam and I decided, virtually in unison. Women treat computers like reliable station wagons: Learn how to make them take you where you want to go, and as long as they're functioning properly, who cares about pistons and horsepower? Computers are useful but unexciting. When something goes wrong, you call a mechanic.

Whereas guys, even those who never learned how to change an oil filter, are enamored of computers, want to play with them, upgrade them, fix them when they falter, compare theirs with the other guys'.

As an admitted technoklutz, I initially figured this observation might simply reflect my own prejudice, not to mention a small sample size. Computers, after all, were initially thought to be a field in which women would triumph. Computers had no history of discrimination. They had no history at all. They did not require biceps. They wouldn't be, to adopt the social science term, gendered.

Well. It turned out—as I started looking into the whole evolving subject of women, computers, on-line communications and other matters I had previously been unconcerned about-that computing is even more of a guy thing than I knew. That's worth paying attention to, not only for women but for our daughters (mine's 12). Yet I would also learn, as I ventured hesitantly into the computer communications realm dubbed cyberspace, that things don't have to stay this way.

Warning: The following article contains assorted generalizations and risks gender stereotyping.

For there are, no question, numerous males who are phobic about or merely uninterested in computing. And there are plenty of techie females, women who know their algorithms, who run major software companies, and who can clean the cat hair out of a trackball in 30 seconds or less.

But it's hard to overlook the stats. Who studies computer science? The Chronicle of Higher Education's latest numbers show that fewer than 30 percent of the people getting bachelor's and master's degrees are women and that fewer than one in seven doctorates is earned by a woman.

Who works in the industry? The Bureau of Labor Statistics reports that the percentage of women who are computer systems analysts and scientists has barely budged in a decade: It's still under 30 percent, even though nearly half a million more people have entered the field. Fewer than a third of computer programmers are women, as well, another statistic little changed since 1983.

Who pants over those fat, glossy computer magazines (PC World, Byte, MacUser) whose lustinspiring displays of software and laptops have been dubbed, by writer James Fallows, compuporn? Eighty percent of their readers are male, says the research firm Simmons MRI. (So are 85 percent of those who buy the newer and hipper Wired.)

Millions of women use computers at their jobs, of course, though often in routinized ways that leave the machines' more intriguing possibilities unexplored. But home computers, which after several years of significant growth still are found in only 31 percent of American homes, remain largely a male preserve. (And a middle-class preserve, but that's another story.) LINK Resources, a New York consulting firm, has found that in only a quarter of those homes is the primary user a woman.

As for cyberspace, about which more later, no one's hung a "No Girls Allowed" sign on the door. It's often a male clubhouse nonetheless, one girls can enter provided they are willing and able to scramble through the briers, shinny up the tree, ignore the skinned knees and announce that they can spit a watermelon seed just as far as the guys inside can. Figuratively speaking.

All of this reflects attitudes toward computers that form at unnervingly young ages.

Ten years ago, not long after Time magazine had declared the computer its Person of the Year, education journals started to fill with reports about the way schoolaged boys embraced computers while girls avoided them. Boys were more likely to have home computers and use them, to enroll in computer camps and summer programs, to take advantage of school computer labs, to elect high school computer courses. Academics who pay attention to these things say they haven't seen much dramatic change since.

So much for parents' assuring themselves that kids who've grown up in the Super Mario Era won't inherit their elders' anxieties and biases. The old patterns show considerable staying power. As early as first grade, according to a 1990 study in the Journal of Research and Development in Education, computer use is seen, by both boys and girls, as masculine. Reading and writing, on the other hand, have no perceived gender associations.

Researchers offer various explanations, including the well-documented aversion that many girls develop to math and science, the ever-popular lack-of-role-models theory, and the fact that many boys are introduced to computers through those kill-and-maim computer and video games that girls very sensibly disdain. (Who dubbed the control a joystick, anyway?) The disparity, however triggered, intensifies with age; by high school, girls may use computers to write their term papers (tests show that they're as competent at it as the guys), but deeper interest is suspect.

Computing's male aura may be one of the enduring legacies of the mythic hackers and nerds who patched together the early personal computers, hammered out breakthrough programs and invented computer bulletin boards. (A notorious few also dabbled in phone and credit-card fraud.) They were true trailblazers. In addition, they and their descendants are, as a subculture, so unappetizing—pale geeks without social skills who lose themselves in binary code, sci-fi sagas and chess gambits—that women develop "computational reticence" in response.

This, at least, is the theme developed by well-known MIT sociologist Sherry Turkle in an essay that's part of a 1988 collection called *Technology and Women's Voices.* Basing her analysis on interviews with college women who were doing well in computer courses but resisted identifying themselves as "computer science types," Turkle says that women "observe [the hackers'] obsessions, observe their antisensuality, observe the ways in which they have put things rather than people at the center of their lives and count themselves out."

It's not hard to understand why an adolescent boy might find computing seductive. At a time when sexual pressures and social demands loom threateningly large, the hacker culture offers autonomy, mastery, safety. "The hook is the feeling of power that it gives you: You control a world of your own making," says my friend Steve Adamczyk, an MIT grad who owns a software company called the Edison Design Group. (I'd call Steve a former nerd except that, he explains, "it's like being an alcoholic: You're always a nerd but you're a recovering nerd.") Staying up all night coding software in FORTRAN, as Steve did in high school, was "terrifically appealing to people who don't do so well at controlling the real world, maintaining relationships and all that."

Girls, though of course also buffeted by adolescence, have by that point been culturally programmed to maintain relationships. And those who withdraw generally seem to find safe havens other than computer labs.

As a small but influential cadre, hackers are also something of an alien species to non-nerd men. But men, Turkle writes, are apt to view hackers' achievements with admiration. Women, however many magazine stories they read about Bill Gates's net worth, are more likely to bolt.

The good news is that unlike some stubborn power imbalances requiring generations to redress (the composition of the U.S. Congress comes to mind), computer attitudes appear to be rather dramatically revisable. And such attempts are underway: This year, the National Science Foundation has more than tripled its funding for programs aimed at pulling girls and women into science, math and engineering. The boys-will-be-nerds paradigm "is just a throwback to separate spheres, simply a vestigial anachronism," announces Jo Sanders, of the Center for Advanced Study, City University of New York.

Sanders ran the NSF-funded Computer Equity Expert Project, a 30-month-long guerrilla campaign to increase girls' participation in math, science and technology by, well, gently but firmly smashing sexism. Sanders convened 200 teachers and administrators, representing every state, for week-long seminars on the causes and consequences of the gender gap and strategies for closing it. Back in their middle and high schools, these people taught computer equity workshops to their own faculties and recruited girls with everything from guest speakers to pizza parties.

The project, which ended last year, got results with startling speed. Reports flooded in:Within a year, an all-male advanced PASCAL class in Virginia turned 50 percent female and an all-male elective computer course in Oklahoma was nearly a third female, while a West Virginia computer club increased its female membership tenfold. "When you change attitudes," Sanders concludes, "the resistance just evaporates."

As for us grown-up women no longer facing math and science requirements, our resistance is also susceptible to change. What has been missing until recently, however, isn't just spine-stiffening; it's a motivation, some reason to acquire or cozy up to a computer, an incentive to struggle past the inevitable glitches.

For years, if you didn't need a computer for work, it has been hard to see what it would do for you. No one really needs to make that sort of investment in time and money to balance her checkbook, file her recipes (to cite one early personal-computer application that was supposed to turn us on) or handle ordinary correspondence. The love of gadgetry and tinkering that draws some men to computers as a hobby hasn't had much measurable impact on women.

What's been missing is the Killer App.

That's the term Silicon Valley types use for the breakthrough use, the irresistible application that finally makes a technological advance not just a toy but a useful tool, so that ordinary people look at it and say, "We need one of those." The Killer App for the desktop computer itself was the Lotus 1-2-3 spreadsheet. The Killer App for microwave ovens, now in 80 percent of homes, was probably reheating leftovers, or maybe popping corn.

The Killer App that draws women into computer use in significant numbers, researchers tell me, will be communication. With a cheap modem and a few commands that connect you to a network, you can reach out and touch people you know and hundreds of thousands of people you don't and discuss everything from breastfeeding to foreign policy. This isn't technology, this is expression, relationships, community, all the things women are taught to be skilled at.

Cyberspace isn't as brave-new-world as the name makes it sound. Reva Basch, whom I've recently met-by-modem on a computer conferencing system called the WELL, told me this story: "My mother-in-law, who's 80, was visiting and expressed curiosity about the WELL. I showed it to her, showed her some of the conferences. She said, 'Why, honey, it's just talking, isn't it?' She got it."

My daughter, Emma, was my guide at first. Growing up with parents who use computers (however rudimentarily) and encourage her to do likewise, plus hours of playing Nintendo and computer games with friends who are boys, seems to have immunized her against computer-aversion. She's not fascinated by the things, exactly, but she's entirely unthreatened by them. So, six weeks before I began writing this essay, I nervously sat down at the Macintosh bequeathed to her when my husband, partly for that very reason, bought his latest. She patiently showed me how to log on to America Online, the country's third largest computer communications system.

America Online is easy to use, even for a neophyte. It has a welcoming "interface," a display of onscreen symbols to point to and click at, so that you can read highlights from USA Today and the Atlantic, send electronic mail ("E-mail") to friends and strangers, scroll through 406 messages from fans of Smashing Pumpkins and add your own in the RockLink Forum, or join as many as 22 other users all typing away at each other in "real time" in each of dozens of "lobbies" and "chat areas." It's gotten so popular and grown so fast that the system grew temporarily choked and sluggish this winter from overuse by its 600,000 subscribers.

I found AOL reassuringly simple but not particularly simpatico and so, two weeks later, I logged onto the WELL, a Sausalito-based network founded in 1985 by the folks who published the Whole Earth Catalogue. This was not simple, and resulted in the humiliation of repeatedly having to dash down two flights of stairs to ask my husband (already a WELLbeing), "How do you get to an OK prompt?," then dash back up. But I've figured out enough to be able to send and receive E-mail and join in the conversation. I've entered cyberspace.

It's become part of the daily routine: I brush my teeth; I go to my aerobics class; I dial the WELL. Once there, I check my E-mail box (an on-line friend from Massachusetts says revisions on her novel are going well; an on-line friend and new dad in California says the baby slept five hours last night). I usually visit Women on the WELL first (no guys allowed) to learn the latest depressing or exhilarating details of the lives of women I've never met but am coming to know anyway, to commiserate or cheer them on, to complain that I've gained three pounds.

Then I venture out to see who's arguing about what topic in the media conference and who's soliciting advice in the parenting conference. If I care to, I add my own comments, stories, jokes, requests for information and general two cents' worth. If I had hours to spend at this, as some folks seem to, I could join conferences where people are yakking about politics, bicycling, sex, Judaism, AIDS, the Grateful Dead and a zillion other passions and problems.

I haven't yet dared the next step, which is using the WELL to access the Internet, the vast global aggregation of computer networks that would allow me to use countless libraries and databases, join hundreds more conferences, and tell *millions* of people that I've gained three pounds. But I could. And someday, depending on how much of the prattling about the "information superhighway" and its services one chooses to believe, I'll use a computer (attached discreetly to my television) to make rental movies pop up on my TV screen, buy everything from groceries to mutual funds, take the courses I need to finish my master's degree. It all looks quite prosaic at this point—just lines of text appearing on my screen—but it feels very exciting.

At the moment, cyberspace is populated primarily by—did you guess this?—men. The WELL has only about 15 to 18 percent women among its 8,000 subscribers, its managers believe, a proportion considered representative of most conferencing or "bulletin board" systems (BBSs). Even the big on-line services that spend bundles on advertising and direct mail have drawn few female subscribers (though they believe that many women and children log on using men's accounts). Most of CompuServe's 1.5 million subscribers are guys (90 percent) and so are most of America Online's (85 percent); Prodigy claims to be the most egalitarian of the big on-line services with a 30 percent female membership.

Yet these are numbers that could change quickly and dramatically, as women learn that even those who don't know bauds from broads can use a BBS (believe me when I tell you) and—more significantly—learn that there are reasons to.

I give you Sarah Randolph, the poet who co-hosts the WELL's writers conference, who lives in a small seaside town and was "just really hungry for conversation and life" when she bought a modem and joined this odd little community. Through it she's made friends, picked up writing jobs, and learned how to increase her garden's broccoli yield. It isn't a substitute for having real people around, yet it has its own rewards. "In the real world, there's your body. Your body is shy and needs something to hold on to at a party," she muses. On-line, "I feel fairly transparent . . . I feel like I can go anywhere in that world."

I give you Patrizia DiLucchio, who read about the WELL a few years ago while writing her dissertation "on an extremely dry topic" and thought "it sounded like having pen pals . . . like putting messages in bottles and sending them out to alien shores." Now, because she lives in the San Francisco area, the WELL's home port, "half the people I hang out with in real life I met on the WELL." She also had a heavy-duty romance of several years' duration with a fellow WELLperson, and she's hardly the only one: "To some extent, all bulletin boards are interactive personals ads."

I give you Ellen Pack, president of a new on-line service that reverses the usual stats (10 percent of its members are male) called Women's Wire. Along with the databases on women's health, the updates on legislation and such, Women's Wire lets Pack, a San Franciscan, stay in touch with her parents and sisters in New York via E-mail. "My mom is 65 and not particularly computer-literate, but I got her a Mac and now she logs on," Pack reports. "It doesn't replace face-to-face or the occasional phone call, but I communicate with them so much more now because it's sooo easy." E-mail is cheaper and more convenient than long distance telephoning, and, Pack points out, "it lets you have all the incremental communications, things you wouldn't pick up the phone for."

I give you, moreover, my friend Pam, who sallied into cyberspace about the same time I did and is busily researching her new book via America Online. We agree that our most serious current problem with computer networks is that work and family obligations can really cut into the time we spend on-line.

And yet. The thing about cyberspace is that although sometimes it feels like a sophisticated graduate seminar or a good-natured pub, it can also, for women, feel like a walk past a construction site or a wrong turn down a dark street. Like life itself, it requires tactical decisions about how to proceed in a not-always-welcoming sphere: Do you opt for a strategic retreat into protected bunkers? Lobby for reform? Take a deep breath and wade in swinging?

For cyberspace is not an alternate, genderless universe. College women report dopey sexist limericks and images of breasts sent via computer nets. Women can be publicly propositioned or stalked by E-mail suitors who hurl abuse when they get rejected. My daughter, visiting an America Online gathering called Teen Chat, is regularly invited by the teenaged boys who predominate therein to enter a private "room." Sometimes she sees whether they have anything interesting to say. Sometimes she Just Types No.

I have watched as someone named Stacey logged onto an AOL book discussion group, introduced herself as a newcomer, then disappeared from the screen for a while. She came back long enough to type out, "What are all these messages?" She'd been flooded with IMs—instant messages directed only to her. The other women in the group pointed out that her female ID had made her a target for attention. It was at this point that, although I had not encountered such treatment, I changed my own ID to something offering no gender clues. The problem, hardly limited to America Online, is widely reported. "You seek out your friends and places you know are safe and harassment-free," an AOL subscriber named Citywoman tells me via E-mail.

You don't have to sit still for such annoyances, of course. Many on-line systems have some sort of recourse, hosts or monitors who chastise offenders, or policies that can toss a persistent harasser off the net. On the WELL, a "bozofilter" command allows you to simply never hear from a given user again, an option I'd find useful in everyday existence. You can change an ID like Citywoman to a string of numbers or to JackSpratt. You can confront jerks.

Still, if cyberspace were a workplace, this stuff would qualify as creating a hostile environment. "Hearing that incidents happen probably discourages some women who haven't even tried going on-line," worries Reva Basch, who co-hosts the cozy Women on the WELL conference. "They'll say, 'Oooh, you'll get cruised and hit on. Who needs it? I get enough of that on my job.'"

It was Basch who alerted the WELL at large to another way in which cyberspace can mirror life: the discovery last summer that a "cybercad" had been romancing several WELLwomen simultaneously, exchanging erotic E-mail with each of them without the others' knowledge, going so far as to visit one woman using a plane ticket she helped pay for. The incident, first reported in this newspaper, sparked weeks of heated discussion about whether and how this sort-of community should respond. The cad eventually resigned his account voluntarily, but left behind a lot of unanswered questions about what the differences between behavior on-line and behavior IRL (in real life) are and ought to be.

And if it's tough to figure out what to do about virtual knavery, what to do about a virtual rape? It happened in a computer-generated environment developed by Xerox researchers in Palo Alto, Calif., reachable through the Internet and called LambdaMOO. In this fantasy domain, a kind of multi-authored fictional work-in-progress known to its denizens as "the MOO," a motley array of characters glide through many rooms, doing and saying what users sitting at their terminals (mostly college and graduate students in their late teens and early twenties, three-fourths of them male) tell them to do and say. Last year, in an incident vividly reported in the Village Voice, a crude jester named Mr. Bungle sexually assaulted several other LambdaMOO characters in a rampage of intensifying verbal violence. The ensuing sociopolitical debate was fierce and prolonged.

Civilization—as designed by Pavel Curtis, who heads the Xerox Social Virtual Reality Project—has now come to the MOO. An arrangement of petitions and ballots allows users to modify the system, request arbitration, seek justice. In the on-line world, Curtis concludes, "the medium is different, but the people are the same."

Less dramatic than rape or harassment, but a deterrent nevertheless to bringing women into cyberspace, is the matter of style. Here again, the hackers of yore have left their fingerprints all over the world they helped create. Hackers were known for a strong anti-authoritarian streak, a libertarian philosophy that resisted rules, controls, the restrictive codes of real life. They also adopted on-line a style of expression that reflected all the maturity, nuance and nurturing qualities of 17-year-old boys. (A recent press release about a book on women and information technology, for example, posted on a University of Illinois network, brought immediate and snarky attacks on the woman who'd written the release. "Who is she, a cow who belongs to NOW?" "A member of Dykes on Bikes?")

This is the clubhouse atmosphere that greets the tentative newcomer of either gender. Nets and conferences have their own varying personalities, but many of them offer no-holds-barred arguments and aggressive put-downs, a rambunctious interplay (known as "flaming") in which women, vastly outnumbered, find their contributions derided or simply ignored. Academics analyzing "netiquette" have pointed out that both men and women respond more to men's messages. Some women charge in and give as good as they get; others retreat.

The WELL, for instance, seems a reasonably civil place with an egalitarian tradition, where conflict-avoidance abbreviations like "imho" (in my humble opinion) and "YMMV" (your mileage may vary) abound. Yet even here, there are women who feel more comfortable in the supportive confines of the women's conference and rarely leave it (though others find it earnest and too polite and rarely enter). During an on-line flap about "male discourse," a woman named Tigereye kept the history conference at a boil for weeks with remarks about the "traditional male style of communication involving gratuitous one-upmanship, insult and posturing we can readily observe on the WELL."

What if women dominated the net and set the tone? To find out, Nancy Baym, a University of Illinois doctoral candidate, has immersed herself in a Usenet group called rec.arts.tv.soaps, devoted to discussion of soap operas. (And referred to as RATS, which is why Baym hopes to title her dissertation "Of RATS and Women.") Its participants are largely female engineers, techies and academics who like to break up their workdays with discussions on such topics as, "Is Dixie a Ho'?"

Wading through 7,000 posted messages on the subject of "All My Children," Baym found a language of elaborate courtesy. "They use a lot of politeness strategies to make disagreement nonthreatening," she reports. "They'll try to build the esteem of the person they're disagreeing with: 'Jane, I see your point of view, but I must say . . .' Alternately, they'll diminish the force of their disagreement, qualify things: 'I could be wrong but . . .' In the soap group, the netiquette is, don't insult people. If you look at groups discussing 'Star Trek,' they'll say, 'Stay off the 'Net, you Nazi!' "

Groans all around. Somewhere between enforcing Nice Networks for women, and having women set upon by wolf packs roaming the Internet, there must be a workable middle ground. I count myself among the optimists, partly because there are systems that demonstrate the possibility of egalitarianism. It doesn't happen by accident, but it does happen.

ECHO, a New York-based bulletin board, is more than 50 percent female, an achievement attributed to its founder's determination to lure women in by means of tutorials, a mentoring program and reduced rates. Arlington's Meta-systems Design Group operates the Meta Network, a conferencing system that is also more than half female—and aspires to be a no-flame zone.

"We do all the things good moderators do in person," says Metasystems partner Lisa Kimball. On the Meta Net, new members get buddies, flamers get a private talking-to, welcomes are issued the first time someone speaks up on-line, yet the opinions fly. "It's like arriving at a big party with lots of people," Kimball says. "One issue is finding out where the bar is, but it's even better when the hostess says, 'I'm so glad you're here. There's someone over on the other side of the room I think you'd like to meet.' "

One of the elders of cyberspace, who has founded bulletin boards in many places, is Dave Hughes, a k a the Cursor Cowboy. He now runs the Old Colorado City Electronic Cottage, based in Colorado Springs, from which perspective he can see the analogy between that onetime frontier and this one. "It's the same as going into the gold rush towns," the Cowboy observes. "Males jump onto their horses, set up these roistering places, saloons and all. As soon as you begin to approach one-third to one-half of the population being women . . . you still have the saloons and the hoop-de-doo, but you also have the schools.

"It's the same in the on-line world, dominated by men, their language, their interests . . . The moment a woman goes on-line, she's a target for all sorts of things, like the gal that came into town on the stage . . . [On-line women] have to be like frontier women, a little tougher-skinned . . . They have to master all kinds of skills they didn't know before. But as the numbers increase, the language changes, the subjects begin to reflect a more balanced society."

Does it matter? I vote yes.

True, people of either gender can still live meaningful lives without computers. If I never progressed beyond the half-dozen commands necessary to send my stories to The Washington Post, I might suffer little handicap. I don't think that will be true for my daughter, though, or any of our daughters. They're entering a world in which card catalogue drawers have already vanished from the public library, replaced by terminals and keyboards.

Perhaps they won't need to be whiz-bang programmers (though it wouldn't hurt). But they can't afford to see computers as toys for boys, to see ignorance as feminine, to wring their hands over the keyboard and worry that they'll break something.

"A sense of yourself as a technologically competent person is no small shakes in this world," Jo Sanders of City University says. "It builds confidence in yourself as a problem-solver. It's important on a résumé whether or not the job you're interested in uses computers . . . It's proof that you are able to learn things, a certificate of capability."

I recall, 20 years ago—as women were trying to free themselves from a set of social expectations that has already changed startlingly—a brief vogue for feminist courses in auto repair. Whether or not you could afford to have someone change your oil or your tire, a sense of independence and mastery of the world demanded that you take on the guy things. You wanted to demonstrate to yourself and others that you could change spark plugs even if, once having proven it, you went back to dropping your VW Bug off at the local garage.

More and more, the computer world feels like that. Women have to be in it because incompetence is an unattractive trait. Women have to be in it because decisions about language and culture and access are being made and we should be involved in making them. Women have to be in it because, although nobody really knows what form all this technology will take, there shouldn't be any clubhouse we're afraid to climb into.

I think that because of timely early intervention, Emma will handle the clubhouse just fine.

As for myself, I'm not afraid of the guys inside, but I dread the technical challenge of climbing the tree. Still, a couple of weeks ago, I logged on and typed in "support" and ordered the WELL User's Manual, Version 5.1a. It arrived recently, a fat and daunting volume that tells you when to use "!sz -a*" as opposed to "!xm stky my*." I'm sure there are dozens of elegant functions in it that I don't need and may never master, just as I doubt that I'll ever drool over the compu-porn in Byte or order RAM-doublers by mail.

But I need to know how to download. I've got to learn how to move files around. So I'm going to wade in. It was sort of a kick, late the other night, when Tigereye taught me, via E-mail, how to extract. It wasn't so difficult; I just typed "!extract -u tigereye history" and the stuff poured forth in waves.

---

1 Span uses a variety of means to support her characterization that the computer culture is male-dominated. What statistics support her assertion? How does the discrepancy between male and female interests stem from childhood? In Span's view, what explains why girls' attitudes toward computers are functional, while boys get more deeply involved with them? What do they represent for boys that they do not represent for girls? How is this difference illustrated in its most extreme form by the hacker?

2 How did the WELL offer Span a portal into cyberspace without the downside of harrassment by males that is so prevalent elsewhere? What form did this harrassment take and what is Span's explanation for it? How does the WELL make it possible to share her experiences and exchange opinions with people all over the country?

3 Have you ever logged onto a "chat room" or BBS? Based on your own experiences, is Span's assessment accurate regarding the way conversations are conducted, the topics that are discussed, the male-female ratio, and the queries made and questions asked? Have you encountered punters or flamers, exchanged pics, read member profiles, or had to activate privacy preferences to shut out IMs? Discuss your answer in relation to the question Span poses in the title.

4 Span has synthesized information from a variety of sources including academic surveys and studies (*Journal of Research and Development in Education,* MIT sociologist Sherry Terkle, among others) and her own experiences. Do you find the conclusions she reaches based on objective sources to be more or less credible than those based on her own experiences ? (Glossary: *Evidence, Objective/Subjective.*)

5 What means does Span use to keep her vantage point consistent throughout the entire narrative? Where does she allow the reader to hear what people said or wrote to each other as a way of making her narrative more immediate and lively? (Glossary: *Narration.*)

6 Do you believe women should be granted special protections on the Internet? What governmental regulations now exist or should be established to protect Internet users, whether male or female?

The Electronic Palimpsest   *Brian Hayes*

◆ BRIAN HAYES writes for *The Sciences,* a magazine aimed at a broadly informed audience. This essay first appeared in the September/October issue of 1991.

Without a doubt, computers permit a more convenient form of writing in which you can rearrange sentences or paragraphs and generate as many drafts as you wish. The problem is that preliminary drafts that might have contained good ideas are normally erased as new versions are generated. By contrast, paper drafts have always served as a record of the composing process. Hayes makes this point to illustrate how scholarship has changed, and will preclude the kind of study scholars have done of, for example, manuscripts of Lord Byron and William Wordsworth. Moreover, there is no foolproof method for verifying when an electronically produced document was composed, even when encryption devices and time-stamping services are used. Lastly, given the rapid change in hardware

---

Brian Hayes, "The Electronic Palimpsest" from *The Sciences.* This article is reprinted by permission of *The Sciences* and is from the September/October 1991 issue. Individual subscriptions are $28 per year. Write to: *The Sciences,* 2 East 63rd Street, New York, NY 10021.

and software, there is no guarantee that anyone in the future will be able to retrieve and read any electronically stored documents of the past.

TO CONSIDER   How has computer-based writing changed the way you compose, revise, and think about what you write? Do you find it makes a difference that your earlier drafts disappear and you are left with only the final draft?

---

pal-imp-sest (pal' imp sest'), n: a parchment from which writing has been partially or completely erased to make room for another text

The Random House Dictionary, 1980, p. 634

As a writing instrument, the computer is not so much a better pencil as a better eraser. Although it serves well enough to put words on the page, where it really excels is in wiping them out again. Writing with a computer affords you the luxury of changing your mind, again and again, without penalty. The excised word leaves no scar; the page never becomes gray or tattered from rubbing; the margins do not fill up with afterthoughts; there is no tangle of arrows showing how sentences are to be rearranged. When you write on the glass screen, the world need never know how you labored to achieve that easygoing prose style. Indeed, this very paragraph conceals the tortured history of its own composition: you the reader cannot see in the space between the lines how I have revised it, a dozen times or more, until hardly a word of the first draft survives.

When I got my first chance to write with a computer, it was an exhilarating experience. I would insert a word into the middle of a paragraph and marvel as all the following words automatically rearranged themselves to make room, cascading from line to line in a kind of domino effect. Or I would hold down the delete key and suck up whole sentences like spaghetti. Suddenly prose became a kind of clay that never hardens, a medium that one can always reshape yet again.

But if the plasticity of electronic text is a great liberation for the author, it can also license the forger, the plagiarist, the swindler, the impostor; and it is not an unmixed blessing for the scholar, the historian or even the ordinary reader. Words stored in electronic form are in certain ways less secure and less permanent than words on paper. When writing is inscribed in the magnetic domains of a spinning disk, can one trust its integrity? Fifty years from now, will anyone even be able to read it? As more of the world's documents migrate from memo pads and filing cabinets and bookshelves into computer memories, those questions are going to take on considerable importance.

One way of exploring the issues is to imagine a world without paper, in which all documents are electronic. Such a world is not far off. True, the "paperless office" has so far turned out to be a bad joke, as office paper consumption doubles every four years. But all those pages spewing out of all those laser printers are coming from computers. In many cases the computer files are already the primary versions of the documents, and the printouts are just a means of distribution or archival storage. In the long run, paper will surely be supplanted in those roles as well.

The first thing you notice in a paperless world is that certain awkward situations become even more awkward:

You receive a letter (in the form of a computer file) in which your long-lost sister claims she is being held in a Turkish prison for crimes she didn't commit: Please send her $20,000 to bribe the prosecutor. How do you establish that the letter was written by your sister?

A Washington friend asks you to take a discreet look around someone else's office late one night. In case you get into any trouble, he gives you a letter, stored on a computer disk, that explains the importance of your work to the nation's security. When you are charged with burglary, however, the friend disclaims all knowledge of the letter—and of you. How can you prove the letter is not a forgery? Note that this task is harder than the first one. With the letter from your sister, you need only convince *yourself* of its authenticity; to avoid jail—or at least to take your friend with you—you must convince a judge and a jury of the letter's provenance.

You pick up a hitchhiker in the desert, and in gratitude for that small kindness he gives you a floppy disk bearing a promise of millions of dollars upon his death. How do you prove the bequest is from Howard Hughes? Again, you must demonstrate to others that the document is genuine. Furthermore, you may well have to show not only that Hughes wrote the note but also that you have not altered it (changing "two million" to "two hundred million," say).

In the world of paper documents the primary tool for settling such controversies is the examination of handwriting. You know the letter is from your sister because you recognize her hand; experts compare your cover letter from the White House or your note from Howard Hughes with specimens known to be authentic. But the bits and bytes of a computerized document are all alike, with none of the idiosyncrasies that might identify individual authorship. Anyone could have typed those letters, on almost any computer.

The introduction of "pen"-based computers, which substitute a stylus for a keyboard, will not solve the problem. On such a machine one might confect an ornate and quite inimitable signature, ending with the most swashbuckling paraph, but a document signed in that way offers only a weak warrant of authenticity. The reason is that such a digitized signature—or any other graphic object—can be copied in an instant with the help of a computer. Give me one "signed" electronic document, and I can forge your name to anything I please. As a matter of fact, the widespread availability of high-resolution scanning and printing equipment raises questions about the security of signatures on paper. There is nothing the modern forger might need that can't be found at the local Kinko's.

Digital documents can be signed, however; what is needed is not a digitized signature but a truly digital one. A technique for creating such signatures was proposed in 1976 by Whitfield Diffie and Martin E. Hellman, both then at Stanford University, as part of their ingenious public-key cryptosystem; the idea was refined a few years later by Ronald L. Rivest, Adi Shamir and Leonard Adleman (a triumvirate known as RSA), all then at MIT. In the RSA cryptosystem each user has two keys, one of which is made public and the other is held in secret. A message encrypted with the public key can be decrypted with the private key, and vice versa.

When the system is used for secrecy, a message is encrypted with the recipient's public key (which anyone can look up in a directory); then only the recipient can decrypt the message with the corresponding private key. A simple variation on the protocol yields highly secure digital signatures. To sign a document, you encrypt a copy of it with your private key. Anyone can then verify the signature by decrypting it with your public key. The mechanism works like Cinderella's slipper: whoever owns the key that fits must be the author of the document.

A further refinement has since been added to the digital- signature protocol. If you encrypt an entire document in order to sign it, the signature is as large as the document itself. To reduce the bulk, and at the same time avoid a subtle weakness lurking in the original scheme, the document is collapsed to a "digest" of just 160 bits, and then only the digest is signed. The digesting is done in such a way that even the slightest change to the document is almost certain to yield an entirely different digest. The recipient verifies the signature by applying the digesting algorithm to the document and decrypting the digest with the sender's public key; the result should match the supplied signature.

The National Institute of Standards and Technology is at work on a digital-signature standard based on the public-key principle. The standard-setting process has been going on for years, buffeted by much controversy, but it now appears to be nearing a conclusion.

Digital signatures would probably deal quite well with the three situations described above. If signatures accompanying the letter from the Turkish prison and the note from Howard Hughes could be decrypted with the appropriate public keys, that would count as strong evidence for the documents' authenticity. Similarly, your Washington friend would have a hard time disowning a letter that had been signed by means of encryption with his own private key. The signatures also protect against after-the-fact tampering. There is no way you could have exaggerated Hughes's generosity in the signed bequest without knowing his private key.

Although digital signatures are dashed clever, they fall short of solving all the problems of the paperless society.

It might seem at first that digital signatures would provide all the security necessary for a system of electronic checks. To pay your rent, you would merely type a note on the computer, or fill in a template, stating the date, the amount and the payee and identifying your bank and your account number; then you would sign the check with your private key and send it off by electronic mail; the recipient would sign it as an endorsement and mail it on to his own bank. You would be confident that your unscrupulous landlord could not alter the amount, because the bank would detect the change when it verified your signature. Unfortunately, you would remain vulnerable to a cruder kind of fraud. The computer is not only a good eraser but also a flawless copier, and your landlord could simply duplicate your check (along with its signature) and deposit multiple copies, all of which would appear equally authentic. Rivest, Shamir and Adleman suggest including a unique serial number in each signed check and requiring banks to accept only one check with a given serial number. But that puts the onus of vigilance and record keeping on the banks, which may be reluctant to accept it.

Another problem arises when readers must verify not only the authorship and the integrity of a document but also its time of composition. In your computerized laboratory notebook you record the discovery of a new comet or a new virus, and you apply a digital signature to the entry. Later, a rival challenges your claim to priority. Naturally you included the date in your signed notebook entry, but your opponent is not much impressed by that evidence. He points out that the digital signature prevents others from tampering with the document, but since you know your own secret key, you could alter the date—or alter other parts of the document—at any time, then resign it. In other words, the signature proves that you wrote the notebook entry, but it cannot establish when you wrote it.

With paper documents there are at least two ways of dealing with the problem. First, important documents are witnessed as well as signed, and the witnesses can later be called to attest to the dating of the material. That practice can be adopted just as easily with digital signatures. Second, laboratory notes are generally kept in a bound volume with numbered pages, so that sheets cannot be inserted or removed. When disputes arise, the notebook will be credible evidence only if it can be read as a complete, continuous and contemporaneous record of laboratory activity. The pages must be filled up in sequence, without leaving gaps where back-dated entries might be inserted. In the recent controversy over the work of Thereza Imanishi-Kari of Tufts University, the U.S. Secret Service was asked to examine certain notebooks in an attempt to verify the chronology of the entries.

A laboratory record kept on a computer is more like a loose-leaf notebook than like a bound volume. New entries can be inserted anywhere in the sequence, or existing entries can be moved around; dates can be misstated or changed after the fact. But a solution is at hand. Inspired by the Imanishi-Kari case, Stuart A. Haber and W. Scott Stornetta of Bell Communications Research (Bellcore), in Piscataway, New Jersey, have devised a time-stamping service for electronic documents. The scheme is conceptually similar to public-key cryptography. When your notebook needs to be validated, you submit a digest to the time-stamping computer, which returns a "certificate" that encodes the time of receipt and other information.

But what if the time-stamping service itself cannot be trusted? For example, someone might tamper with the time-stamping computer, perhaps resetting the clock for long enough to create a fraudulent certificate, then restoring the clock to the correct current value. As protection against such deceptions, each certificate is combined with others issued at about the same time in a treelike structure; the single certificate at the root of the tree, whose value depends on all the individual certificates, is publicly posted. During preliminary trials of the service, documents are being time-stamped in weekly batches, and the root certificates are being published every Sunday in the Public Notices section of *The New York Times*. A certificate for any document stamped in the past week can be verified by rederiving the published root value. (A question that remains for the future is what will happen when *The New York Times* is published electronically instead of on paper.)

Even documents that no one would dream of having time-stamped or witnessed sometimes come under scrutiny. For example, George Bush has made public some of his private diaries in an attempt to establish what he didn't know (and when he didn't know it) about the sale of arms to Iran during his vice-presidency. Suppose Bush had kept his diary on a computer instead of on paper: he would have had great difficulty convincing his critics that no entries had been altered, deleted or back-dated.

Of course another major cache of documentary evidence in the Iran-Contra affair was in electronic form: the electronic mail messages of Oliver North. Curiously, those messages were accepted as authentic and unaltered precisely because North had deleted them (or rather had tried to delete them) from the disk memory of his computer. They were recovered through a sector-by-sector examination of the contents of the disk. If North had instead copied all the files onto floppy disks and voluntarily handed them over to congressional investigators, the messages would surely have been viewed with greater skepticism. (The hard-core conspiracy theorist knows that the supposed deletion and subsequent recovery of the messages was all a carefully staged means of increasing the credibility of concocted evidence. That some of the recovered messages were incriminating counts for nothing, apart from demonstrating that the real messages must have been much worse.)

The handling of legal documents is certainly not the only domain in which a conversion to electronic storage and transmission will change the nature of writing. Even personal correspondence is affected. For example, consider the art of the deft postscript. At the end of a chatty letter home, below the signature, you add, "P.S. I've just heard from Stockholm. Good news." Now, it may be that word of your Nobel prize reached you in the moments after the letter was finished but before it was sealed, but it's also possible that you turned the announcement into a casual afterthought purely for rhetorical effect. With a letter on paper, the recipient could never be quite sure. But with an electronic letter, "P.S." is almost certainly an artifice. After all, with a word processor it is no more trouble to add a sentence at the beginning than at the end.

Other rhetorical devices also lose a bit of their impact. In a letter on paper you might write, "Say hi to ~~dreary~~ dreary old Dad," where the strike-through is very much a part of the joke. With a computer, since any mistake can be silently and invisibly corrected, the same trick seems more contrived, less spontaneous.

When a manuscript is being prepared for publication, the kind of invisible mending made possible by computers is often a handicap. Traditionally an editor would return to the author a marked-up copy of the original manuscript, showing all the proposed changes and corrections. When the editing is done with a computer, that record of alterations generally disappears. In fact, software solutions are available for that problem; they are just not widely used. Many word-processing programs offer a "red-lining" mode, which displays insertions and deletions explicitly (though seldom as clearly as they can be with a red pencil). There are also special-purpose programs for annotating text, and the contributions of multiple editors are identified by color.

Such tools may capture an editor's changes, but what about the author's transformations of the work during its composition? Few writers have the patience to document every stage in the creation of a novel or a poem (much less a love letter or a business memorandum). Indeed, some authors would cite as an advantage of computerized writing the end of old drafts and scribbled notes; all that remains of those scraps is now seamlessly integrated into the final text. From the scholar's point of view, however, a valuable source of information is being lost.

Take William Wordsworth's long autobiographical poem *The Prelude*. Fragments of the poem are known from as early as 1798; several versions were composed between 1799 and 1804; Wordsworth made sporadic revisions until 1839; various further emendations were introduced by others before a new edition was published soon after the poet's death in 1850. Dozens of manuscript sources survive, and they have enabled scholars to reconstruct the poem's compositional history in detail. There is no consensus among modern readers that the final state of the poem is the best; indeed, the 1805 version has many partisans. Yet if Wordsworth had had a PC, the history of the poem would probably be lost.

Lord Byron is another intriguing case. He presented himself to the world as an aristocrat of letters whose verses were casual, offhand productions, which he would not deign to correct or revise. Had he been writing with a computer (I imagine him toting the latest laptop model across the Alps into Italy), he might have gotten away with that fib. But recently published facsimiles of his manuscripts show just how labored his process of composition was. A reviewer describes the manuscripts as "bristling with added stanzas, overwritten crosswise, with false starts, impatient deletions, emendations, and adjustments of rhymes." A modern Byron can readily conceal all signs of such unseemly labor, and as a result readers of the next century will likely find that manuscript sources for authors of the 1990s are rather scanty. Information that might well have been preserved on paper is being lost on disk.

The loss is not inevitable, and the cause is not really technological. As a matter of fact, keeping a complete archive of a life's work is surely easier with a computer than it is with a filing cabinet. One approach—one of many—is the WORM drive: a disk memory that can be written on and read from but never erased. (WORM stands for "write once, read many.") WORM drives have ample storage capacity; a single disk would hold all the versions of all the works of a Wordsworth or a Byron, along with all his journals and correspondence. The trouble is, adopting such a device amounts to a declaration that one's every word is worth preserving—which is even more obnoxious than the pose of the poet who claims he never cancels a line.

Still, somewhere in America today there must be a writer of merit who is either meticulously or absentmindedly saving her complete oeuvre as a series of computer files. Fifty years from now some lucky scholar will sit down in a library carrel to unseal the treasure. There they'll be, packed in a cardboard carton: 600 eight-inch floppy disks from a Radio Shack TRS-80 Model 1. What is the probability anyone will be able to read them? Even supposing the information encoded on the disks has survived, where would one go in the year 2043 to find a working TRS-80? And a copy of the Electric Pencil, the word-processing program the author used to create her works?

It is curious that archival longevity seems to be the last thing anyone worries about when choosing computer hardware and software. In picking a word processor for my own use, for example, I have focused mainly on ease and speed of editing, and the elegance of the on-screen display; I've thought very little about how I will read my own files a few decades from now, when I will have gone on to another computer, another word processor, another disk format (if indeed the very notion of "word processor" or "disk format" is still meaningful). I should know better. I've changed computers five times in ten years. Every few months I need to resurrect a document from some long-gone system, and I spend an exasperating hour puzzling over cryptic formatting commands that were once intimately familiar. What does "@ |" mean again? And "♦HYØ♦"?

I'm not the only one with such a narrowly constrained time horizon. The computer I'm writing on at this moment thinks the world will end in 2040.

Both buyers and sellers of software pay a good deal of attention to the transfer of information between different programs and computer systems, but the emphasis is on synchronic rather than diachronic transfers. We worry about how to move a WordPerfect file on an IBM PC onto an Apple Macintosh equipped with Microsoft Word; we don't pause to ask how our descendants will read any of those files in a century or two, when WordPerfect, IBM, Apple Computer and even Microsoft are only dim memories.

Given all the drawbacks and disadvantages of electronic documents, why not just stick with paper? The best way of answering that question is to look back on the one other occasion in human history when a writing medium was replaced. To societies accustomed to writing on stone or clay, paper must have seemed terribly ephemeral stuff, vulnerable to fire and water, with inscribed marks that all too easily smudged or bleached away. And yet paper prevailed. Moses' tablets were stone, but the story of Moses was told on paper. The economic incentives were just too powerful to be ignored: with paper, information became far cheaper to record, to store and to transport. Exactly the same considerations argue that a transition to paperless, electronic writing is now inevitable.

In any case, eternity is too much to ask of any storage medium. Libraries are full of disintegrating paper books; graveyards are full of stone tablets eroded to illegibility; even languages die. Perhaps the best advice, if you must write for the ages, is this: Write very well. In the centuries to come no one will be reading your verses or your novels because they are stored as WordStar files on 1.2

megabyte floppy disks; but maybe someone will preserve the equipment needed to decipher those files and disks if that's the only way to read your deathless works.

1　How has the ease with which writers can rearrange sentences or paragraphs on computers created a problem for scholars—a problem they never faced before in creating a history of the evolution of a literary work, such as those by Lord Byron and William Wordsworth (para. 27–28)?

2　Why has authenticating a document's author and time of composition become unreliable because of computers? What procedures have been instituted to rectify this problem? How reliable are they? Why might the work of an author stored in electronic form in the present be difficult to read in the future?

3　How have computers changed the methods you use in the way you write? Do you save previous drafts for good ideas that did not get developed in the final paper? Do you revise as you write? Have you encountered problems with a mismatch of programs and incompatible formats used to retrieve documents that were saved in another form? If you were to extrapolate from your experience into the future, why wouldn't what Hayes describes occur?

4　Hayes invents a number of scenarios ("you receive a letter . . . ," "a Washington friend asks you . . . ," "you pick up a hitchhiker . . ." para. 6–8) which he then uses as evidence for his thesis. How credible did you find these scenarios and the conclusions he draws from them? (Glossary: *Evidence*.)

5　How does Hayes use the comparison and contrast format to disclose startling differences in the ways in which traditional documents and electronic files are created and stored? What verbal cues does Hayes use to signal similarities or differences? (Glossary: *Comparison and Contrast*.)

6　In what fundamental ways have computers altered questions of who is an author, who owns a particular piece of writing, how writing is reproduced and disseminated, and how it is stored and retrieved?

How the Web Destroys the Quality of Students' Research Papers

David Rothenberg

◆ DAVID ROTHENBERG is an associate professor of philosophy at the New Jersey Institute of Technology. He is the author of *Hand's End: Technology and the Limits of Nature* (1993) and the editor of *Terra Nova: Journal of Nature and Culture*. The following article appeared in the *Chronicle of Higher Education* (August 1997).

The process by which students write research papers has, Rothenberg believes, been dramatically altered by the greater convenience of using the web. Whereas before students might have gone into libraries looking for information and informed viewpoints from books, periodicals, and other reference sources, now they can simply type a few key words into a search engine that does the searching for them, click from one website to another, download whatever information—however skewed, unsubstantiated, or outdated it may be—and arrange it into an acceptable format. In essence, the web promotes a passive attitude toward research and encourages papers that are little more than patchwork quilts of summaries, slanted opinions, and very little original thought or analysis.

> **TO CONSIDER**   How does the Internet make it possible for sloppy researchers to take whatever is available in lieu of continuing to search for exactly what they need?

S OMETIMES I look forward to the end-of-semester rush, when students' final papers come streaming into my office and mailbox. I could have hundreds of pages of original thought to read and evaluate. Once in a while, it is truly exciting, and brilliant words are typed across page in response to a question I've asked the class to discuss.

But this past semester was different. I noticed a disturbing decline in both the quality of the writing and the originality of the thoughts expressed. What had happened since last fall? Did I ask worse questions? Were my students unusually lazy? No. My class had fallen victim to the latest easy way of writing a paper: doing their research on the World-Wide Web.

It's easy to spot a research paper that is based primarily on information collected from the Web. First, the bibliography cites no books, just articles or pointers to places in that virtual land somewhere off any map: http://www.etc. Then a strange preponderance of material in the bibliography is curiously out of date. A lot of stuff on the Web that is advertised as timely is actually at least a few years old. (One student submitted a research paper last semester in which all of his sources were articles published between September and December 1995; that was probably the time span of the Web page on which he found them.)

Another clue is the beautiful pictures and graphs that are inserted neatly into the body of the student's text. They look impressive, as though they were the result of careful work and analysis, but actually they often bear little relation to the precise subject of the paper. Cut and pasted from the vast realm of what's out there for the taking, they masquerade as original work.

Accompanying them are unattributed quotes (in which one can't tell who made the statement or in what context) and curiously detailed references to the kinds of things that are easy to find on the Web (pages and pages of federal documents, corporate propaganda, or snippets of commentary by people whose credibility is difficult to assess). Sadly, one finds few references to careful, in-depth commentaries on the subject of the paper, the kind of analysis that requires a book, rather than an article, for its full development.

Don't get me wrong, I'm no neo-Luddite. I am as enchanted as anyone else by the potential of this new technology to provide instant information. But too much of what passes for information these days is simply *advertising* for information. Screen after screen shows you where you can find out more, how you can connect to this place or that. The acts of linking and networking and randomly jumping from here to there become as exciting or rewarding as actually finding anything of intellectual value.

Search engines, with their half-baked algorithms, are closer to slot machines than to library catalogues. You throw your query to the wind, and who knows what will come back to you? You may get 234,468 supposed references to whatever you want to know. Perhaps one in a thousand might actually help you. But it's easy to be sidetracked or frustrated as you try to go through those Web pages one by one. Unfortunately, they're not arranged in order of importance.

What I'm describing is the hunt-and-peck method of writing a paper. We all know that word processing makes many first drafts look far more polished than they are. If the paper doesn't reach the assigned five pages, readjust the margin, change the font size, and . . . voila! Of course, those machinations take up time that the student could have spent revising the paper. With programs to check one's spelling and grammar now standard features on most computers, one wonders why students make any mistakes at all. But errors are as prevalent as ever, no matter how crisp the typeface. Instead of becoming perfectionists, too many students have become slackers, preferring to let the machine do their work for them.

What the web adds to the shortcuts made possible by word processing is to make research look too easy. You toss a query to the machine, wait a few minutes, and suddenly a lot of possible sources of information appear on your screen. Instead of books that you have to check out of the library, read carefully, understand, synthesize, and then tactfully excerpt, these sources are quips, blips, pictures, and short summaries that may be downloaded magically to the dorm-room computer screen. Fabulous! How simple! The only problem is that a paper consisting of summaries of summaries is bound to be fragmented and superficial, and to demonstrate more of a random montage than an ability to sustain an argument through 10 to 15 double-spaced pages.

Of course, you can't blame the students for ignoring books. When college libraries are diverting funds from books to computer technology that will be obsolete in two years at most, they send a clear message to students: Don't read, just connect. Surf. Download. Cut and paste. Originality becomes hard to separate from plagiarism if no author is cited on a Web page. Clearly, the words are up for grabs, and students much prefer the fabulous jumble to the hard work of stopping to think and make sense of what they've read.

Libraries used to be repositories of words and ideas. Now they are seen as centers for the retrieval of information. Some of this information comes from other, bigger libraries, in the form of books that can take time to obtain through interlibrary loan. What happens to the many students (some things never change) who scramble to write a paper the night before it's due? The computer screen, the gateway to the world sitting right on their desks, promises instant access—but actually offers only a pale, two-dimensional version of a real library.

But it's also my fault. I take much of the blame for the decline in the quality of student research in my classes. I need to teach students how to read, to take time with language and ideas, to work through arguments, to synthesize disparate sources to come up with original thought. I need to help my students understand how to assess sources to determine their credibility, as well as to trust their own ideas more than snippets of thought that materialize on a screen. The placelessness of the Web leads to an ethereal randomness of thought. Gone are the pathways of logic and passion, the sense of the progress of an argument. Chance holds sway, and it more often misses than hits. Judgment must be taught, as well as the methods of exploration.

I'm seeing my students' attention spans wane and their ability to reason for themselves decline. I wish that the university's computer system would crash for a day, so that I could encourage them to go outside, sit under a tree, and read a really good book—from start to finish. I'd like them to sit for a while and ponder what it means to live in a world where some things get easier and easier so rapidly that we can hardly keep track of how easy they're getting, while other tasks remain as hard as ever—such as doing research and writing a good paper that teaches the writer something in the process. Knowledge does not emerge in a vacuum, but we do need silence and space for sustained thought. Next semester, I'm going to urge my students to turn off their glowing boxes and think, if only once in a while.

1 Why would students' reliance on the web instead of libraries produce inferior research papers? How do the way searches are conducted on the web and the form and kind of information that appear produce papers where students gain little if any knowledge from the research process?

2 What factors directly attributable to doing research on the web explain skimpy and skewed bibliographies, unattributed quotes, slanted or superficial summaries, out-of-date or limited references, and the use of attractive visuals to make up the required page length of the paper?

3 If you have ever done a research paper in the traditional way and one using the web, compare the two methods and the results you obtained. Do your experiences support Rothenberg's thesis?

4 How does Rothenberg organize his article to point out the differences between the way in which traditional research papers were done with those now being done using the web? (Glossary: *Comparison and Contrast.*)

5 Has Rothenberg established a clear causal connection between students' use of the Internet and the declining quality of research papers? Explain the possible reasons for the decline in quality Rothenberg has observed. Are these effects superficial, in your opinion, or the inevitable consequences of reliance on the Internet? Why or why not? (Glossary: *Cause and Effect.*)

6 How has writing on a computer changed the nature of the writing process? Describe some of these changes in a short essay. Which writing tasks would be better with computers and which would be better without them? For example, what is the consequence of writing on a page that never ends, in a blank space that never gets filled? Are writers less inclined to edit what they write (and decide what should go and what should stay) when writing on computers than they would on a single page of paper in a typewriter?

Christmas Unplugged   *Amy Bruckman*

◆ AMY BRUCKMAN is a doctoral candidate at the Media Lab at MIT, where she specializes in virtual communities. She has created several role-playing games that take place in imaginary or virtual spaces on the Internet. These

Amy Bruckman, "Christmas Unplugged," from *MIT's Technology Review Magazine.* Reprinted with permission from *MIT's Technology Review Magazine,* copyright 1995.

include MediaMoo, a MUD (multiuser dungeon fantasy game) designed for media researchers, and MOOSE Crossing, a MUD designed to serve as an innovative learning environment for children. The following essay originally appeared in the January 1995 issue of *Technology Review*.

The extent to which our everyday lives are dependent upon computer technology becomes more comprehensible when we consider how ubiquitous electronic communications have become and consequently how hard it is to unplug from the Net. This is exactly Bruckman's predicament when she decides to leave her laptop behind to visit her parents during Christmas in Miami. As a result, she has to reevaluate her obsessive reliance on its "seductive, engrossing world."

TO CONSIDER   Have you become addicted to e-mail and chat rooms to the point where you cannot conceive of taking a vacation without taking your computer with you?

If I had a network link, I'd be home now.

From my chaise lounge on the terrace of my parents' Miami Beach apartment, I see a grid of four-lane roads with palm-treed median strips, yachts moored on the inland waterway, a golf course, and a dozen tall white condominiums. The hum of traffic is punctuated by the soft thunk of racquets striking tennis balls somewhere below. The temperature is in the 70s and a breeze blows through my toes. I am a long way from Boston. If I had a net link, I'd know exactly how far.

I'd know the weather forecast for Miami, and, if I cared, for Boston too. Just about anything you might like to know is out there on the worldwide computer network—the Net—if you know where to look.

It's Christmas day in Miami, but I'm not sure it would really be Christmas or I would really be in Miami if I were plugged into the Net. I would be in my virtual office, a "room" in the text-based virtual reality environment where I do most of my work. I have a desk there, piled with things to do, and a fish tank—just like my "real" office. Except that the virtual fish don't need to be fed—they're just a program I created one day while procrastinating from real work. My virtual office is just some data on a computer housed at MIT that I can tap into from anywhere, but it is a place to me. When I log onto the network, I am there.

And I would be there right now, if not for a difficult choice I made two days ago. I was packed for my trip south and had called a cab. I had the important things: airline ticket, wallet, bathing suit. I stood in the hall staring at a padded gray bag, the one containing my Macintosh PowerBook computer. I grabbed the bag, double-locked the door, and started to walk down the hall. I stopped. 5

I went back, opened the door, and put down the gray bag. I stood in the doorway, feeling foolish. The taxi honked. The honk gave me courage: I locked up again, leaving my computer—my office—behind.

A vacation should be about escaping from routines; going somewhere else provides a new perspective. But when I travel with my PowerBook, I bring many of my routines with me. I can readily gain access to all my familiar tools for finding information. It's as if I never left. And that's the problem. Had I brought my computer, I would not have written this essay (for which I am using a pencil). Instead, I would have logged onto the network and entered its seductive, engrossing world. By now I would have read the newswire and Miss Manner's column, answered a dozen questions from friends and colleagues, and possibly posted my thoughts on a movie I saw last night to a public discussion group. It would be as if I never left home.

The network destroys a sense of time as well as place. Daily and seasonal rhythms are subtle at best. As morning turns to evening, I am more likely to bump into my friends in Hawaii, less likely to encounter my friends in England. In the summer, things quiet down. April 1st is the only real network holiday—don't believe anything you read that day! Beyond that, life on the Net proceeds at an even, unpunctuated pace. There are no holiday decorations on the Net.

On my flight down here I saw a young boy carrying a sleek black bag on his shoulder. He held it naturally, but with a hint of importance. It took me a moment to see the logo: it contained his Nintendo Game Boy. His generation sees nothing remarkable about traveling at all times with a computer. It is already possible to connect to the network from a palm-sized computer with a cellular link. As computers get smaller and cheaper, we will lose even the excuse of the weight of that black bag or the cost of losing it.

The Net is becoming an important part of the lives of a broader segment of the population. Its spread presents a worrisome challenge: is it ever possible for us to take uninterrupted time off any more? The new technologies of connectedness are pushing people to blend their many roles into one: personal mail is mixed with professional correspondence, and work crises arrive on a cellular phone during leisure time. If our coworkers and competitors have made themselves perpetually available, we feel all the more pressure to do the same, lest we be left behind. One of my colleagues deliberately vacations in places so remote that getting a Net connection is almost impossible—it's the only way she can get a real break, and, for a little while at least, be a carefree newlywed instead of a world-renowned researcher. But such exotic locales are getting harder and harder to find.

10   I love the network and the people and places I find there. But sometimes I find it important to disconnect—to leave the cellular phone and the beeper in a desk drawer, leave that padded gray bag at home. To be out of touch, not for hours but for days. To leave behind routines, both virtual and real.

---

1 Why was the decision not to take her laptop computer such an agonizing one for Bruckman?

2 In what way, in Bruckman's opinion, does the existence of the Net alter one's sense of time in general and leisure time specifically, and impinge on areas of life that used to be seen as private?

3 In your experience, are Bruckman's concerns about the growing inability to disconnect from one's professional life well founded? To what extent do you share her conclusion about the value of leaving behind routines, both virtual and real?

4 Would Bruckman's essay have been just as effective if she had written it from a third-person point of view? Why or why not? (Glossary: *Point of View.*)

5 Of what advantage is it to Bruckman to use a point-by-point method of comparison in her account of what life was like without her laptop computer? How does this rhetorical strategy make it possible for her readers to understand the consequences of disconnecting from all electronic forms of communication? (Glossary: *Comparison and Contrast.*)

6 In a short essay, discuss the impact that high-tech paraphernalia (computers, beepers, e-mail, fax machines, cellular phones, etc.) have had on your life. Describe a day in your life without any of these devices. What would this day be like? Would it seem like a vacation or would you experiences stress and a sense of deprivation?

The Personal Touch   *Chet Williamson*

◆ CHET WILLIAMSON is the author of a number of works including *Soulstorm* (1986), *Ash Wednesday* (1987), *Dreamthorp: A New Novel* (1989), *Lowland Rider* (1988), and *Reign* (1990). This story first appeared in *Playboy Magazine*, August 1983.

If you have ever received a seemingly personalized letter that projects a tone of warmth and intimacy while being electronically produced, you have experienced the unnerving result of mass-marketed publishing hooked into vast computerized databases. They seem to know everything about you (except when they spell your name wrong)—and they do. Everyone knows how it is almost impossible to have your name removed from these lists. Williamson ingeniously weaves

---

these elements together to create an absurd scenario that becomes more likely every day.

TO CONSIDER   Have you ever wished you could take your name off every computerized mailing list and mass-market and telemarketing lists, or that you never had to receive junk e-mail again? Have you become accustomed to the deluge of printed and electronic communications you receive? What is the worst case scenario you can imagine involving being on all these lists?

SEED CATALOG—TOSS; Acme flier—keep for Mary; *Sports Illustrated*—keep; phone bill, electric bill, gas bill—keep, keep, keep. Damn it. Subscription-renewal notice to *Snoop*—toss. . . .

Joe Priddy tossed, but the envelope landed face up, balanced on the edge of the wastebasket. He was about to tip it in when he noticed the words PERSONAL MESSAGE INSIDE on the lower-left front.

Personal, my ass, he thought, but he picked it up and read it.

Dear **Mr. Pridy,**

We have not yet received you subscription renewal to SNOOP, the Magazine of Electronic and Personal Surveillance. We trust that, after having been a loyal subscriber for 9 months, you will renew your sub-scription so that we may continue to send SNOOP to you at **19 Mer-rydale Drive.**

We do not have to remind you, **Mr. Pridy**, of the constant changes in surveillance technology and techniques. We are sure that in your own town of **Sidewheel, NY**, you have seen the consequences for yourself. So keep up to date on the latest in surveillance, **Mr. Pridy**, by sending **$11.95** in the enclosed prepaid envelope today. As one involved and/or interested in the field of law enforcement, you cannot afford to be without SNOOP, **Mr. Pridy.**

Best Regards,

David Michaelson
Subscription Director

P.S.: If you choose not to resubscribe, **Mr. Pridy,** would you please take a moment and tell us why, using the enclosed post-paid envelope? Thank you, **Mr. Pridy.**

Joe shook his head. Who did they think they were fooling? "Pridy," said Joe to himself. "Jesus."

Mary's brother Hank had given Joe the subscription to *Snoop* for his birth-day. "As a joke," he'd said, winking at Joe lasciviously, a reference to the evening he and Hank had watched the Quincy girl undress in the apartment across the courtyard with the aid of Joe's binoculars. It had taken some imagination to satisfy Mary's curiosity about Hank's joke, and Joe still felt uncomfortable each time *Snoop* hit his mailbox. And now they wanted him to resubscribe?

He was about to toss the letter again when he thought about the P.S. "Tell us why." Maybe he'd do just that. It would get all his feelings about *Snoop* out of his system to let them know just how he felt about their "personal message."

Dear MR. MICHELSON,

I have chosen not to resubscribe to SNOOP after having received it for 9 MONTHS because I am sick and tired of computer-typed messages that try to appear personal. I would much rather receive an honest request to "Dear Subscriber" than the phony garbage that keeps turning up in my mailbox. So do us both a favor and don't send any more subscription renewal notices to me at 19 MERRYDALE DRIVE in my lovely town of SIDEWHEEL, NY. OK?

Worst regards,

Joseph H. Priddy

P.S.: And it's Priddy, not Pridy. Teach your word processor to spell.

Joe pulled the page out of the typewriter and stuffed it into the postpaid envelope.

Two weeks later, he received another subscription-renewal notice. As before, PERSONAL MESSAGE INSIDE was printed on the envelope. He was about to throw it away without opening it when he noticed his name was spelled correctly. "Small favors," he muttered, sitting on the couch with Mary and tearing the envelope open. Could they, he wondered, be responding to his letter?

Dear **Mr. Priddy,**

Christ, another word-processor job. . . . At least they got the name right. . . .

We received your recent letter and are sorry that you have chosen not to resubscribe to SNOOP, the Magazine of Electronic and Personal Surveillance. We hope, however, that you will reconsider, for if you resubscribe now at the low price of **$427.85** for the next nine issues

$427.85? What the hell? What happened to $11.95?

we will be able to continue your subscription uninterrupted, bringing you all the latest news and updates on surveillance technology and techniques. And in today's world, *Mr. Priddy,* such knowledge should not be taken lightly. You'll learn techniques similar to those that led New York City law-enforcement officials to the biggest heroin bust in history, that told members of the FBI of a plan to overthrow the state government of Montana by force, that alerted us to your own four-month affair with **Rayette Squires.**

Wha—Joe could feel the blood leave his face.

You'll get tips on photographic surveillance, as well, and learn techniques that will let your own efforts equal that of the enclosed 2 by 2 showing you and **Miss Squires at The Sidewheel Motel** in the lovely town of **Sidewheel, NY.**

Joe dove for the envelope, which was lying dangerously close to Mary's *McCall's*. He peeked as surreptitiously as possible into the envelope and found, between the slick paper flier and the return envelope, a well-lit color photo of him and Rayette in a compromising and fatiguing position. His wife looked up in response to his high-pitched whine, and he smacked the envelope shut, giggled weakly, and finished the letter.

We sincerely hope, **Mr. Priddy,** that you'll rejoin our family of informed subscribers by mailing your check for **$427.85** very soon. Shall we say within 10 days?

Regards,

David Michaelson
Subscription Director

Joe got up, envelope and letter in hand, and went to the bedroom to get out the shoe box he'd hidden—the one with the money he'd been squirreling away for an outboard motor, the money even Mary didn't know about.

When he counted it, it totaled $428.05. Which made sense. This time, the return envelope wasn't prepaid.

---

1 How does Williamson's story dramatize the theme of mass-marketing intrusions on personal privacy that the computer has made possible, and which have become an annoying feature of contemporary life?

2 How does Williamson structure his story so that the stakes escalate for Joe Priddy, the narrator? Why is the amount $427.85 significant?

3 Describe your own experiences, although one hopes they were not as gruesome as those dramatized in this story, with mass marketing by phone, fax, letter, or e-mail (known as spamming). For example, have you ever responded to a Publisher's Clearing House notification, or truly believed for a split second that you had won a prize or vacation? What happened?

4 How would you characterize the narrator? How is the story shaped as a confrontation between the narrator and the mail order company? (Glossary: *Characterization, Fiction, Protagonist/Antagonist.*)

5 How does Williamson use irony in his short story? What exactly is being satirized— computer-driven mass mailings, the narrator's naiveté, or something else? Explain. (Glossary: *Satire, Humor.*)

6 What problems—ethical, financial, etc—are involved in online searching? Under what circumstance would individual rights come into conflict with new information technologies, especially in areas of privacy?

◆ CONNECTIONS: CYBERTALK

LynNell Hancock, "The Haves and the Have-Nots"

1. To what extent do Paula Span's experiences provide a complementary perspective on the generation gap discussed by Hancock?
2. Compare the predicament of a computer illiterate person with that of a person who cannot read or write, as discussed by Jonathan Kozol in "The Human Cost of an Illiterate Society" (Ch. 8).

Sven Birkerts, "Into the Electronic Millennium"

1. Which of the probable trends mentioned by Birkerts seem borne out by Brian Hayes's analysis?
2. How, according to Birkerts, has the advent of electronic communications changed the basic relationship between the self and the world that David Abram (see "The Flesh of Language," Ch. 3) describes?

David Angell and Brent Heslop, "Return to Sender"

1. Angell and Heslop appear to believe that cautionary advice about how one should conduct oneself on the Net will solve most of the existing problems. Do Paula Span's experiences seem to support their analysis?
2. How has e-mail changed protocols of interpersonal communication in ways that are radically different from conversation held face to face or over the telephone, as discussed by Peter Farb in "Verbal Dueling" (Ch. 4)?

Paula Span, "Women and Computers: Is There Equity in Cyberspace?"

1. Did Span's experiences on the Internet change her perception of time and impinge on areas of her life in ways that she had not expected, as described by Amy Bruckman?
2. Is it likely that Julia Penelope (see "The Glamour of Grammar," Ch. 7) would characterize the computer culture experienced by Span as revealing an adolescent mindset that is implicitly sexist? Why or why not?

Brian Hayes, "The Electronic Palimpsest"

1. To what extent are Hayes's concerns about the effect of computers on academic research borne out by David Rothenberg's experiences?
2. How would the ability to create a historic record of the transformations of the English language of the kind offered by Paul Roberts (see "Something

About English," Ch. 7) be altered or even circumvented if Hayes's worst fears came true?

David Rothenberg, "How the Web Destroys the Quality of Students' Research Papers"

1. What predictions made by Sven Birkerts as to the effects of computers on literacy are borne out by actual experiences described by Rothenberg?
2. How do trends in the reporting of news on television sound curiously similar to the trends in the increasing shoddiness of research papers done using the Internet, as discussed by Rothenberg (see Neil Postman and Steve Powers "How to Watch TV News," Ch. 10)?

Amy Bruckman, "Christmas Unplugged"

1. How do Bruckman's experiences illustrate what Sven Birkerts identifies as "the waning of the private self"?
2. To what extent do Bruckman's experiences illustrate the kind of disconnection from reality that David Abram discusses in "The Flesh of Language" (Ch. 4)?

Chet Williamson, "The Personal Touch"

1. How does the narrator's discovery in Williamson's story that rather than knowing nothing about him other than his name, *Snoop* knows much more than he would want them to know correspond to what Sven Birkerts calls "the waning of the private self" in his essay?
2. How are both this story and Aldous Huxley's "Propaganda Under a Dictatorship" (Ch. 10) based on the concept of an all-knowing "Big Brother" type of intrusiveness into the private life of the average citizen?

◆ WRITING ASSIGNMENTS FOR CHAPTER 11

1. How do databases change the way you do research or locate information? What advantages do databases have over books and what advantages do books still possess over computer databases?
2. How does the form and speed with which researchers can share their latest results with each other differ from the traditional dissemination of findings through journals and books? Why would the ability to make data electronically available be an advantage? Would there be any foreseeable disadvantages?
3. If you had to state something that, in your opinion, computers would never be able to do, what would it be (for example, have faith in God)?
4. In some libraries, new money is allocated exclusively for acquiring computer terminals and on-line services and subscriptions to databases instead of buy-

ing books. How do you feel about a trend that might lead to libraries in which there are no books, newspapers, journals, or any printed media?

5. In your experience, have you found that women are treated differently in cyberspace? If so, in what way? Would this help explain the much larger proportion of men who are part of this world?

6. The computer/language connection has taken a number of fascinating turns. In the Human Genome Project, computers are being used to decipher the language of human chromosomes. Biblical scholars have used computers to discover hidden meanings in the language of the Old Testament (*Bible Codes,* 1997), and computers are routinely used to translate texts from one language to another, to analyze stylistic characteristics of authors' works, and to enable autistic children to communicate. Choose any of these or another application and discuss the role computers play.

7. The following exchange was reported in an Ann Landers column. What experiences have you had with spell checkers? Do you find that since relying on them your spelling has improved, gotten worse, or remained the same? Take a paragraph you have recently written and reformulate it using phonetic sound-alikes that a spell checker would not recognize as being misspelled. What words do you commonly confuse in your own writing that a spell checker would not know were being used incorrectly—for example, "peace" for "piece," "too" for "to," "their" for "there"?

> **Dear Readers:** What follows is something for computer buffs who rely on spell checkers to contemplate:
> **Dear Ann Landers:** Sum won tolled me wee wood knot knead two learn how too spell because computers wood dew it four us. Eye disagree. Dew ewe?
> —P.E. in St. Louis Park, Minn.
> **Dear St. Louis Park:** Ewe our write. Thank ewe four a good clothes look at what "progress" has dun fore education.

8. How does the following ad manufacture images for NEC monitors? Consider how the ad describes the way computers helped a nonverbal autistic child communicate with others. As a research project, you might look into the new ways computers are being used to help those with various language impairments.

9. What new verbal constructions have come into existence as a consequence of the computer's impact on the language?

10. Which of the following terms do you recognize and use? Have you or someone you know created additional terms or extended these to apply to new situations? If so, what are they?

     In each case, discuss the significance of any of the following terms you recognize and its impact on the language:

   a. barf

   b. bozo filter

   c. ftr

Christian Murphy was non-verbal. He lived with a wall between himself and the world.

1 THIS IS CHRISTIAN.
He can see, hear, feel, touch,
but he cannot speak. He was born
with autistic tendencies that cut
him off from the world around him.

NEC Technologies, Inc.: MultiSync, Copyright 1997. Reprinted with permission from
NEC Technologies, Inc.

    d. imho (and) imnsho

    e. rtfm

    f. chips and salsa

    g. cuspy

    h. dead end users (DEUs)

    i. flame mail

    j. 404

    k. gigo

    l. killer app

    m. munge

    n. Smileys

    o. trap door

11. How has the shift from printed to electronic media changed relationships between readers and writers in general and changed your reading habits in particular? Do you learn differently when you rely on written texts than when you are using electronic media? How has the existence of electronic media made the kind of education you are receiving different from what it would have been? Write an essay in which you explore some of these issues and your reactions to them.

12. Have you ever participated in a discussion group, bulletin board, or chat room to meet with others to discuss common interests? What experiences did you have and what social consequences do you foresee? What are your views regarding attempts to censor material that goes across the Net?

Glossary of Rhetorical and Linguistic Terms

Abstract: Designating qualities or characteristics apart from specific objects or events; opposite of concrete.

Accent: A mode of pronunciation involving pitch, tone, emphasis, pattern, or intonation characteristic of the speech of a particular person, group, or locality. For example, foreign accent or Southern accent.

Acronym: A word formed from the initial letters or groups of letters in a set phrase. For example, NATO (North Atlantic Treaty Organization).

Allusion: A brief reference in a literary work to a real or fictional person, place, thing, or event that the reader might be expected to recognize.

American Sign Language (ASL, Ameslan): A method of communicating as a substitute for speech, derived from hand gestures, that preserves English structure and syntax. This was brought to the United States from France by T. H. Gallaudet.

Analogy: A process of reasoning that assumes if two subjects share a number of specific observable qualities then they may be expected to share qualities that have not been observed; the process of drawing a comparison between two things based on a partial similarity of like features.

Argument: A process of reasoning and putting forth evidence on controversial issues; a statement or fact presented in support of a point.

Attitude: The writer's emotional stance toward the subject.

Audience: The group of spectators, listeners, viewers, or readers who are reached by a performance or written work.

Biased Language: Language that reflects a preconceived opinion usually designed to cause prejudice toward a person or group.

Bilingual Education: A method by which children are instructed in their primary language, which may vary from the dominant language used in the mainstream culture.

Black English: The ordinary, everyday variety of English spoken by some African Americans.

Cause and Effect: A method of analysis that seeks to discover why something happened or will happen.

Characterization: The techniques a writer uses to create and reveal fictional personalities in a work of literature, by describing the character's appearance, actions, thoughts, and feelings.

Classification/Division: A method of sorting, grouping, collecting, and analyzing things by categories based on features shared by all members of a class or group. Division is a method of breaking down an entire whole into separate parts or sorting a group of items into nonoverlapping categories.

Cliché: A timeworn expression that through overuse has lost its power to evoke concrete images. For example, "gentle as a lamb," "smart as a whip," "hard as nails," "proud as a peacock," "pleased as punch."

Coinage: A word or phrase made, invented, or fabricated.

Colloquial Expressions: Words or phrases characteristic or appropriate to ordinary or familiar conversation rather than formal speech or writing.

Comparison and Contrast: A rhetorical technique for pointing out similarities or differences. Writers may use a point-by-point method to interweave points of comparison or contrast between two things or a subject-by-subject method to discuss similarities and differences.

Conclusion: The end or closing; the last main division of a discourse, usually containing summation and a statement of opinion or decisions reached.

Concrete: Pertaining to actual things, instances, or experiences; opposite of abstract.

Connotation: The secondary or associative meanings of a word as distinct from its explicit or primary meaning; the emotional overtones of a word or phrase; opposite of denotation.

Definition: A method for specifying the basic nature of any phenomenon, idea, or thing. Dictionaries place the subject to be defined in the context of the general class to which it belongs and give distinguishing features that differentiate it from other things in its class.

Denotation: The literal explicit meaning of a word or expression; opposite of connotation.

Description: Writing that reports how a person, place, or thing is perceived by the senses. Objective description recreates the appearance of objects, events, scenes, or people. Subjective description emphasizes the writer's feelings and reactions to these subjects.

Descriptivism: The study of the grammar, classification, and features of a language as they are, not as they should be. (See *Prescriptivism.*)

Dialect: A variety of a language that is distinguished from other varieties of the same language by features of phonology, grammar, and vocabulary, and by its use by a group of speakers who are set off from others geographically or socially.

Dialogue: Conversation between two or more persons or between characters in a story.

Diction: The choice of words in a work of literature and an element of style important to the work's effectiveness.

Doublespeak: In general, language used to distort and manipulate rather than to communicate.

Downplaying/Intensifying: Methods of drawing attention and diverting attention.

E-mail: Electronically transmitted communication that has evolved its own style and conventions.

Ethnocentricity: The belief in the inherent superiority of one's own group and culture.

Euphemism: From the Greek word meaning *to speak well of;* the substitution of an inoffensive, indirect, or agreeable expression for a word or phrase perceived as socially unacceptable or unnecessarily harsh. For example, "private parts" for sexual organs, "slumber robe" for shroud, "disadvantaged" for poor, "full-figured" for fat.

Evidence: All material, including testimony of experts, statistics, cases (whether real, hypothetical, or analogical), and reasons brought forward to support a claim.

Examples: Specific incidents that illustrate, document, or substantiate a writer's thesis.

Exposition: Writing that seeks to clarify, explain, or inform using one or several of the following methods: process analysis, definition, classification and division, comparison and contrast, and cause-and-effect analysis.

Fallacy: Errors of pseudoreasoning caused by incorrect interpretations of evidence and incorrectly drawn inferences.

Fiction: A mode of writing that constructs models of reality in the form of imagined experiences that are not literally true.

Figurative Language: The use of words outside their literal or usual meanings, used to add freshness and suggest associations and comparisons that create effective images; includes elements of speech such as hyperbole, irony, metaphor, personification, and simile.

Grammar: The study of the formal features of a language, such as the sounds, morphemes, words, and sentences.

Humor: A comic quality causing amusement.

Hyperbole: An extravagant statement or figure of speech not intended to be taken literally ("to wait an eternity").

Idiom: An expression whose meaning cannot be derived from its constituent elements (for example, "kick the bucket" in the sense of "to die").

Illustration: (See Examples.)

Imagery: Use of language to convey sensory experience, most often through the creation of pictorial images through figurative language. For example, "Shall I compare thee to a summer's day."

Indo-European Languages: A family of languages characterized by inflection, grammatical number, and, typically, gender, and ablaut, and by basic vocabularies that have many correspondences, jointly in sound and in meaning. Typically, this refers to languages thought to have originated from a common prehistoric parent language including those spoken in Europe, North and South America, Australia, New Zealand, and sections of India and the Middle East.

Introduction: A preliminary part (as of a book) leading to the main part. The function of the introduction is to engage the reader in the central issue and present the thesis regarding the question at hand. Writers may engage the audience's attention with an anecdote, apt quotation, personal narrative, or definition of key terms, or by posing a thoughtful question.

Irony: A mode of speech in which words express a meaning opposite to the intended meaning.

Jargon: From the fifteenth-century French term *jargoun,* meaning *twittering* or *jibberish;* usually refers to a specialized language providing a shorthand method of quick communication between people in the same field. Often used to disguise the inner workings of a particular trade or profession from public scrutiny.

Language: A body of words used in common by people of the same community or nation, the same geographical area, or the same cultural tradition.

Lexicography: The writing or compiling of dictionaries.

Linguistic Relativity Hypothesis: The view that the structure of a language has a profound influence on the way speakers of that language view reality. (Also known as the Sapir-Whorf Hypothesis.)

Logical Fallacies: Methods of pseudoreasoning that may occur accidentally or may be intentionally contrived to lend plausibility to an unsound argument. These include:

Ad Hominem: An attack against the character of the person instead of the issue.

Begging the Question: A pseudoargument that offers as proof the claim the argument itself exists to prove; also known as circular reasoning.

False Analogy: An unwarranted assumption that two things similar in some respects are also similar in all other ways.

Hasty Generalization: An erroneous judgment based on too few instances or on atypical or inadequate examples.

Loaded Question: A question posed in such a way as to suggest that an implicit question has been answered.

Non Sequitur: The introduction of irrelevant evidence to support a claim.

Post hoc, ergo propter hoc: The incorrect inference that because B follows A, A caused B.

Red Herring: Use of an irrelevant point to divert attention from the real issue.

Slippery Slope: Failure to provide evidence showing that one event will lead to a chain of events of a catastrophic nature.

Straw Man: An easily refuted objection used to divert attention from the real issue.

Logical Reasoning: Principles governing correct or reliable inferences.

Metaphor: A figure of speech that implies comparison between two fundamentally different things without the use of "like" or "as." It works by ascribing the qualities of one to the other, linking different meanings together, such as abstract and concrete and literal and figurative (For example, "couch potato").

Narration: The story of events and/or experiences that tells what happened. Effective narratives in both fiction and nonfiction tell what happened, when it happened, and to whom it happened; relate events from a consistent point of view; organize the account with a clear beginning, middle, and end; and employ events and incidents that dramatize important moments in the action.

Objective/Subjective: A point of view that emphasizes the external appearance of objects, people, events, or scenes—in contrast to a subjective point of view, which communicates personal feelings and permits readers to empathize with reactions toward scenes, objects, or events.

Onomastics: The study of the origin and history of proper names.

Organization: The order of presentation that best fulfills the writer's purpose;

may be chronological, least familiar to most familiar, simple to complex, or arranged according to some other principle deemed appropriate.

Paradox: A seemingly self-contradictory statement that may nevertheless be true.

Personification: A usage in which human characteristics are attributed to nonhuman things ("an amusing little wine").

Persuasion: According to Aristotle, the act of winning acceptance of a claim achieved through the combined effects of the audience's confidence in the speaker's character (*ethos*), appeals to reason (*logos*), and the audience's emotional needs and values (*pathos*).

Phonetics: The study of speech sounds and their production, transmission, and reception, as well as their analysis, classification, and transcription.

Poetry: A literary form that emphasizes rhythm and figurative language, often expressing personal emotion.

Point of View: The relationship between the speaker and events he or she narrates in an essay or story. Events may be related in either the first person (I) or the third person (he, she, they).

Prescriptivism: Giving directions or injunctions with regard to linguistic matters as they should be, not as they are. (See Descriptivism.)

Process Analysis: A method of clarifying the nature of something by explaining how it works in separate, easy-to-understand steps.

Propaganda: Information or ideas methodically spread to promote or injure a cause, group, nation, etc.

Protagonist/Antagonist: Main character in a short story, play, novel, or poem, opposed by an adversary or antagonist who may be another character, nature, fate, society, or any combination of these.

Purpose: The writer's objective. More formally, refers to the goals of the four basic types of prose: narration (to tell or relate), description (to describe), exposition (to explain or clarify), and argument (to persuade or convince).

Racist Language: A form of discriminatory labeling by which one race is stigmatized. (See Biased Language.)

Rhetorical Question: A question asked solely to produce an effect and not to elicit a reply, such as "When will genetic engineering fulfill its promise?"

Sapir-Whorf Hypothesis: Named after Edward Sapir, German-born American anthropologist and linguist, and Benjamin Lee Whorf. (See Linguistic Relativity Hypothesis.)

Satire: A technique that ridicules both people and societal institutions, using irony, wit, and exaggeration.

Semantics: The study of linguistic development by classifying and examining changes in the meanings of words.

Sexist Language: Discriminatory labeling that presumes the inherent superiority of one sex over the other.

Simile: An element of speech involving a direct comparison between two unlike things and using the words *like* or *as* ("as high as a kite").

Slang: Very informal usage in vocabulary and idiom that is characteristically more metaphorical, playful, elliptical, vivid, and ephemeral than ordinary language.

Speaker: The narrator in a poem, created for the purpose of relating events from a consistent point of view.

Specific/General: The linguistic spectrum, ranging from an individual item (for example, Winesap apple) to the class or group to which it belongs (apples, or, more generally, fruit).

Standard English: The English language as written and spoken by literate people in both formal and informal usage that is universally current while incorporating regional differences.

Stereotype: Labeling a group in terms of a perjorative character trait.

Style: The author's characteristic manner of expression. Style includes the types of words used, their placement, and distinctive features of tone, imagery, figurative language, sound, and rhythm.

Symbol: Something concrete (such as an object, person, place, or event) that stands for or represents something abstract (such as an idea, quality, concept, or condition). For example, the caduceus or staff carried by Mercury as a messenger of the gods is used as the universal emblem or symbol of the medical profession.

Syntax: The pattern or structure of the word order in a sentence or phrase; the study of grammatical structure.

Taboo Language: Proscribed by society as improper and unacceptable language.

Technical Language: Peculiar to or characteristic of an art, science, profession, trade, etc.

Theme: An important underlying idea, either stated or implied; used in both fiction and nonfiction.

Thesis: The position taken by a writer, often expressed in a single sentence, that an essay develops or supports.

Tone: The voice the writer has chosen to project to relate to readers. For example, serious, light-hearted, etc. Tone is produced by the combined effect of word choice, sentence structure, and purpose, and reflects the writer's attitude toward the subject.

Topic Sentence: The sentence that expresses the central idea in a paragraph, which other sentences in the paragraph clarify, support, or explain.

Transitions: Signal words or phrases that connect sentences, paragraphs, and sections of an essay to produce coherence. These can include pronoun references, parallel clauses, conjunctions, restatement of key ideas, and expressions such as "furthermore," "moreover," "by contrast," "therefore," "consequently," "accordingly," and "thus."

Usage: Customary manner in which a language is spoken or written.

Voice: The implied personality the author chooses to adopt. In fiction, the voice may reflect a *persona* who projects views quite different from the author's.

Index of Authors and Titles

Index